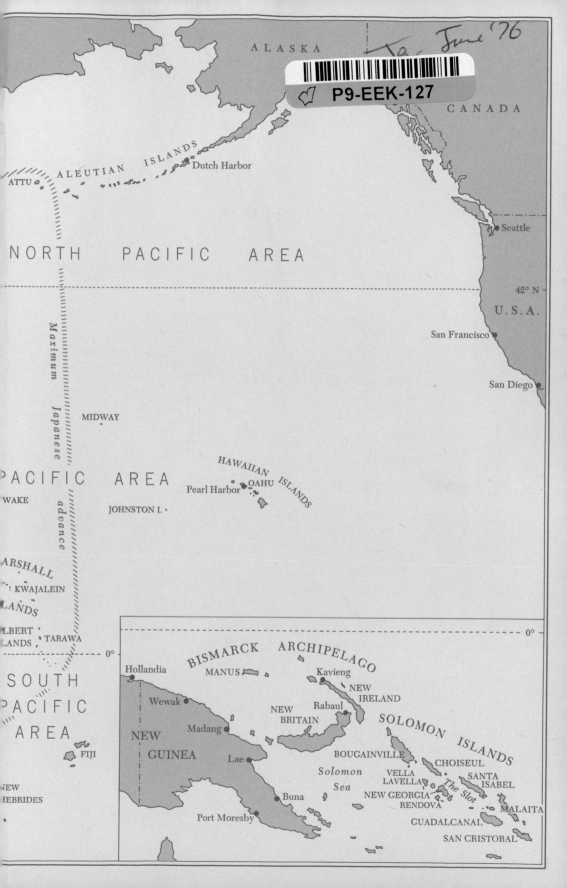

ALASKA

June '76

P9-EEK-127

CANADA

ALEUTIAN ISLANDS

Dutch Harbor

ATTU

NORTH   PACIFIC   AREA

Seattle

42° N

U.S.A.

San Francisco

San Diego

Maximum Japanese advance

MIDWAY

PACIFIC   AREA

HAWAIIAN ISLANDS

WAKE

Pearl Harbor   OAHU

JOHNSTON I.

ARSHALL

KWAJALEIN

LANDS

LBERT

LANDS   TARAWA

0°

BISMARCK   ARCHIPELAGO

0°

SOUTH

Hollandia   MANUS

Kavieng

PACIFIC

Wewak   NEW IRELAND

Rabaul

AREA

Madang   NEW BRITAIN

SOLOMON ISLANDS

NEW   GUINEA   Lae

BOUGAINVILLE

CHOISEUL

FIJI

Solomon Sea

VELLA LAVELLA   SANTA ISABEL

NEW   HEBRIDES

Buna   NEW GEORGIA   The Slot

RENDOVA   MALAITA

Port Moresby   GUADALCANAL

SAN CRISTOBAL

GEORGE C. MARSHALL

* *

ORDEAL AND HOPE

1939-1942

By the same author

GEORGE C. MARSHALL

*

EDUCATION OF A GENERAL

1880–1939

GENERAL GEORGE C. MARSHALL

1942

GEORGE C. MARSHALL:
ORDEAL AND
HOPE

By FORREST C. POGUE
DIRECTOR OF THE RESEARCH CENTER
GEORGE C. MARSHALL RESEARCH FOUNDATION

Foreword by General Omar N. Bradley

NEW YORK: THE VIKING PRESS

COPYRIGHT © 1965, 1966 BY GEORGE C. MARSHALL RESEARCH FOUNDATION.
ALL RIGHTS RESERVED.

FIRST PUBLISHED IN 1966 BY THE VIKING PRESS, INC.,
625 MADISON AVENUE, NEW YORK, N.Y. 10022.

PUBLISHED SIMULTANEOUSLY IN CANADA BY
THE MACMILLAN COMPANY OF CANADA LIMITED.

LIBRARY OF CONGRESS CATALOG CARD NUMBER: 63–18373.

SET IN BASKERVILLE, WEISS AND TRAJANUS TYPES.
MBG
PRINTED IN U.S.A. BY H. WOLFF BOOK MANUFACTURING CO.

A PORTION OF THIS BOOK FIRST APPEARED IN *Look*.

SECOND PRINTING FEBRUARY 1967

Thanks are due to the following publishers for permission to quote from the books named: The Devin-Adair Company for *The Untold Story of Douglas MacArthur*, by Frazier Hunt; Doubleday & Company, Inc., for *The Turn of the Tide*, by Arthur Bryant, Copyright 1957 by Arthur Bryant, and for *Triumph in the West*, by Arthur Bryant, Copyright © 1959 by Arthur Bryant; Harper & Row, Publishers, Inc., for *Roosevelt and Hopkins: An Intimate History*, by Robert Sherwood; Holt, Rinehart and Winston, Inc., for *The Watery Maze: The Story of Combined Operations*, by Bernard Fergusson; Houghton Mifflin Company for *The Grand Alliance* and *The Hinge of Fate*, by Winston Spencer Churchill, for *The Reckoning*, by Anthony Eden, and for *Years of Urgency, 1938-1941* (Volume II of *From the Morgenthau Diaries*), by John Morton Blum; *Life* for "This Is What the Soldiers Complain About" (from the issue of August 18, 1941); Tupper and Love, Inc., for *Annals of an Army Wife*, by Katherine Tupper Marshall; William Sloane Associates, William Morrow and Company, Inc., for *The Stilwell Papers*, by Joseph Warren Stilwell, Copyright 1948 by Winifred A. Stilwell.

TO THE MEN AND WOMEN
WHO SERVED WITH GENERAL MARSHALL
IN BUILDING AMERICA'S DEFENSES
IN THE YEARS
1939-1942

Illustrations

Contents

Foreword

BY GENERAL OF THE ARMY OMAR N. BRADLEY

WHEN General Marshall became Chief of Staff in 1939 at the outbreak of war in Europe I was privileged to serve directly under him as one of three members of the secretariat of the General Staff. Our duties, among others, were to present to the General the staff papers from the various divisions, after digesting the contents of each paper along with the recommendations for action it contained.

At the end of the first week General Marshall called us into his office and said without ceremony, "I am disappointed in all of you." When we asked why, he replied, "You haven't disagreed with a single thing I have done all week." We told him that it so happened we had been in agreement with every recommendation presented to him thus far. But the very next day we presented to him a staff study with a recommended course of action which seemed questionable, and we told General Marshall so. He said with approval, "Now that is what I want. Unless I hear all the arguments against something I am not sure whether I've made the right decision or not."

It was this reaction of a true commander or executive who did not want a staff of "yes men" which is what made General Marshall an outstanding leader. I was to see his qualities of leadership repeatedly put to the test in the crucial years between 1939 and 1942, when the Chief of Staff's remarkable vision brought our fighting forces to combat strength, and attained a state of preparedness in a minimum of time. I am convinced that by his ability and foresight General Marshall saved this country at least a year. Invasion of Europe a year later surely would have jeopardized our chances of winning. This is the year that may well have rewritten history.

It would be pleasant to record that, once we were actively en-

gaged in it, World War II was fought and won by ourselves and
our allies with no differences of opinion and no injured feelings
or bitter statements. But this would be expecting too much of
human beings at any time, and particularly at such a period of
extreme tension and stress. The British, with their commitments
around the world, saw the strategy of the war in a slightly different
light from that of the Americans. An officer in the Philippines,
Australia, London, Cairo, or Algiers was likely to have a perspective different from that of one sitting in Washington. There were
times when commanders felt they were being forgotten or ignored.
Frustrations, disagreements, misunderstandings created frictions
that were difficult to bridge over the gap of miles. Under the heavy
pressure of battle, differences flamed into controversy that in some
cases has persisted to the present day.

The various controversies discussed in this book all have been
revealed in prior biographies and memoirs, diaries, and official
histories. General Marshall's views on strategy have been criticized
by some of his former colleagues and subordinates and by a number of his foreign contemporaries. He personally kept silent on
these issues, but his attitude toward his critics was consistent with
his usual readiness to consider all sides of a question. He agreed
there had been mistakes, and opportunities missed, but he insisted
it was necessary to judge the decisions in the light of the knowledge
commanders had at the time, and of the paucity of their resources.
His advice to his biographer was to keep before the reader the circumstances, the atmosphere, and the personalities involved with
the decisions and operational orders. An historian or biographer
cannot properly evaluate the trials of leadership by ignoring the
personal factor, any more than he can write reliable history by
ignoring the fact that controversies did exist.

It would be unfortunate, however, if the reader were to conclude from the attention paid to such matters that controversy
rather than agreement marked the progress of World War II.
Despite differences of viewpoint, the Allied Commanders were
in accord on the broad issues and worked unusually well together
in attaining their common aims. There were disagreements over
the emphasis to be placed in various theaters, and there were disagreements on how the war should be fought. Nevertheless, the
American as well as the British commanders ended by finding poli-

cies on which they could agree, and they dropped their personal differences to cooperate in the most successful joint effort in which American arms ever participated.

In my Foreword to the first volume of this biography, *George C. Marshall: Education of a General,* I described the circumstances under which the biography was undertaken. After refusing many sizable offers for his memoirs, among them one estimated at a million dollars, General Marshall in 1953 at the urging of President Truman and other friends decided to give his papers to a Research Library at Lexington, Virginia. The George C. Marshall Research Foundation was organized that year by Mr. John C. Hagan, Jr., to collect the General's papers and to raise funds for a building in which to house these papers and memorabilia. President Truman directed the General Services Administrator, the Secretary of State, and the Secretary of Defense to cooperate by making available to representatives of the Foundation records pertaining to General Marshall. The project has been made possible through the backing and support of three other Presidents, Dwight D. Eisenhower, John F. Kennedy, and Lyndon B. Johnson. My own esteem for General Marshall's contributions and the desire that his records be preserved and the story of his service be presented to the public led me in 1959 to accept the presidency of the Foundation.

In 1956, General Marshall agreed to furnish interview material on tape and in recorded notes to a historian for use in a biography to be published after his death. Among the stipulations made by the General were (1) that the biographer be selected by the board of directors without reference to him for comment or concurrence, and (2) that any funds accruing from the sale of books or articles based on the interviews or his papers should remain with the Foundation. Dr. Forrest C. Pogue was selected in 1956 on the basis of his experience as a combat historian in World War II and as the author of *The Supreme Command,* the Army's official volume on General Eisenhower's command in Northwest Europe, 1944-1945. In preparing that volume, Dr. Pogue had worked among General Marshall's papers and in the files of the Combined and Joint Chiefs of Staff and had interviewed many of General Marshall's associates in the United States, Great Britain, and France. He was given access, at the General's suggestion, to the former Chief of Staff's files in his Pentagon office and to other pertinent records as a basis for the interviews he conducted with General Marshall in 1956 and 1957. In preparing the present volume, Dr. Pogue has drawn also on several diaries, including that of Secretary of War Henry L. Stimson, and on the recollections and private papers of a number of General Marshall's World War II associates.

In accordance with the directive given him by the board of directors of the Marshall Foundation, the author is attempting in this multi-volume biography to cover all of General Marshall's activities with a broad stroke, emphasizing specifically the man, his problems, his method of operating, and the outstanding personalities with whom he dealt. Dr. Pogue has been permitted in this account of the 1939-1942 period to exercise his discretion in presenting the story as it is unveiled in his interviews with the former Chief of Staff, with his associates, and in his papers.

In *Ordeal and Hope,* as in *Education of a General,* Dr. Pogue has attempted to capture the spirit of his subject. Although noting that General Marshall could be aloof and austere, he shows the human side of the man—an officer with great consideration for the common soldier, with intolerance for red tape and inefficiency and indifference, with a concern for those who must bear the heat of battle coupled with the determination to make the men with whose welfare he was charged ready for the fight and equipped with the means to win. Desiring to give his troops the best leaders possible, he could be ruthless in eliminating officers not up to the rigorous test of battle.

The book shows the way in which a fine officer handled the delicately triggered assignments of dealing with the powerful leaders of Great Britain and the United States, with the leaders of Congress, and with brilliant and bold commanders, all with forceful minds of their own. In the midst of unprecedented pressures and shattering difficulties, General George C. Marshall developed the largest and most successful fighting force this country has ever seen.

Preface

GENERAL MARSHALL believed that history could be depended on to furnish a full and accurate answer to all questions regarding his role in World War II. He declined, therefore, to write his memoirs, feeling that unless his account could be put into proper perspective and based on careful study of the documents, it would stir controversy without settling anything. In 1956 he yielded to pressure from friends and scholars to the extent of furnishing background material for the writing of a biography based on significant personal and official documents dealing with his career. I was selected by the George C. Marshall Research Foundation to conduct the interviews and to write the biography.

My assignment proved especially difficult because of the General's reluctance to become involved in controversy. I have explained in my bibliographical note the basis on which he finally agreed to make information available. I am certain that he would have preferred that I omit all reference to controversial matters. I was aware of his reticence, and I made the point to him more than once that if he did not reveal his side of the story history could not do full justice to his career. For this reason he left me with final discretion on statements that I could print.

In attempting to deal fully with the many subjects pertaining to General Marshall's activities as Chief of Staff in the period 1939-42, I produced a number of early chapters that seemed to duplicate the official volumes on this period. The publishers insisted, and the Foundation's directors accepted the view, that we prepare an account for the general reader, concentrating on the wartime Chief of Staff, showing how he operated, describing the individuals with whom he worked, and weighing his influence on strategy and command. We propose later to supplement this account with a number of monographs that will give in greater detail General Marshall's contributions to such important matters as the development of new weapons, his efforts to increase war pro-

duction, the reorganization of the Army, and relations with Latin
America.

The decision in January 1966 to split a rather bulky volume on
the war years has created certain problems in the presentation of
material. Many activities in which General Marshall was vitally
interested, such as the establishment of the Women's Auxiliary
Corps (established in 1942), the development of the Air Force, the
establishment of various commands throughout the world, have
been omitted or lightly sketched in Volume II. They will be covered in greater detail in the next book.

General Marshall considered the period 1939-42 the most difficult period of his tour as Chief of Staff in that the country was slow
in awakening to the dangers threatening it. His efforts to establish
an adequate national defense program in the prewar years required
a constant campaign to gain the support of the White House, the
Congress, and the general public. When money was provided for
defense needs, he faced the problem of building the Army and
Army Air Corps while making arms available to friendly powers
abroad.

Once war began, he worked to establish the principle of unified
command and to shape a strategy that would bring the defeat of
the principal enemy, Germany, while dealing effectively with
Japan's threat in the Pacific. His efforts to advance his views at
conferences with the President, the British, and his American colleagues are the theme of the later chapters. As the background for
a third volume, I have developed in some detail the bases of his
selection of key commanders around the world and the nature of
the relationships between him and the brilliant leaders who would
lead the fighting in America's far-flung theaters of war.

I have attempted to keep the emphasis on General Marshall
throughout the book. As a result I may have slighted contributions by some of his colleagues and may have given him more
credit than he ever claimed for himself. Since I have drawn
heavily on his papers I have sometimes seen his viewpoint more
clearly than views of his associates. In dealing with some of the controversies I have probably stressed his side of the argument more
strongly than that of other individuals involved. For these reasons
I have called attention to the memoirs and biographies dealing

with the careers of most of his contemporaries as a corrective to any bias that may exist here.

Collecting the material on General Marshall and his career has required the efforts of several people besides myself. Miss Eugenia Lejeune, Archivist-Librarian of the Foundation, has had the difficult task of acting as my chief research assistant while supervising the collection of books and documents in Arlington and the preliminary work on the library in Lexington. The assistance of the other members of my staff, in Arlington and Lexington, is acknowledged on page 439.

I was fortunate in obtaining the editorial assistance of Mr. Joseph Friedman, the Editor-in-Chief of the Office of the Chief of Military History. Working in his free time, he has brought to his task the knowledge and experience gained over more than fifteen years as editor of the official volumes on the Army's wartime role, *United States Army in World War II*. Mr. Friedman edited my volume, *The Supreme Command,* in that series, and we established a rapport that made our current association exceedingly pleasant and productive. I am deeply indebted to him for many suggestions for improving the presentation of material in the book. I have profited greatly from his counsel and have been stimulated by his reminders that there is a limit to the amount of information the general reader wants on some involved questions. Needless to say, neither he nor the Army is in any way responsible for the interpretations in this volume. General editorial direction has been exercised by Denver Lindley of The Viking Press. His task has been made more difficult by the delays imposed on my writing schedule by numerous other duties I have performed as Executive Director of the Marshall Foundation and as Director of the George C. Marshall Research Library. I wish to thank him and The Viking Press for their forbearance.

Elsewhere in the volume I have listed the names of those individuals who have contributed directly through interviews, letters, documents, photographs, and advice. I have also listed those individuals and foundations that made contributions specifically to the research program that produced this book. As a privately supported organization, the Marshall Foundation is also heavily indebted to hundreds of individuals who have given generously to the drive for funds to erect a library and to defray our operating expenses. Limitations of space have prevented me from listing the names of those who have given this assistance. I wish, however, to acknowledge here that our program and this book would not have been possible without them.

The work on this volume, amid fund-raising activities and the building and dedicating of the Marshall Library, was made possible only by the assistance and understanding of my colleagues. I hope that the book will repay them in some part for their efforts. For infinite patience, tolerance of bad temper, and sound suggestions for improving the book, I wish to record a special word of thanks to my wife, Christine.

—FORREST C. POGUE

Arlington, Virginia
May 1966

GEORGE C. MARSHALL

✳✳

ORDEAL AND HOPE

1939-1942

The New Chief

IN mid-April, 1945, the Commander of Allied troops in Europe paused in his preparations for the final drive to the heart of Germany to write a warm and gracious letter to his chief in Washington, General of the Army George C. Marshall. Come over for a visit, urged General Dwight D. Eisenhower, and "see in visible form the fruits of much of your work over the past five years." Even in a short visit, he added, "I am sure you would see things that would be of great satisfaction from now on." [1] The Chief of Staff made no response; the war ended in Europe without his observing at its peak the great Army he had created and trained. Later, he brought the triumphant commanders home for tumultuous receptions, sending each man to a different city where he would be certain of fresh acclaim. The only public cheers the organizer of victory received were those of 1919 when, as General Pershing's aide, he rode through the cheering throngs of Paris, London, New York, and Washington.

Marshall missed the plaudits he would have gained as leader of the Allied forces in a successful invasion of Europe. But he had won a greater triumph. Starting in 1939 with an Army and Army Air Corps of fewer than 200,000 men, he had directed their growth until in the spring of 1945 they numbered nearly eight and one-third million, ranged round the globe, tested in the operations he helped to plan, victorious on every front. In the brilliant performances of the troops he had inducted, trained, and equipped lay all the "satisfaction" that he craved. Three months after the Japanese surrender concluded the Second World War, President Harry S. Truman bestowed on the retiring General the nation's accolade:

"In a war unparalleled in magnitude and horror, millions of Americans gave their country outstanding service. General of the Army George C. Marshall gave it victory." [2]

General Marshall began his duties as Chief of Staff in a period of international turmoil. "My day of induction was momentous," he wrote a friend, "with the starting of what appears to be a world war." [3] And so it proved to be. Hitler attacked Poland on September 1, a few hours before the General took his oath of office. Two days later Great Britain and France entered the war against Germany. Within a week the countries of the British Commonwealth joined the mother country. In mid-September, as Germany rocked Poland with furious ground and air assaults, the Russians poured in from the east to complete that hapless country's ruin. In early November the brutal successors of Russian tsars and Prussian kings again partitioned Poland, turning back a page of European history by nearly a century and a half. This quick victory, revealing both the power of Germany and the weakness of the western democracies, swept away the last of the comfortable fictions by which the United States justified its neglect of defense preparations in a period when Germany, Italy, and Japan were demanding that the world order be changed to their liking.

For twenty years the United States had managed to stay at peace while achieving the contradictory ends of rejecting the system of collective security offered by the League of Nations and of failing to make adequate provisions for a self-maintained system of national defense. In 1920, after refusing League of Nations membership, Congress passed a national defense act authorizing a peacetime Regular Army with a strength of 280,000 and an effective reserve program. In the economy drives of the prosperous 1920s and the stress on welfare programs during the lean years that followed, Congress declined to appropriate sufficient funds to put even these modest plans into full effect. The regular forces averaged from 130,000 to 190,000 between 1922 and 1939. Not until after the fall of France was the figure set by the original act attained. By the Five-Power Naval Treaty of 1922 the United States gave up an extensive construction program designed to produce a two-ocean navy, in order to escape a possible naval race with Great Britain and Japan and freeze the status quo in the Pacific. In a period of vaunted self-reliance, Americans were able to sleep quietly only because of their trust in the strength and resolution of Great Britain and France, the ability and willingness of the League of Nations to prevent aggression in Europe and Asia, and Germany's peaceable acceptance of the Treaty of Versailles.

In the first decade and a half after World War I the United States was interested less in what might be needed for its future protection than in whether it had been duped by the Allies or by "merchants of death" in the conflict that had passed. The writings of revisionist historians, revelations by congressional inquiries, and refusals of former allies to pay their war debts helped persuade the general public that the nation's great mistake of 1917 was sending troops to France.

When the Ethiopian conflict and the Spanish Civil War threatened to involve the United States again in the affairs of Europe, Congress hastily adopted a series of laws designed to keep the country out of the first World War. Isolationist proposals reached their peak in 1938 when the House of Representatives approved by 209 to 188 the proposed constitutional amendment offered by Representative Louis Ludlow of Indiana to require a national referendum before the United States could go to war. Although the measure failed to get the necessary two-thirds vote, it obviously had the support of a large segment of the population.

Fortunately for the Army and Navy, the same month that saw the vote on the Ludlow amendment also heard vigorous presidential warnings that the United States was living in a rapidly changing world. Alarmed by the Japanese abrogation of the Five-Power Naval Treaty, renewed Japanese expansion in Manchuria, and anti-American incidents such as the Japanese attack on the U.S.S. *Panay* in Chinese waters, President Franklin D. Roosevelt in 1938 pushed through Congress a bill allowing a 20 per cent increase in the Navy. Early in 1939 he called for one and one-third billion dollars for the armed services, a considerable increase over appropriations for the preceding year. Less than a week later he asked for an additional half-billion dollars, specifying that three-fifths would go for the procurement of military aircraft. It was clear that he intended part of the expanded airplane production to aid Great Britain and France.

By the summer of 1939 the President became alarmed lest, if war came, the Neutrality Act of 1937 prevent the United States from making munitions and planes available to Great Britain and France. To his dismay Congress refused to consider a series of qualifying amendments before the outbreak of war. He had no choice when the fighting began but to proclaim American neutrality. Three days later he announced a state of limited emergency and with it a ban on the export of war materials to belligerents. Before the month's end he called in congressional leaders and repeated his earlier plea for the lifting of the embargo on arms shipments.

Germany's swift defeat of Polish forces as Britain and France looked on helplessly shocked the West. Suddenly it seemed that instead of being able to depend on the democracies to hold the line at the Rhine, the United States might have to defend London and Paris against assault. No longer was it possible to dismiss as mere evidences of war weariness or internal discord the recent diplomatic defeats of Great Britain and France. Obviously the countries on which America counted for protection, while letting its own defenses deteriorate, had also failed to keep pace in the rearmament race with Adolf Hitler.

Thus, like France and Britain, the United States in 1939 suffered from the twin ills of complacency and unpreparedness. Fortunately its fighting forces, weak as they proved to be, and the breadth of the oceans gave General Marshall and Admiral Harold R. Stark, the Chief of Naval Operations, a little time in which they could shore up America's defenses. Certain cherished national fallacies hampered their efforts. Since Bunker Hill, congressmen as well as schoolchildren had accepted the concept that the patriot, armed with little more than the righteousness of his cause, could quickly take his place behind the country's breastworks or even man a foreign trench. Forgetting the bitter experiences of the Civil War and World War I, many American leaders opposed military training and relied on the simple cry of danger to fill the ranks of the Regular Army and the National Guard. Perhaps most disturbing was the most recently born myth that America's tremendous industrial complex and special "know-how" in the fields of production and supply made unnecessary costly programs of developing and stockpiling military weapons and equipment.

The hallowed fallacies fitted comfortably into the framework of political demands for economy and general national distrust of military preparedness. For ten years Marshall's predecessors had requested critical items desperately needed by the Army and Air Corps but had ended by cutting their lists to a point acceptable to the President and Congress. Convinced that one day the Army would be asked why it had left the country unprepared for war, War Department planners in the late 1930s began to assemble evidence that they had at least warned of the country's military weakness.

Despite the clear evidence that the United States could no longer expect its friends in Western Europe to contain German aggression or rely on Russia to serve as a counterweight to Nazi designs, the nation still delayed taking the strong measures needed for hemispheric defense. Congress went so far as to show its sympathy for the Western Powers in November 1939 by permitting the shipment of arms on a "cash-and-carry" basis, but it adopted no long-range plans to build up the armed forces. American thinking was still obsessed by the fear that large defense appropriations would lead to intervention; well-known figures warned against this eventuality. Colonel Charles A. Lindbergh, eminent airman and national hero, spoke in mid-September for many of his fellow countrymen in warning that participation in the war would mean the loss of the nation's democracy.

General Marshall had watched with deep concern as the country seemed to follow its familiar pattern of neglecting defenses until crisis forced it to start arming overnight. And the outbreak of war in Europe did little to reverse this trend. Looking back at these troubled days seventeen years later, he spoke of his "tragic feeling" that the United States could have "shortened the war by at least a year" and saved "billions of dollars and 100,000 casualties" by initiating a speedy rearmament program in the fall of 1939.[4] He attributed part of the blame to the President's failure to press Congress for larger defense appropriations and to his delays in appointing a board with broad powers to manage war production. But, recalled Marshall, Roosevelt was aware "that the Middle West was so solidly against him that if he moved into a large military effort he would encounter such opposition he wouldn't be able to manage [it]." Under these circumstances his policy of acting "carefully and in a very restrained manner" proved to be politically sound.[5]

In stressing the role of the Middle West in the isolationist move-

ment of 1939-41, General Marshall overlooked the strong opposition to Roosevelt's rearmament policies in other parts of the country. Teamed against the President in the period before the Pearl
Harbor attack was an uneasy alliance of conservatives, liberals, and
radicals brought together in temporary collaboration. At the hard
core of the movement were isolationists of the 1914-17 variety, who
clung fondly to George Washington's admonitions to stay clear of
entangling alliances, and the disillusioned internationalists, who
believed that their idealistic crusade of 1917-18 had been grossly
betrayed by the Treaty of Versailles. Joining them briefly, until
Germany attacked the Soviet Union in the spring of 1941, were
those Communists or fellow travelers who on the announcement
of the Nazi-Soviet Pact in August 1939 had flopped overnight from
a militant anti-German stand to support of American neutrality.
Out of place in this company was a newer group consisting of
businessmen apparently frightened by all of Roosevelt's policies.
Loathing his domestic program and determined to block any development that would increase his control over taxes, production,
prices, and labor, they furnished much of the cash and effective
leadership for a bitter last-ditch fight against any weakening of
neutrality legislation or increase in aid to the Western Allies.

Marshall's program for strengthening the Army was caught in
the cross fire. Accustomed to the opposition of traditional isolationists, he was astonished to find some old acquaintances from
conservative business circles fighting his proposals and, in time,
accusing him of being a Roosevelt tool. The appropriations he
believed essential to raise the Army to a passable state of efficiency
he heard described as the first moves by the President to involve
the United States in conflict abroad. Increased airplane production, preparation of special forces to protect the Western Hemisphere, and the early proposals for selective service were carefully
searched for evidence that they were steps toward war. Marshall
knew America's weaknesses too well to favor warlike measures
against Germany, but he was convinced that more men, training,
and equipment were needed to defend the Western Hemisphere
against possible aggression.

The task confronting the Chief of Staff in the fall of 1939 was
staggering. Seventeenth in rank among the world's armed forces,
the United States Army retained from World War I only the luster

of its fighting reputation. Weapons effective in the Meuse-Argonne were obsolescent; many officers lacked proper training or had stagnated; the allotment for training in the late thirties, amounting to approximately two per cent of the Army's appropriations, was insufficient to keep the Regulars in shape or give the National Guard a real concept of field duties; and the lack of equipment and personnel for existing units held them below authorized peacetime strength. Worse still, Congress in its legislation reflected the national conviction that enforcement of the neutrality laws was sufficient to prevent war from touching the Western Hemisphere.

In meeting the tremendous challenges of his new job, Marshall himself moved unobtrusively and deliberately toward his goals. He was not of the breed of officer who announced his arrival on a new post by moving the flagpole, changing the flower beds, or enlarging the space allotted for his office. While Acting Chief of Staff during the summer, he had been able to fit smoothly into his new responsibilities. He and Mrs. Marshall had slipped quietly into the Chief of Staff's quarters at Fort Myer in late August, and the War Department had completed its transfer from the old State, War, and Navy Building next to the White House to part of the Munitions Building on Constitution Avenue shortly before he took up his new duties. He was pleased with the new offices, finding that "doing business in this building has increased the efficiency of operations very materially, for now it is a simple thing to bring in the people you want and talk things over." "I have the Assistant Chiefs of Staff in here frequently," he added, "and it only costs them a minute or two to get here, and we settle things in a hurry and then they are back at work." It was helpful, too, to be little more than two miles across Memorial Bridge from his quarters, so that he could go home at noon. His secretary telephoned from his office when he started, "and I walk right to the lunch table—on the glassed-in porch—from the car, and then I have a half hour or more to relax in a more restful atmosphere than here at the office or at the Army and Navy Club." [6]

He especially liked the way that his staff had smoothly made the transition from one chief to another. In July he had brought in as his successor in the Office of Deputy Chief of Staff, Brigadier General Lorenzo D. Gasser, a tremendously effective administrator, linked with Marshall back in 1935 before either had received a general's star as one who was eminently fitted for two-star rank. The Chief of Staff reported to his predecessor in September his immense gratification "with the efficient, quiet manner in which the Staff has gone about business. We were well prepared to extend ourselves immediately, so there is no necessity for our rushing here and there and deciding things on the spur of the moment. . . . Gasser has been splendid; I could not have done a wiser thing than bring him in. He has relieved me of a tremendous load, and as a matter of fact I have walked out of about 75 per cent of the normal business and left it completely to him, without even knowing what was going on in that connection." [7]

He also relied heavily on his Secretary General Staff, Lieutenant Colonel Orlando Ward, a quiet, studious type, who resembled a teacher more than a future armored division commander. Ward and his assistant, Stanley R. Mickelson, were the first of a remarkable group of officers who served Marshall in the exacting job of handling correspondence, collecting statistical information, and keeping up with the entire flow of business between the Chief of Staff and his various assistants. In the course of the war this staff was to include a number of top officers, destined to become high-ranking generals, such as Omar N. Bradley, Maxwell D. Taylor, J. Lawton Collins, and Walter Bedell Smith. As the war progressed he brought in younger reserve officers in order that the older men could have a chance at high command. Among them were two sons of the Virginia Military Institute, Frank McCarthy and Merrill Pasco, who remained with him during most of the war.

In taking over, the General saw that some changes would need to be made in the administrative organization in order to handle the growing responsibilities of the Army. He was disturbed by a number of practices, "age old in custom but inappropriate to the war office of a great power," that he saw about him. While still Acting Chief of Staff he had told Gasser, "Gradually and without any publicity and undue stirring up of people, I wish to eliminate such features of the War Department as are a continuation of the old days when the Army was a very small affair." [8] But he moved slowly. For the moment he retained the General and Special Staff sections and the various chiefs of arms and administrative services as they had existed between the two wars; a thorough reorganization would await the shock of Pearl Harbor.

The number of activities calling for the Chief of Staff's personal attention was astounding. In addition to taking part in the unscheduled meetings with the President, members of the Cabinet, the Secretary and Assistant Secretaries of War, the unofficial advisers, such as Harry Hopkins and Bernard Baruch, members of boards and committees that dealt with production, allotments, and economic policy, and officers of his own staff, he sat in regular conferences that helped determine military policy. He was a member of the President's War Council, which included the Secretaries of State, War, and Navy, and the Chief of Naval Operations: a member together with the Undersecretary of State and the Chief of Naval Operations of the Standing Liaison Committee, which dealt mainly with military and political planning for the Western Hemisphere; and a member of the Joint Army-Navy Board, which coordinated policy for all matters requiring joint action of the services.

Inside the War Department, Marshall regularly attended the Secretary of War's conference, made up of the top civilian and military heads of the department, and his own conference with the deputy chiefs of staff and the assistant chiefs of staff for personnel, intelligence, operations, and supply and the head of the War Plans Division. The list of officers with whom he had to deal ran on through chiefs of arms (Infantry, Cavalry, Field Artillery, Coast Artillery), chiefs of services and administrative bureaus, corps area commanders, and commanders of overseas establishments. With the expansion of the air and ground forces, the number of problems requiring Marshall's attention grew alarmingly. By 1941 some sixty officials of the War Department and Army theoretically had access to the Chief of Staff. In the quiet days that Marshall had known as Pershing's aide, when the Chief of Staff could stay abroad from two to six months out of the year without disturbing the even flow of the War Department's work, there had been time for him to give personal attention to minor proposals. But in the months after war began in Europe new responsibilities threatened to overwhelm the Chief of Staff before he could institute drastic reforms. In his first two years as head of the Army, Marshall had to struggle to keep his head above water.

In the midst of all these duties and administrative pressures Marshall managed to make his presence felt. A superb staff officer, he worked best with groups of advisers. He exerted his influence in casual discussions with division heads in initiating new studies or by criticizing their proposals. Seldom expressing a specific opinion in conference with his subordinates, he would shape the discussion by the nature of his questions. Papers brought to his desk started a chain reaction in which he penned comments and pointed queries and made copious revisions. Many of them were sent back with specific directions for further study. The process might go on through several changes until at last he made the proposal or paper his own by barking, "Do it," to a staff member or writing the key words, "Send this out."

Marshall began his work as Acting Chief of Staff in the summer of 1939 by pushing projects already recommended by General Malin Craig, the outgoing Chief of Staff. The first major venture on his own was a modest request for an increase in Army strength after the outbreak of the war in Europe. In mid-September he summarized his proposal for his predecessor: "We are headed to full peace strength of 280,000, and a total increase of 126,000 for the National Guard, with about double the number of pay drills and two rations a month—one for weekend shooting and one for weekend field training." "Unfortunately," he went on, "there is little that can be done regarding munitions which we lack which can be remedied quickly." [9]

In approaching Congress the Chief of Staff and his associates measured their demands, as General Marshall put it, on the basis of "what we might be permitted to do rather than . . . what should be done on the basis of national defense." [10] Having presented his budget for the fiscal year beginning July 1, 1940, shortly before Germany invaded Poland, he now had to go back and ask for an increased appropriation. Marshall was placed in the unhappy position of a college freshman who, after telling his stern father that he could get by on a slightly larger allowance next term, has to return a week later to the irate parent to ask for a much greater increase as well as for funds to pay an oversized bar bill that had unexpectedly come due.

Marshall was questioned sharply on his request when he appeared in November before the House Subcommittee on Appropriations. Representative George W. Johnson, West Virginia Democrat, spoke for many of his colleagues in asking why it was necessary to increase the Army during a period when the Euro-

pean countries were too busy fighting one another to be concerned
with the United States. Marshall flared up when the congressman
warned that the warring countries might regard the sudden defense build-up as an unfriendly act. The Army was not building
up, Marshall said sharply, but trying to catch up to the level that
had been authorized as long ago as 1920. He assured the subcommittee that the War Department had "an earnest desire, a desperate desire, to keep out of trouble, and no one is more sincere in that desire than the Chief of Staff." [11]

The years 1940-41, Marshall said later, were his most difficult
of the war. At the beginning of 1940 he wrote a friend of the
"terrific strain" he and his colleagues felt as they worked practically
on "a wartime basis with all the difficulty and irritating limitations
of peacetime procedure." [12] He was well prepared physically and
mentally for the ordeal ahead. The two warnings of the danger
of overwork he had received before World War I had convinced
him that he must conserve his strength. From sad experience, he
counseled a hard-working officer in 1937 to make "a studied business of relaxing and getting to the office late, taking trips, and
making everybody else work like hell." [13] He drove his staff hard.
"Once in the machine here, it is very difficult to spare anybody,
because I have to work fast and rather ruthlessly," he warned a
friend in 1940.[14] But he came early to work and left his desk cleared
before he left at the end of the day. Not by avoiding work but by
organizing it and his life and adhering to a fairly strict routine did
he keep his health and sanity.

Fellow officers met him as he rode regularly in the morning or
afternoon, or both, near Fort Myer, at first with his stepdaughter
Molly and later alone, determined to keep down the "desk belly"
the doctor had warned him against in the spring of 1939. When
he rode in the morning he returned to Quarters I for a shower,
ate an ample but simple breakfast, took a quick look at several
newspapers (these often included the *New York Times, Washington Post,* and *Christian Science Monitor*), and arrived at the Munitions Building usually by 7:30, ready to start his morning briefings.
Although his dictum that no one had an original thought after
three o'clock was widely quoted in Washington, he seldom finished
his tasks at that early hour. The afternoon stint in the office was
ended by four or five o'clock whenever possible.[15] Members of his

staff were less lucky. They complained that occasionally after his requests for a staff study by the next morning had kept them up most of the night, he looked at their drawn faces and glazed eyes and told them solemnly that they shouldn't work so hard.

On returning to Fort Myer he often started at once for an afternoon ride, using it to think over his problems or to review decisions that faced him. In the summer when he had the chance he would, like many another resident of the sticky Washington area, slip away with his wife to a point near Georgetown, where the two could rent a canoe and drift slowly down the river. Often on long evenings they walked in the quiet of nearby Arlington Cemetery. Although no teetotaler—he liked a weak old-fashioned or a bourbon highball—he made a practice of shunning cocktail parties and holding attendance at formal dinners to a minimum. Customarily he and Mrs. Marshall kept their evenings free; the General found relaxation in casual conversation from which he excluded all mention of office matters. He enjoyed watching a movie, particularly westerns, at the Fort Myer post theater, where they usually arrived just after the lights were lowered, or spending the evening with magazines and books. His reading, as always, was extremely varied. Of the many magazines to which they subscribed, he preferred the *Saturday Evening Post* and *Reader's Digest*. The books ranged from a current western—a preference he shared with Eisenhower —to a new biography or a volume of history.

Long before 1939 Marshall had formed the habit of retiring early. Like many successful executives, he had the faculty of going to sleep quickly and soundly, leaving to the light of day the examination of puzzling problems. In an effort to discourage business calls at night he normally declined to answer the telephone after dinner. All evening messages were relayed to a member of his staff, who decided whether the General should be disturbed—a practice that undoubtedly saved his physical and mental stamina for the following day but made his subordinates unduly reluctant to inform him of critical matters at night.

As the harsh pressure of the war mounted, Marshall gave up many of the personal contacts he once treasured. He had never made close friendships easily; now he seemed more and more distant. Some officers who met him for the first time during the war concluded that he had no confidants. It was not true—old friends such as Philip B. Peyton, Charles D. Herron, and Frank McCoy could attest to that—but the number of long talks with old friends and the chats with younger officers of his staff dwindled as the strain increased. The reserve, aloofness, and austerity that had long been obvious traits of his personality became more intense. One wise officer, still on a "Dear George" basis in private letters, followed the course of avoiding all allusions to personal matters when he called in connection with official business. One day, he recalled, he left without remarking that he and his wife were looking forward to seeing the Marshalls at their home that evening for dinner.

There were exceptions to the rule. Even in the busiest season he found some time for old friends visiting in Washington unless he suspected that they intended to ask for a special favor. Until the war made it impossible to squeeze in casual visitors who arrived unannounced, the door was open to VMI classmates, associates from Fort Leavenworth days, and especially veterans of the 1st Division in the First World War. An orderly or chauffeur who had once worked for General Pershing needed only to mention that fact to gain admittance to the office.

To save time the General used a no-nonsense approach with subordinates that sometimes frightened the uninitiated into tongue-tied confusion. An officer, on being ordered to report at the General's office, was expected to enter at the appointed time, walk uninvited to the chair placed in front of the General's desk, and without speaking or saluting take his seat. The Chief of Staff, absorbed in a document or letter, would finish his reading and quickly raise his head, looking fixedly at the visitor. On that cue the officer was expected to start talking. The General, completely attentive, would lean forward to follow the discussion. Unless the speaker bored him or continued to labor a point Marshall remained silent until the officer had finished. Then with swift verbal jabs he probed for further information. Once he had satisfied his curiosity, he abruptly ended the session and turned to the next item of business.[16]

Unwilling to tolerate windy explanations, he cut in mercilessly on tedious talkers and suffered fools not at all. Capable of great patience in hearing a case, he developed a brusqueness in manner and a sharpness in questioning that sometimes bordered on rudeness. Never completely rid of a violent temper, he managed usually to keep it under the tight control he had developed since World War I, even though he found that "forbearance and self-restraint are very wearing on the individual and probably do more harm than violent exercise." [17] Occasionally, tried beyond his patience, or perhaps to score an effect, he let himself explode. Then, whitefaced and shaking, he burned "the paint off the walls." But hot anger was a rarity. More often, it took an icy form. Those who crossed him learned that freezing as well as blazing wrath could remove the hide.

His insistence on articulateness in his assistants proved unnerving to the clumsy of speech and the unprepared. More than one officer who had chanced going into the chief's office without doing his homework paved the way for quick reassignment by pawing the air as he struggled for words and information to answer the General's questions. His almost brutal emphasis on clear presentations was unduly hard on officers whose powers of expression were unequal to their store of information. Their services were often saved by more coherent colleagues who saw to it that these otherwise capable officers presented their views by memoranda rather than in personal reports. They learned to watch for signs of the chief's displeasure and explained why an officer had not done well. For it was well known that if he concluded an officer was below the mark, it was extremely difficult to eradicate that impression from his mind.

His assistants extended this watchfulness to cases where some misinterpreted comment might prejudice the future chances of a promising officer. In one such instance, someone reported to the General that if Colonel Ray W. Barker, then in London, could get back to the United States he would get his star. Assuming that the colonel had instigated the suggestion, the General muttered, "He won't get his B. G. and he won't go back." An officer who knew the facts of the case risked Marshall's displeasure by insisting that he hear the full explanation of the remark. "I knew," he said afterward, "if I didn't get it straightened out then and correct it in the Chief of Staff's mind, Barker would lose his promotion." The matter was soon properly adjusted, and Barker went on to get not only his first but a second star. But there had been a close shave.[18]

As Marshall entered the Munitions Building each morning he

looked lean and fit. In the civilian clothes that he usually wore
in the days before the Pearl Harbor attack—a holdover from his
duty with Pershing when congressmen had made "acrid comments" about the number of men in uniform they saw around
Washington[19]—he could have passed for a vigorous leader in any
profession. The suggestion of frailness evident at the time of the
1937 operation was disappearing as his knobby face filled out
slightly, softening the two somber lines that ran from nose to
mouth. His eyes, cool and very blue, seemed gentle to those who
knew him best but alarmingly cold and hard to those who stirred
his displeasure. As he strode from his car to his office with head
erect, step quick, he was obviously a man of unconscious and un-
questioned authority. Although often deliberate in his movements,
sparing in his use of gestures, he conveyed a quality of force and
action—and a youthfulness that belied his fifty-nine years and the
gray hairs that had replaced the former flicker of red. Visitors
noted his fine, expressive hands, his direct gaze, his air of command. His voice, normally quiet and soft, changed quickly to a
sharp bark as he corrected a blunder or questioned an ill-advised
proposal. With few exceptions those members of his staff who knew
him best mingled their affection with a touch of awe.

The aura of authority that he had gradually acquired over the
years became pronounced by the end of his first two years as Chief
of Staff. Few people could put their finger on it, but every subordinate and most of his colleagues were impressed by the air of command he exuded. "He made you want to do your best," said one
assistant. Others have recalled that they never really felt that they
had done quite enough since he clearly expected of them their
best—exacting it by patient expectancy rather than by loud demands or poundings of the desk.

Marshall personally never knew how he developed the art of
command. Some of it he had achieved by the time of his second
year at the Virginia Military Institute. Fellow cadets from that
period have recalled his ability to lead and the firm voice that
obviously expected to be obeyed. A mastery of his profession, born
of extremely hard work and dedication rather than striking power
of intellect, impressed all who worked with him. A knowledge of
detail and the ability to bring together from a mass of recommendations an effective plan for action made him a splendid staff

officer. And, especially, there was his formidable self-discipline. In a perceptive appraisal, Kenneth Davis spoke of the self-mastery "which gave to him his rare distinction, causing associates to trust him as they did few men." [20]

There was integrity—a disdain for false speaking and dissembling and an unwillingness to become a pawn of any man. "The thing that stands out in everybody's recollection of General Marshall," Dean Acheson has said, "is the immensity of his integrity, the loftiness and beauty of his character." [21] The General treasured traditional values and a good name and simple virtues and was not embarrassed by possessing them. When he first came to Washington in 1938 newsmen and politicians and soldiers alike saw in him a highly skilled practitioner of his profession. By the end of 1941 they recognized him as one of the few men who made Washington tick and a leader whose aspirations and inner sureness were desperately required by a country in the midst of war.

For all his strength and authority, his appeals to Congress early in 1940 met little success. The sense of urgency that pervaded the country in the first weeks of fighting in Europe relaxed in the late fall and winter of 1939-40 as Hitler regrouped his forces. Congressmen and commentators talked of a "phony" war whose theme song was nothing more martial than "we'll hang out our washing on the Siegfried Line." Members of Marshall's own War Plans Division reflected the changed climate of opinion when they concluded in late December that so long as full-scale fighting continued in Europe and Asia the Western Hemisphere was not in danger.[22]

In Britain and France, where frenzied efforts had been made to prepare against attack from the air, the people recovered their confidence as weeks passed with no threat of immediate action by Hitler. Their chief anger at the end of 1939 was directed, as was America's, against the Soviet Union for invading Finland and reducing the Baltic states to satellite status. To those Americans who had fought to amend the Neutrality Act to permit sales of airplanes and other commodities of war to the western democracies, the British and French seemed unduly slow about placing orders.

Marshall's dominant problem was getting approval of his request for funds to complete the equipping of 227,000 men in the Regular Army and 235,000 in the National Guard, and to provide the critical items of equipment for another 500,000 who would be called to service in an emergency. Anticipating a strong fight in Congress on the 850 million-dollar budget, the Chief of Staff used every opportunity offered to explain the importance of his requests. In a speech to the American Historical Association at the end of December, deploring the failure of schools to teach military history, he grabbed headlines by announcing that the Army was less than 25 per cent ready to fight.[23] In mid-February he warned a radio audience that time was running out for America. Modern warfare, he reiterated, could not be improvised, and there was a time lag of one or two years between the initial order and the delivery of the finished product to the soldier.[24]

Despite these public warnings he proceeded cautiously with both President and Congress. In explaining his budget he carefully avoided challenging the limits set by the White House, making clear that the Army was asking only for the items absolutely necessary to meet existing demands. He advised his staff members in mid-February 1940 to be patient in their approach to Congress, saying that their bills might fare better if left to the last possible date since it was probable "that events in Europe will develop in such a way as to affect congressional action." [25] He recognized that he would need help. "The trouble is," he wrote Douglas S. Freeman, "we have no fat meat that permits of heavy cuts without serious damage, yet the pressure from home is so heavy for economy that the legislators are genuinely embarrassed and they have my sympathy." [26]

On February 23 he begged the members of the House Appropriations Committee to allow the armed forces to proceed "step by step to prepare ourselves against the possibility of chaotic world conditions" in order to deter any nation or group of nations from menacing the Americas. Fixing his eyes on the congressmen who listened attentively to his words, he warned dramatically, "If Europe blazes in the late spring or summer, we must put our house in order before the sparks reach the Western Hemisphere." [27]

While hearings continued on the appropriations bill he flew to Hawaii on a long-delayed inspection tour, spending nine days as the guest of his onetime classmate at Fort Leavenworth, Major General C. D. Herron, commander of the Hawaiian Department. On his return in mid-March he was told that his bill was in trouble.

Not only was the House Committee hostile, but there was growing opposition in the Senate. General Hugh Johnson reported that one member of the Upper House had said that they were going to cut the hell out of the Army's appropriations. In his "thank you" note to Herron, Marshall described the backfire he was trying to build against the Senate action as "really hard work, because I have to see so many people, convince them, provide them with arguments, and then see that the whole scheme of defense dovetails together." [28]

He was not fully successful in his efforts. Europe was not yet ablaze and some members saw only the warning lights of the approaching elections. On April 3 the House Committee cut the budget of the armed forces by almost 10 per cent, striking from Marshall's list an air base at Anchorage, Alaska, and all but 57 planes from a request for 166. Six days later Germany invaded Denmark and Norway.

II

Europe Blazes

THE strange quiet of the phony war was sharply broken. Within hours after the enemy moved, Denmark surrendered and Norway was plunged into an unequal struggle that could end only in defeat. As details of the German attacks poured from clattering teletype machines in Washington pressrooms newsmen recalled Marshall's February prophecy. They found him on Capitol Hill, waiting to testify on a promotions bill before the House Military Affairs Committee. When they stopped him in the corridor near the hearings room to ask if Hitler's offensive was the "blaze" in Europe of which he had so recently warned he fought off a moment of temptation. "I told you so," almost came from his lips, but he stifled the impulse. Remembering where he was he replied politely that "it appeared at the moment" to be what he had in mind. The new fire was of course exactly what he had warned of, and the flimsy defenses of the Western Hemisphere had indeed to be put "in order." His first move was to urge Secretary of War Harry H. Woodring to demand restoration of the military items recently cut from the appropriations bill and the addition of new items to the budget for 1940.

There was no gratifying response, no sudden easing of Marshall's difficulties in getting immediate aid. For his efforts were hindered by the same administrative paralysis that had already crippled the War Department during General Craig's final months as Chief of Staff. Particularly in the early period, when President and Congress hesitated to move as quickly as events in Europe demanded, a scandalous feud between Woodring and Assistant Secretary of War Louis Johnson deprived the department they headed of effective civilian leadership. On Marshall fell the main burden of pleading the Army's case.

The Woodring-Johnson fight, characterized by Secretary of the Interior Harold L. Ickes as a "holy show," grew out of Roosevelt's unfortunate habit of sweeping embarrassing administrative problems under the rug. Woodring had won the President's attention in 1931 by capturing the governorship of Kansas, a rare feat for a Democrat in that midwestern stronghold of Republicanism. On the expiration of Woodring's term, Roosevelt named him Assistant Secretary of War under George H. Dern. In 1933, when the low price of corn in the Middle West and the high unemployment rate throughout the nation constituted Washington's chief concerns, this seemed to be one appointment that could not cause trouble.

By 1936, when the death of Secretary Dern brought Woodring to the post of Acting Secretary, Roosevelt's attention was fixed increasingly on troubles from abroad. He was warned against keeping Woodring, but after the elections—in which the Democrats carried Kansas as they did nearly every other state in the country—the President named him to fill the War Department vacancy. He had talked things over with the new appointee, he explained, and Harry understood that his tenure would be short. Instead Woodring held on tenaciously for nearly four years, giving the President ample time to regret naming as head of the War Department, where his approval and cooperation would be needed to implement plans for aiding Great Britain and France rearm, a man whose views were more isolationist than interventionist.

Roosevelt made confusion certain by selecting the politically powerful Johnson for the post of Assistant Secretary of War. Louis A. Johnson of West Virginia, former national commander of the American Legion and chairman of the National Democratic Advisory Committee—ruthless, energetic, ambitious—strongly disagreed with Woodring's peace views. Determined to have the number one job, he was quoted as saying that he had the President's solemn promise, seven times repeated, for the succession. It seemed only a matter of finding something suitable for Woodring.[1]

When Woodring became especially obstructive the President spoke to friends of several stronger candidates for the job. Washington columnists and White House intimates played a little game of finding something else for the Secretary of War, but it turned out that his eye was fixed on the ambassadorship to London, a post filled just then by the rather formidable figure of Joseph P. Kennedy, a generous contributor to party coffers in the past, whose support would be needed in 1940. A week after the war began in Europe, Secretary Ickes tried to move the President to action by suggesting that everyone in the Cabinet resign, thus allowing Roosevelt to retain only those he wanted to keep. The realist in the White House called it an absurd idea and indicated that he was going to solve the problem by firm action. Ickes retorted that he had proposed it only because he knew that Roosevelt was too "tender-hearted" to use direct methods. He knew his man.[2] The winter passed and spring came and the voice of the turtle was heard but Woodring remained.

With an unwanted pilot at the helm of the War Department the President resorted to the familiar device of bypassing him whenever possible, handing matters of plane production to Johnson and the coordination of airplane sales to Great Britain and France to Secretary of Treasury Henry Morgenthau, Roosevelt's neighbor from New York. Woodring complained to Brigadier General Edwin M. ("Pa") Watson, White House military aide, that Johnson was "running away with the War Department," and there were reports that the Assistant Secretary was planting attacks on his boss in Washington newspaper columns. Still the President took no action, Woodring held on grimly to his post, and the War Department stagnated.[3]

The sorry spectacle of the open fight seriously embarrassed General Marshall in his relations with his two civilian chiefs. As Deputy Chief of Staff he had worked closely with Johnson. He praised his efforts for strengthening the Army and Air Corps and was grateful to him for supporting his candidacy for the Chief of Staff post. But he would not desert the Secretary of War. Marshall told Henry Morgenthau: "Everybody in town is shooting at Woodring and trying to put him on the spot and I don't want to see him get on the spot. Everybody is trying to get him out of there and I am not going to be a party to it."[4] Johnson later reproached the Chief of Staff: "You clouded up on me; I thought you were for me." A stickler for loyalty to civilian and military superiors, Marshall replied, "Listen, Mr. Secretary, I was appointed Chief of Staff and I think you had something to do with it. But Mr. Woodring was Secretary of War and I owed loyalty to him. . . . I can't expect loyalty from the Army if I do not give it." [5] Johnson could not see his argument. But only Marshall's firm refusal to be caught up in the departmental fight and his concentration on the Army's needs helped the War Department escape serious damage in this critical period.

General Marshall felt especially isolated during his first months in office when his chief had no standing at the White House and he himself felt that he lacked Roosevelt's full confidence. The President, Marshall explained later in a characteristic demonstration of his ability to see the other man's point of view, was "accustomed to dealing with many political factors where you have to be so careful and [must] possess such a wide . . . knowledge of the people involved that . . . he rather hesitated about taking me into his confidence. Also I had not been proven. He appointed me without any large war experience, except being with General Pershing in the First World War and for a time chief of operations of an army of about a million men. . . . [So] it was quite a while before he built up confidence in me anything like the extent he apparently had in the last year of the war." [6]

Marshall was conscious too of Roosevelt's preference for the Navy over the Army. As Assistant Secretary of Navy in World War I and as an ardent yachtsman who loved the sea, the President took a personal interest in the development of the fleet. Marshall recognized that there were compensations in that Roosevelt gave him a free hand in naming even theater commanders while intervening actively in the selection of Navy bureau chiefs. But the President never let the Chief of Staff forget on which side of any service argument his sympathies were likely to lie. Marshall once broke up a discussion in which the President was showing his customary lack of impartiality by pleading good-humoredly, "At least, Mr. President, stop speaking of the Army as 'they' and the Navy as 'us.' " [7]

The surprising thing is not that initially the two men held each other at arm's length but that Roosevelt had ever selected Marshall as Chief of Staff. In temperament, methods of work, approach to domestic and international problems, general viewpoints, even forms of relaxation, they differed remarkably. Roosevelt's mercurial nature, flashy intuitiveness, and helter-skelter handling of administrative problems contrasted sharply with Marshall's reserve, careful judgments, and passion for orderliness. Regarding clearly defined channels of authority and tidy organization almost as articles of faith, the Chief of Staff was appalled by Roosevelt's policy of retaining subordinates who quarreled among themselves and who gave only a dubious loyalty to the President himself. The proposition that any administrator—particularly the Chief Executive—should keep in office men he regarded as incompetent merely because he disliked firing them was highly repugnant to one steeped in Army traditions. Not fully understanding at first the political problems faced by the head of a party, General Marshall at times doubted the President's capacity to lead the country in a great emergency. He admitted later that not until after Pearl Harbor, when he saw him act swiftly and decisively, did he conclude that Roosevelt was a great man. "I hadn't thought so before. He wasn't always clearcut in his decisions. He could be swayed." [8]

A soldier who favored quiet and almost solitary forms of recreation, preferring the company of a few friends to large parties, Marshall failed to share Roosevelt's delight in political gatherings, picnics, and poker. He winced at first-name familiarity and was not won to it because it was practiced by the President of the United States. Learning that his air of reserve sometimes cut short some of the persiflage used by Roosevelt to evade ticklish topics, the Chief of Staff carried his stiffness to the point of declining to laugh at the President's jokes. It is doubtful that Roosevelt ever enjoyed Marshall's company. From the General's standpoint the important thing was that the President respect him and accept his advice in military affairs.

"I never haggled with the President," Marshall said later. "I swallowed the little things so that I could go to bat on the big ones. I never handled a matter apologetically and I was never contentious. It took me a long time to get to him. When he thought I was not going for publicity and doing things for publication—he liked it." [9]

Strongly committed to the principle of civilian leadership in the making of national policy, Marshall determined, if at all possible, to follow the President's lead in military matters. Despite his discomfiture at the administration's cautious policy on Army appropriations, Marshall supported it in public while vigorously arguing

his service's needs at White House conferences. Only in those cases
where the President faced trouble in getting the funds for which
he had already asked did the Chief of Staff feel justified in approaching congressional leaders or appealing to the public for support. The General said in later years: "While it would be difficult
at times and [there] would be strong pressures for me to speak to
the public, I thought that it was far more important in the long run
that I be well established as a member of a team and try to do my
convincing within that team than to take action publicly contrary
to the desires of the President and certain members of Congress. . . ." [10]

In attempting to gain full presidential favor Marshall found invaluable the strange friendship he had developed with Roosevelt's
close adviser, Harry Hopkins. Army associates of the Chief of Staff
marveled at his ability to find a common meeting ground with one
so different in public and personal outlook. Reared in a family half
Republican, half Democratic, and educated in an Army that for
more than a generation had avoided participation in politics, Marshall refrained from voting all his life. Basically he was a moderate
conservative on most political issues, ill at ease with extremism of
any kind. As Pershing's aide, he had been impressed by General
Charles Dawes and Bernard Baruch, men who wore different political labels but were capable of working with broad-gauged associates
of either party. In international affairs he had been attracted by
Woodrow Wilson's proposals for a league, and he preferred the
foreign-policy views of Theodore Roosevelt and Henry L. Stimson
to those of Colonel Robert R. McCormick or Senator Robert A.
Taft. He agreed with Franklin Roosevelt's desire to aid the foes of
the Axis but felt that his first concern should be for the Army under his command. Although favorable to any program designed to
prevent waste of human and natural resources, he had strong
doubts about many of the President's domestic reforms. Accustomed to careful handling of his own finances, he disliked schemes
that were poorly administered or purely political. Politicians, civilian or military, who set up projects or who judged issues solely on
the basis of their own profit or advancement repelled him. There
was quite a touch of the stereotyped New England Yankee in Marshall's reserved, orderly habits, his distaste for flamboyance, his personal frugality, and his methodical planning.

Hopkins was unlike the General in many of these characteristics;

he was the totally disorganized man, following no system in his own affairs and no regimen for preserving his meager physical resources. His public life had been a strange mixture of welfare worker and ward politician. With the intent of building him up for the presidential nomination in 1940, Roosevelt had given him the position of Secretary of Commerce despite shocked protests of Democrats and Republicans, some of them Marshall's close friends. To many critics of the President, Hopkins was the evil genius of the administration. But Marshall held no such view. On Christmas Eve, 1941, he wrote Roosevelt's adviser, "You have been a source of confidence and assurance to me ever since our first meeting and conversation in December 1938." One Christmas later he wrote, "Your presence in the White House and with me in England has always been a great reassurance and I pray for the continued improvement in your health, and damn your indiscretions." At the end of 1943, with the final decision to stage the cross-Channel invasion at last made, he thanked Hopkins for his "stalwart and invaluable support" and expressed his admiration "for the gallant and self-sacrificing manner in which you have carried on, under every possible degree of misrepresentation, while rendering one of the most outstanding services of any individual to the country in this emergency." [11]

To Marshall, even as to Roosevelt and Churchill and the members of the Combined Chiefs of Staff, Hopkins was indispensable in the grim days of the war. An honest broker, a necessary catalyst for men of different nationalities and temperaments, the impudent poser of hard questions, the relentless driver in rearmament programs, Churchill's "Lord-Root-of-the-Matter," the gadfly of the Grand Alliance, Hopkins pushed the war effort when at times it seemed that he survived on drugs and will and a flickering vital spark. Marshall, who had known him so worn by exhaustion and refusal to save himself that he literally had to crawl up a stairway he lacked the strength to climb, affectionately chided him from time to time for his failure to care for his health. At the end of 1944, even when he no longer needed Hopkins to plead the cause of his armies at the White House, he begged him to remember his health. "My hope for you personally," he said, "is that for once in your life you will be reasonably prudent and give the Good Lord and nature a chance." [12]

They had first met in late December 1938 when Hopkins, still hopeful that he might build up his candidacy for the Democratic presidential nomination in 1940, had taken Bernard Baruch's advice to study the military situation. But long before Marshall was sworn in as head of the Army, Hopkins' health had given way, and instead of trying for the Presidency he was fighting for his life. Not until May 10, the day Germany invaded the Netherlands and Belgium, did he recover sufficiently to return to his office. For the next three and one-half years he remained there as Roosevelt's closest adviser. A critical physical condition that left him only half alive burned out his ambition for personal advancement, and he looked about for ways to serve the President. Once a pacifist, he became wholly dedicated to the fight against the Axis Powers. It was in this role that he earned the gratitude of the United States and in this role that Marshall came to be his friend.

Marshall had no doubt of Hopkins' effectiveness. In 1957, when Hopkins' standing with many of Marshall's friends was perhaps even lower than it had been during the war, the General spelled out exactly what their relationship had meant: "He was invaluable to me. I didn't see Hopkins very often, because I made it a business not to go to the White House [often]. . . . But whenever I hit a tough knot I couldn't handle . . . I would call him up and he would either arrange a meeting with the President for me or he and I together would see the President. He was always the strong advocate, it seemed to me, of almost everything I proposed, and it required quite a bit of explanation [to make] the President see that the set-up could not be handled [as] he sometimes suggested. And there had to be a firm position taken in these matters. So he was quite invaluable to me and he was very courageous. I couldn't get at the President with the frequency he could, nothing like it, nor could I be as frank nor could I be as understanding. . . . He supported me strongly and he made the technique . . . of the military position . . . plainer to the President than I could possibly have done myself." [13]

A friend in the White House was not enough for Marshall's immediate needs in early April 1940. The power of the purse was vested elsewhere. Having failed to persuade the House of Representatives to restore the recent cuts in the President's requests for the Army, the Chief of Staff asked a friend of long standing to arrange a meeting with key members of the Senate Appropriations

Committee. The man he turned to was Bernard Baruch, whose counsel and friendship had been freely bestowed on Marshall since his service as General Pershing's aide.

Independently wealthy from shrewd speculation in the stock market and careful investment of his gains, Baruch had effectively used his money and the opportunity it gave him to play the role of adviser to those in the seats of power. Marshall had learned that the tall, deaf, white-haired confidant of Presidents had many sound ideas and was equally valuable as a pipeline to centers of influence. He was aware of his friend's egotism and his extreme touchiness if his counsel was being neglected. Unable to drop what he was doing at a moment's notice to go to New York or sit in on a conference in Washington or give proper attention to a lengthy memorandum, the Chief of Staff arranged for some trusted member of his official family to listen carefully to all suggestions and to see that they were brought at once to his attention. It was understood that Baruch was to be kept informed of the Army's needs and flown occasionally to Army exercises and training centers so that he could be informed personally of the current developments. Since he was a close friend of congressional leaders, such as James F. Byrnes, powerful Democratic member of the Senate, it was possible to funnel information through him to White House and legislative circles. It seemed that the time had now come for a more direct approach.

For nearly a year Baruch had pressed President and Congress for larger appropriations. Fearful of Nazi power, he believed that the United States must hasten its defense preparations. When in early April 1940 Baruch asked if he could be of help, the Chief of Staff stressed the importance of putting back into the budget the air base at Anchorage. Marshall forwarded a copy of the argument he was sending the White House, adding that it would be helpful if Baruch would mention it to the President. The New Yorker promised to get busy. "The Army has never gotten its real story over," he said. "Maybe this is the time to do it." Baruch decided to take the matter up with his good friend Jimmy Brynes and shortly afterward reported happily to Marshall that the South Carolina senator was arranging a dinner with several key senators so that Marshall could explain what he wanted. On the evening of April 10 Marshall and Baruch sat down with a dozen or more influential senators, including Alva Adams, powerful Democratic leader **from**

Colorado, who although personally friendly to Marshall still had serious reservations about military preparations. The Chief of Staff wanted particularly to get his vote.[14]

In a session that lasted until two or three o'clock in the morning Marshall was given a chance to state his case. The Chief of Staff suggested that Baruch start off the discussion with a statement of the Army's needs. Suddenly, moved by the strongest emotion his friend had seen him display, Marshall interrupted. "Let me take over, Baruch," he said as he rose to his feet to plead the Army's cause. Eloquently he outlined the situation. At the end he said, "I feel culpable. My job as Chief of Staff is to convince you of our needs and I have utterly failed. I don't know what to do." Adams, who had been carefully following the arguments, laughed as he said, "You came before the committee without even a piece of paper and you got every damned thing you asked for." It was, Baruch wrote afterward, "a turning point in convincing such critics of preparedness as Senator Adams of the urgent need for speeding the rebuilding of our defenses." [15]

In his wide-ranging efforts to restore the items cut from his budget, Marshall also sought the backing of one of the most powerful and influential members of Roosevelt's inner circle. Secretary of the Treasury Morgenthau had worked for months to expedite shipment of planes to Great Britain and France. Interested in the Army's budgetary problems, he invited the Chief of Staff to explain his immediate needs. Feeling that the War Department was making a mistake in "feeding the President little pieces here and little pieces there," he asked Marshall for a balanced proposal for American national defense that they could sell to the President and Congress. On May 11, as news flowed in of Germany's success in its attacks on Holland and Belgium launched the day before, the Chief of Staff outlined his case.[16]

The turmoil of emergency was an effective backdrop for Marshall's presentation. "Just remember it is all new to me," Morgenthau declared as the General began.

The Chief of Staff minced no words. In addition to increases in the Regular Army, sufficient planes to build a modern air force, and plants for the manufacture of ammunition, he wanted reserve equipment and munitions for a Protective Mobilization Plan force, including Regular Army and National Guard troops, that would ultimately total nearly one and one-quarter million men. Additional troops required pay, shelter, rations, clothing, and maintenance; the Air Corps must have planes of all descriptions, trainers, fighters, and bombers, all in short supply; the Regular Army and the forces later to be called would need rifles, field artillery, anti-aircraft guns, and all types of ammunition. The bill, heavy when placed against earlier estimates, ran upward of 650 million dollars.[17]

Appalled by what he had heard, the Secretary said gamely, "I don't scare easily. I am not scared yet." It was an old story to the General, but he confessed, "It makes me dizzy." "It makes me dizzy," Morgenthau replied, "if we don't get it."

Encouraged at this reaction, the General outlined the strategy he hoped to follow on Capitol Hill. It was essential, first of all, to avoid stampeding Congress with the Army's demands. The legislators must distinguish carefully between full mobilization, to be considered sometime in the future, and the vital requirements of the Army. Morgenthau agreed and added that Marshall should make the same point clear to the President. He was also convinced that "only one person [should go] on the Hill and that is General Marshall." If the Chief of Staff went up alone the congressmen would realize that they were receiving a balanced military build-up. "We can't have the Air Corps," warned the Treasury chief, "asking for 400 heavy bombers, as though that were going to solve the whole picture." [18]

The problem, as both the Chief of Staff and the Secretary of Treasury realized, was to convince both President and Congress that something more was needed than the manufacture of additional planes. Eager to expand air production in order to make available more planes for the foreign market, Roosevelt had been inclined to discount Marshall's insistence on the need for pilots and training facilities for the Air Corps and to minimize the need for additional ground elements. Assistant Secretary Johnson, whose special interest was the development of airplane production, tended to favor the President's view.

Thoroughly committed to Marshall's cause, the Secretary of Treasury arranged for a meeting at the White House. On May 13 Morgenthau, Marshall, Budget Director Harold Smith, Secretary Woodring, and Assistant Secretary Johnson sat down with the

President to consider the plight of the Army. Marshall asked for funds to expand the Regular Army to 280,000 by the end of September 1940, and the mobilization with complete modern armament and equipment of 750,000 men with replacements by the end of the following year. The 657-million-dollar appropriation that he requested at once would not buy everything he needed but would pay for the increase in the regular forces and provide all items for the 235,000 men now in the National Guard. It would also supply the critical items needed for the larger combined force when it was called into service.[19]

The White House meeting developed into an incredible performance. Roosevelt was uncertain about the proposals, and the War Department representatives disagreed among themselves. Even Johnson and Marshall differed on some of the suggestions, while Woodring sat apart, lending no help to the Chief of Staff. In a situation where the President wished to postpone or avoid a decision, he followed the practice of dominating the conversation in an effort to prevent the introduction of a subject he did not want to discuss. His approach that morning was to concentrate his fire on his friend Morgenthau.

In a bit of byplay that Marshall at first interpreted as an act put on by the two associates, Roosevelt greeted Morgenthau's defense of the Chief of Staff's proposals with a sort of "smile and sneer." The President said, "I am not asking you. I am telling you." When the Secretary retorted bluntly, "Well, I still think you are wrong," Roosevelt brushed the remark aside with, "Well, you filed your protest." Morgenthau's suggestion that Marshall go up alone to the Capitol got no better reception. "Why do you want to go up on the Hill?" Roosevelt shot back. "Tell them to wait. I am going to have a message. Don't go up and tell them anything." [20]

Marshall had seen Roosevelt in action before, but he was annoyed by this reception. Two days earlier he had seriously discussed with the Secretary of Treasury the best way of getting his program before the President, adding that although Admiral Stark had been going to the White House to discuss his proposals, he personally hesitated to take this step. The Secretary agreed but suggested that in case Marshall ever got a chance to present his views to the President, "Stand right up and tell him what you think and stand right there. There are too few people who do it and he likes it." At the end of what appeared to be a fruitless session, as the President started to wave the conferees out, Morgenthau and Marshall decided to act on that advice. "Mr. President," asked the Secretary, "will you hear General Marshall?" Still in a bantering mood, Roosevelt replied, "I know exactly what he would say. There is no necessity for me to hear him at all." Nettled by the answer, the Chief of Staff strode over to the President's chair and, looking down, demanded with quiet intensity, "Mr. President, may I have three minutes?" In a complete change of mood Roosevelt said graciously, "Of course, General Marshall."

His voice sibilant with frustration, anger, and intense concern, Marshall exceeded his allotted time in pouring forth the Army's critical requirements. More money, better organization of production, effective control of defense developments—these were all set forth before the astonished President, quiet before the force of an unsuspected torrent. The Chief of Staff finished heatedly, "If you don't do something . . . and do it right away, I don't know what is going to happen to this country." [21]

"He stood right up to the President," an impressed Morgenthau wrote in his diary. He thought that Marshall would get 75 per cent of what he asked.[22] Knowing Roosevelt, he assumed that there would be some scaling down of the request. And so there was. The President told Marshall that he could recommend only a 15,000 increase in army manpower at the moment but said confidentially that later he would issue an Executive Order to permit him to add the remaining 38,000 men needed to raise the Army to its authorized strength before the end of July. This would create a deficiency in the Army's appropriations, but he would seek funds to make that up later in the year.[23] Once more, he held back from hitting Congress with the full force of his budget demands.

As Marshall was leaving, Roosevelt asked him to return on the 14th with a detailed list of his requirements. The President's main interest was in increasing plane production, which he now set at the seemingly impossible figure of 50,000 a year, but he listened attentively to the Chief of Staff's insistence that they must also have money to train pilots and to strengthen the ground forces if the Army was to have a balanced program. At last, Roosevelt set down in his slashing penmanship those items that he was willing to request—funds to buy 200 B-17 bombers, an even larger sum for

pilot training, and money to purchase essential supplies for existing units and critical items that would be required later when the
Protective Mobilization Plan force was called up.[24]

Although he had approved the request the President worried
over the reception it would meet on Capitol Hill. "I know you can
get them to accept it; they can't evade it," Marshall urged. He
himself wrote out the first draft of a presidential message to Congress; Roosevelt changed it in language but not in essentials and
sent it to the Capitol two days later. "The developments of the past
few weeks," he declared, "have made it clear to all of our citizens
that the possibility of attack on vital American zones . . .
[makes] it essential that we have the physical, the ready ability to
meet those attacks and to prevent them from reaching their objective." He asked for the sums he had approved earlier in the talk
with Marshall, requests that ran to nearly 900 million dollars in
direct appropriations and 300 million dollars in contract authority. The sum of 250 million dollars had been included for the
Navy, but the greater part of the supplemental request was intended for the Army.[25]

Marshall always spoke of this action afterward as the breaking of
the log jam. In April, he recalled in later years, he had struggled to
get 18 million dollars restored to the budget; in May the President
asked for a billion for defense. It was, of course, only the beginning
of a constant escalation of demands that would still require labori-
ous efforts by Marshall to sell the President and the members of
Congress.

Even in the changed atmosphere Marshall proceeded with caution. In his frequent appearances before the committees of Congress in the next eighteen months he gained ground steadily in the
role of the Army's most persuasive advocate. Drawing on the experience gained as Pershing's aide during the hearings on the National Defense bill of 1920, he impressed congressmen by his frankness, his grasp of bedrock essentials, and his refusal to be drawn
into partisan discussions. He found useful illustrations from his
early experiences and knew the art of easing tension with an anec-
dote. In one of Marshall's first appearances before a congressional
committee the chairman said, "I imagine that you are not accustomed to dealing with members of Congress." The General wryly
explained that as a boy in Pennsylvania he and a friend had

once written their representative for free seeds to plant in their greenhouse. When the packets arrived they opened them in great excitement, but they were amazed to find that their prize packages contained cotton seeds. Respecting the superior wisdom of a legislator in Washington, they planted the contents; to their dismay the plants produced no cotton. Scoring his point, Marshall concluded, "So you see I have been knowing about Congress for a long time." [26]

Accompanied usually by one or more officers who had prepared the preliminary studies for his proposals, he turned to them for detailed information on specific points, retaining for himself the delineation of the principal items, which he presented without reference to notes. In time his technique became so thoroughly polished that some subordinates thought his quiet manner had a studied effect. By lowering his voice to impart a prosaic piece of information, as if it were a secret shared with members of the committee alone, and by reminding them of the accounting history would require of them, he "mesmerized" them. Perhaps his performances were artfully prepared. But his strength with Congress lay not in rehearsed lines or confidential asides but in the assurance he gave legislators that he was telling the truth as he knew it and that he served no party in his recommendations.

General Marshall was greeted cordially when he appeared before the Senate Appropriations Committee in mid-May. Some of the members pointedly reminded him that two weeks earlier, before the attack on France, they had expressed a strong interest in "what ought to be in the bill in order to meet the situation which confronts us." The Chief of Staff had been encouraged by some members of the committee—Carl Hayden, Democrat of Arizona, Millard E. Tydings, Democrat of Maryland, and Henry Cabot Lodge, Republican of Massachusetts. But he recalled other vocal senators, such as Democrat Burton K. Wheeler of Montana and Gerald P. Nye of South Dakota, who spoke for many of their colleagues in opposing large increases in the armed forces. Both to keep within the bounds set by the President and in the hopes of winning some of the former isolationists to his cause, Marshall steered a moderate course. Recalling that he had gone through one war and did not want another, Marshall assured Senator Adams, "I am more of a pacifist than you think." He demonstrated his mild-ness by telling the committee that he would be "embarrassed at the moment by more money for matériel alone." [27]

In mid-June the Chief of Staff was sorely tempted when Senator Tydings pressed him to go beyond the presidential request for troop authorization and ask all that he really wanted from Congress before it met again. The Maryland senator held out the alluring offer of an additional 100,000 men to cover emergencies that might arise while Congress was not in session during the approaching summer or fall recess. The General prudently decided to wait until President and Congress were ready to move.

To later charges that in this period he had asked for too little and moved too slowly toward rearming, Marshall replied, "People have forgotten today what a difficult time we had raising an army, how bitter was the opposition to raising it, how strong was the influence of the Middle West. . . . We had to move cautiously. If I had ignored public opinion, if I had ignored the reaction of Congress, we would literally have gotten nowhere. I had to be very careful, I felt and I still think, not to create the feeling that I, as leader of the military portion of affairs at that time, was trying to force the country into a lot of actions which it opposed. I was trying to get Congress to do it and get the public to do it. Of course," he conceded, "there may have been excessive caution at that time by both the White House and the military. I did everything I could to stir the President's appreciation of the vastly critical military situation which we had to cure. It was not a question of imagination; I had too much imagination around. Members of the staff were terribly concerned, and they spent their time trying to force me to take open action contrary to the administration, which I declined to do. In the end it paid because all through the rest of the war I had the backing of the administration . . . and the backing of the conservative Congress." [28]

The late spring and summer of 1940 were filled for Marshall with appearances before congressional committees, speeches, and trips of inspection. At the end of April he made a trip to Fort Benning, where he picked up a cold, nursed it along at Charleston, where he stopped to speak at a luncheon and inspect General Charles P. Summerall's cadet corps at the Citadel, and then returned to Washington for a short rest before he started testifying. "By the time I got to Washington," he wrote General Stanley D. Embick, "I was pretty well shot, but next morning—yesterday, I spent two hours before the Senate Appropriations Committee, return again this morning, and go before the House Military Affairs Committee Thursday morning. There is not much rest and relaxation about this business. . . ." [29]

He feared that his inspection schedule, involving a trip in June to Alaska, would make impossible his attendance at the approaching wedding of his stepson, Allen Brown.[30] This dilemma was solved by a worsening of the situation in Europe, which made it unwise for him to go outside the country. As a result he was able to get away with Mrs. Marshall and the other members of the family to Chappaqua, Westchester County, New York, for Allen's marriage to Margaret Goodman Shedden on June 22.

The Chief of Staff had always felt especially close to Allen, who was barely in his teens when the General and Mrs. Marshall were married, and he achieved a close father-son relationship with the younger boy that he never reached with Clifton. Marshall showed great interest in Allen's various jobs, gave him advice on proper use of his time, and was delighted when the young man became interested in Madge Shedden and began talking of marriage. Playfully chiding Allen for going away with his scarf on an earlier visit, and for missing their New Year's party, he wrote on January 2, 1940, to wish for him in the coming year "a wife, a home, and a tremendous business success, and a muffler all your own." [31]

By spring Allen was engaged, and plans were being made for a June wedding. The General, who had been concerned for the past two years over the young man's inability to settle on any special line of work, was pleased. He had seen Madge, he wrote, and thought she would be a "splendid stabilizer." [32] He took pleasure in the first letters from the young couple; he wrote Allen in mid-July with proper fatherly pride and paternal candor:

> Your mother has been excited over the reports of your initial experience at housekeeping, and I gather that so far there have been none of the preliminary battles over toothpaste in the bathroom, the shirt on the floor, and other casual gestures common to men, about the house. If you can prevent the superficial irritations from annoying you, the remainder of the adjustments should be very simple of management.[33]

Marshall's trip to New York was a brief personal interlude snatched from a crowded official schedule in a hectic summer. War and fire and plunder and desolation had stalked through western

Europe in May and June. Little more than a quarter-century after the 1940 debacle in Holland, Belgium, and France, the state of shock inflicted by the magnitude of German victory is almost impossible to describe. The shattering in a few confused weeks of the French Army, widely accepted to be the best in Europe, the reduction of the British Army to a virtually unarmed force whose troops were snatched from German vengeance at the beginning of June by the miracle of Dunkerque, and the sudden prospect of enemy occupation of key ports on the Channel and the North Atlantic coasts of France stunned American leaders as they hurriedly revised their military and diplomatic assumptions. Hitler was no longer merely a mad dictator disturbing the quiet of Europe; suddenly the Nazi threat loomed over the Western Hemisphere.

Italy attacked France on June 10. That evening at the University of Virginia, President Roosevelt characterized Mussolini's thrust as a stab in a neighbor's back. But for all his sense of hot outrage and righteous anger he could do little more than bid France be of good cheer and keep a stout heart.

Marshall was depressed by the heavy blows inflicted on Great Britain and France; he was more deeply troubled than ever by the terrible weakness of his own country. The United States at last faced the responsibility it had so long avoided; in its hands now rested the ultimate fate of the Western Powers. He thought of the new order in which he must have a leading part as he drove down to Lexington, Virginia, to address the cadets of his alma mater. It was thirty-nine years after his own VMI graduation, shortly after the close of the War with Spain, which had set the United States on the way to becoming a world power, and nearly twenty-one years since he had ridden down the Champs Elysées in a celebration of the victory American troops had helped the Allies win over a German army. The Great War to save democracy had not finished the job; greater efforts than his country had ever exerted before must be made if the old balance was to be restored.

This day, he told the graduating class, whose members sat with military stiffness, uncomfortable in their tight uniforms, might be "one of the most fearful" in world history. It was an old prophecy, often made in the past to college graduates about to venture on uncertain futures, but the perspiring cadets sensed that these were honest rather than rhetorical passages as the Chief of Staff spoke

hurriedly, rushing to finish his short remarks so that he could hasten back to his desk in Washington. Had he known a few weeks
before what was to come, he would not have agreed to speak. Now
that he was here, he wanted these graduates to have no illusions
about the future. He was especially moved that these young men,
with special military training, would be mobilized early in any call
to arms. No man, he warned them, could foresee the outcome of
the tragic struggle in Europe or assess the eventual effect on the
fortunes of the Americas. "The world we have known may be revo-
lutionized; the peaceful liberty we have accepted so casually may
be a hazard in this ghastly game abroad." [34]

The "ghastly game" haunted him and other Americans as they
watched the death agonies of the Third French Republic. Premier
Paul Reynaud implored Great Britain and the United States to
send troops and weapons to stop the advancing German armies.
With only the men and planes of the Royal Air Force between the
British Isles and almost certain bomber attacks, Churchill refused
to risk them in a futile gesture. With nothing to give, Roosevelt
could only beseech the aggressors to curb their appetites. The British Prime Minister made a gallant effort on June 16, offering at the
last a plan of union between France and Britain. Reynaud saw no
hope in what was clearly an alliance of weakness. In a desperate
effort he reorganized his cabinet, bringing in old Marshal Pétain
and aging General Weygand, ghosts from earlier wars, in the hope
that their prestige, if not their wisdom, might somehow save the
situation. Their proposed solution, favored by Pierre Laval and
Admiral Jean Darlan, lay in a quick armistice to salvage what remained of the French Army and save the country from further
destruction. When Roosevelt and Churchill could offer no clear
alternative, Reynaud handed the government over to Pétain.

Marshal Pétain had won his reputation by standing firm at Ver-
dun and by combining force and understanding to quell the mu-
tiny that had threatened to destroy the French armies after the failure of Nivelle's unsuccessful offensive. Now he had no magic left.
This time he knew only how to sue for terms. After the war he
would be condemned to death for using the presence of Hitler's
armies on French soil as an excuse for ridding the nation not only
of the Communist Manifesto but also of the Declaration of the
Rights of Man. Remembering the Pétain of a brighter hour, the

Chief of Staff was pleased when the sentence was commuted to life imprisonment. Although deeply saddened by the actions of the Marshal's government at Vichy, he remained convinced that the hero of World War I had never ceased to think first of France's salvation.

By late June, France could do no more. Hitler summoned the French emissaries to the same spot where the Germans had been forced to sign the Armistice more than twenty years before. His representative dictated the terms of surrender. The boundaries of German-held France were carefully designed to shut off Vichy from the Atlantic and give the Nazis a corridor through which their troops could conceivably pass through a friendly Spain to North Africa. Among the frightening prospects for the United States were the surrender of the French fleet to Germany, a Nazi drive to a point on the western bulge of Africa nearest the most easterly bulge of Brazil, and German attempts to take over French and Dutch possessions in the New World. Congress, suddenly aware of foreign peril, and the President, fearful of what he saw and nonetheless still resolved not to go too far ahead of public clamor, looked for means to strengthen American defenses. The legendary man in the street saw nothing but trouble ahead. Public-opinion polls indicated that although a majority of those interviewed still opposed involvement in the spreading conflict nearly 50 per cent doubted that the nation could avoid it.

From Great Britain, now alone, facing the might of Hitler, there came a roar of defiance. There the May offensive had forced the resignation of Neville Chamberlain and the formation of a coalition government under Winston Churchill. Foe of appeasement, witty scourge of his own party's timorous leadership, vigorous First Lord of the Admiralty since the early days of the war in Europe, he was the obvious choice to reanimate the British will to win. Master of the challenging word and preacher of positive action, the Prime Minister summoned all democratic nations to his aid. Even those American leaders who shook their heads over his World War I indiscretions and feared his lead in military strategy had their hearts lifted by his eloquence and blazing courage.

Britain's plight enlisted the backing of many outstanding Americans who had already worked effectively to repeal the arms embargo. They now demanded that Congress sweep away all neutrality legislation and give all aid short of war. William Allen White, famed Republican editor of Kansas, a leader in the earlier fight, proposed the formation of a Committee to Defend America by Aiding the Allies. His group attracted a number of interventionists of World War I, who had then fought for the Allied cause under the leadership of Theodore Roosevelt. It also included those liberals who repented of their onetime criticism of the militant preachers and teachers of World War I and now insisted that Fascism was more dangerous to democracy than Kaiserism. Their efforts were strongly countered by the isolationists, who redoubled their attacks on the President and watched the armed forces carefully for any signs of interventionism. The tide was against them, but they battled to the very morning of Pearl Harbor.

The news from Europe was devastating enough to ring down the curtain at last on the Woodring-Johnson "holy show." President Roosevelt finally decided to take action. In the place of Secretary Woodring and Secretary of Navy Charles Edison he selected Republicans who would vigorously support his policies for aiding American friends abroad and, hopefully, strengthen his position in dealing with Congress. On June 22 he named Colonel Frank Knox, Chicago publisher, onetime Rough Rider, and Republican vice-presidential candidate in 1936, to the Navy vacancy. The War Department assignment went to Colonel Henry L. Stimson, friend of Theodore Roosevelt and Elihu Root, Secretary of War under William Howard Taft, Governor General of the Philippines under Calvin Coolidge, and Secretary of State under Herbert Hoover. Their former military service, their impeccable party records, their devotion to public service, combined to make them ideal choices for the key defense posts in the bipartisan cabinet that Roosevelt proposed to form. Republican political leaders, on the eve of a national convention, looked upon the measure as a Rooseveltian trick to steal headlines. Party members assailed the two men for accepting the appointments, and prominent isolationists in the Senate prepared to handle them roughly when they came up for confirmation.

Nor did Marshall escape attack. He was not consulted about the appointment of the chief with whom he would serve the next five years, nor did he expect to be. But that he welcomed the change was so clearly evident that both Woodring and Johnson suspected

him of influencing Roosevelt's decision. On this issue the two opponents found at least one point of agreement. To the open embarrassment of some of his friends, Woodring in 1954 wrote that
Marshall "would sell out his grandmother for personal advantage" [35]; less publicly Johnson accused him of ingratitude and spoke
of his feet of clay. Without reflecting adversely on either man, the
General could only feel a monumental relief at the change. At last
he had an end of open strife in the department and a chief he could
respect and gladly serve.

Stimson was a late-comer among the prospective nominees for
the job—Frank Murphy, William Donovan, and Lewis Douglas
had been among those considered. Normally his age—seventy-two
—would have kept his name out of consideration. But his uncompromising support of aid to Britain and strong advocacy of compulsory military training commended him to old friends such as
Grenville Clark and Justice Felix Frankfurter, who were pushing
the President to speed up American defense preparations. They in
turn convinced Roosevelt that Stimson was the man to choose. The
Chief Executive demurred only on the question of health, and
when that point was satisfactorily settled offered the post to Stimson on June 19. The elder statesman knew thoroughly the drawbacks of the job and chanced them; knew the possible points of
difference with Roosevelt and demanded their settlement before
going further. The President agreed that Stimson could stay clear
of domestic politics and pick his own subordinates. He also knew
and approved of Stimson's intention to ask for compulsory military
training.[36]

Although thirteen years younger than Stimson, Marshall found
much in common with him, and they successfully collaborated for
more than five crucial years. They shared the same fondness for the
Army and the belief that in its strength lay the country's safety;
agreed on the same qualities of leadership; respected the same kind
of fighters and administrators. More important, they had the same
views on duty, loyalty, and integrity. There was a decent regard for
the opinions of others; a code of the gentleman to be observed.
Both resented invasion of their privacy and shunned self-publiciz-
ing. They were men of firm opinions, and occasionally they argued
heatedly when one thought the other had invaded his domain. But
mutual respect, common purpose, and a saving sense of humor

dominated their councils. A photograph of them standing by the door that divided their Munitions Building offices, captioned "The door that was always open," became a symbol of their cooperation.

By choice a lawyer, Stimson made a profession of public service; Marshall had known no other vocation since his commissioning in 1902. For both of them duty was something one performed without advertising it; one did not deny a call to give service to the state. Thus Stimson, although tired and old, delayed accepting Roosevelt's offer only long enough to consult his wife and partners. Ten years later, when nearly as old and equally as weary, Marshall accepted the post of Secretary of Defense as a duty his country had a right to expect.

At seventy-two Stimson had no further rewards to seek and no interest in playing politics. He expected his appointment to be of short duration, at most twelve to eighteen months. His sole interests were in preparing the United States' defenses and helping its friends. He did not propose to wait on Roosevelt's lead or to give him soft answers. Member of a generation that expected the "better element" to give sound advice to newspaper editors and to the rulers of the nation, he had long exercised the prerogative of pointing out sternly the right direction. As a private citizen, he had recently told congressional committees, the President, and *The New York Times* what he thought should be done; as Secretary he could do no less. Marshall saw the flaw as well as the virtue in Stimson's approach. The Secretary of War, ever the lawyer, developed one brief at a time to the point of exhaustion. Roosevelt would stop listening before Stimson had finished. The General tactfully suggested that the Secretary prepare memoranda brief enough for a busy man to read. Stimson accepted the counsel, bombarding Roosevelt with hard-hitting recommendations that could not be ignored.

As a public servant who assumed that one appointed his advisers on the basis of their ability to perform a specific job rather than for their value in past or future campaigns, Stimson was a trial to politicians. Roosevelt and members of Congress knew that the Secretary's resignation on grounds of political interference or disagreement with the President's policy would probably lose more votes for the administration than could be gained by granting some political favor in Army matters that Stimson opposed. He thus became the perfect buffer for the Chief of Staff against congressmen who wanted camps located in their districts or promotions for constituents and a guardian against White House attempts to meddle in purely Army affairs. After the war Marshall said that "keeping the politicians off me" was one of Stimson's great contributions in the war.

Stimson was determined from the outset to establish firmly the position of the Secretary of War and to make clear that he and Marshall were the President's chief advisers on Army matters. He found that the position of the Secretary had deteriorated under Woodring, who had not only lacked the power to appoint his chief assistant but was unable to dismiss a subordinate who actively opposed him. Early in his term of office, therefore, Stimson resolved to make his authority clear. He had been promised before his appointment that Judge Robert P. Patterson would be his chief assistant. Stimson allowed Roosevelt a decent period of time in which to remove Johnson. When the matter dragged on without being settled he insisted that the change be made. Recognizing a new tone in communications from the War Department, the President sent up Patterson's name for confirmation.

The duties of the Secretary of War as chief adviser to the President on military affairs were limited by Roosevelt's Executive Order of July 5, 1939, permitting direct contact between the Chief Executive and the Chief of Staff on matters dealing with "strategy, tactics, and operations." The wording could have created a ticklish situation between the civilian and military chiefs, but Marshall carefully avoided a clash of authority inherent in this divided responsibility. The General went beyond the letter of the law to keep the Secretary informed of the full military picture, by asking his advice and seeing that he approved major changes.

Another of Stimson's great contributions to the War Department was the assembling of a splendid staff. First member to arrive was Judge Patterson, a product of Plattsburg in World War I. The new Assistant Secretary had fought well in France and was proud of having killed a German in combat. Eager to get into action in 1940, he offered to resign from the bench to enlist as a private if given a chance to fight. A determined supporter of the civilian military training program, he was serving a two-week stint as a private in a training camp when he was chosen as Stimson's assistant. In office, Patterson pushed his program as if he were attacking an enemy line, resolved to drive over those who got in his way. When his actions bruised the soldiers' feelings, Marshall intervened.

Once when Patterson persuaded Stimson to sign an order affecting matters under Marshall's control, the General filed the paper. Weeks later, during an argument, when the Secretary observed that his office never interfered with Marshall, the General quietly produced the document. Stimson's temper flared for a moment and he demanded, "Well, what is this? What is it doing there?" Marshall replied, "You were just talking about how you supported me in all these things. It hadn't anything to do with Judge Patterson's responsibility. Yet he takes the initiative and writes this thing and you sign it. . . . So I just put it in the drawer. That's a good place to solve these difficult questions." Stimson barked, "I never saw anything like that." The Chief of Staff retorted, "I never saw anything like that either. But it didn't go any farther than my drawer." "Well," Stimson said, "just give it to me." Determined not to yield, Marshall answered, "Just hold on, I have an Executive Order from the President that I have the matter of organization in my sole control. Now you are going to take this out and start it all over again." The Secretary of War calmly rejoined, "No, I am going to give it to Judge Patterson and tell him to tear it up." With his simple gesture he turned away the General's wrath; his acceptance of Marshall's action helped to demarcate the line of War Department responsibilities.[37]

The trouble shooter of the department, John J. McCloy, came in as a consultant on counterintelligence. Friendly, ebullient, enormously energetic, he gave a bounce to the War Department that it had hitherto lacked. As an attorney who had made his reputation in investigating the Black Tom case, involving German sabotage in World War I, he was an expert on enemy subversive action. Later he was employed on Lend-Lease procurement matters, the relocation of the Japanese on the west coast, and other knotty problems. In April 1941 he became Assistant Secretary of War, taking the place vacated by Patterson, who had been moved up to a new Under Secretary of War post a few months before, and was handed questions dealing with civil affairs, military government, and postwar occupation policy. Marshall depended on him heavily. When asked about his recollections of matters under the Assistant

Secretary's special care, the General would say, "Ask McCloy, I took his recommendation." [38]

For the post of Assistant Secretary of War for Air, Stimson brought in Robert A. Lovett, a Navy flier in World War I who remained devoted to the air service. Son of the former president of the Union Pacific Railroad, Lovett was a successful banker in Wall Street. Quiet, witty, widely read—he could couple quotations from Dorothy Parker and George Santayana in the same paragraph —Lovett brought to policy meetings a calm appraisal and intellectual balance that Marshall highly prized.

Stimson's closest personal assistant was Harvey H. Bundy, one-time Assistant Secretary of State. A man of great tact and discretion, he saved precious hours for the Secretary by listening carefully and patiently to a flood of callers and examining their suggestions and proposals. He was Stimson's special representative to scientists and educators and coordinator of matters pertaining to the atomic bomb.

These advisers provided the Secretary of War with one of the most gifted staffs in Washington. They learned how to work with an elderly man accustomed to his own way, often tired and exasperated by the problems of Washington, unlikely to be at top form in the late afternoon or near the end of long meetings. Well established in their own professions and serving at great financial sacrifices, they were completely at ease. They were prepared to roar back at him when he scolded them and to treat with humorous tolerance his more peremptory orders. He in turn could laugh with delight when they recounted to his wife some of his more impossible performances. It was a congenial office, and the entire war effort benefited as a result.

Although attached to Stimson's office, the four men and their later associates spread their influence throughout the entire War Department. Some of Marshall's military advisers viewed them with suspicion, but at the end Lovett and McCloy were as close to Marshall as to their civilian chief. Less involved with operational matters than the other two assistants, Patterson and Bundy still won the Chief of Staff's admiration and aided him immeasurably in bearing his burdens in the war.

Above all else, it was the relationship with Stimson that Marshall remembered. Despite age and weariness, the Secretary brought authority, public reputation, and independence to his post. He did not have an old man's caution; often he wanted to go faster than Marshall thought the Army was prepared to go. On most issues they were in clear accord. The Secretary's revealing diary is amazingly detailed on Marshall's actions and decisions and almost as full on the Chief of Staff's opinions as on his own deeds and views. The similarities of their characters and convictions and the deep respect they held for each other gave the War Department in the crucial years 1940-45 a degree of close coordination between civil and military chiefs never surpassed in the annals of their country.

III

"The Hungry Table"

THE German sweep through northern France in the spring of 1940 brought General Marshall face to face with his first crucially serious international problem. He was in his sixtieth year, an age when most men are set in their habits of thought and action, and the fall of France in June ripped the orderly pattern he had carefully traced through the decades of his career. His hope of concentrating on purely American defenses was ended; his future thinking now had to be directed beyond the seas.

He must respond to outside pressures now rather than force the issue as world events beyond his control spawned day-to-day crises that had to be dealt with in spasmodic fashion. Looking back, he could see that he had expected the deluge since that September morning in 1939 when he had taken his oath as Chief of Staff. Catching his breath after a hectic day of considering the Army's position in the new state of world affairs, he had dictated his reactions to an old friend he had known at Fort Benning. "I wish above everything else that I could feel that my time was to be occupied in sound development work," he wrote plaintively, "rather than in meeting the emergencies of a great catastrophe." [1]

In spite of pressures from home and abroad he attempted to hold to his ideas of "sound development"—the careful building and training of the Army and Air Corps to meet future demands—while keeping sight of the constantly changing world picture. Agreeing with Roosevelt and his supporters that heroic efforts must be taken to sustain Britain and, later, the Soviet Union, he steered a course between stripping American forces of their "seed corn" and making mere token gifts from their meager stores to keep Hitler's enemies in the fight. Above all, he sought a long-range plan that would determine what American policy should be in case of war and the number of men and the amounts of matériel that would be required to enforce it.

If one period can be singled out as the most significant growing season in a man's life, it was for Marshall the chaotic eighteen months that spanned France's downfall and Pearl Harbor. During the fourteen years between his two tours of duty in Washington he had grown accustomed to thinking in terms of the small Regular Army established by the National Defense Act of 1920. In his busy round of seeking ways to spur the interest of officers who saw little chance for advancement and to make do with severely limited budgets and obsolescent weapons, he had few incentives to think in terms of world problems or possible American collaboration in international conflict. Even in his assignments as Chief of War Plans and Deputy Chief of Staff he had not gone beyond considering how to maintain American neutrality and strengthen hemispheric defense in case of trouble abroad. The fall of France suddenly demanded that he plan and act on a global level. At last empowered to expand the Army, he was forced to measure the critical needs of his own ground and air forces against the desperate requirements of potential Allies in different corners of the world. The long months in which he strove to place arms and munitions where they would best serve the Allied cause left a permanent mark on his thinking. In this forcing house of international chaos he quickly grew in national stature and his mental horizons expanded to embrace the globe. In 1940 and early 1941 he made the great transition from the role of an able soldier intent on making an efficient force of United States troops and fliers to that of a planner and leader charged with considering the problems of armies and strategies other than his own.

The dreadful problem of supply that was to bedevil the leaders of the West for the next three years arose simply from the fact that Britain, France, and the United States had not started soon enough to prepare their great industrial machinery for the tremendous demands of a modern war. France and Britain had made a start after Munich and had placed orders for military planes in the United States early in 1939, but war came before their own factories were in full production and long before the United States was finding its stride. In the tragic days of early June 1940, when the British saved their Army from annihilation in France at the cost of leaving in German hands almost all of its weapons, vehicles, and munitions, there was only one immediate source of supply. Only American reserve stocks saved from an earlier war, and planes and tanks and ammunition on order in United States factories, could arm their home reserves in time to deal with the theatened German invasion in the fall. Britain thus became the first guest at what Winston Churchill aptly called "the hungry table." Before another year had passed, China, Soviet Russia, and countries of Latin America would clamor for a place at the crowded board.

The most troublesome phase of Marshall's supply problem came from the competition between his air force and that of Great Britain, and later Russia, for the fighters and bombers that were beginning to come off American assembly lines. The problem was complicated in the case of the British because funds from Great Britain and France in the form of direct investments or new contracts had given a needed impetus to the growth of the United States aircraft industry at a time when Congress was providing little encouragement for expanding the American Army Air Corps. Significantly, foreign orders at the end of 1939 were ten times as large as the Air Corps' appropriation for new aircraft for that fiscal year. Of the total 630 million dollars' worth of aircraft orders at the end of 1939, approximately 400 million dollars represented foreign purchases.[2] The arrangement at first seemed ideal. Foreign governments supplied funds for the development of new plants and placed orders to foster expansion of those in operation. The War Department encouraged cooperation with British and French purchasers by deferring deliveries on its contracts in their favor.

The scheme worked well until the fall of France. Then, at a time when an aroused nation was prepared to support a greatly expanded Air Corps, the War Department found that the British, who had absorbed the French orders, had contracts for nearly 11,000 planes as opposed to 4500 for the Army and Navy. Moreover the foreign orders were for five times the number of airplanes produced in the United States in 1939. Within a few weeks additional orders pushed the total number of planes to be delivered by April 1942 to 33,500, of which more than 14,000 were scheduled to go to Great Britain. As production rates fell behind expectations, it was the competition of the British for 50 per cent or more of the planes coming off the assembly lines that created a constant nightmare for General Marshall in the last six months of 1940.[3]

The Chief of Staff's difficulties multiplied as his own airmen steadily increased pressure for larger appropriations and an expanded role for the Army Air Corps. Sentiment for a separate air corps was reawakened with the outbreak of war in Europe as strong supporters of air power insisted that the war would be won in the air. General Marshall was uneasily aware that a failure to consider the pressing needs of the Army Air Corps could stimulate the movement for independence. He met the challenge by giving its chief, General Henry H. Arnold, an increasingly important role in War Department planning and by placing airmen in key places on the department staff. But this recognition was no substitute for additional planes and the training of new pilots. It was more than a natural desire to secure aircraft for his own airmen that prompted his efforts to retain for the Army a substantial portion of American airplane production. Early in 1939 he had formulated a policy to cover the handling of foreign orders for munitions. Speaking of French contracts, he had said that no objection would be raised to the placement of such orders "unless our current procurement program would be seriously delayed thereby." It was in accordance with this principle that he later questioned some of the President's efforts to make available to Britain and Russia a large share of American aircraft production.[4]

The first supply crisis came in mid-May 1940. Scarcely a week after he became Prime Minister, Winston Churchill submitted an almost endless want list for ships, planes, anti-aircraft guns, rifles, ammunition, steel, and tools. To furnish a tenth of what he needed would delay even the extremely modest plans for an expansion of the ground and air forces that had been approved by Congress. Listening to Secretary Morgenthau, his strong supporter of a week before, present the British requests, the Chief of Staff was torn between sympathy for Great Britain and the necessity of meeting his own defense obligations.

In a conference at the Treasury on May 22, the General turned to Arnold and asked how much training time his forces would lose if he agreed to turn over to the British 100 planes then held by the Air Corps. The Chief of the Air Corps replied that this number of planes, sufficient to replace aircraft lost by the Royal Air Force in three days, would cost six months of training time. At the moment, Marshall knew, the Air Corps had only 160 pursuit planes for 260 pilots and 52 heavy bombers instead of the 136 it required. He did not see how the planes could be released.

"We have got to consider the psychological effect on both sides of the water," the Chief of Staff had told Morgenthau on May 17. At first he thought it was a simple question of a political matter on this side of the Atlantic and a military one on the other. At a second glance he could see that it was "a military consideration to us that the Allies succeed in stopping this flood."

Marshall continued: "And this whole thing [has] a tragic similarity to the pressure for American men in 1917. They wanted men in their outfits and they didn't want us in the divisions. Their purpose at first was purely business. Later it was something else. We have got to weigh the hazards in this hemisphere of one thing and another. I have taken the risk of not concentrating our talent in the immediately operating squadrons, excepting the more desirable, the symmetrical development of the whole program to avoid setting it back. If I do this, that accentuates the ineffectiveness of the air force. It is a drop in the bucket on the other side and it is a very vital necessity on this side and that is that. Tragic as it is, that is it." [5]

Seemingly he had written off the British requests. But he could not forget Churchill's plight. Although Morgenthau had promised, "There will be no pressure from me," Marshall seemed to feel that he must justify his position. On May 18th he cited the dangers to the Western Hemisphere in arguing that the United States could not submit "to the delay and consequences involved in accommodating the British government in this particular manner." A week later he reminded Morgenthau that American air defenses in Hawaii, Puerto Rico, and Panama were outmoded because of the serious shortage of bombers. If the administration could ignore the Neutrality Acts and unfavorable political reactions, there were some items in Army reserve stocks that might be spared. Even here he saw little encouragement. "The shortage is terrible, and we have no ammunition for anti-aircraft and will not for six months. So if we give them the guns they could not do anything with them. . . . Anti-tank guns, the situation is similar, a shortage. . . . 50-caliber, our situation is the same." [6]

Meanwhile he had his supply officers looking through the musty inventories of the War Department. Left in Army warehouses from World War I were rifles, machine guns, and field pieces of British manufacture that on transfer could be easily put to use by British soldiers. They were obsolescent and therefore capable of being disposed of as surplus. Yet they could be used by American units for training. Marshall asked for a list of what could be made quickly available. In a survey that gave every benefit of the doubt to the British, his supply officers included as surplus 500,000 Enfield rifles, 500 field pieces, 35,000 machine guns, 500 mortars, and a limited amount of ammunition for each weapon. For a country already contemplating the impounding of pikes from local museums for the use of the Home Guards, these weapons would be a godsend. It was these items the British asked for in the dark hours after Dunkerque.[7]

Surplus stocks were available, but the neutrality regulations that Roosevelt had vainly tried to change were still on the books. The question was, "Could they be shipped legally?" Half the Cabinet was soon involved in a search for a formula that would not violate American neutrality laws. After a period of soul-searching in which he weighed the Army's needs against those of Britain, Marshall was caught up in a matter of conscience that would not be completely settled until the passage of the Lend-Lease Act the following year. Acting Attorney General Francis Biddle, Secretary of the Treasury Morgenthau, and Undersecretary of State Sumner Welles all worked with the Chief of Staff in early June to find an acceptable solution. The legal impasse was finally broken; Marshall decided that he could sign a statement certifying the items as surplus Army property that could be sold to American firms. They, in turn, could dispose of them to British representatives on a "cash and carry" basis. By June 24 the arms and munitions, in amounts exceeding the initial estimate, began to move to English ports.[8]

Transfer of American destroyers to Great Britain, arranged later that summer, posed a tougher problem for the Navy. It was less easy for Admiral Stark to certify that his ships were surplus than for General Marshall to authorize sale of Army reserve stocks. In the end the Prime Minister and the President found a means of clothing the transaction in legal dress. Churchill announced that Great Britain was helping to strengthen Western Hemisphere defense by giving the United States bases in Newfoundland and Bermuda and leasing others in the Bahamas, St. Lucia, Trinidad, Antigua, Jamaica, and British Guiana. In turn, Roosevelt said that he was making fifty destroyers available to the British as a means of aiding American defense. The bargain was sealed officially on September 2, 1940.

Through the months of ostensible neutrality Roosevelt called the arms assistance tune, and his service chiefs, believing further diminution of their resources unwise and dangerous, hopped to it with something less than wholehearted enthusiasm. Marshall and Stark appealed to Roosevelt to judge Britain's newest requests solely on the basis of their effect on the United States armed forces. They opposed further releases from their reserve stocks and suggested that private manufacturers decline foreign orders that might interfere with the American arms procurement program. Roosevelt took a broader view. If a little more help would see the British through the year, he argued, it would be worth sacrificing some of the services' basic stocks.

The President had chosen to ignore the main point of their argument. For them it was not an issue of whether the British would fight but if they could survive. One of Marshall's officers put it brutally in a conference in June: the United States could assume that it would have six months to gather its strength after the British were defeated; that the British would count in strategic matters after another six months could not be assumed. Thus the President's desire to aid the British was countered by War Department fears, similar to those Churchill had shown when he withheld RAF squadrons from the Battle for France, that munitions and supplies sent from America's meager reserves would not suffice to save Britain and would leave the country naked. Marshall joined Stark in asking that any future sales be backed by evidence that they would materially aid Britain's survival.

As if anticipating their argument, Congress at the end of June forbade the sale of additional surplus matériel unless the Chief of Naval Operations and the Chief of Staff certified that it was not "essential" for American defense. Marshall was distressed by the provision. He explained to the United States Ambassador to Canada, Jay P. Moffatt, that "had the adjective been 'expedient' he would feel far freer to make such certifications than he does today." It was possible, he contended, but not "provable" that the nation would improve its defensive position by sending additional aid to

Great Britain and Canada. If they were defeated, he warned, "the Army and the administration could never justify to the American people the risk that they had taken." Major Walter Bedell Smith, a man noted for plain speaking, had put the matter more succinctly several weeks earlier: "If we were required to mobilize after having released guns necessary for this mobilization and were found to be short . . . everyone who was a party to the deal might hope to be hanging from a lamp post. . . ." [9]

The supply crisis, unfortunately, did not end there. Crowding Great Britain at the hungry table were the republics of Latin America. Marshall and Stark had invited trouble in the first weeks after the German invasion of the Low Countries by urging the State Department to determine at once which American republics could furnish aid or would accept armed support in case of an emergency. Their idea was sound, but they lacked the munitions to meet the demands of needy neighbors. Short of modern weapons, the means to produce them, and the money to purchase them elsewhere, the Latin-American countries asked for military assistance if they were to share effectively in hemisphere defense. Jefferson Caffery, the Ambassador in Rio de Janeiro, reported bluntly that unless Washington provided such aid the United States could not hope to maintain its position in Brazil.

Seeing nothing but outstretched hands around them, Marshall and Stark in July set strict priorities for supplying arms. They placed at the head of the list those countries whose defense was essential to American security: Brazil and Mexico in the first category; Ecuador, Colombia, and Venezuela in the second; Central America and the islands of the Caribbean area in the third. At the time the priorities were almost meaningless. Often the United States had nothing to sell. When it did, as in the case of some anti-aircraft and coast-defense weapons the Army was authorized to release, the countries to the south had no funds to buy them. For months the most that Marshall could do was to look hopefully to the future. In these lean days he helped create the Joint Advisory Board of American Republics to provide machinery for processing requests for arms. Later he helped win from Congress authorization for the expenditure of 150 million dollars on munitions for these countries. Unfortunately the United States was at war before the funds could be made available.

If the Latin-American countries lacked the means to provide for their own defense, Marshall and Stark had to find ways to help. Hitler presented them with a dilemma in May and June when his conquest of the Low Countries and France raised the question of his possible claim to French and Dutch possessions in Latin America. Admiral Stark provided a measure of protection by acquiring from the British use of facilities in some of their Caribbean bases—some that would figure in later negotiations—for the maintenance of a Western Atlantic patrol. Marshall's staff suggested a protective occupation of European possessions to forestall German attempts to seize control.

These prudent moves, innocent in themselves, were charged with political dynamite. For a decade Roosevelt and Cordell Hull had worked to quiet century-old Latin-American fears of Yankee domination; protective gestures in the Caribbean could easily be interpreted as imperialistic encroachments under a guise of benevolence. In a gesture of reassurance, the State Department inspired the calling of a consultative conference of American states in Cuba in July. Rising to the occasion, the Latin-American representatives approved the Convention of Havana, which gave the United States exactly what it wanted. They preserved the amenities by providing that an inter-American authority would administer any protective occupation required in Latin America, while agreeing that the United States could act on behalf of the signers.

Next to the Caribbean, the most vulnerable spot in South America was Brazil. Marshall had seen firsthand evidence of that country's weakness on his trip south in the spring of 1939. President Getulio Vargas had the unhappy task of defending an area larger than the United States with a virtually outmoded navy, an air force lacking modern planes, and an army of 65,000 poorly equipped men. Most of the troops were concentrated along the southern borders of the country to meet potential threats from large numbers of Italian and German settlers in the southern states of Brazil and in nearby Argentina and Uruguay. As a result the coast north of Rio de Janeiro was almost defenseless.[10]

It was in the north, the Chief of Staff knew, that possible trouble could come from Germany. Across the South Atlantic, some 1600 miles from the Brazilian port of Natal, lay French-held Dakar. A German army, if allowed by Spain to move from Occupied France into West Africa, could find there a point from which troops conceivably could be airlifted in force to the Western Hemisphere.

The Brazilian situation fed alarm with rumors. Suddenly disturbed by the possibility of a German attack, President Roosevelt in late May directed the Armed Services to make immediate plans to move 100,000 troops to Brazil. The lack of men, airlift, and landing fields in that country reduced his order to a futile planning exercise.[11] A year later Europe's rumor market reported that a German force, with Admiral Darlan's blessing, was on the way to Dakar. The Chief of Staff rushed Colonel Matthew Ridgway of his staff to Rio to win Brazil's consent for the dispatch of 10,000 soldiers. Although eager to get Yankee arms and munitions, Brazil wanted no American soldiers on its soil. Despite the rebuff, the War Department continued to study the possibility of moving troops, estimated at 64,000, to northeast Brazil in case of emergency.

Roosevelt's critics later accused him of magnifying the German danger to South America in order to push the American people into war. When Hitler's records were examined in the postwar period they revealed that the threat had indeed been a hollow one. Nevertheless, as late as October 1941 Colonel Ridgway and General Leonard T. Gerow, given the task of preparing plans against possible enemy attack and lacking the hindsight that access to enemy documents later gave, expressed a commonly held War Department view when they warned General Marshall that the German threat to Brazil was still extremely serious.[12]

Elsewhere in the Western Hemisphere the United States moved ahead in 1940-41 to strengthen ties with a neighboring country that was at war with Germany. Because a threat to Canada was a serious threat to his own nation, President Roosevelt had promised that country in October 1938 that the United States would not permit a foreign power to touch its soil. After the outbreak of war in Europe, he renewed his pledge. In the summer of 1940, as Canada stripped her troops of arms to aid embattled British forces across the seas, General Marshall at the President's request scraped the bottom of his reserve barrel for weapons to replenish part of the Canadian stores.

To coordinate American defense efforts, the President and the Prime Minister of Canada met at Ogdensburg, New York, in mid-August 1940, and agreed to establish a Permanent Joint Board on Defense, made up of military and civilian leaders from the two countries. Secretary Stimson thought that the signing of the agreement marked "the turning point of the tide of the war." To General Marshall, who had to implement this and the other defense agreements, the change in the fortunes of the Western Powers could not come until greater production and vastly larger sums of money were made available for the needs of the United States and those American and European nations that depended on the United States for aid. The production to meet these enormous demands could be achieved only by a degree of American commitment to the Allied cause that the country had not yet made.

American public opinion was still months away from accepting all-out intervention on the side of the British. Thus far the mythical man in the street and his representative in Washington, the average congressman, had reacted in spasms of panic at each dark turn of events in Europe, accepting as necessary the shipments of guns that might stave off an immediate disaster. But not yet were they willing to bear the costs of a long-term siege or the risks of possible involvement in war. Until the election of November 1940 secured his return for four more years in the White House, President Roosevelt himself dared not go beyond a policy of improvised aid—piecemeal, uncoordinated, and incomplete.

At the end of the trying summer of 1940, as the United States searched for extra rifles and machine guns to help its desperate friends, Congress took a surprising giant step forward by passing a Selective Service Act and calling into national service the eighteen divisions of the National Guard and the officers and men of the Organized Reserves. To the demands of Great Britain, Canada, and Latin America were now added the heavy new requirements of an expanded American force. General Marshall's satisfaction at the passage of the new legislation was submerged in the task of finding how many more slices he could cut out of a rather smallish pie.

For a variety of reasons the administration had not taken the initiative in proposing the act. Leading the fight for the draft, as he had the drive for Stimson's appointment as Secretary of War, was a remarkable New York lawyer, Grenville Clark. A lifelong sponsor of worthy causes, he gave the same single-minded efforts to military preparedness that other equally sincere men gave to vegetarianism, the single tax, and planned parenthood. He buttonholed generals, congressmen, and like-minded associates, organized dinners, wrote letters to editors, recommended—as in the case of Stimson—the appointment to key positions of men friendly to his cause, and helped draft legislation for presentation to Congress. Father and midwife to numerous brainchildren in the course of a long career, he had helped develop the Plattsburg camp movement in 1915 for training civilians as future officers. In the years that followed he was a leading figure in the Military Training Camps Association, whose supporters included Colonel Stimson, Judge Patterson, and Brigadier General William J. Donovan. He began lobbying for universal military training in the spring of 1940. On seeking the active backing of General Marshall and administration leaders in Congress in May of that year, he was told that the Army was not yet ready to give public support to the proposal. Clark then turned to his own friends in Congress as a means of forcing the hands of the President and the Chief of Staff.

Conscription, the ugly name for selective service, was no stranger to the Army. In the Civil War and World War I it had been resorted to after the volunteer system proved ineffective. Long before the outbreak of war in Europe, War Department planners had devised schemes for raising men again by this method, should it ever prove necessary. But they preferred to creep cautiously toward the issue. Realizing that even in time of war strong opposition had always greeted such legislation, Marshall did not expect the public to welcome the draft in time of peace.

The General was impatient afterward with friends of Clark's who suggested that he opposed the plan. "No one had to tell me how much it was needed—I knew that years before—but the great question was how to get it. It wasn't for me to establish a reputation because I asked for selective service legislation." There were good reasons other than the avoidance of political controversy, he believed, against rushing an overnight expansion of the Army. He was in the process of bringing his five Regular Army divisions up to full strength. He dreaded diluting them with new men or taking from them the instructors he would need for new units. A sharp rise in the size of the Army without corresponding increases for equipment and matériel would mean stripping the National Guard divisions of vehicles and weapons. In this situation his War Department planners continued to finger their draft proposals while recommending an appeal by governors of the states for an increase in volunteers. Thus the initiative for proposing selective service legislation passed to civilian leaders. "I wanted it to come from others," Marshall declared later. "Then I could take the floor and do all the urging that was required. But if I had led off . . . I would have defeated myself before I started, and I was very conscious of that feeling. If I could get civilians of great prominence to take the lead, . . . then I could take up the cudgels and work it out."

"You might say," he continued with a candor that did less than justice to his motives, "that the Army played politics in this period. That is a crude expression. Actually, we had regard for politics. We had regard for the fact that the President did not feel assured he would get the backing of the people generally and in the Middle West particularly and had to move with great caution." Undoubtedly these problems existed, but Clark and some other proponents of the draft movement believed that Marshall and the President underestimated the readiness of the American people to prepare for war.[13]

Unwilling at the outset to sponsor Clark's measure or to pressure the President into supporting it, Marshall limited his assistance to sending three officers to New York to help prepare a bill. (One of them was Major Lewis B. Hershey, who would still be helping to draft men twenty-five years later.) In June, as news from Europe grew worse, the Chief of Staff's support of the bill grew bolder. Prompt passage of the Selective Service bill was included by Marshall and Stark in their memorandum called "Basis for Immediate Decisions Concerning the National Defense," which they discussed with the President on June 24.[14] Meanwhile, without waiting for the President or the War Department to act, Clark had made his own arrangements with friends in Congress. On June 20, shortly before the French armistice went into effect, Senator Edward R. Burke, conservative Democrat from Nebraska, and Representative James W. Wadsworth, Republican of New York, who as a senator had helped frame the National Defense Act of 1920, introduced the Clark-supported measure.

With a civilian-sponsored bill before Congress, General Marshall gladly appeared before the Senate Military Affairs Committee in July to give the War Department's blessing to legislation for the draft and for federalizing the National Guard for at least twelve months.[15] This was the first of a series of visits to Capitol Hill for this purpose in which he strengthened the good relations he had already established in the spring. Although he had excellent legislative liaison officers in Colonel Wade H. Haislip, Colonel R. H. Brennan, and Lieutenant Colonel Wilton ("Slick") Persons, the General was his own best advocate in dealing with Congress. Few of his contributions to the Army were greater than those he rendered in 1940 and 1941 in explaining and selling the nation's defense program as something above party politics and the bickering of inter-service rivalries.

In his first testimony on the draft measure before the House Subcommittee on Appropriations, the Chief of Staff accepted the major provisions of the Burke-Wadsworth bill and asked for funds to arm and equip the men who would be brought into the service on its passage. Though expecting only 1,400,000 men by the following summer, he urged the stockpiling of critical items needed for a force of 2,000,000. His earlier estimates were too low, he admitted, because the War Department had vainly hoped in May for another miracle of the Marne. Now with France under German rule, the United States faced "a tragic shortage of time." It was an hour for plain speaking. He asked for another billion dollars to cover expansion in the coming fiscal year but added bluntly that the money could not buy immediate results. As startled congressmen gasped, he declared that from one and one-half to two years would be required to complete his program and show results.[16]

He repeatedly warned in the weeks that followed against being caught in the predicament of those European countries that had made preparations "too late and too little." Assuming that all his hearers could read the warning proclaimed by the fate of France, he was amazed to find congressmen who doubted that a crisis existed. One representative asked guilelessly if the Army was not asking for more than was needed to meet the current situation. Marshall snapped, "My relief of mind would be tremendous if we just had too much of something besides patriotism and spirit." [17]

In his efforts to smooth out opposition to the Burke-Wadsworth bill the General laid the basis for later trouble by failing to make clear that men called into service might be retained for more than a year. He preferred that the legislation provide for a tour of eighteen months but settled for a twelve-month draft accompanied by a statement that in case Congress declared a national emergency at the end of a year the men might be retained.[18] The fine print of the agreement specified conditions under which selectees and National Guardsmen could be kept on beyond one year; the headlines mentioning twelve months were later cited as evidence of the administration's bad faith.

Marshall returned to Capitol Hill on July 30 to warn members of the Senate Military Affairs Committee that there was "no conceivable way" to secure "the trained, seasoned men in adequate numbers" for the country's defense except by the draft.[19] He was aware that he would meet heated opposition. One senator had already told him baldly that the draft was "one of the most stupid and outrageous things that 'the generals' have ever perpetrated on the Congress." Senator Adams, who in recent weeks had thawed considerably toward the Army's requests, placed his objections on a different basis. Fearing the hazards of financial collapse as much as the dangers of war, he asked for proof that they were not "shoveling out money with undue liberality, following our fears a little too closely." A few days later at a second hearing he asked if it might not be possible to reduce the size of the Army after the current crisis had passed. The Chief of Staff declined to sugarcoat his reply. It was tragic, he agreed, for the nations of the world to expend their wealth on "non-productive war-making purposes," but he saw no alternative if the democratic powers were to heed history's warnings that peace-loving nations were destroyed by neighbors "guided by the policy of force of arms." He doubted if military requirements could ever be reduced to the point they had reached before 1939. He prophesied all too accurately that conditions after the war would "probably never be again as they have been." [20]

The President, intent on his campaign for a third term, remained aloof from the selective service fight in its early stages. The isolationists nevertheless attacked the bill as part of a Roosevelt plan to "fan war hysteria" and promote his re-election.[21] Although opposition from both the left and right was extremely noisy, the measure gained strength across the nation. Public-opinion polls taken during the spring and summer showed a constant upswing in favor of a bill requiring compulsory military service for one year. Less than two weeks before the final vote the percentage of individuals supporting such legislation stood at an astounding 71 per cent of those expressing an opinion on the issue. More astonishing were the views of young people of draft age. The American Youth Conference, once sponsored by Mrs. Roosevelt, claimed to speak for the youth of the nation in opposing conscription. The polls indicated, however, that 65 per cent of males between the ages of sixteen and twenty-four favored one-year service. Mrs. Roosevelt's comment that the American Youth Conference sounded as if "they have done an awful lot of talking and not enough thinking" seemed to have support.[22]

General Marshall was drawn into the controversy in the final stages of the debate by a "colossal boner," as he called it, of the War Department staff. A subordinate officer in the Adjutant General's Office discovered that the current issue of an Army publication, *Recruiting News,* about to be released, contained a message from General Marshall commending recent recruiting efforts. Assuming that the Chief of Staff's optimistic statement on the rise in recent enlistments would hurt the bill's chances of passage, the officer destroyed the page containing the letter. The inevitable leak occurred, and the Army's inept attempt to hide the facts became the subject of an attack on the War Department by Senator Wheeler, who had recently been roughly handled by President Roosevelt and welcomed the opportunity to hit back at the administration. Marshall was rushed into the breach. With the aid of numerous charts and his reputation for candor, he managed to convince a Senate Committee that the current rate of recruiting, although praiseworthy, was not sufficient to fill the Army's demands.[23]

The bill picked up momentum in late July when the President publicly went on record in favor of the draft. A few weeks later the Republican candidate for President, Wendell Willkie, announced his support in his acceptance speech. By mid-August there was little doubt of the bill's passage. The danger lay in the possibility that it would be crippled by amendments. The Senate defeated by only one vote a provision forbidding the use of the National Guard outside the United States, and the House of Representatives adopted Representative Hamilton Fish's proposal to postpone registration of selectees until after the election.

On August 27 Congress authorized calling the National Guard

and the Organized Reserves to federal duty for twelve months. The Burke-Wadsworth bill was delayed for another two weeks as proponents of the measure struggled to substitute the Senate-approved measure for the amended bill passed by the House. The Fish amendment proved so attractive to representatives apprehensive over retaliation from voters upset by the draft that Stimson and Marshall feared that only a compromise measure had a chance to pass. They were relieved when the House finally accepted the Senate version on September 14. Two days later at the White House, as Stimson and Marshall stood watching with the chairmen of the Senate and House Military Affairs Committees, Senator Morris Sheppard and Representative Andrew J. May, President Roosevelt with a grand flourish signed the bill giving the War Department the means of raising an effective Army. Marshall at last was on his way.

Indefatigable opponents of the administration still hoped to make capital of the draft issue. Ignoring the fact that Mr. Willkie had approved the legislation while it was being debated, some of his isolationist supporters continued to denounce it as a war measure. A Democrats-for-Willkie Committee circulated a photograph of the signing ceremony, showing Secretary Stimson and General Marshall standing by solemnly as the President and the Democratic leaders hammed it up with broad smiles. The strongly anti-administration *New York Daily News* was pleased that the War Department leaders realized the seriousness of the situation but disturbed "that anyone should laugh at such a moment, and most of all a President of the United States." [24]

Perhaps an instinct for the politic gesture had saved Marshall and Stimson from clearly expressing their glad relief at the end of the long fight. They did not doubt that prompt passage of the measure was the key to an adequate national defense. As later events proved, it was the Selective Service Act of 1940 and its subsequent modifications that made possible the huge United States Army and Air Force that fought World War II. By making all American males between the ages of twenty-one and forty-five liable for military service, Congress provided a pool of 16,500,000 from which soldiers and airmen could be drawn. Before the war's end the number reached 32,000,000, and the Navy and Marine Corps, unable to get sufficient volunteers for their purposes, also tapped this source of manpower.[25] It permitted General Marshall, as Chief of Staff, to call up enough men, not to exceed 900,000 annually, to bring to war strength nine Regular Army infantry, four armored and two cavalry divisions, and to raise to peacetime strength the eighteen National Guard divisions that were brought in to federal service. Until the limit was removed entirely some months later, the size of the Army was regulated by the size of appropriations rather than by the periodic raising of the ceiling by Congress.[26]

The bill's passage coincided with a stepped-up air assault on London. In September, Hitler, while postponing indefinitely Operation Sea Lion, the projected sea assault on Britain, launched an all-out effort to destroy British resistance from the air. For sixty-nine nights without a break, the bombers of the Luftwaffe swarmed over the British capital. When temporary respite came, it meant only that the attack had shifted to nearby industrial centers. Throughout that dread winter, as friends of England watched the mounting toll in lives and property and wondered how much longer London could "take it," Roosevelt demanded that the Army allocate to Britain a larger share of American plane production.

At a time when Marshall had the heavy responsibility of equipping and training hundreds of thousands of selectees and National Guardsmen and expanding his budding Air Corps, the President's requirements were almost more than he could bear. Stimson, sympathizing with his problems, invited him out to Woodley, his Washington home, for lunch on September 23. Afterward they sat out on the porch of the large rambling house that looked out on Rock Creek Park and quietly explored ways by which they could better regulate the handling of war supplies.

Stimulated by the talk, Marshall dropped into the Secretary's office next day to suggest that a survey be made of all requirements of the War and Navy Departments and the British services, including a statement of what would be required in case of possible emergencies. It was essential, they both agreed, to chart their course carefully "so that we will not make the decisions, these vital decisions, as to what we give or do not give to the British, too haphazard and under the emotion of a single moment." [27]

The need for an orderly plan was evident, but the President's only approach to the problem was to order the Army and Navy to release everything that could be spared to the British at once. On September 27, he summoned his advisers to the White House to urge that B-17s be made available to Churchill. Seeing that Marshall was itching to get into the argument, Stimson let him state the War Department's case. "On the Flying Fortresses, I let him do the talking, and he did it well." When the General said that he had only forty-nine bombers, outside of those in the insular possessions, fit for duty, "the President's head went back as if someone had hit him in the chest." Stimson was pleased at the day's work, believing that the President and the Secretary of the Treasury, who had been present, "finally saw the situation we were in." [28]

Marshall had not ruled out an additional share of bomber production for Great Britain. He in effect offered a horse trade: if the British wanted bombers they must release items they had on order to help the United States meet its own pressing problems. In exchange for 120 engines to be used by the United States in finishing B-17s for current American needs, the Chief of Staff would release six B-24s at once and deliver an additional twenty within the next six months. Stimson showed the memorandum to Morgenthau, saying that this was as far as they could go.

On October 2, the Chief of Staff sent the Secretary of Treasury the War Department's recommendations for untangling the confused state of war supply. In an analysis of the current strategic situation, he explained that the United States might have to defend the Western Hemisphere from a strong threat from abroad within the year. To meet its responsibilities, the Army must have arms and equipment to train large units now.

Unfortunately United States industry did not have the capacity at the moment to supply all of Britain's demands and the most pressing American needs. It could increase its output, Marshall thought, by having more shifts, working more hours, and setting up rigid priorities to eliminate bottlenecks. He also wanted to make adjustments in favor of the Army. Foreign orders that interfered with delivery of airplane engines, ammunition, and fire-control equipment needed by the United States should be strictly rationed, and the export of machine tools should be entirely stopped. These policies he believed should be supervised by a committee consisting of the Secretaries of Treasury, War, and Navy

and a representative of the Council of National Defense. Morgenthau liked the idea and helped set up a committee in which he
joined with Stimson, Knox, and William S. Knudsen, then commissioner of industrial production for the National Defense Advisory Commission, to review American and British requirements.[29]

The next step was to standardize those items to be manufactured
for both countries in the United States. It was agreed that American factories would fill existing contracts for items that were completely British in design but that in the future orders would be
accepted only for items standard for the United States. The Army
also agreed to the placing of orders to equip and maintain ten British divisions with standard United States equipment so long as
these did not interfere with the equipping of the initial Protective
Mobilization Plan force.[30]

The allocation of airplane production remained unsettled. In a
casual statement in September, interpreted as a hint of future policy rather than as a directive, the President mentioned that he
wanted the plane output divided on an "even-Stephen" basis.[31] But
in November, Secretary Morgenthau announced that the President
definitely wanted every other B-17, the Flying Fortress, complete
with all equipment including the bombsight, turned over to the
British as it came from the assembly line. Marshall wearily concluded that all his efforts to explain his problems to the President
and the Secretary of Treasury had been in vain.

Marshall recognized the uselessness of sheer opposition. He
asked General Arnold to investigate the situation thoroughly. "See
if there is anything more we dare do? What will this do in blocking
training of pilots?" Troubled by the effects on British morale of
the continued bombings, he pondered the consequences of the
Royal Air Force's defeat. "If the British collapse there are certain
things of theirs we can seize," he remarked, "but we can't seize
trained pilots. We will be the sole defenders of both the Atlantic
and Pacific. What do we dare do in relation to Britain?" [32]

As pressure was renewed from the White House for release of
the B-17s, Secretary Stimson warned the President of the legal tangle Marshall would face if he allowed the shipment of planes the
British had never placed on order. They had initially distrusted
the B-17 and wanted others instead. Now that they had changed
their minds they found that the bombers had either passed into the

possession of the United States or that the parts in them were Air Corps property. There was no argument on this point; the Department of Justice had ruled flatly that these planes could not be shifted to the British without congressional authorization.[33]

Months of practice had made the President expert in finding loopholes in congressional regulations and Department of Justice interpretations. If transferring B-17s to the British served a good cause, then there must be a lawful way of accomplishing this end. He suggested to the Chief of Staff that the Air Corps send a limited number of the bombers to Britain to be tested under combat conditions. Clearly no better laboratory could at the moment be found. It was a fine point of casuistry, and Marshall had a tough tussle with his conscience before he agreed to approve it. As much to convince himself as to sell the argument to his chief airmen, he told General Arnold and General Brett, "Battle tests will enable us to eliminate errors sooner. Battle tests are better than years of peace tests." [34]

General Marshall clearly recalled this development in 1957: "We turned over fifteen Flying Fortresses, I think it was, to the British for experimental purposes. I was a little ashamed of this because I felt that I was straining at the subject in order to get around the resolution of Congress. Actually when we got into it and did it, it soon became apparent that the important thing was exactly that—to let them have planes for experimental purposes. And we should have done it much earlier. Because we found difficulties with the planes the Air Corps had not perceived at all and they could hardly be used. . . . There were things of a similar nature . . . which involved me in the difficult business of deciding whether a certain thing should be done for the British or not—deciding with or against the President—and Mr. Stimson would become very much worried—he was intensely desirous of assisting the British and he would speak to me as a man of high honor, trying to find some way for me to do these things. . . . It was a very peculiar situation when the Chief of Staff of the Army can turn down the President and the Secretary of War—to my mind wholly unconstitutional. Nevertheless it had to be carried out until it was proved unconstitutional and I felt it incumbent on me to be extremely exacting in observing it. Because I thought in that way we would get an earlier repeal of the law which we did."

"The matter of the Flying Fortresses was very illuminating to me—that we could be so far off center on the matter and not realize it at all. We got into somewhat a similar thing on the question of tanks. Our tanks were easily the most mobile, the most perfectly controlled of all the tanks. But they were deficient, very decidedly, in their fighting qualities, in the arrangement of the tank so they could be fought with efficiency. So we had the British disapproving our model, and ourselves being very contemptuous of theirs. When the issue was: the British had it right on the fighting part and we had it right on the mobility of the tank, and not until I got a prominent, informed Britisher in my office and told him, 'Now just what, confidentially between you and me, . . . is wrong about the tank affair'—and he told me what they saw and I looked into it and found out about our side of it and that we were both wrong. Then it was comparatively easy to get the matter adjusted—doing it all behind the scenes.

"Well that was the case in so many things. We just didn't understand them and they certainly didn't understand us. And they had information as to the battle efficiency of things that we just refused to accept. And yet we were without experience in the matter. We did have experience in the mobility of tanks because we could do that without a battle, but in the fighting of the tank we had that quite wrong. So I tried to follow a scheme, very confidentially, of getting certain Britishers to give me their side behind the scenes." [35]

Having shown his willingness to stretch a point by sending bombers to Britain "for experimental purposes," Marshall felt entitled to press his case for saving enough aircraft from current production to train American pilots. He attacked the President with considerable boldness in an interview at the White House in late November, asking him to clarify his earlier proposal of "even-Stephen" division of bombers with the British, an arrangement that seemed, he went on to say, "to be based on a political speech." Exhibiting a chart showing that only a third of the tactical planes planned for the current month had been manufactured, he asked if the British were to have 50 per cent of the number produced or 50 per cent of those promised. Either believing that he was being ribbed or conscious that he was being scolded, Roosevelt retorted, "Don't let me see that chart again." [36]

There was no easy solution of the problem. Marshall continued to show his charts to others. In mid-December, while discussing what could be done to aid China with representatives of the State and Navy Departments, he disclosed that out of the November production the Army had received almost nothing as against 400 planes exported to foreign purchasers. Secretary Stimson added sadly that unfortunately it would be impossible to get sufficient planes to fill British needs until the following fall, too late to have an effect on the expected crisis of the spring and summer. "Everybody wanted to get planes from us and the bone was dry. They couldn't get them." [37]

Stimson advocated a cure more radical than Marshall wanted. The Secretary of War attempted to drive home to his associates "that the U.S. was up against wartime measures if it was going to try to save Great Britain."

The Secretary's way was not the President's way, and there would be no outright war for another year. Meanwhile Marshall continued to save as much of the American share of current arms production for the Army as he could while making maximum concessions to the British. His task was indirectly made easier in the coming weeks by the President's measures to help finance Britain's purchases in the United States.

Lord Lothian, British Ambassador to the United States, created a sensation, on returning from a trip to London in late November, by making public what was already an open secret at his press conference. His country, he announced, was rapidly coming to the end of its financial resources. Secretary Morgenthau, busily seeking ways to provide merchant ships and essential ordnance items for the British, whirled quickly to the vexing problem of financing the sales. A sympathetic President suggested to him that the government build additional plant facilities to manufacture what the British needed and then sell the matériel to Great Britain. Roosevelt left for a two-week vacation at sea, leaving members of his official family to find ways to implement his proposal.

Thus far in its dealing with the British, the administration had managed to avoid the tangled thicket on Capitol Hill. The time had now come when congressional approval had to be obtained. At Secretary Morgenthau's luncheon meeting on December 3 with administration advisers, Secretary Stimson accepted gladly the

President's proposal to build new facilities and place orders for munitions to be sent to Great Britain. But he informed his listeners that the War Department could not act without authority from Congress. As other colleagues around the table expressed agreement, Morgenthau replied, "You can't get an argument out of me about not going to Congress." Knowing the searching questions they would be asked, he proposed that they review the military situation before going to the Capitol.[38] Marshall, sitting quietly by up to now, was invited to take the floor.

He had already been studying British ordnance requirements. "We have just finished a first estimate on availabilities and types and have gone back into . . . just what time elements are . . . as related to our situation." He considered foreign orders "useful to us because they carry us beyond the two-million-man point in production of critical material . . . [to] around three million men, I think, something we would probably have to do anyway." [39]

At a second meeting of military and political advisers the following week Treasury representatives announced that British orders would total at least 5 billion dollars, a sum far beyond their ability to pay. If Britain should be defeated, they asked, would the orders help the U. S. Army? Marshall again said yes. The recent standardization agreements reached by the United States with Great Britain had greatly simplified production. The United States would benefit from new plant capacity created by the orders; if Great Britain had to drop out of the fight the additional weapons and munitions thus provided would be indispensable for American defense.

Marshall's vigorous support of increased British purchases puzzled some members of his staff who had seen him wrestling for months with foreign demands on his meager reserves. Secretary Morgenthau, delighted at his backing, apparently considered that he had made a recent convert to the British cause. Marshall's position in fact had remained consistent. He had firmly opposed an unequal division of his stocks of weapons and munitions with the British; he welcomed a carefully planned program calculated to increase the productive capacity of American industry. With that understanding he threw his full weight into the fight for a plan to supply Great Britain with the means to survive.

The issue before the President when he returned from the Caribbean in mid-December was sharp and clear: how far was he prepared to commit the United States to Britain's cause? It was no longer possible to cover aid to Britain by talk of West Atlantic patrolling or sale of surplus stocks. Yet he remained hesitant to make a decision. With one eye on public opinion and the other on British importunities, he called for increased aid but stopped short of the firm commitment that the interventionists demanded. On December 17, he outlined for reporters his concept of lending or leasing American equipment to a neighbor in great distress. In his "Arsenal of Democracy" speech near the month's end, he identified American interests more closely with those of Britain, arguing that if the United States permitted the British to be defeated it would have to fight the Axis alone. But he still drew back from the logical next step. Vigorously denying the "deliberate untruth" that he planned to send troops to Europe, he insisted that the nation would restrict its action to sending guns, ships, and planes for the British to employ.[40]

The House of Representatives passed the Lend-Lease measure by a vote of 260 to 165 on February 8, 1941. In the Senate, where a number of restrictive amendments were introduced to insure strict congressional supervision of the assistance program, the debate dragged on for another month. Battling to keep the bill's original provisions, Stimson arranged a special meeting between interested members of the Cabinet and three Senate leaders, Alben W. Barkley, Majority leader of the Senate, Walter F. George, chairman of the Senate Committee on Foreign Relations, and the General's old friend, Jimmy Byrnes, one of the floor managers of the bill and sponsor of one of the amendments opposed by the administration. At Stimson's suggestion, Marshall dropped in at the meeting after it was well under way. At the psychological moment the Secretary of War called on him to present the Army's view of the bill. Marshall impressed Barkley and George by his incisive analysis of the situation in a "ripping speech," according to Stimson, "showing what we gained and stood to gain." [41] Perhaps the General shored up their determination to push the administration bill or furnished them effective ammunition to combat the restrictive proposals. The record shows only that a version acceptable to the administration was adopted. The bill was passed on March 11 and signed by the President the same day. A few hours later Roosevelt asked Congress for 7 billion dollars to finance the Lend-Lease program.

For the British the legislation meant a glimpse of final victory. For the military leaders of the United States it meant that the armed services were able to proceed in an orderly manner with military procurement. The contracts were now placed and payments made by the United States. Weapons and munitions were then allotted in accordance with agreements worked out by representatives of the countries concerned. Marshall had the satisfaction of feeling that future orders for weapons and equipment would be carefully coordinated and the expansion of industrial production carefully planned.

On the significance of Lend-Lease and its workings, General Marshall commented in 1957: "I think the passage of the Lend-Lease Act plainly declared our relations with Great Britain and our friendship with them. It didn't necessarily indicate we were going to war with them, but it made it a probability rather than a possibility. I don't know what the result would have been if we had not had Lend-Lease. I think it would have been exceedingly difficult for the British [to survive], maybe not as difficult for the Russians. Though they were seriously lacking in many, many things." [42]

Before the new system could be put into effective operation, Fate, or Hitler, for the two could be considered synonymous at the moment, upset all the careful calculations with a totally unexpected stroke. Three months after the Lend-Lease Act went into effect his armies invaded the Soviet Union.

The Führer's bold gamble changed the direction of the war and forced another importunate guest to approach the hungry table. It also ended the threat of an immediate assault across the Channel or South Atlantic and provided an opportunity for Great Britain to bolster its defenses. British and American leaders who detested the Soviet Union now began to look more tolerantly at the Russians. Winston Churchill, no friend of tsars or commissars, told his colleagues that if the Devil himself fought against Hitler he would manage to say a good word for him in the House of Commons.

Eager to use any diversion that might liberate Europe from Nazi control, the President announced that Soviet funds in the United States would be unfrozen and that the neutrality laws would not be invoked against Russia. He disagreed with those Americans who believed that the Germans and Russians should be allowed to destroy each other, and he saw no reason to worry over "any possibility of Russian domination" for the future.[43] At Russia's call for arms and supplies at the end of June, Roosevelt directed Marshall and Stark to rush as much assistance as possible to the Soviet Union by October 1. If the Russians could be kept in the war until late fall there was a chance of tying up large numbers of Germans throughout the winter so that the West would have its first breathing spell in a year.

Marshall's intelligence experts held out little hope for the Russians. The poor showing of their troops in the early phases of the Russo-Finnish War made them downgrade Soviet fighting ability. It seemed inevitable that the Axis would add one more victory to its recent lightning successes in the Balkans, Crete, and Libya. Few American or British observers believed it possible for the Russians to survive the winter. Indeed, six weeks was looked upon as a sufficient interval for the Germans to complete their conquest.

General Marshall was more cautious in his forecast. He may have recalled that other conquerors had been swallowed by the vastness of Russia. Soviet survival, he predicted, depended on whether the Red commanders "were wise enough to withdraw and save their army, abandoning their people, if necessary, and whether they have arranged in an efficient manner for sabotage of oil production." His prediction was prophetic: it was the skillful use of strategic withdrawal and scorched-earth tactics that saved the Red armies from defeat.[44]

The President laid the Russian requirements for arms and planes, running to nearly 2 billion dollars, before his Cabinet in mid-July. He asked the War and Navy Departments to furnish him, in twenty-four hours, lists of those items that could be shipped by the first of October. Since the Soviet wanted planes at once, these would have to come from aircraft allocated to the United States or in the hands of the British. Marshall received the request as he was drawing up plans for maneuvers in Louisiana. Determined to continue his training program, he tried to persuade the President to moderate his demands by playing on his concern with public opinion. Marshall did not think the public would be indifferent to the news of plane shortages in the Air Corps. "Can the President survive the political attacks which will come if we undertake maneuvers this fall without airplanes?" he asked.[45]

The President was unworried. Elated over possibilities rising from the dramatic shift in the conflict in Europe, he ordered everything available into the battle. The daily bulletins proclaiming new German advances made him impatient at the Army's slowness in filling Russian requests, and he suspected that the Red forces were being given a "runaround." He "pranced in" during the cabinet meeting of August 1 and laid into Stimson for the War Department's failure to help the Soviet Union.[46] The Secretary of War was not only simmering over the new demands on the Army, he was thoroughly disgusted with Russian Ambassador Oumansky, whom he considered "nothing but a crook" and "a slick, clever little beast," who differed greatly from the two generals, "two honest and straightforward Russian peasants," who had come to arrange for shipments. Fretting about Marshall's harassment over the Air Corps needs, the Secretary of War wrote irately in his diary of those who were "just hellbent to satisfy a passing impulse or emotion to help out some other nation that is fighting on our side" and had "no responsibility over whether or not our own army and our own forces are going to be left unarmed or not." [47]

Stimson and Marshall were particularly disgruntled because the Russians insisted that the only available planes, then in crates in Britain, be shipped back to the United States and then reshipped to Vladivostok. Stung by the President's insistence that they stop stalling, Marshall arranged for a token flight from Fairbanks in Alaska. Stimson indicated that the Army would send pilots to train the Russians who were to fly the aircraft across the narrow strip of water between Alaska and the Russian mainland, "and then God bless 'em down Siberia as far as they could get them." Before they could try this plan the Soviet representatives changed their minds and agreed that the British could ship the planes via Archangel.[48]

The President soon stepped up his demands. The Office of Emergency Management, then handling Lend-Lease shipments, notified the War Department in October that the President wanted that month's deliveries to Russia to take precedence over all other shipments of defense materials. Intent on having mechanics sent to provide maintenance for war equipment, he ordered that Army personnel be provided if no civilians could be found for the jobs. To keep the record straight, General Marshall asked Stimson if he was expected to order soldiers to go or to ask for volunteers. Second, he inquired, "what is the political repercussion at the present time, and what would it be if they were lost to us, as very easily can be the case? And what will be the repercussion if we order them, and they themselves wish to avoid such detail?" Stimson wisely settled this issue by deciding that they must seek volunteers.[49]

For all his questioning, Marshall carefully avoided a negative approach to Russian aid. Although irritated with Oumansky and concerned over this new drain on his resources at a critical time in his own defense preparations, he managed always to find something he could send. Stimson pointedly reminded Roosevelt in September of "Marshall's courageous and generous attitudes" in supplying bombers and war matériel to the Soviet Union. He was delighted when the President said that he had only praise for the War Department's recent efforts.[50]

This agreeable state of mutual satisfaction was short. In early November the Soviet Union was brought fully under the Lend-Lease program and was promised at least a billion dollars' worth of aid within the year. The President gave Harry Hopkins the job of speeding up Lend-Lease shipments. As the Russian Ambassador, backed by the White House, increased his demands, General Marshall had reason to recall his earlier statement that "Mr. Oumansky will take everything we own if we submit to his criticism." [51] The pressure increased as the Germans drove to the gates of Moscow in late November; Roosevelt's constant plea to Hopkins was "Hurry, hurry, hurry." [52]

"Hopkins had power in representing the Russians," Marshall later recalled. "His power could always override mine because of his closeness to the President. Fortunately we were good friends or we would have had open battle down the line." On another occasion he added: "Hopkins' job with the President was to represent the Russian interest. My job was to represent the American interest and I was opposed to any, what I called, undue generosity which might endanger our security. I thought we gave too much at times and Hopkins thought we gave too little, which would always be the case. I thought the administration dealt very generously with the Russian complaints. The Russians demanded everything, criticized everybody. The point was they were fighting and they were fighting hard. And we needed their fighting to keep the enemy engaged as much as possible. But their complaints were continuous and always have been. No matter how much you gave them, they didn't hesitate at all to complain bitterly about the whole thing." [53]

Hopkins exerted his influence in selecting Colonel Philip R. Faymonville, gifted Russian-speaking expert, as Lend-Lease representative in Moscow over strong State and War Department objections. General Marshall regarded him as being unduly favorable to Russian demands. He added that the Army had experienced great difficulty recently in controlling the colonel while he was serving as a guide to the Russian group in the United States. "He was quite oblivious to instructions and almost defiant of regulations." Recognizing that Hopkins wanted someone who would have the confidence of the Russians, he did not press the arguments against sending the officer and indicated that if he went he should have general officer's rank. [54]

As one of the few Americans who had predicted that the Russians would not be beaten, at a time when the Army intelligence experts and the United States military attaché in Moscow believed that the end of Russian resistance was not far away, Faymonville was in a strong position with Roosevelt and Hopkins. Despite strong opposition to him in Army circles, he became the United States Lend-Lease representative and was at once promoted to Brigadier General.

Marshall must have realized that in the extremely difficult days of 1941 the President suspected that, without the active intervention of the White House and Hopkins and Morgenthau, the Army in its preoccupation with its own problems would have sold Britain short and left the Russians to the tender mercies of the Wehrmacht. Roosevelt's constant demands that more be done, even at the price of taking essential weapons and equipment from the Army for enterprises that often seemed hopeless, undoubtedly created confusion and delays in General Marshall's program, but they encouraged America's future allies to stay in the fight. The General recognized that the Army's extreme pessimism on the staying power of the British and the Russians weakened its arguments with the President. He admitted later that the British were quite right and the Americans wrong in their views on the feasibility of holding the Middle East. He conceded that they took a terrible gamble, but they were right.

The administration's insistence on rushing aid to Russia and Great Britain regardless of its effect on the Army's development bred War Department suspicions that the President had no major role for the ground forces in his future plans. General Marshall was alarmed in late September when Walter Lippmann, in his widely read column, suggested that "All popular doubts, political confusions, all ambiguity would be removed by a clear decision to shrink the Army and concentrate our major effort upon the Navy, the air force and lend-lease." In "The Case for a Smaller Army," the writer explained that the program of a large army was born out of the dangers of encirclement that threatened the United States in the summer of 1940 when it seemed that Britain might fall and the Navy would be unable to carry the burden of defending the country by itself. This danger had passed. "Today," he argued, "the effort to raise such a large army so quickly is not merely unnecessary but undesirable. It interferes with our Lend-Lease and naval policy, obscures the nation's understanding of American national policy. It is, in fact, the basic cause of most of the discontent which exists in the Army and spreads its infection beyond the camps." He believed that the "complex of circumstances" that centered on "the great expansion of the Army" had become "the cancer which obstructs national unity, causes discontent which subversive elements exploit, and weakens the primary measures of our defense, which are the lend-lease program and the naval policy. I think that a surgical operation is indicated—an operation to shrink the Army which will at the same time increase its efficiency." [55]

Lippmann's punditry, reflecting views then current of "the Navy, the Lend-Lease authorities, the British, and even the anti-French agents then in Washington," apparently stirred the President near the end of September to invite Marshall to the White House to discuss the possibility of cutting the size of the Army.[56]

Speaking of this period later, General Marshall declared: "The opposition to a large army was very widespread and there was a feeling that such an army was possibly no longer needed and therefore the other proposals from the Navy and the Air demanded first action. . . . Everybody was fighting for something. Each service wanted to get an increase—each service wanted more money—and we had the regrettable state of one service working against another. The British, for example, were very intense in their efforts to get more metal, to get more tanks from us, to get more weapons from us—and they opposed a lot of our proposals—particularly my proposals. So we had the peculiar situation of the British and the Navy, . . . [and] to a certain extent the Air, working together to prevent the ground forces from being organized. I was very conscious of this and it required a good deal of self-restraint not to become unduly irritated by the business.

"All of it had a background, of course, of public misunderstanding. The airplane is very photogenic, the Navy is very photogenic. . . . It was not at all dramatic to ask for the force we needed in the ground army which was going to be compellingly needed once the real fighting started. . . . We had to have infantry divisions and the call from our commanders was for infantry divisions. . . . [In time] it became evident if you wanted to get an air base, you used the ground troops. If you wanted to hold an air base, you used these ground troops. And without them, you were in a sense impotent.

"So the fight . . . [in the fall of 1941] . . . was conducted without any real understanding of the question by the columnists, by the various writers, and certainly not by the public. They all played to the dramatics of the thing—which was the budding air force. Of course we had to have an air force. But if we didn't have an army—and a ground army—we didn't have anything. Therefore the fight was to maintain a ground army. And all the advice and pressure that we were getting was against a ground army. . . . I notified the British—their representatives—confidentially once or twice—that if they didn't stop this business I would have to come out and pillory them publicly. But that was about the last thing I wanted to do because it would be so much to the advantage of the Germans and so much to the harm of the international Allied accord.

"This was a very serious affair and it remained serious until the real fighting began and the people's understanding of the situation grew to a proper appreciation of what was needed in a balanced force. We used too many general terms like that in discussing these matters. 'A balanced force'—well, that didn't mean anything to the average man—it meant little to a congressman—and it was not at all convincing. You had to find some other way to explain it. I found these difficulties in dealing with the President. All his advice was coming in from the Navy [which] needed the steel and material of that nature—and needed men too—and he was personally, intimately, of course, familiar with the Navy and naturally very responsive to its requests or, I might better say, demands. The Air people had plentiful backing from outside. We had certain columnists who could tell you exactly what to do and how to do it—with regard to air. There were a great many phases of the matter they did not touch on; as a matter of fact they did not understand at all. So I regarded this period as very serious and very difficult to handle. . . ." [57]

In retrospect the idea that anyone in authority in Washington two months before Pearl Harbor would have suggested a sharp reduction in the Army seems absurd. Marshall seems to have credited it because of the President's repeated assurances that American contributions would be in arms and not in men. In asking his staff for studies to present at the White House, the Chief of Staff called for strong arguments against slashing the Army, cutting its allocations of material, or reducing the overseas garrisons. On the positive side he wanted additional studies to show the need of filling vacancies in existing units and of creating larger forces for possible action against the Axis.

In the welter of material he carried with him to the White House one of the most important documents was a memorandum by Assistant Secretaries McCloy and Lovett. They argued vigorously that reduction in the size of the Army would be disastrous in view of Russia's desperate situation, Japan's aggressiveness, and Germany's current preparations for an offensive in the Middle East. Such a step would be looked upon abroad as an attempt to limit the American commitment. "Abandonment of maximum effort in any form would be considered a step toward appeasement, for a negotiated peace is at the root of the Lippmann article—not a complete victory." [58]

Afterward Marshall was never sure whether he had been needlessly apprehensive or if the President had changed his mind with characteristic abruptness. When the General appeared at the

White House fully armed for battle, Roosevelt denied that he had ever considered any reduction of the Army. He ended by suggesting that an increase in the strength of garrisons at some of the overseas bases might be necessary.

The War Department settled for the President's disclaimer. Believing the moment ideal to explain the Army's importance to the nation's defense, Stimson made that the theme of his next press conference. Well briefed by Marshall, the Secretary on October 1 roundly denied the current rumors. To a newsman who asked if the size of the present ground forces was adequate for national defense, he casually replied that United States Army forces were now almost equal in strength to the Belgian and Dutch armies—twenty-odd divisions in all—when they were crushed by the Germans in 1940.[59]

To a later generation, familiar only with the huge, well-equipped Army and Air Force of 1945, the episode can serve as an illustration of Marshall's enormous problems in 1940-41. America's provision of aid to nations in death grips with the Axis threatened to stunt, if not strangle, the growth of the United States Army and Air Corps. Not the least of the Chief of Staff's accomplishments in the trying months before Pearl Harbor was that he managed to preserve a balance between the demands from abroad and the appeals at home from the Army and Air Forces. Somehow he made of "the hungry table" a hospitable board at which his own gaunt charges could get daily rations and still share a portion with their starving guests.

IV

The Power to Lead

T H E Selective Service Act of 1940 was written by the glare of burning English cities. Even as General Marshall labored to train and condition the forces now provided, Axis armies were on the move. They threatened British control of Egypt and the Suez Canal, toyed with possible advances into western Africa, menaced the Azores and Cape Verde Islands, conquered the Balkans in a few brutal thrusts, and swept into the Soviet Union with massive forces that seemed destined to destroy the Red armies in a matter of six to eight weeks. On the horizon, scarcely discernible at first, was the specter of Japanese aggression in the Pacific. Not knowing how soon or where he might have to put up a fight, the General could only pray for time to prepare his untried forces for battle.

The magnitude of his task in the first eighteen months as head of the Army was best summarized by Marshall himself near the end of 1940:

A year ago last summer our active Army consisted of about 170,000 soldiers, 56 squadrons of combat planes, and some 2500 pilots. There were two small regiments of mechanized troops.

From a purely organizational point of view, the Regular Army had only three half-organized infantry divisions. As for larger organizations, the basic battle unit is an Army Corps and there was not one in our Army.

Today there are 500,000 men in the field undergoing intensive training, and within a very few weeks this total will approach 800,-000. Instead of three incomplete infantry divisions, there are today eighteen under training, with nine more soon to come. The two weak mechanized regiments have grown into an armored corps of two divisions, each of about 12,000 men. . . .

The Air Force of 56 squadrons has been increased to 109, and the number of pilots to 4000 a year.[1]

As Army Chief of Staff, Marshall dealt with the President and the Secretary of War, the General and Special Staffs, and the chiefs of arms and services. As commanding general of General Headquarters (GHQ), he directed a far-flung empire that included four armies, nine corps area commands, the tactical air forces, the Armored Force, harbor defense units, and GHQ reserves. Wearing his Chief of Staff hat, he also controlled troops and supplies of units abroad through four departments: Hawaii, the Philippines, the Panama Canal area, and Puerto Rico. Later the last two were incorporated into a Caribbean Defense Command, and an Alaskan Defense Command was added. Not surprisingly, the overlapping jurisdictions created confusion. His supply division in the War Department was often at odds with the field armies he commanded under GHQ.[2]

The air set-up was almost equally complicated. Early in 1939 the air headquarters assigned to control combat operations when GHQ went into action was assigned to the Air Corps. Near the end of 1940 Marshall shifted it to General Headquarters, giving it some supervision of air-ground support. That change in control was more apparent than real since the Chief of the Air Corps, as one of Marshall's three deputies, had responsibility for coordinating all Army air activities.

General Marshall's machinery for handling training in the new Army was a curious affair devised in 1920 to deal with a war fought along the lines of World War I. When the United States entered that conflict President Wilson had organized an American Expeditionary Force, selected a commander, and sent it overseas to show the flag while the troops were prepared for action. The early divisions were organized from independent regiments on shipboard, and the units were trained in France. To direct the training and fighting abroad, a general headquarters (GHQ) was established under General Pershing, which seemed to be independent of the War Department in all matters except promotions and supply.

At the close of the war Pershing, along with former members of his staff, including Colonel Marshall, proposed to a congressional committee considering a National Defense bill that a new GHQ be created in case of future war. Thinking solely of a one-theater conflict, soldiers and legislators alike assumed that on the outbreak of war the commanding general of the Army (perhaps the current Chief of Staff) would sail away with his headquarters for the theater of operations. The staff remaining in Washington would oversee the procurement and forwarding of supplies, leaving to the commander in the field the training of troops and the making of operational decisions.

The passage of the Selective Service Act in 1940 destroyed this meticulous pattern. The concept had to be scrapped as soon as the peacetime Army began to take shape and it appeared that fighting in two or more theaters of war would require a more effective command organization in Washington. For the foreseeable future, the commanding general of GHQ would have no overseas assignment.

Whether Marshall would or would not hold that post, it became apparent that as Chief of Staff he would have to function for many months in at least two capacities—first in his current position as military adviser to the President and second as chief of the field forces that were being raised and trained. In the first assignment he continued to direct the activities of the General and Special Staffs in the War Department. For the second, he activated General Headquarters, provided by law, in the summer of 1940, directing it through his GHQ chief of staff Major General Lesley J. McNair.

Even before he became Army Chief of Staff, General Marshall had discovered McNair's special gifts for organization and training. In 1939 he had concluded that the short, wiry Scot was the type of single-minded driver he needed to reform the stuffy halls of Fort Leavenworth. He had summoned him from his experiments with the new triangular division at Fort Sill and directed him to take over the Command and General Staff School. "I selected him very hurriedly . . . to give him control of Leavenworth, which I thought was following a very antiquated [policy] particularly in regard to the Air Corps," General Marshall said of this appointment. Before all the desired changes could be made, the Chief of Staff called McNair to GHQ to handle the even tougher assignment of creating divisions in one or two years from units consisting of a hard core of Regular Army officers and noncoms, partly trained National Guardsmen and Reservists, and completely untrained selectees. This part of the program was still being debated when McNair arrived in Washington, but before he and his tiny staff could complete their plans Marshall dropped into their laps the federalized National Guard and the first batch of selectees.

"McNair was a very able officer, a conscientious officer, and he had a good staff headquarters at the War College," General Marshall said later. "And he is entitled to vast credit for what he did." Preaching that "time is short" and that sweat shed in training was preferable to blood shed on the battlefield, McNair drove the competent and harried the unfit. Demanding strict discipline and firm leadership, he compiled long lists of officers found wanting in action for Marshall to remove. More important, he kept the Chief of Staff informed of those promising officers to whose leadership divisions and corps could be entrusted in case of war.[8]

Helping McNair in his training tasks was another selection of the Chief of Staff, Lieutenant Colonel Mark Wayne Clark, who came to GHQ as chief of operations in the summer of 1940 and within a year was deputy to McNair with the rank of brigadier general. While commanding at Vancouver Barracks, Marshall had met and liked Clark, then chief of operations of the 3rd Division at Fort Lewis. Impressed by his work as a planner in the Joint Army-Navy exercises at Monterey in 1940, Marshall ordered him to the Army Staff College as an instructor and then, when classes were suspended, directed Clark to report to the GHQ commander as a member of his staff.

Because of his deafness, McNair often sent Clark to represent him in meetings with the Chief of Staff. Intelligent and persuasive, the younger officer grew in Marshall's favor as he exercised his role in developing the Army's training program. "General Clark played a very determining part," said General Marshall. "As a matter of fact, the method of raising these divisions, building them up, was largely worked out by General Clark. He would sit across the desk from me up in the Chief of Staff's office and we would work out the details."[4]

To members of the Personnel and Plans divisions of the War Department, already upset because their functions were being shifted to GHQ, the Chief of Staff's tendency to listen to this newcomer was especially frustrating. They, as well as many generals in the field, blamed "the palace guard" for unpopular changes in ground-force organization and training methods and growled as Clark rose rapidly toward the top in the Washington hierarchy. Like many men near the source of power, Clark grew both in self-confidence and in capacity to exasperate his contemporaries and former superiors, gaining many powerful enemies. But his position was safe. In a later fight over the nature and control of GHQ, he was pitted against Brigadier General Harry J. Malony, a witty, able officer, who believed GHQ should direct the forces it was deploying. Clark, who wanted to emphasize the training side of GHQ, was on the winning side.[5]

Except on training details, which McNair and Clark handled directly, Marshall kept in direct touch with the four Army commanders. As a result of their seniority—all of them had outranked Marshall before he became Chief of Staff—the four officers wielded broad powers over troops assigned to their control. Staff officers at GHQ approached them with the same deference they showed the Chief of Staff. Like Marshall, the four field commanders were non-West Pointers: Lieutenant General Hugh A. Drum of First Army and Lieutenant General John L. DeWitt of Fourth Army had been commissioned from civilian life, and Lieutenant General Walter Krueger of Third Army and Lieutenant General Ben Lear of Second Army had entered the Army as privates. All had served in the Spanish-American War, and all save Lear had held important posts overseas in World War I.

Marshall's chief airman was an old friend he had first met in the Philippines in 1914. Pennsylvania-born "Hap" Arnold had begun his career in the infantry after being graduated from West Point in 1907. After four years as a foot soldier, he had replied eagerly to an invitation in 1911 to take flying instruction. He was promptly sent to Dayton, Ohio, where under the personal supervision of the Wright Brothers, he learned how to be a pilot.[6]

Arnold's service in World War I was confined to Washington, where he ended the war years as a temporary colonel and as executive officer of the Air Division. In the period between wars he backed General William Mitchell's arguments in favor of the development of the Air Force and found himself temporarily in hot water because of his activities. In 1935, after the creation of the GHQ Air Force at Langley Field, Virginia, he was given command of one of its three wings with headquarters at March Field, California. He was called from that post to Washington in 1936 to become Assistant Chief of the Air Corps under Major General Oscar Westover, and on the death of that officer in an air crash in the fall of 1938 he became Chief of the Air Corps. Thus, he was the chief airman in Washington when Marshall became Deputy Chief of Staff.

Arnold and his air-minded friends lost no time in instructing General Marshall in the needs of the Air Corps. The airman's former boss at Langley Field, Frank M. Andrews, who had gone back to his permanent rank of colonel after completing a tour of duty in a major general's slot, accompanied Marshall while he was still Deputy Chief of Staff on a cross-country trip to airfields and airplane plants. Andrews also took the opportunity to explain the nature of the disagreement between air and ground officers of the Army.

General Marshall found "that Air had almost no representation . . . on the General Staff and . . . that the General Staff officers had little interest in the Air, mostly antipathy, and it was quite marked. . . . I found everyone on the staff hostile to Air, and the young air officers were going to Congress and stirring up everything—and the [situation] was in a general muddle. They had something to complain about because they were not getting recognition, and the General Staff at that time had little understanding of the Air." [7]

Shortly after he was named Chief of Staff, General Marshall asked that Andrews be made a brigadier general and brought into the War Department as chief of the G-3 Division, which dealt with training. "For the first time that I remember, Woodring, Johnson, and General Craig all acted as a unit in opposing action." After a stormy session they finally gave in to Marshall's demands and approved Andrews for both appointments. [8]

Arnold later wrote of this period that Marshall needed "plenty of indoctrination" about airpower but learned rapidly. "The difference in George, who presently was to become one of the most potent forces behind the development of a real airpower," he declared, "was his ability to digest what he saw and make it part of as strong a body of military genius as I have ever known." [9]

Arnold's praise for General Marshall's contributions to the development of the Air Corps was later echoed by General Laurence S. Kuter, who was assigned to the War Department as a major on July 1, 1939, and rose in the next few years to high command in the

Air Force. Kuter was first impressed by General Marshall's instructions to the young officers reporting to the War Department in the summer of 1939 that they should consider their jobs "as war assignments" and approach their problems as if they were at war. He was to find other indications of the General's realistic approach to America's problems in the months to come.

In 1940 Kuter, as project officer for the G-3 Division, had the task of presenting a proposal for expanding the Army Air Corps to fifty-four groups. At that time it seemed extremely expensive and almost out of the question. When his study was complete he outlined it to Marshall, who sat quietly trying to weigh the arguments for and against the plan. At the end Marshall asked only one question: "Why is it only fifty-four?" Kuter was surprised. "Every other question [raised by others] had been focused on reducing the air effort, that it was beyond any reason, it was imaginative, beyond any common sense. . . . General Marshall approved the program there. There was no further discussion or debate . . . It became the War Department's directive that day. I therefore attribute to him in 1940 full credit for the vision and imagination that led [ultimately] to an increase to 286 groups from a force which at that time consisted of about three that were worth mentioning . . ."[10]

The Chief of Staff also made an effort to go part of the way toward meeting demands from airmen and some air-minded civilians for an independent Air Corps. Although convinced that the Air Corps had too few graduates of the Army schools to furnish an adequate staff for an independent force and believing that at this stage it was essential to have an air force that would support ground action rather than act independently, he embarked on a policy of granting increased autonomy to the Air Corps. In the fall of 1940 he created, in addition to the post of Deputy Chief of Staff, then held by Major General William Bryden, two new deputy slots: one for supply, which he gave to Major General Richard C. Moore, and one for air, which he handed to General Arnold in addition to his position as Chief of Air Corps. He also gave Arnold a voice in the meetings of the War Council, where Arnold sat as a deputy while meeting with the representatives of the Navy. Marshall's admiration for Arnold's abilities did not diminish; in later years he said of him, "He was always loyal"—one of the tributes he reserved for those he trusted most.

With McNair, Arnold, and the four Army commanders in charge of a reorganized program of training, Marshall in the fall of 1940 began a strong effort to prepare his ground and air forces for battle. As one of the Army's best-known troop instructors, he never lost sight of the training program. After the summer of 1940, when the time to train the Army's soldiers and fliers for future tests of arms became "tragically" short, he speeded up the efforts in this field.

General Marshall particularly wanted more time to prepare the ground force. He said later: "I never saw it properly trained except during the latter part of the war. Everything you do is under extraordinarily difficult circumstances, which is not the case with the other services. For example, in the Navy, I think it was the ship's custom that everyone should take a bath before going into action and put on clean underwear. The probability was that he had a night's sleep in his regular bunk. With the Army it was quite the other way round. The probability was that he had been in a series of marches—some of them forced marches. He had been pushed to the verge of exhaustion. He was wet—because it always seems to rain in such cases—and muddy and he had to sleep in those clothes. He had no chance to get a change of garments on the eve of action or a long time after that. And yet the moment when his high courage was necessary came as a rule at dawn, when he woke up half-frozen to deal with an enemy he couldn't see and [when his own] machine guns and artillery [could be seen only] through the eyes of a single observer. The artillery which had to furnish close support was out of sight. All of this required a very high state of training, higher than that of any other force I know of." [11]

In his early days as Chief of Staff, Marshall had flown to Puerto Rico, Hawaii, and Panama to inspect the training of those distant garrisons. Now, he stole away at every opportunity to observe the efforts of his commanders to iron out the shocking weaknesses of command and execution in the field. In one busy week he left Washington for Minnesota at six on Saturday morning, arrived in the afternoon, and left next morning for Fort Lewis, Washington, where he spent a quiet Sunday. On Monday he visited units in the field between Fort Lewis, near Seattle, and Vancouver, Washington. From nearby Portland he flew to Alexandria, Louisiana, where he arrived on Wednesday morning and spent the day watching maneuvers then in progress. Next morning he was in

Montgomery, Alabama, to inspect forces on an air base, and that afternoon, at Fort Benning, he inspected two new divisions being organized there. He left Fort Benning at 5 p.m. and was back in Washington by 9.[12]

His frequent whirlwind visits, essential to a commander of a far-flung Army, were possible only in an air age. Marshall flew whenever possible and insisted that all of his principal commanders and staff officers fly, relieving those officers who declined to do so. His airplane visits speedily changed established protocol for receiving the Chief of Staff at subordinate headquarters. Desiring to make full use of his time, the General bluntly directed that no honors, ceremonies, or parties be scheduled for him.[13] (An exception was made infrequently when he accompanied important visitors on special inspections.) He made many of the trips too rapidly to form careful judgments, and some of the commanders complained that he neglected the morale factor to be gained from showing himself to the men. In a sense he was conducting the type of sampling he received from reading representative letters each day from soldiers and their families. He was stimulated by hearing from different commanders firsthand accounts of their problems, and he gained an advantage over his assistants in Washington by seeing more of the Army than they.

As he moved about the country the Chief of Staff looked in on recruit training at division level, at flying instruction at distant fields, or watched while larger ground and air units engaged in maneuvers across the territory of entire states.

To the new recruit, training meant hours of hated drill in heat or cold, marches with full field pack down dusty or muddy roads, memorizing the names of hundreds of parts of unfamiliar weapons and reciting them in a sort of dreadful litany, interminable cleanings of rifles and bleachings of equipment, enforced by unpredictable inspections. The greatest problem of wartime instruction, General Marshall believed, was to continue long enough with basic training. "It is dull and it is long and it is very strenuous, and unless it is well done, thoroughly done, the troops are going to be lacking in discipline and performance from that time on. And yet it is very hard to have them see the reason for it. I remember I had some professional fact-gatherers go around for me. They saw the men in training in this country and asked them about what they thought of it. . . . [Later] they found the same men on the front, after they had been engaged [in action], and [nearly everything] the men objected to in this country . . . they now said they had not had enough of." [14]

It was Marshall's belief that one could best judge the preparation of men for battle by testing them in prearranged maneuvers. Most civilians failed to agree. They saw them as confused and expensive affairs in which troops and vehicles moved haphazardly along the highways, interfering with traffic and disturbing honest working people, or across fertile fields, knocking down fences, ruining cornfields and frightening cattle, as they played at war.

The General talked with one senator who objected to the money that was being spent on maneuvers. The senator was particularly upset because the troops had made numerous mistakes, and he asked why maneuvers were held with so many errors. The Chief of Staff replied, "My God, Senator, that's the reason I do it. I want the mistake down in Louisiana, not over in Europe, and the only way to do this thing is to try it out, and if it doesn't work, find out what we need to make it work." [15]

Here for the first time, General Marshall explained later, it was possible to train the High Command. "Eisenhower, for example, was chief of staff of General Krueger's [Third] Army in the South. All of them learned a great deal. I remember in the 500,000-man maneuver down in Louisiana, I directed that they change their bases on each side. They told me it would take a month for something like that and be very, very expensive. Well, I said, they would have to do it anyway. They would have to do it in Europe and they would have to do it here. So they changed the bases. I remember in one case it took ten days and cost 40,000 dollars. That seems a large sum for a maneuver like that. But it was a very economical sum when it came to the efficiency it developed in the troops. That is the reason that Patton and Hodges and Bradley were able to move as rapidly as they did across the face of Europe."

Before 1940 field exercises were usually staged by opposing divisions. In 1940 and 1941 the War Department used rival corps and finally large peacetime armies. When properly equipped and led, units in maneuvers improved their tactical effectiveness and developed their supply and communications systems. Even when many weapons were obsolete or completely unavailable and many rules of ground warfare violated, life in the open, the conditioning of bodies, practice in shifting large numbers of troops across great distances, and the attainment of some degree of cohesion within competing units constituted a high return on the Army's initial investment.

Irked by caustic criticisms of the 1939 maneuvers that had been ordered before he became Chief of Staff, General Marshall moved at once in the fall of that year to plan more effective training exercises for 1940 and 1941. To get additional officers to train his expanded Regular Army units, he suspended classes at the Command and General Staff School, Fort Leavenworth, in February 1940. As a means of providing training aids for the enlarged units he retained the faculty at the school to prepare or revise training manuals to meet his new requirements. In later years he liked to boast that whereas American officers in 1917 had had to borrow training guides from the British in order to start instruction in France, the Army in 1940 was able to start its expanded program with manuals that incorporated the newest military doctrines.[16]

Despite his initial efforts General Marshall was disappointed by the ragged performances of officers and troops and the lack of realism in the 1940 exercises. In the May maneuvers conducted by the Third Army, the commanding general, General Henry J. Brees, was so critical of his principal commanders in the presence of their subordinates that the Chief of Staff barred junior officers from similar critiques in the future.[17]

Of the maneuvers held by the four armies in 1940, General Drum's attracted the greatest publicity. Having called performances in the 1939 maneuvers "inexcusable," the First Army commander opened the 1940 exercises by listing his woeful shortages in manpower and weapons. He dramatically illustrated his lack of equipment by labeling iron pipes as "cannon," trucks as "tanks," and using light planes to simulate bombers. Possibly his publicity campaign was designed to alert the American public to the need of more equipment, but the Chief of Staff's friends thought he was trying to embarrass Marshall and McNair.

Marshall's old friend, Fox Conner, wrote a biting article on the conduct of the exercises in New York, saying that the Army must re-establish the fundamental conceptions of "what war is." He forwarded the clipping to the Chief of Staff, adding that he would have been even more critical if he had been making an official report. Current conceptions, he thought, were "completely haywire and cockeyed." In extenuation of the situation, he remarked that Marshall and McNair had many more difficult training problems than Pershing and his staff had faced in 1917.

The Chief of Staff replied softly that his staff was carefully studying recent errors and making sweeping changes in organization and tactics for the 1941 exercises. He was hopeful, he said, of showing the nation something better in the future. "Our intensive training program, the additional equipment which will soon become available, and a realization by all concerned of the seriousness of the times and our weaknesses will contribute toward the end in view." [18]

When training and operations went badly Marshall examined first the quality of leadership. In 1940 he took another hard look at a problem that had concerned him during all the years he had been training troops. He was haunted by recollections of the droves of unfit commanders sent in World War I by General Pershing to "Blooey" (Blois)—as the French used to send theirs to Limoges —for reclassification, and of his chief's almost frantic efforts on eve of battle to find suitable officers for combat assignments. Having personally fought the dead hand of promotion by seniority in the period between wars, he concentrated now on finding the right man for the right job.

Even while he was still Deputy Chief of Staff, Marshall had campaigned to improve Army command by seeking to reform the promotion system. Since the peacetime Army had no permanent rank higher than that of major general, the seniority system dictated that the senior corps commander in each Army area automatically succeed to the vacant Army command. As a result the position was sometimes filled by generals with only months or even weeks to serve before retirement. Officers with fine records often reached their goal just in time to stage their final reviews, or mediocre officers moved upward to high command only because they had stepped on the escalator of rank a few months before an abler colleague.

Marshall determined to change the system. "I wanted to be able to put my finger on the man I wanted," he recalled, "so he would work like the devil and be interested in something besides the two cars and the [extra] bathroom for his wife he wanted." [19] With General Craig's consent, he lobbied for temporary lieutenant-general ranks to be established for the commanders of the four armies. Thereafter the Chief of Staff could make his own selection without bowing to the rules of strict seniority.

His efforts to create four new lieutenant generals brought him into collision with Senator Tom Connally, powerful member of the Senate Committee on Military Affairs. Silvery-maned, Texas tall, devastatingly sarcastic, formidable in debate, "Old Tawm" proceeded to tear "the Army to ribbons" when Marshall tried to present his case. Winded at last by his tirade, he stopped for breath long enough for Deputy Chief of Staff Marshall to inquire innocently what state he hailed from. Indignant, Connally replied, "Why, I'm from Texas." "I thought so," rejoined the General as he turned from current history to the experiences of an earlier war. Recalling that the South at the beginning of the Civil War had given the titles of general and lieutenant general to its top commanders, Marshall spoke of the mistake made by the Yankee government in restricting its commanders initially to major general rank. Stretching history slightly, he suggested that not until Lincoln had made Grant a lieutenant general did the North begin to defeat the armies of the South. Connally listened and agreed finally not to oppose the measure when it came to a vote. He kept his word, and the measure passed. In a committee hearing some months later, when Marshall referred to the earlier discussion, the Texan growled that he hadn't changed his mind.[20]

The increase in the number of general officers, soon to be a continuing process, solved only a part of the command problem. As the Army expanded in 1940 and 1941, the Chief of Staff was shocked and saddened to find that many of his contemporaries, with fine records in peacetime or in World War I, could not meet the heavy demands of new command responsibilities. For some of the early appointments he had reached back in his memory and recommended for high place old friends from Fort Leavenworth or First Army. He was aghast when many of them broke under the pressure of their new duties.[21]

Many problems arose, as Marshall pointed out, because men had been held in relatively junior rank for so many years that on finally reaching colonel or brigadier general rank they were unprepared for their responsibilities. Often a ludicrous incident suddenly revealed an officer's weakness. More than once, Marshall's younger advisers would say to him than an officer he had pushed for advancement "no longer had it." In one case it was an intimate friend, once "very able," who failed to measure up when, soon after the United States entered the war, Marshall selected him for an overseas post. Directed to proceed at once to his new assignment, he replied that he couldn't leave because the furniture wasn't packed and his wife was away for a month. Scarcely believing the answer when informed of it, Marshall took the telephone and asked the officer if he had been correctly quoted. When the old friend placidly replied in the affirmative the Chief of Staff blurted out, "My God, man, we are at war, and you are a general." To the reply, "Well, I'm sorry," Marshall could only say, "I'm sorry, too, but you will be retired tomorrow." [22]

The General was particularly affected when able officers, nearing retirement, had to be relieved so that he could replace them with much younger men. In several cases he had the unpleasant task of telling them that the star they had sought for several years would go to an officer better fitted for the rigorous demands of field duties. As often as possible he softened the blow by finding a place where the officer could still serve competently. Many of the men understood and were grateful; others were convinced that Marshall was paying off old grievances. They formed a small, bitter band within the ranks of the Army, eager to listen to personal attacks on Marshall and to offer their views later as ammunition for campaigns against him.

To those who had survived the years of poor pay and slow promotion, the prospect of being removed from the list just as they had reached the door of promise seemed incredible, and to the wives who had waited impatiently for the golden moment it was monstrous. In the end it was the ladies who tore at him violently in letters, reminding him of long personal friendships, recalling their fondness for his first wife, pleading that he spare their husbands lest they lose their interest in life. Others coaxed and wheedled, adding that their husbands would kill them if they knew they were writing. Marshall developed special methods for dealing with this painful raking over of old memories and treasured friendships. To letters filled with unaccustomed praise or sweetness he was friendly but cautious; to the begging letters he was distant; to heartbroken letters there were reminders of the superior claim of the Army's welfare or a suggestion that the husband could still render service in his present rank; to the letters with barbs and edges he gave no further answer. Folders of correspondence, running over fifteen or twenty years, contained pleasant memories of early service together, photographs of children now grown tall, invitations to weddings, congratulations, felicitations and good wishes, and then pleading for "George" to remember the friend of his youth.

Occasionally a dark, unforgiving letter, written after a loved one had died, stabbed at the General with its accusations of ingratitude. On these he would sometimes write the words, "This is an old matter; goes back some years. File." Some of the postscripts to friendship he did not hear or read, but the tragedy is contained in comments to a biographer—"I have no further interest in General Marshall" or "he was once our dear friend, but he ruined my husband." Marshall resolutely rose above the insinuating demands of friendship as colleagues shivered over his cold-blooded willingness to make former associates walk the plank along with others he did not know if they failed to measure up. But the knife turned in the wound. Only rarely did the feelings show through, but his chance remarks showed the hurt. There is conscious agony in a memorandum he penned for an aide during the war: "Please draft a letter for General —— on the death of his second son. I had to relieve him, and I am afraid I broke his heart."

Possibly at times his scales of justice were a little askew. Just as he seldom permitted the doubt to be resolved in favor of a friend, he occasionally weighed too heavily against those who had come under his disfavor for a long-remembered defect in personal conduct or leadership. He was not deaf to appeals and, if the evidence warranted, sometimes changed his mind. But if a man pressed too hard he could destroy himself. One officer, convinced that he had lost a promotion by failure to accept an assignment that Marshall had proposed, wrote to beg the General's forgiveness, saying that he had already been made to pay heavily enough for his error. As if offended by this self-abasement, Marshall sent back a curt reminder that advancement was based on performance. When the officer persisted the Chief of Staff slashed across the paper, "He is a whiner. File." The man remained a colonel until the war's end. In this instance Marshall's only feeling seems to have been one of irritation.

In another case, involving the removal of an officer who had once been a close personal friend, there was obviously personal regret. He had known the man since World War I and had been a close friend of his family. When Marshall became Chief of Staff he had singled out his old friend for an important post, had praised his initial efforts, and then had removed him when he found that serious difficulties were developing between his appointee and another officer in the same command. The officer returned to Washington, where he expected to get another assignment. Days passed and then weeks and there was no word from the War Department. At last he asked about his situation. There was no response. Finally, in anguish that permeated his letter, he appealed to his old friend to remove his hand. "You need only [say] that you want me usefully employed without humiliation." He could find slots in several War Department offices, he added, but "they are all afraid to touch me so long as I am manifestly under your displeasure." Marshall made no reply, and in a short time the former friend retired, bitter against the General who could have saved him but would not. It gave Marshall no joy to wield such power, and he said later, while agreeing to the harsh reproach that he was ruthless in removing officers from command, that no task he performed pained him more. But he was preparing an army for war and felt that the selection of those who could lead in battle was a duty he owed the state.

Feared throughout the Army was Marshall's little Black Book, which he kept in the drawer of his desk. Members of his staff watched with fascination as he took it out from time to time, crossed off a name and moved up or added that of another. The Black Book was a little-needed crutch to a well-charged memory that still contained the names of classmates from Fort Leavenworth, colleagues in France, instructors and students at Fort Benning, dozens of men whom he saw on every visit to maneuvers, the names advisers and old friends counseled him to remember, men of good report whose achievements were chronicled again and again in his mail.

Balanced against the cases of men suddenly advanced because of Marshall's recollection of a single fine performance were the names of those held back because he recalled a black mark from the past. Widely repeated in the Army was the case of Colonel (later General) James A. Van Fleet, whose name was similar to that of another colonel listed among the rejected in the Black Book. Each time Van Fleet was recommended for a star, his name was crossed off. Only after he had proved himself in the Normandy fighting did the Chief of Staff concede that he had been holding back the wrong man.[23]

By 1941 certain names recurred regularly in his listings for important commands. In addition to those who had been generals when he became Chief of Staff he put down again and again the names of younger officers destined for the highest ranks the Army had to offer—Bradley, Patton, Eichelberger, Hodges, Collins, and Eisenhower.

Marshall stirred up bitter controversy with his early efforts to hack at the "hump" caused by the number of men of approximately the same age and rank who became Regular Army officers at the close of World War I. Marshall had suffered from the stagnation in promotions caused by a similar "hump" created at the end of the Spanish-American War and his testimony in behalf of his proposed bill was strongly shaped by his personal history.

Out of the depths of his former frustrations he demanded that officers be saved from the spirit-destroying effect of being held for years in the same grade without hope of reaching one of the higher posts in time to be of service to the Army. More effective was his argument that men retained in lower grades were being deprived of needed experience in handling large numbers of men. In emergencies they would suddenly succeed to command of large units without knowing how to perform their duties.

From the need for experience he turned to the need for youth: "It took a great deal of imagination; it took a great deal of vigor in order to lead the vast Army we were starting to build up. . . . The whole point was not that everyone of that age was lacking; but it was the average of that age that was lacking. For example, General Patton was up in years and, incidentally, would always talk to me about the age question all the time for fear we would apply it to him. Well, he was the epitome of vigor and leadership and that sort of thing. He was the exception, and there were not many like him. . . ."[24] Marshall reminded his hearers that the maneuvers had demonstrated that only leaders of great physical stamina could command the maximum exertions from their men. "In my experience in the war—and I saw about twenty-seven of twenty-nine divisions in battle," General Marshall told members of the House Military Affairs Committee in 1940, "there were more failures, more crushed careers of officers of considerable rank that grew out of physical exhaustion than [from] any other one cause." [25] One acquired judgment with the years but lost "the resiliency of tendons and muscles." "Leadership in the field," he repeated, "depends to an important extent on one's legs, and stomach, and nervous system, and on one's ability to withstand hardships, and lack of sleep, and still be disposed energetically and aggressively to command men, to dominate men on the battlefield." In World War I many men had had to be relieved because "their spirit—their tenacity of purpose, their power of leadership over tired men—was broken through physical fatigue. They became pessimistic. They became nervous impossibilities in positions of leadership. . . ." [26]

"You have to lead men in war by requiring more from the individual than he thinks he can do," he argued. "You have to lead men in war by bringing them along to endure and to display qualities of fortitude that are beyond the average man's thought of what he should be expected to do. You have to inspire them when they are hungry and exhausted and desperately uncomfortable and in great danger; and only a man of positive characteristics of leadership, with the physical stamina that goes with it, can function under those conditions." [27]

Marshall emphasized advancement of younger men, but the point that caught the eye of the armed services journals and the general press was the provision to retire colonels who failed to measure up to the new exacting demands. "I was accused," Marshall recalled, "of getting rid of all the brains of the Army. I couldn't reply that I was eliminating considerable arteriosclerosis." [28]

To insure fairness in the elimination Marshall selected for the task a committee of six retired officers—a "plucking board" as it was called—headed by his immediate predecessor, General Craig. The officers, after examining records and recommendations as to performance, were empowered to remove from line promotion any

officer for reasons deemed good and sufficient. He would then be
subject to removal one year after the action was taken. As a guide
Marshall passed on to the board, with his approval, G-1's statement
that cases were to be decided not on an officer's past record but on
his value to the Army. "Critical times are upon us," he warned,
and the standard had to be "today's performance." [29]

It was not enough to weed out the incompetent; it was even
more important to see that younger officers of exceptional ability
were advanced quickly to higher rank. On this problem the Chief
of Staff found himself blocked by Chairman Andrew May of the
House Military Affairs Committee because of pressure brought by
officers Marshall did not plan to promote. Frustrated by the pi-
geonholing of his bill, the Chief of Staff went to Senator Byrnes of
South Carolina to see what could be done in the upper house.
Byrnes, an old hand at parliamentary maneuver, suggested that
Marshall have his staff draft an amendment that could be added to
the appropriations bill on the floor of the Senate. An innocuous
statement—"In time of war or national emergency determined by
the President, any officer of the Regular Army may be appointed
to higher temporary grade without vacating his permanent appointment"—was quickly prepared and handed by the Chief of
Staff to the Senator. When the appropriations bill was reported
from the Senate Committee to the floor, Byrnes offered the Army's
amendment. No questions were asked, and it was quickly adopted.
The bill was sent to a joint conference with members of the House
Appropriations Committee. There the South Carolinian got the
cooperation of friends, who also accepted his amendment. The
amended measure sailed through both houses without May's learning until later that he had voted for a bill containing the provision
he thought he had blocked. Byrnes in his memoirs proudly recalled
Marshall's statement that the legislation had permitted him to
jump Eisenhower over more than 350 senior officers and that
others moved up rapidly as a result were Clark, Patton, Kenney,
and Spaatz. "In Congress nothing just happens," remarked Byrnes,
"somebody must make it happen." By helping to "make it happen," Marshall had taken one more step toward strengthening the
leadership of the Army.[30]

His task of weeding out senior officers not only embarrassed him
but at last led him to wonder, since "no man would agree to him-

self that he was not quite up to the punch," if perhaps he himself were too old for his position. In the face of growing attacks from congressional and military circles he took a surprising action. Before the plucking board started its work, the General called on the President to explain that the process of eliminating older officers could be done faster if the Chief of Staff were a younger man. He proposed that he resign. Roosevelt heard him through without comment. Two weeks later, when Marshall mentioned it to Harry Hopkins, the latter replied, "The President just laughs at you. He says no politician ever resigns a job and that's just talk." Marshall returned a second time, proposing that he select a younger man for his successor, carefully groom him for the position for two or three months, and then step aside. Roosevelt again heard him through and said nothing. Little more than a year younger than Marshall, he may have thought it was dangerous to start a wave of self-denying ordinances in the government. A call to Hopkins brought the same jesting response that the President had never known a man in high position to resign.[31] Marshall's gesture had done nothing more than reveal the depth of his feeling on the necessity for thorough reorganization of the officer corps.

Inasmuch as no congressional authorization was necessary for forced retirements or reshuffling of the command organizations of the National Guard and the Reserve Officer Corps, General McNair began to shift officers in these groups before the Regular Army board started its work. Consequently many non-Regulars charged discrimination. A check of the statistics refuted the charge. The percentage of field-grade officers retired in the National Guard was somewhat less than in the Regular Army. The highly publicized shifts in the National Guard took place at division and regimental levels, where command and staff positions had often gone to men with political backgrounds or to able World War I officers who had gained little experience in command since that time. General McNair found little difficulty in showing evidence of poor administration or ineffective troop handling to justify his requests for the transfer of many officers.

In dealing with the National Guard removals, Marshall found that he had to tread warily. Many of the higher-ranking officers had powerful political connections in their states, and members of Congress were quick to intervene in their behalf. In the case of one such officer, General Marshall received a protest from the entire congressional delegation from the general's home state. He discussed the heavy demands of divisional command, the lack of opportunity of many officers to get proper training, the necessity of having the best-trained men possible for field leadership. When these arguments failed to move his listeners, he declared firmly: "I'll put it this way, gentlemen. I don't understand your position because I should think that your constituents should be your principal interest—and here it seems to me that you are only considering one constituent and ignoring all [your] other constituents who are members of the division. I am concerned with them. . . ." While they considered the political implications of that blast he added with some heat, "I am not going to leave him in command of that division. So I will put it to you this way—if he stays, I go, and if I stay, he goes." That, recalled the General, "broke up the meeting."

The incident had a poignant ending. One of the senators went home, perhaps a little angry at the rebuff he and his colleagues had received. He returned to the War Department next day in a better frame of mind. "I told my wife about the meeting yesterday," he said. She had reminded her husband of their special interest in one of the many constituents the Chief of Staff had claimed as his own. Their son was in the service. She for one was very happy, she told the senator, that the boy was in the Army and that General Marshall was at its head.[32]

One of the hottest controversies to arise over National Guard leadership came in the summer of 1941 in the case of General Lear's disciplinary measures against the 35th Division, a National Guard unit commanded by Major General Ralph Truman, a veteran of the Spanish-American and First World Wars and an insurance executive of Missouri. For some months General McNair had been criticizing Truman's handling of the division, and Lear, commanding general of Second Army, had been cracking down on deficiencies in that unit. During the maneuvers in Tennessee that summer, criticisms reached Washington from local citizens complaining of depredations by various units in their areas. Lear was quickly peppered with directives to tighten up on the discipline of units going to and from the maneuver area in his Army. Shortly afterward men of the 35th Division, while passing a golf course in

Memphis, proceeded to utter wolf whistles—described as "yoo-hoos"—at several young ladies on the course. Unrecognized, one of the older golfers in civilian clothes happened to be General Lear, who promptly ordered them to stop their whistling. They told him to shut up. Boiling mad, he returned to his headquarters and ordered that the men be brought back from their home station at Fort Robinson, Arkansas, and required to walk back part of the forty-five miles to their post. Judged against later drill requirements for infantry, his penalty of fifteen miles' hiking, followed by fifteen miles' riding, was less than criminal. At the time it was widely condemned as a Prussian act of brutal callousness, and letters were addressed to the hapless general as "Hitler" and "Von Lear."

The incident coincided with the fight then going on over extension of selective service legislation and retention of the National Guard in federal service. A public and press inflamed over the congressional fight magnified the case out of all proper proportion. When McNair and Lear proposed in the wake of the furore that the 35th Division commander be transferred to another assignment Truman applied for retirement. A mild storm arose some months later. Lear's name came up for temporary promotion to lieutenant general, and the senior senator from Missouri, Bennett Clark, objected on the ground that Lear had treated Truman improperly. However, the junior senator, a cousin of the former division commander, declined to join in the protest, and Lear's nomination was confirmed.

Throughout the extended controversy over Regular Army versus National Guard, Marshall retained the respect of the National Guard. During his long association with state militias and Guard units he had developed an understanding and sympathy for their problems that made it possible for him to keep the friendship of their commanders. As Chief of Staff he insisted that their officers be given full opportunity to prove that they were as efficient as Regular officers. He held that their weaknesses were due to lack of experience and insufficient time for training and not to any lack of capacity for leadership. To avoid charges of favoritism he directed that no vacancy in a Guard unit be filled by a Regular officer if a qualified National Guard officer could be found.

Marshall's effort to put into effect his particular theories on the training of officers brought him into a painful conflict with Secretary Stimson in the spring of 1941. At issue were two different concepts of officer procurement and training. In World War I the Army had copied the British system of commissioning college-trained men after a short period of military training in the belief that they would excel in leadership qualities. Marshall had accepted this system at that time and during the period between wars had backed the civilian military-training camp program, sponsored by the Reserve Officers Training Organization and by Stimson, Grenville Clark, Patterson, and others. Once selective service was adopted, he proposed a different method of procuring officers. Believing that every officer should have a taste of a private soldier's life, he recommended that candidates be selected by officers under whom they had trained.

At the urging of Grenville Clark and Under Secretary Patterson, Stimson raised the issue in 1941. The matter of officer training was soon lost in the larger question of whether the Chief of Staff or the Secretary of War's civilian advisers were to determine War Department policy. In late March, Marshall called in his staff and requested advice on ways to battle the proposal. He asked them to study various other methods, pressing the importance of answering the argument that the Army should adopt the Navy's practice of awarding commissions to college-trained specialists. His military assistants spread the word that the boss was set for a showdown with the civilian authorities who were trying to run the War Department.

Armed with sage advice, Marshall bluntly told Secretary Stimson that he must decide whether he intended to follow the views of his Chief of Staff and the General Staff in military matters or listen to Grenville Clark and other civilian advisers. The General reviewed his arguments for selecting officer candidates from outstanding selectees. He offered to open commissions to qualified men outside the service who would volunteer for officers' school after they had taken basic training. Stimson was startled at Marshall's vehemence. In the midst of the argument the Chief of Staff suddenly declared that he would resign if the Secretary insisted on holding civilian military camps.

Seeing that the Chief of Staff was troubled "far out of proportion to the importance" of the issue, Stimson quietly assured him that he "would not have him unduly worried" and made clear that he would follow his advice. His assistants were displeased by Stimson's surrender. Patterson and McCloy criticized the Army's opposition, calling it "simply a mark of incompetence and narrowmindedness." The General later expressed regret over his offer to resign, saying incorrectly that it was the only time that he had used this threat to get his way. Undoubtedly Stimson's civilian advisers would have liked to recall their aspersions on the Army. Stimson, at least, conceded that "the solution reached was a better one than any of them had anticipated." [33]

With this background General Marshall watched closely over the first class of officer candidates at Fort Benning. He insisted that they be chosen for mental aptitude and qualities of leadership from units throughout the Army and then carefully trained and tested for their knowledge of weapons and tactics. He recalled again his insistence at the Infantry School that officers must be taught to fight the brutally tough battles of the first six months of a war when properly trained troops and adequate weapons were often lacking.

He was on hand to deliver the graduating address when the first class finished in the fall of 1941. His remarks were brief, but they went straight to the heart of what he wanted from his future combat leaders. "Warfare today," he reminded them, "is a thing of swift movement—of rapid concentrations. It requires the building up of enormous firepower against successive objectives with breathtaking speed. It is not a game for the unimaginative plodder."

Marshall spelled out for them the difficulties of commanding American troops. Their characteristics of individual initiative and independence of thought, which made them potentially the best fighters in the world, could become possible sources of weakness without good leadership. Lacking the homogeneity of the British people, Americans did not have their ability to "glorify a defeat by their stubborn tenacity and dogged discipline." The American soldier's unusual intelligence and resourcefulness could become "explosive or positively destructive . . . under adverse conditions, unless the leadership is wise and determined, and unless the leader commands the complete respect of his men."

His mind went back to his experience in the Philippines, on the battlefields of France, and in China during the trying days of the 1920s as he tried to picture for the young lieutenants about to receive their first gold bar of rank all the things he had learned from rugged old sergeants and tough old colonels and the other leaders who had won the love or respect of the men they commanded. He recalled for them how soldiers changed their minds, once they hit combat, about officers they had once regarded as "tough" or "easy." The great task of leadership, he said, would come "during the long and trying periods of waiting and marching here and there without evident purpose, and during those weeks or months of service under conditions of extreme discomfort or of possible privations and isolations." Then the true leader must surmount the difficulties, maintain his discipline, and develop his training.

Marshall then ticked off alertness and initiative as qualities he expected of them as well of his senior officers: "Passive inactivity because you have not been given specific instructions to do this or to do that is a serious deficiency." He charged the first of the Army's ninety-day wonders with the care of the small units of the great army with whose command they would be entrusted—whose quality, discipline, and development would depend on them. In an effort to make them see the awful demands of true leadership he recalled that the failures of the units, great or small, would be charged to their incapacity. After underlining their responsibilities he cautioned his listeners: "Remember this: the truly great leader overcomes all difficulties, and campaigns and battles are nothing but a long series of difficulties to be overcome. The lack of equipment, the lack of food, the lack of this or that are only excuses; the real leader displays his qualities in his triumph over adversity, however great it may be." [34]

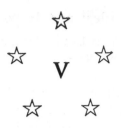

Civilians in Uniform

MARSHALL'S speech at Fort Benning articulated his strong feelings on the subject of leaders for his enlarged Army. He was equally concerned with those who would have to follow the leaders. The task of making an efficient force, of maintaining morale, and of developing discipline in all the soldiers now entrusted to his care was more than an obligation for the Chief of Staff. It was an article of faith.

In 1939, when the Chief of Staff had enlisted volunteers to fill vacancies in the Regular Army, he had been able to find a sufficient number of them who could adjust fairly easily to pay of twenty-one dollars a month, primitive housing, and inadequate recreational facilities. The National Guardsmen, many of whom had signed up for weekly training sessions in their hometowns to make a little extra money or because they enjoyed the two weeks of field training each summer, and the new selectees, called from every walk of life, were of a different breed. They resented the great gulf that existed between their former status in the community and the low estate they now held as recruits. Especially galling was the gap between their Army pay and the rising salaries men with exempt status or uncalled draft numbers were drawing at home. The problem, as General Marshall knew, was that in wartime most soldiers recognized their duty to the nation and raised no outcry since most of their contemporaries were engaged in similar service. The Army now faced the resentment of men who felt that the luck of the lottery had imposed on them an unfair sacrifice. In their discontent they had the sympathy of their families, their hometown newspapers, and local political leaders, all prepared to blame the Army.

Marshall saw clearly the risks that he faced as soon as the Selective Service Act was passed. Rather wryly he wrote General Craig in September 1940: "You were good enough to predict that the coming twelve months will not be so hard, but I rather anticipate the next three months as being the hardest of all because it will be the first experience of a troop concentration of the National Guard and probably compulsory service trainees in the time of peace." He expected trouble from the press and that "captious criticisms" were bound to come his way. "However," he added, "I will continue to follow your scheme of 'doing my damnedest and to hell with the result.' " [1]

The next four months proved him to be a more accurate prophet than Craig. In one of his occasional informal reports to his old mentor and longtime friend, General Pershing, he wrote of the rapid increase of the Army and the problems it had brought. "We had about 600,000 Jan 1; we have about 775,000 at the present time, and I understand we should approach 950,000 by the end of February." Problems had multiplied even faster than men. "With rain, mud, storms, peacetime press supervision, 'flu, new National Guard units of varied efficiency and preparation, and a tremendous battle on the Hill, things are pretty busy." [2]

Of all his difficulties, the greatest in the early months of preparations was housing. For months before the passage of the Selective Service Act he had struggled in the toils of post construction, a constant barrier to progress until near the end of the war. The temporary buildings on World War I posts still owned by the Army had so deteriorated during a long period of nonuse or neglect that Marshall complained that an umbrella was often "as useful inside a building as it was outside." With thousands of men coming in weekly, even these inadequate buildings were soon overrun.

Soldiers in the field can and often do sleep in the open, in tents, ditches, or improvised shelters. After months of hardening, men can live and even thrive under extremes of discomfort and exposure that ordinarily would be intolerable. But the transition from decent homes to the rigors of the field would scarcely have been tolerated by draftees and National Guardsmen even if the Army had been willing to risk the serious outbreaks of illness and the chorus of protests that would come from the men and their families. Marshall warned congressmen as the Selective Service bill neared passage in the summer of 1940 that "shelter is a serious problem." To all who would listen he argued: "We have known for some time where we want to put these people. We [have] decided on the type of shelter to be erected and have plans and specifications for it. . . . We have neither the authority nor the funds, and time is fleeting." [3]

As he spoke it was already too late to let contracts for buildings to be completed that fall. In September when the legislation was finally approved, he was faced by bad weather and poor working conditions, which imposed endless delays and vastly increased the costs estimates. An attempt to speed up the construction program led inevitably to rising expenditures, and unexpected requirements for roads and streets and laying of drains added to the outlays. The War Department had escaped censure during the winter of 1939, Marshall believed, only because he was dealing with Regulars who were old-timers and "didn't make any reclamers to the press and nobody heard about it." [4] The new men were more vocal, and the Army was soon under attack. In the spring of 1941 Marshall was forced to delay inductions until new barracks were completed, and he faced the unpleasant task of telling Congress that he had to have more money for camp construction. It was a ticklish subject, and he discussed in detail with his staff the best way to approach the committees waiting for him on Capitol Hill. Realistically he decided that the only course was one of complete frankness. With the candor that usually disarmed his toughest critics he accepted the blame for the delays and the increased cost. But he reminded the congressmen of their failure to act speedily on his requests when some of the delays might have been avoided.

The success of his appeal was not lost on Mrs. Marshall. In the following year when she took advantage of the General's absence to make major repairs on their home in Leesburg, she found that costs rapidly outran her largest estimates. On the General's return she showed him the improvements and then added shrewdly, before showing him the bills, ' Remember your testimony . . . on the construction of camps. It costs more to do things in a hurry." In her case candor also paid off. "There isn't going to be any investigation of this job," he said with a grin. [5]

The mounting criticism of the Army's construction program led indirectly to the establishment of the Senate Special Committee to Investigate the National defense program, which brought to public recognition its chairman, Senator Harry S. Truman, Democrat of Missouri. Concerned over charges of waste and favoritism in the building of Fort Leonard Wood in his home state, the Missourian in March 1941 proposed his special committee. Roosevelt, Stimson, and Marshall recalled the Joint Civil War Committee, established by Congress to oversee the conduct of that war, which had ended by interfering actively with operations. Recognizing the problems that a politician intent on advancing his own fortunes could create by irresponsible charges and indiscriminate hauling up of military and civilian leaders before the committee, the White House and the War Department were alarmed by the proposal. On reflection, General Marshall argued that it was not prudent for the Army to take a defensive attitude toward the Truman Committee or any other that might be established by Congress. "It seems to me," he declared, "that a free and easy and whole-souled manner of cooperation with these committees is more likely to create an impression that everything is all right in the War Department, than is a resentful attitude, and that it must be assumed that members of Congress are just as patriotic as we. . . . My guess is that in the current investigations, no one is going to hurt the Army and I do not believe that we should adopt an attitude of official nervousness." [6]

His healthy attitude toward Congress and Truman's handling of his duties created an atmosphere in which the Special Committee helped protect the War Department against outside attacks and found and permitted the correction of many abuses before there was chance of scandal.[7] What might have been a serious embarrassment became an asset, and the responsible action of Senator Truman helped to place him in line for the vice-presidential nomination in 1944. His cooperation with General Marshall in this period helped lay the basis for mutual trust between the two men that resulted in the closest friendship of Marshall's later career.

Delays in construction and excessive costs severely tried the patience of the Chief of Staff, but he saved his choicest profanity for the War Department system and the lack of imagination of a staff that permitted generations-old inertia and an antiquated set of regulations to delay the movement of matériel to troops in the field. His first showdown with the foot-draggers of his own organization came during his first winter as Chief of Staff.

The explosion grew out of a visit to Fort Benning soon after units of the 1st Division had moved there from New York and attempted to adapt to the rigors of an unusually cold winter. Seeing the men standing around in the cold, he ordered rough lumber sent down so that the men could build shacks "where they could open their mail or have a first-aid shelter." As he visited various units during his inspection, his orderly—Sergeant James W. Powder—was approached by one of the first sergeants for aid in getting extra blankets or quilts to meet the severe shortage that they faced.[8] The General at once promised to see that additional covers were shipped and instructed Powder to remind him of the matter on their return to Washington. Some weeks later, once again at Benning with the General, Powder was approached by the same first sergeant, who said, "You're a helluva of a fine friend." When he asked, "Why?" the sergeant retorted, "We are still waiting for them quilts." As the Chief of Staff was going into dinner that evening Powder told him of the incident. The Chief of Staff's mouth hardened and his cheeks grew red. "That was the first time I had ever seen anger in his face," Powder recalled. "We'll find out why they weren't sent," Marshall snapped.[9]

Back in Washington a few days later, Marshall called in members of the Quartermaster staff. He was "outraged" to find that the officials, unable to find proper authorization for the blankets and quilts, had handled the matter in a routine way, demanding through the frozen channels of normal communication that proper requisitions forms be submitted. When he asked for a report, one of the officers responsible for the delay said that he had "fixed up" the matter and nothing more would be heard of it. This combination of formal washing of hands and sweeping the dirt under the rug infuriated the General. "I am not worried about not hearing any more about it," the General exploded, "I want the matter arranged." Bluntly he ordered, "Get these blankets and stoves and every other damn thing that's needed out tonight, not tomorrow morning, and not two weeks from now. I don't care what regulations are upset or anything of that character. We are going to take care of the troops first, last, and all the time."

When his anger subsided he concluded that the trouble lay less in bureaucratic indifference than in "the pinchpenny policy" the Army had been forced to follow for years. Many of the officers had become so sensitive to criticism directed at them by congressional committees that they seemed convinced that "the main purpose of the War Department was to operate in a way that no congressman could possibly criticize [the Army] for 'spending any money.' " [10]

Until the reorganization of the Army in 1942 permitted him greater control over the situation he pounded unceasingly at his supply staff to move clothing and equipment to the field. He laid down his most famous dictum on supply when he learned during one of his trips to the field that most of the units had shortages in supplies of clothing. When he complained to his supply chiefs they showed him inventories of well-stocked warehouses and stacks of requisitions being processed. He was not impressed by the lists, reminding them that recently, after he had been told by the Quartermaster that the Fort Myer Post Exchange had socks, he had been unable to buy a pair for himself. He suggested that they deal with units in the field as if the War Department were a mail-order company trying to dispose of surplus stocks. He declared crisply, "I am interested in the soldier having his pants." [11]

From the major task of moving basic supplies to field units he turned to the knotty problems of meeting complaints over food and clothing and recreation. He was haunted by the recollection that thousands of soldiers at the close of World War I had believed the Army had no interest in their welfare and made no effort to better their conditions. Their bitterness remained with them on their return to civilian life, where they became critics of the peacetime Army. He wanted no battalions of discontented veterans to fight the War Department in the years to come. Some officers misread his purpose, saying that he listened too much to "cry-babies." But he was not being naïve or soft-headed. He had served long enough in the sun and the cold and the battle to know the difference between a private's "beefing" and justified protests. All soldiers complained about their food, the hours of drill, the unfairness of inspections, and the stupidity of their officers. This type of complaint he took for granted and joked about it with civilians who took it seriously. He took great pleasure in informing anxious parents and clucking congressmen that the "starving" recruits over whose waistlines they were worrying had gained fifteen or twenty pounds during their early weeks in service. Propaganda to get a cake or cookies from home, he laughingly told members of the American Legion in 1941, was responsible for many of the complaining letters.[12]

His natural skepticism as to the seriousness of complaints so long as they remained on the level of those expressed by college students or boys away at summer camp for the first time did not blind him, as it did many of his subordinates, to the importance of guarding against subtler causes of discontent. "Soldiers will tolerate almost anything in an officer except unfairness and ignorance," he told his colleagues. "They are quick to detect either." [13]

From long experience and instinctive sympathy for the feelings of the individual he struggled to eliminate small things that could build dissatisfaction and resentment. He protested when a member of his staff suggested that the War Department save on construction costs by following the World War I practice of leaving barracks unpainted.[14] Years before, as a young officer in Oklahoma, he had been able to develop pride among the sergeants' wives who lived on Soapsuds Row by offering to paint kitchens in return for clean front yards. He said in 1940 that soldiers in World War I, moving rapidly through camps to overseas billets, had paid little attention to the nature of the barracks. In these times of peace when they might have to live for months in the same drab buildings, it was essential to provide some element of dignity in the men's surroundings.

Having been burned black by the sun in a Texas summer and nearly frozen in northern New York and in unheated quarters in France, he knew at first hand the discomforts men had to suffer. He saw no reason, while there was no fighting, why the Army should not eliminate those unpleasant elements of training that added little or nothing to the soldier's preparation. When pertinent, he authorized and praised training in the California deserts or in the mountains of Colorado for men who were to fight in these environments. But in the prewar period, when a well-wisher proposed that men wear steel helmets in training, he wrote that this article of apparel "was developed and worn in the climate of Europe, and you can fry eggs on it in Arizona and could have broiled a steak on it in August at Manassas." For the moment he preferred to forgo this item of realism.[15]

He recognized the soldier's distaste for uncomfortable and ill-fitting clothing, and he campaigned for tailor shops on each post to make uniforms less ridiculous in appearance; he also encouraged experiments with caps and jackets and shoes that combined comfort with neatness. In these efforts he and his associates were often defeated by cost or tradition or the sheer lack of time. He sometimes received officers while sitting on the floor, with members of the Quartermaster Corps, examining a new shoe or a jacket that had been ripped open so that he could check it personally for service and comfort.

From the time of his first command in the Philippines when, as a twenty-one-year-old second lieutenant, he had tried to find means of providing amusement for a company in a remote part of Mindoro, he knew the importance of proper recreation to morale. Shortly before he came to Washington, when he was dealing daily with discipline problems at isolated camps of the Civilian Conservation Corps in Oregon, he drew up a recommendation that places be provided reasonably close to posts where men could get away briefly from the routine of barracks life. His transfer to the War Department came before he could put the plan into effect, but he recalled it two years later as men began to flow into Army camps throughout the country. Often located in isolated areas or near small towns because of the need of placing them in sparsely settled country that afforded open fields for training and maneuver, the camps at the beginning provided no recreational facilities. Often the nearby towns were helpless to cope with the thousands of restless soldiers who came on pass over the weekends. In 1940, before the large expansion of the Army began, the Chief of Staff ordered the construction of tented recreational camps some miles away from large posts. These simple accommodations were free, and their meals set at prices ranging from fifteen to thirty cents. Nearby communities cooperated in providing local entertainment. The first camps were located along the Gulf Coast of the United States; by midsummer 1940 plans were on foot for similar centers in other parts of the South and in the Middle West. By mid-July *The New York Times* was praising General Marshall for solving the Army's recreation problem, announcing that by fall he would be able to provide room for 20,000 men.[16]

Before the end of the year the Chief of Staff had an alarming situation on his hands. His modest recreational centers were hopelessly inadequate to accommodate the tremendous influx of National Guard and selective service troops. Soon the General was confronted by the same problems of drinking, prostitution, and disorder that he had fought in Tientsin as a regimental executive fifteen years before.[17]

In an effort to judge the seriousness of the situation for himself, Marshall had set off some time earlier on a Haroun al Rashid trip to a small southern town near a large military base. Wearing civilian dress, he checked into a downtown hotel and then at about 6:30 that evening walked out to find a place to eat. Milling crowds of soldiers jammed every restaurant, and scores of men stood waiting for every available seat. It was nearly four hours later before he found a place at a lunch counter where nothing was left save "some warmed-over biscuits and things of that sort." After finishing his unpalatable meal he sought fresh air in the central part of the town. Every bench in the city square was filled, and hundreds of men wandered about aimlessly. Marshall was disturbed at this complete lack of any recreational facilities. He returned to Washington convinced that without some improvement there would soon be "an outbreak of some sort or other" in towns overwhelmed by thousands of soldiers on pass.[18]

Near Christmas, 1940, Marshall and Stimson took the first step toward solving the problem by appointing members of a War Department Community Service Committee to plan recreational activities for soldiers. Frederick Osborn of New York, an old friend of Franklin Roosevelt's who had worked with the Army Red Cross in World War I, was selected as its head. He joined the Secretary of War, the Chief of Staff, Lieutenant Colonel William Draper, and Charles P. Taft on January 3, 1941, in a careful survey of what had been done in World War I and what could be set up to meet current problems. To achieve coordination on the broadest basis possible, Secretary Stimson and Secretary of Navy Knox appointed a Joint Committee on Welfare and Recreation. Out of their efforts eventually grew the United Services Organization—the USO— with its program for providing halls where servicemen on leave could buy light refreshments at reasonable prices, find a congenial spot to write letters, listen to records, or dance with partners selected by local committees. Later the organization sent out traveling shows to camps throughout the country and eventually to every theater where American soldiers, sailors, fliers, and marines were in combat. Once the program was established, General Marshall left the supervision of the Army side of it to Secretary Stimson and his civilian aides, but he never lost interest in its activities or discounted its tremendous importance in maintaining morale.[19]

The USO was a brilliant triumph, but Marshall never forgot that the morale of troops in training and headed for combat had other more basic foundations. Matters of health, food, promotion, mistreatment by superiors, housing—any one of these could cause sullen resentment within the ranks and ultimately break out in severe criticism by parents, congressmen, and the press. By the spring of 1941 he had concluded that many commanders in their proper concentration on training had allowed it "to cloud the issue of cause and effect as to morale." To stress the degree to which he valued this function, he made the Morale Officer, formerly an assistant to the Adjutant General, a brigadier general and head of a special branch. "Morale," he reminded his generals, "is primarily a function of command," putting them on notice that they would be held strictly responsible for eliminating those issues that created special problems.[20]

Marshall warned the members of his own staff in Washington that they must be vigilant in removing causes for complaint and in improving conditions at posts throughout the country. No matter how hurried his visit to a distant camp, he asked what Washington could do to improve conditions. He deliberately tried to find at every headquarters some deficiency he could correct or some item that could be supplied. A part of his technique, as he stood near his plane ready to depart, was to question a commander, penciling the request in his pocket memorandum book. On the day of his return to Washington the items were transferred to a list that was quickly circulated to the staff sections concerned. "I reached my office this morning," he wrote one division commander in a typical communication, "and have immediately taken up the matter of getting some additional authorization for construction at your camp."[21] He did not add that his staff knew that the best way to gain forgiveness for its previous sins of omission was to break all records in filling the request.

At the end of one of his quick sweeps across the country in late

March and early April he showered on the chiefs of his principal staff divisions demands for investigations of complaints or corrections of problems that he personally had spotted. His questions were sharp, pointed, and demanded immediate action: Why was there a shortage of shoes at the Reception Center at Monterey, a shortage of hospital equipment at Fort Sill, a delay in the delivery of laundry machines at Camp Beauregard, a delay in construction of recreation facilities for Negro troops at Camp Claiborne—a service club, a tent theater, and a guest house—a failure to reply to the 367th Infantry's request for field manuals, a lack of basic issues for the 18th Field Artillery, and no books for the new recreation halls at Camps Livingston and Claiborne? He had also noticed conditions that could be improved or solutions adopted to improve morale and passed them on for further study. Was it feasible to have air-conditioning in hospital rooms in the Louisiana camps? How about more general use of the shoulder patch to improve unit pride? Send some oil to Camp Bowie, Texas, to keep down the dust. Look into the matter of sun helmets for flying cadets and, while checking on that, note that newly inducted men at various camps are showing severe sunburn for lack of proper field headgear. On trip after trip, the list grew in length and diversity.[22]

He was equally vigilant in dealing with complaints from political sources. One evening the wife of a Rhode Island senator leaned across the dinner table to say she had heard that 80 per cent of the men in Camp Stewart, Georgia, were sick. Next morning he requested a report from the commanding officer. By the following day he was able to assure her that there were forty sick out of an enlisted strength of 1516.[23] A congressman called to report that visitors to the headquarters battery at Fort Hancock, New Jersey, had found the men were being served bad eggs, not allowed cereal for breakfast, and fed from unsanitary kitchens. At once he demanded an investigation and improvement of conditions.[24]

Few complaints received the special care that he and Secretary Stimson gave those forwarded by Mrs. Roosevelt. Although interested in any case of neglect or mistreatment, the President's wife acted as the special advocate of Negro troops. Hundreds of Negro parents considered her office a special court of appeal for their problems. She made no effort to pass on the correctness of their complaints but quickly sent them on to the War Department for proper action. On arrival, all such letters were "flagged" with a distinctive slip of paper, indicating that these must be acknowledged immediately and action taken at once to investigate the matter. If basis was found for the complaint, the report also had to indicate what corrective measures had been taken. As the Army grew and the number of complaints increased, with Mrs. Roosevelt's extension of her inquiries to cases of alleged discrimination against enlistees formerly active in liberal or radical organizations who were now seeking commissions in the Army, General Marshall assigned one or two members of his staff to see that all complaints from the White House were carefully examined.

In order to sample for himself the woes and complaints of men in uniform General Marshall early in his tour at the War Department directed the Secretary, General Staff, to prepare a summary of all messages received from men in the service and from their families, giving names and addresses and the main points of their letters. He estimated that he spent twenty minutes a day on these in the prewar years and personally answered at least six of them daily.[25] If a gripe had merit he sent it on to the soldier's division commander, directing an investigation and correction of any abuses that might be found. Perhaps the high point of his leniency came when a soldier mailed him a tough steak as undeniable evidence of the poor cooking inflicted on his company. In passing on the letter to the man's commanding officer, Marshall said that he could not send the steak since it had reached a point "where it has to be disposed of" but that it hinted at a poorly run mess "for which I find few excuses." Noting that he was putting the man out on a limb by revealing his name, he warned the officer that there might be something in the complaint, adding, "So do not kill him until you have looked into it." [26]

Until the coming of war the General went to amazing lengths to grant what he considered to be reasonable requests for changes in stations, for transfers to positions offering better opportunities, and even to requests by former patients of an Army doctor that he be transferred to a hospital where he could practice his specialty. On the day before Pearl Harbor he forwarded to a divisional commander the moving letter of a sergeant formerly assigned to Pershing's headquarters who admitted that he had been badgered by his daughter and her mother-in-law into asking that his young son-in-law be assigned to a base near home. Marshall wrote that the War Department usually kept its hands off individual assignments but that the letter appealed to him "as rather pathetic" in view of the fact that the poor sergeant was being actively besieged by the two women. Marshall said if there was a vacancy in Florida and the man could fill the bill, to send him down.[27]

It was not enough to correct ills and watch for telltale indications of discontent. Marshall was convinced that men fought better and were less inclined to protest if they understood why they were in the service and what they were contributing to the nation's defense. "Do they know what is going on and why?" he asked his Inspector General in the spring of 1941. He directed the various Army commanders to make a spirited effort to explain to all soldiers the nature of the heritage they were defending, and why it was necessary that they do their part. Special textbooks were developed on American history and international relations, and officers were appointed in each headquarters to lecture once a week or oftener in the School of the Citizen Soldier. The program was beset by difficulties in the prewar period, and General Marshall proceeded warily for fear of "being charged with conducting a propaganda service under the power of military control and in opposition to the minority group in Congress." [28] It suffered also from the inability of commanders to find effective speakers in many units and the deadly effects of prepared lectures indifferently read to bored troops. A strenuous effort was made to improve the program by sending out special lecturers and by instituting discussion groups. General Marshall continued to be dissatisfied with the results until after the coming of war, when it was possible to prepare a series of movies on "Why We Fight" that proved to be almost universally popular and effective in putting across the message he desired.

The question of morale, as Marshall knew, did not stop with removing the negative factors that created complaints. There was a need for leadership and discipline and spirit to supply the element that made men fight. In a speech in June of 1941 at Trinity College, Hartford, Connecticut, he declared: "Today war, total war, is not a succession of mere episodes in a day or week. It is a long-drawn-out and intricately planned business and the longer it continues the heavier are the demands on the character of the men engaged in it." It was true that war was fought with "physical weapons of flame and steel," but it was not the possession of the arms or use of them that decided the issue. "It is morale that wins the victory." This intangible element, he continued, is a state of mind. "It is steadfastness and courage and hope. It is confidence and zeal and loyalty. It is *élan, esprit de corps,* and determination." Above all, "It is staying power, the spirit which endures to the end—the will to win." [29]

The elements that went to make up morale depended heavily on the new type of discipline he wanted for the citizen army he was developing. The older type of discipline, he declared, "was the ob- jective of all that monotonous drilling which, to be honest, achieved obedience at the expense of initiative. It excluded 'thought' of any kind. As an old drill sergeant put it one day, 'Give me control of the *instinct* and you can have the *reason.*'" But that type of Army was gone. "Theirs not to reason why—theirs but to do or die" did not fit a citizen army. The new discipline was based on "respect rather than fear; on the effect of good example given by officers; on the intelligent comprehension by all ranks of why an order has to be and why it must be carried out; on a sense of duty, on *esprit de corps.*"

To the cynical among his hearers, it may have appeared that he was still saying that soldiers must do what they are told. And in- deed that was what he meant. But the individual must be given a reason for his obedience. "From a moral standpoint," Marshall argued, "there is no question as to which of the two disciplines is finer if you admit that respect is to be preferred to fear; the white flame of enthusiasm to the dull edge of routine; the spiritual to the instinctive." It was a large order but worth trying.

In the days when the United States was finding it difficult to prepare for war in time of peace, General Marshall's patience and his understanding of the problems of the civilian turned soldier eased the process of raising the Army. An able historian, Dr. Kent R. Greenfield, chairman of the Department of History at Johns Hopkins University, listening to Marshall explain his program at Baltimore in the spring of 1941, found his skepticism about some of the Army's program being swept away as the tall soldier care- fully explained what he was trying to do. Impressed by his sincerity and his humanity and understanding, the scholar who one day was to direct the Army's historical program recorded the impact made by this unusual officer. "If he represents our Army, the American Army is yet a part of the American people," Greenfield wrote. "He pointed out the time consumed by working in a democracy, but with no impatience. He evidently thinks the advantages are worth the waste of time." [30]

The willingness of the Army Chief of Staff to listen to the complaints of the newest recruit and, more important, to correct them if they were well founded was the essence of democracy. And that, as Marshall and Stimson never let their colleagues and subordinates forget, was what the fighting was about.

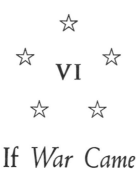

If War Came

IN a rare complaint about General Marshall, Secretary Stimson
once said that at times he was too diplomatic. A staff officer who
watched him daily during the confused days of 1940-41 said the
same thing in a slightly different way: "He stuck to his job and did
the best he could, playing politics with the rest of them, and ultimately proved himself as good as the best. He was thus able to be of
great service to his country. If he had been born with less self-
control and tact he would have become ineffective in his job and
would have been replaced." A third observer, Sir John Dill, Chief
of the Imperial General Staff, remarked after his first meeting with
Marshall in the fall of 1941 that the American was less interested
in strategy than he had hoped. He found him absorbed in details of
war production and Army organization rather than operational
planning.[1]

His three colleagues were disappointed that the American Chief
of Staff had not stepped out more vigorously in the framing of
United States strategy for the war. Stimson desired a more positive
commitment to British victory; the staff officer wanted a bold stand
against the President's dispersions of American military effort; and
Dill hoped to find him ready with plans for active collaboration in
the European war. General Marshall's hesitance was due neither to
lack of interest nor to excessive caution. He believed that without a
larger and better-trained Army detailed strategic plans were almost
purely academic. Until the early fall of 1941 at least, he held serious reservations about the wisdom of American entrance into war.

If an administration critic, who pictured the War Department as
an incubator of militarism prolifically hatching designs for war,

had looked in on the activities of the planning staffs or the discussions during coffee breaks, he would have been surprised by the strong element of isolationism and the absence of militancy in their deliberations. Many of Marshall's colleagues had come out of World War I convinced that United States intervention had been an error and that Wilson had been duped into furnishing men for a victory that failed to advance American interests.

By 1940 one could find as many different views on American foreign policy among those military leaders who expressed opinions as among the general population. Some shared the view of the America First Committee that true patriotism enjoined strict adherence to Washington's admonition to stay clear of foreign quarrels. A thoroughly prepared America could successfully resist any outside power or combinations of powers; American democracy could be preserved only by staying out of alien wars.[2]

Another group was willing to assist Great Britain in its struggle for survival but only on the firm understanding that American viewpoints would be considered first. The Joint Army-Navy planners spoke for this element when they issued instructions to American representatives engaged in conversations with the British in the spring of 1941. They warned that "we cannot afford, nor do we need, to entrust our national future to British direction." Since British postwar interests, commercial and military, were never absent from British minds, "we should likewise safeguard our own eventual interests." [3]

With reservations, General Marshall belonged to the latter group. Although he had been repelled by "treaty-port" British that he had met in Tientsin, Marshall escaped the anti-English bias nursed by some of his associates. From his service abroad in World War I he retained a lively sympathy for France during the worst of her disasters. He was no German-hater, but he was disturbed by the rise of Hitler and seriously alarmed about a possible Nazi challenge to the United States' special interests in Latin America. He shared the typical military distrust of the Japanese but saw them as less of a menace than the Germans. In any war with Britain and France on one side and Germany and Japan on the other, his sympathies were solidly with the Western Powers. But in 1940 he stopped short of favoring war. In 1941 as the flames of war grew hotter he avoided full commitment to the Allied cause, hoping still for time to create a strong Army and Air Corps before becoming completely immersed in Europe's struggles.

Dominant in Marshall's thinking during this prewar period, as Dill correctly saw, were two themes: the organization of the Army and the spurring of war production. Still he did not neglect the broad outlines of American strategy or the examination of military collaboration with Great Britain *if* the United States found itself at war with the Axis Powers. The key to his thinking about American involvement was always *if* rather than the *when* that the more militant interventionists such as Stimson, Morgenthau, and Knox increasingly employed.

The guidelines of Army and Navy cooperation in case of war had been laid down long before he became Chief of Staff. In the pigeonholes of the War Plans Division were carefully revised and recently formulated plans to cover future American military actions. They were the product of the interservice consultation that since 1903 had been centered in an agency called the Joint Board, whose members were charged with considering "all matters and policies involving joint action of the Army and Navy relative to the national defense." The membership had changed occasionally through the decades, but in Marshall's time it consisted of the Chief of Staff and the Chief of Naval Operations, their deputies, their Chiefs of War Plans, and representatives of the air services. This board in turn had its joint planners.[4]

Few officers in the large aggregation of faithful and anonymous "staffs" that make the War and Navy Departments function are more faceless than those who "plan." Some of them—Marshall and Eisenhower are examples—find their way to high command, but during their period as planners they usually are overtired workhorses writing and rewriting hundreds of papers, produced often at a moment's notice and at late hours, in which their contribution is often unrecognized. Their identifying initials, scrawled on thousands of pages of legal-sized documents, reveal little more than the amazing energy of the inscribers.

Beginning with a single thread furnished by the President or the Chief of Staff or the superior next in line, the planner carefully weaves in additional threads from old material in the files, strands that had been knitted into other patterns and then unraveled for further use, and fresh skeins picked from recent reports and newer "appreciations." The design that emerges may never be used but only stored for emergencies that may never arise. It is an inert piece of material waiting for someone with the power of decision to convert it to utility.

Historians who write about the plans of diplomats and generals often pull out old files and engage in dusty explanations of projects that never saw the light of day. Although dull to read, these plans serve a vital function in the development of governmental policy. A chance phrase, a clever concept, a useful formula, may survive dozens of changes over a period of years in departmental musings on what would happen in case of foreign shifts of policy or of war. A proposed solution to meet a specific situation in the 1920s may survive a generation of broad turnings in policy to reappear in totally different surroundings, the threads of its identity still verifiable in spite of a radically new environment.

So it was with the work of the anonymous planners who had begun before World War I to formulate color plans, among them ORANGE for the Rising Sun of Japan and RED for the color Great Britain had used to mark out its dominion on the maps of the globe, outlining general steps for joint Army-Navy action if the United States were attacked by any one of these powers. After World War I the plans were carefully revised, the chief emphasis being placed on plan ORANGE, the only one that seemed likely to be used. Imaginative planners also produced a two-color combination, ORANGE-RED, to deal with an improbable collaboration of Japan and Great Britain against the United States. The plan was academic, but one basic idea stuck in their minds and was repeated in later outlines. Assuming that the United States with a one-ocean Navy would have to deal with enemies in two oceans, the American planners proposed to fight the stronger power in the Atlantic before turning to deal with the ORANGE forces in the Pacific. When Germany replaced Britain as a likely partner in the two-power color scheme, this concept remained.

Fight the strong Atlantic power first, advised the strategists of the Joint Army-Navy Board in 1939 when, turning and re-turning the pages of possible combinations, they pitted the United States and Great Britain and perhaps France against Germany and Italy in the Atlantic, or against all three Axis Powers in both oceans. All the basic colors were mingled to produce several somewhat differ-

ent RAINBOWS. Five separate variations on the theme were handed
to the Chief of Staff and the Chief of Naval Operations shortly
before Marshall took over his War Department duties. Covering
nearly every possible contingency, from defense of the Western
Hemisphere to the defense of the western Pacific, the color wheel
came to rest finally on RAINBOW 5. In case of a two-ocean war between the United States and Great Britain and the Axis partners,
American forces would be concentrated first against Germany,
while maintaining a defensive posture in the Pacific. In the years
that followed the plan would be modified, but when the United
States at last entered the war it sought its eventual victory at the
end of that particular RAINBOW.

In 1939, during the early period of American neutrality, the
United States concentrated on strengthening the defenses of the
Western Hemisphere in the Caribbean and the Atlantic. The fol-
lowing spring, as Japan showed signs of expanding in the Pacific,
President Roosevelt shifted his attention to that ocean, ordering
the fleet, then holding maneuvers in Hawaiian waters, to remain at
Pearl Harbor rather than returning to the west coast bases.

So long as the British and French fleets held the Atlantic it was
possible for the United States to shift its emphasis to the Pacific.
The defeat of France demanded a new look at the problem. On the
mid-June morning that Marshal Pétain asked the Germans for an
armistice, General Marshall summoned his advisers to an early
conference to consider the implications of the Allied defeat. Although he was immediately concerned about the prospect of a Japanese raid against Hawaii to create a diversion that would prevent
the shift of American naval strength to Britain's aid, his chief
thought was of the danger in the Atlantic area. If the French Navy
went to Germany and Italy, he foresaw the possibility of the Nazis
rushing "the South American situation to a head in a few weeks."
It was necessary, he believed, to review the nation's war plans.
"Are we not forced into a question of reframing our naval policy,"
he asked, "that is, purely defensive action in the Pacific, with a
main effort on the Atlantic side?" [5]

The Chief of War Plans Division, Major General George V.
Strong, was pessimistic. He feared that Britain's capitulation might
soon follow that of France. If such a disaster developed, the only
ray of hope was that the British would move their fleet to Ameri-

can ports. Facing the prospect realistically, he thought that the United States must bolster its Atlantic defense.

Marshall nodded agreement. "We have to be prepared," he said, "to meet the worst situation that may develop, that is, if we do not have the Allied fleet in the Atlantic." Looking about the room at his advisers, he spoke of the possible mobilization of the National Guard and an attempt to guarantee the protection of South American countries by occupying and holding certain key ports. These actions, if they became necessary, would obviously prevent further shipment of arms and supplies abroad as "we have scraped the bottom so far as the Army is concerned." [6]

Washington's pessimism gave way to cautious hope during the summer as the British continued their gallant fight. To assess their long-term chances of holding out and their requirements for a prolonged conflict, General Marshall and Admiral Stark in August sent representatives to London. After a quick tour of inspection Major General Delos C. Emmons of the Air Corps and General Strong of the War Plans Division reported to the Chief of Staff that the battle was going well and the people of Great Britain seemed in the fight to win. Rear Admiral Robert L. Ghormley, the Navy representative, remained in London on an extended tour of duty, discussing informally with British naval officers the bases of cooperative action in case the United States should enter war. None of these guarded actions constituted a formal agreement or the suggestion of an alliance, but tracks were laid along which a future partnership might run smoothly.

Gradually Stark and Marshall began to consider rather definite outlines of combined action in case war came. As the commander of the only American force then capable of taking effective action outside the United States, Admiral Stark assumed the lead in sketching this course of future cooperation.

Friend of Franklin Roosevelt since World War I, the white-thatched, bespectacled, scholarly looking Chief of Naval Operations had served during part of that conflict on Admiral William Sims' American headquarters staff in London and had a sympathetic understanding of Britain's problems. Selected by the President as head of the Navy over several of his seniors, Stark was regarded in Washington as an able officer unduly responsive to Roosevelt's views. While perhaps as unfair to the admiral as a similar judgment made on Marshall at the time of his appointment, this view of his status was accurate in the sense that the President kept the Navy more completely under his thumb than he did the Army. Although this paternal relationship was undoubtedly irksome at times, it gave the Chief of Naval Operations an easy entree to the White House that Marshall never gained.

By late fall of 1940 Stark believed that the time had come for the United States to explore with the British, Canadians, and the Dutch possible courses of future American military action. In one of the key strategic documents of the war he examined carefully four alternatives reminiscent of possibilities suggested earlier by the RAINBOW planners: that the United States (a) concentrate on hemisphere defense only; (b) maintain equal vigilance in the Atlantic and the Pacific; (c) build its chief defense in the Pacific; or (d) pursue a strong offensive policy in the Atlantic as an ally of Britain. Agreeing that Plan A was the only one that the United States could accept for the present, he urged that Plan D (Plan DOG as it was known in the code language of the services) be accepted as the ultimate policy for the future.[7]

At first General Marshall was almost noncommittal. Lacking a fighting force that could contribute heavily to any offensive policy within the next eighteen months, he preferred to proceed cautiously. Recognizing that the services required "some vague idea of what we could expect from the British—what sort of help they would want and what sort of help they should get from us," the Chief of Staff "acquiesced" in the proposal for a conference with them that winter. Otherwise, he said, "we would start with no basis at all if war developed later on." [8]

Although unready to consider any alliance with Great Britain at this stage of the war, General Marshall saw the advantages of stressing American defense activities in the Atlantic. Assistance to the British there helped keep a strong ally in the fight, strengthened hemisphere security, and laid a sound basis for eventual collaboration with Britain in case the United States entered the war. Having accepted the Atlantic as the crucial theater, Marshall frowned on further naval build-up in the Pacific. In late November he urged Admiral Stark to concentrate on aiding the British to survive by avoiding dispersion of the Navy. He was against accepting a British invitation to send naval reinforcements to Singapore. A better plan, he thought, was for the United States Navy to free the British of some of their Atlantic responsibilities in order that they could shift forces to the Far East.[9]

A full year before Pearl Harbor the Chief of Staff committed himself to the Europe First strategy. His and Stark's views were reflected in the Joint Planning Committee's report of December 21, 1940, summarizing the American position for guidance of United States representatives in the forthcoming conferences with the British. After urging that the armed forces be increased rapidly, while avoiding actions that would provoke war, the planners declared that a firm decision should be made "not willingly to engage in any war against Japan." If the United States was forced into war with that country, Pacific operations should be restricted "so as to permit use of forces for a major offensive in the Atlantic." [10] Marshall and Stark promptly approved the recommendations. Except for modifications in the summer of 1941 to permit a strengthening of the American position in the Philippines, the General maintained these views consistently until after the Pearl Harbor attack.

The American-British Conversations (ABC), suggested by Stark in November, took place between United States and British Army and Navy representatives in Washington, January 29 to March 29, 1941. Elaborate precautions were taken to keep the meetings secret and to remove any possible suggestion of official commitment by the United States. The President carefully took no part in the proceedings, and Marshall and Stark, after appearing briefly at the opening session, stayed aloof from the remaining deliberations.[11]

The report of the British and American representatives was later approved by the British government, although President Roosevelt declined to give it his formal blessing. Treated as a fairly specific understanding by the service leaders of both nations, it became the basis of the new United States RAINBOW 5 plan.

Much of what the Americans had to say had been set forth earlier—the United States was interested primarily in hemisphere defense and the maintenance of Britain's position in Europe. Running through their conclusions were threads of Churchillian strategy: operations to knock Italy out of the war, a major air offensive and minor amphibious raids against German-held areas, and the encouragement of resistance groups in occupied Europe. Still painfully short of men and arms, the two powers had few other courses open. Only for the undetermined future could they speak of a build-up for a final offensive against Germany.

By taking a hand, even unofficially, in these deliberations, Marshall opened himself to later charges that he had worked with Roosevelt to bring the United States through the back door to war. The General vigorously denied the accusation, adding in retrospect: "It was a question of knowing what we might run into and what [the] conditions would be under which we met it. . . . We needed to know what sort of response they would like and what sort of assistance they could give. . . . I don't feel that in any way we committed the United States to take specific military action unless we were attacked. The advantages of the talks were—they were done without regard to the President. . . . It was done to find out what we needed to know without in any way involving him in any commitments of any kind." [12]

The American representatives had indeed made no pledge to enter alongside the British. But they had gone far toward specifying the type of war the country would wage if it entered the conflict with Germany. Robert Sherwood concluded correctly that the conversations and exchange of opinions "provided the highest degree of *srategic perparedness* that the United States or probably any other nonaggressor nation has ever had before entry into war." [13]

Whatever the future, Marshall agreed with Stimson and Stark that the United States should continue its dialogue with Great Britain. Soon after the meetings ended in Washington he sent Major General James E. Chaney to London as "Special Army Observer, London," to join Admiral Ghormley. His instructions reflected the current combination of caution and confusion. Marshall warned Chaney to avoid any commitments in his discussions with the British while informing him that, in case American forces should be sent later to the United Kingdom, he would serve either as commander or chief of staff.

Chaney went to London at a tragic time. In the Atlantic, the Mediterranean, and the Middle East, the war was going badly for the British. German submarines were taking an increasing toll of British shipping throughout that spring. Losses were so heavy by April that Stark considered the situation hopeless, "except as we take strong measures to save it." [14]

Foreseeing the necessity for United States action, the American

Navy as early as January had established a force to convoy merchant ships and shortly afterward instituted antisubmarine training. On February 1 Stark directed the establishment of an Atlantic Fleet, placing it under the command of Admiral Ernest J. King. With the preliminary measures settled, the President in the next two months considered plans for escorting convoys at least as far as Iceland and perhaps to Great Britain, or, as an alternative, patrolling the western Atlantic to gather information on German submarine movements that could be passed to the British. In early April, after favoring the Navy's convoy plan, Roosevelt veered back to a more cautious course. On April 10 he proposed to establish a line in mid-Atlantic, west of which the Navy would send out patrols. These ships would have the task of following convoys and of alerting them and British warships to the presence of German vessels discovered in the area. Dropping his earlier plan to make a public announcement of the establishment of a patrol, the President told Stimson on April 15 that he had decided just to give the Navy its orders.[15]

It was less easy for the United States to aid Great Britain in the Mediterranean and the Middle East. Even as Roosevelt and his advisers discussed schemes for patrolling the Atlantic, the Axis forces were pushing the British out of Greece and Libya and threatening Egypt. Like many other American leaders, General Marshall feared that recent reverses might bring the fall of the Churchill government. The War Department's chief intelligence expert on Germany horrified Stimson by declaring that Churchill's diversion of troops from Libya to Greece, an action that failed to save the Greek Army while seriously weakening Wavell's forces, was the most disastrous interference by a political leader in military strategy since the Civil War. The shocked Secretary told Marshall he wanted no more statements reflecting on Churchill. The safety of the United States depended on the British fleet, and the fleet depended on the preservation of the present government. Marshall strictly enjoined all his advisers from open criticisms of the British leader.[16]

The news of the most serious reverses in Libya reached General Marshall while he was on a five-day inspection trip through Kentucky, Texas, Louisiana, and Oklahoma. In a typical whirlwind trip he visited the Armored Force headquarters at Fort Knox, the

Field Artillery School at Fort Sill, a replacement center, a Regular Army and four National Guard divisions and an Air Corps depot, squeezing in an overnight visit with General Pershing at San Antonio and stopping at Texarkana for the funeral of a stanch friend of the Army, Senator Morris Sheppard, chairman of the Senate Military Affairs Committee. He returned to his office on April 14, tanned and fit if a little tired, reporting that the Army was "in bloom now, after a hard winter." [17] His good news was tempered by the thought that the defeats in the Middle East would require him to send weapons and equipment to the British and perhaps dispatch expeditions to relieve their garrisons in the Atlantic or to occupy islands that would be menaced by the Germans.

Marshall met with the President and his chief political and military advisers on April 15 in an atmosphere murky with gloom. After the meeting Harry Hopkins asked the Chief of Staff if he could get information from the British on their military dispositions and plans for future action. With an instinctive distaste for lacerating the raw wounds of an old friend, the Chief of Staff explained, "It would be cruel to probe the British within the next twenty-four hours. They are in a tragic dilemma." Later he added that if he were the Chief of Staff of the British Army he would be very loath to give out secret data. "If they give us information," he said wryly, "the next thing that would happen is that it would be in Kintner and Alsop's column. It is asking a lot to have them give us information of future plans." [18]

A few hours after the White House conference Secretary Stimson called Marshall into a meeting with Hopkins to discuss the value of sending weapons and equipment to the hard-pressed forces in the Middle East. The General corroborated his chief's view that military aid could not arrive there in time to affect the issue. He did not agree with his intelligence experts that the situation was virtually hopeless. Predicting that Rommel might get "bogged down by an adverse climate and the difficulties of the terrain in the North African desert," he gave the Germans only a fifty-fifty chance to take Alexandria.[19]

Stimson had become upset in recent weeks by the tendency of the intelligence experts to overrate German military capabilities. Two days after his discussion with Marshall and Hopkins he told the Chief of Staff that he couldn't stand the attitude of the officers any longer and that Marshall must "tincture up G-2 with some men who have a little broader vision." Refusing to believe that a rosy report would help a tangled situation, the General "slammed back" at Stimson, "as we sometimes do in our conversations," but agreed that he would think over the problem and talk it over with the Secretary again.[20] The issue was postponed, and Stimson was to renew his attack later when the same experts predicted the quick collapse of the Soviet Union in the face of Hitler's armies.

Short tempers and pessimistic reports were symptomatic of growing nervousness over the situation abroad and general confusion in connection with the administration's policy. Hopkins told Stimson that he was trying to introduce some order into White House decision-making by persuading the President to take his military advice from not more than six men instead of listening to the first person who came into his office with an idea. He hoped to arrange a series of discussions to inform the President on national strategy for the future "without regard to politics." Marshall and his staff, already unhappy because "every man who slept in a tent during the last war is a military authority," were delighted at the prospect of getting the President to rely on his Secretary of War and his Chief of Staff for military policy.[21]

They were amazingly optimistic in assuming that Roosevelt could be persuaded overnight to change lifelong habits of picking up advice wherever he found it. General Marshall may have had some doubts, but he decided to act immediately on Hopkins' suggestion. He instructed his chief war planners to discuss ways of beginning "the education of the President as to the true strategic situation—this coming after a period of having been influenced by the State Department." His initial conferences for this purpose were more useful for clarifying his own views and those of his staff than for any immediate effect on the President.[22]

At his early morning meeting with members of his staff on April 16 Marshall asked that they consider whether the country had reached a point where it had to be placed on a war status and if immediate action was necessary. He then asked them to study his questions and report back shortly before noon with their recommendations. They must tell the President if he had "to make a decision now" and what "he has to work with." [23]

The planners were joined at the second meeting by a remarkable officer, Major General Stanley D. Embick, whom General Marshall had summoned from out of town. Former Chief of the War Plans Division and later Deputy Chief of Staff, Embick had been appointed recently by the Chief of Staff as the Army's representative on the Joint Defense Board that had been organized with Canada. More recently he had served as one of the American representatives, along with General Gerow and General Miles and Colonel McNarney, in the conversations with the British. He had gained a reputation as an expert on strategic planning and collaboration with Allied forces in World War I while attached to the American delegation on the Allied War Council.

Embick's experience with the Allies during World War I had made him skeptical of their military judgment. In the spring of 1939 he had warned Marshall that Prime Minister Neville Chamberlain was running a risk of incalculable consequences in intervening either in the Balkans or Poland. If war came, he predicted that the Axis Powers would speedily overrun both areas and that neither the Western Powers nor the Soviet Union would be able to influence the course of events. He had also foretold the period of "the phony war" in which "military activity would become largely restricted to aerial and submarine warfare after stabilization of the western front." [24]

Apparently recalling these accurate forecasts but forgetting the General's accompanying caustic remarks on American interventionists (Embick had said that his views on Stimson would scorch the paper and that those who supported intervention showed less historical sense than the average European peasant, repeating the same fallacies that led to "our being duped twenty years ago"), Marshall asked him to attend the pre-briefing conference and go with him to see the President.

From the standpoint of American national interests, General Embick admitted that the United States could not permit the Germans to conquer the British Isles. But any assistance offered by this country must be carefully hedged lest the American people be committed to "they know not what." He dreaded American involvement in peripheral operations that would sap the country's strength without contributing to its defense. Above all he distrusted the strategic judgment of Winston Churchill. His British friends in France in World War I had been unimpressed by the future Prime Minister, fearing his impulsiveness and his fondness for diversions from the main effort. Embick was still under their spell. Totally ignoring the vital contributions made by the British statesman in one of England's most desperate hours, he concluded that Great Britain might profit if the current crisis resulted in the fall of the Churchill government.[25]

Normally Embick's bias might be dismissed as illustrating the views of only one school of thought in the War Department in 1941. It became highly significant because General Marshall had high regard for his military judgment and later appointed him as the Army member of the future strategy planning staff. Embick's influence was exerted through his own reports and through the views of his son-in-law, Colonel (later General) Albert C. Wedemeyer, a member of the War Plans Division. Embick represented the conservative Army position, watchful always of British schemes and dubious about any policy based on political rather than military considerations. Though more friendly to Britain than Embick and his associates, Marshall never completely rid himself of a certain wariness in dealing with strategy that he believed to be motivated by purely British political interests.

General Marshall questioned his colleague closely when he suggested that the United States stand aside from the conflict, asking at one point, "For the American people is that all you have to say?" When Embick said that increased American participation in the war might decrease sinkings of Allied shipping but that was about all, Marshall got him to agree that such action was, after all, "the vital thing." There is no evidence that he shared Embick's view that Churchill's leadership could be spared at this critical stage of British history. He again admonished his advisers about their criticisms of the Prime Minister, saying that Stimson believed Churchill to be the one British political leader who would continue to wage war and refuse to appease the Nazis.

Most of Marshall's planners at the meeting that morning definitely favored action against the Axis. Colonel Joseph T. McNarney, the blunt airman who had recently returned from an observation trip to Great Britain, put the issue simply: If the British Isles fall, the whole task of opposing the Germans would devolve on the American people. "If we wait," he warned, "we will wind up standing alone and internal disturbances may bring on Communism." McNarney put his finger on the only contribution the United States was then capable of making: naval patrolling of the North Atlantic. Here was the means of insuring that planes and matériel reached the vital center of opposition to Hitler—the British Isles—and of assuring the British people that they could count on American aid. Although the United States ran the risk of provoking the Germans to war, it could keep the British in the fight and at the same time give its own people the time they needed to prepare for action.

The opposing viewpoints expressed by General Embick and Colonel McNarney represented two contradictory elements in General Marshall's own thinking. He recognized the dangers of permitting Great Britain to succumb to Hitler's attacks as well as the risks involved in committing the United States too heavily to British strategy. During the conference the General remarked that Churchill had been influenced in his decision in the Near East "by success against Italy, which was gained after overriding his military advisers." In later years, as he sat at the council table with Churchill, he recalled clearly General Embick's point that it was almost impossible to get the volatile English leader to concentrate on the main battle.

At his meeting with the President on the afternoon of April 16 General Marshall had no opportunity to discuss the broad issues that he had raised with his War Department advisers that morning. The President seemed interested instead in exploring a number of immediate steps to aid the British. He directed Marshall and Stark to examine cargoes ready for shipment to Greece and Yugoslavia to see if any could be diverted to General Wavell. He also asked them to reanalyze the situation in the Eastern Mediterranean, the possible relocation of British ground forces if they were withdrawn from that area, and the potential field of action for the Eastern Mediterranean fleet after its withdrawal. He lingered for a moment on the importance of Dakar, setting off a discussion of the importance of West Africa to future American strategy.[26]

In the week that followed, the Navy outlined for its forces in the Atlantic a Western Hemisphere Defense Plan that put into effect the President's mid-April decision on patrolling. Admiral King indicated that the Western Hemisphere extended from approximately 26 degrees West (a boundary that ran just west of Iceland

and included most of the Azores), westward to the International Date Line in the Pacific, to include the Hawaiian Islands and the Aleutians. The territorial extension was not so important as the reminder that "Entrance into the Western Hemisphere by naval ships or aircraft of belligerents other than those powers having sovereignty over territory in the Western Hemisphere is to be viewed as possibly actuated by an unfriendly interest toward shipping or territory in the Western Hemisphere." [27]

Secretary Stimson was disappointed that Roosevelt had not gone further. He wanted not only escorts for ships but early shifting of a large part of the Pacific Fleet to Atlantic waters. His wishes were contrary to the firm convictions of the Secretary of State, who believed that the Pacific Fleet had to stay at Pearl Harbor to exercise a calming effect on the Japanese. Deeply involved in negotiations with Japan, Hull was certain that the removal of part of the Navy from the Pacific would be interpreted as a sign of weakness. For more than two months, during which the Secretary of State urged postponement of the transfer and Admiral Stark, to Stimson's dismay, blew hot and cold on the proposition, the Secretary of War worked doggedly to encourage the President to make the shift. In this effort he relied heavily on Marshall's current high standing with the White House and the State Department to win his point.

When Stimson told General Marshall on April 23 that the President now was convinced that the Pacific Fleet had to remain at Pearl Harbor, the Chief of Staff strongly dissented. "Marshall felt," recorded Stimson, "that with our heavy bombers and our new fine pursuit planes, the land force could put up such a defense that the Japs wouldn't dare attack Hawaii, particularly such a long distance from home." On the following day the Secretary took the Chief of Staff with him to the White House to assure the President that Hawaii was impregnable. The land defense, Marshall said, was sufficient to keep off the Japanese, and the air defense could be reinforced from the mainland if necessary. Knox agreed. Stimson felt that these arguments "completely exploded the President's reason, which he had given me the night before, for not taking any ships from Hawaii in order to reinforce the main area—the main theater of war in the Atlantic." Roosevelt argued that the United States had always held the fleet in Hawaii as a striking force and that its very presence had protected the Southwest Pacific, including Singapore, Australia, New Zealand, and the Dutch East Indies. He felt that the British should be asked about the effect of the withdrawal of capital ships. Stimson reminded him that Churchill had said that Britain could take care of Singapore if the United States would reinforce the Atlantic.[28]

Roosevelt, strangely cautious about the action in the Atlantic he had favored a few days before, replied that the Navy was merely going to look for aggressors and report them to Washington. The Secretary of War, far more realistically, pointed out that the Navy would be in the Atlantic for the purpose of warning the British fleet about the presence of hostile vessels. "I wanted him to be honest with himself," Stimson wrote. "To me it seems a clearly hostile act to the Germans and I am prepared to take the responsibility of it." [29] Stimson disliked the President's "rather disingenuous" attitude in facing the facts and his refusal to admit that since the action would probably bring a clash with the Germans it did not make much difference what it was called.

"Marshall was particularly strong in thinking that I had done a great thing in getting the chance of having the main fleet sent over to the Atlantic," the Secretary of War recalled. "He was strongly of the opinion that the psychological benefit of moving the fleet to the Atlantic would far outweigh any encouragement it would give to Japan. Japan would recognize that we meant business and would be just as cautious about getting down to Singapore as if we stayed there." [30]

With Marshall's assistance Stimson kept up pressure on the President during the next five weeks. They made it even stronger when they learned that the British would not oppose the shift of a substantial part of the fleet to the Atlantic.

In an effort to have Marshall available for discussions with State Department representatives, Stimson asked him to cancel his plans for visiting Alaska in early May. A few days later, when Ambassador Norman Davis dropped by the War Department to offer his services in ironing out differences between Stimson and Hull, the Secretary of War requested General Marshall to present the arguments for shifting additional ships to the Atlantic. Impressed by his presentation, Davis asked him to repeat his views to Secretary Hull. Next day Davis pleased Stimson by saying that the Secretary of State seemed "to be coming around" under Marshall's influence.

Deciding to leave no avenue unexplored, the Secretary of War then urged Marshall to use his persuasive powers on Robert Sherwood, one of the President's speech writers, apparently hoping that some of the General's ideas would seep through this channel to Roosevelt.[31]

The War Department's vigorous support of a shift of a substantial part of the Pacific Fleet to the Atlantic contrasted sharply with Admiral Stark's own doubts during May. The upshot was a compromise between Hull's position and Stimson's position: the President returned to his earlier more modest plan for transferring almost one-fourth of the Pacific Fleet to the Atlantic.[32] The proposal to move other ships later was dropped when Japanese moves in the Far East made such a step dangerous.

These discussions of late April and May took place against a bleak backdrop of the final German conquest of Greece, a Nazi airborne landing in Crete, and Rommel's drive to the Egyptian border. In mid-May an announcement of increased collaboration between the government at Vichy and Germany started rumors that France was opening the way for Nazi advances into West Africa. On May 27 the President warned the country of possible German aggression in the Atlantic. Announcing that he had extended American naval patrols to North and South Atlantic waters and hinting that the Navy was carefully watching the Cape Verde Islands, the Azores, and Dakar, he proclaimed an unlimited national emergency.

General Marshall was unhappily aware that the Army was still far from ready to do its share in protecting the Western Hemisphere. Part of his strong support for increased naval strength in the Atlantic had been based on this realization. For several weeks he had attempted to raise a force that could cooperate with the Navy in a proposed Army-Navy expedition to the Azores. In late May he had to admit with considerable embarrassment that the Army could not meet its proposed target date. Although the operation was later dropped when the Portuguese government postponed an invitation to the United States to occupy the islands, the experience was a bitter one for the General.

Compounding Marshall's problems was Roosevelt's offer in early June to relieve the British garrison in Iceland. Neither Stark nor Marshall liked the commitment, but, at Churchill's insistence, agreed reluctantly to go on with it. Already feeling the pressure of having to furnish equipment for a Marine unit scheduled to take part in the expedition to the Azores, Marshall complained to Secretary Stimson that he didn't know "whether we shall have anything left after the British and Marines get theirs."

The General's fears were not exaggerated. After trying vainly to gather a force to garrison Iceland, he again had to concede the Army's weakness by recommending that the job be left to the Marines. The Army was now so short of weapons, he warned, that he would have to use dummy pieces in maneuvers scheduled for the summer. This situation, he added, was so potentially damaging to the administration that he was being advised to suppress statements about their use.[33]

Marshall's woes were merely a small part of the somber background of the military situation the early part of June. Information carefully collected by War Department intelligence experts raised the serious possibility that the British would lose the Suez Canal and the Straits of Gibraltar in three to six months. If those painful events occurred before late fall, they said, the Army would have to meet the crisis with a small unbalanced force that lacked adequate combat aviation.

Then, almost miraculously, Adolf Hitler relieved the pressure on the West. Deciding that he had to deal with Russia before finishing with the British, the German Führer on June 22 sent his armies against the Soviet Union. As the Nazi forces drove farther and farther, that summer and fall, into a land where distance, weather, and tenacious partisans disrupted their timetables of conquest, the United States was able to draw breath, assess its position and that of Britain, and plot its way more carefully for the future.

VII

Plan for Victory

GIVEN the Hitler-sent reprieve, Marshall redoubled his efforts to see to first things first. Though *if* rather than *when* continued to dominate his thinking about American involvement, he knew that the production of war matériel and the training of men had to come before anything else. The forming of bucket brigades might quench small blazes; it would take a well-organized fire department with the most modern equipment to deal with a world conflagration. The General had never forgotten the confusion created in World War I by the sudden summoning of scattered regiments that were rushed aboard transports and organized while on the high seas. In 1941 he was no less disenchanted by frenzied efforts to mount haphazard expeditions against the nation's potential enemies. What he sought was order—the shape of an over-all plan for victory.

Two lieutenant colonels (later generals) on his staff innocently got a lesson on the dangers of coming to him with an ill-conceived plan. As a staff exercise, they casually outlined a scheme for occupying the Cape Verde Islands to forestall their seizure by the Germans. By accident their tentative draft found its way to the Chief of Staff's desk. A few hours later a young staff officer informed them that the "Old Man" wanted to see them personally. Marshall greeted them with elaborate courtesy and invited one of them to sit behind his large desk. "Now you be General Marshall and I will be the President," he said. Pausing to let the implications of that statement sink in, he continued, "Now, 'General Marshall,' I should like to have you explain to me briefly and clearly why you propose to launch an attack upon the property of a neutral, which

United States divisions you had planned to use in this expedition, where you propose to get the several hundred ships necessary to transport it, and whose navy you have in mind to escort it." Luckily, as the officers were trying to think of a conciliatory reply, Stimson's aide summoned the General to a conference. The officers were allowed to slip away, glad to forget their grand design.[1]

The episode pointed up a situation that cried out for correction in the spring of 1941. The time had passed when it was enough to improvise a plan that might briefly bolster British morale or discomfit the Germans. If the United States merely intended to build up the Army to Protective Mobilization Force strength, Marshall wondered if the War Department was justified in seeking funds for matériel beyond that needed for the stipulated 2,800,000 men. He believed that any expansion must be based on carefully defined strategic requirements. In late May he asked his staff for a "more clear-cut strategic estimate of our situation," which might provide a "base of departure" for an orderly expansion of production capacity from a ground, air, and naval viewpoint.[2]

Under Secretary of War Patterson, who had the task of procuring supplies for the War Department, had paved the way for Marshall's request. A tenacious man who, like Marshall, kept his eye on the main point of a discussion, he had asked Stimson in mid-April to determine how much production was necessary to achieve victory, keeping in mind "probable enemies, and friends and theaters of operations." [3]

The Army planners had scarcely settled down to their task when the President entered the picture. He directed the Army and Navy to prepare studies of production needed to defeat America's enemies.[4] Marshall's earlier request was now incorporated in this larger requirement. The work already begun became in time the hard core of the Army's Victory Program.

Ironically, the task of drawing up the estimate was entrusted to one of the members of the War Plans Division least in sympathy with aid to Great Britain or participation in the current war. The assignment went to Major Wedemeyer, a Marshall protégé who later became one of his most caustic critics as a result of their disagreements over the General's China policy. A West Point graduate, the major was a Nebraskan of German, Irish, and French descent. His father's teachings and his own study had persuaded him that the United States was "propagandized into World War I," a view that made him sympathetic to the aims of the America First organization. As an exchange student at the German War College (Kriegsakademie) in Berlin in 1936-38, he became an expert on German tactics and military organization. Newly returned to Washington in the summer of 1938, he met General Marshall, who had recently become Chief of the War Plans Division. Unlike many officers in the War Department who wished only to gossip about Göring or Hitler, Marshall read Wedemeyer's report on his experiences and then questioned him at length on his views of German strength. The Major believed this contact was responsible for his assignment to the War Plans Division in 1941.[5]

While the Army and Navy planners gathered statistics on their needs and those of potential allies, Marshall was busily occupied with current developments that threatened to involve the United States in a shooting war. Throughout June he continued to urge the President to move more ships to the Atlantic; in July the Japanese menace to Thailand led him to develop a plan for strengthening the air and ground forces in the Philippines. In early August, as events threatened to make the careful estimates obsolete before they could be presented to the President, he found himself discussing world-wide strategy with the British.

The first of a series of high-level Anglo-American conferences grew out of the situation created by Hitler's attack on the Soviet Union. Wanting a firsthand view of the changed situation, Roosevelt had sent Hopkins to London in mid-July to arrange a conference with Churchill. The Prime Minister had accepted the idea at once and agreed to come in early August to Argentia at Placentia Bay, Newfoundland.

Notifying General Marshall of the forthcoming meeting, President Roosevelt suggested that he bring General Arnold and two other members of his staff. Hurriedly the Chief of Staff recalled the airman from an inspection trip, informing him only that they would be gone about ten days and that he should take heavy clothing. He told Mrs. Marshall no more than this, but she surmised from the clothing he packed and the inordinate security precautions taken by members of the party that he was going northward with the President.[6]

In elaborate secrecy the Army and Navy representatives were

brought together in New York. In Long Island Sound, where they were taken by destroyer from the Hudson River docks, Marshall and Stark joined Admiral King aboard his flagship, the *Augusta*, and the other officers were transferred to the *Tuscaloosa*. Farther along the coast, they were joined on the following day by the presidential yacht, which carried President Roosevelt and his military and naval aides. This party was also brought aboard the *Augusta*, while the *Potomac*, still flying the President's flag, continued to sail within sight of shore, giving the impression that an announced fishing trip was still in progress.

Early on the morning of August 7 the Americans arrived just off the entrance to Argentia, where they anchored to await the coming of the British delegation. The President and his advisers thankfully seized on the forty-eight hours before the British arrival to make hurried preparations for their discussions.

Marshall later described the situation: "I think the best answer to those who feel that we were planning the war in detail ahead of time would be the fact that we had so little basis for planning at the time of the meeting on the *Augusta*. . . . The British would have liked to have gone much further. They were at this business every day—all day—on a very definite warmaking basis. We were in the position of mobilizing and equipping an Army. Just how this was to be handled on our side largely remained to be determined. Therefore we were not prepared to give them any fixed advice." [7]

Murky was the word for the American position. More interested in covering the Allied situation in a broad sweep than in detailed examination of possible Anglo-American collaboration, the President paid little attention to the issues that harassed his service advisers. It was left to the purely military sessions for Marshall and Stark to explore such troublesome questions as the amount of aid to be furnished Great Britain and Russia and the problems involved in escorting British convoys. The service chiefs agreed that future assistance to the European powers must not be at the expense of American forces. If the United States was drawn into war, they emphasized, the American people would demand action and not excuses from their military leaders.

For all their stern resolve about straight talk to the British, the American representatives could not avoid a feeling of excitement at the thought that they would soon be sitting down with leaders of a country that for almost a year had singlehandedly defied Adolf Hitler. The crews of the American ships watched eagerly through the morning mists of August 9 as the *Prince of Wales,* newest of Britain's battleships, still bearing the marks of its battle in late May with the *Bismarck,* sailed into Placentia Bay. At 11 a.m. the Prime Minister and his party were welcomed aboard the *Augusta* by the President.

Churchill, broad and stocky, wearing the blue uniform of an Elder Brother of Trinity House, had changed considerably from the dapper figure dressed in morning coat and top hat whom Marshall had escorted during the review of American troops in Hyde Park twenty-two years before. Following closely behind him were two military leaders with whom Marshall would be intimately associated in the months to come, Admiral of the Fleet Sir Dudley Pound, the First Sea Lord, limping and showing the effect of overwork as the head of Britain's busiest service; and a tall, sinewy man whose alert eyes transmuted a long-boned "British" face into a handsome one—General Sir John Dill, Chief of the Imperial General Staff.

The day was taken up principally by Admiral King's luncheon for the British and American military representatives, and the evening by the President's formal dinner. Between lunch and a courtesy call to the *Prince of Wales* by the Americans, Marshall and Dill found time for their first military talks. The two officers, immediately attracted to each other, formed a friendship that ended only with the British leader's death in Washington late in 1944.

At the first general meeting that evening Churchill eloquently outlined Britain's gravest problems and asked for men, ships, planes, and tanks. As the Americans had expected, he called on the United States to assume the task of escorting convoys in the North Atlantic, thus releasing British ships for service elsewhere. Expressing deep concern over Japanese aggression in the Far East, he proposed that the United States, Britain, and Russia warn Japan of their opposition to movement of troops into the Malay Peninsula or the Dutch East Indies.

During the next three days Churchill and Roosevelt and their political advisers evolved the declaration of principles later known as the Atlantic Charter. As they expanded their ideas as to the proper course to be followed in the Far East, Marshall, Arnold, and Stark examined other proposals on strategy handed them by the British Chiefs of Staff. Stressing the weakness of their position in the Atlantic, the British suggested American intervention to reduce serious shipping losses, prevent German movements into Morocco and Western Africa, and relieve the Royal Navy of heavy commitments in the Atlantic.

Possibly with the intention of making intervention more palatable to the Americans, the British advanced the theory that the Germans could be defeated without an Allied landing on the Continent. Referred to hopefully at every Anglo-American conference until the late fall of 1943, this assumption rested on the alluring possibility that bombings, blockades, and propaganda would so weaken the German will to fight that an invasion would not be needed. The British also declared that even in the case of a landing the large infantry forces of 1914-18 would not be required to defeat Germany. Instead, armored units equipped with the most modern weapons would be used to overrun territory. Once the penetration was achieved, the Allies could hand over to armed resistance groups the task of holding the conquered areas.

From the first, Marshall doubted the accuracy of these views. Convinced that victory depended on closing with the enemy, he believed there must be large ground armies if the United States went to war.

At a time when Marshall was trying to find enough troops to replace the Marine brigade in Iceland, the question of whether he would send a large or small force to Europe was completely unrealistic. He stated bluntly that existing American commitments rather than British needs must control future shipments of weapons and equipment. He and Stark took a sharper tone on August 12, charging that the British had created serious procurement problems by their failure to coordinate their purchases with the United States and to respect the priority system. General Arnold had privately told the British air representative that there was little hope of sending the British a large number of heavy bombers in the near future.

When the conference ended on August 12 the British had failed to win promises of increased assistance. In some respects the American military chiefs seemed less generous than they had been earlier in the year. Churchill was comforted, however, by Roosevelt's agreement to put teeth into his warnings to Japan. From a practical standpoint the conference gave the leaders of Great Britain and the United States an opportunity to know one another better and to discuss frankly their points of difference—thus serving as a rehearsal for later wartime collaboration. In the Atlantic Charter the conferees appealed dramatically for the support of world opinion by proclaiming a set of principles that the English-speaking peoples were prepared to defend.

Back in Washington two days later, Marshall and Arnold briefed Stimson on what had happened at the conference. The British did not realize, they reported, how bare the American cupboard was. They were interested in four-engine bombers, once disdained, which they now wanted faster than these could be supplied. Next day Harry Hopkins gave the Secretary of War a further report, saying that the Navy would never fight Germany if it could help it and adding, tantalizingly, since there were no details, that Marshall was "the dominating figure" at the meeting.[8]

The Secretary also had some exciting news to relate. On the evening of the same day that the Atlantic Conference ended, the House of Representatives had concluded one of the hottest fights of the year by passing the extension of the draft and the federalization of National Guard units. One vote (203 to 202) had made the difference. Two days later the Senate approved the House bill by 36 to 19. Stimson knew that Marshall would relish the details of the final debates, not only because congressional action preserved an Army for future training, but also because Marshall had played a crucial role in the measure's passage.

In this year of growing tension General Marshall had found his greatest test in the battle to extend the Selective Service Act. Doubtful at the time of its passage as to whether he would be able to release the men at the end of twelve months' service, he grew increasingly skeptical of the possibility as the menace from abroad expanded with every Axis victory. The situation in Europe and in the Pacific failed to conform tidily to a year's enlistment, a dilemma that became evident to officers in the War Department within three months after the passage of the legislation. Selectees were distributed throughout the National Guard and the Regular Army, and Reserve officers filled key posts in these units. Wholesale release of men and officers therefore meant the destruction of the battle-worthiness of nearly every American division.

Marshall found no enthusiasm on the part of the President and the leaders of Congress for a renewed debate over the draft. The *Chicago Tribune* had warned in 1940 that President Roosevelt would renege on his promise to release the troops at the end of a year's service, and few congressmen cared to join him in the face of the storm that they knew would break over the administration if he tried to extend the draft. With the approach of spring, nervous selectees and Guardsmen began to inquire if they would be returning to their businesses and jobs in the fall. There was no clear answer, and they spoke to friends in Congress. Marshall was interrupted in the midst of testimony on an appropriations bill in March 1941 by a congressman who bluntly demanded if the Army intended to keep its word to the troops. Leaving the matter in the hands of Providence, the Chief of Staff replied simply, "If the Lord is good to us, they will be returned to their homes." [9] War Department planners proceeded as if Hitler instead of a higher authority would make the decision—and that it could go either way. Since December 1940 they had counted on keeping the troops for a longer period than a year, while acting on the assumption that the first National Guard units would have to be demobilized in mid-September 1941 and the first selectees discharged two months later.

The matter dragged on until mid-June with no one daring to bring it up in Congress. Finally on the 19th, while discussing the possibility of sending troops to Brazil, Stimson and Marshall urged the President to ask Congress to extend the terms of military service. They suggested that he make the request at the time troops were sent to Iceland. On further reflection, Marshall concluded that there would be less opposition if the War Department took the initiative in recommending the action, subject to presidential and congressional approval. Secretary Stimson agreed and called Hopkins to say that he was making the statement on his own responsibility.[10]

Although by nature chary of airing his problems in the press, General Marshall had gradually learned the importance of getting his side of the story before the public. As he considered the uphill fight the Army faced in extending the Selective Service Act, he decided in late June on a bold stroke. For many years the Chief of

Staff had submitted an annual report on the Army, often dull and replete with dreary tables of statistics. General Marshall had made no report in 1940, and the deadline for the second year was approaching. Near the end of June he decided to use the report not only as a statement of the Army's accomplishments but as an argument for the extension of the Selective Service Act. Calling on his assistants for a ten-day burst of speed, he set them to work preparing summaries of their activities while he sketched in simple, effective English a statement of the Army's problems. By working day and night he had the report in print on July 3, almost two years to the day since he had become acting Chief of Staff.

In fewer than forty pages, illustrated by simple charts and maps that replaced the usual formidable statistical tables, the General told how the Army had grown eight times its initial size in two years. The bulk of the report described the nature of that growth and commented on problems such as housing, training, and morale. In the pages devoted to the draft Marshall made his strongest plea. Once completely unprepared, the United States Army was reaching the point where it could provide the country with an adequate defense. That force, unfortunately, would soon be in danger of falling apart. At a time when Nazi units were at full strength and equipped with what seemed to be the most modern engines of destruction, the workings of the draft law threatened to nullify what had been accomplished in the last twelve months. He spelled out the possible consequences. From 75 to 90 per cent of the officers in the Regular Army units were reservists whose service was soon to end. Under existing legislation, some 600 officers in each division could return home within a few months, leaving the Army without suitable replacements. As for enlisted men, the outlook was no less grim. In all but two Regular Army divisions, the number of selectees ran from 25 to 50 per cent of the total strength. Hardest hit if the twelve-month period of service prevailed would be organizations on which Marshall was now depending for special support units such as engineers, heavy artillery, and anti-aircraft. The Chief of Staff faced the prospect of seeing National Guard members, reserve officers, and trained selectees melt away within a few months.[11]

For all his skill in preparing a report, the General was still an amateur in dealing with the press and Congress. In his haste he

failed to get the full exposure he needed from the country's newspapers—an error he corrected handsomely two years later in a report that made banner headlines in nearly every city—and, a more
serious omission, he neglected to brief administration leaders in
Congress on what he had in mind. Caught flat-footed, Speaker Sam
Rayburn blew up over what he regarded as a crude attempt by the
Army to force his hand on a draft-extension measure that had little
chance of passing. After careful explanations the Chief of Staff
managed to repair the damage. A few days later Rayburn showed
that he harbored no hard feelings by throwing his full weight into
the fight. Gradually, too, the War Department press section managed to feed the General's arguments to friendly correspondents in
Washington. The report remained a handy summary of the Army's
case for use by its friends in the Senate and the House.

They needed all the assistance available. The opposition papers
pictured Roosevelt as bent on dictatorship. Stimson was alternately
described as a tired old man and a demonic warmonger and more
warlike than the President. In the face of this assault the Chief
Executive was of little use in winning recalcitrant members of
Congress to the bill's support. Stimson and the members of Grenville Clark's group, so effective in the passage of the 1940 bill, now
found themselves tarred with the "War Party" brush. Of the administration leaders, only Marshall had grown in favor with Congress since the hearings of 1940. As a result he assumed a heavy
share of the burden of selling the resolution to its foes.

His first efforts moved few administration critics. Vainly he
pointed to the language of the act of September 16, 1940, that had
added to the twelve months' service clause the words, "except that
whenever Congress has declared that the national interest is imper-
iled, such twelve-month period may be extended by the President
to such time as may be necessary in the interest of national defense." Marshall's liaison officer at the Capitol reported the remark
of an experienced congressional secretary to the effect that in forty
years on the Hill he had never seen such fear of a bill.

Miscalculating the strength of the opposition, the Chief of Staff
made his task harder by trying to persuade Congress to remove restrictions on use of selectees and National Guardsmen outside the
Western Hemisphere. Without such action, he would have trouble
getting troops for Iceland or for expeditions to islands in the At-

lantic. The President agreed but assigned Marshall the "laboring oar" in getting the ban lifted. In his arguments before the Senate Military Affairs Committee on July 9 the General was effective, carrying its members "all with him," according to Stimson.[12] The story was different in the House. Rayburn soon reported that only strong pressure by the President would bring enough Democrats in line to pass the amendment. To encourage Roosevelt, Stimson and Marshall lectured him on July 14 and came away under the impression that they had won his "warm support." [13] He was in fact weakening under the intense opposition that continued to build up. Fearing that insistence on the provision would endanger the whole measure, Roosevelt dropped the effort to get the ban removed.

As it became clear that much of the violent opposition in Congress was directed against the President personally, Marshall appeared before the Senate Military Affairs Committee in an attempt to shift responsibility from the White House to the War Department. He assured members that he and Secretary Stimson had pressed for the extension on their own responsibility and without the knowledge of President Roosevelt. Rather than trying to build a large Army, the President was unduly conservative in his requests for troops.

From the cordial reception he received and the nature of the questions addressed to him on this and other visits to committees on Capitol Hill, the Chief of Staff came to an astounding conclusion. Many of the doubtful congressmen were willing to back the resolution if he rather than the President would state the administration's case. As the world crisis had deepened during the past twelve months, Marshall's stature had grown steadily. Members of Congress who recognized that the country had to face up to its defense problems listened gladly to an expert who could give hard answers with arguments that they could pass on to constituents and headline writers at home.

Marshall acted and talked the way they believed a leader should. There was the appearance of great power under full control in this quiet, patient gentleman, carefully dressed in a well-cut civilian suit of conservative design, who looked more like a prosperous businessman than the tough commander of the nation's Army. Obviously he was not trying to carve an empire for himself, and he was dedicated to efficiency and economy. Sensing that he could accept authority gracefully, they gave him more. They realized that he was devoid of political ambition and trusted his counsels. Preferring his word to that of the President—a situation that always disturbed him—they listened to his recommendations with a confidence they denied to Roosevelt. Wanting a convincing explanation for those voters in the hinterland who hated "that man in the White House" and the war and higher taxes and the draft, they found a convenient man to hide behind. Invited to provide them with arguments, Marshall obliged.

The change in his tone was clearly discernible. Where he had previously deferred to the judgment of congressmen, he now claimed the right to speak as an expert on military matters. Insisting that there was no doubt "whatever about the existence of an emergency," he invited a senatorial committee to "depend on our judgment and good faith." The recent German attack was merely the latest in a series of carefully timed actions by which "we have seen nation after nation go down, one after the other, in front of a concentrated effort, each one lulled, presumably into negative action, until all the guns were turned on them and it was too late." [14]

Emboldened by his discovery that the committee members craved his advice, he fought proposals to shift responsibility for action to the President or to limit the Army's requests. He questioned the suggestion that responsibility be left to Roosevelt to retain the troops by declaring a national emergency. He opposed efforts to restrict the extension of the draft to six months or some other precise limit.

Current plans to reinforce garrisons in Hawaii and Alaska, he explained, were blocked by the one-year service provision. Certain units earmarked for these assignments were filled with National Guardsmen or selectees. Under existing legislation he would have no choice but to tear up these units when terms of service began to expire in three to six months. Exasperated by the suggestion that he send overseas only those soldiers willing to volunteer for one or more years, he retorted impatiently, "We must not line up a military force to vote" on whether or not the individuals will participate in a military operation. Knowing well that Soviet practices were anathema to many critics of the draft, he blandly noted that to ask for volunteers in such a situation meant adopting the system of "another country which . . . I do not think we are prepared to copy. An army is an army. It is not a political group. It is not a citizens' meeting." [15]

When the committee chairman, Senator Robert Reynolds of North Carolina, often critical of the administration, expressed concern over the resolution's probable bad effect on morale unless it could be shown that the measure was needed, Marshall argued that the discontent would be short-lived. "I think world happenings will rapidly shock us into unity, as it has in the past. . . . To be perfectly frank, I have timed a great many proposals with the actions of Hitler's government. Hitler's actions have always appeared to be convincing to the public."

The General was in a state of mind similar to that he had reached at the time of his famous confrontation with General Pershing, when he had decided that he was already up to his neck in hot water and might as well swim for it. "I cannot, for the life of me," he concluded, "see how anyone can read what has happened, can see the analysis of the situation of the Army, and not agree that we have to take such measures as I have recommended."

Testifying a few days later before the House Committee, he reminded the congressmen of the failure of the volunteer system in the War of 1812, the Mexican conflict, and the Civil War. In a mischievous allusion to the Union defeat at Bull Run, where fleeing soldiers had knocked down congressmen who had come out to see a great Federal victory, he recalled that General McDowell had fought the action prematurely because he knew the enlistments of most of the men would soon expire. War plans, he warned, must not depend on short-term enlistments or commanders be put at the mercy of the calendar. Sending troops abroad under such conditions would be less a matter of defending the country than of "running excursions." [16]

Marshall's "right combination of tact and firmness," as Grenville Clark put it when he congratulated the General on the "magnificent" way he handled "a very delicate and also very arduous task," won plaudits from members of the House. Representative Charles I. Faddis, Pennsylvania Democrat, spoke for many of his colleagues at the end of the General's testimony when he said that the House Committee on Military Affairs should "express itself as having the fullest confidence in the sincerity, patriotism, ability, and professional qualities of the Chief of Staff." [17]

Respect for the General's patriotism did not automatically guarantee votes for the bill. Mindful of next year's elections, members from strongly isolationist areas of the country were weighing their desire to back the Army against their chances of returning to Washington. In most cases Washington won.

Representative James W. Wadsworth later blamed the situation in the House on deep hostility to Roosevelt and the cowardice of members facing re-election. For the effectiveness of the opposition, considerable credit belonged to the America First Committee, headed by one of General Marshall's old acquaintances from Chicago, Major General Robert E. Wood, chairman of the board of Sears, Roebuck and Company. One of Marshall's former associates in the Illinois National Guard, Brigadier General Thomas J. Hammond, testified against the measure. The America First Research Bureau denied the Chief of Staff's contention that failure to extend the length of service would leave the country with only a skeleton army.[18] In its steady fire on the administration the *Chicago Tribune* avoided attacking Marshall by name. But as the opponents of the President's measures came to realize the importance of the Chief of Staff's role in pushing legislation through Congress, they ultimately included him among the "conspirators" who helped Roosevelt drag the United States into war.

The battle for extension of selective service went on into August, and it became clear that Republican votes could be essential to carry the resolution. Votes from that side of the aisle were hard to glean in face of Minority Leader Joseph W. Martin's decision that a party vote against the draft extension was the type of issue "that might yet funnel the winds into our sails and blow us back again to the commanding position the Republican Party had enjoyed in the 1920s." Although he personally wanted the bill to pass, his desire to put the party on record as "keeping faith with the men who had been drafted for one year" meant that neither he nor most other Republicans would be likely to vote with the President.[19]

In the state of mind that prevailed in the House of Representatives, presidential intervention could change few votes. Marshall decided to put his prestige on the line and appeal personally to a group of Republican congressmen. He arranged with his old friend Representative Wadsworth to call together some forty fellow Republicans who might be willing to listen to his arguments.

Meeting them at the Army and Navy Club, Marshall led a discussion from seven until midnight, rehashing the statements he had made a few days before. Logic, statistics, and patriotic appeals left most of his listeners unmoved. One stalwart isolationist said bluntly, "You put the case very well, but I will be damned if I am going along with Mr. Roosevelt." The man's statement hit Marshall like a blow in his face. He retorted angrily, "You are going to let plain hatred of the personality dictate to you to do something that you realize is very harmful to the interest of the country." [20]

Indeed, most of the men present were of the same persuasion. Of the forty-odd at the meeting, Marshall found that he had reached perhaps a dozen who were willing to risk their seats to vote the extension. A few told him they would support the measure although it would cost them re-election. Deeply moved by their action, he resolved, if his help was needed, to go on the platform when they ran in 1942 and defend their patriotism.

In the late phases of the debate the opposition used a familiar device to discourage supporters of the legislation. Senator Wheeler, one of the strong opponents of draft extension, mailed out under his congressional frank one million postcards, printed at America First Committee expense, to voters, asking them to "write today to President Roosevelt that you are against our entry into the European War." Some of the cards turned up in the hands of soldiers, and Stimson assumed that they were being deliberately sent to draftees. In a blistering statement to the press he said that it was an act of near treason. When assured by Wheeler that no effort was being made to send them to men in uniform, the Secretary apologized. But Marshall was seriously concerned by reports that groups outside the Army were trying to persuade soldiers to send members of Congress petitions opposing extension of the draft. He told the House Committee on Military Affairs that he could not allow trainees to get involved in politics. "We must treat them as soldiers; we cannot have a political club and call it an Army. I regard these disturbing activities from outside the Army, gentlemen, as sabotage of a very dangerous character. . . . Without discipline an Army is not only impotent but it is a menace to the state." [21]

By August 6 Majority Leader John W. McCormack had to report that defections were developing in his ranks to the extent that forty-five Democrats were definitely opposed to the measure and thirty-five were undecided. He and other administration leaders were particularly alarmed by an opposition amendment intended to embarrass Roosevelt. By its provision all selectees would be put into the Reserves and the President authorized to call them back for additional duty at the end of a year's service. It was a means of dodging an issue that Congress should decide. Stimson, who denounced the suggestion in his Diary as "cowardly," accurately added that the same men who voted to shift the responsibility to the Chief Executive would be the first to denounce him if he exercised that authority. The proposition had a broad appeal, and only with difficulty was it shelved.[22]

In an atmosphere smoldering with anti-administration feeling and growing discontent among selectees and Guardsmen in the service, the House brought the draft extension to a vote on the very day the German Army reached the Black Sea, east of Odessa, threatening the defeat of the Russians and the outflanking of the British in the Middle East. Speaker Rayburn and Majority Leader McCormack counted Democratic noses but were short of the votes needed for passage. An appeal to the American Legion brought a strong statement in favor of extension that steered a few fence-sitters into line. Representative Wadsworth called on his faithful band of Republican supporters and they stood firm, delivering to the administration's support twenty-one votes on the final roll call. In one of the most crucial actions in the prewar period, less than four months before Pearl Harbor, the House agreed to the extension of the enlistment of men in service by a majority of one. Although many political leaders, Democratic and Republican, could properly claim a share of the credit, there was no denying that Marshall's firmness and personal standing had provided the slim margin of victory.

The violent campaign against the administration's proposals had incited strong resentment among selectees and Guardsmen and their families against the President and the Army. Soldier agitation for quick release from service flared up across the land in the closing days of the debate. The letters "OHIO" began to appear on walls of latrines and artillery pieces. Translated, they threatened, "Over the Hill in October," suggesting that a wave of desertions would follow the end of the initial twelve months' period of service.[23]

In reporting the appearance of the signs at a National Guard division camp, *Time* magazine declared that a low state of morale affected two-thirds of the 1,500,000 men under arms. It stated that only the Regulars, the men in the Air Forces, mechanized troops, Negro regiments, and Texas units had managed to escape this prevailing feeling. During the previous week in a Mississippi camp men in uniform watching a film had booed when pictures of President Roosevelt and General Marshall were shown.

The editors of *Life* sent a roving reporter to interview 400 privates in five National Guard regiments. He reported that 50 per cent of this number "say they will desert ('go over the hill' in army slang) when their year's period of service is over. Actually most of these will do nothing so drastic, but there definitely will be trouble with deserters." National uncertainty, disbelief in the existence of a national emergency, dissatisfaction with officers, old-fashioned training methods, lack of equipment, inability to get ahead, absence of recreational facilities, and the unfavorable comparison of their lot with the life of civilian contemporaries were among the reasons cited for their anger at the White House and the War Department. One infantry private was quoted as saying, "To hell with Roosevelt and Marshall and the Army and especially this goddam hole and the Germans and the Russians and the British. I want to get the hell out of this hole." Out of thirty other men called into this man's tent, all but one agreed wholeheartedly with his opinions. The exception feared an eventual German attack on the United States but was set on getting out of the Army within a year. The men seemed particularly aggrieved at Army attempts to picture them as happy with their lot. In a typical reaction, one Quartermaster private declared, "No guy wants to be a sucker. Hell, that's what we'll be if we get into this goddam mess. Marshall and the other generals who say we like it are liars." [24]

The Chief of Staff knew that he was in for a hard winter. He wrote Bernard Baruch that it was "quite tragic" to watch the violent changes in the Army commencing with the recent debates. Until June, when the first discussions had begun, the troops had maintained a remarkable state of morale, but the vehement arguments had stirred up parents and "individual soldiers were taught to feel sorry for themselves." [25]

"I have always felt surprised that in our democracy we were able to achieve a selective service system late last summer, but I guess it was hoping too much to think that we could continue the strenuous preparation to meet this emergency without great difficulties. There is no more delicate problem than troop morale, and with such a slender margin of public approval to back us, it is no easy matter to build up the highly trained and seasoned fighting force that we must have available as quickly as possible. However, we are going to do it if too many of us do not lose our tempers."

The storm continued into September. At the end of the first week the Chief of Staff wrote the President of his worry over home influence on men in the service. Parents had been so confused as to the facts of the situation that something had to be done to bring them to an understanding of the national emergency and the necessity for a highly trained Army. While the President sought for some means to reassure the families of troops the War Department attempted to still some of the loudest clamor by announcing that it would release all men over twenty-eight at the end of a year's service and give special attention to hardship cases.

Acutely aware that a self-pitying soldier desires nothing better than a willing listener, be he newsman or bartender, the Chief of Staff strengthened the Army's Press Relations organization and set it to work telling the positive side of the Army's training program. The Morale Branch was enlarged and more camp shows were organized to entertain men at the various posts. But press clippings from the hometown paper and two hours of music and dancing were insufficient to still the anger of selectees and their families over what they regarded as a flagrant breach of contract by the government. Not until the attack at Pearl Harbor made evident that the release of selectees and Guardsmen in the late fall of 1941 would have destroyed almost all the gains in military preparations made since 1940 were the damaging effects on Army morale finally repaired.

The feeling of general uneasiness in the Army and in the country was part of something much broader than the controversy over the extension of the Selective Service Act. Strong supporters of the administration, such as Stimson, believed that there was a dangerous state of drift, a lack of national purpose, a failure by the President to provide a plan and a stirring call for united action. Much of it went back, as General Marshall explained to Secretary Morgenthau later, to Roosevelt's unwillingness to look at the problem whole. "First the President wants five hundred bombers a month and that dislocates the program. Then he says he wants so many tanks and that dislocates the program. The President will never sit down and talk about a complete program and have the whole thing move forward at the same time." [26]

The editors of *Fortune* in August explored carefully the failures in American war preparations. They concluded, after examining the various facets of the problem, that the "United States is not merely falling short, it is failing spectacularly, in nine different ways and nine different places." The list boiled down to lack of a proper plan for waging war politically and economically and the fact that Americans had "not yet been asked to do what is necessary to win." [27]

The armed services were already hard at work on a part of the plan the country required. Their proposals were delivered in late September to General Marshall and Admiral Stark, who sent them on, with their approval, to Secretary Stimson and Secretary Knox for transmission to the President. To get the answers needed by Marshall and Stark, the Army and Navy planners tried to determine what would be expected of them if the United States entered the war, or if Great Britain and Russia were knocked out and the United States had to defend its interests alone. Both services agreed that Germany was the one power capable of affecting American interests in the Atlantic and the Western Hemisphere. Assisted feebly by Italy, German armies held the Continent from the Atlantic coast of France to the Ukraine, the doors of Leningrad, and the shores of the Black Sea. Only Spain, Sweden, Portugal, and Switzerland remained fully outside the Axis camp, and Spain was extremely friendly to the Axis. Germany held Crete, menaced Cyprus and Malta, threatened the Middle East and Egypt, and appeared on the verge of knocking Russia out of the war. Not since Napoleon had one country so completely controlled the fate of Europe. To establish a realistic basis for estimates the Army planners recited the list of requirements for the defeat of Germany. For any hope of success the Allies would have to create air superiority, strengthen naval forces, create industrial production sufficient to arm the defenders of the Western Hemisphere, outfit task forces for operations in the Atlantic and in the European Theater, and furnish weapons and supplies for friendly powers wherever they might be.[28]

The services had no false hopes about the length of time such a program would take. From one and one-half to two years would be needed between the planning and carrying out of operations if, as they thought likely, the Russians were defeated west of the White Sea-Moscow-Volga line by the summer of 1942. Only if the Soviet armies could hold firm or, even better, launch a counterattack could the Allied timetable be revised.

No estimate was harder to make than the requirement for adequate invasion forces. In 1914-18 the French had had a large army and friendly harbors through which Allied troops and munitions could easily flow to the front; now the British and Americans would have to seize a foothold on hostile shores and perhaps restore the transportation system. It was doubtful that the Anglo-Saxon powers could provide the two to one superiority in ground strength considered necessary to force a landing. As a consequence the American planners resorted to the ideas already advanced by the British. Whether they reflected the recent suggestions made by the British Chiefs of Staff at Argentia or, more probably, the harsh counsels of necessity, the joint planners fell back on a blockade of Germany, aid to resistance forces in occupied countries, and a powerful air offensive as the necessary preliminaries to any final attack on the Continent. Small task forces could, meanwhile, harass the enemy in North Africa, the Middle East, and along the coasts of France and the Low Countries.[29]

In the course of their general planning the Army and Navy had agreed on the broad outlines of strategy. They soon differed over the division of tasks. Although General Marshall realized that the estimates were purely for planning purposes he objected strenuously to Navy proposals that either gave the Army tasks it did not want or neglected the Army altogether. He had balked at early Navy suggestions that the War Department arm a number of potential allies around the globe and supply troops for small operations in North and West Africa. Believing that his combined Army and Air Corps forces of 1,500,000 were scarcely sufficient to defend the Western Hemisphere, he avoided commitments that he might later have to hand over to the Navy and Marines to carry out. The Chief of Staff was equally sensitive to the notion that the air and naval forces could handle most of America's future fighting. He informed the Navy, as he later did the British, that the battle of Europe would ultimately be won by ground forces. It was essential that the process of procuring, training, and supplying the Army be stepped up.

Unfortunately, by the early fall of 1941 Marshall could show little promise of Army preparedness. On re-examining their estimates in late September, the War Department planners had to admit that only one infantry division, two bomber squadrons, and three pursuit groups would be ready for combat by October 1, 1941. The most they could promise in the next six months was a force of three infantry divisions, an armored corps (of one motorized and two armored divisions), seven bomber groups, and seven and one-half pursuit groups. The Army's official historians have written of this period: "The Army's own plans in the late summer of 1941 called for release of the older selectees and replacement of all selective service and National Guard enlisted men after eighteen or twenty months' service. Indeed, the Army was planning to retire all National Guard units from federal service, though it hoped to recruit by enlistment as many trained men as possible from their ranks. Army personnel plans in September contemplated only about a 10 per cent increase in future ground force strength. As late as November, General Marshall and his advisers assumed in their planning that no more than sixteen divisions would be made ready for overseas employment so long as the nation remained at least technically at peace." [30]

The planners continued to recommend that the United States remain on the defensive in the Pacific. They suggested a mixture of carrot and stick in dealing with the Japanese—negotiations to discourage collaboration with the Germans and deployment of forces in Hawaii and Alaska to deter aggression in the Pacific. Forces in the Philippines should be augmented but "without heavy commitments." Success in a Pacific war, they stressed, "would be at a cost incommensurate with other American interests." [31]

Having sketched in bold relief the possible commitments of the United States around the world, the War Department planners prepared to produce some educated guesses on the size of the Army and Air Corps needed to mount and launch successful operations. Without the aid of sophisticated computers or careful surveys, they found a number by estimating the number of physically fit males of draft age available for duty. After subtracting the share needed

for the Navy, industry, and agriculture, they assigned the remainder to the Army and Air Corps. Oddly enough the number
that came up, 8,800,000, was only a half million more than the
peak strength attained by forces under Marshall's command. The
planners did less well in their initial calculations on divisions, estimating that they would need 215, or more than double the number
of units finally organized during the war. This misjudgment, it developed, arose from the assumption that the Russians would be
knocked out of the war and the United States would have to contribute an extremely large Army to the Allied offensive effort.[32]

Inevitably rumors of secret War Department planning for possible action abroad crept into print in the fall of 1941. General
Marshall innocently created a three-day furore in mid-November
by suggesting that volunteers be sought for a Regular Army task
force that could be held ready for emergency duty outside the
United States. Directed by the President to be prepared to forestall
possible Nazi attacks on islands in the Atlantic, Marshall faced
the unpleasant truth that he could not send selectees, reservists,
or National Guardsmen outside the Western Hemisphere without their permission. He therefore had to fall back on the use
of a volunteer force that he had previously ruled out. When a
newsman revealed that he was recruiting such a unit, critics of the
administration charged him with organizing an overseas invasion
as part of Rooseveltian warmongering strategy. The War Department quickly denied any such intention, pointing out that Marshall's action was entirely a defensive move. When the details of
the Victory Program were published a few weeks later, critics
quickly charged the Chief of Staff with misrepresenting the facts.

As the United States extended its support to British merchant
ships in the Atlantic and warned the Japanese against aggression in
the Pacific, the isolationist press and the America First organization increased the tempo of their attacks on Roosevelt. As a thun-
derous climax, the *Chicago Tribune* and the *Washington Times-
Herald* on December 4 published Chesly Manly's exposé of the
Victory Program, described as "a blueprint for total war." Under
the screaming headline, "F.D.R.'S WAR PLANS," the *Tribune* pictured the victory plan as an actual timetable for conflict. Instead of
making clear that July 1, 1943, was the first date on which the
planners believed that the United States could be prepared for ac-

tion, Manly wrote, "July 1, 1943, is fixed as the date for the beginning of the final supreme effort by American land forces to defeat the mighty German army in Europe." [33]

Stimson's reaction was, predictably, one of flaming anger. In his press conference on December 5 he hotly defended the War Department for drawing up tentative war plans and attacked the *Tribune* and *Times-Herald* for revealing them to the nation's possible enemies. Instead of waiting for questions he asked rhetorically, "What would you think of an American General Staff which in the present condition of the world did not investigate and study every conceivable type of emergency which may confront this country and every possible method of meeting that emergency?" His second question was more pointed: "What do you think of the patriotism of a man or a newspaper which would take these confidential studies and make them public to the enemies of the country?" [34]

President Roosevelt set the Federal Bureau of Investigation to track down the individual responsible for the leak, and Stimson hoped that there might be a great trial to put an end to "this infernal disloyalty we now have in America First and the McCormick family papers." Their attacks on the publisher of the *Chicago Tribune* and certain key members of its staff strengthened the animus of that journal against the administration. Colonel McCormick and his paper supported the war effort but lost no opportunity to charge that the President bore a large share of the responsibility for the war. Once a friend of General Marshall's, Colonel McCormick ended by dropping the Chief of Staff from this list.[35]

As Japan's forces were already moving in for attack, the revelation of the plans had little effect on their action. In Germany the intelligence agencies gratefully noted the free information for which they would have gladly paid. Yet it seems that the publication of the plan gave little assistance to the Axis. For Stimson and Marshall the episode underlined the difficulty of preserving security when some trusted staff members were bitterly opposed to the administration's policy. Then, as in later years when inside information was furnished Senator Joseph R. McCarthy and favored columnists, no secret was safe if powerful newspapers and members of Congress appealed to individuals sympathetic to their policies to hand over material that could be used against presidential policy.[36]

Marshall was calm about the warmongering charge. He agreed

with Stimson that the War Department, which existed to develop
the military forces of the United States, had to prepare for all eventualities and that a Chief of Staff would be negligent if he did not
see to it that all necessary plans were made.[37]

Although he admitted that the United States was engaged in a
form of warfare in the Atlantic, Marshall did not envisage early
offensive efforts against Germany. In November 1941 he reacted as
he had at the ABC conversations and at Argentia: *if* the nation
went to war the principal showdown must come in Europe. At a
time when he had fewer than 1,500,000 men in arms, when sentiment in Congress still favored the prompt return of selectees and
Guardsmen to their homes, and when lack of shipping limited
movements overseas for many months to come, any realistic plan
for landing troops in Europe revealed a blueprint of American un-
readiness for war rather than a grand design for conquest.[38]

Marshall's real concern in the fall of 1941 was to prepare his still
puny force for maximum defensive duties. Fearing the possible defeat of the draft extension, he had ordered extensive field exercises
while he could still be certain of having enough fully trained units
to participate. As part of this program, corps exercises were staged
separately in late August in General Lear's Second Army and General Krueger's Third Army areas. Both commanders were dissatisfied with the performances of their forces; Krueger blistered his
troops for their "stupid disregard" of air attacks.[39]

The grand climax of a summer of maneuvers came with the
Army exercises held in September in Louisiana and Texas. After
ironing out many of the deficiencies noted in the earlier performances, Lear and Krueger put on a military show that captured
headlines throughout the country. An armored corps was committed in the most extensive use of tanks ever seen in the United
States; parachute troops were used in exercises for the first time;
and more than 1000 planes saw action. At least 400,000 men, double the strength of Marshall's army two years earlier, took part.[40]

In the final phase of the exercises Lear had the thankless task of
holding off General Krueger's larger and more mobile units in
Louisiana. As the armored columns closed in, almost capturing the
Second Army commander, General Marshall's attention was focused on the brilliant planning of the Third Army Chief of Staff,
resourceful Colonel Dwight D. Eisenhower, and the slashing at-

tacks of the 2nd Armored Division commander, Major General George S. Patton. To most Americans and, indeed, to many officers in the Army, Eisenhower was relatively unknown. The Chief of Staff had met him only twice, but his attention had been called to the officer three months earlier when Krueger, newly assigned to the Third Army Command, had spoken to Marshall about the qualities he wanted in a new chief of staff: "a man possessing broad vision, progressive ideas, a thorough grasp of the magnitude of the problems involved in handling an Army, and lots of initiative and resourcefulness." He was describing Eisenhower, his candidate for the job. For his outstanding performance in the maneuvers the colonel was to be promoted to brigadier general before the end of September.[41]

The second star of the maneuvers, Patton, a friend of both Stimson and Marshall since World War I, had made his mark in the first Tank Corps in the earlier conflict. His reputation for profanity and flamboyance was matched only by his ability to fight. As early as 1936 Marshall had assured Patton that if he ever reached a position of high command he would want his services, since Patton was the type of man who would go through hell and high water. It looked as if Patton would soon be needed; Marshall was to give him the Armored Corps before the year's end.[42]

Despite the serious errors committed by divisions in the maneuvers Marshall and McNair were pleased at the improvement they saw in the ground forces. At the close of the first phase the Chief of Staff told members of the American Legion at their convention in Milwaukee that it was difficult to overemphasize the importance of the recent exercises. "The present maneuvers," he declared, "are the closest peacetime approximation to actual fighting conditions that has ever been undertaken in this country. But what is of the greatest importance, the mistakes and failures will not imperil the nation or cost the lives of men." The maneuvers constituted a field laboratory to test new methods of applying fundamental tactical principles and permitted experimentation in the employment of tanks and in finding a defense against them. In some cases, had they been at war, entire divisions would have been annihilated or captured. By means of these exercises they were able to correct errors, replace ineffective leaders, and gain field experience without suffering casualties.[43]

In the last exercise of the year and, as it was to prove, the last in peacetime, the First Army and IV Armored Corps spent the last half of November maneuvering in the Carolinas. With great quantities of anti-tank guns, whose "killing" power was overstressed, the Blue force successfully countered Red's armor and then established its superiority with eight infantry divisions against Red's three infantry and motorized divisions.

Like the earlier maneuvers in Louisiana, these attracted national attention. Marshall watched them closely, slipping away from Washington on November 26 to see the last phase of the exercises. He and his associates still found great need for improvement. General McNair, the GHQ Chief of Staff, deplored the lack of strict discipline and reprimanded commanders for their disregard of air threats, imperfect reconnaissance, and the tendency to stick to highways. He called for leaders who would make troops willing to return to the tedium of elementary exercises. Not by "pep talks and verbose programs" but by skill in the practical conduct of training would they make men ready for battle.[44] While agreeing with the criticisms General Marshall saw significant improvements over the Louisiana maneuvers a few weeks earlier. The troops, he believed, had proved to the country that a powerful and highly trained army could be developed with amazing speed.

He based his praise of the ground forces not on troop performance as judged against that of professional fighting abroad, but against what had been done with the time and materials available. General Arnold was more critical of air-ground cooperation, which he described as largely ineffective. He charged that in spite of lessons available from abroad the ground forces had failed to utilize their air support fully. Every top commander could cite similar examples in the handling of armor or of infantry. To an extent that they did not tell the general public, Marshall and his assistants realized that months of tough training still were required before they would be willing to test their forces against a battle-hardened enemy.

Answering the rhetorical question, "Are these troops ready for war?" General McNair on the eve of Pearl Harbor underlined the task still confronting the American ground forces. If completely equipped, he thought that the units he had trained would fight effectively. "But," he added with emphasis, "the losses would be unduly heavy and the results of action against an adversary such as the Germans might not be all that could be desired." Marshall in a short time and with inadequate means at his disposal had done an amazing job in preparing a semblance of a fighting force. But with war less than a week away, his forces were tragically unprepared to meet an experienced enemy.[45]

VIII

Pacific Outposts

IN June 1940 General Marshall foresaw the possibility of a sneak attack by the Japanese on Pearl Harbor and warned his staff that an enemy could be four-fifths of the way to Hawaii before "we knew that they had moved." [1] At the end of the staff conference of June 17 at which he made this announcement he called in the Chief of War Plans Division and with him prepared a message to General Herron, commander of the Hawaiian Department. In the first of a series of warnings that were to go out from Washington in the next eighteen months he ordered:

> Immediately alert complete defensive organization to deal with possible trans-Pacific raid to greatest extent possible without creating public hysteria or provoking undue curiosity of newspapers or alien agents. Suggest maneuver basis. Maintain alert until further notice. Instructions for secret communication direct with Chief of Staff will be furnished you shortly. Acknowledge.[2]

General Marshall's abrupt warning reflected the tension that for months had been building up between the United States and Japan in the Pacific. Since 1937 Americans had watched with mounting anger as the Japanese encroached on China, bombing her larger cities without mercy and seizing the main ports along the coast. America's best wishes and modest help went out to Chiang Kai-shek as he withdrew far inland along the Yangtze to Chungking to plot ways to stay in the fight.

Japan, with better planes and guns and munitions, should have been able to score a knockout blow long before the beginning of the European conflict. But the punch-drunk giant would not quit.

The military clique grew first angry and then outraged, as if its honor were somehow besmirched by China's refusal to succumb. Obstinacy, reinforced by assistance sent in from the West over the Burma Road and the railroads of French Indochina, kept China in the fight.

When the European war came, Japan saw her chance for victory. With Great Britain and France under heavy attack by the Nazis, she hoped to settle the China Incident without fear of their interference and expand her new order throughout Greater East Asia. She would need to be sure of Russian quiescence, but that could probably be arranged now that the Soviets were friendly with Hitler. And even Chiang Kai-shek might yield if Berlin applied extra pressure on Chungking.

The unknown factor was the United States. The Japanese expected crude warnings and harsh words from that quarter. Secretary of State Stimson had preached vigorously against Japanese aggression in Manchuria at the beginning of the 1930s. There had been angry rumblings from Washington in 1934, when Japan indicated her intention of renouncing the limitations of the Five-Power Naval Treaty at the end of 1936. President Roosevelt had threatened a quarantine of aggressors in 1937, started a new shipbuilding program in 1938, and given notice in July 1939 that the commercial treaty with Japan would be allowed to expire in 1940. There was an increasingly sharp edge to America's opposition to Japan's dreams for a new order in East Asia. But Washington was not yet prepared for a two-ocean war. If Japan could act quickly the issues might be settled before the United States could be stirred to effective action.

Meanwhile there were quick rewards that could be won in French Indochina and the Netherlands East Indies by iron-gloved diplomacy that did not openly invite American intervention. France's hard-pressed government was in no position to refuse the use of airfields and bases in northern Indochina. The Dutch East Indies administration, thousands of miles away from a capital already marked for capture by Hitler, might be persuaded to grant special concessions in the sale of oil and other critically needed resources. The haughty British, once apparently secure in Singapore, were on the defensive. Possibly that great naval base itself might be bypassed or taken and the way opened to the riches of Malaya.

Some of these gaudy dreams were for the future. But a beginning could be made in the spring of 1940 with the French and Dutch. As early as January the Japanese made polite requests of the Dutch East Indies; the German invasion of France in May was the signal for tougher Japanese demands on French representatives in the Far East.

Tokyo's latest moves were closely watched in Washington. Suddenly, in early May, President Roosevelt decided to exert counterpressure in the Pacific. He directed a detachment of ships in the Atlantic, which had expected to visit New York during the World's Fair, to return to the Pacific. A few days later he ordered the Pacific Fleet, then completing annual naval maneuvers in Hawaiian waters, to remain temporarily at Pearl Harbor rather than return to its permanent bases on the west coast. To the fleet commander, Admiral James O. Richardson, who questioned the arrangement, Admiral Stark explained, "You are there because of the deterrent effect which it is thought your presence may have on the Japs going into the East Indies." [3]

Less than six weeks later the rapidly deteriorating military situation in Western Europe presented the President with a new dilemma. He had to assume that Germany would demand the French fleet in the terms of surrender. With the British Navy spread out around the world, American ships might have to be shifted to the Atlantic.

While the necessity of this transfer was being weighed in Washington, General Marshall's intelligence experts reported the alarming news that after years of bickering the Russians and Japanese had suddenly reached an agreement on some of their differences. That these traditional antagonists should be at peace seemed incredible, yet war had already seen stranger sights. There were few surprises left after August 1939, when Nazis and Communists had agreed to a nonaggression pact. Russia's earlier action had freed Germany for an attack in the west; the new agreement might help both Germany and Japan. Had the Japanese made concessions in order to get a free hand for action in the Pacific? To General Marshall pondering these possibilities on June 17, the morning that Marshal Pétain asked Hitler for surrender terms, the sudden thaw in Russo-Japanese relations had a sinister sound. The accord seemed timed "to permit Japan to undertake a trans-Pacific raid against Oahu, following the departure of the U. S. fleet from Hawaii." He presumed that such a raid would be in the interests of Germany and Italy, "to force the United States to pull the Fleet back to Hawaii." [4]

Only in the strange world of June 1940 could one imagine that the Japanese would stage a raid to hold the American fleet at Pearl Harbor. But if it would help her larger program, Japan might be willing to take pressure off her German partner in the Atlantic. So Marshall reasoned. In a world situation "so troubled and changing so rapidly," he thought it foolhardy not to take special precautions and put the Hawaiian Command on its guard.[5]

He was not seriously disturbed about Oahu's defenses if American forces there had sufficient warning. Since 1908, when the Army and Navy had agreed that Pearl Harbor would be America's chief naval base in the Pacific, the island of Oahu had been heavily fortified and garrisoned to make it secure against any likely attack. In 1920 the Army had been given the mission of protecting the base against sea or air bombardment, sabotage, or an expeditionary force. By 1940 the troops under the Hawaiian Department, stationed mainly on Oahu, constituted the Army's largest overseas detachment, amounting to more than one-tenth of the Army's total strength.[6]

In March 1940 General Marshall had flown to Hawaii to see the state of its defenses for himself. Shortly after completing a similar inspection tour to Puerto Rico and the Panama Canal Zone, he accepted General Herron's invitation to observe the four-day military exercises designed to test the command's ability to meet an enemy attack.

Marshall's visit was the first made to Hawaii by a Chief of Staff during his term of office, and the Islanders made a spirited effort to make him welcome. The Army Air Corps sent an escort of sixty planes to meet his Clipper one hundred miles out, and the military and civilian leaders of the Islands arranged a series of dinners and receptions in his honor. During his ten-day visit he sampled the laughter and gaiety that made Hawaii the happy paradise known to American moviegoers. But he did not stop there. In a strenuous inspection tour of Oahu, which included the base at Pearl Harbor and several of the outlying islands, he got a close look at what he had come to see—the iron muscles of Hawaii. On his return to the United States in mid-March he announced that the Hawaiian department needed some additional anti-aircraft units but otherwise was in "excellent shape." [7]

To make certain that Hawaii was ready for any eventuality he issued his alert of June 17. It differed sharply from the more crucial warning on the eve of the Pearl Harbor attack some seventeen months later in that his initial message was more explicit and the response more complete. Without alarming the public the Hawaiian Department commander put his command on full alert, bringing out his artillery units, issuing live ammunition, taking adequate precautions against sabotage, and preparing to meet the enemy by sea or air. General Herron's model alert may have been too successful. It may have given General Marshall a false sense of security about Hawaii's readiness to meet a future attack.[8]

After two days General Marshall directed a gradual lessening of the alert. Several weeks later he authorized Herron to relax it completely except for precautions against sabotage and for arrangements that would permit re-establishment of air patrols on short notice. The President's decision in July to leave the fleet indefinitely at Pearl Harbor lessened the War Department's fear of a sudden attack. Still cautious, General Marshall warned Herron to stay on guard for a lunge from an unexpected quarter. Herron reassured him in September: "As things now are, I feel that you need not have this place on your mind at all." [9]

In February 1941, when General Herron handed over his command to Lieutenant General Walter C. Short and Rear Admiral Husband E. Kimmel took Admiral Richardson's place as commander of the Pacific Fleet, General Marshall could boast that Hawaii's defenses had been heavily strengthened during the year that had passed. The presence of the fleet in itself seemed to insure Pearl Harbor's protection. In addition he had sent out an anti-aircraft artillery regiment at Herron's request, and on the day before Short was sworn in the Chief of Staff ordered eighty-one pursuit planes to be dispatched to Hawaii at once.[10]

In General Short, General Marshall had picked an officer with a fine record for training troops. Nearly the same age as the Chief of Staff, the new Hawaiian Department commander came out of the University of Illinois at the same time Marshall was completing his courses at VMI. They were commissioned as lieutenants of infantry in 1902, only a month apart. They had first met at Fort Reno in 1906 and had later served together in the 1st Division in France. In 1940 Marshall advanced Short from division to corps command shortly before giving him the largest United States overseas command. Some of Short's contemporaries later blamed Marshall for selecting an officer who did exactly as he was told, using little imagination, for a key post where great flexibility was required. The Chief of Staff had been impressed by his excellent record with troops in World War I and his command experience in the years between the two wars. Perhaps most important, he had done an outstanding job as assistant commandant at Fort Benning, the job Marshall had once held.

The Chief of Staff left no doubt in Short's mind as to the importance of his task and the necessity of his close cooperation with the Navy. He carefully spelled out the fact that the Army's mission was "to protect the base and the naval concentration" and that the "fullest protection of the fleet is *the* rather than *a* major consideration for us." He also directed him to work closely with Kimmel, warning him not to let "old Army and Navy feuds engendered from fights over appropriations" confuse issues of national defense. In order that Short could see "with whom you are to deal," he forwarded a statement of Stark's to the effect that Kimmel, a man of great ability, could be brusque and undiplomatic. "We must be completely impersonal in these matters, at least so far as our own nerves and irritations are concerned," Marshall advised. "Fortunately, and happily I might say, Stark and I are on the most intimate personal basis, and that relationship has enabled us to avoid many serious difficulties." [11]

General Short saw in his cordial reception by Admiral Kimmel and Admiral Claude C. Bloch, commander of the Fourteenth Naval District, an indication that there would be no difficulty with the Navy. Later he stressed his pleasant social relations and golf games with Kimmel as evidence that they had worked closely together. The assumption confused cordiality with close cooperation. Despite numerous instances of mutual affability, the Navy did not trust the Army with some of its secret information and made no special effort to inform the Hawaiian Department of some of its changes in operating procedure. The lack of complete coordination of plans and exchange of information that was to be criticized later in reports on the Pearl Harbor attack was attributable more to basic organizational differences than it was to clashes of personality.

The new Hawaiian Department commander set about his task with enthusiasm, covering Marshall's desk with proposals for strengthening the island's defenses. He compiled a formidable list of requisitions as he outlined plans for cooperating with the Navy, dispersing and protecting aircraft, and improving the anti-aircraft defenses.[12] General Short's reports in the spring and summer of 1941 stressed particularly his preoccupation with the possibility of surprise from the air. At the beginning of March he informed General Marshall that his principal requirement was an air-warning system; a week later he said his chief worry was the vulnerability of the airfields.[13] In requests for radar equipment, additional planes, and more anti-aircraft artillery, the emphasis was on the need to prevent surprise.

In view of this continued emphasis, the wonder is that Japan was so overwhelmingly successful in its assault of December 7. A War Department survey of Pearl Harbor defenses in January 1938 had included the prediction that in case of hostilities Japan would strike without notice, and "there can be little doubt that the Hawaiian Islands will be the initial scene of action." [14] In 1941 the staffs of Short and Kimmel in preparing plans to cover Army and Navy action in case of trouble underscored the possibility of a surprise attack. Noting the past history of Japan in this connection, they predicted that without any prior warning from naval intelligence a fast raiding carrier force might arrive in Hawaiian waters. They estimated that "the most likely and dangerous form of attack on Oahu would be an air attack" and "would most likely be launched from one or more carriers which would probably approach inside of 300 miles." [15]

Short's air commander was even more specific. In outlining the requirements for adequate air protection in August, Major General Frederick L. Martin declared that the most favorable plan of action for the enemy, "upon which we should *base our plans* of operation," would be to launch his planes "233 nautical miles from Oahu at dawn the day of the attack"; the worst situation that could arise was "the employment of six enemy carriers against Oahu simultaneously, each approaching on a different course." He was getting exceedingly close to the language in the enemy script for December 7.[16]

Despite his warning of mid-June against a sneak attack General Marshall shared the views of most of his colleagues that the Hawaiian defenders could successfully deal with an enemy raid. In his February 1941 instructions to Short he had indicated his belief "that if no serious harm is done us during the first six hours of known hostilities, thereafter the existing defenses would discourage an enemy against the hazard of an attack. The risk of sabotage and the risk involved in a surprise raid by Air and by submarine constitute the real perils of the situation. Frankly, I do not see any landing threat in the Hawaiian Islands so long as we have air superiority." [17]

He was even more positive in late April in describing the impregnability of the Island of Oahu to attack. After explaining his intention to send Short thirty-five heavy bombers and additional medium bombers and pursuit planes, General Marshall assured Roosevelt that, when the build-up of men, planes, and weapons then in progress was completed, they need not fear a successful landing. An invader would face more than 35,000 troops backed by coast defense guns, anti-aircraft artillery, and infantry weapons. With an adequate air defense, the American defenders could attack an enemy task force 750 miles away; if by chance a task force came within 200 miles it would be hit by all types of bombers and the most modern pursuit planes. He was convinced that the island's fortifications, garrison, and physical characteristics made it "the strongest fortress in the world." [18]

In speaking of the Pearl Harbor attack in later years General Marshall emphasized the fact that, in at least one respect, General Short had no basis for defense against the charge of being caught off guard. The very purpose of the Hawaiian Command was to protect the naval base and fleet at Pearl Harbor. Given the growing tension between the United States and Japan, a prudent commander had to assume that his garrison—however remote from the enemy—might be a target. Indeed, the commander had made that assumption, drawn up the necessary plans to counter an attack, and asked for weapons and equipment to meet the danger. Under these circumstances, the sending of a series of warnings, however ambiguous they might be, indicating a possible attack somewhere in the

Pacific, should have sufficed to put the garrison on full alert.

General Short could and did argue effectively in his defense that despite the numerous warnings sent out by Washington in 1941 General Marshall and the War Department did not give him the impression that they feared a crippling attack on Pearl Harbor. Not only did the air strength initially envisaged by the Chief of Staff for Hawaii not materialize but the emphasis on the Pacific build-up shifted in the late summer and fall of 1941 from Hawaii to the Philippines, Malaya, and the Dutch East Indies. Senator George pressed this point in his interrogation of Admiral Stark in the postwar Pearl Harbor Inquiry, saying, "I have been unable to escape the conclusion that little emphasis was placed upon the possibility of an air attack at Pearl Harbor late in the year 1941." [19] He accepted Stark's assurance that he and General Marshall kept up their interest in strengthening the defense plans and preparations already in effect. The fact remained, however, that from the spring of 1941 onward the attention of Washington turned increasingly toward the Far East. Significantly, when General Marshall sent his final warning message on the morning of December 7, priority was given to the Philippines.

The shift came slowly, and there was little indication until the end of 1940 that the United States would make any major change in the strategy decided on more than three decades earlier. Army and Navy planners had concluded in 1907 that it was impossible to get appropriations sufficient to maintain an outpost in the Philippines powerful enough to defeat an enemy invasion in force. They proposed instead a garrison that could put up a desperate fight until reinforcements could be sent from Pearl Harbor or the west coast of the United States. To give the defenders a fighting chance, strong fortifications were constructed over a period of years in and around Manila Bay—on the key island of Corregidor, whose name was to pass into the history books, and on the smaller islands, El Fraile, Carabao, and Caballo, which young Lieutenant Marshall had visited by small boat in 1903 to tack up "No Trespassing" signs.

The Army was never comfortable at the idea of leaving a small force to a desperate fate 7000 miles from home. After World War I, when the Treaty of Versailles assigned Japan control of the mandated islands—the Marianas, Carolines, and Marshalls—lying across United States lines of communication from the Central Pacific to the Philippines, Army officers periodically proposed that the United States either enlarge its garrison in the Far East or fall back to a better defended line. In the 1930s General Marshall's old friend Major General Ewing E. Booth, then commander of the Philippine Department, warned that by leaving a weak garrison in the Philippines the United States exposed the troops to the risk of suffering a humiliating defeat or invited an outraged public to "force our Navy to proceed with an attempted relief expedition before complete and satisfactory preparations had been made for such an expedition." [20] He agreed with his subordinate, General Embick, then commanding the detachment at Corregidor, that unless much larger sums of money were spent on the defense of the Philippine Islands the United States should try to neutralize them, withdraw from the Far East, and accept the Alaska-Oahu-Panama line as its line of defense.[21]

Initially rejected by both Army and Navy planners in Washington, the concept gained adherents in the Army, especially after 1935, when the Tydings-McDuffie Act, designed to give the Philippines their independence in 1946, went into effect. Wanting to keep bases there, the Navy insisted on hanging on. The Army went along with the Navy but limited its commitments. During the 1930s the War Department decided to confine its policy to keeping up existing strength in personnel and matériel and providing harbor defenses at Manila Bay and to limit further expense for permanent improvements "unless thereby ultimate saving will result." [22] Until 1935 the defense of the Philippines was vested in the forces of the Philippine Department, some 10,000 men, half of whom were American Regulars and half Philippine Scouts under American command. In that year an interim Commonwealth government designed to pave the way for complete independence was established. The President-elect, Manuel Quezon, who was to share executive control during the transitional period with the United States High Commissioner, promptly appointed a military adviser to start building and training a small, balanced force that could assume the task of defending the Islands when the Americans withdrew in 1946.

In the course of representing the Philippines in Washington during the long fight for independence, Quezon had become ac-

quainted with many of the capital's distinguished figures. He persuaded one of them, General Douglas MacArthur, the outgoing
Chief of Staff of the United States Army, to assume the post of
military adviser for the next six years. More than a decade and a
half would pass before MacArthur returned home to stay.

With the aid of his senior assistant, Major Dwight D. Eisenhower, who had previously served with him in Washington, General MacArthur planned a force in keeping with the limitations of
Quezon's budget. He proposed a small regular army, a ten-year
training program to create thirty reserve divisions, a small air
force, and a fleet of thirty to fifty small torpedo boats. When this
plan was completed he felt confident that he could oppose successfully "any conceivable expeditionary force." [23]

Beset by many demands on his meager resources, Quezon found
it difficult to allot sufficient funds to push the Commonwealth
Army as fast as Eisenhower and his colleague, Major James B. Ord,
desired. As a result, when General Marshall became Chief of Staff,
he found the defense of the Islands still resting mainly on the
forces of the Philippine Department.

Waiting on General Marshall's desk when he took the oath as
head of the Army in September 1939 was a reminder from the
Chief of the War Plans Division that a decision was needed on
Philippine defenses. With more pressing problems staring him in
the face at home, the new Chief of Staff came down in favor of the
status quo by holding the memorandum until spring. The question came up again in February 1940, when the Navy Department
proposed that both services expand their air forces in the Philippines. Any hope that the Army would consider the proposition
went out the window when the War Plans Division reported that
large outlays of money and manpower would be required and the
number of planes would have to be increased from the thirty-seven
now based there to 441. At a time when Congress had just cut all
but fifty-seven replacement planes from his request, Marshall saw
no prospect of carrying out such a plan. The proposal was shelved
but not the idea behind it.[24] In 1941 the Chief of Staff would return to the key point made by the Navy: a build-up of sufficient
airpower in the Philippines could deter Japanese aggression in the
Far East.

Disturbing developments in Japan during the summer and fall

of 1940 forced the Chief of Staff to take a second look at American defenses in the Pacific. The fall of the comparatively peaceful Yonai cabinet in July and its replacement by a government headed by Prince Fumimaro Konoye troubled President Roosevelt and his chief advisers. The new Prime Minister was no violent militarist, but two of his appointments were not conducive to Washington's peace of mind. The new Foreign Minister, Yosuke Matsuoka, was the American-educated firebrand who had led the Japanese out of the League of Nations in 1933, and the new War Minister, General Hideki Tojo, former chief of staff of the Japanese army in Manchuria, was a leading advocate of increased Japanese military power. Their presence in positions of power created the fear that the new regime would soon embark on a period of expansion to the south.[25]

Konoye's government moved quickly to strengthen Japan's bid for a free hand in the Far East by concluding a tripartite agreement with Germany and Italy on September 27, 1940. Japan recognized the special leadership of her two new partners in establishing a new order in Europe; they in turn recognized Japan's special position in Greater East Asia. Taking dead aim at the United States, the Axis Powers pledged their aid to any signatory "attacked by a power at present not involved in the European war or in the Sino-Japanese conflict." [26]

Rumors that negotiations were in progress and reports of an agreement between Japan and the French government at Vichy by which Japanese troops were to move into northern Indochina stirred President Roosevelt to action. On the day before the actual signing of the Axis accord, he stopped foreign shipment of iron and steel scrap except to Great Britain and the countries of Latin America.[27]

The President's embargo served notice on Japan that American patience was wearing thin. But he risked inciting the Japanese to seize available resources in the Pacific before the United States could bring additional economic pressure to bear. Marshall's new Philippine Department commander, Major General George Grunert, saw the danger and asked for reinforcements. A plain-spoken, cocky officer who knew Marshall well enough to call him "George" in official correspondence, Grunert peppered the War Department with requisitions for new weapons and equipment and warnings that the United States could not depend on the readiness of MacArthur's Commonwealth forces. Instead of being able to defend the Islands as the local newspapers boasted it could, the Commonwealth Army then consisted of one skeletonized Regular division of fewer than 500 officers and 3700 men and ten Reserve divisions in which 15 per cent of the officers had no active duty training and 50 per cent had no training whatever. There were serious shortages of clothing and equipment, and ammunition was almost completely lacking. Grunert proposed mobilizing the Commonwealth Army for one year under his supervision as a means of stepping up preparations. He also urged the United States to heed President Quezon's appeals for American support of the Islands' training program.[28]

As a soldier who had served his first tour of duty in the newly occupied island of Mindoro and who had won his first reputation as a staff officer in a simulated attack on Luzon, General Marshall knew and loved the Philippines. His last duty there, in 1916, had been in planning a staff ride over the routes between Lingayen Gulf and Manila that an invading army might take. He was moved by Grunert's earlier pleas for strengthening the United States forces and by his warnings that citizens of the Commonwealth were growing restive as it appeared that the United States would not or could not defend the Islands.[29]

Sympathy was not enough. The War Department simply could not fill all the demands on it. In late November, Marshall's advisers concluded that General Grunert's proposals would contribute little to the defensive strength of the Islands and "might result in involving us in action in that theater which we are not prepared to sustain." [30] Believing that a serious commitment of the United States in the Pacific "is just what Germany would like to see us undertake," the Chief of Staff hesitated. At the end of the month he suggested to Stark that the Army and Navy resist all proposals that did not have for their immediate goal the survival of the British Empire and the defeat of Germany. He was certain that they must avoid dispersions that might lessen their power to act effectively and perhaps decisively in the Atlantic.[31]

By stressing the Atlantic role of the United States, General Marshall and Admiral Stark could sidestep British requests for American reinforcement of the British base at Singapore. Help for China was far less easy to refuse as the signing of the tripartite agreement threatened renewed agony for that unfortunate country. When Germany began applying pressure on China to accept Japan's demands for a settlement and the Japanese redoubled their air efforts, Generalissimo Chiang Kai-shek accelerated his efforts to get American aid.

To bolster China's morale the British agreed to reopen the Burma Road—closed at Japan's insistence a few months earlier— and the United States offered additional credits for the purchase of nonmilitary goods. The Chinese countered with a recommendation that Washington provide 500 military planes, part of them bombers, to be used against Japanese targets. Although they realized that furnishing that number of planes was impossible, both Secretary Hull and Secretary Morgenthau backed a proposal for supplying 24 four-engine bombers to the Chinese. In meetings on December 22 and 23, 1940, General Marshall strongly opposed the proposal. American aid served no useful purpose if China, lacking trained pilots and adequate fighter support, ended by losing valuable bombers without inflicting any appreciable damage on the Japanese. Recently he had examined a promising proposal to remedy the lack of experienced pilots by recruiting volunteer groups to serve in the Far East. The plan appealed to him, but it would take time to implement. Meanwhile, he was willing to help China arrange a deal by which she would get 100 pursuit planes allocated to the British.[32]

The end of the year also saw a surprising shift in American thinking concerning the Philippines. Completely reversing the War Plans Division's recent recommendations, the War Department decided in late December to increase sharply its support of General Grunert. As a belated Christmas present, General Marshall approved doubling the Philippine Scouts (from 6000 to 12,000), increasing the 31st Infantry Regiment, shipment of additional antiaircraft guns and allotment of funds for construction of airfields and buildings for the air force.[33]

Problems from around the globe swirled across Marshall's desk as the holidays approached. Until Christmas Eve he struggled to find planes and weapons and men. Then he hastened to Quarters One, Fort Myer, for one of the happy events in the life of the Marshall family. Some months earlier Mrs. Marshall's daughter, Molly, had become engaged to a field artillery captain, James J. Winn of Alabama, currently stationed in Panama. The wedding, the first to be held in the quarters of the Chief of Staff, was set for December 25.

The gay occasion brought all the family members together for one of their infrequent gatherings, adding the spirit of reunion to the natural excitement of Christmas and the wedding. Not wishing to save all the celebration for one day, they opened their gifts on the evening of December 24. General Marshall had noted the headaches that marked the busy preparations for the wedding and had planned one of the practical jokes that he sometimes sprang on friends and members of the family. With proper ceremony a special present was brought in for Mrs. Marshall. Unwrapping the large package carefully tied up in silver paper, she found a large bottle of Bromo Seltzer, a foot high. The laughter that followed was typical of the warmth and joy that made that Christmas especially memorable. It was the last time all of them would be together for a Yuletide celebration.[34]

The gladness of late December did not last. After a short holiday over the New Year, General Marshall returned to the War Department in a troubled mood. Secretary Stimson noted: "He is very gloomy about what is going to happen during the coming winter, and I think he has good reason to be." [35] To the recurrent problem of Britain's security had been added the deepening crisis in the Far East.

During the next two months reports multiplied of Japanese preparations for new attacks. Rumors bred and spread alarm in far separated capitals. One day in early February, as he was trying to find heavy guns for MacArthur to guard the straits between Luzon and the islands to the south, General Marshall was startled by alarming messages from London. The Japanese, perhaps in conjunction with a German assault on the United Kingdom, planned within a week to attack Indochina, the Malay Peninsula, or the Netherlands East Indies. Next came reports that a Japanese naval force was concentrated off Saigon and that ground and naval forces were being assembled at Hainan, 100 miles east of Indochina. Wild accounts from London that members of the Japanese Embassy staff were clearing out of the city added to the confusion.

Fresh alarms on February 10 prompted the President to call a

White House conference of his military and diplomatic advisers. The meeting did little to dissipate their gloom. When asked what he could do to restrain the Japanese, General Marshall could point only to current efforts, still weeks or months away from completion, being made to strengthen the defenses of the Philippines. In a gesture that revealed the nakedness of the Army in the current crisis, the Chief of Staff ordered sixty officers, due to return to the United States, to remain at their posts in the Philippines. The President had little more to suggest. He spoke of several "moral steps" that might be taken—the recall of women and children from China, the Philippines, and Malaya; sending some cruisers on a good-will mission to the southern harbor of Mindanao; and arranging a conference between the President and Hull and Ambassador Nomura in which they would "pull very long faces and give him a very serious talk." [36]

Watching the storm warnings during the spring of 1941, General Marshall prepared to take positive action in the Philippines if the situation grew much worse. At least as early as May, he told Stimson that in case of further Japanese threats he proposed to recall General MacArthur to active duty in the United States Army and put him in command of all Army and Navy forces in the Philippines.

The same solution had occurred to the former Chief of Staff now watching impatiently on the sidelines as a field marshal in the Commonwealth Army. He broached the subject to the President in late May and in early June informed Marshall of the suggestion. Unwilling to be rushed, the Chief of Staff replied that he and Stimson had agreed earlier "that your outstanding qualifications and vast experience in the Philippines make you the logical selection for the Army commander in the Far East should the situation approach a crisis." At the proper time, he added, Secretary Stimson would recommend the appointment to the President.[37]

The time for stepped-up military preparations was almost at hand. Two days after Marshall's message to MacArthur, Germany invaded Soviet Russia. With one of her possible enemies now thoroughly occupied, Japan prepared to move rapidly to get her way in the Far East. Just when Roosevelt was pressing Marshall hardest for more planes for Great Britain and all-out assistance to Russia, the Chief of Staff had to give his attention to the Philippines.

On July 2, 1941, the Japanese military and political leaders lit the slow-burning fuse of a bomb that was to explode five months later with tragic results. In a fatal hour the Privy Council in Tokyo approved a policy of aggression sketched a few days earlier by representatives of the Army and Navy. Emboldened by Britain's problems and by Russia's plight, the Japanese government resolved to proceed against all obstacles to the establishment of the Greater East Asia Co-Prosperity Sphere, the settlement of the China Incident, and the possible solution of differences with the Soviet Union. It made crystal clear its determination to get complete control of Indochina even at the cost of war. Although Washington did not receive intercepts confirming the broad outlines of these decisions for nearly a week, President Roosevelt was sufficiently disturbed by hints of impending Japanese action to issue a warning to Prime Minister Konoye on July 4. Japan's future efforts at conquest, said the President, would "render illusory" American hopes that peace in the Pacific area might be strengthened and made more secure.[38]

In mid-July, Konoye made a bow in the direction of moderation by replacing the strongly pro-Axis Foreign Minister, Matsuoka, with Admiral Teijiro Toyoda. The effects of this gesture were dissipated almost at once when Tokyo, profiting by France's weakness, pressured Vichy into granting Japan the use of eight airfields in southern Indochina and naval bases at Saigon and Camranh Bay. From these positions the Japanese could attack supply lines into China and threaten the Dutch East Indies, Malaya, and the Philippines. These actions spoke louder than any proposals Konoye or his successors could make thereafter for peaceful settlement of differences with the Western Powers.

The President at last resolved to take the step long urged by some of his advisers. Stark and Marshall on July 25 alerted their overseas commanders to his action and warned of the possible consequences:

> You are advised that at 1400 GCT July twenty-sixth United States will impose economic sanctions against Japan. It is expected these sanctions will embargo all trade between Japan and the United States subject to modification through a licensing system for certain material. It is anticipated that export licenses will be granted for certain grades of petroleum products, cotton and possibly some other

materials and that import licenses may be granted for raw silk. Japanese assets and fund[s] in the United States will be frozen except that they may be moved if licenses are granted for such movement. . . . CNO and COS do not anticipate immediate hostile reaction by Japan through the use of military means but you are furnished this information in order that you may take appropriate precautionary measures against possible eventualities. . . .[39]

Although no immediate military action was expected, Stark warned that an embargo might provoke the Japanese into attacking Malaya or the Dutch East Indies. General Marshall did not go on record at the time. Later he testified that he and Stark wanted "to do all in our power here at home, with the State Department or otherwise, to try to delay this break to the last moment because of our state of unpreparedness and because of our involvement in other parts of the world." [40]

Of one thing Marshall was certain. It was now time for the Army to reorganize its defenses in the Philippines. On July 26, the same day that Roosevelt announced the imposition of economic sanctions, Marshall notified MacArthur that he had been named commanding general, United States Army Forces in the Far East (USAFFE), and that the Commonwealth armed forces had been called into the service of the United States.[41]

General MacArthur's new command consisted of some 22,000 Regulars and Philippine Scouts of the Philippine Department and his own Commonwealth Army, which was scheduled to reach a total of 120,000 Regulars and Reserves by mid-December 1941. Since the Commonwealth Army was far below the state of readiness predicted nearly a year earlier, General Grunert's units had to furnish the effective ground defense of the Philippines in the current crisis. It was a weak force to challenge the might of the Japanese.

In recalling General MacArthur to active duty, Marshall brought back to the service of the United States one of the outstanding military figures of American history. Reared in a splendid military tradition, number one student and First Captain at West Point, brave and brilliant fighter in World War I, able superintendent at West Point, and a forceful Chief of Staff for five years under Hoover and Roosevelt, he was a legend before he came to the Philippines in 1935. To these credentials he added special qualifications for the role he was to play in the Pacific area for the remainder of his active career. Son of General Arthur MacArthur, a Civil War hero who had won added fame as commander in the Spanish-American War and as first military governor of the Philippines, he early developed a special interest in the Far East. A nine-month trip with his father in 1905 from Tokyo to India and then back by way of Ceylon, Java, Siam, and Indochina to China proper had convinced him that America's destiny was more closely tied to the Pacific and the Far East than to Europe and the Atlantic. Two tours of service in the Philippines in the 1920s and his six years as military adviser merely strengthened his view.[42]

From the day that MacArthur succeeded to the Far East Command, his story became intertwined with General Marshall's. Soon exaggerated accounts of an old feud lost in the early mists of their Army careers were related around far-scattered bars. In later years friends of the Philippine Commander would charge Marshall with failure to give proper support to the Far East Command.

Although the messages between Washington and Manila and later between Washington and MacArthur's various Pacific headquarters were usually couched in correct military language, the return of General MacArthur to active duty created a difficult situation. Having served as Chief of Staff for a longer period than any of his predecessors, he naturally found it awkward to accept directives from men who were colonels or even captains when he was Chief of Staff. For six years as field marshal of the Commonwealth Army, he had enjoyed a close relationship with the Philippine President and struggled with high commissioners sent out from Washington; now he found it galling to defer to the judgment of civilians he regarded as mere politicians or of an Army Chief of Staff who attempted to carry out the policy of these civilians.

There is evidence that in discussions with his staff General MacArthur sometimes talked freely of his likes and dislikes. Comments arising from frustrations apparently were often taken as evidence of deep-seated antagonism to Marshall and the administration. Some of the inner circle developed the view that anything withheld from General MacArthur—an additional division or control over Admiral Thomas C. Hart's naval forces in Philippine waters—was based on personal bias and that any strategy that failed to put his operations first was dictated by forces subversive of the best interests of the United States. To what extent General MacArthur shared these bizarre conjectures that spice the pages of several of the biographies written by his friends or former aides is not completely clear. Certainly, several officers who were close to him managed to reconcile their great respect and admiration for him with the realization that the allotment of men and supplies to the European and Pacific Theaters was based on strategy and not on personal animus. In conversation with Marshall's biographer in 1961, General MacArthur sought to minimize the personal differences that existed between the two.

In speaking of MacArthur to his staff, Marshall avoided personalities. Although he sometimes showed by tone of voice or gesture of impatience or stiffness in a letter his reaction to some communication of MacArthur's, he avoided personal bickering. As a result his staff did not develop the bitter feeling toward the Pacific commander that some members of the latter's staff have exhibited in their comments on the wartime Chief of Staff.

The differences between Marshall and MacArthur lay more in their temperaments and styles than in ancient quarrels and fancied injuries. In a revealing aside to an old friend who had done his portrait, Marshall once protested: "You have endowed me with more of a MacArthur personality than my own less colorful characteristics, and I fear you strove too hard to make good my deficiencies." [43] It was his way of saying that he lacked the florid touch and the flair for self-dramatization that helped make the Pacific commander a striking and effective figure. These were not qualities that the Chief of Staff held against his brother officer—Marshall recognized that showmanship could be a valuable asset to a field commander—but they were not to his taste.

So far as Marshall was concerned, MacArthur was the officer best suited for the new Far East Command in the time of crisis. He had been on the spot for six years, he had the confidence of Quezon and the people of the Philippines, he was thoroughly cognizant of the problems of the Pacific, and he was a gifted soldier. The Chief of Staff regretted the necessity of shifting General Grunert just as his program was beginning to move, but there was a place for only one commander.

Marshall's establishment of the Far East Command was initially a purely defensive move in keeping with the past efforts of Grunert and MacArthur to prepare the Philippines to ride out a storm. Soon this concept changed radically. Between the Far Eastern commander's oversanguine estimates of the strength of his forces and General Marshall's overrating of the current capacity of the heavy bomber, Washington and Manila developed the theory that the Philippines could play a key role in deterring further Japanese expansion toward the south.

The air reinforcement of MacArthur's command began quietly in early August when General Arnold allotted to the Far East Air Force four heavy bomber groups consisting of 272 planes with 68 in reserve and two pursuit groups of 130 planes each. With Marshall's approval, the Air Chief transferred units from commands in the United States and Hawaii and earmarked 165 of the 220 bombers scheduled for production in the United States by the end of February 1942 for delivery to the Islands.[44]

Before this basic build-up could get properly under way, two events stirred Marshall and his associates to dream of a greater role than they had hitherto envisaged for the Philippines. On a visit to the Boeing works in Seattle in late August, the Chief of Staff and the Secretary of War were deeply impressed with the increased potential predicted for the improved B-17s then in production. Little more than two weeks later, a history-making flight of nine heavy bombers from Hawaii to Manila demonstrated that the Philippines could be reinforced by air by way of Midway, Wake, Port Moresby, and Port Darwin. The way seemed open to bypass the hostile Japanese bases in the mandated islands. Stimson reflected the excitement created in the War Department by the flight when he wrote that the United States now had a chance to "get back into [the] Islands in a way it hadn't been able to for twenty years." [45]

General Marshall moved at once to establish a ferrying route to the Far East and to provide air bases in the Southwest Pacific. At the end of September the Chief of Staff directed General MacArthur to arrange for regular use of the British airfields at Port Darwin, Rabaul, Port Moresby, and Singapore, to secure emergency use of airfields in the Dutch possessions, and to request the British to develop a field in northern Borneo for American planes. The War Department also issued elaborate plans for stockpiling ammunition, bombs, gasoline, and oil in the Southwest Pacific for future operations.[46]

In briefing the new commander of the Far East Air Command, Major General Lewis H. Brereton, who stopped in Washington for final orders in October before leaving for Manila, the Chief of Staff pointed up the increased strategic importance of the Philippines. Fearing that the Japanese would learn of the steady build-up and act promptly to knock out the bomber force before sufficient fighter protection arrived, the airman expressed his alarm. Unperturbed, General Marshall calmly acknowledged that he and General Arnold were taking a calculated risk and were moving quickly and quietly to forestall a premature attack.[47]

In the new stress on airpower, General Marshall kept firmly in mind the importance of strengthening MacArthur's ground defenses. In early September he had assured the Far East commander that he was giving him the "highest priority for equipment including authorized defense reserves for 50,000 men." The Far East commander reacted enthusiastically, proposing on October 1 that his mission be enlarged from defense of the Manila Bay area to defense of the entire Philippine Archipelago. In a burst of optimism he wrote that his total force would soon be equivalent "to an army of approximately 200,000 men" and that the "strength and composition of the defense forces here are believed to be sufficient to accomplish such a mission." So contagious was his confidence that the War Department momentarily overlooked Grunert's warning regarding the readiness of the Commonwealth forces for combat.[48]

Now that they were working closely together toward a common goal the leaders in Washington and Manila seemed to forget how quickly time was running out and how many months were still needed to prepare an adequate Philippine defense. The quickening flow of planes and equipment swept away the strong doubts that the War Department had held only a few months before. Caught up in the excitement, General Gerow of the War Plans Division in early October dramatically announced that the air and ground forces scheduled for delivery within a few months had changed "the entire picture in the Asiatic area" and might well "have a vital bearing on the course of the war as a whole." If Japanese vessels moved west of the Philippines in a drive toward Malaya, they exposed themselves to air and naval attacks from the Islands; a swing to the east would open them to assault by the United States fleet. If the enemy foolishly undertook to move against eastern Siberia, he ran the risk of bringing the United States into war and suffering air attacks by Russian and American bombers that would be stationed in Siberia. Thus by threats of air and naval action the United States could stay out of the war and still restrain the Japanese. Although completely unrealistic at this stage of the Far Eastern build-up and current bomber capabilities, the concept fired the imagination of the Joint Board. Among the revisions recommended in the RAINBOW plan for the Pacific was Army support of the Navy in raiding Japanese sea communications, destroying Axis forces, and conducting air raids against "Japanese forces and installations within tactical operating radius of available bases." [49]

General MacArthur was delighted when General Brereton arrived in Manila in early November with secret instructions and directives foreshadowing Joint Board action. Reacting boyishly to the promise of speedy reinforcement, he embraced the air officer, saying, "Lewis, you are just as welcome as flowers in May." To his chief of staff, Brigadier General Richard K. Sutherland, he shouted happily, "Dick, they are going to give us everything we have asked for." [50]

General Brereton was less elated when he saw how little had yet been done. Lack of money and equipment still made difficult the basic implementation of the Far East commander's plans. He recalled later that he found few indications that officers and men were aware of the imminence of war. MacArthur was proceeding on the assumption that nothing would happen before April 1, 1942, to disrupt the mobilization, training, and equipping of units.[51] General Marshall would have been satisfied with a month or so less, but he too seemed unaware how short a time still remained.[52]

Determined to take advantage of the days of grace that remained, Marshall drove his staff to rush reinforcements to the Philippines. Units were shifted at short notice from maneuver areas to ports on the Pacific coast and sudden levies were imposed on scarce stores in commands across the country to speed the build-up. To his great disappointment, weapons and equipment accumulated at west coast warehouses quicker than ships could be found to transport them. In offering a National Guard division to MacArthur in September, he had to explain with embarrassment that its immediate shipment would constitute a heavy strain on shipping. The problem was compounded when the worsening of American relations with Japan forced him to move forward the delivery dates of critical items. Thus, in late September, he had to intervene with Admiral Stark to postpone the conversion of three transports to carriers in the hope that he could deliver scheduled reinforcements in Manila by December 10 instead of the end of February. Increasingly aware of MacArthur's vulnerable position, he directed in October that he be personally informed "as to [the] certainty that MacArthur can be sure that one or two [tankers] will always be within reach." By giving the Philippines top priority and by continually hammering away at the movement of reinforcements, General Marshall was able to advance shipments slated for the Islands from January to mid-December.[53] Although the attack on December 7 would find crated planes on ships in mid-Pacific and unarmed bombers ready to touch down at Hawaii en route to the Philippines, the movement of supplies and equipment after September was impressive. Aided by the eager cooperation of Army and Navy commanders on both sides of the Pacific, Marshall shifted to the Philippines before Pearl Harbor one-half of all heavy bombers (35 B-17s) and one-sixth of all fighters (175) stationed in overseas bases.[54]

During that fall of 1941 General Marshall became painfully aware of the Army's severely defective administrative organization. Still geared to the demands of a small peacetime Army, working at a normal bureaucratic pace, the War Department lacked the personnel and the methods to insure prompt execution of the Chief of Staff's directives. These failings had been obvious as early as the fall of 1940 when the passage of the Selective Service Act was followed by embarrassing delays in providing housing and clothing for the newly inducted men. Marshall's investigations into the difficulties and his tightening up of control over shipments met the immediate problems, but the necessary sweeping reorganization still remained in the future. Hampered by the dead hand of tradition and beset by problems at home and abroad, the Chief of Staff had failed to find time to put his administrative house in order. Now when every day was at a premium, he was shocked not only at the unnecessary delays but at the fact that his staff did not know why they had occurred. In early November he growled at his assistants in a staff conference that he had been "paralyzed" to find that through "command failures" a cargo of bombs shipped to Singapore at the end of September would not reach its destination until after mid-December. Exasperated by a clear failure to follow up his directives, he stated that "we can have no more of this." One month before Pearl Harbor he cried out in frustrated anger, "This is the poorest command post in the Army and we must do something about it." [55]

The marvel was that he managed to keep a sense of proportion as each afternoon seemed to reach "a peak of new difficulties." The General's simplest efforts to relax were often disturbed by threatened catastrophe. Finding a quiet weekend one Saturday in early September, Marshall slipped down to Leesburg for the first time since July 4, hoping to prune some of his apple trees. Climbing one of them, he was just reaching for a dead limb when he was called to the telephone by an officer from the War Department. There was news of a German raider in the Caribbean and the danger of an attack on Dutch oil refineries on the islands of Aruba and Curaçao. The General called the President at Hyde Park, asking him to get permission from Queen Wilhelmina of the Netherlands for the United States to install guns and an air base on the islands. His call completed, he returned to his task. A second time the telephone rang, and he wearily came down from his perch. This time the President wanted more information. When this was furnished, the General, determined not to give up, retraced his steps and succeeded in sawing through part of the limb before an orderly summoned him for the third time to the telephone. This time the War Department wanted more specific directives. Knowing he was licked, Marshall called for his car and set off for Washington. The island defenses were ready when war came in December; the half-severed limb hung there until spring.[56]

When his stepson Allen, within a week of becoming a father, wrote him of his problems in buying a new house and the failure of his employer to come through with a promised pay raise, General Marshall passed on his own philosophy for dealing with difficulties. "To my mind, self-control and a certain endurance of unsatisfactory conditions are ever the supreme test, and certainly have been so in my case," he wrote. Allen's perplexities were soon forgotten in his delight over the birth of a son, Tupper, for whom Marshall served as godfather. There was nothing to make the General's problems vanish so easily.

In September, Marshall hoped to go to the Canal Zone before

Christmas both for a long-delayed inspection of defense installations and a short visit with Molly and her husband, who were expecting a child. By late October any hope of getting away seemed to have vanished. "Last week was worst of all," he complained, "a combination of Russian affairs, the Japanese situation, supplies to England, the political pressures, developments in relation to National Guard and some Regular officers over relief from command, the development of the next period of training for the Army, the approaching hearings on Lend-Lease, etc., etc." [57]

The world's woes were temporarily shoved to the back of his mind a few days later when Mrs. Marshall slipped in their Fort Myer quarters and broke four ribs. Still upset over the accident after a week, the General wrote Molly, "The moral of this tale is, get rid of those damned high-heeled bedroom slippers, with leather soles." Sadly he confessed that he knew his words would go unheeded. He had given the same advice to her mother a few days before her fall, and his reward had been the remark that he was becoming more difficult to live with. Even the stenographer, he added, was defending women "with a cynical smile" as she took down his words.[58]

Running through all of his thinking now was the question of the Japanese. The brief September hope for some understanding with Japan after Matsuoka's replacement by Togo disappeared in October when Premier Konoye resigned and was succeeded by General Tojo, one of Tokyo's most aggressive leaders. From the Japanese capital, Ambassador Joseph C. Grew warned that the change of government might mean the opening of the road to war. Secretary Stimson despaired of reaching any settlement with the new government, hoping only that the United States could gain time enough to strengthen American forces for tests in the Philippines and the South Pacific. Of late, he had discussed the build-up repeatedly with General Marshall. If time was on their side, they believed they might yet discourage Tojo from challenging the West.[59]

That possibility rapidly faded. The worsened situation was clearly expressed in the warning of October 16 sent by Stark to commanders in Hawaii and the Philippines:

The resignation of the Japanese Cabinet has created a grave situation. If a new Cabinet is formed it will probably be strongly nationalistic and anti-American. If the Konoye Cabinet remains the effect will be that it will operate under a new mandate which will not include rapprochement with the United States. In either case hostilities between Japan and Russia are a strong possibility. Since the U. S. and Britain are held responsible by Japan for her present desperate situation there is also a possibility that Japan may attack these two powers. In view of these possibilities you will take due precautions including such preparatory deployments as will not disclose strategic intentions nor constitute provocative actions against Japan.[60]

The reference to possible hostilities between Russia and Japan reflected a belief that had been growing in Washington and Hawaii since spring that war when it came would be closer to Manila than to Pearl Harbor. General Short, who had been watching the stream of planes and weapons bound for General MacArthur's command, might be pardoned for taking the alert rather calmly. He testified later that he recalled taking no specific action on the receipt of the October 16 message. After receiving the July warning on the occasion of the imposition of economic sanctions against Japan, he had tightened his guard against sabotage and subversive activities. These measures had never been relaxed. As a result, "I figured when I got that message that we were all right . . . and I was probably just a little more watchful." [61]

In its own concentration on the dangers to the Philippines, the War Department failed to see that Hawaii had dropped its guard. General Short reported no precautionary actions taken and no report was required of him. Washington's apparent acceptance of his reasoning that the danger lay elsewhere than in his part of the Pacific was to have fateful consequences when warnings were sent in November.

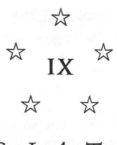

So Little Time

"YESTERDAY we had time but no money and . . . to-day we have money but no time." Since the summer of 1940 when General Marshall made that rueful remark, he had struggled against deadlines set by approaching conflict. At the beginning of November 1941 he feared that he would be unable to complete his reinforcement of the Philippines in time. "'Until powerful United States forces have been built up in the Far East," he realized, "it would take some very clever diplomacy to save the situation." During the days of grace remaining, he and Admiral Stark spent their hours and energies encouraging diplomacy to do its best.[1]

Since late July when American attention focused on the Philippines, the Chief of Staff had worked doggedly at the seemingly impossible task of deterring attack while preparing for it. "If we could make the Philippines . . . reasonably defensible, particularly with heavy bombers in which the Air Corps at that time had great faith," Marshall testified later, "we felt that we could block the Japanese advance and block their entry into war by their fear of what would happen if they couldn't take the Philippines, and we could maintain heavy bombers on that island." [2]

Only a weakening of resolve in Tokyo or a mood of acquiescence in Washington could have gained the time he wanted at this stage of developments. He saw little prospect of concessions by Japan. General Tojo was too strongly committed to strengthening his country's control of the Far East and to gaining a speedy settlement of the China Incident to turn back. His aggressive views tensed nerves throughout the Far East.

Two weeks after the new cabinet came to power in Japan,

Chiang Kai-shek warned Washington and London of an impending attack through Yunnan province, designed to capture Kunming and cut the Burma Road. He saw no hope of meeting the
threat without support from the United States and Great Britain.

The State Department, as always, was sympathetic. But Hull and
his advisers had found the War and Navy Departments cool in the
past to active intervention on the mainland of Asia. The Secretary
of State said quite firmly on November 1 that he saw no point of
sending further warnings to Japan "if we can't back them up."
General Marshall and Admiral Stark immediately resisted the pressure for action. Both, said the General, were trying "to do all in
our power here at home, with the State Department or otherwise,
to try to delay this break to the last moment, because of our state of
unpreparedness and because of our involvements in other parts of
the world." [3]

The Chief of Staff knew that China would carry its pleas from
the State Department to the White House. It was necessary then
for the Army and Navy to make their own appeal to the President.
As a beginning Marshall asked his colleagues: How far should the
United States commit itself in the Far East and the Pacific? How
far should the country go in trading concessions to Japan for time
in the Philippines? At what point would the United States have to
say "thus far and no farther" to the Japanese?

Deciding that a massive build-up in the Philippines was more important to peace in the Pacific than piecemeal aid to China or
Singapore, he argued vigorously at a Joint Board meeting on November 3 in favor of sticking to the current schedule. With the Far
East taut with tension, he and Stark deplored any word or action
by the administration that might precipitate a crisis.[4]

On November 5 the American service chiefs took their case to
Roosevelt. They began by restating basic American policy. The
primary strategic objective of the United States was the defeat of
Germany. "If Japan be defeated and Germany remains unde-
feated," they warned, "decision will still have not been reached."
An unlimited Allied offensive against Japan would greatly weaken
the combined effort against Germany, "the most dangerous
enemy." [5]

After refocusing the President's attention on Europe, Marshall
and Stark turned to the possibilities opening up in the Pacific. If

they could continue the build-up in the Philippines until mid-December they could threaten any Japanese operations south of Formosa; if they had until February or March, when the air forces reached their projected strength, the planes might well be "a deciding factor in deterring Japan in operations in the areas south and west of the Philippines." British naval and air reinforcements, now being rushed to Singapore, would reach impressive proportions by March.[6]

While the build-up was in progress, war between the United States and Japan must be avoided unless strong national interest was involved. They ruled out American entry into war to prevent a Japanese attack on Kunming, on Russia, or on those areas of Thailand that did not threaten the British position in Burma or Malaya. Although favoring more material aid for China and an accelerated development of the American Volunteer Group, they opposed sending United States armed forces to intervene in China against Japan.

If war with Japan could not be avoided, it should follow the outlines of existing war plans in that "military operations should be primarily defensive, with the object of holding territory and weakening Japan's economic position." They emphasized that America should go to war only if Japan attacked or directly threatened territories "whose security to the United States is of very great importance." These areas included the holdings of the United States, the British Commonwealth, and the Netherlands East Indies; those parts of Thailand from which a hostile force could threaten Malaya and Burma; and certain French and Portuguese islands in the South Pacific. In no case, they argued, should an ultimatum be delivered to Japan.[7]

The President heeded his service chiefs. Next day he told Secretary Stimson that he was trying to think of something that "would give us further time." He suggested a six months' truce during which there would be no movement of troops and the Chinese and Japanese would have a chance to come to terms. Stimson, as interested as Marshall in completing the Philippines build-up, threw cold water on the idea. The proposed truce would stop any reinforcements to the Far East and give the impression that the United States was deserting China. Roosevelt conceded that he would have to look for a different formula.[8]

As Marshall said, it would indeed take "clever diplomacy" to keep the peace. Even as he and Stark argued for moderation and more time, their counterparts in Tokyo, General Hajime Sugiyama and Admiral Osami Nagano, were setting rigid time limits on their Foreign Office in its search for agreement. Since the Imperial Conference of July 2 when Japan's political and military leaders had decided to settle the China Incident even at the risk of war with the United States and Great Britain, the diplomats had worked under impossible restrictions. They continued talks in Washington, knowing that the Army had ordered studies of operations against the Philippines, Malaya, and the Dutch East Indies and that the Navy was practicing for an attack somewhere in the Pacific.

The details of Japan's military preparations were not known in Washington, but reports from Tokyo by Ambassador Grew were sufficient to indicate the growing danger. When Prince Konoye's government fell in mid-October, Grew described the situation as extremely delicate. He warned the State Department against "any possible misunderstanding of the ability or readiness of [Japan] to plunge into a suicidal war with the United States." The time had come when neither "clever" nor "tough" diplomacy would suffice. Only if the United States yielded on several debated points could peace be saved. General Marshall was prepared to make such a gesture to Tokyo. "It appeared that the basis of United States policy should be to make certain minor concessions which the Japanese could use in saving face," he said in early November. "These concessions might be a relaxation on oil restrictions or on similar trade restrictions." [9]

He was seriously mistaken about the Japanese. Having embarked on a campaign to win their place in the sun, the military masters of Japan were unwilling to settle for a simple gesture. On November 5 the members of the Imperial Conference in Tokyo approved two proposals to be presented to the United States. These were less plans for negotiation than terms of surrender of the basic United States position. Plan A, providing for a settlement of the chief issues between the two countries, was so one-sided that Foreign Minister Togo recognized that it was unacceptable. Plan B, to be presented if the first was rejected, provided for a short-term truce. The Japanese would agree to stop their expansion in the Pacific if the United States would lessen its economic pressure in the Far East.

The diplomats were given little chance to negotiate. Not only would the plans create additional friction; the time limit virtually decreed failure. The three weeks allotted the Foreign Office on November 5 for closing a deal gave neither room nor time for diplomatic maneuver.

Troubling the Japanese Ambassador in Washington, Admiral Kichisaburo Nomura, was the knowledge that his nation's military leaders did not expect a peaceable solution to the crisis. He probably did not know that as early as November 3, the Japanese Chief of the Naval General Staff had approved the plan for attacking Pearl Harbor. He was almost certainly aware that on November 5, the same day Marshall and Stark asked the President not to issue an ultimatum to Japan, the Japanese Army and Navy commanders had alerted their subordinates to the likelihood of conflict with the United States, Great Britain, and the Netherlands East Indies. Two days later they tentatively set the date of December 8, Tokyo time, for the outbreak of war.[9]

At this point the Foreign Office dispatched Saburo Kurusu to Washington to help the ambassador in the final discussions with Secretary Hull. The Japanese representative could not have been too hopeful about his mission; unless the United States was prepared to make concessions, there would be a violent explosion by early December.

In this ominous period numerous problems beset General Marshall and Admiral Stark. The three most persistent were: how to gain time, how to continue the build-up, and how to make certain their commanders overseas were not taken by surprise. The Chief of Staff was comforted by the secret knowledge Washington had of Japanese diplomatic activities. He had said confidently to his staff in late November, "We know a great deal that the Japanese are not aware we know and we are familiar with their plans to a certain extent." [10]

The General was speaking of a secret asset possessed by the United States. Over a period of years military monitoring stations throughout the country had been plucking from the airwaves wireless messages sent by Japan's Foreign Office to its representatives in the United States and abroad. Many of them were sent in cipher or code which could not be read and the result was a collection of gibberish. In other cases cryptographic experts were able to solve the secret and produce decrypted diplomatic messages which were known to the initiated as MAGIC.[10]

The most valuable single source of information in the collection consisted of messages sent from Tokyo's Foreign Office in the diplomatic cipher known as PURPLE. Sixteen months before Pearl Harbor, Lieutenant Colonel William F. Friedman, Chief Cryptanalyst of the War Department, in a brilliant piece of work had uncovered this tremendous secret. Complicated machines were built to pick up the messages and turn them back into the language in which they had been originally written. Installed in Washington, London, and Corregidor, they poured forth a mass of data on those Axis designs known to Japanese diplomats and such details of Japan's military plans as its Army and Navy commanders were willing to disclose to the Foreign Office.

This was the source on which Washington depended for the final warnings of an attack. Yet the last crowded weeks before Pearl Harbor tell the story of a magic that somehow failed. The PURPLE machines produced marvels but did not reveal all the American Army and Navy needed to know to put their houses in order before the storm. The whereabouts of the Japanese fleet, the target for the attack, the hour of bombing, were never sent in diplomatic cipher. Read later in the light of the burning ships and the blazing barracks of Oahu, there were warnings that pointed toward Pearl Harbor. Some of these were either never disseminated or sent so guardedly that the recipients misread their meaning; or, when received, either because of complacency or confusion, they were not properly acted upon.

The cracking of the PURPLE secret generated its own complexities. The volume of traffic in intercepts, the preponderance of chaff in the mass of messages, and the limited number of translators combined to build backlogs of material. Some items remained untranslated for more than a week after they were received. A more serious weakness was that recipients were not permitted to keep a file of the copies for comparison and careful study. The intercepts had to be returned to the central file as soon as they were read and all but a master copy destroyed. As a result the cumulative evidence of Japanese intent was never spread out for examination at one time.

The elaborate secrecy surrounding the use of the material also limited its usefulness. Considering American ability to read Japan's secret diplomatic messages one of the most potent weapons the United States could have in case of war, intelligence officials demanded the most rigid safeguards to prevent the Japanese from knowing that the cipher had been broken. The intercepts were decoded and translated on alternate days by the Army and Navy and the messages delivered to the small list of authorized officials by carefully selected officers of the two services. Distribution was limited to the President, the Secretaries of State, War, and Navy, the Chief of Staff, the Chief of Naval Operations, Chiefs of the Army and Navy War Plans Divisions, Chiefs of Army and Navy Intelligence, and a few other experts in the two departments. Not even General Arnold, Marshall's chief airman, was on the list.

Possibly the Army and Navy came to depend too heavily on the intercepts. In their warnings of July and October 1941, neither Marshall nor Stark had to go beyond the information available through normal sources of intelligence. Japan's aggressive intentions were evident in the national press and in reports sent by American diplomats from Tokyo. An intelligence officer reading *The New York Times* could be almost as well informed on Japan's future policy as another officer scanning a number of random diplomatic messages coming off the decoding machines.

Few students of the Far East doubted that Japan intended to use the opportunity offered by the plight of Russia, Britain, France, and the Netherlands to grab the oil and other critical resources she desperately needed. The question was where and when a frustrated and fanatic military clique would choose to strike.

There were some tough questions to answer. Would Japan dare drive southward for raw materials as long as a powerful United States fleet was at Pearl Harbor and an Army garrison in the Philippines? Would the pressure of economic sanctions and a ban on oil exports force even the moderates among Japanese leaders to approve attacks on the oil fields of the Netherlands East Indies before economic strangulation set in? Or would they choose the moment of Soviet Russia's greatest weakness to settle old accounts with Japan's most feared neighbor and seize points in eastern Siberia that would both remove Russian pressure and give Japan a point from which to threaten Alaska? Intelligence officers in the War Department read intercepts of continuing troop and ship movements southward but kept Siberia high on the list of Japanese goals.

Throughout the summer of 1941 danger signals kept going up. Despite soft words from Premier Konoye, the intercepts between Tokyo and Berlin indicated that Japan would risk war in order to profit from Germany's European conquests. There was no specific indication in any of the messages that Pearl Harbor would be a target. In the summer and early fall, perhaps only an intelligence officer forced to rely on intuition, a clever assessment of Japanese psychology, and American reports from Tokyo would have reached that conclusion. With the MAGIC intercepts at hand, the tendency was to rely on them for the positive statement of Japanese movements. Inasmuch as the Foreign Office was kept ignorant of details of military plans, no orders were picked up showing Pearl Harbor high on the list of targets.

For years writers in Sunday supplements had alternated articles on invasions from Mars with warnings of the "yellow peril." The two favorite journalistic targets for the Japanese were Pearl Harbor and the Panama Canal. Characterizing the Japanese as a "sneaky" people because of their earlier surprise attacks on the Chinese and the Russians, the prognosticators assumed that Japanese planes and ships would come out of the mists just at dawn on a Sunday morning when defending crews and troops were asleep. Intelligence officers regularly included such attacks in their lists of possible enemy actions. They just as regularly ruled them out because some other alternative seemed more the type of attack they would make if they were running the Japanese armed services.

General Marshall always felt that his Intelligence Division, for all its expert knowledge, let him down in 1941. He was aware of Stimson's strong dissatisfaction with many of the intelligence reports. Several times he had intervened on his experts' behalf, although he later admitted that the organization of the division was bad and that it was short of people. He said in 1956 that he should have made necessary changes but "I didn't know enough about where they were wrong to relieve them." [11] Despite his confidence in some of the officers in the organization, he shared the field officer's unfavorable view of G-2. Beset by demands for officers for training and command assignment, he neglected to strengthen adequately the division on which he had to depend for accurate enemy information.

Critics of the War Department G-2 Division aimed their shafts at its chief, Brigadier General Sherman Miles, son of a former commanding general of the Army, Nelson Miles, and nephew of General William Tecumseh Sherman. Although Miles' post-World War I service had included three years as chief of the Plans and Projects section of the War Plans Division, his critics remembered that he had been five times a military attaché. This association with the "pink tea" set was almost fatal to the ambitions of an officer in the old Army. Too many attachés had been selected for their social graces and their personal incomes and had spent too much of their lives as social aides to ambassadors to impress their colleagues. General Marshall knew better than to make any such generalizations. His own knowledge of Germany and Central Europe had come from extremely well-informed attachés such as Colonel Truman Smith in Germany and Colonel John Winslow in Poland. Nevertheless he was dissatisfied with the functioning of G-2 and he had considered bringing in a new Chief of Intelligence several months before Pearl Harbor.[12]

Despite shortcomings of the organization and mistaken estimates, the Intelligence Divisions of the Navy and War Departments in Washington and in Hawaii collected an impressive amount of accurate information. There could be no question in the minds of General Marshall or General Short or General MacArthur that the Japanese were daily growing more restless or that war might come suddenly. The trouble lay in the fact that all signs pointed to pressure points in the Far East rather than to Pearl Harbor.

Assuming that the Japanese would continue to push southward until they were stopped by the British or the Americans, General Marshall believed as late as mid-November that the Army still had a chance to influence the decision in the Far East. Knowing that Kurusu was on the way from Tokyo, he hoped that the talks could be spun out for at least a few more weeks. His main concern on November 15, as he prepared to leave for several days to see the Carolina maneuvers, was that nothing be leaked to the Japanese of his plans for the Philippines. With planes being shifted from various parts of the country to west coast ports, it was only a matter of time until an enterprising reporter would break the story. A premature announcement might either destroy the shock value of the build-up or trigger Japanese action.

The Chief of Staff had learned that the best way to keep a secret out of the newspapers was to reveal it to responsible newsmen and then explain why it could not be printed. Growing uneasy about how much rumor might reveal of his plans, he called an extraordinary Saturday morning briefing on the 15th. Seven newsmen, representatives of the chief wire services and the *New York Times, New York Herald Tribune, Time,* and *Newsweek,* received early-morning invitations to meet General Marshall at the Munitions Building.

On their arrival the puzzled newsmen were shown to the Chief of Staff's office. Looking about for a clue as to the nature of the meeting, they saw a huge map of the Pacific with large circles marked on it representing the range of aircraft from various fields and bases. When they were seated General Marshall explained that what he had to tell them would have to remain secret. If they did not wish to remain under the circumstances, they were free to go. No one moved, and he started his briefing.

When he had their attention Marshall announced calmly that the United States and Japan were on the brink of war. He then listed the reinforcements that had been sent and were waiting to go to the Philippines. If the United States was allowed time to complete the build-up, he said, the President would then suddenly reveal to the moderate leaders of Japan the extent of the vast air force that menaced them. Perhaps, if they were allowed to save face, they would desist from their aggression.

The General stressed the defense potential of the Philippines set forth by his War Plans Division in late October. It was an ambitious program, requiring luck and time, but within the realm of possibility.

As reported by one of the newsmen, Robert Sherrod of the *Time-Life* Bureau, who kept notes on the briefing, the remainder of Marshall's talk was somewhat fanciful. He seemed to believe that heavy bombers would greatly reduce the role of the Navy in the Far East and to suggest that the outbreak of war would be followed almost at once by bombing attacks from the Philippines on the cities of Japan. Perhaps in his efforts to emphasize the importance of secrecy about the air build-up, he exaggerated what he expected of the B-17s. Only ten days earlier he had stated that "the main involvement in the Far East would be naval," and his current directives for air action envisaged no strikes against the civilian population of Japan.[13]

His briefing was successful in gaining secrecy if not in reporting accurately all of his plans. In his main point—the need for time—he was merely stating a somewhat exaggerated version of what he was attempting to do in the Philippines. Not by threatening to burn Japan's cities but through menacing Japanese expeditions that must pass near the Philippines on their way south did he expect to exert pressure on Japan. He was no Billy Mitchell proclaiming the end of naval power and hailing the triumph of air. In whatever hopes he held for the Far East Air Forces in November 1941, he was deceived. The new B-17, much improved as it was, still could not perform the major miracles that he expected of it.

On the day after his press conference General Marshall left for a short trip to Florida and to North Carolina, just as the newly arrived envoy, Kurusu, was preparing to open talks with Secretary Hull. Marshall returned to his office on the 18th to clear away papers that had accumulated over the weekend and left again the following afternoon. He was bound for the Stettinius cottage at Pompano Beach to spend a long Thanksgiving weekend with Mrs. Marshall. He was thus away from Washington during the preliminary skirmishes between the Japanese envoy and the Secretary of State.

On the 24th the Chief of Staff returned from the warmth of Florida to the chill of Washington, where signs of winter were beginning to appear. The contrast was even greater between the lazy calm of the Florida resort and a city on edge with apprehension. The negotiations had not gone well.

Even before Kurusu's arrival Secretary Hull had ruled out Plan A. Having read the terms of Plan B through MAGIC intercepts before he met the new envoy, he was inclined to distrust both the plan and the emissary. In both he sniffed the odor of deceit. In Plan B, Tokyo talked of halting its advances into southeastern Indochina. But the price was outrageously high. It required America's virtual abandonment of China and the relaxation of economic pressures being exerted on Japan by the West.[13]

Old, ailing, worn out by his exertions to reach a settlement with the Japanese, Hull was sickened by the proposed negation of a policy that he had tried for months to establish. His patience at an end, he might have dropped the conversations altogether but for the pleas of Marshall and Stark for a little time. Piecing together various suggestions that had been considered in the State Department and making use of a draft developed in the Treasury Department, he considered briefly the possibility of presenting two counterproposals to the Japanese.

As the State Department sketched these offers Nomura and Kurusu watched anxiously the approach of the fatal deadline. For more than two weeks Tokyo's instructions to Nomura had stressed the need for haste and the dangerous passage of time. The Foreign Office's response of November 22 to the ambassador's request for an extension of the period for further negotiations produced a chill that matched the season. Negotiations were almost at an end.

The Foreign Office was explicit in its warning: "There are reasons beyond your ability to guess why we wanted to settle Japanese-American relations by the 25th, but if within the next three or four days you can finish your conversations with the Americans; if the signing can be completed by the 29th (let me write it out for you—twenty-ninth); if the pertinent notes can be exchanged; if we can get an understanding with Great Britain and the Netherlands; and in short if everything can be finished, we have decided to wait until that date. This time we mean it, that the deadline absolutely cannot be changed. After that things are automatically going to happen." [14] There were two other highly important messages from Tokyo the same day. MAGIC missed Japanese Navy announcements that the task force bound for Pearl Harbor would depart November 26 and that X Day would be December 8, Tokyo time, but it did flash a clear signal of danger.

The deadline rang a warning bell in the Navy Department. Always conscious of keeping the fleet on the alert, Admiral Stark over a period of months had peppered Kimmel with wires concerning the course of negotiations and chatty personal letters revealing his private reactions to Japanese intentions. In accordance with this practice he had a proposed message prepared to show the Chief of Staff when the latter returned to his office on the 24th. With General Marshall's approval, Stark that afternoon warned Navy commanders in the Pacific (with instructions to show the message to their Army colleagues) that:

> There are very doubtful chances of a favorable outcome of negotiations with Japan. This situation coupled with statements of [Japanese] Government and movements of their naval and military forces indicate in our opinion that a surprise aggressive movement in

any direction, including an attack on the Philippines or Guam is a possibility. . . . Utmost secrecy is necessary in order not to complicate an already tense situation or precipitate Japanese action.[15]

The Chief of Naval Operations later argued that the message should have alerted Pearl Harbor to a possible attack, but his specific listing of Far Eastern targets lessened its impact on Admiral Kimmel. It had even less effect on General Short. He testified later that he never saw it. Contradictory evidence was presented as to whether or not it was forwarded by the Navy. The salient point that impressed the probers was that information sent to the Navy did not flow automatically to Army headquarters at Fort Shafter.

The calm of Hawaii did not prevail in Washington. The knowledge of a deadline and the continued movement of Japanese forces weighed heavily on the minds of the President and his advisers. At the White House meeting on November 25 General Marshall heard Roosevelt announce that "we were likely to be attacked perhaps next Monday for the Japanese are notorious for making an attack without warning." In a much publicized description of the discussion that followed Secretary Stimson recorded: "The question is how we should maneuver them into the position of firing the first shot without allowing too much danger to ourselves." [16] There was nothing sinister in this traditional American formula for keeping the record straight—it was written into the next day's warning as "permit the Japanese to commit the first overt act"— but it would serve one day as a basis for the charge that Roosevelt and his advisers were conspiring to get the United States into war.

His patience wearing as thin as Hull's, Secretary Stimson thought that another warning to the Japanese was now in order. He recalled that after the Atlantic Conference the President had taken the first step toward reminding the Japanese that if they crossed the border from Indochina into Thailand they violated "our safety." Stimson suggested that the President need only point out that their current movements were in violation of that warning. At the end of the meeting he and Hull went to work to prepare such a statement.[17]

General Marshall was of two minds about the proposal. He had recognized for some time that if the Japanese appeared in the Gulf of Siam "war was inevitable and [that] we would be in a very critical situation if we didn't immediately take some action to try to control it." But he shied away from a final break. On the 25th or the morning of the 26th, he apparently discussed the situation with Admiral Stark, and they decided to rush to the President a second appeal that their staffs were already writing. As the Philippines seemed to be the American possession in the Pacific most threatened by current developments, he also directed his Chief of War Plans Division to draft a warning to MacArthur.[18]

The situation grew still worse on November 26. For several days Hull had been considering the possibility of presenting the Japanese with a proposal for a three months' truce, a *modus vivendi,* at the same time that he delivered his Ten Point Program for a permanent settlement. Disturbed at criticisms of the truce by the Chinese and their strongest backers, he decided to drop the *modus vivendi* and present the Ten Point Program as his final offer. He handed his reply to the Japanese representatives on the afternoon of the 26th.

General Marshall and Secretary Stimson had already agreed that the terms of the *modus vivendi* were too stiff. Even Secretary Hull conceded that there was only one chance in three that the Japanese would accept them. There was still less reason to believe that Tokyo could or would agree to the Ten Point Program. This demanded withdrawal from Indochina, which the Japanese might have considered, and withdrawal from China and the recognition of Chiang Kai-shek's government, which would nullify their gains of the past four years. In exchange for these concessions the United States offered to unfreeze Japanese assets and enter into a liberal trade agreement with Japan. Hull saw nothing in the memorandum "that any peaceful nation pursuing a peaceful course" would not be delighted to accept. It is possible that his analysis was correct. But the existing Tokyo government could not have approved the program and survived. It confirmed the view of the military party that the United States had no wish to reach an understanding.[19]

In submitting the stronger proposal Secretary Hull did not consult the Army and Navy leaders, who so recently had asked for minor concessions to Japan and the avoidance of an ultimatum at this critical point in their preparations. Some of Hull's friends saw the righteous indignation of a man who had lost all hope of reaching an agreement and was merely restating for the record the basic

American position on issues in the Far East. Others, including his biographer, Professor Julius W. Pratt, concluded that his action "was a petulant one by a tired and angry old man." [20]

Before learning of Hull's intentions General Marshall held a morning conference with his advisers, Arnold, Bundy, Gerow, and Handy, to determine what action they should take in view of the fact that the President and Secretary Hull expected an attack on the Philippines. Marshall said that he did not see it as a probability. The oversanguine estimates of General MacArthur and his own overoptimistic predictions of the rate of airplane build-up in the Islands had done their work. The hazards of such an assault, he held, "would be too great for the Japanese." [21]

As a prudent man, however, he took no chances. He proposed to send instructions to MacArthur "in spite of the fact that a break will not necessarily mean a declaration of war." The United States could not justify ignoring any Japanese convoy that might be a threat to American interests. "Thus far we have talked in terms of the defense of the Philippines," he added, "but now the question is what do we do beyond that." As a means of furnishing a guideline for MacArthur, he devoted much of the conference to revising draft instructions that Gerow had hurriedly sketched before the meeting. They were the basis for the wire sent the next day while Marshall was out of Washington.

In his later discussion of the November 27 message General Marshall indicated that it was probably he who had passed on to General Gerow the President's demand that the United States must not commit the first overt act of war. Marshall was equally responsible for removing inhibitions on MacArthur's freedom of action. At his morning conference he asked specifically about the nature of the Far Eastern commander's mission under current directives. When reminded that MacArthur was to defend the Philippine Archipelago, support the Navy, and attack threatening convoys, the Chief of Staff instructed Gerow to make clear that the Far East commander was "authorized to take such action as might be necessary to carry out that part of his mission which pertains to the defense of the Philippine Archipelago."

General Marshall went still further in authorizing action that conceivably could lead to war. Determined to allow General Mac-Arthur complete freedom, the Chief of Staff ruled that the Far East commander was free to fly reconnaissance missions over the Japanese mandated islands. To remove any doubts as to the decisive moment for MacArthur to begin operations, Marshall declared that MacArthur should start with "actual hostilities" rather than "a state of war." War, he told his subordinates, existed in China and in the Atlantic, although no one had bothered to declare it.

Significantly, no one throughout the morning conference raised the question of General Short's mission in Hawaii. On the contrary, General Arnold spoke of transferring pursuit planes from that command to strengthen the garrisons at Midway and Wake and the possibility of sending two Army battalions from Hawaii to relieve Marines in the two islands was discussed. Marshall stipulated that the Navy would have to agree to the transfers. Otherwise there would be no air strength in the Hawaiian Islands until replacements could arrive. In the end Marine Corps planes were substituted for those offered by the Army, but the action confirmed the point that neither the Army nor the Navy considered Pearl Harbor in danger of attack.

The news from the Far East, while threatening, was not considered dangerous enough by the Chief of Staff to prevent him and several members of his staff from flying down to North Carolina on the 27th to observe the final phases of the maneuvers. Later, Senator Homer Ferguson questioned Marshall's judgment on leaving the city at the height of the crisis. Forgoing the obvious rejoinder that the President and other top government officials were still in the city, the Chief of Staff rested his defense on one episode of the trip. He recalled with relish the splendid performance of one of the armored force commanders, a certain George S. Patton. As a result he had set that fiery soldier on the road to high command. So far as the warning message was concerned, Marshall's absence was not crucial. He had expressed his views on the 26th and they were included in the message sent out the following day.

The imminence of war hung over deliberations in the State Department and the War Department on the 27th. During the long, trying day Secretary Stimson became perturbed as reports reached Washington that the large Japanese expeditionary force was continuing to move south. With Marshall away, he called the President and got his approval to send a final warning to General MacArthur "that he should be on the *qui vive* for any attack and telling him how the situation was." [22]

Stimson felt Marshall's absence "very much." The Secretary

found Stark, "as usual, a little bit timid and cautious when it comes to a real crisis, and there was a tendency, not unnatural on his part and Gerow's to seek for more time." Nevertheless Stimson called on Stark, whose staff was already preparing a message to commanders in the Pacific, and Gerow, who brought the draft that Marshall had discussed on the previous day, to help with the drafting of the wire. Intended primarily for MacArthur, it was to go, with a significant amendment, to Hawaii, the Canal Zone, and San Francisco.[23]

In a long session, marked by many interruptions, they spelled out the warning. Stimson made a final check with Hull as to the state of negotiations. Although pessimistic in general, the Secretary of State held out a faint hope that talks might continue. That slight glimmer of optimism caused Stimson to modify his warning, making it weaker than Marshall had intended and much milder than the message Stark was to send.

During the afternoon of November 27 the War Department informed commanders in the Pacific:

> Negotiations with Japan appear to be terminated to all practical purposes, with only the barest possibilities that the Japanese Government might come back and offer to continue. Japanese future action unpredictable, but hostile action possible at any moment. If hostilities cannot, repeat cannot, be avoided, the United States desires that Japan commit the first overt act. This policy should not, repeat not, be construed as restricting you to a course of action that might jeopardize your defense.[24]

This part of the message was straightforward and left no chance for confusion. The chance for trouble lay in the next sentence, which was changed in three of the four wires. All of them contained the statement General Marshall had stressed the previous day: "Prior to hostile Japanese action you are directed to take such reconnaissance and other measures as you deem necessary." This was left in its original form in the wire to MacArthur. In the directives to Hawaii, the Canal Zone, and San Francisco, someone added, "but these measures should be carried out so as not (repeat not) to alarm civil population or disclose intent." General Short was later to call it a "do-don't" message and claim that it prevented him from taking more positive action in Hawaii.[25]

Before many hours passed, Short saw a stronger warning. On the heels of the Army message Admiral Stark sent an additional alert, which he instructed Kimmel to show his Army colleague. Opening with the explicit admonition, "This dispatch is to be considered a war warning," it could scarcely have been more pointed. But Stark weakened his alert by adding too much. Unaware that Japanese carriers were on their way to Hawaiian waters and with no hint that Pearl Harbor rather than Thailand was the prime target, he listed as likely "an amphibious expedition against either the Philippines, Thai or Kra Peninsula or possibly Borneo." He then confused matters by writing Admiral Kimmel that he did not expect an attack against the Philippines but had thrown that in. His danger flare fizzled out without alarming Kimmel or Short.[26]

General Short reacted to the Army message with amazing speed. Foreseeing no threat to Pearl Harbor and believing that subversive activities by Japanese inhabitants of Oahu constituted his major problem in case of war, he ordered Number One Alert, the defense against sabotage. Within minutes after receiving his warning he confidently notified Washington, "Report Department alerted to prevent sabotage. Liaison with Navy reurad [reference your radio] 472 27th." He had not interpreted his warning properly and he was in line for a reprimand in case of trouble. But he had made his report, referring specifically to the War Department directive by number.[27]

No one in Washington noticed that fate, persistently against the United States in this period, had thrown dust in the eyes of the officials in Washington. Shortly after the message signed in General Marshall's name had gone out, General Miles, the Army Chief of Intelligence, sent another message to Short, directing him to take proper precautions against sabotage. When the War Department received the Hawaiian Department commander's assurance that he had taken proper action, apparently everyone who saw the message —Marshall, Gerow, Stimson—assumed that it was an answer to Miles' warning and not to the important earlier message. Washington felt assured that Short was on guard, and Short assumed that the War Department was satisfied with his alert.[28]

The confusion between headquarters in Hawaii and Washington was matched by that between Army and Navy headquarters in Pearl Harbor. In the curious lack of coordination that existed in Hawaii, the Navy commander did not know that Short's Number

One Alert, meaning that he was on guard against sabotage, now was totally different from the Navy's, calling for a full alarm. When the naval officers heard that Short had proclaimed a Number One Alert and saw his trucks and troops moving to stations, they concluded that Short was in a full state of readiness.

General Marshall was impressed by the fact that three of the four recipients of the November 27 warning responded by taking positive action. In the Canal Zone, at San Francisco, and in the Philippines, the commanders reported that they had gone on full alert, specifying the steps they had taken to meet an enemy attack. General Short's failure to react in the same fashion weakened his later defense that if he had been shown additional intercepts, available in Washington, he would have been fully prepared for attack.

After all the facts were known, General Marshall had no doubt that General Short had failed to carry out his instructions. "I feel that General Short was given a command instruction to put his command on the alert against a possible hostile attack by the Japanese. The command was not so alerted." [29]

Later he spelled out some of the steps the Hawaiian commander should have taken. "His planes should have been—he should have been in full contact with the Navy; the arrangements should have been so far as he could manage them through the Navy for the conduct of overwater reconnaissance, of which the Navy would have the direction; his own planes, his fighter and interceptor planes in particular, should have been ready for action. They were flying anyway. They should have been armed. Pilots sufficient for the first flight should have been ready; planes, presumably, might have been in the air in the early morning; the radar [which was used only three hours a day] should have run 24 hours a day as they did in Panama." [30]

Marshall recognized that the warning not to alarm the civilian population might have prevented the full alert of ground troops. But he saw no "particular reason why there was any difficulty in relation to the restrictions . . . in the message toward the water reconnaissance, overwater reconnaissance, toward radar activity, toward the handling of the fighter planes, toward the manning with ammunition ready of the anti-aircraft guns."

Up to a point his arguments were sound. General Short had misunderstood the directive and had not carried out instructions. But the War Department could not escape its share of responsibility. Short had reported as ordered and the War Department had nodded momentarily, overlooking his failure to go on full alert against attack. Four years later the Army Board investigating the causes of Pearl Harbor blamed the Hawaiian Department commander for command failure. It also censured General Marshall and General Gerow for failing to see that he had not responded properly to their instructions. General Gerow assumed the blame for not recognizing the import of the reply from Fort Shafter.

General Marshall declined to allow Gerow to take the rap for the War Department. As Chief of Staff, he had to answer for the faults of his commanders in the field and "for the actions of the General Staff throughout on large matters and on the small matters." Although he did not initial Short's wire he assumed that he had seen it. It had been his opportunity to intervene and he had not taken it. Therefore, he thought "General Gerow had overstated it when he said he had full responsibility. . . . He had a direct . . . but . . . I had a full responsibility." [31]

Having assumed the responsibility in this phase of the Pearl Harbor affair, he claimed some indulgence from history. "I am not a bookkeeping machine and it is extremely difficult . . . for me to take each thing in its turn and give it exactly the attention that it had merited." It was a reasonable defense from an overworked Chief of Staff, but it did not exonerate him. [32]

General Marshall's direct responsibility in November 1941 for the failure to follow up on his orders stemmed from his neglect to reorganize the War Department staff in 1940-41. He had attempted to hold too many threads of operations in his hands and had spread himself so thin between administering the War Department staff, overseeing training, appearing before Congress, selecting officers, dealing with soldier morale, and puzzling over the demands of Lend-Lease operations, that he could not closely follow the day-by-day reports of his intelligence officers or check adequately on the response of his various commanders to orders. It was not that he was unwilling to delegate authority. Over a period of years his habit had been to give his subordinates full powers and allow them to find their way. But as the War Department was then organized he had found it difficult to divest himself of authority. The reform of the staff system was to be one of his first major projects after the initial shock of Pearl Harbor.

Beyond the question of poor organization there was the simple fact, indicated repeatedly in October and November, that both Pearl Harbor and Washington had been blinded by the glare of Japan's fireworks in the Far East. For months American political and military leaders had watched anxiously as the Japanese extended their control over Indochina. They speculated that Thailand, Burma, Malaya, the Dutch East Indies, or even the Russian Maritime Provinces might be attacked. Since General Marshall's alert of 1940 Washington had never again included Pearl Harbor in the list of probable targets.

In a memorandum to the President on November 27 Marshall and Stark emphasized the degree to which the Far East now dominated their thinking. In their second appeal within a month, again reminding President Roosevelt that "the most essential thing now from the United States viewpoint is to gain time," they enumerated the problems in the Far East that caused them concern:

> Considerable Navy and Army reinforcements have been rushed to the Philippines but the desirable strength has not yet been reached. The process of reinforcement is being continued. Of great and immediate concern is the safety of the Army convoy now near Guam, and the Marine Corps' convoy just leaving Shanghai. Ground forces to a total of 21,000 are due to sail from the United States by December 8, 1941, and it is important that this troop reinforcement reach the Philippines before hostilities commence. Precipitance of military action on our part should be avoided so long as consistent with national policy. The longer the delay, the more positive becomes the assurance of retention of these Islands as a naval and air base. Japanese action to the south of Formosa will be hindered and perhaps seriously blocked as long as we hold the Philippine Islands. War with Japan certainly will interrupt our transport of supplies to Siberia, and probably will interrupt the process of aiding China.[33]

Their pleas for moderation were made against a background of increasing Japanese boldness. Alarmed by November 28 intelligence reports of continued movements southward, Secretary Stimson rushed to the White House, breaking in on a conference between Roosevelt and William Donovan, to announce a new crisis. Already under pressure from the British for a statement of the American position in case of continued trouble, the President summoned his advisers to a noon meeting to consider what should be done.

Deeply concerned over a possible Japanese attack on the Isthmus of Kra, the narrowest part of the long finger of Thailand that thrusts southward to separate Malaya from Burma, the British commander-in-chief at Singapore (Brooke-Popham) had drawn up plans to land troops to forestall a Japanese threat to that area. Told of these plans, Roosevelt's advisers agreed that circumstances had completely changed since their meeting two days before.

In speaking of Thailand on November 26 General Marshall had thought it possible to wait until the Japanese actually invaded the country before issuing an ultimatum. Now with a force of 25,000 Japanese on the high seas, headed southward, he recognized that the situation had changed. As Stimson recalled the discussion, "It further became a consensus of views that rather than strike at the Force as it went by without any warning on the one hand, which we didn't think we could do; or sitting still and allowing it to go on, on the other, which we didn't think we could do—that the only thing for us to do was to address it a warning that if it reached a certain place, or a certain line, or a certain point, we should have to fight." [34]

Hoping that diplomacy might still yield some small delays, the President suggested that the Japanese be asked for an explanation of their troop movements and their reasons for continuing the build-up in Indochina. If the answer was not satisfactory he proposed as a last resort to appeal to Hirohito. Stimson demurred. One did not send warnings to an Emperor. A better course was to advise Congress of the perils facing the American people and of measures that might have to be taken to meet those dangers. As for Hirohito, it was better to send a separate and secret plea. The President agreed. On the assumption that there would be no attack until after the Japanese returned an answer to the Ten Point Program, Roosevelt directed his advisers to work on a message to Congress while he slipped away to Warm Springs, Georgia, to share a belated Thanksgiving dinner with the patients at the Infantile Paralysis Center.

Meanwhile the commanders in Hawaii seemed blandly unperturbed by the danger facing them from Japan. Stimson and Marshall later charged them with forgetting the main duty of a sentinel guarding an outpost. In the absence of specific directives, the general orders of a sentry required that he be constantly on the alert. Time and perspective have mellowed these stern judgments of the past. It is easy now to feel sympathy for the two commanders in Hawaii who were to be relieved of their posts for sharing Washington's mistaken notion that trouble was coming in the Far East rather than the Central Pacific.

General Marshall and Admiral Stark were to have their uncomfortable innings before the Congressional Inquiry of 1945 because certain messages, indicating undue Japanese interest in ship traffic at Pearl Harbor, were not forwarded. Kimmel and Short listed as critical a Tokyo directive to agents in Hawaii in September 1941, dividing the harbor into five areas and requesting weekly reports on arrivals and departures of ships in each area. General Marshall replied that the Japanese showed similar interest in ship movements throughout the world and that no specific danger to Pearl Harbor was indicated by the request.

In later years the Hawaiian commanders cited the list of intercepts that had not been passed on from Washington: the deadline messages indicating that Tokyo's patience was wearing thin and that only a few days were left for decision; messages in late November and December ordering the evacuation of Japanese nationals from the United States and Great Britain; precise instructions about the burning of codes; and finally orders to destroy code machines.

All the faults of omission were not in Washington. The Navy headquarters at Pearl Harbor did not always make certain that all warnings from Washington were passed on to all of their key officers and to General Short. A properly coordinated Army-Navy organization would have made the Army commander aware that the Navy was not conducting long-range reconnaissance on December 7. Someone at Navy headquarters should have known that General Short's Number One Alert was not a state of full readiness against attack.

There were also telltale messages intercepted in Hawaii that were misread. Analyzed more carefully, they could have pointed toward undue curiosity in Tokyo about ship traffic and the anchorage of ships at Pearl Harbor. There might have been more concern about the fact that Kimmel's chief of fleet intelligence did not know the location of the Japanese carrier fleet or that little importance was attached to reports (later proved false) of the arrival of two Japanese carriers in the Marshall Islands.

Through all the debate over what information was given and

what withheld, one point stands out. If the attack had come just after the "war warning" of November 27, as Roosevelt had predicted it might, the commanders in Hawaii could never have justified their position. They were to base their most effective defense on the failure of the War and Navy Departments to pass on numerous intercepts that flowed into Washington during the last week before the attack. It was easy enough for Kimmel and Short to say afterward: if we had received this message or that we would have been adequately prepared. The hard fact is that more imaginative commanders might have done more with what they had.

Believing that the commanders in Hawaii were on the alert, General Marshall ceased to worry about Pearl Harbor. Over the last weekend in November he thought mainly about problems in the Philippines.

He also had personal concerns. Mrs. Marshall's ribs still gave her trouble. Earlier in the month, after her side was healing nicely, she had made a sudden misstep that had pulled loose some of the incompletely knitted cartilage. The General had taken her to Florida over Thanksgiving so that she could get some rest. He gave her physical state and "critical matters" pending at that time as reasons for canceling his plans to attend the Army-Navy game on November 29. His tickets were not wasted. Allen and Madge Brown enjoyed sharing Marshall's box with General Arnold during a closely fought contest which the Navy won 14-6. Washington newspapers dutifully recorded that General Marshall had been kept at home by the international situation.[35]

The short vacation in Florida had made General Marshall aware that he was nearly exhausted. On December 1 he wrote the head of the Army Hospital at Hot Springs, Arkansas, that he was thinking of coming out—a day or two before Christmas—"to stay there ten days or two weeks and give myself an opportunity to rest up" and give Mrs. Marshall a chance to recuperate completely. Realizing that he was indulging in wishful thinking, he added: "Of course, all my plans are dependent on the international situation and the President's desires at the time." But it was good to think about two unhurried and unharried weeks.[36]

He realized that there was a direct correlation between his own state of health and Mrs. Marshall's. On the day before Pearl Harbor he wrote Mrs. Winn that he feared her mother was "going too strong" and might collapse. He was not certain he could bear that added burden. "I have just about enough steam to do this job," he declared, "and if I am involved in her being down with an illness in addition to the job, it quickly goes beyond my strength." [37]

His anxieties were soon to be submerged in a sea of international woes. This weekend of the Army-Navy game marked the watershed between peace and war. Many who celebrated Navy's victory on November 30 mourned its losses ten days later. But with disaster little more than a week away, Washington and Pearl Harbor still showed no immediate alarm about America's danger.

X

The Fatal Week

A motion picture depicting the final tense week before Pearl Harbor would interrupt footage on the serious conferences, the speech drafting, the Army-Navy game, and the G-2 briefings with shots of Japan's carriers steaming purposefully toward Pearl Harbor while life there and in Washington went on much as usual. Lights burned a little later in the nation's capital, and there was increasing tension as reports came in that the Japanese were ordering various embassies and consulates to burn their code books. But at top levels the emphasis was on what the United States intended to do when the Japanese got south of Formosa or turned into the Gulf of Siam. Nothing in the MAGIC intercepts warned Marshall and Stark of a Japanese foray into the Central Pacific; the charts in the war room at Pearl Harbor gave no whereabouts of the Japanese carriers. In late November, Admiral Kimmel's war plans officer discussed with his chief the possibility of the danger from Japan. Asked when he thought there would be an attack on Pearl Harbor by air, Captain McMorris answered, "Never." [1] As for the missing carriers, Admiral Kimmel joked about them with his fleet intelligence officer, Captain Edwin Layton, on December 2. "Do you mean to say they could be rounding Diamond Head [just east of Pearl Harbor] and you wouldn't know it?" Captain Layton replied he hoped they would be sighted before that.[2]

"November 29 arrived and passed," General Marshall recalled later, "and we entered into December without anything happening other than the continuation of these movements which we could follow fairly well, down the China coast and Indochina and headed quite plainly toward Thailand and the Gulf of Siam." [3] Of course he and Stark were concerned. If the Japanese went into the Gulf of Siam, "that meant that they were on the back door of Singapore, and could have, in our opinion, only a direct hostile motive." But the move in itself was not sufficient grounds for immediate alarm. "It was still possible for them, of course, to have turned north and then east, and establish themselves . . . on the west coast of Thailand. That was still a possibility." [4] His only basis for assurance was the fact that the President had not yet sent his warning. Since Marshall and other Washington officials believed that war would come with the Japanese when they crossed a line in the Pacific drawn by the United States, there still seemed to be some time left.

The form of this declaration to Japan was widely discussed in Washington the week before the attack. Secretary Stimson went into specifics with General Marshall on December 1, "going very carefully over the question of whether or not we should include China in our warning—whether we should warn Japan that we would take as a vital attack on us any further aggression against China in the direction of the Burma Road." [5]

The suggestion drew fire from General Marshall. On no point had he argued more strongly than on the danger of getting involved in the sticky morass of Chinese operations. He made clear his repugnance as he restated all his arguments. Secretary Stimson heard him through carefully and backed off. "Perhaps his position is safer," he wrote. Whether this view was passed on to Roosevelt is not clear. On December 4, however, the President told the British Ambassador, Lord Halifax, that he doubted the wisdom of including the Burma Road in any warning the United States sent.

Apparently neither Stimson nor Marshall knew that the President had discussed with Lord Halifax action the United States might take if the Japanese continued their movements in the Far East. In case of a direct attack on the British or the Dutch, the President declared, "We should obviously all be together." Great Britain could also count on American support if it undertook a defense of the Kra Isthmus against Japanese attack. He suggested that London promise the Thai government its sovereignty and independence. As President he could not constitutionally give final guarantees of armed support to Great Britain, but he left no doubt that in case of war in the Pacific the British would have the backing of the United States.[6]

Roosevelt had not completely given up hope of reaching a temporary agreement with the Japanese. He would wait for Tokyo's reply to his recent request for an explanation of its most recent moves. If it was not satisfactory, he would appeal to the Emperor. Before issuing his final warning to Japan he intended to hear from Hirohito.

The civilians and officers who daily pored over the intercepts and agent reports predicting Japan's future action could now almost smell an imminent clash. So could those without top secret clearance who depended for their information on a good daily newspaper. The carefully briefed expert and the reasonably well-read nonexpert saw the same point: war was near because the United States and Great Britain were preparing to challenge Japan's future advances.

Later, in Army, Navy, and congressional inquiries, interrogators asked why during the last week before Pearl Harbor, Washington did not send more specific warnings to Hawaii pointing toward an attack on the fleet. General Short and Admiral Kimmel claimed that if some of the pertinent information had not been withheld, by negligence or design, they would have been fully alerted. One naval officer insisted that he knew, through a special Japanese signal, called an "execute winds message," received three days before the attack, that there would be a raid and that it would be against Pearl Harbor. Several brother officers recalled hearing of such a message but denied seeing it. Others declared that a "winds message" arrived but not in a form pointing to war with the United States. Even the Navy officer who insisted that the message meant war with the United States finally admitted that it did not say Pearl Harbor.

Of great significance were orders for the destruction of codes that began to flutter through PURPLE in early December. Although all of these did not reach Pearl Harbor, Admiral Kimmel was informed on December 3: "Highly reliable information has been received that . . . urgent instructions were sent yesterday to Japanese diplomatic and consular posts at Hong Kong, Singapore, Batavia, Manila, Washington, and London to destroy most of their codes and ciphers at once and to burn all other important confidential and secret documents." Kimmel also knew that Stark on

December 4 had directed Navy authorities in Guam to destroy classified publications.[7] On the 6th Stark instructed the Pacific commander-in-chief:

> In view of the international situation and the exposed position of our outlying Pacific islands you may authorize the destruction by them of secret and confidential documents now or under later conditions of greater emergency.[8]

Tokyo's answer to Roosevelt's inquiry concerning Japanese activity in Indochina arrived on December 6. Finding it evasive and unsatisfactory, the President followed through with his final message to Emperor Hirohito. It went out that evening, destined to be delayed in Tokyo more than ten hours through design or, more probably, bureaucratic interference until shortly before the time set for the attack. It reached Tojo on the way to the Emperor just as planes from the Japanese carrier force were taking off to attack Pearl Harbor.[9]

Having dispatched his appeal to Tokyo, the President continued to work on the speech he expected to deliver to Congress on December 8 or 9. Apparently to discuss this statement and the possible showdown that might follow in the Far East, he called for a meeting of his advisers at the White House for 3 p.m., December 7.

The conference was never fully explored in the 1945 inquiry. Congressmen wondered why Secretary Stimson on December 6 asked for information as to the location of British and American naval forces in the Pacific. They also read into the record a statement by a member of General Marshall's staff, Colonel John R. Deane, saying that the Chief of Staff informed him on the morning of the 7th, before he heard of the attack, that he was to go to a White House conference at 3 p.m. that afternoon.

Overlooked was the fact that on the 6th the Chief of Staff directed members of the War Plans Division to collect studies and documents dealing with the Far East and the Southwest Pacific that he would want for the Sunday afternoon meeting. The material was assembled by a staff headed by Colonel C. K. Gailey, executive officer of the War Plans Division, and placed on the General's desk the next morning. The covering note, dated December 6, 1941, indicated that the documents were for the Chief of Staff's use at the White House meeting.[10]

The General was not to read them. Before he had a chance to

examine the folder on the 7th, the intercepts from Tokyo claimed his attention. He was to use only one of the carefully prepared documents from the file. Colonel Gailey had thoughtfully included a directive to be sent to General MacArthur in the event of war in the Far East, leaving the date blank. It was a copy of this document, with proper date inserted and a penned promise from the Chief of Staff that all possible aid would be sent, that General Marshall dispatched to Manila after the news of Pearl Harbor.

On the last day before the attack Secretary Stimson longed to get away to his home on Long Island for a brief rest, "but as the morning went on, the news got worse and worse and the atmosphere indicated that something was going to happen." He shared General Marshall's concern over the reinforcements they were sending to the Far East. Adverse winds had held up planes scheduled to reach the Philippines several days earlier. As a last resort the Chief of Staff had sent General Arnold out to the west coast to see if he could get the bombers on their way. Arnold had arrived at Hamilton Field, California, on the 6th and was prepared to send out thirteen B-17s by way of Hawaii to the Philippines before the end of the day. During the morning Marshall discussed with Stimson whether he should send them on and risk having them attacked over the Pacific. After weighing the dangers against their value to the Islands he finally allowed them to leave on the afternoon of the 6th. It was this flight that arrived at Pearl Harbor in the midst of the Japanese attack.[11]

In the course of the day General Marshall found a few moments to write Molly Winn in Panama. (Colonel Morrison Stayer, an old friend from Fort Benning days, now stationed in the Canal Zone, had stopped by two days earlier to tell them of the Winns' young son, Jimmy, born in November.) Marshall filled Molly in on the state of her mother's health and then wrote of his current problems and anxieties:

My Panama dates are still uncertain. I had thought I might be able to make the trip between the 12th and Christmas, but conditions here will prevent that. Now it appears that I will get down some time in January. It is probable that I will go to the West Coast before Christmas, though that will depend on the international situation. Everything is so unsettled that it is out of the question for me to make additional plans. In addition, I am taking a rather heavy political beating these days, as a result of the large appropriation bills, regarding which I must testify, and the acute battle between the isolationists and the administration supporters. Added to these are a few bouquets that come from those who have been relieved from command. Most of this last has been quietly carried out, but the repercussions are severe and numerous nevertheless, and I am the target.[12]

These difficulties had been in his mind the day before when he wrote Allen's wife, Madge, apropos of the daily walks he and Mrs. Marshall took through the quiet of nearby Arlington: after "some of the stormy days and weeks here, I think a cemetery would be pretty nice." In addition to the peaceful promenades, one other relaxation remained for him: "I get in a ride almost every day, and Fleet is now an accomplished coach dog when it comes to following and obeying." [13]

Tired by a week of crises, he spent the evening of December 6 at his quarters. Although an orderly was at hand to take calls, the General was not disturbed. Despite the later importance attached to the intercepted Japanese message that was received at the War Department that evening, his subordinates who saw it believed that it was unnecessary to notify him until the following morning.

Because vagueness of testimony in the Pearl Harbor Inquiry in 1945 was often regarded as an indication of sinister conduct, critics of General Marshall continue to repeat that he could not remember where he was on the night of December 6.[14] In his mind and that of Mrs. Marshall there was no doubt that they were at home that evening. He was equally positive that he was not at the White House. However, he thought it proper to establish the fact that he was at home. His testimony is worth rereading:

I can only account for [my movements on the evening of December 6] by sort of circumstantial evidence. The only definite thing I have is that I had no dinner engagement. I found our engagement book, or Mrs. Marshall's engagement book, and between the 1st of November and 7th of December I had one dinner engagement, that was the 2d of December.

Also they checked on the post movie. It was about our only recourse for relaxation, and I had never seen the picture. So I was not there.

We were not calling. We were leading a rather monastic life.

There was also in that record the affairs of the day for her, which involved, I think, an old-clothes sale, I think, all day long, to raise money for one of these industries they had down there, so the probability is that she was tired and we were home.[15]

Elsewhere in Washington and across the seas in Pearl Harbor, many of the General's friends and associates were enjoying a Saturday evening of relaxation. In Hawaii, Admiral Kimmel dined with a classmate, and General Short and his chief of intelligence and their wives attended an Army benefit dinner. As Short's party was preparing to leave, his assistant chief of intelligence arrived with an intercept of a telephone call from Tokyo to a local Japanese dentist indicating an unusual interest on the part of the caller in the arrival and departure of ships in the fleet. Short paused briefly to read the message but took no further notice when his assistant proved unable to explain its significance.

In Washington, President and Mrs. Roosevelt entertained old friends at dinner at the White House. A few blocks away, at the National Theater, Admiral Stark and his wife, accompanied by his aide and wife, were attending a performance of *The Student Prince*. Over in Arlington the Naval Chief of Intelligence, Rear Admiral Theodore S. Wilkinson, was entertaining a group that included the Army Chief of Intelligence, General Miles, and the President's naval aide.

At the War and Navy Departments intelligence and signals experts labored over important MAGIC intercepts that had been coming in since afternoon. First to arrive was a "pilot" message from the Foreign Office in Tokyo notifying the Japanese Ambassador that a fourteen-part answer to Hull's Ten Point Program was on the way. No hint was given as to what it would say, and no time was set for its presentation. The Embassy was told only to make a copy and put it in the safe until further instructions arrived. Lieutenant Commander Alwyn D. Kramer asked his staff to work overtime to keep up with the intercepts as they arrived.

Apparently the "pilot" message was delivered to Marshall's office during the afternoon. Neither the General nor any members of his staff recalled seeing it. If they did, they probably shared the view of nearly everyone else who examined it that there were no grounds for immediate alarm.

In the late afternoon and early evening the first thirteen parts of the Japanese reply were intercepted and deciphered. Copies were then handed to Colonel Rufus Bratton, chief of the Far Eastern Section, War Department G-2, who shared with his assistant, Colonel Carlisle C. Dusenbury, the responsibility of delivering MAGIC intercepts to the offices of the Chief of Staff, the Chief of Intelligence, the Chief of War Plans, and the Secretary of State. Commander Kramer assumed the task of delivering copies to the President, the Secretary of Navy, and the naval officers on the list.

At 10 p.m. Colonel Bratton was informed that the fourteenth part would not be in until the following morning. Realizing that he would have to be at the War Department early to deal with this final section, he decided to deliver the intercepts already received to the State Department duty officer and then go home for the evening. In later testimony he gave several confused versions of his actions, ranging from a positive statement that he delivered the intercepts to everyone on his list to an admission that he may have stopped after his visit to the State Department. Positive statements were made by Generals Marshall, Gerow, and Miles, as well as by their assistants on duty at their offices that afternoon and evening, that they received no copies of the intercepts on December 6. Only one of them, General Miles, was to know that evening that the thirteen parts of the Japanese message had arrived.[16]

Commander Kramer managed to reach most of the officials on his list. In the course of a busy evening he took a copy to the White House, the Secretary of Navy, and the residence of the Chief of Naval Intelligence. As Admiral Stark was at the theater, he made no delivery at his home but showed the intercepts to the Assistant Chief of Naval Operations, Rear Admiral Royal E. Ingersoll, and the Chief of the Naval War Plans Division, Rear Admiral Richmond K. Turner.

President Roosevelt's dinner party had ended and he was in his study with Hopkins when Lieutenant Lester F. Schulz brought in the message delivered by Commander Kramer. The thirteen parts, containing point-by-point rejections by the Japanese government of Hull's proposals, included no positive statement that diplomatic relations were broken off. The President assumed, however, that all hopes of peaceful negotiations were at an end. When he finished his reading he remarked, "This means war." Roosevelt critics saw in his words the gloating of a master conspirator who had succeeded in tricking the Japanese into war with the United States. Lieutenant Schulz saw them as meaning that the President saw no way to escape a showdown with Japan.

Roosevelt attempted to telephone Admiral Stark. Learning that the Chief of Naval Operations was attending the theater, he decided against having him paged for fear it might cause alarm. Later in the evening Stark returned the call and apparently learned for the first time of the Japanese message.

On reading his copy of the intercepts, Colonel Knox also attempted to call Stark. Unable to reach him at home, the Secretary of the Navy made no further effort to get in touch with him. It is not clear if Secretary Stimson and Secretary Hull received their copies that evening or even learned of the message until the following morning.

Commander Kramer notified both the Navy and Army Chiefs of Intelligence of the message when he reached the former's home in Arlington that evening. The two officers discussed the significance of the reply with the President's naval aide, who was also a guest at Admiral Wilkinson's dinner party, and took no further action. Later that evening Colonel Bratton called General Miles and found that he had seen the intercepts and was not seriously alarmed. Miles' reaction was typical of all the officers who saw the reply that evening. For his failure to inform General Marshall, General Miles later took full responsibility. On the Navy side, every officer on the distribution list either got a copy or was made aware of the receipt of the thirteen parts of the Japanese message on the evening of December 6. Not one considered it necessary to take action.

Until the final section arrived there was nothing more than intemperate language and threats—fairly standard elements in diplomatic correspondence then as later—to indicate that war was at hand. Even the rupture of diplomatic relations did not necessarily mean an outbreak of hostilities. Much of official Washington had never expected the Ten Part Program to be accepted, but it always entertained the possibility that the door would be left open for a little longer.

In view of the incomplete state of the message and the lack of a fixed time of delivery, it is doubtful that General Marshall would have proposed any action on the evening of December 6 if he had received the intercepts. The important difference was that he would have checked with the War Department early the next morning. Unaware of the recent intercepts and assuming that he would hear of any new developments from the President during the scheduled midafternoon conference, he made no change in his usual Sunday routine. Like many other Americans on December 7, he had his breakfast an hour or so later than usual. Then, after eating, he sent for his horse and set out on his accustomed leisurely Sunday ride.

Methodical in his habits, the General rode along the same trails nearly every day. He did not use the bridle paths in Rock Creek Park across the river but rode on the Virginia side of the Potomac. Recalling his rides in later years, he declared that they "took me almost invariably down to the site of the present Pentagon Building, which was then the site of the government experimental farm." The average time of his rides was "about fifty minutes because I rode at a pretty lively gait, at a trot and a canter and at a full run down on the experimental farm." [17]

At the time Marshall was on his ride, Secretary Stimson and Secretary Knox were at the Munitions Building arranging to meet with Secretary Hull at the State Department to discuss Japanese movements in the Far East and the draft of the President's statement to Congress.[18] Admiral Stark was already at his office working out a new distribution of the ships of the fleet in order to find additional vessels for the Atlantic.

The fourteenth part of the Japanese message, revealing that diplomatic negotiations were terminated, was placed in Colonel Bratton's hands at about 9 a.m., before the General returned to his quarters. A few minutes later, another message from Tokyo to the Embassy in Washington instructed Ambassador Nomura to deliver the Japanese reply to Secretary Hull at one o'clock. As if released by a spring, Bratton sprang into frenzied action. Although unusual, formal delivery of messages to the Secretary of State on Sunday was not unknown. It was the specific timing of the reply that appeared significant: to Bratton and his colleagues, 1 p.m. in Washington corresponded to early morning in the Far East and daybreak in Hawaii. The colonel assumed it coincided with a possible attack on the Philippines and hastened to the telephone to summon General Marshall to his office.

The super-secrecy surrounding the MAGIC intercepts had served well to conceal the fact that the United States had broken the Japanese code; that same elaborate secrecy now prevented rapid transmission of vital information. Colonel Bratton called Fort Myer and reached General Marshall's orderly. Apparently the colonel was unable or unwilling to give him enough information to emphasize the extreme urgency of the situation. No one went to summon the General. Not until he returned to his quarters around 10 a.m. did he receive Bratton's call. Bratton obviously failed to communicate anything but his state of excitement. The Chief of Staff calmly replied that as soon as he could shower and change clothes he would be at the War Department, some seven minutes away. Bratton later described his hand-wringing state. Although he reached General Miles, who offered to go to the Chief of Staff's quarters if it would prove helpful, neither Bratton nor Miles attempted to reach other officials in the War or Navy Department who could have taken the action they were waiting for Marshall to initiate.

General Marshall's Sunday ride and his delay in reaching his office gained a permanent place in the story of the Pearl Harbor attack because he was the only individual in Washington, with access to MAGIC information, who took steps to alert American commanders in the Pacific after seeing the intercepted messages. By the time he saw the intercepts, they had been seen and discussed by the President, the Secretaries of State, Army, Navy, the Chiefs of Army and Navy Intelligence, the Chiefs of Army and Navy War Plans Divisions, and the Chief of Naval Operations. On November 27, in Marshall's absence, the Secretary of War, the Chief of Naval Operations, and the Chief of the Army War Plans Division had drafted an alert and sent it out over Marshall's signature. Later that same day the Chief of Naval Operations had dispatched an even stronger "war warning," and the Chief of Army Intelligence, prompted by Colonel Bratton, had alerted General Short against sabotage. Now, with the exception of General Marshall, every individual in Washington on the distribution list for MAGIC intercepts had seen the fourteen-part message and was in his office thirty minutes or more before the Chief of Staff arrived. It is absurd to suggest that history had to stand still until he turned his horse's head back to Fort Myer or took a quick shower.

Shortly after General Marshall reached the Munitions Building,

General Miles and Colonel Bratton came to his office to find him slowly reading the fourteen-point message. Marshall said in 1956 that when "they got to the office on December 7, they didn't show me the last and important part first but let me read all of it." [19] Bratton insisted in his later testimony that they tried to direct his attention to the fourteenth part but that he wouldn't listen. Perhaps he could not conceive of a colonel interrupting a four-star general. Whatever the reason, the reading continued through a seeming eternity until Marshall reached the final section and looked up to ask for an interpretation of the significance of the 1 p.m. delivery time.

When Bratton explained that it might coincide with an early morning attack somewhere in the Pacific, General Marshall acted swiftly. (It was now more than two to two and one-half hours since the colonel had started to worry about the timing.) The Chief of Staff quickly penned a dispatch to the various American commands in the Pacific:

> The Japanese are presenting at 1 p. m. Eastern Standard Time to-day what amounts to an ultimatum. Also they are under orders to destroy their code machine immediately.
> Just what significance the hour set may have we do not know, but be on the alert accordingly.[20]

The message was not as specific as the "war warning" sent by the Navy on November 27, nor did it in any way indicate that Pearl Harbor was in danger of attack. When Marshall asked Admiral Stark if he wanted Navy commanders included in the wire, the Chief of Naval Operations replied that he thought enough alerts had been sent. After a moment's reflection he called back and asked that "Inform Navy" be added to the message.

Stark also offered the use of Navy wireless facilities to send the dispatch. Out of mistaken confidence in the War Department's communications system, Marshall replied that it would go all right by Army channels. He handed the draft to Bratton at 11:50 a.m. As the colonel was leaving the office for the Signals Room, General Gerow called out to say that, if a priority had to be set, the message should go first to the Philippines. Bratton, a Far East expert, usually credited with being the only Army officer aware of the full significance of the intercepts on December 7, did not question the priority. He too believed that a Japanese attack would come in the Far East rather than Pearl Harbor.

Tragicomedy rather than grand tragedy marks the rest of the story. A War Department not yet prepared for a major challenge bumbled on the threshold of war. Bratton took Marshall's draft to Colonel Edward F. French in the Signals Room, and the two officers lost several precious minutes deciphering the General's usually legible handwriting. Assured at last that the warning would be on its way in thirty minutes, Bratton returned to report to Marshall. The Chief of Staff sent him back to recheck. "They didn't tell me they couldn't use their regular communications," Marshall later complained. Yet French knew that the Army signal system was unable to contact Hawaii at the moment and that it would be necessary to use commercial telegraph. No one suggested using the scrambler telephone. If anyone had, Marshall would not have risked revealing that the United States had broken the Japanese diplomatic code by relying on the dubious security of the scrambler then in use. When questioned on this point, the General explained that if he had been willing to use that instrument he would have called Manila rather than Pearl Harbor.

Sent out finally by commercial telegraph, the warning to Pearl Harbor, listed third in priority after Manila and Panama, reached the telegraph station in Honolulu about the time the Japanese planes were leaving their carriers. As the messenger boy, a Japanese on a motorcycle, rode out to General Short's headquarters with the message, he could hear anti-aircraft guns firing at enemy planes. The message had not been marked "priority," and he ran into roadblocks and suspicious soldiers along the way. The Japanese had carried out their work of destruction and General Marshall was in touch with Short's headquarters by telephone before a copy of his warning message finally reached its destination.[21]

To the Philippines, the target General Marshall expected to be hit first, the delivery service was better. Both the initial warning and the official announcement of the attack on Hawaii reached General MacArthur nine hours before the Japanese attacked Clark Field, near Manila, destroying half of his planes on the ground.

December 7—the day that would live in infamy—was also a day of misread warnings. At Pearl Harbor the report of the early-morning sinking of a Japanese submarine within the harbor was still being investigated when the attack began. In another part of Oahu two soldiers who were operating the radar apparatus after time to close it down saw the blips caused by the approach of the first Japanese planes. The lieutenant to whom they reported the incident was not surprised; American planes were expected from the west coast that morning. He suggested they forget it and head for morning chow.

Meanwhile at the State Department, Hull, Stimson, and Knox continued to discuss the message that Roosevelt should send Congress indicating America's intentions to support Great Britain against continued Japanese aggression. Shortly after noon Secretary Stimson went home for lunch. A little later Marshall drove the short distance across Memorial Bridge to Fort Myer for a bite to eat before returning to his office to prepare for the conference he still expected to attend at the White House. While at his quarters he received the announcement that was soon blaring forth from radios across the land: "Air Raid on Pearl Harbor. This is not a drill." [22]

XI

Pacific Ordeal

TWENTY-FOUR hours after the first planes left the Japanese carriers off Oahu, General Marshall's plans and hopes came to grief along with the Pacific Fleet. The way was opened for Japanese expansion to the south, Hawaii's safety could no longer be assumed, the west coast of the United States appeared vulnerable, and the means to send immediate aid to the Philippines ceased to exist. The nation fell back on a generation-old concept of leaving the garrison to fight a last-ditch stand. But the script differed from the assumptions of the 1920s and the 1930s. Instead of being able to sail with troops and supplies at the start of the conflict, the fleet had to dress its own grievous wounds.

Marshall's hopes and MacArthur's plans for defending the Philippines were also smashed. They foundered on the Navy's losses, the lack of air strength in the Islands, and the ineffectiveness of the defense force MacArthur had been building since 1935. Hampered by insufficient funds, lack of weapons, and poorly trained men, the Far East commander had to depend mainly on the force of United States Regulars he had inherited from General Grunert. As that officer had predicted shortly before he left Manila for home, the Philippine Army was not yet prepared for a trial of strength.

The blow was doubly hard to General Marshall because his chief efforts in the weeks before Pearl Harbor had been spent in strengthening the defenses of the Islands. No less than MacArthur, the Chief of Staff had emotional ties to the Philippines. He had many good friends among the defenders and a commander's pride in saving the members of a brave garrison from defeat and capture. His first thought on reading the intercepted Japanese messages on the morning of December 7 was to get a prompt warning to Mac-Arthur.

Like his message to Short, Marshall's wire to the Far East commander was delayed for several hours. As a result General MacArthur received his first news of the attack on Pearl Harbor by commercial radio at about 3 a.m. Manila time (December 8). The Chief of Staff's initial warning and official announcement that hostilities had begun arrived two or three hours later. Still later, but several hours before the Japanese attacked Clark Field, General Gerow talked to the Far East commander by telephone.

Writing in 1964, General MacArthur recalled hazily that, until he was himself attacked, he knew only that Pearl Harbor had been bombed and was under the impression that the Japanese had possibly suffered a setback. A record of his conversation with the War Department shows that General Gerow reported that considerable damage had been done to planes and installations in Hawaii and that he "wouldn't be surprised if you get an attack there in the near future." General Arnold also definitely warned General Brereton to expect an air attack.[1]

In announcing the commencement of hostilities General Marshall directed General MacArthur and other commanders in the Pacific to put into effect RAINBOW 5, a plan that included air raids against Japanese forces within tactical operating range of available bases. Inasmuch as this wire arrived several hours before the Japanese attack, it should have removed any doubts that the Far East commander had about freedom to act. In fact the message of November 27, while warning MacArthur against committing an overt act of hostility, had specifically added, "This policy should not, repeat not, be construed as restricting you to a course of action that might jeopardize the successful defense of the Philippines. Prior to hostile Japanese action you are directed to take such reconnaissance and other measures as you deem necessary."[2]

Heated and highly contradictory statements by air and ground officers in the Philippines have obscured the precise orders given at Manila for dispersion of aircraft, an attack on Formosa, or defense of Clark Field. The Far East commander and his staff have also insisted that the planes available were so few in number as to be relatively unimportant in Philippine defense. Whatever their worth, the Japanese caught and destroyed half of them on the ground, permitting enemy planes to strike the Philippines almost at will. The point that nagged at both General Marshall and General Arnold was that the destruction came nine hours after clear warning was given. Meeting Robert Sherrod of *Time* two weeks later, General Marshall declared: "It's all clear to me now except one thing. I just don't know how MacArthur happened to let his planes get caught on the ground." [3]

The twin disasters—and the one in the Philippines, while not as overpowering as the one at Pearl Harbor, was far more damaging than realized at the time—were the most staggering blows sustained by General Marshall in the course of the war. Hawaii, which he believed impregnable, seemed in imminent danger of invasion; the air organization on which he had staked his hopes of changing the balance of power in the Far East ceased to exist as an effective force a few hours after the opening attack. Yet those who talked with him then saw no signs that he was shaken.[4] He was obviously surprised at the attack on Hawaii but otherwise showed no emotion during that period.

Marshall may have recalled Pershing's statement that during the trying days of World War I he never allowed himself to appear worried or gloomy lest it discourage his staff. But he could not hide his feelings from Mrs. Marshall. That evening she noticed a grayness of expression that she had seen formerly only when he was extremely depressed. Withdrawn and silent, Marshall made no mention of the tragedy and encouraged no talk as he went to his bedroom. Recognizing the evidence of great inner tension and unable to think of anything she could say to help, Mrs. Marshall wrote later, "I passed his door and went into my room." [5]

If Marshall and those with whom he worked in Washington were self-possessed, most of the nation was not. The west coast was in a ferment of fear and rumor. Japanese were reported off the coast; innocent speculations were magnified into wild fantasies. Requests poured in on the President and War Department for more troops and anti-aircraft artillery to defend the cities of the Pacific Coast.[6]

The heavy losses at Pearl Harbor created bewilderment and anger among a people unaccustomed to defeat. Harsh charges, subsequently discredited, soon circulated that officers and crews were drunk, that Kimmel and Short scarcely spoke, and that sabotage by the Japanese on Oahu was widespread. To clear up the situation the President dispatched Secretary Knox to Honolulu. General Marshall sent Colonel Charles W. Bundy, chief of the plans group of the War Plans Division, to check into the Army side of the attack. His death in a plane crash en route to Hawaii forced the War Department to rely entirely on Knox's report.

On Knox's return to Washington in mid-December he stopped first to talk with Secretary Stimson before reporting to the President. The two Cabinet members agreed that both the Army and Navy had been remiss and that they must avoid recrimination and insist on inflexible responsibility and punishment. Apparently on the basis of Secretary Knox's report, the President directed that both Kimmel and Short be relieved. The two officers were replaced officially on December 17—Short by Lieutenant General Delos C. Emmons and Kimmel by Admiral Chester W. Nimitz—and were returned to the United States to await further orders. Several weeks later they were permitted to retire, subject to possible court-martial proceedings after the war.[7]

The relief of the Hawaiian commanders came during a period of tremendous confusion as leaders in Washington tried to brace their outposts against further attack and to lay down a course of effective action for the future. The uncertainty remaining as to Japanese intentions and the whereabouts of the enemy fleet stymied initial efforts to reinforce Hawaii and the Philippines. Naval officials responded warily to General Marshall's proposals to rush planes and men to Oahu, as they checked on reports that Japanese ships were headed for the Panama Canal and the west coast of the United States. In the Far East, Admiral Hart concluded that his squadron must withdraw from the Philippine area—a decision firmly opposed by MacArthur as denying him the use of submarines against invading transports.[8]

In a meeting of the Joint Board on December 10 the Navy representatives strongly insisted that the *Pensacola* convoy, bound for the Philippines with planes, men, and supplies, be returned to Hawaii. Reluctantly General Marshall went along with the recommendation. Next day he was "much relieved" when the President's opposition to the plan made it possible to reverse the decision. Although the situation in the Philippines was still too uncertain to permit the ships to continue to their original destination, they were diverted to northern Australia in the hope that their cargoes could later be sent to Manila.

Aware that the threat to the Philippines grew hourly, Secretary Stimson and General Marshall sought hard for something they could send to MacArthur by air or by sea before the Japanese blockaded the islands. They met many obstacles, the Secretary grumbled, "particularly because the Navy has been rather shaken and panic-stricken after the catastrophe at Hawaii." [9]

Having spent nearly ten years abroad—seven and one-half years in the Far East—Marshall was deeply moved by the plight of a garrison, beset by a strong enemy force, halfway around the world from home. As a lieutenant in 1902 in south Mindoro, where only one ship a month came to preserve contact with the outside world, he recalled that a delay in arrival of mail and supplies suggested that officers taking their ease in Manila were uninterested in the fate of the tiny garrison. He realized that men in the Far East might think the same of officials in Washington. He worried aloud in his morning conference about the unpleasantness of having to inform MacArthur "in the midst of a very trying situation that his convoy had to be turned back," and he told his staff that he wanted to send some news "which would buck General MacArthur up." [10]

In their frustration, it is clear why Stimson, Marshall, and Mac-Arthur blamed the Navy for some of their problems. MacArthur's feelings were so strong that he still claimed near the end of his life that the Navy "might well have cut through" the Japanese block-ade with planes and supplies. In retrospect, it is difficult to question the Navy's reluctance to send out the bulk of its fighting strength nearly 5000 miles away from the base at Pearl Harbor when the safety of the Hawaiian Islands was still in question. As the sole effective protecting force of the west coast and of the American position in the eastern Pacific, the Navy had excellent grounds for opposing a move through Japanese-dominated waters to an area where the enemy had absolute air superiority. Any doubts about the deadly menace of Japan's air strength should have been dissipated on December 10 when the British warships, *Prince of Wales* and *Repulse,* recently sent out to Singapore to strengthen that base, were sent to the bottom of the sea after an air attack that lasted for only two hours.

If Marshall could have started a relief expedition to the Philippines the day after the attack it might have evaded enemy ships. That opportunity was lost when the *Pensacola* convoy was diverted to Australia. Every day that passed intensified the danger. The Navy's inability to set a date when it could reasonably undertake the task asked of it by the Army settled the fate of the Philippines. But MacArthur's dogged determination, demands of an outraged American public, and the intense desire of Roosevelt, Stimson, and Marshall to get assistance through to the embattled garrison kept hope alive for another two months.

Aiding Marshall at the most frenzied period of the crisis was a fifty-two-year-old brigadier general, Dwight D. Eisenhower, who had served for six years with General MacArthur in Washington and the Philippines. As a member of the Philippine Mission, 1935-38, he knew better than any other Army officer in the War Department the state of MacArthur's defending force and the nature of his needs.

Marshall had first met and been favorably impressed by this unassuming, friendly Kansan in 1930, when he had talked with him in the office of the American Battle Monuments Commission in Washington. He ended by inviting the young officer to join his staff at Fort Benning. Although another assignment made it impossible for him to accept, Eisenhower won a favorable entry in Marshall's little Black Book and his name was listed with those of Bradley, Patton, Hodges, and Clark as available for service when leaders should be needed. The two men met only once more, briefly during maneuvers, before Mashall summoned Eisenhower to Washington. Undoubtedly the Chief of Staff had been impressed by General Krueger's list of the officer's strong points and by his service as Third Army Chief of Staff in recent maneuvers. It seems likely that Eisenhower had been strongly boosted by his West Point classmate, General Clark, and his former classmate at Fort Leavenworth, General Gerow, head of the War Plans Division in which the new officer was to serve. Gerow was aware that his friend had been number one at the Command and General Staff School and had an excellent record as a staff officer.

The new general was only one of several top men Marshall brought into the War Department in the first few weeks of war to take from his shoulders some of the burdens he had been bearing alone. Even before Pearl Harbor, Stimson and Hopkins had become concerned about the duties the Chief of Staff was handling personally. On December 11 the Secretary of War had a long talk with General Marshall about the need of giving him additional help for his staggering task. The Chief of Staff, Stimson recorded, was called on for everything from answers to strategic questions to the details of organizing the American Army for training. "I told him that it was more important that his life and brain should be kept going, than anything else that I could see on the horizon." [11]

Eisenhower arrived by train at Union Station in Washington early Sunday morning, a week after the Pearl Harbor attack. A few hours later he was seated in Marshall's office in the Munitions Building. Quickly the Chief of Staff outlined the desperate situation in the Pacific. Although the Navy's carriers, which had been away from Pearl Harbor at the time of the attack, were intact, the remainder of the Pacific Fleet would not be ready for months to play a part in Far Eastern operations. Hawaii desperately needed additional air and ground strength. The Philippines Air Force had been hard hit, although it was not known at the time just how badly. The question then was what to do.

After describing the seriousness of the situation in some detail Marshall suddenly asked, "What should be our general line of action?" It was a large order to dump in the lap of an officer who had just arrived. Wishing to give a careful judgment, Eisenhower replied, "Give me a few hours." Marshall dismissed him with a simple "All right" and turned to his next item of business.[12]

Marshall had already settled on his basic policy. Before meeting with Eisenhower that morning he had discussed with Stimson the problem in the Far East. They were alarmed by messages from General MacArthur indicating that Admiral Hart, commander of the Asiatic Fleet, had virtually told him that the Philippines were doomed instead of doing his best to keep the lifelines open. Marshall agreed with Stimson "that we could not give up the Philippines in that way." [13]

That afternoon Marshall traveled out to Walter Reed Hospital on one of his customary visits to his former chief, General Pershing, to bring him up to date on current developments. On the way home he stopped at Woodley to ask Stimson the outcome of the Secretary's visit to the White House earlier in the day. The Chief of Staff was "much relieved" to find that Roosevelt supported their position against the Navy. The President had told Assistant Secretary of Navy James Forrestal that they were going to help the Philippines.[14]

Meanwhile General Eisenhower had examined the alternatives in the Pacific. After a short study of the situation he returned to report that major reinforcements could not be sent to the Philippines for a long time, "longer than the garrison can hold out with any driblet assistance, if the enemy commits major forces to their reduction." Nevertheless he believed it necessary to do everything humanly possible. General Marshall nodded agreement. "His tone implied that I had been given the problem as a check to an answer he had already reached," Eisenhower recalled. Underlining the gravity of the situation, the Chief of Staff said quietly, "Do your best to save them." [15]

In their efforts to apply maximum pressure on the enemy MacArthur, Roosevelt, and Marshall proposed that Russia launch an immediate attack on Japan.[16] President Roosevelt specifically invited Marshal Stalin to call an Allied conference in Moscow to discuss possible joint action. Hard-pressed by the Germans, the Russian leader indicated that he preferred to wait until spring before making a decision. On studying Stalin's reply, General Marshall agreed with Admiral Stark that it was best not to press the Russians.[17] They found a similar reaction in London.

War Department leaders wanted to provide bases at Vladivostok and in the Maritime Provinces from which the Allies could launch air attacks against Japan. Fearing retaliatory raids, Stalin also denied these requests. In later years critics of the administration accused Roosevelt of softness and lack of political realism for failing to use his control over Lend-Lease supplies to force the Russians to meet United States demands. At a time when it appeared that the United States might have to divert supplies and planes earmarked for the Russians to other parts of the globe, it did not seem wise to raise that issue. Lest the Germans turn their full fury of their attack on the British Isles and intensify their effort in the Middle East, the British also strongly opposed any measure that might lead to a weakening of Russian resistance to the Germans.

The debate over use of pressure to force the Russians into the war is part of a larger argument that includes two hardy questions: "Why didn't the United States let Germany and the Soviet Union kill each other off?" "Why did the United States permit the balance of power to be destroyed in Europe and the Far East?" The argument assumes that the United States in 1942 was free to follow a course of *Realpolitik* in its relations with the totalitarian powers. Ideologically it was difficult to choose between Nazism and Communism. Militarily, the choice was simple. A beleaguered Soviet force faced a German war machine that held all Europe between the Atlantic and the gates of Moscow and Leningrad and threatened British control of the Middle East and the Mediterranean. At the beginning of 1942 Marshall's intelligence advisers still doubted if the Russians could last through the rest of the winter. With his forces beset by the Japanese in the Pacific, the General was content to follow the British policy of sustaining the only power then capable of engaging the Germans on the Continent of Europe. Even if he had held the power of political decision, the Chief of Staff would have hesitated at a time of fearful peril for the West to disturb the delicate equilibrium by which a severely mangled Soviet Army managed to fight off an enemy that had already penetrated deep into Russian territory.

Manila stepped up its demands for aid. As the Japanese swarmed ashore on various islands, including Luzon, during the first two weeks of fighting, High Commissioner Sayre and General MacArthur warned the President and General Marshall of growing Filipino discontent. Belatedly Washington realized that what military planners had considered to be a question at most of rescuing a garrison had now become a political problem of saving a people. Bound to the Philippines through strong emotional ties, General MacArthur sternly reminded Washington of American political obligations to its inhabitants.

Arguing that the Japanese blockade of the Islands was paper thin, the Far East commander demanded that the Navy bring in reinforcements. Failing this, he proposed that commercial ships be chartered to run supplies to his troops through enemy-controlled waters and that planes be flown in from British or Dutch bases. These expedients had already been considered by Marshall and Eisenhower, who were speedily building up supply depots in Australia from which shipments might be made to the Philippines.

In war, fortune seldom favors the weak and usually coldly spurns those who must have all the breaks to win. Just as an underdog athletic team frequently succumbs to simple errors and misplays, so a military force on the defensive often attracts calamity. Planes turned back at the outbreak of war from the Philippines and then diverted to Australia, in the hope that they could be ferried to MacArthur, arrived just before Christmas. An unfortunate error in unpacking prevented them from being flown to the Philippines. The solenoids, essential to the proper functioning of the firing mechanism, had been thrown away with the crates to which they were attached. Unwilling to risk pilots in planes whose guns would not shoot, American officials left the aircraft on the docks while frantic cables went back to Washington for spare parts. Stimson, for whom the great jumble of new military terms was sometimes overwhelming, exploded to Assistant Secretary of War Lovett: "They have a name that sounds like a bad word. They are some kind of an 'oid'—they remind me of a bad word—something like hemorrhoids." [18]

In time additional parts came by air and by ship, enough to outfit the planes three times over, but the slim chance that had existed of getting them to MacArthur had gone. They were not useless; the bombers played a crucial role in the early battle for the Southwest Pacific. Given the situation in Luzon, they might have vanished as quickly as the planes at Clark Field. But to the defenders of Manila, and to General Marshall desperately longing to send something to the Philippines, fortune seemed never to favor the hard-pressed.[19]

Marshall quickly followed up the original shipment of aircraft with fifty-five pursuit planes in the *Polk* and seventy in the *Coolidge*. Both ships sailed for Australia before Christmas. The senior officer with the initial convoy, Brigadier General Julian F. Barnes, was designated temporary commander of U. S. Forces in Australia and directed to make every effort to get the planes to the Philippines. In an unusual burst of prodigality the War Department gave him "unlimited credit from the Treasury" to speed the planes to their destination. The week before Christmas, Marshall notified MacArthur that fifteen B-24 heavy bombers were being diverted from their original destination to the Southwest Pacific in the hope that they might reach Manila.[20]

Help was on the way, but the tightening of the Japanese blockade around the Philippines made the possibility of its getting through increasingly unlikely. General Marshall tried another tack. Appointing Major General George H. Brett, an outstanding airman then in the Far East, as commander of United States Forces in Australia, the Chief of Staff ordered a build-up in Australia and the Philippines of a sixty-day allotment of supplies of all categories, giving "highest priority" to accumulating and forwarding provisions requested by the Far East commander. He authorized Brett to purchase locally any items that were available, allotting 10 million dollars from special funds and promising more cash when needed.

As far as credit, cash, directives, and grants of broad authority could go toward providing assistance in the critical period after Pearl Harbor, the Chief of Staff went, in his strenuous efforts to move planes, ammunition, and supplies to MacArthur. In those dreary December days he failed not for lack of overriding interest in the fate of the Philippines, but for lack of ships to run supplies through the Japanese blockade and inability to fly planes through enemy-dominated skies. Washington's encouraging cables to Manila listing the weapons and equipment intended for the Philippines raised the hopes and expectations of MacArthur and his staff. When the reinforcements did not arrive some of them charged the President and Chief of Staff with indifference to their fate. Later they accused them of cruel deception.[21]

Clutching at any means to fill the Far East commander's requests, General Marshall explored MacArthur's proposal for using carriers to take planes to the Islands. Two days before Christmas, Admiral Stark dispelled this illusion of holiday cheer. He ruled impracticable under the existing strategic situation the diversion of these ships from their proper combat functions. This decision left the Army with the staggering task of securing commercial ships in Australia for blockade running. General Marshall handed the job to General Brett, reminding him that his primary mission was "forwarding vital equipment to Philippines as expeditiously as possible." [22]

In the midst of these trials the Chief of Staff wired that MacArthur had been promoted to four-star rank. The Far East commander, restored to the temporary grade he held as Chief of Staff and now second only to Marshall in rank in the Army, wryly recalled the remark of an old sergeant on another occasion, "Thank God, Captain, we're holding our own." [23]

As late as December 28 Marshall and Arnold still saw a glimmer
of hope for the Philippines. The Chief of Staff was pleased that
MacArthur was not falling back as fast as his first reports indicated
he might be forced to do; the Air Chief believed that once he got
heavy bombers operating out of Borneo, he could cover both Saigon and the Philippines.[24]

A close look at enemy progress could not have encouraged optimism. The initial Japanese landings were made on December 10
in northern Luzon—in the region over which Marshall and other
members of Liggett's staff had ridden horseback in 1916. A few
days later the enemy came ashore in southeastern Luzon and was
soon pushing toward Laguna de Bay—a name that recalled to the
Chief of Staff his dismal days of guarding prisoners in 1903. Shortly
before Christmas a Japanese force captured Davao in Mindanao in
preparation for an early attack against Borneo to the south.

Although MacArthur's forces outnumbered the enemy almost
two to one during the period of the landings,[25] he was severely
hampered by untrained and poorly equipped Reserves and the absence of air support. Before the first week of fighting had passed,
the Far East commander made preparations to move the government and his headquarters to Corregidor and to declare Manila an
open city. He made the transfer on a cheerless Christmas Eve; on
the day after New Year's the Japanese entered Manila without opposition.

From central and southern Luzon, the American commander
pulled back his forces to the Bataan Peninsula, where he proposed
to make a determined stand against the enemy. He handled his
withdrawal skillfully, but he lacked time to bring into the restricted area many of the supplies stockpiled elsewhere. Within a
few weeks his troops were on extremely short rations. As he concentrated his forces for a last-ditch defense he demanded more
strenuous efforts of Washington. He urged the Chief of Staff to
rush air and sea forces from Australia by way of Borneo and the
Netherlands East Indies to establish a base in the southern Philippines.

In Washington, where the British and United States Chiefs of
Staff had been meeting since Christmas Eve in the hope of finding
a formula for dealing with German and Japanese threats, there was
now firm agreement on holding the Malay barrier and Burma and
Australia, but somewhat less emphasis on saving the Philippines.

Nonetheless President Roosevelt broadcast a cheerful, indefinite New Year's message, which both American newspapers and officials in the Philippines accepted as promises of immediate aid. General Marshall wrote hopefully to MacArthur on January 2 that the rapid development of overwhelming airpower on the Malay barrier might cut Japanese communications south of Borneo and open the way to Allied attack on the enemy in the southern Philippines. This prospect became more remote hourly as the Japanese advanced.

Even as Marshall sought to assure MacArthur of support, his War Department planners were outlining cogent reasons why he should not reinforce the Islands. Showing that half of the air force and the major part of the naval force needed for an effective effort would have to be transferred from other theaters, they concluded that a plan to drive from Australia northward would require an "unjustifiable diversion" of forces from the principal Allied theater in the Atlantic area.[26]

Both strategy and logistics now worked against the Philippines. Yet Marshall continued to try desperate expedients to send something to American and Filipino fighting men. Seizing on General MacArthur's proposal that anti-aircraft ammunition be sent by submarine, the Chief of Staff persuaded the Navy to dispatch one northward with this cargo. He also made funds available to General Brereton, temporarily commanding ground and air forces in Australia, to hire commercial ships to make the dangerous run.[27]

Marshall's last major effort to speed supplies to the Philippines came near the end of January with the sending of Patrick J. Hurley to Australia to try his hand. A fiery Irishman from Oklahoma, known for a loquacity that forced even Winston Churchill to stop talking and listen, and for a pugnacity that had led him as a cabinet officer to stalk out of a congressional committee hearing when he felt that a senator had reflected on his veracity, Hurley had the persuasiveness, determination, and the touch of the pirate needed for the job. An officer in World War I, colonel in the Army Reserves, and Secretary of War under Herbert Hoover, Hurley had volunteered his services in a military capacity at the beginning of the war. Soon afterward the President offered him the post of Minister to New Zealand. On Hurley's insistence that he wanted military service, Roosevelt sent him over to see General Marshall.

"Hurley saw a message from MacArthur there, appealing for something at Corregidor," General Marshall recalled. "And he said, 'If I can just help Doug.' I said, 'All right you can help him.'" The Chief of Staff proposed that Hurley accept the diplomatic appointment but go out first as a temporary brigadier general, representing the Army in Australia. He was authorized funds in addition to those already given to the commander in Australia for the purpose of hiring ships to break the blockade of the Philippines. Lest the ebullient Hurley talk too much before leaving, Marshall sent him around to the War Plans Division. "Then I telephoned and said he was coming; that I was sending a letter of instructions; and they were to keep him there and take him to the plane and not to let him get out of the Department." General Gerow and General Eisenhower took Hurley in tow. After allowing him a short time to complete final arrangements in the city, each donated a star for his uniform and then put him aboard a plane shortly after midnight.[28]

Hurley was firmly committed to his mission. As Secretary of War under Hoover he had stressed the vital role of the Islands in American defense. It was he who had proposed the name of MacArthur for the post of Chief of Staff and had shared with him bitter attacks from those who opposed their handling of the bonus marchers in 1932. His appointment gave MacArthur new hope.

Delayed two weeks by bad weather in California, Hurley arrived in Australia in early February 1942, eager to cut through red tape and delays and mountainous obstacles to help his friend. Meanwhile Marshall was hammering at the commanders in the Southwest Pacific to accelerate their efforts. On the day that he started Hurley on his way he charged Brereton to use his funds "without stint" to organize groups of bold and resourceful men to buy supplies and charter ships for blockade running. Prices were to be set high enough "to insure utmost energy and daring" on the part of ship commanders. Two days later he demanded redoubled efforts.[29]

In urging the use of blockade runners, both MacArthur and Marshall were apparently thinking of their use in the American and Spanish Civil Wars. But in 1942 Australia failed to provide the daring freebooters that Bermuda, the Caribbean Islands, and the Mediterranean had afforded in earlier conflicts. Not only were few ships available at any price, but the risks discouraged most sea captains who could be found. Despite liberal offers and feverish activity, Hurley got only six ships started for the Philippines. Of these, only three got through, one to Mindanao and two to the island of Cebu. Of the 10,000 tons landed in the southern Philippines, only 1000 tons finally reached the garrison in Luzon.[30]

After weeks of trying to aid his old friend Hurley saw why the Army and Navy commanders in Australia had failed to get results: "We did not have the ships, the air force or ground forces necessary to make the operation successful. We were out-shipped, out-planed, out-manned, and out-gunned by the Japanese from the beginning." [31]

Watching his half-starved forces being battered by Japanese bombings, low on badly needed medical supplies, and facing the reproaches of the Filipinos, MacArthur bombarded the War Department with demands for stronger American measures. Apparently convinced that Roosevelt would certainly act if he knew the situation in the Philippines, he pointedly reminded Marshall that he expected his messages to be shown to the President. He assailed as diversions from the main business of the Allies in the Pacific current efforts to establish a base in Australia and to restore naval lines of communication. Only immediate direct attacks on the Japanese lines of communications, he advised Marshall, would bring results.[32]

Marshall explained patiently that the United States Navy lacked ships for such attacks. Until additional forces could be brought to the Pacific, the Navy, temporarily crippled by the Pearl Harbor blow, could only try to contain the Japanese advance and deny the enemy access to areas that the Allies would need later for mounting their offensives.[33]

It was as if a man dying of thirst were told that he must wait for a drink of water until a well could be dug and a water main laid. Thoughts of well-dressed officers sitting in comfortable offices and sleeping in clean beds excited the anger of the battlers of Bataan and deepened their suspicions of a faceless enemy called Washington.

If the situation was galling to the Far East commander, it was intolerable to the President of the Philippines, desperately ill of tuberculosis, lying on his cot in the crowded tunnel of Corregidor. Forgetting his long fight to break away from the United States and ignoring his inability to give MacArthur the funds needed to build an independent Philippine defense force, he blamed Washington for his plight. His mind recoiled at the thought of the Japanese in the presidential palace in Manila, at the constant menace of enemy planes, and at the almost certain prospect that he would not live to see his country a free republic.

A few days after President Quezon and Vice-President Osmena were sworn in for a second term in a simple but moving ceremony at Corregidor, Quezon decided on a policy of shock action. Bitingly he charged that the United States and Great Britain had failed to aid the Philippines and had purchased a breathing space for themselves by dooming the Islands to virtual extinction. His suggested remedy was absurd on its face, in view of Japanese occupation of his capital and Japan's long-established ambition to own the Philippines. If no aid was to be sent, he proposed to President Roosevelt, the United States and Japan should be invited to withdraw their forces and the Islands should be neutralized. High Commissioner Sayre approved the proposal if no further relief was forthcoming.

According to General MacArthur, Quezon recognized that the plan was impractical and that it would be unacceptable to either country. In his *Reminiscences,* General MacArthur later recalled arguing against it and declaring that he would not endorse it. But not averse to using shock treatment on Washington, MacArthur in forwarding the Quezon plan failed to note his own disagreement and neglected to indicate why President Quezon had recommended it. His covering letter to General Marshall said that, from a military standpoint, the question was whether the plan of Quezon "might offer the best possible solution of what is about to be a disastrous debacle." He suggested that if the Japanese accepted the idea the United States would lose no military advantages, and if Japan rejected it her action would strengthen the American position psychologically in the Philippines.[34]

The Chief of Staff and the Secretary of War were much concerned by the message and by the fact that General MacArthur's telegram "went more than halfway toward supporting Quezon's position." When they showed the message to President Roosevelt on February 9 he declared, "We can't do this at all." His firmness in a situation that Stimson called "ghastly in its responsibility and significance" impressed General Marshall. "I immediately dis-

carded everything in my mind I had held to his discredit. . . .
Roosevelt said we won't neutralize. I decided he was a great
man." [35]

In a strong cable, drafted by General Marshall and General Eisenhower, the President authorized MacArthur to arrange for the
capitulation of the Filipino units, but declined to consider the
neutralization of the Islands. Making clear that he was issuing his
orders in complete understanding of the military estimate that accompanied Quezon's message, the President directed American
forces to keep the flag flying "so long as there remains any possibility of resistance." Without reminding MacArthur that the Army
had long assumed such last-ditch activity to be the lot of the garrison in the Philippines, he emphasized that the duty and necessity
of resisting Japanese aggression to the last transcended in importance any other obligation facing the United States in the Philippines. He expressed his sympathy for the extremity to which they
might soon be reduced and declared that the service MacArthur
and the American members of the command could render to the
country in the struggle then developing "is beyond all possibility
of appraisement." [36]

Stung by the Roosevelt-Marshall version of Nelson's message at
Trafalgar, the Far East commander retorted that he had no
thought of surrendering the Filipino forces under his command.
He intended to fight on until destruction of his forces in the Bataan Peninsula and then wage a last-ditch stand at Corregidor.[37]

Dismayed at MacArthur's suggestion that he planned to go down
with his troops, Marshall discussed with his colleagues how best to
save him for future service to the nation. As the best-informed
American officer on the Far East and the heroic defender of the
Philippines, MacArthur exhibited a leadership and example that
were essential to future campaigns in the Southwest Pacific. His
capture would damage the Allied defensive effort and give the Japanese a psychological victory. No one in Washington was willing to
consider such an ending to the MacArthur story.

So far had distrust of Washington's motives developed in the
Far East Command that Marshall's efforts to arrange for the evacuation of General MacArthur and his family were regarded with deep
suspicion. On Febuary 4 the Chief of Staff sounded out MacArthur
on his course of action if Bataan could not be held and only Correg-

idor Island remained. He advanced the possibility of General Mac-
Arthur's transferring to Mindanao, where he might organize guer-
rilla warfare in the central and southern islands before proceeding
farther south to resume command of United States Forces in the
Far East. As an alternative, he suggested that General MacArthur
might go directly to Australia. Asking for a confidential statement
of MacArthur's views, he added that any order for his withdrawal
would come directly from the President.[38] This request produced a
strange effect at the Philippines headquarters. Writing nearly fifteen years later, General MacArthur's aide and personal friend,
General Courtney Whitney, asked: "Was Marshall threatening
ahead of time to use the Commander-in-Chief on him?" In asking
MacArthur to speak freely, "was he setting any kind of a trap? Mac-
Arthur could only guess at the answers." [39]

Rather than threatening General MacArthur, General Marshall
was following the advice of the Far East commander's friends.
Colonel J. Munroe Johnson, who had served with the Pacific commander in World War I, said that MacArthur would not obey the
orders to withdraw if they came only from the War Department.
Later, this view was confirmed by Pat Hurley, who cabled General
Marshall that the President must "definitely order MacArthur to
relinquish his command and proceed elsewhere." [40]

A few days later, when plans were being made to evacuate
President Quezon and High Commissioner Sayre and their families, General Marshall proposed that the Far East commander
send his wife and son along lest he later have to withdraw under
"conditions impossible for them." At MacArthur's reply that they
would share the fate of the garrison, the Chief of Staff again urged
him to send them away, adding that he might have to be separated
from them "under circumstances of greatly increased peril." [41]

Meanwhile, sentiment was growing in the United States to
bring MacArthur out of the Philippines. In February former Republican presidential candidate Wendell Willkie proposed that
MacArthur be summoned to head United States efforts in the Pacific; a bill was introduced in Congress by Representative Knute
Hill, Democrat from the State of Washington, to establish a Supreme War Command over all armed forces with MacArthur as
their chief. Senator Millard Tydings, chairman of the Senate Military Affairs Committee, argued that MacArthur would oppose leav-

ing his men and that it would take a peremptory order to get him out.[42]

The plight of the Philippines occupied the central stage in American thinking while the Japanese swarmed into British and Dutch possessions in the Southwest Pacific, thus accomplishing the real object of their Pearl Harbor attack. In mid-January the ABDA Command, of which the Dutch East Indies, New Guinea, Malaya, Burma, and the Philippines formed a part, had been established under General Sir Archibald Wavell. Australia was excluded from the command, although Australian forces in the ABDA Command area were placed under the supreme commander, and United States Forces in Australia were directed to support his operations. By mid-January when General Wavell joined his American deputy commander, General Brett, and other members of his staff in Java, the defenses of the command had already begun to disintegrate. The far-ranging Japanese forces had isolated the Philippines, captured Hong Kong, forced back the British in Malaya, and were storming ashore in Borneo and the Celebes. With his forces widely separated and completely off-balance in the face of a coordinated Japanese attack, Wavell was unable to organize an effective defense. Within a month the enemy took Singapore and was threatening Java and Sumatra. Convinced that there was no hope of defending these possessions, Wavell proposed that two Australian divisions being brought from the Middle East to defend Java be sent instead to Burma or Australia. He gained permission to turn the ABDA Command over to the Dutch and return to India.

At this point General Marshall directed the small American ground and air force on Java to continue its support of the desperate Dutch defenders. The possibility of putting up an effective fight ended at the close of February with the defeat of the Allied naval forces in the Battle of the Java Sea. On March 1 the Japanese began landings on Java. Eight days later the Dutch army surrendered. Elsewhere the story was the same. When in early March Rangoon was taken, the Japanese held the land and sea area from central Burma to New Guinea, threatening northwest Australia with attack. In the Philippines a battered American-Filipino force still held out, but its prospects of surviving dimmed with the passage of each day.

As the ABDA Command began to fall apart, General Marshall

and Secretary Stimson became convinced that General MacArthur must be ordered out of Luzon. Their first discussions of his future role pointed in the direction of establishing a force in Mindanao which would prepare for a later return to Manila. As the Japanese extended their conquests the American officials abandoned this prospect and turned to the establishment of a new headquarters in the Southwest Pacific. The approaching fall of Java made a strong organization in Australia essential. On February 22 General Marshall drafted orders for the Far East commander that were signed the same day by the President. MacArthur was directed to leave for Australia as soon as possible. He was to stop briefly, not to exceed a week, in Mindanao and then go southward to assume command of American forces in the Southwest Pacific.[43]

A proud man, unaccustomed to defeat, saddened by reverses, MacArthur considered the possibility of disobeying the order and remaining with his troops in a futile but courageous last-man stand. His senior advisers urged him to take the new command, arguing that he could do more there to aid his embattled forces in the Philippines than by allowing himself to be killed or captured at Corregidor. In deciding to comply with the presidential order, he asked and was granted permission to select the psychological time for departure.[44]

On March 11 General MacArthur selected seventeen members of his staff to accompany him and his wife and son by PT boats to Mindanao and then by bombers to Australia. After a dramatic journey, which he described as "undoubtedly unique in military annals," the party on March 17 reached Batchelor Field some forty miles south of Darwin. There MacArthur was greeted by reporters, to whom he gave the salutation that thrilled the world: "I came through and I shall return." Soon afterward members of the party flew on to Alice Springs, where they boarded a train for Melbourne. A few days later he drove to Canberra for his first meeting with Prime Minister John Curtin. In this conference MacArthur received the impression that Curtin was solely responsible for bringing him out of the Philippines and for his selection as supreme commander in the Southwest Pacific. Apparently he was completely unaware that the basic decisions had been made in Washington as part of a plan for reorganizing the Allied commands throughout the world.[45]

The Japanese capture of Singapore in mid-February foreshadowed the split of the ABDA Command and with it the possibility of keeping Southeast Asia and the Pacific area under a single commander. As early as the 15th, President Roosevelt began to think in terms of dividing that part of the world into two command areas with the United States accepting responsibility for Australia, New Zealand, and China, and the British controlling the India-Burma defense. The President suggested this solution to Prime Minister Churchill on the 18th. Before any conclusion could be reached, the political and military leaders of Australia and New Zealand, in a series of meetings between February 28 and March 2, turned their attention to a new Pacific command to include their areas. Fearing that British generals were more interested in the defense of Burma and India than in the Southwest Pacific, they favored an American as allied commander for the area. Apparently assuming that General MacArthur was committed to the Philippines, they considered General Brett, then commanding American forces in Australia and deputy supreme commander under Wavell, for the post.[46] In late February Brett received intimations from Marshall that Washington was considering MacArthur for the appointment.

Wishing to avoid any appearance of American pressure and believing that the open shift of MacArthur to Australia would bring protests from the Filipinos, General Marshall suggested to General Brett that the Australian and New Zealand governments make a specific request for an American commander. On March 8, still without knowledge of American plans for MacArthur, these governments proposed to Churchill that a United States commander be named. Their request was submitted more than two weeks after the President's directive to MacArthur to proceed to Australia to take command of a reconstituted ABDA area.[47]

On the day the Dutch surrendered in Java, President Roosevelt proposed to Churchill the division of the world into three major command areas. The British would have the chief role in the area from Singapore and India to the Mediterranean and the Middle East, the United States would be responsible for the Pacific, and both countries would share responsibility for the Atlantic area.[48] Although Churchill and Curtin approved an American for the supreme command in the Pacific, their reservation about boundaries and organization of the Pacific command area required rather extensive negotiations with Washington. These were still being discussed at the time MacArthur left Corregidor. Delays in obtaining final acceptance of the draft directive of March 30 by the governments concerned prevented MacArthur from assuming formal command until April 18.

Because premature announcement of MacArthur's departure from the Philippines might endanger the safety of his party, General Marshall withheld even from Curtin information on the journey until MacArthur had actually landed in Australia. On the day the Far East commander stepped aboard the PT boat in the Philippines, Marshall directed General Brett to inform Prime Minister Curtin the moment MacArthur arrived that he was assuming command of the United States forces in that area. Brett was then to propose, in the name of the President, that MacArthur be selected as supreme commander of the Southwest Pacific. He was also to inform Curtin that Washington was announcing that the Australians had asked for the transfer. The Prime Minister enthusiastically nominated MacArthur for the new post, and his statement was included in a news release of March 18.[49]

Possibly in the excitement of welcoming MacArthur, Curtin overstated his own role in naming the General as supreme commander. He may have assumed that the new arrival was completely informed of Washington's prior arrangements. Apparently MacArthur was never informed of Marshall's key role in his transfer to the new command.

Besides stressing Australia's demand for MacArthur's transfer from the Philippines, the Chief of Staff took a second step to offset Japanese propaganda attacks on the Philippine commander. On January 30 Marshall directed Brigadier General Richard Sutherland, MacArthur's chief of staff, to report promptly any action of his chief for which the Medal of Honor could appropriately be awarded. No reply was received and no further action was taken by Marshall until bills were introduced in Congress in February by J. Parnell Thomas, Republican of New Jersey, and James Van Zandt, Republican of Pennsylvania, to authorize the presentation of the Medal of Honor to MacArthur. When asked for comments by the chairman of the House Military Affairs Committee, General Marshall directed that Sutherland be asked again "to furnish a basis for the award," adding that it would mean more if it came from the War Department than from Congress.[50]

General Sutherland followed Marshall's directive and urged that the award be given at the time of MacArthur's arrival in Australia. He suggested, in particular, that MacArthur be decorated for refusal to take cover during an air attack. General Marshall recalled, "I asked them [MacArthur's staff] to write it, but they asked us to, so I did it." The Chief of Staff's citation acclaimed MacArthur's gallant defense of the Philippines and praised him for his "utter disregard of personal danger under heavy fire and aerial bombardment," and for "his calm judgment in each crisis [which] inspired his troops, galvanized the spirit of resistance of the Filipino people, and confirmed the faith of the American people in their armed forces." [51]

Although realizing that there was no specific act of MacArthur's that called for the award under "literal interpretation" of the statutes, Marshall believed that MacArthur deserved recognition beyond that given by any other decoration the War Department had to award. He justified the proposal on the basis of the presentation of a Medal of Honor to Colonel Charles A. Lindbergh in 1927. "I submit the recommendation to you," he wrote Secretary Stimson, "not only because I am certain that General MacArthur is deserving of the honor but also because I am certain that this action will meet with popular approval, both within and without the armed forces, and will have a constructive morale value." The conferring of the medal in the name of Congress by the President was announced on March 25. Nearly two weeks later, on being asked by Representative May for comment on the pending resolution in his committee, Stimson replied that inasmuch as the Medal had been conferred there appeared to be no further need of congressional action. [52]

After being welcomed with wild acclaim in Australia, General MacArthur received from Marshall the first official appraisal of his new command. The boundaries of his Southwest Pacific theater were still being debated by the Combined Chiefs of Staff and the President and Prime Minister. The Chief of Staff explained that the forces and planes available to him were small, the limits being fixed by shortages of shipping "of the utmost seriousness" and critical situations elsewhere. To secure his lines of communication, one division had been sent to New Caledonia and small units to nearby islands. Small garrisons and airplane squadrons were being stationed along the line between Hawaii and Australia to protect the movement of troops and supplies. [53]

MacArthur was profoundly shocked to discover that widely publicized Australian statements of large forces and stockpiles of supplies were merely propaganda statements to fool the enemy. He was sorely disappointed at the badly battered air force at his disposal and the scarcity of American troops in his theater. Unsympathetic with the Navy's insistence on protecting its line of communications to Australia and with demands by the Free French that their Pacific islands be properly defended if they were to furnish airfields for the Allies, he was appalled to hear that troops which he believed to be intended for Australia had been landed there briefly and then transshipped to New Caledonia.[54]

Command arrangements had to be worked out between Roosevelt and Churchill and then between the British and the governments of Australia and New Zealand before the Joint Chiefs of Staff could agree on their own division of responsibilities. MacArthur was already concerned over delays that had occurred before the final directive was issued in mid-April. He was more than concerned when the Pacific area was divided between his command and that of the Navy. General Marshall, a strong advocate of unified command, was inclined to agree with the Army commander's protests. He had told Stimson back in February that he thought MacArthur's "dominating character is needed down there to make the Navy keep up their job in spite of rows which we shall have between them." [55] He recognized, however, that Admiral King, the new boss of the Navy, would not accept Douglas MacArthur as over-all commander. Disagreements between the Philippine commander and Admiral Hart about command of naval forces in the Islands had already aroused Navy Department opposition to placing its ships under Army command. More important, King felt that the Pacific was primarily a Navy responsibility, that troops and supplies must be moved by his ships, that bases must be seized, maintained, or defended by the Navy, and that ground operations must have close naval support. Marshall saw that if MacArthur was to retain command of a substantial part of the Pacific he had to agree to a division of responsibility. In the end the Central, South, and North Pacific came under Admiral Nimitz, who wore the hats of Allied commander of these areas and of commander-in-chief, Pacific Fleet, with headquarters at Pearl Harbor. From him came the ships that were assigned to General MacArthur. The arrangement was made to work because of strenuous efforts by Marshall and

King, but friction continued throughout the war, leading to re-
criminations on both sides in the Pacific.

Nearly everything that Marshall and his staff touched in connection with the Philippines and the Pacific command during the
early months of 1942 seemed to create friction. In preparing to
leave the Philippines on March 11 the Far East commander proposed to establish four commands in the Islands, giving the one in
Luzon to General Jonathan M. Wainwright but retaining at Corregidor a deputy chief of staff, Brigadier General Lewis C. Beebe,
through whom he expected to exercise command over the Islands.
Although other messages concerning the situation in the Philippines got through to Washington during this period, MacArthur
neglected to notify the Chief of Staff of this arrangement.[56]

On the assumption that Wainwright had been left in command,
General Marshall directed his orders to that officer as "Commanding General, U.S. Army Forces, Far East," specifying that MacArthur's new command would retain supervisory control over Wainwright's forces. Caught in the middle in this situation, General
Beebe urged MacArthur to explain his plight to Washington. On
the 20th Marshall notified Wainwright that he had been promoted
to lieutenant general and that he was to assume command in the
Philippines. Next morning Wainwright carried out his directive
and appointed Beebe as his chief of staff. Promptly General MacArthur asked Wainwright on what authority he had based his action.
For the first time MacArthur notified General Marshall of his intention to control operations in the Philippines from his Australian headquarters.[57]

General Marshall was not impressed with the proposed command set-up. He explained to President Roosevelt in March 1942
that it would be difficult for MacArthur in Melbourne, 4000 miles
away, to control operations through a deputy chief of staff and
that such an arrangement would have a depressing effect on General Wainright, on whose leadership the United States now had to
depend. Furthermore General MacArthur, as supreme commander,
was not supposed to exercise direct control of any national force.
This restriction, imposed on General Wavell several weeks earlier
with the purpose of preventing him from devoting his attention
too closely to any one phase of his mission, was still in effect. At
Marshall's recommendation, Roosevelt notified General Mac-

Arthur that unless he strongly objected Marshall's order would stand. The Southwest Pacific commander indicated that he understood the problem and would fit into the new scheme of command. He approved Wainright's promotion and described his assignment to the Philippine Command as "appropriate." Later he and some members of his staff sharply criticized the change.[58]

The closing days in the Philippines were especially bitter to Army officials in Washington and the Pacific. During Marshall's absence in London in April, Stimson discussed with General McNarney and General Eisenhower whether they should continue to demand that American forces fight until the end. Believing that the situation had changed completely since February, when there had seemed to be some slight hope that a garrison could hold out, the officials now proposed that the directive be changed. On their recommendation the President sent to General MacArthur, for forwarding to Wainwright, if he agreed in substance and timing, an announcement that the final decision on the action of the Bataan garrison would be left to the commander on the ground. The message arrived shortly after the surrender of Bataan had been announced. Roosevelt hastened to inform General Wainwright that he hoped he could hold Corregidor. Realizing that this course was also almost hopeless, he assured the commander of his full confidence in whatever decision he might make and permitted him complete freedom of action.[59]

General MacArthur was less lenient. He notified Wainwright that he had made no comment on the earlier message because the President's direct cable had already made clear that the final decision was left to the Philippine commander. But he emphasized to Washington that he was utterly opposed to the capitulation of the Bataan command. He believed that it should fight to the last on the field of battle while taking full toll of the enemy. He was equally set against the surrender of Corregidor, now left in Wainwright's hands.[60]

In Washington, as in the Islands, it was evident that once Bataan surrendered, Corregidor could not long survive. Despite shortened rations, the damage of shelling, and heavy bombing, the garrison miraculously managed to last nearly a month more. The original defense plan for the Philippines had asked a six months' defense by the garrison to prepare the way for a relief expedition to return.

By superhuman effort the defenders got within sight of that goal. But the prospect of a relief expedition seemed farther away than ever.

The landing of a large Japanese force at the northeastern end of the island on the evening of May 5 made it obvious that resistance was hopeless. In this situation General Wainwright on May 6 decided to ask for terms. His efforts to restrict the surrender only to the garrison at Corregidor proved fruitless as the Japanese commander demanded that Wainwright order all forces under his command elsewhere in the Islands to lay down their arms before an armistice to Corregidor would be granted. With this threat of annihilation hanging over his troops, Wainwright broadcast an appeal for his commanders to cease their resistance. MacArthur attempted until the last to save units in some of the islands from the capitulation, indicating that they could ignore orders from Corregidor.

Unable to aid the commander and his fighters, the Chief of Staff wrote into the message sent Wainwright by the President the words: "In every camp and on every naval vessel soldiers, sailors, and marines are inspired by the gallant struggle of their comrades in the Philippines. The workmen in our shipyards and munitions plants redouble their efforts because of your example." [61]

Profoundly touched by the defense the forces had put up in the last hopeless days, General Marshall proposed to recognize General Wainwright's efforts by conferring on him the Medal of Honor. Forwarding several affidavits sent him by officers in the Philippines, he asked General MacArthur, for whom he had arranged a similar award, for his recommendation. The Pacific commander replied sharply that the men who made the sworn statements were not in a position to know the facts, that the citation as proposed did not represent the truth, that Wainwright's actions fell far short of those needed to win the award, and that if he received it the action would constitute an injustice to others who had done far more than the Philippine commander. [62]

"His animosity toward Wainwright was tremendous," General Marshall recalled. Distressed by MacArthur's reaction, the Chief of Staff asked General McNarney to investigate the recommendations for the award and the basis of the opposition to it. He also presented the case to Secretary Stimson. Impressed by Marshall's belief that the evidence would support the decoration, the Secretary of War strongly favored overriding MacArthur's opposition. On General McNarney's warning that a persistence in their course might bring a public airing of a bitter dispute in the Army, the two officials agreed to suspend the matter temporarily until a better time. Neither Marshall nor Stimson changed his mind. The Secretary became especially indignant several months later when a member of the Southwest Pacific headquarters staff, while visiting in Washington, made a number of derogatory remarks about Wainwright. Stimson pointedly asked if he was acting on MacArthur's instructions and apparently was not wholly convinced by the officer's negative reply.[63]

Of all the prisoners of the war, General Marshall was most deeply moved by the plight of those from Corregidor or Bataan. In the dreary months that followed the surrender he made a special effort to send on to families of imprisoned men any hopeful bits of information that might filter through from Japanese prison camps. He was particularly attentive to General Wainwright's family. In 1943, when Stilwell, Patton, Somervell, and McNarney (temporary lieutenant generals) were recommended for permanent two-star rank, he added Wainwright to the list. On August 20, 1945, when the war was won, Marshall cabled MacArthur: "It seems to me that it would be most appropriate to have General Wainwright present at signing of capitulation. This also appears to be the general view in U. S. as expressed in the press. Please let me have your reaction." MacArthur responded that he would be delighted to have him, and General Wainwright was present for the ceremony.[64]

General Marshall also resurrected the idea of a Medal of Honor. At a special reception in the White House garden in 1945, President Truman presented Wainwright with the medal that Marshall had wanted him to have three years before. Apparently Wainwright bore no grudge against his former chief. In 1948 at the Republican National Convention, he was to present the name of Douglas MacArthur for nomination as a candidate for the presidency of the United States.

The Wainwright matter and the question of command in the Philippines were relatively minor points of difference. The issue that counted was the decision of Roosevelt and the Joint Chiefs of Staff to stand firm on a Europe First strategy. Apparently MacArthur was never reconciled to this action.

Implicit in all Army and Navy planning since early 1941, this course was plotted before MacArthur became commander in the Far East. Although Marshall and Stimson had modified their views in the fall of 1941 in the hope of building up a threat to Japan in the Philippines, their emphasis on the Atlantic never changed. On the declaration of war, MacArthur attempted to alter the basic Allied strategy. Calling the Philippines the key to the Far East, he insisted that the Army make a major effort in that area. When he was transferred to the Southwest Pacific he urged that the United States place first the war against Japan.

Marshall could not ignore the feelings of his Pacific commander and the substantial backing he gained in the United States. MacArthur's constant demand for greater support undoubtedly left an imprint on the Chief of Staff's thinking in his strategic planning. Never absent from his mind was the fact that peripheral operations in the European Theater drew shipping and supplies from the Pacific without significantly hastening the winning of the war. The strategy of grappling directly with the main German forces on the continent of Europe, which he had favored from the beginning, gained added impetus as he sought to get on with the war in Europe so that he could turn his full force toward the Pacific.

XII

Arcadia

SIMPLE and serene, ancient Arkady was an untroubled haven. Its rustic charm knew no harsher noise than the soft songs of birds and shepherds' sweet pipings. Either by the blind workings of bureaucratic choice that bestows on hurricanes the gentle names of Hazel and Dulcie or by Winston Churchill's conscious efforts to express his pleasure at having the United States at last as an ally, the first Anglo-American conference after Pearl Harbor was christened Arcadia. As the ominous thunder of enemy attacks rumbled half a world away, the leaders of Great Britain and the United States came together in Washington from December 22, 1941, to January 14, 1942. In their deliberations George Catlett Marshall was to come into his own.

Wrestling with the tasks of sending aid to General MacArthur, moving troops to the west coast, and scraping up scarce men and equipment, General Marshall—like his colleagues—would have preferred waiting until after the first of the year for a meeting. It was almost as if he hesitated to assume the vital role that he would hereafter play on the world stage. He had already taken his place in the councils of the President and established his leadership in the anterooms of Congress, but except for a brief appearance at Argentia he had not yet matched his wits with the political and military leaders of Great Britain. In the approaching conference he would bear the main responsibility for presenting the American military case. Although Stark was oldest of the Chiefs of Staff in point of service, he was already on his way out as the dominant figure in the Navy. General Arnold, beginning his full participation as a partner in the United States Chiefs of Staff at this confer-

261

ence, kept in the background, speaking up only when technical matters arose pertaining to the Army Air Forces. Admiral King, although an active participant in the meeting, had only recently arrived on the scene.

Even had he craved a star's role, Marshall would have been handicapped in trying to speak for the United States Chiefs of Staff. Despite the efforts made over several decades to develop close-knit collaboration among the President, the cabinet, and the Chiefs of Staff, no integrated system of defense control existed in Washington. Sir John Dill was not far wrong when he reported to General Brooke in 1942 that "the country has not—repeat not—the slightest conception of what the war means, and their armed forces are more unready for war than it is possible to imagine." He attributed these problems to the lack of regular meetings of the United States Chiefs of Staff, the absence of a Joint Secretariat, the President's haphazard way of consulting with his military advisers, and the lack of a system for regular sessions attended by the President, the service secretaries, and the Chiefs of Staff.[1]

In pointed contrast to the American lack of organization was the British system of military collaboration. For eighteen months Churchill, as Minister of Defence, had met almost daily with his Chiefs of Staff, whom he alternately bullied and cajoled. They had long since agreed on basic issues and acted together in international conferences with a sixth sense of understanding common to partners in a long and harmonious marriage. In the early meetings with the Americans they displayed a careful preparation of proposals and a singleness of purpose that gave them a decided advantage in debates. They were always conscious of the Prime Minister's control of policy even when he was absent from the scene.

The Arcadia meeting was suggested by Churchill. Sitting at Chequers on December 7 with United States Ambassador John G. Winant and the President's Special Representative, W. Averell Harriman, pondering ways to block a Japanese attack on Malaya, he had heard the staggering news of the attack on Pearl Harbor. His first reaction was enormous relief that the United States at last marched side by side with embattled Britain; his second was fear that, in their fury, the American leaders would shift their central interest from the Atlantic to the Pacific. He immediately proposed to President Roosevelt a meeting before the year's end to nail down Allied policy.

Within a week he and his chief advisers were aboard the *Duke of York* and headed for Hampton Roads. With him went Lord Beaverbrook, member of the War Council and chief of war production, and most of his top military advisers: Admiral Pound, the First Sea Lord; Field Marshal Dill, until recently the Chief of the Imperial General Staff; and Air Chief Marshal Sir Charles Portal, Chief of the Air Staff. Left behind to mind the store in London was Dill's successor, General Sir Alan Brooke. Aboard ship, the indefatigable Prime Minister dashed off brilliant minutes to his advisers, confident that the Americans were still stunned by their sudden precipitation into war and consequently unprepared for the conference. He proposed a basic agenda that the conference followed and an outline of global strategy that was to be accepted by the Americans with few important changes.

Arriving off Hampton Roads on December 22, the Prime Minister canceled plans to proceed to Washington by water and flew instead to National Airport in the early evening. The day was cloudy and warm and the temperature still stood above freezing when the British arrived and were greeted by the President. When Press Secretary Stephen Early notified White House correspondents that Churchill was in Washington, he was almost trampled in the rush of newsmen to nearby telephones. Morning newspapers reminded their readers that Churchill was the first British Prime Minister to visit Washington in wartime and the only head of a great nation to cross the Atlantic while his country was in the midst of conflict. Indeed, only two previous Prime Ministers, David Lloyd George and Ramsay MacDonald, had made the trip at all. Churchill himself was no stranger, having visited the country before the turn of the century and on lecture tours before and after World War I.[2]

General Marshall and his colleagues looked with mixed feelings on this meeting with the visitors from overseas. So long as they were out of the war, they had been able to resist many British proposals for arms and material. Committed now to a common cause, the Americans wanted to make certain that they were not used to carry out a purely British strategy. Harry Hopkins had tried to avoid trouble by warning Churchill not to bring a cut-and-dried program to Washington. As Hopkins feared, the Prime Minister's proposed outlines for the conference raised dark suspicions among many of the American military planners.

After the war General Marshall conceded that there "was too much anti-British feeling on our side; more than we should have had. Our people were always ready to find Albion perfidious." He was amused at the lengths to which their doubts led some of his subordinates. "On one occasion our people brought in an objection to something the British wanted. I didn't see anything wrong with the British proposal, but our planners . . . explained that there was an ulterior purpose in this thing. So . . . I had our rebuttal to the proposal. Portal . . . read this memorandum from my planners. Portal said that he drafted the proposal and that it was taken from a memorandum of ours. And it was a fact; he showed it to me. I told him I would do anything in way of reparation. Our own paragraph was the key of our objection." [3]

The General found the British far less suspicious of American aims. "This may not have been a compliment," he said with a chuckle. "They may have just felt we weren't smart enough to cause them trouble." [4]

Fortunately for the British, Marshall seldom took an extreme position. "I made it my business to be on a very warm and understanding basis with the British, and they were appreciative of that," he recalled. He was aware that some of his more isolationist officers and friends believed that he was being overpersuaded by Roosevelt, Hopkins, and other pro-British leaders in the government. [5]

The Prime Minister's installation as a guest and temporary occupant of the White House contributed further to American doubts. Of necessity, he set up his office, map room, and command post near the President's own bedroom. The proximity of his quarters made it possible for him to confer with the President early and late. The continuous flow of advisers and couriers contrasted strangely with the activities of the small American military staff. An arrangement that could only make for closer relations between American and British political leaders created anxieties in the minds of the American military leaders. Because the President failed to keep his staff advised on his discussions with the Prime Minister, the British Chiefs of Staff, who were briefed regularly by Churchill, were often better informed on Roosevelt's thinking than the American service chiefs.

The Prime Minister wasted no time in beginning his person-to-person campaign with the President. On his first evening in Washington as he, Lord Halifax, and Lord Beaverbrook dined at the White House with the President, Secretary Hull, Secretary Stimson, Hopkins, and Undersecretary of State Welles, Churchill outlined his strategy. In an expansive mood and without his military advisers at his elbows, the President seemed to agree to most of his visitor's proposals. It was the sort of situation Marshall and his colleagues dreaded most when the two men were together.

In retrospect General Marshall could see why the British had to take the lead at a time when the Americans, shocked by Pearl Harbor, were looking little beyond the day-to-day problems of saving the Philippines and rushing aid to beleaguered garrisons around the world. Their mistake lay in the assumption that they could draw on United States manpower and weapons as if these had been swept into a common pool for campaigns tailored to suit the interests and convenience of Great Britain. From the British standpoint it was easy to conclude that a course of action favorable to their national interests was simply good strategic sense and that failure of the Americans to agree showed inexperience, immaturity, and bad manners.

A disturbing incident, created by Churchill's aggressiveness and the President's impulsiveness, occurred shortly after the visitors arrived. General Marshall and his staff learned on the morning of the 25th that the President on the previous evening had been wheeled into a meeting with the Prime Minister and some of his advisers. There Roosevelt had agreed to discuss the possibility of turning over to the British reinforcements intended for the Philippines if it proved impossible to get them to MacArthur. Although a practical solution on its face, it could be interpreted as a British effort to write off the Philippines in favor of Singapore. Tempers flared when the head of the British secretariat called for a meeting of the Combined Chiefs of Staff to consider the proposal. Marshall, Arnold, and Eisenhower rushed at once to Stimson's office to protest the matter.

Extremely angry, the Secretary of War resolved to force a showdown. He rang up Harry Hopkins and warned that if Roosevelt persisted in this type of decision-making he would need a new head of the War Department. Already disturbed by the President's habit of accepting casually some of the Prime Minister's proposals, Hopkins found a moment when the two leaders were talking together to drop Stimson's bombshell in their midst. Both men denied that any such agreement had been made. When Roosevelt later made a slighting reference to incorrect statements that were going around, Stimson read him extracts from a record made by a British secretary of the informal discussions of the previous evening. Apparently realizing that he had burned his fingers, Roosevelt assured his military advisers that he had no intention of depriving MacArthur of men and supplies.[6]

General Marshall was painfully aware that the British had the feeling, which he thought "fully justified," that American ground forces were of uncertain value for current operations. The Prime Minister aroused his fears by stressing the role of the United States Navy in protecting the lifelines of the Empire and the increase in the United States Air Force to reinforce British offensive and defensive strength in Europe. Underestimating the requirements of ground troops for the defeat of Germany, Churchill seemed to look upon the building of a large American Army as nothing less than a calamity in that it would absorb most of the weapons and supplies the British would need for the next two years.

From the moment that Marshall and Stark learned that the British were coming to Washington, they agreed that the United States should hold to its former agreements with Great Britain that Germany was the main enemy and its defeat "the key to victory." But they were sorely conscious of current demands in the Pacific and the limitations of their resources. With their forces suffering for lack of reinforcements, they could not withhold aid from the Philippines and the threatened possessions of the Southwest Pacific. In the Atlantic they were thrown back to the capabilities of 1940—to protect Latin America against German threats, to maintain lines of communications to Great Britain, to preserve the security of the British Isles, and to look toward a future return to the Continent. The defeat of Germany remained for them the first order of business and nothing could be spared for sideshows.

Only by recalling the weakness of the United States position in December 1941 is it possible to escape a common misconception of early American strategy and plans. It has been popular to find in America's continental position and wealth of resources a large-scale approach to war that demanded head-on assaults on the enemy and the employment of mass armies. Proponents of a theological approach to history have found in America's Puritan past a predilection for great crusades against evil that required a battle unto the death. The fact that this type of thinking has recurred in American statements both during and since World War II should not blind historians to the views of the military planners at the outset of the conflict.

On December 21, as they studied British proposals for an agenda, the Americans were extremely modest in their plans. They assumed that at the moment the British could do no more than maintain their position in the British Isles and the Middle East and attempt to send reinforcements to the Far East. Any operations other than these "must necessarily be of an opportunist nature, executed with exceedingly small forces and with very doubtful chances of success." The prospects for United States action were more modest still. At the moment it was capable of defending its own coasts against air raids, holding Hawaii, the Panama Canal, and other bases, gradually relieving the British in Iceland, possibly reinforcing the Philippines or the Dutch East Indies, occupying Natal, and perhaps some other base, such as the Cape Verde Islands or the Azores, not seriously defended by the Axis or its sympathizers. It might be necessary, the Americans agreed, to send some troops to the British Isles in the winter or spring. Shipping shortages, they added, "preclude the possibility of executing more than one, or at most two, of these operations concurrently." [7]

General Marshall's handwritten notes summarize the proposals of the Prime Minister and the replies of the President at the opening conference at the White House on the afternoon of December 23. The high points of Churchill's views, carefully worked out on shipboard, had been outlined to the President the evening before. Now, as the British and American military leaders listened, Churchill let his mind range round the world on Allied strategy for the future. Encouraged by recent British victories in Libya, he hoped that he could soon shift forces westward into Tunisia. If Italian and German forces could be defeated in the desert, perhaps the Vichy French might be encouraged to invite the Allies into their North African possessions. It was an alluring prospect. Exhilarated by prospects of clearing one shore of the Mediterranean and of uniting British forces in the Atlantic and the Middle East, he asked for American cooperation in preparing expeditions that could move quickly into French Africa, with or without an invitation, if a situation developed favorable to the Allied cause. The British had 55,000 troops ready to load on ship at short notice and capable of landing in North Africa within three weeks. If the United States could support this effort, Churchill thought it might be successful.[8]

In order to release trained British units for service in the Middle East and for strengthening the North African effort, the Prime Minister proposed that the United States dispatch divisions to Iceland and Northern Ireland to relieve his forces. Stressing the value of even a few bomber squadrons in damaging German and aiding French morale, he asked that American units assist in British air offensives against Germany. Basic to the success of his whole plan for the future were continued naval and air superiority in the Atlantic, the maintenance of sea communications between the United States and Britain, and the protection of the British Isles against attack—propositions on which Marshall and Stark were in complete agreement.[9]

The Prime Minister refrained from asking too much at the outset. He pleased General Marshall by agreeing that it was unwise to send American troops to the Middle East. In the Pacific he proffered aid in containing the Japanese advance. He spoke confidently of Singapore's ability to hold out for another six months and of efforts to strengthen Burma and hold on to the Burma Road—an unwarranted optimism about possibilities in the Far East matched only by the confidence of the Americans.

President Roosevelt was also in good form. As he talked, however, the British became uneasily aware that his support of some of the Prime Minister's proposals had weakened since the night before. They assumed that he had been in conference with his advisers. Instead, he seems merely to have returned to Secretary Stimson's outline of December 20 that gave the War Department's views on questions to be considered at the conference. He agreed with Churchill on the value of sending United States bomber squadrons to Great Britain, the importance of substituting American for British units in Northern Ireland, the elimination of a mixed force in Iceland by relieving all other troops there with American soldiers, and the necessity of finding a way to capitalize on favorable developments in North Africa.[10]

The Atlantic Theater

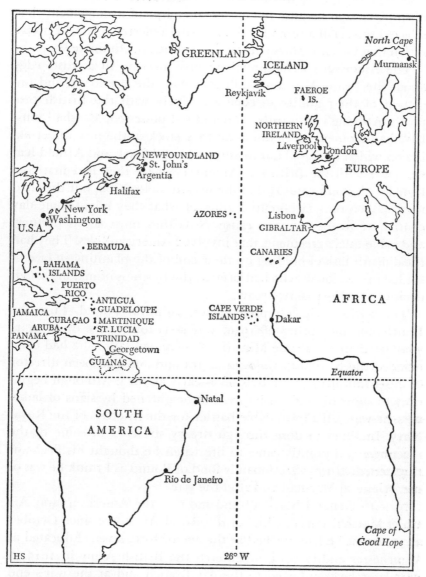

The plenary session was followed on the morning of December 24 by the first formal meeting of the British and United States Chiefs of Staff, which took place in the Federal Reserve Building, clean-cut in its newness and contrasting strangely with the aging and severely utilitarian World War I structures across Constitution Avenue where the War and Navy Departments were located. The staff organization was less than desirable. The delay of the opening session because the officer in charge of arrangements had selected too small a room for the meeting reflected a lack of preparation that General Marshall was determined to eliminate.[11]

The Americans went into their first meeting ill at ease, edgy about the Prime Minister's influence over the President, and uncertain of their ability to cope effectively with the British proposals. Although outwardly calm and self-possessed, Marshall must have had moments of doubt as he took stock of the new undertaking on which he was about to enter. He and Stark and Arnold had sat down with the British at Argentia, where they had first conferred with Pound and Dill of the present delegation, but they had then spoken only as potential allies of what they might some day contribute to the common cause. Now they must act as partners and make final agreements that involved American lives. They had the difficult task of holding up their end of the planning in face of skilled professionals who had been at the business of making tough decisions for the past two years.

The senior British representative, Admiral Pound, First Sea Lord since the spring of 1939, was sixty-four, only three years younger than the Prime Minister. A seasoned sailor, he had commanded the battleship *Colossus* at Jutland and had been director of the Admiralty's plans division as early as 1922. Although beginning to show his age, an impression heightened by signs of lameness, he was still a formidable battler for the interests of the Royal Navy. Inclined to doze through dreary stretches of some of the meetings, he instantly came to life when he thought his fleet was threatened. "I was affectionately fond of Pound as I think he was of me," General Marshall said after the war.[12]

New to General Marshall and most of the Americans was Air Chief Marshal Portal, Chief of the Royal Air Force since October 1940, a post he had reached at the age of forty-seven. Educated at Winchester and Oxford, he entered the British Army in 1915. A year later he transferred to the Air Branch and at the war's end accepted a permanent commission in the Royal Air Force. From March to October 1940 he headed the British Bomber Command, directing attacks on German bases in France and the Low Countries and helping to frustrate enemy plans for the invasion of Britain. "Swarthy, eagle-beaked, and young," keenly alert to everything around him, he instantly gained the respect of the Americans at the conference. Calm, unruffled in argument, with what General Marshall called "the best mind of the lot," he followed the most tedious arguments, prepared to find the defects in a faulty presentation.[13]

Throughout the war in sessions with the British Chiefs of Staff, Portal and Marshall took the lead in trying to reach understandings when matters reached an impasse. General Laurence S. Kuter, who sat in on a number of conferences of the Combined Chiefs of Staff, observed that in later conferences when a controversy reached the boiling point, "with Admiral King red in the neck and inarticulate, General Arnold apparently furious but quiet, Brooke equally red-faced and inarticulate, it was Lord Portal on the British side and General Marshall on the American side that calmed things down in very simple language: 'We can't blow up on points like this. Something has to be done which one side or the other isn't going to agree on. Let's get on with it.' " [14]

Marshall's closest friend among the British was Sir John Dill, who was to serve in Washington until his death near the end of 1944. He came to the Washington conference under difficult circumstances, having been relieved of his post as Chief of the Imperial General Staff only a few weeks before. Although a year younger than Marshall, the Belfast-born field marshal had become a brigadier in World War I. Like Marshall, Dill spent much of his career as a staff officer. He became Commandant of the Staff College at Camberley in the 1930s, where his fine brain impressed many of the future officers of World War II. After two years as Director of Military Plans at the War Office, 1934-36, he became commander of British Forces in Palestine with the rank of lieutenant general. Early in 1940 he was leading the 1st Corps of the British Expeditionary Force in France when Churchill recalled him to succeed Ironside as head of the British Army.

In the most trying days of the war Dill had struggled to prepare the Army for greater sacrifices and to restore the units that had been badly battered at Dunkerque. Worn with anxiety by the mortal illness of his first wife, who had been paralyzed in 1940, he fought a losing battle with the Prime Minister, who insisted on measure after measure that Dill considered impractical. Dill found that he was unable to throw off his cares and incapable of coping effectively with Churchill's vigorous demands. His body and spirit exhausted, Dill as well as the Prime Minister was aware, by November 1941, that he could no longer carry the burden of his post. Churchill replaced him with General Brooke and proposed to send Dill to Bombay as governor. For a dedicated soldier it was a bitter ending to a long career. Then, as he prepared to set off for his new assignment, the Japanese struck at Pearl Harbor and the Prime Minister proposed his trip to the United States. At General Brooke's urging, Churchill included the weary soldier in the British delegation, opening the way to Dill's last and finest assignment.

In suggesting that Dill go to Washington as a possible permanent representative of the Prime Minister in the American capital Brooke may have been merely attempting to soften the blow of the recent demotion. In accepting this advice Churchill may have acted from similar motives. Whatever their reason, nothing they did during the war was more effective in creating good relations between the American and British military staffs. In his sincerity, frankness, and self-discipline Dill in many ways resembled Marshall. The two men had liked each other at once on meeting at Argentia and had agreed before parting to keep in touch with each other. The British commander had written candidly about his supply problems, and Marshall had moved at once to help him. Their correspondence became increasingly cordial and they had disposed of formalities of address before they saw each other again in Washington.[15]

A man of great warmth and charm, Dill later won friends in the United States by his openness and ability to see Allied problems as if he were an American. It was a tribute to his breadth of view that Marshall worried lest Churchill and Brooke would feel that Dill was becoming too thoroughly American in his outlook. The friendship of the two officers grew and flourished and became one of the finest legends of Anglo-American cooperation. By their ability to speak frankly without rancor and by their confidence in each other, some of the sharpest British and American differences were smoothed away and the basis laid for full trust and confidence.[16]

Joining the American representatives at the meeting was Admiral King, who had been named "Commander-in-Chief, United States Fleet" six days earlier. In an Executive Order that greatly increased the significance of the post and relocated it in the Navy Department in Washington, the President gave King "supreme command of the United States Navy and the operating forces of the naval coastal frontier commands . . . directly responsible, under the general direction of the Secretary of Navy, to the President of the United States." [17] Until March, when Stark was sent to London as "Commander, U. S. Naval Forces, Europe," King had the task of planning and directing the actual operations of the Navy's fighting forces while the Chief of Naval Operations dealt mainly with the professional administration of the Navy. On Stark's departure, King also became Chief of Naval Operations.

The first session was remarkable for the variety of topics touched on as the British and American representatives brought forward dozens of projects for consideration. Stark and Marshall stilled British fears on future strategy by announcing that the Japanese attack in the Pacific had not changed the earlier understanding that the Allies should concentrate on defeating Germany first.[18]

Looking toward a landing in North Africa, the British were surprised to find the Americans still worried about the security of South America. Both Stark and Marshall still believed in the existence of a German threat to Brazil and European possessions in the Caribbean. Stark caught the attention of the British with the reminder that the Guianas, particularly vulnerable to German machinations, provided from their refineries 95 per cent of the oil sent to the eastern seaboard and one-half of Britain's Lend-Lease allotment. Admiral Pound at once promised to press for diplomatic action that would permit the United States to move into Dutch Guiana.

Despite dismal news from the Pacific, the United States Chiefs of Staff shared Prime Minister Churchill's optimism about holding on to the Philippines and Singapore. In the face of mounting disaster, they still expected to bar the enemy from the Dutch East Indies, to safeguard the Burma Road, and to develop Australia into an effective base for future operations.

The warm glow of these false hopes shone through the gloom on Christmas Eve in the short ceremony at twilight as Churchill joined the President on the balcony of the Executive Mansion to watch the lighting of the tree in the White House garden. The day had been warm, with the temperature going to about 60 in the afternoon, and a crowd of some 20,000 had assembled. The President spoke briefly, and the Prime Minister won the hearts of his hearers by saying that he could not "feel myself a stranger here in the centre and at the summit of the United States." Next morning he and the President went to Foundry Methodist Church and sang together the hymns of Christmas. For a moment, as Churchill had suggested in his brief address, they caught the joy and promise of the season.[19]

Christmas for the Marshalls, as for many American families, contrasted strangely with the one of the previous year. Only Clifton, soon to enlist in the Army, was to spend the holidays with them. Young Tupper Brown was not old enough for his parents to come down from Poughkeepsie for the holidays. Molly Winn, who had been married only the year before, was in Panama with her husband and not quite two-month-old baby. Mrs. Marshall fretted because there was not sufficient transport to bring her and the other families of service personnel back to the United States. It would be May before the Winns returned.

Instead of members of the family, guests from overseas and Washington joined the Marshalls for the midday Christmas meal. Lord and Lady Halifax, Admiral and Mrs. King, Beaverbrook, Pound, Portal, and Dill made up the list. The dinner was turned into a double celebration when they discovered, belatedly, that it was Field Marshal Dill's birthday. Mrs. Marshall at once suggested a cake with candles, but she realized she couldn't trust her cook's baking capabilities. When she discovered that pastry shops in Washington had been emptied by holiday shoppers, she sent into action Sergeant Powder, the General's resourceful orderly. Using skills in foraging that he had learned through long service in the Army, he not only wangled a cake from a downtown bakery but found the last set of British and American flags, made in Japan, in a five-and-ten-cent store, to add to the birthday candles.[20]

The meal was successful, although interrupted sporadically by London's reactions to a diplomatic incident created the previous evening when Free French Forces loyal to General Charles de Gaulle had occupied the Vichy-administered islands of St. Pierre and Miquelon in the St. Lawrence River. Secretary of State Hull's violent condemnation of the action and demands that the Free French be thrown out of the islands soon had the wires busy between London and Washington. The British Ambassador was summoned frequently to the telephone and then returned to confer with Lord Beaverbrook over the proper course of action to be recommended.

The high points of the day were Sir John Dill's birthday cake, his first, he said, since he was a small boy, and a "singing" Western Union "Happy Birthday" message, which Dill's wife Nancy, whom he had married in October, had cabled from the United Kingdom. Unfortunately the full performance failed to take place when Secret Service agents refused to permit the messenger to enter.

On the day after Christmas the British and United States Chiefs of Staff resumed the discussion of unified command that General Marshall had sprung the afternoon before. He was to consider it one of his major contributions to the winning of the war. Closer cooperation between the United States Army and Navy had been a favorite concept pushed by the General since he became Chief of Staff. He had worked closely with Admiral Stark and impressed on General Short when he went to Hawaii in February 1941 the importance of working closely with the Navy. One of the last problems he discussed with MacArthur before Pearl Harbor was closer relations with Admiral Hart in the Philippines. As recently as December 19 he had helped prepare a directive by which the Army and Navy commands were unified in the Caribbean. He realized that the need for unity between the various commands in the Pacific would be necessary now that several nations were engaged in fighting the Japanese. His views on this subject were strengthened on the 21st by a cable from Lieutenant Colonel Francis G. Brink, American representative at the recently held Allied conference at Singapore, urging the immediate formation of a supreme command over American, British, Dutch, and Australian forces in the Pacific.[21]

Colonel Brink's recommendation gained additional weight as a result of the episode on Christmas Eve when President Roosevelt had lightly agreed to Churchill's proposal that reinforcements intended for MacArthur would be diverted to Singapore if it appeared they could not get through to the Philippines. Although strong action by Stimson and the Chiefs of Staff had headed off this suggestion, General Marshall was convinced that only the appointment of a supreme commander for the Pacific would permit a logical arrangement for dealing with similar proposals in the future. When the British called for a special session on Christmas afternoon to discuss the question of reinforcements for MacArthur, he seized the opportunity to propose a unified command in the Pacific.

After a routine beginning, dealing with North Africa and oil supplies for Australian bases, the question of Allied dispositions in the Pacific was introduced. General Marshall at once grasped the initiative. He took the view "that it was premature to make such a decision." Such questions would come up again and again until unity of command was achieved over all Allied forces and all categories of force in the Far East. No local commander, he believed, could see the situation whole. Only a commander responsible for the whole theater could decide the question of the allocation of defense forces.[22] Explaining carefully that he spoke only for himself, he insisted that the most important consideration before them was unity of command. "I am convinced," he said, "that there must be one man in command of the entire theater—air, ground, and ships. We cannot manage by cooperation. Human frailties are such that there would be emphatic unwillingness to place portions of troops under another service. If we can make a plan for unified command now, it will solve nine-tenths of our troubles." [23]

General Marshall read addresses poorly, but when he spoke without a manuscript and from deep feeling he achieved an eloquence that was never forgotten by his hearers or recaptured in type. Strongly committed to his proposal, he argued that the objections to a single command were "much less than the hazards that must be faced" by the Allies if they did not achieve it. He called for one man, operating under a directive from a combined body in Washington, to direct activities in each theater. "We had to come to this in the First World War," he continued, "but it was not until 1918 that it was accomplished, and much valuable time, blood, and treasure had been needlessly sacrificed. If we could decide on a unified command now, it would be a great advance over what was accomplished" during that war.[24]

If he had hoped that, by raising the specter of divided counsels preceding the appointment of Marshal Foch as generalissimo late in the war, he could win immediate acceptance of his views, General Marshall was mistaken. Admiral Stark was noncommittal when the Chief of Staff ended his appeal. The British were obviously unwilling to discuss the matter without sounding out the Prime Minister. To parry the suggestion, Air Marshal Portal argued that once the highest authority had decided on allocations and issued a directive, everything else would move smoothly. Marshall strongly disagreed. The Americans and British were in complete agreement on allocations, he countered, but unity of command had certainly not been achieved. Portal won his postponement by asking that a study of distribution of forces, based on whether the Philippines held or not, should first be made. This task was assigned to the senior members of the British-American planning committee. On this note of agreement the conference had adjourned for Christmas dinner.[25]

Perceiving that he had made a tactical blunder by failing to prepare the ground for his sweeping proposal, General Marshall moved at once to correct his mistake. He turned to General Eisenhower at the close of the meeting and directed him to draft immediately a letter of instruction for the supreme commander of the Pacific area, outlining his mission, defining his authority, and safeguarding each nation's control over those matters pertaining to national sovereignty. He hoped by this means "to convince the other members of the conference that no real risk would be involved to the interests of any of the Associated Powers, while on the other hand great profits should result." [26]

In the midst of detailed discussions of the proposed expedition to West Africa on December 26, General Marshall found time to outline his command plan to Secretary Stimson and Assistant Secretary McCloy. He confided to them his willingness to give the Pacific Command to General Wavell if that appointment would win British approval.

On the following morning the Chief of Staff dictated a suggested agreement on unity of command for which he hoped to win the President's backing. Delighted with the draft, Secretary Stimson proposed that Marshall and Arnold accompany him to the White House at 10 a.m. "The President fully approved of the plan which General Marshall has fathered and at the close of the conference . . . asked me if I would tell Knox about it," Stimson wrote at the end of their successful session.[27]

At noon the General made his appeal for Navy support in a special meeting with Navy Department representatives in Admiral Stark's office. Only King had spoken up for the proposal in its early stages, and Stimson believed that the bulk of the admirals were "pretty stubborn" in their opposition.[28]

General Marshall first won agreement to a united command in the Pacific. Then he took up the more difficult question of giving the supreme command to a British ground commander. With Australia, New Zealand, Singapore, and British and Dutch islands at stake, it would be difficult for Great Britain to accept an American for this post. Wavell was the logical choice. In Africa and the Middle East he had gained experience in successful campaigns and in those ending with a setback. He was accustomed to moving large bodies of troops and he knew India. Particularly important was the fact that with him in command the Prime Minister's fears that troops would be withdrawn from the defense of Singapore would be quieted.[29]

Some Navy leaders questioned the selection of a British officer for the command but ended by conceding that the step might be necessary to win Churchill's consent. Admiral King clinched the argument by throwing his support to Marshall's proposal. Colonel Robinett, who had accompanied his chief to the meeting, recorded: "When King said this all the other Navy people smiled and concurred in their own way. . . . Admiral Stark finally gave his blessing though I think he had always followed General Marshall's lead. The Chief has gone a long way toward winning his battle." [30]

With his position now clearly outlined and strongly buttressed by presidential and Navy backing, General Marshall on December 27 resumed his plea to the British Chiefs of Staff. Such a scheme had never been imposed on the British Navy before and, in Stimson's phrase, "they kicked like bay steers." [31] The Chief of Staff conceded that it would be impossible to choose anyone for supreme command who would have full technical knowledge of all the services. By selecting an officer of good judgment they could minimize this problem. Marshall cited the safeguards written into the draft directive preventing the commander from exploiting one area of his theater at the expense of another. In the Pacific the Associated Powers were opposed by an enemy possessing unity of command in its highest sense. He warned that in light of the dispersion of

Allied forces in the Pacific, no plan could be "made worse" than the one then existing.[32]

To General Marshall's surprise, the British who had been resisting the entire concept of unified command suddenly shifted their ground and criticized his plan as restricting the supreme commander too strongly. He promptly agreed, saying that he had tried to be a realist in drawing up the paper. Seeing the British yielding, Admiral Stark quickly declared that the important thing was to establish the principle of unified command and then revise it as needed. The conference ended on a happy note with the combined staffs agreeing to prepare a directive for presentation to the President and Prime Minister. General Marshall recalled proudly fifteen years later, "The chief of the naval planners rushed to the door to shake hands with me and put his arm around me, which surprised me. And Dill followed me and threw his arms around me, and still another one acted explosively." [33]

The backing of the Prime Minister still had to be won. On first hearing of the Chief of Staff's plea of December 24 he had expressed strong doubts as to the desirability of the plan. During the evening of the 27th Churchill argued the matter with President Roosevelt at the White House, insisting that there was a great difference between one man's commanding the widely scattered forces in the Pacific and Foch's handling of Allied troops from the Channel to the Vosges in 1918. Instead of Marshall's proposal, he suggested that each service act on its own with its individual commander reporting to the Supreme War Council in Washington. Lord Beaverbrook, who was listening to the discussion, passed a note to Harry Hopkins, advising: "You should work on Churchill. He is being advised. He is open-minded and needs discussion." [34] Hopkins found an opportunity later to beg the Prime Minister not to turn down the proposition until he heard the name of the officer the Americans had in mind for the command.

General Marshall's showdown with the British leader, arranged by Hopkins, came in Churchill's bedroom on the morning of the 28th.[35] The Prime Minister had continued in Washington his practice of staying up late, sleeping late, and then remaining in bed until lunchtime while he dictated letters or talked business with visitors. Marshall found him propped up in bed, ready for action. Aware from his talks with Roosevelt that a man on his feet had an advantage in an argument, the General walked up and down as he talked. Churchill began his attack by observing that a ship was a very special thing and that it was therefore hard to expect the Navy to put its vessels under an Army commander. Once a battalion commander but twice First Lord of the Admiralty, the Prime Minister asked belligerently what an Army officer could know about handling a ship. Marshall hotly retorted, "What the devil does a naval officer know about handling a tank?" He was not trying to enlist sailors as tank drivers, he continued, but to get unified control of the armed forces.

"I told him," Marshall recalled later, "I was not interested in Drake and Frobisher, but I was interested in having a united front against Japan, an enemy which was fighting furiously. I said if we didn't do something right away we were finished in the war." Perhaps the doughty old statesman was aware that he would have to yield, but he continued to hold out. Breaking off the meeting to take a bath, he came out a few minutes later with a towel wrapped around him to declare that Marshall would have to take the worst with the best. With this apparent warning of an unfavorable decision, he summoned the British Chiefs of Staff. As Marshall left the room, he met Portal and Pound coming in and saw that they were both wearing gloomy expressions.[36]

Marshall had in fact won his fight. On the 28th the Prime Minister informed the British Cabinet:

> Last night President urged upon me appointment of a single officer to command Army, Navy, and Air Force of Britain, America, and Dutch, and this morning General Marshall visited me at my request and pleaded case with great conviction. American Navy authorities take opposite view, but it is certain that a new far-reaching arrangement will have to be made. The man the President has in mind is General Wavell. Marshall has evidently gone far into detailed scheme and has draft letter of instructions. So far I have been critical of plan, and while admiring broadmindedness of offer have expressed anxiety about effects on American opinion. Chiefs of Staff have been studying matter all day and tonight I will send you my considered advice after receiving their views.[37]

In the course of the day the Prime Minister decided that he could not wait for an answer from London. After talking further with Roosevelt he cabled: "I have agreed with President, subject to Cabinet approval, that we should accept his proposals, most strongly endorsed by General Marshall." The arrangement included the establishment of unity of command in the Southwest Pacific with Wavell as supreme commander and an American, probably General Brett, as deputy. Wavell's directive would be issued by a joint body responsible to the President and Prime Minister.[38]

Now that he had accepted Marshall's proposal, the Prime Minister pressed the War Cabinet to approve it, saying that "I have not attempted to argue the case for and against our accepting this broadminded and selfless American proposal, of merits of which as a war-winner I have become convinced." He called for quick action, adding that a decision would probably be necessary before he returned from a short trip to Canada on January 1.[39]

Secretary Stimson, eagerly following the course of negotiations, welcomed Churchill's action, a development "due largely—almost wholly—to Marshall's initiative and vigor." Stimson believed that if the example of the Pacific could be followed elsewhere, the Allies could "avoid a year of disaster which . . . attended the Allies in the last war arising out of disunity." [40]

Many of the British were unhappy with the arrangement. Calling the proposal "wild and half-baked," General Brooke condemned it for its emphasis on the western Pacific rather than the Indian Ocean. Sir John Dill, who had accepted the concept of unified command, nonetheless feared that it would be fatal "to have a British commander responsible for the disasters that are coming to the Americans as well as ourselves." [41] A member of General Marshall's staff agreed: "General Wavell has been chosen for supreme commander in the Southwest Pacific. The poor fellow must again plan a defensive role in a desperate situation. What a job he must undertake in an effort to coordinate and fight [with] the air, sea, and land forces of such diverse elements as British, Indian, Dutch colonial, Australian, and American over such a vast area of scattered land masses." [42]

In proposing the command arrangement for the Pacific, General Marshall made no claim that it could assure immediate victory. He was aware that the command "covered a region from Burma and India down to Australia, the Philippines, and so forth, and one man couldn't possibly get at it very well." But as matters stood, "the thing was so messed up that no one was in command anywhere." It was therefore necessary "to do something." [43]

Overlooked by many critics was the fact that the ABDA Command, far-flung and loosely organized as it was, gave some unity to an existing British and American command structure in the Pacific and Far East that reached from Hawaii to India. When a conference in Washington had to be repeatedly interrupted to discuss whether cargoes should be sent to Manila, Singapore, or Australia, it was vital to have that decision considered by a commander who had responsibilities for the defense of all three.

In making his recommendation General Marshall was looking beyond the immediate situation in the Pacific. His hope was to open the way to the establishment of unified command for all theaters to which the United States sent troops. ABDA Command was not ideal, but it served as an opening for over-all acceptance of this principle.

Of equal concern to General Marshall was the nature and composition of the Allied council that would give the supreme commanders their directives. Among the decisions that had to be made was whether there should be two committees of equal authority, sitting in Washington and London; whether all of the Allied and Associated Powers should be represented by political and military officials on such councils; and what the status of British representatives to the supreme council in Washington should be if a decision were made to have one joint body located in Washington.

Early in the discussions the British indicated a willingness to have a single council sitting in Washington to which they would appoint officers to represent the Chiefs of Staff in London. A proposal that their delegation should be headed by Sir John Dill, who would serve as representative of the Prime Minister at a level above the Chiefs of Staff, immediately drew American fire. General Marshall explained gently that if he would accept anyone for such a position it would be Dill. He was unalterably opposed, however, to interposing an additional level of authority between the service chiefs and the political heads of Great Britain and the United States. Embarrassed, Dill suggested that the matter be dropped.

Seeing that an imperfect arrangement might result from hasty action, General Marshall recommended the adoption of a simple provision that directives would be issued by a combined council later to be established. He changed his mind, at Admiral King's insistence that unity of command in the Pacific required agreement on the control organization. Marshall then moved that the conference accept a British proposal for stationing in Washington a Joint Staff Mission that would represent the British Chiefs of Staff in regular meetings with their American counterparts. Without debate the military representatives established a committee called the Combined Chiefs of Staff to direct Anglo-American strategy until the war's end. In international conferences the British Chiefs of Staff would act for themselves. Otherwise they made their wishes known through the Joint Staff Mission, headed by Field Marshal Dill.

The new organization required a change in the American staff arrangement, owing to the need to provide some counterpart for the Royal Air Force representation on the British side. General Marshall had taken General Arnold with him to the Argentia conference in August 1941 and had invited him to be present as a full-fledged member at the Arcadia conference. Thoroughly aware of the dangers of trying to put through a basic change in organization, he resorted to a pleasant subterfuge. Knowing that the President was about to issue a statement about his military advisers, he arranged with Marvin McIntyre, the President's secretary, to include the name of General Arnold among the Chiefs of Staff. Thereafter, without special legislation, "Hap" Arnold sat with Marshall and King as members of the Joint Chiefs of Staff. Technically the first meeting of this body took place on February 9, 1942. No formal document was ever issued establishing such a group. In actuality it was born at the Arcadia meeting.

The larger organization, now called the Combined Chiefs of Staff, provided the Allies in the Second World War with an effective instrument for close cooperation that was completely lacking in the First. Even General Brooke, whose strong criticisms included "the false arrangements made in Washington"—the Combined Chiefs of Staff organization—had to agree finally that it was "the most efficient [organization] that had ever been evolved for coordinating and correlating the war strategy and effort of two allies." [44]

No coalition requiring the combined efforts of two great powers, each jealous of its traditions and prerogatives, ever functioned more smoothly. Much of its success depended on a common purpose and a common language. Equally important was the fact that, in the early stages of the alliance, the two powers contributed much the same in men and matériel to the common venture and commanded mutual respect for their views. Toward the end of the war, when the United States became completely ascendant in manpower and production, the British had no alternative but to go along with American strategic views.[45]

Above all, the Combined Chiefs of Staff organization worked well because of Marshall's close friendship with Sir John Dill, chief British representative in Washington. In an amazing balancing act, Dill was able to represent British wishes to the Americans without antagonizing them and to warn London of the limits of American forbearance without arousing suspicion on the part of his own chiefs that he had become a captive of his hosts. For his part, Marshall continued to be more favorable to the British than most of his advisers and was willing to listen sympathetically to Dill's presentation of Britain's case. His respect for the Field Marshal's mind, fairness, and integrity grew rapidly as their intimacy increased.

Although Dill never permitted himself to reach the point attained by United States Ambassador Walter Hines Page in World War I, when he would read a protest by his government to the British Foreign Secretary and then suggest they work together on a reply, he rapidly evolved a formula that permitted him to pass on to his chiefs the full flavor of the Chief of Staff's studied wrath. "He would bring his stuff to me and read it," Marshall recalled, "but not say that Churchill had asked him for my reactions. I would react, I am ashamed to say, with curse words. Dill would write it down. Then he would say that Churchill had asked for my views. He would show me the notes and we would strengthen the language. . . ." Dill then reported that the Chief of Staff had been very rude when he heard of the message. But the reaction had been recorded outside regular channels and the chance of friction had been reduced. On the British side, Dill smoothed away the rough edges of some of the official messages entrusted to his care and explained to the Chief of Staff the compelling reasons his colleagues in London had for insisting on some of their demands.[46]

To some British observers it seemed that Dill was educating Marshall to the realities of world strategy; to some Americans it appeared that Dill was taking advantage of his friendship with Marshall to lead him into British traps.[47] So far as Marshall was concerned, there was no question of Dill's great worth. As the British representative, Dill defended his country's position in conversation with the American Chief of Staff. But he went no further than Marshall wanted him to go. Early in their relationship, Marshall sensed what Dill could give him and his value in explaining the American position to the British. Instead of being worried about Dill's pro-British influence, he feared that London would decide that the Field Marshal was too pro-American in his views. If, as Marshall believed, only his strenuous efforts saved Dill's job during the last year of the Britisher's life, his intervention served both the cause of the United States and Great Britain.[48]

General Marshall's final service to the cause of Allied cooperation during the conference came in the debate over the establishment of the special board under the Combined Chiefs of Staff to allocate production. For months before the conference the British had been seriously alarmed over American failure to decide on an orderly method of allocating munitions to the military services of the United States and the Associated Powers. They were equally concerned over the delay in developing an industrial program that would insure the production needed for victory.

The American military leaders welcomed British pressure for a more effective machinery of control. As early as August 1941 Marshall and Stark had tried vainly to place the allocation of military matériel under the Joint Chiefs of Staff. After Pearl Harbor the President attempted to meet their request by appointing Hopkins, Marshall, and Stark as members of a strategic munitions board to establish programs for allocating munitions to the United States and the countries receiving defense aid. They had not held any formal meetings before the Arcadia conference.

At the end of the first week of January 1942 a British representative suggested a combined committee in Washington to make bulk allocations to Great Britain and British protégé nations (the Dominions, France, Netherlands, Egypt, and Turkey), with the actual distribution to be made by a British committee. Few propositions could have been devised that would more quickly arouse

American suspicions that the British were planning to use United States supplies to serve purely national interests.[49]

On the next to last day of the Arcadia conference the British delegation formally presented a plan authorizing the establishment of guidelines to govern the distribution of available weapons of war. General Marshall agreed with the proposal but insisted that there be no duplication in London of the controlling agency. He had no objection to the parallel allocation committees in London and Washington but held that "there could be only one Combined Chiefs of Staff" to give broad directives on the allocation of matériel.[50]

At strong British urgings the United States Chiefs of Staff finally agreed that "finished war matériel should be allocated in accordance with strategic needs." They rewrote a draft agreement to emphasize Marshall's point that allocating committees in Washington and London would be under the Combined Chiefs of Staff.[51]

Although the United States Chiefs of Staff signed the statement reluctantly, it gave General Marshall a weapon in his later discussions with the President and Prime Minister. Having won his battle at the Chiefs of Staff level, he found that he had to wage another with his political superiors. Much earlier in the conference Hopkins had suggested the creation of a two-man civilian board, with an American and a British member, to advise on the allocation of war matériel. Beaverbrook had gone further and asked for a supreme command over supplies as well as strategy, with Hopkins coordinating production in the United States, Great Britain, and Canada. By mid-January these two ideas had been merged in a proposal by which a board of two parts, one in Washington and one in London, would report directly to the President and Prime Minister and be independent of the Combined Chiefs of Staff.[52]

Marshall found himself back in a debate that he thought ended. Although ever the stanch supporter of civilian control of grand strategy and national policy, he was firmly set against the establishment of a civilian body that could interfere with established plans by refusing to allocate matériel. As a former aide of Pershing, he was thoroughly aware of the World War I commander's views on keeping control of supply operations. Possibly Marshall also feared that a civilian director would be inclined to grant the British a degree of control over American military activities that they could not get from the Combined Chiefs of Staff.

A few minutes before British and American representatives filed into the President's White House office for their last meeting, Roosevelt summoned Marshall for a brief chat. In the presence of Harry Hopkins, the Chief Executive handed the Chief of Staff a proposed draft of an order setting up boards under Hopkins and Beaverbrook and making them independent of the Chiefs of Staff. Marshall quickly made clear that his views had undergone no change. He added that if control of supply matters by the Combined Chiefs of Staff in Washington was not accepted, he could not continue to accept the responsibilities of his office. Although it seems likely that his hint at resignation was rhetorical rather than deeply serious, he impressed Roosevelt by his earnest opposition. The President turned at once to Hopkins, apparently expecting that Hopkins would support the two-board proposal. To Marshall's surprise and pleasure, Hopkins agreed completely with the Chief of Staff.[53]

In the conference that followed, the President presented the General's case, calling on Marshall and Hopkins to repeat their arguments. When Churchill and Beaverbrook debated the question, pointing to the possibility of disagreements, Hopkins suggested that in case of disputes the civilian board members could appeal to the President and Prime Minister. Reluctantly Churchill agreed to try the arrangement for one month. Pleased at this concession, Roosevelt quickly closed the bargain by saying, "We will call it a preliminary agreement and try it out that way." As a result, Munitions Assignment Boards were set up in Washington and London shortly after the meeting and continued in operation during the rest of the war. Marshall's stand was firmly upheld.[54]

For a third time in three weeks, Marshall had appeared as the most forceful proponent of Allied command unity and of a strong Combined Chiefs of Staff organization centered in Washington. The Prime Minister now singled him out for special treatment. When Churchill flew down to Florida on January 5 for a short vacation, he begged the President to send Marshall along. He used the opportunity to become better acquainted with the American Chief of Staff and to explore a number of questions that had been raised at the conference.[55]

Churchill had found that in every showdown between British and American representatives over the issues of command, the President had supported his Chief of Staff. But he was too clever to have missed the basic point on which Roosevelt and General Marshall differed. In speaking of the proposed North African operation, the Chief of Staff had emphasized that a "failure in this first venture would have an extremely adverse effect on the morale of the American people." [56] The President took a slightly different view. As noted by General Marshall, the President in the first conference "considered it very important to morale, to give the people of this country a feeling that they are in the war, to give the Germans the reverse effect, to have American troops somewhere in active fighting across the Atlantic." [57] Roosevelt agreed with his Chief of Staff on the need for victory, but his emphasis was on action soon. By playing on the divergence between the two approaches, Churchill was to find the means of winning Roosevelt to his strategy of invading North Africa in the fall of 1942.

XIII

Streamlining for Action

WEEKS before Arcadia General Marshall had called the War Department the poorest command post in the Army. Within hours after war began he told the members of his secretariat that "the time was long past when matters could be debated and discussed and carried on *ad infinitum.*" He ordered them to "get action where action was needed with or without reference to the deputy chiefs of staff but . . . with a brief note to the [Chief of Staff] on the action taken in his name." [1] This was the opening move in a whirlwind campaign that was to shake the War Department as it had not been shaken since the turn of the century.

The General demanded "a drastically complete change, wiping out Civil War institutions" in the agency.[2] The General Staff, established in 1903 as the War Department's planning and coordinating organization, had, he said later, "lost track of its purpose of existence. It had become a huge, bureaucratic, red-tape-ridden operating agency. It slowed down everything." [3] To cure these ills he decided in late November to order General McNarney back from London to head a committee to reorganize the War Department.

Since 1940 there had been clear signs that the machinery meant for use in case of war was geared to a World War I situation, not to the new conflict that loomed on the horizon. It was painfully evident that the War Department was not up to the demands of a rapidly growing Army and Air Force. General McNair had been reminding Marshall for several months that General Headquarters must make radical changes, and General Arnold was pushing the Air Force's claims for greater autonomy. Amid the General Staff divisions, the Chiefs of Arms, the Technical services, and the numerous commands and agencies that appealed to him for decisions, Marshall was drowning in a sea of papers.

Students of the War Department's organization on the eve of World War II have estimated that at least sixty-one officers had the right of direct access to the Chief of Staff and that he had under him thirty major and 350 smaller commands. Over a period of years a number of semi-independent agencies and offices, as jealous of their privileges as a clutch of feudal barons, had grown up. As a result the Chief of Staff and his three deputies were completely submerged in details. General McNarney graphically described the situation: "If a decision had to be made that affected an individual doughboy it had to be referred over to the Chief of Infantry, get his recommendation on it, and back to the General Staff section; it went up to one of the Secretaries, General Staff, and they had at least eight assistant secretaries . . . who did nothing but brief papers so that they could be presented to the Chief of Staff and . . . the three deputy chiefs of staff." [4]

In the end it was the Air Force that brought matters to a head. Since 1940 support had been growing in Congress and the press for an independent air corps. Urging patience on proponents of the idea, Marshall and Arnold continued to make adjustments that gave a larger share of autonomy to the Air. "I tried to give Arnold all the power I could," said General Marshall in 1957. "I tried to make him as nearly as I could Chief of Staff of the Air without any restraint although he was very subordinate. And he was very appreciative of this. My main difficulties came from the fact that he had a very immature staff. They were not immature in years, because they were pretty old, but I used to . . . say [they were] antique staff officers or passé airmen—passé fliers, I guess—because they were not trained at that kind of staff work and they were busy taking stands . . . about promotions. They were already getting more rapid promotions than anybody else. . . . But his staff was always agitating about that. And the less [rank they had] the more they were busy talking about a separate air corps. Well, that was out of the question at that time. They didn't have the trained people for it at all. . . . When they came back after the war, the Air Corps had the nucleus of very able staff officers but that wasn't true at all at the start.

"I gave Arnold his head as much as I possibly could, but my

main trouble was when his staff would get him in trouble. He would always take it very well. In fact, Arnold's disposition to cooperate with me was a very wonderful thing. Because I had to be rough time after time. And he was splendid about the matter and there weren't many difficulties. . . . He had great success in getting the following of the young airmen. They all liked him, they all respected him, and they [felt] he represented their interests. . . .

"Arnold's role was a very difficult one because he had a budding air force. It had a terrific expansion rate to it. And the upper stories of the Air Corps had a great many of these elderly pilots who were not trained in staff development. They had kept away from that in a sense in order to make certain that they didn't lose their flying qualification pay. It was very hard to handle because they would always be senior to any group that we would form to study some particular set of circumstances.

"These young fellows hadn't yet come into any great prominence, like 'Tooey' Spaatz, Vandenberg, and other fliers of that category. So we had a hard time. . . . I know one young officer [General Laurence S. Kuter] who right now is in a leading position in the Air Force. I was very much impressed with him when Arnold brought him in as a major. I said why don't you make that fellow [a general] and he said he couldn't, he would lose all his staff. They would all quit on him if a man that young was made. And he just couldn't do it. So the next list that came in, I just wrote the officer's name on it. Within one month he was a lieutenant colonel. A month after that he had his first star. General Norstad, who is now the supreme commander [in Europe], was another one of the young men I regarded with great respect. . . ." [5]

In the late summer of 1941 General Arnold and Brigadier General Carl Spaatz, Chief of the Air Staff, recommended three separate commands, directly responsible to the Chief of Staff, to control the ground, air, and supply forces of the Army. Suggested months earlier by Colonel William K. Harrison of the War Plans Division and ruled too drastic by his chief, General Gerow, the idea now struck a responsive note.

Gerow thought Marshall could solve his problem by reorganizing General Headquarters. Having tinkered with the workings of that headquarters to give it control over organizing certain task forces for proposed operations in the Atlantic, General McNair disagreed. The air representatives also insisted that only a full-scale reorganization would meet the demands of a rapidly growing air and ground force. This pressure from Arnold and McNair as well as his own desire for a more effective organization led Marshall to come to grips with the problem early in 1942.

Asked why he had settled on General McNarney as the man to put the reorganization into effect, General Marshall replied: "I selected him because he had been an outstanding member of the War Plans Division, was familiar with General Staff procedure and, of course, with the Air Corps, had been close to active operations, at least of the air; had seen British governmental machinery at work, had been in Moscow and Cairo." [6]

Marshall may also have been influenced by an incident that had marked his first meeting with the airman some months before. McNarney had brought in a plan for the General to consider. When the Chief of Staff suggested some change his subordinate disapproved, McNarney blurted out, "Jesus, man, you can't do that!" Marshall shot a startled look at him but said nothing. On the way out of the office the air officer mentioned the incident to the Secretary General Staff. Colonel Ward reassured him, saying, "Don't worry. He likes for people to speak up." [7]

It was not candor alone that won McNarney the assignment. Marshall needed a tough hatchetman with a rhinoceros hide and the nerve to push through the reorganization in the face of the rugged infighting that was almost certain to follow. He was not mistaken in his man. Slight of build, dark of feature, singleminded, a man of few words and those plain-spoken, General McNarney let nothing get in his way when given an assignment. Pennsylvania-born, a classmate of General Eisenhower's at West Point, he was commissioned in the Infantry in 1915. Entering the Aviation Section of the Signal Corps the following year, he helped organize and command several observation groups in France in World War I. Between wars he combined command and staff work with study at the Command and General Staff College and the Army War College. He served one tour in the Intelligence Division and then came to the War Plans Division at the time General Marshall became Chief of Staff. As a member of the Joint Army-Navy Planning Committee, he got a chance to show his toughness by trading epithets with the redoubtable Admiral Kelly Turner. In the spring of 1941 he had gone to London as chief of staff to the Special Observer Group. It was from there that he was summoned near the end of November. He left London on December 6 and was on the way to Lisbon to catch a plane for the United States when he heard the news of the bombing of Pearl Harbor. He arrived in Washington, without his luggage, just in time to be sent to Hawaii as an Army member of the Roberts Commission investigating the Japanese attack. Not until the commission returned to the United States and finished its report near the end of January 1942 did he learn why General Marshall had sent for him.[8]

Realizing that the reorganization was doomed if he gave its opponents time to organize, General Marshall depended on careful planning, minimum publicity, and complete ruthlessness in execution of his plan. He called McNarney in on January 25 and said that too many people were reporting to him. "It was taking too long to get a paper through the War Department. Everybody had to concur. About twenty-eight people had to pass on matters. I can't stand it." He asked for "some kind of organization that would give the Chief of Staff time to devote to strategic policy and the strategic aspects and direction of the war." [9]

It was not a task to be undertaken lightly. The plan Marshall was considering meant downgrading the General Staff divisions, eliminating the Chiefs of Arms, subordinating to a supply chief the Chiefs of Services, and abolishing General Headquarters. A great many proud officials would have their prerogatives diminished or abolished. They were individuals with powerful friends and traditions on their side. If Congress intervened and the press raised an outcry, the resulting battle might be bloody.

For decades the Chiefs of Infantry, Cavalry, Field Artillery, and Coast Artillery—major generals—had exercised great power in training and equipping troops assigned to their particular arm. Jealous of their rights, they insisted on being consulted about any order that might conceivably pertain to their special preserves. They stood for hallowed service loyalties and a special parochialism that made change and speed and development especially difficult to achieve. Integration of the arms and the services into a fighting force was what Marshall wanted and he intended to get it, at the expense of cutting away much that was deeply embedded in the War Department's past.

Careful preparations won much of the battle before the showdown was reached. Marshall told an old friend: "I timed the matter so that two of the Chiefs of Arms and the Adjutant General's tours would expire, and fortunately the two remaining Chiefs of Arms were suited perfectly to more important positions. . . . Chief of Infantry Courtney Hodges, in charge of all Schools, Training Centers, etc., and Joseph A. Green, Coast Artillery, to command the anti-aircraft forces. They would have been too loyal to have opposed in any event; however, with such future prospects there was slight possibility of any opposition." [10]

Because much of the preliminary planning had already been completed, McNarney was soon proceeding at top speed. His assistants, Lieutenant Colonel Kuter (who was shortly to jump to brigadier general) of General Marshall's staff, Colonel Harrison, who had drafted the initial reorganization plan, and Lieutenant Colonel Otto Nelson, who had written his thesis at Harvard in 1940 on the organization of the War Department, were chosen for their expert knowledge and ability to work under pressure. In less than a week they had their recommendations for thoroughgoing change in General Marshall's hands. A few days later they informed him that the President under recently granted war powers could put the changes into effect by Executive Order.

After approving the general outline the Chief of Staff had the plan explained on February 5 at a full-dress meeting attended by the chiefs of the General Staff divisions (G-1, G-2, G-3, G-4, and War Plans), representatives of GHQ and the Air Forces, and the deputy chiefs of staff. The Chiefs of Arms and Services were carefully excluded. General Marshall followed the arguments closely, defending the cuts in the General Staff as necessary to the success of the program, and insisting that the new arrangement would not interfere with the development of weapons. He gave those present forty-eight hours to file complaints and appointed an executive committee with McNarney as chairman to put the plan into effect.[11]

Marshall wrote a friend: "It might amuse you to know that this committee, to which I gave complete power, was referred to as the 'Soviet Committee.' Also, what the public is not aware of, we had completed the major portion of the proposed organizational readjustment before the plan was even submitted to the Secretary of War or the President." [12]

When the changes were fully outlined they were explained to the Secretary of War, who gave his general approval. With solid War Department backing General McNarney drove full speed ahead. At a meeting on February 16 with representatives of the General Staff divisions, General Headquarters, the Army Air Force, and the offices of the Under Secretary of War, Adjutant General, Inspector General, and Judge Advocate General, he defined the role of the committee in a manner that cut off argument and full discussion: "It is not a voting committee. It is not a debating society. It is a committee to draft the necessary directives. It will prepare directives and such other papers as may be necessary so that the new organization may be prepared to function as early as March 9, 1942, if so ordered by the Secretary of War." [13]

The audacity of his approach and the full authority of the Chief of Staff removed the major roadblocks to the most sweeping reorganization of the War Department since Secretary of War Elihu Root had undertaken the job in 1903. Only under the pressure of war and the shock of Pearl Harbor would it have been possible to stifle the heated protests of the officers whose authority was being eliminated or sharply curtailed. Only because he believed ruthless changes were vital to the effective waging of war did General Marshall demand the immediate adoption of a program that might otherwise have been debated for months.

The Chiefs of Arms, whose established prestige might have gained them a day in court, were ignored. All but one protested orally. The fourth, Major General Robert M. Danford, Chief of Field Artillery, sorrowfully and with great dignity, filed a brief. General Marshall returned a kind reply and received a second moving appeal. The Chief of Staff was not moved, inasmuch as Danford's arguments for preserving branch consciousness in the War Department were "largely my arguments, paradoxical as it may seem, justifying the necessity for change." He forwarded the letter to General McNair, also a field artillery officer, and Secretary Stimson, who had commanded a field artillery unit in World War I, for comment. Both officials upheld General Marshall.[14]

The word went out that efficiency, tighter control, reduction in the number of General Staff officers, and a wholesale cut in the number of individuals having direct access to the Chief of Staff from some sixty to about six were essential to a successful war effort. General McNarney moved relentlessly toward his target date. He had given himself three weeks. On February 28 he received President Roosevelt's approval of an Executive Order authorizing the changes. It was formally published in a War Department circular on March 2 and become effective on March 9.

In his zeal McNarney almost alienated Roosevelt's support. Instructed by General Marshall to get the President's approval, the airman took the paper personally to a White House secretary to get the President's signature. His insistence on priority treatment overimpressed the young lady. She broke in on the President while he was in the dentist's chair to say she needed his signature at once. Shortly afterward an irate President complained to General Marshall. The Chief of Staff defended his subordinate, saying, "When I find people who get things done, I won't fire them." The President calmed down and approved the changes.[15]

They were drastic indeed. General Headquarters was eliminated completely. A new Operations Division (OPD), set up in late March in the place of the old War Plans Division, was to serve General Marshall as a command post for directing the war. "It really is GHQ," he told a friend.[16] Three of the General Staff sections, G-1, G-3, and G-4, which formerly had combined staffs of 304 officers, were cut back to twelve officers each and restricted to planning functions. The operational portion of the G-2 Division (Military Intelligence Service) was allowed to keep a large staff, but its planning section was sharply reduced.

Instead of the numerous agencies and commands that once had access to the Chief of Staff, three commands were substituted: Army Ground Forces under General McNair, Army Air Forces under General Arnold, and Services of Supply (later called Army Service Forces) under Lieutenant General Brehon B. Somervell. Army Ground Forces swallowed the staff of General Headquarters and what was left of the Chiefs of Arms. It was to control administration, organization, and training of ground forces. In return it gave up any part in planning operations for overseas theaters. The Air Forces headquarters was to have similar control over air units plus the development and procurement of aviation equipment. The Services of Supply organization was to have nearly everything else. In addition to being the procurement and supply agency for the Army, taking over many duties formerly assigned to the office of the Under Secretary of War, it handled personnel, communications, hospitals, the training of service troops, the direction of recreational and morale services, the supervision of military justice, the delivery of mail, the spiritual welfare of troops, and on and on. Nearly everything not obviously part of the other two commands was funneled into Somervell's domain. His sprawling headquarters grew swiftly in size and power until it became one of the most powerful agencies in the country.[17]

In picking General Somervell to head the Services of Supply, General Marshall chose one of his most gifted subordinates, a lean, dynamic engineer, who had gained recognition between 1936 and 1940 for turning the Works Progress Administration agency in New York City into an efficient organization. Called to Washington late in 1940 to speed up the Army construction program, which was falling behind at a time when draftees were beginning to flow into the service, he had won a reputation as the kind of tough, uncompromising, ruthless expediter that Marshall needed for a nasty job. "He was efficient; he shook the cobwebs out of their pants," General Marshall declared after the war.[18] Somervell's temper and his tendency toward empire building created trouble, but his ability to get projects moving made up for the faults. "Of course I had to fight Somervell down or he would have taken the whole damn staff," said Marshall. And the Chief of Staff had to ride herd on his protégé's temper. "I told him once not to insult the Navy. I said, by God, don't do it again."[19]

Absolutely cold-blooded in removing officers who failed to deliver and capable of running down those who got in his way, Somervell pushed reorganization plans to rapid fruition. Taking as his motto, "We do the impossible immediately. The miraculous takes a little longer," he reveled in rough assignments, driving through projects without rest and without regard for costs.[20] As long as his efforts helped win the war he received General Marshall's backing. In later years, the wartime Chief of Staff left no doubt about the value of Somervell's work: "He was one of the most efficient officers I have ever seen. And he got things done in Calcutta as fast as he did in the meadows there around the Pentagon. Whenever I asked him for something he did it and he got it. He was very forcible. He reformed, and I am using the word accurately, he reformed the adjutant general's department and others. He found conditions there were just intolerable and naturally they were all bitterly against him. And I think all the [postwar] reorganization so far as supply and services were concerned was built on avoiding any future development of a man like General Somervell. If I went into control in another war, I would start out looking for another General Somervell the very first thing I did and so would anybody else who went through that struggle on this side." [21]

Three days after the reorganization of 1942 was completed General Marshall revealed the strategy he used to put it through: "I started on reorganization a year and a half ago to see what might be done—or rather to work out a means of doing it, as there was not a great deal of doubt in my mind in general what the basis of organization should be. Of course the difficulty was how to bring it about without so much . . . discussion and opposition within the Army and on the Hill and in the press that I would be stirring up a most unfortunate morale situation at a critical moment and also would be defeating my purpose." [22]

No such radical surgery on the War Department as that announced in early March could be performed without blood-letting and violent reactions. Some of the displaced never forgave General Marshall. Others were convinced that the General Staff system had been improperly used, and that the Army lost valuable benefits that would have followed from keeping the older organization intact. General Marshall never regretted the change. In his view the reorganization made possible the effective waging of war by leaving him free to concentrate on strategy and major operations abroad.

Before the new structure of the War Department was completed General Marshall took up with the President one other reform that he thought essential to strengthen the system of military command. In February he suggested that Roosevelt appoint a chairman of the Joint Chiefs of Staff.[23]

When it became clear later in the month that Stark would leave for the United Kingdom early in March, General Marshall grew concerned over King's likely reaction to the Army's having two votes to his one. "I therefore thought it would be wise if we had a chairman and one from the Navy, if one could be found that I thought was entirely impersonal and a man of good judgment," the Chief of Staff recalled later. With what Stimson described as "great magnanimity and self-effacement," Marshall nominated for the post Admiral William D. Leahy, former Chief of Naval Operations and currently United States Ambassador to the French government at Vichy. "I thought," he said, "the Navy couldn't resist this, and from what I had learned I was willing to trust Leahy to be a neutral chairman. . . ." [24] Stimson favored the unified command idea but felt that "Marshall is a far better man than any man in sight" for the appointment.[25]

In his postwar account of his motives for making the proposal and of the manner in which the President altered the original design, General Marshall declared:

> I thought that it was very important that we, in effect, have a neutral agency because we would have had trouble with the Naval Air and the Army Air and the Naval-Army disagreements through the years—which were . . . exaggerated [at first] . . . by the fact that the Navy had a fleet; the Army had no army. It had little detachments around the United States and in . . . places [such as] Hawaii or Panama. . . . But the Navy actually had a navy. They had an Atlantic Fleet [and] a Pacific Fleet. . . . We had nothing like that. The real term of "Army" as we used it later in the war could not be applied properly to the scattered troops we had except as an administrative reference to all the individuals who were in the military service. Therefore, I thought it was particularly important to have Leahy in the chair. . . .
>
> I continued to press for Leahy being returned and made chairman of the Chiefs of Staff. The President always answered my proposals regarding Admiral Leahy by saying, "But you are Chief of Staff." But I said, "Mr. President, I am only Chief of Staff of the Army and, in a sense, of the Army Air. There is no Chief of Staff of the military services." "Well," he said, "I am the Chief of Staff. I'm the Commander-in-Chief." And I explained to him in great frankness that it was impossible to conceive of one man with all of his duties as President being also, in effect, the Chief of Staff of all the military services. That it was a superman job and I didn't think that even the exaggeration of the powers of Superman would quite go far enough for this. And I know he was not very well pleased with my statement.
>
> But the trouble was he didn't quite understand what the role of the Chief of Staff would be.[26] While I was in England [on July 21] Leahy . . . was announced as . . . coming on the Chiefs of Staff.[27] But the President said he was going to be his "leg man." And when I arrived in Washington, Leahy was very much at a loose end. He didn't quite know where he stood. He called on me because he had

learned that I proposed his name. I was the one who urged his re-turn.

I had an office fixed for Leahy over in the building where the Chiefs of Staff met [initially the Public Health Building, then the new War Department building, which became the State Department building] and showed him the chair where he should sit, which was unoccupied at the time . . . because I always sat at one side al-though I was the senior on the American side. I proposed to him that when the next meeting came, which I think was the next day, he just calmly sit down in that chair. . . .

I thought it was particularly important to have Leahy in the chair, and I incurred, possibly, Admiral King's displeasure, but . . . Ad-miral Leahy functioned from that time on [July 30] as the chairman. The matter became very much confused later on because he became more what you might call the Chief of Staff of the President, which was not my intention in making the proposal and urging that he be brought home. It was excellent to have him in contact with the White House. It would have been excellent if he had kept us straight on all of the political goings-on, like Yalta, for example. . . . But anyway, he became more the Chief of Staff of the President and less the chairman of the Chiefs of Staff as time went on. And, for ex-ample, at Potsdam he was almost exclusively engaged in attending the political meetings. I know on one occasion we had been trying to get an answer out of the Russians regarding certain things we wanted them to concede. The Navy was particularly anxious for some sta-tions . . . up near Petropavlovsk. The Russian Chief of Staff finally made a written statement of the commitments they would make on this thing. When we went to the next meeting they expected an an-swer and we didn't have the paper. It had gone to Admiral Leahy and he was away with the President. We had to answer all of these comments without having seen the paper.

Even though Leahy's time was more completely given to attending the President in his political meetings, nevertheless it was quite essen-tial to have the arrangement as it was, because it would never have done to have tried to have gone right straight through the struggle with Admiral King in a secondary position and me as the senior where I was also the senior of the Air. It was quite essential that we have a neutral agency, and Leahy, in effect, was that so far as the Army and Navy requirements and positions were concerned.[28]

The reorganization of the War Department and the changes in the Joint Chiefs of Staff came during a trying period for General Marshall. Demands piled up for men and supplies from every corner of the globe. Under the new War Department organization the Chief of Staff could leave the details of training and supply to other hands and turn his attention to the making of strategy. It was to be a busy season as British and American political and military leaders virtually commuted between London and Washington in an effort to plot a successful course of action for 1942.

London in the Spring

"GEORGE MARSHALL was the most self-confident man who ever wore pants," a newsman once said of the Chief of Staff. So it seemed when he spoke from serene Olympian heights at news conferences. To Secretary Stimson who saw him in his undressed moods, the General occasionally showed a troubled face, fretted with gnawing doubts. On March 24, 1942, as he looked for ways to stiffen the President's stand against granting all the insistent demands from Churchill, Stalin, MacArthur, Curtin, and King that poured across the White House desk, Marshall confessed somewhat dispiritedly to the Secretary of War that he felt unready for the following day's conference with the President.[1]

To this wholly uncharacteristic hesitation to close with a tough assignment was added a small but nagging disquiet about Mrs. Marshall's health. The daily concern that he had displayed about his first wife's semi-invalidism was extended to the well-being of the second Mrs. Marshall. The broken ribs that had made her life miserable for several months had now at last healed, but still he worried because she constantly ignored the limits of her strength. Overtaxed by a round of what she felt were obligatory public activities, from Red Cross drives to receptions for newspaperwomen, she was near exhaustion. The day before his talk with Stimson he had coaxed and cajoled until she promised to leave Washington for a rest. "The trouble is," he wrote his stepson, Allen, "I cannot persuade her to lighten her own burdens, telephone, mail, and committees. She resents my ideas of procedure and suffers accordingly. Her mail has become voluminous, telephone calls more numerous than ever, and demands on her to attend meetings a daily matter. Added to this are her own affairs, those normal to the house, and her unremitting concern regarding you and Clifton and Molly and Allene, Nona, Clara, Tris, etc." [2]

Marshall possibly thought that she might profit from his own example in handling encroachments on his time. Almost completely indifferent to the social whirl of Washington, he became expert in avoiding it and the deluge of requests for public appearances that followed his elevation to Chief of Staff. For those parties at which he felt his attendance was obligatory he perfected a serviceable routine. He arrived early for cocktails, chatted briefly with the hostess, greeted one or two friends, then unobtrusively vanished. At dinners, except with old friends or state guests, he usually arranged to be called away. In time this action became suspect. Noticing his restlessness, one evening, a dinner partner said mischievously to Mrs. Marshall, "I hear the phone calling your husband." [3]

With a few friends who knew the art of relaxed conversation he would stay the entire evening, but the rarity of the Marshalls' social appearances came to make their presence a distinction for any party. Justice Felix Frankfurter liked to tell of the time when he wished to repay in proper style the social debts he and his wife had incurred. Knowing that he could not compete in lavish hospitality with most of his hosts, he hit upon the idea of persuading the Marshalls to be guests of honor. They came, and the General regaled the group with tales of his early Army life and his views on baseball. No mention was made of world politics or military strategy, but Justice Frankfurter knew, at the end of the evening, that he had given one of the outstanding parties of the season. [4]

The attack on Pearl Harbor not only further curtailed General Marshall's social activities but accentuated an aloofness that already seemed extreme to some of his associates. When he went with Mrs. Marshall on one of their frequent walks, it seemed to her that as he chatted quietly he was really talking to himself. "It was as though he lived outside himself and George Marshall was someone he was constantly appraising, advising, and training to meet a situation." The standards he set for himself were rigid. "I cannot afford the luxury of sentiment," he told her, "mine must be cold logic. Sentiment is for others." Again he said, "I cannot allow myself to get angry, that would be fatal—it is too exhausting. My brain must be kept clear." Mindful of his two early collapses under the strain of overwork, he was careful of his health. "He watched it," Mrs. Marshall remarked, "as though he were a runner in training for a long race." [5]

Every ounce of his stamina and every particle of his logic was needed to cope with the monstrous difficulties that followed in the train of Pearl Harbor. Every fresh disaster turned on Washington frantic appeals for help that threatened to disrupt all of Marshall's careful preparations. Churchill, to still the clamor of the alarmed governments of Australia and New Zealand for return of their fighting units enlisted under Britain's banners in various parts of the world, begged for one or two American divisions and additional naval units for the Southwest Pacific. Looking at the Far East, he proposed that the United States supply shipping to transport British reinforcements to the Indian Ocean area as well as opening air offensives against the Japanese from China, Northeast India, and the Aleutians.[6]

Marshall looked on this kind of piecemeal scattering of Allied forces, vividly described by Stimson as the stopping up "of urgent rat holes," as a dangerous dispersion of resources. General Eisenhower vigorously expressed the War Department's thinking in late January:

> We've got to go to Europe and fight—and we've got to quit wasting resources all over the world—and still worse—wasting time. If we're to keep Russia in, save the Middle East, India, and Burma; we've got to begin slugging with air at West Europe; to be followed by a land attack as soon as possible." [7]

It was this concept of concentration on an offensive in Europe, an operation that would focus the efforts of the Allies on a decisive effort, that Marshall was to present to the President on March 25.

Like most War Department plans, this one had a mixed parentage. Many hands had helped nurture it. The basic concept that a large ground force operation in Western Europe would be necessary to topple Hitler from power went back to early Army and Navy discussions at the beginning of 1941. Germany held the nations of Western Europe in thrall and threatened to turn the remaining resources and industrial potential of the occupied lands into a powerful engine of destruction that could complete the subjugation of Britain and Russia and then threaten the Western Hemisphere. From the windows of Washington and London it was easy to see which enemy must be conquered first.

The detailed work on the plan was under the direction of General Eisenhower, recently appointed by Marshall to succeed General Gerow as Chief of War Plans Division. Completely in accord with the Chief of Staff's thinking, Eisenhower at the end of February proposed that the United States "at once develop, in conjunction with the British, a definite plan for operations against Northwest Europe." He believed that "it should be sufficiently extensive in scale as to engage, from the middle of May onward, an increasing portion of the German Air Force, and by late summer an increasing amount of his ground forces." [8]

To Marshall and his planners the United Kingdom was the logical point for the United States to concentrate men and resources for the final assault on Hitler. Anchored off the coast of France and Belgium, the British Isles provided the most convenient staging area for an attack on Germany. At a time when shipping was at a premium, the North Atlantic route put the least burden on the United States. Inasmuch as supply lines to the United Kingdom were already being kept open with the aid of the Atlantic Fleet, no dispersion of effort would be required. The airfields of Great Britain afforded the best base from which to give air support to an invasion force. The air and ground build-up in the British Isles in itself would constitute a threat to Germany and give some indirect aid to the Soviet Union. Europe was the only place in which the bulk of British ground forces could be committed to a general offensive in cooperation with American forces.[9]

The crowning merit of the operation from the Army's standpoint was that it saved American forces from involvement in subsidiary operations of little interest to the United States. If the Western Allies had no fixed plan for opening a second front, Americans would see their resources being siphoned off in driblets to every threatened part of the globe without saving the Red armies from defeat and without making progress toward a decisive result.

General Marshall presented these arguments to Roosevelt at a White House luncheon on March 25 that he attended with Stimson, Knox, Arnold, King, and Hopkins. The President proved difficult.

"Roosevelt had a habit of tossing out new operations," General
Marshall once declared. "I called it his cigarette-holder gesture." [10]
Stimson on this occasion called it "a dispersion debauch" in which
Roosevelt toyed with possible operations in the Middle East and
the Mediterranean. Only by strenuous exertions did the Army
leaders steer him back to the Atlantic. In "a very fine presentation" Marshall won the President's backing for a cross-Channel
effort. Finally Roosevelt asked that a detailed plan be prepared for
his examination. Hopkins, who wanted prompt action by the British, recommended that as soon as the plan was made and approved
someone take it directly to London, bypassing the British Mission
in Washington." [11]

On the same day Marshall spoke with the President, General
Eisenhower put into the Chief of Staff's hands a memorandum urging that Great Britain and the United States agree as soon as possible that a major offensive against Germany constituted their eventual aim. If, said Eisenhower, commitment on this point was not
firm, the United States should turn its back on the Atlantic area
and go full out against Japan.[12] Marshall agreed completely with
this reasoning. He shared the conviction that Stimson expressed to
President Roosevelt two days later that "so long as we remain without our own plan of offensive, our forces will inevitably be dis-
persed and wasted." [13]

On April 1 General Marshall presented the plan worked out by
Eisenhower and his assistants. With the aid of Stimson and Hopkins he succeeded in getting the President's approval. At the close
of a lengthy session Roosevelt directed that Hopkins and Marshall
take the plan to London and win British agreement.[14]

To keep Hopkins going physically, Roosevelt sent along a Navy
doctor and later directed Marshall "to put Hopkins to bed and
keep him there under 24-hour guard by Army or Marine Corps"
while he got some rest. As his assistants Marshall took along Colonel Howard A. Craig, an Air Force planner, and Colonel Wedemeyer, the Operations Division's most militant proponent of the
cross-Channel operation.

During the flight from Baltimore on the morning of April 4 one
of the plane's engines went out, and the party was forced to pro-
long its scheduled stop in Bermuda over Easter Sunday until another engine could be brought from New York. Despite Marshall's

distaste for plans that went awry, he conceded that this delay could not have come at a pleasanter place or at a more delightful season.

Hearing that General Marshall would attend Pembroke Church for Easter Services, Lord Knollys, the Governor-General, asked if he would read the Second Lesson. Not wishing his chief to come suddenly on an unfamiliar text, Wedemeyer—who was acting as aide during the trip—found a Bible and brought it along to the General, having marked what he believed to be the assigned passages. A wise soldier who had learned that the best improvised maneuvers are those that have been carefully rehearsed, General Marshall used part of his time at breakfast in reading the Lesson to Hopkins and Wedemeyer. They agreed at the end that he had done well, and the General felt amply prepared for his morning assignment. Consternation and confusion awaited him at church. As he confidently waited to hear his name called, he was dismayed when Lord Knollys handed him a slip of paper listing several additional verses that he had not seen.

When his eyes searched out the unpracticed lines he found the names of the seven churches of Asia Minor—Ephesus, Smyrna, Pergamum, Thyatira, Sardis, Philadelphia, and Laodicea. Though scarcely justifying Marshall's later description, "more unpronounceable words than I have ever seen collected in one chapter," they were definitely a nasty surprise for an unwary soldier. "At the end of a long list of tribes," he later wrote a friend, "I found the familiar name *Philadelphia,* which I intoned in such an impressive manner that on my arrival in England the Prime Minister told me that he had learned I had made a profound impression by my reading. . . . The exact character of the impression he didn't go into." Apparently Churchill had heard of the effect produced by the General's fervid stress on the blessed name of Philadelphia after hurried fumblings in the catalogue of alien cities. An elderly native of that Pennsylvania city, sitting in the church, rushed up to him afterward to say, "I'm from Philadelphia too." [15]

Marshall's party resumed its trip early on April 7 in the repaired flying boat, which put down at Lough Erne in northern Ireland the following morning. The General broke the tedium of the long flight by reading a twenty-five-cent copy of H. G. Wells' *Outline of History,* which Mrs. Marshall had thrust into his hands at his departure. Forerunner of the historical volumes of the Eveyman

series that he later carried in his plane, this capsule summation of
world development kept him occupied for several hours until
"Hopkins and some of the others got their hands on it" and he
turned his thoughts again to the present.[16]

From Ireland the travelers flew by a landplane to Hendon Airport near London, where they were met by the Prime Minister
and the British Chiefs of Staff. On the way into the city Marshall
was moved by evidence of what war had brought to England. Piles
of rubble marked the scenes of recent bombings, and carefully
cleared empty spaces denoted the paths of destruction made by
Luftwaffe raids in the frightful fall and winter of 1940. The rigidly
enforced blackout, noisy screams of sirens, the constant sweep of
powerful searchlights, and irregular outbursts of ack-ack fire soon
reminded the General that terror from the air was still a menace.
These first glimpses left their mark on Marshall, fresh from a capital where even the shock of Pearl Harbor had failed to eliminate
stress on creature comforts or stop the whinings of individuals in-
convenienced by production demands of the Army and Navy. In
all of his debates over strategy with Churchill and his staff, he
never minimized the fighting spirit of the British people or their
leader.[17]

As the climax to a long and crowded day, which included an
afternoon meeting with the Prime Minister and a press conference,
Churchill entertained his visitors at dinner. Ignoring the world's
latest conflict for the moment, the British leader talked authorita-
tively and well of the United States Civil War and World War I.
More immediate matters were left to General Brooke, who
promptly told Marshall of his distaste for the American plan.[18]

Marshall's first important encounter with his British counterpart started badly. Perhaps in unconscious resentment at Brooke
for having supplanted Dill as Chief of the Imperial General Staff,
Marshall later told Hopkins that Brooke might be a good fighting
man but that he lacked Dill's brains.[19] Brooke was equally restrained in his compliments. "I liked what I saw of Marshall, a
pleasant and easy man to get on with, rather overfilled with his own
importance. But I should not put him down as a great man." Both
men later revised their estimates upward.[20]

To most Americans, as to some of his colleagues, Brooke was icy,
imperturbable, and condescending. Four years younger than Marshall, he was smaller in stature, delicately boned, and with large

dark eyes that had a shining, impenetrable stare. Precise, methodical, abrupt to the point of rudeness, he lacked Dill's charm. Marshall later saw a pleasanter side of Brooke, an officer who loved nature, a field marshal who could ease the strain of command by slipping away for an afternoon into the British countryside. Near D-Day, a colleague recalled, Brooke broke off a conversation on landing preparations to tell of the rare photograph he had made of a marsh tit. Some Americans sneered at his bird watching, but Marshall felt at home with a soldier who liked birds, gardening, and fine horses. Both men later recalled that Marshall had presented him with a copy of James Lane Allen's *A Kentucky Cardinal*.

As a soldier, Brooke had impressive credentials. Descended from an Anglo-Irish family known for its fighting qualities, he had served bravely in World War I, winning decorations and commendations for his work as an artilleryman. Ending the war with the temporary rank of lieutenant colonel, he embarked on a peacetime service that made him one of the best-informed officers in the British Army. Eight of the years between the wars were spent as student and instructor in the Staff College and Defence College, working with many of the officers who later held key posts in World War II. Then, as commandant of the School of Artillery, brigade commander, Inspector of Artillery, Director of Military Training, commander of the first mobile division, and first commander of the newly formed Anti-Aircraft Command, he gained a thorough knowledge of the organization of the British Army.

At the outset of World War II he was taken from his recently acquired post at Southern Command to lead the II Corps in France. In the fighting that followed he had under him for a time two outstanding division commanders, General Harold Alexander and General Bernard L. Montgomery. Skillful handling of his forces in the Dunkerque evacuation gained for him the appointment to organize the expeditionary force that was sent back briefly into France. Returning with his forces intact, he was given command of the units organized to deal with a possible German attack. As Commander-in-Chief of Home Forces for almost one and one-half years, he began the training of divisions that would one day return to the Continent to help defeat Germany. From this post he was summoned by Churchill in November 1941 to the post of Chief of the Imperial General Staff.[21]

General Marshall was aware that Brooke looked upon the Amer-

ican leaders as green newcomers in the fight. "I can understand his
thinking," the Chief of Staff declared in 1956. "He had led a corps
in battle, while my experience—dating back to the First World War
—was [as chief of operations] on an Army staff." There were officers on Marshall's staff who believed that the British commander's
service in the costly campaigns in Flanders in World War I and in
two evacuations of troops from France in World War II were not
conducive to the aggressive strategy that they believed necessary
for victory.[22]

The Americans counted in Brooke's favor his ability to stand up
to the Prime Minister. Although in disagreement with the British
commander's strong advocacy of the Mediterranean strategy, Marshall was aware that General Brooke blunted some of Churchill's
more impractical schemes. In the combined conferences, however,
Brooke supported loyally the proposals presented by his chief, arguing bravely for measures that he had sometimes opposed in
purely British meetings. As a result he later lamented, "I think
that Marshall sometimes thought I was double-crossing him." [23]
From his British colleagues Brooke got top marks. Although dep-
recating many of Brooke's claims in his diary, General Ismay, after
surveying the work of eight Chiefs of the Imperial General Staff
with whom he had worked over a period of eighteen years, declared, "I would unhesitatingly say that Brooke was the best of
them all." [24]

Despite strong disagreements and heated arguments throughout
the war, Marshall retained great respect for Brooke. For two other
British leaders that he met for the first time on this trip, General
Hastings Ismay and Lord Louis Mountbatten, he had affection as
well. "Pug" Ismay, whose nickname derived from the conforma-
tion of his friendly features in which large, slightly protuberant
liquid brown eyes dominated a very short nose, aroused Colonel
Wedemeyer's suspicions initially because of his ingratiating manner. An excellent raconteur with a rich fund of stories and a gift
for mimicry, particularly of the mannerisms of his chief, he seemed
at times to be merely a court jester whose chief function was to
reduce tension at staff conferences. Actually he was an extremely
hard worker who formed an effective buffer between the Prime
Minister and his Chiefs of Staff. Early years of soldiering in India
and Africa were followed in the mid-twenties by an assignment to

the staff of the Committee of Imperial Defence for five years. After two years as Military Secretary to the Viceroy of India he returned to England as deputy to Sir Maurice Hankey, brilliant secretary of the Imperial Defence Committee from 1912 until his retirement in 1938. At the outbreak of war Ismay became head of the military wing of the War Cabinet secretariat. On Churchill's accession to power and assumption of the Defence Ministry, Ismay became head of the Office of the Minister of Defence and representative of the Prime Minister in the Chiefs of Staff Committee. Prepared to say "no" to his chief when that proved necessary, capable at times of persuading the Prime Minister to soften some of his harsher judgments, willing at heavy cost to his own rest to share the lonely watches of the night, he ably served Churchill and the Allied cause.[25] General Marshall considered him "ideal" for his position. "He straightened out things for us time after time. I was fond of him." [26]

Ismay was a great public servant and an invaluable aide. Mountbatten belonged to a breed accustomed to command. His father was Prince Louis of Battenberg, who had served as First Sea Lord in World War I until bitter anti-German feeling in Britain had led him first to give up his post and then his German titles. His mother was Queen Victoria's granddaughter, and he was thus a cousin of the King. He looked far younger than his forty-one years, and he projected a "bred-in-the-bone" handsomeness that caused many Americans to fear he was better fitted for the role of playboy than that of a serious and hard-working member of Britain's high command. His fondness for imaginative experiments and fads led both foreigners and fellow Englishmen to distrust his soundness. Conventional officers complained of the "long-haired" scientists with whom he surrounded himself.

Shortly before Hopkins and Marshall arrived in London, Mountbatten had been named Chief of Combined Operations. To make certain that Mountbatten would not be snubbed in dealing with the various services, Churchill made him a vice-admiral, lieutenant general, and air marshal and let him sit on the Chiefs of Staff Committee. Thus, to the disadvantages of being junior in years and rank to the heads of other services on which he had to depend for assistance, he added the burden of being described as the Prime Minister's favorite.

Having no basis for prejudice against him, General Marshall liked Mountbatten from the start. At the General's first meeting with the Chiefs of Staff Committee, the British officers invited him to visit their headquarters. To Mountbatten's delight, Marshall singled out Combined Headquarters as the one he wanted most to see. General Marshall learned how the young commander got representatives of the various services to work closely together—an arrangement of which he had often dreamed. The Chief of Staff accepted Mountbatten's invitation to send American service representatives over to work with the Combined Operations staff. From the meeting also flowed a second important result. To Marshall's question, "What do you most need to get ahead with planning and training?" Mountbatten replied, "Double your orders for landing ships and craft in the United States and develop even a larger type of landing craft to carry infantry troops." On his return the General put his full strength behind the proposal.[27]

Of all the British leaders with whom Marshall came into contact on this trip to London, it was Churchill who interested him most. This was his first opportunity to get to know him well and to learn just how tough the old campaigner could be. In their previous conferences the Chief of Staff had been one of the supporting cast; now he had a major role in the main production. The change in the billing was not without its drawbacks.

To the amusement of Brooke, deadly tired from the Prime Minister's fondness for late hours, Marshall was startled by Churchill's working habits. On his first visit to Chequers, country house of the prime ministers of Great Britain, Marshall sat with the group at dinner long past his hour for eating. Churchill's evening was just beginning. Near ten o'clock he started a review of the current conflict that lasted until nearly two. Then, needing diversion, he turned to a film that continued for almost an hour. Marshall's face "was a study," Brooke wrote. "He was evidently not used to being kept out of bed until the small hours of the morning and not enjoying it much. . . ."[28] Marshall sympathized with Ismay, who often sat until almost dawn with the Prime Minister, only to be told if he yawned or yearned for bed, "There you stand loaded down with honors by your country and now you betray her. Go to bed if you like, but I expect to do my duty." Only Hopkins delighted in the Churchillian pace. His fondness for conviviality and late hours took its toll as he continually ignored his doctor's instructions.

On this April visit the Chief of Staff worked with Churchill more closely and over a longer period of time than on any other occasion during the war. Attempting to win the fight for his strategy, he was able to observe the master of the Allied cause at close range. Marshall admired his gift for language, his knowledge and sense of history, his splendid contempt for the enemy, his capacity for boldness. He was appalled by swift changes of plans, a flexibility that brought chaos in planning, a daring that brushed aside careful details. Most of all he dreaded the Churchillian influence on Roosevelt, who also delighted in the dramatic and the unexpected and who was determined, now that he was in the war, to strike a sudden and vital blow at the Nazis.

Descendant of the great Marlborough, twice First Lord of the Admiralty, former Secretary of State for War, author of popular books on past conflicts, Churchill could more than hold his own in any military gathering. As a student of English and world history, friend of the great and near great in political and military realms since the 1890s, veteran of political fights in the House of Commons over half a century, scarred battler for British preparedness, masterful foe of the Fascist "jackals" for whom he saved his choice invective in Britain's most trying hours, he embodied a living legend that was difficult to combat. Those who challenged him had to meet not only his alert mind and sure mastery of debate but the fact and myth of a glorious past. Like Brooke, Marshall learned that his best weapon against his opponent was sheer doggedness. Throughout the sessions, in which winning charm, cold persuasion, rude insistence, eloquent flow of language, flashes of anger, and sentiment close to tears were called on by Churchill to advance his cause, the Chief of Staff stuck to his basic contentions for a strategy that suited the interests of the United States, carefully reiterating American problems, American pressures, and American determination. Again and again he won what he believed to be firm agreements, only to find them dissolved in a matter of hours. The most solid victories became hollow when the Prime Minister, finding that Marshall backed by Hopkins was too much for either his cajolery or bite, simply went around them to their more pliable Commander-in-Chief.

The basic difference between them on strategy arose from the point at which they looked at the map. Forced to protect a lifeline that stretched from Britain by way of Gibraltar through the Mediterranean and Middle East to India, Churchill saw the Southwest Pacific operations as peripheral and action in northern Europe as merely part of a larger whole. Seated in Washington, Marshall saw two great battles being fought at opposite extremes from the United States. Pressured hourly to send men and resources to two divergent theaters, he saw the Middle East and the Mediterranean as peripheral areas. For Churchill, any battle with the Axis helped to destroy forces that might have to be fought later on the Continent. Bedeviled by defeats in the desert, German threats to the Middle East, and Japanese incursions into the Indian Ocean, the Prime Minister dreaded the rigidity that would be imposed on his actions by a commitment to all-out attack across the Channel in 1943.

No less than the British chief, Marshall understood the value of flexibility in planning. But as he watched the final phases of Wainwright's heartbreaking defense of Corregidor, he feared the prospect of starving his forces in the Pacific to build up reserves in Britain that might be swallowed up in enterprises in Norway, North Africa, and the Middle East or in small raids along the coast of Europe. To demonstrate that the United States was not in the war merely to furnish men and matériel for any plan the Prime Minister might devise, no matter how advantageous it might appear to the British, he demanded concentration on the one operation that Americans would list above an offensive against Japan. It was this rather than American fondness for large-scale operations and American dislike of improvisation that lay behind his insistence on a large-scale 1943 cross-Channel attack, with a smaller emergency landing for 1942 if it proved necessary.

The United States proposal, usually referred to as the Marshall Memorandum, was formally outlined by the Chief of Staff on April 9. Pulled together by General Eisenhower and his staff from many earlier proposals—some British in origin—the statement envisaged three operations. The differences between them were clear-cut, but their names were sometimes confused, to the bewilderment of contemporary leaders and later historians. It is important to sort out their identities.[29]

The name BOLERO was applied to the build-up of men and matériel in the United Kingdom for a 1943 cross-Channel attack. The main invasion was to be called ROUNDUP, a name selected earlier by the British and criticized as pretentious and boastful by the Prime Minister. Fifty-eight hundred combat planes and forty-eight divisions, of which thirty were to be contributed by the United States, were to be used. Here at last was a broad concept for action on the Continent. Even British opponents of the plan had to admit that the Americans were approaching ROUNDUP on the proper scale. "We had come to be daunted by figures and had got into the habit of planning everything on the improvised and shoestring basis to which circumstances had condemned us," wrote the historian of Mountbatten's headquarters. "Here were the Americans coming along to say that there was no shortage of manpower, and that there need be no shortage of anything else. The British planners gulped when they saw their modest twelve divisions neatly multiplied by four to make forty-eight, and their hundreds of landing craft translated into thousands; and it took them a little time to raise their sights." [30]

Prior to the main operation Marshall proposed a limited attack, originated by the British and still being studied, usually known as SLEDGEHAMMER, to be launched in the fall of 1942. He thought of it as "justified only in case" German successes became "so complete as to threaten the imminent collapse of Russian resistance unless pressure is relieved by an attack from the west by British and American troops." It would thus be considered "as a sacrifice in the common good." The BOLERO build-up would help to make the small invasion possible in the fall of 1942 or provide a force that could be sent to the Continent in the unlikely event that Germany appeared to be on the point of collapse.

Marshall carefully labeled SLEDGEHAMMER an emergency measure with the secondary purpose of keeping the emphasis on planning for 1942. In time the British would discard both schemes in favor of a Mediterranean strategy dictated by their national interests and by distaste for an operation whose costs in its early stages would have to be borne by Great Britain. By a peculiar chemistry of history, this strategy that developed gradually under the pressure of events was later described by General Brooke and others as a careful plan set forth from the beginning for a series of orderly operations from the south that would be capped by the cross-Channel operation. Viewed in that light, Marshall's emergency attack has become a rather simple-minded proposal by an ill-informed and even obstinate American leader.

Undoubtedly Churchill had wanted to strike back at Germany since the time of Dunkerque, but in the face of enemy attacks on British cities from the air and enemy threats of invasion by sea there was no possibility of early offensive operations. Only with American entry into the war and the pressing need to aid the Russians did the possibility of a cross-Channel attack for 1942 or 1943 revive. In January 1942, as Churchill and his advisers were discussing strategy in Washington, the British Chiefs of Staff were examining proposals for a landing in force on the Continent.[31]

Aid to the Russians appeared in cross-Channel planning in two different lights. At times the British staff argued that no landings should be attempted unless the Soviet forces could pull sufficient German strength from the western front to make an invasion likely of success; on other occasions some members talked in terms of an emergency landing to pull Hitler's armies away from the Russian front. What appeared in one case to be the exploitation of an opportunity became in the other a dangerous sacrifice play. Less than ten days before the American mission arrived in London, the Combined Commanders (Home Forces, Combined Operations, and Fighter Command) concluded that such an operation should be carried out in 1942 only if German forces were extended in Russia or if a Russian victory seemed likely. On the day Hopkins and Marshall arrived General Brooke asked the Commanders to consider the more important question of what should be done if the Russians were hard-pressed. From this meeting he and his colleagues went to the airport to welcome the American visitors.[32]

Thus, at the time Marshall arrived to argue for ROUNDUP and an emergency SLEDGEHAMMER, there were evidences of considerable British support for the former and possible backing for the latter operation. But there was a fatal weakness in SLEDGEHAMMER that Marshall later conceded. Since execution of the plan depended largely on British men and supplies the operation had to have the warm approval of the Prime Minister, who was in no mood to risk the blood baths of World War I. Weary of costly evacuations and sacrificial efforts that ended disastrously, the Prime Minister became cautious. When he looked at the fields of northern France he thought of the generation of leaders that should now be leading Britain—lost in the mud of Flanders. Churchill's doctor warned Marshall that he was fighting the ghosts of the Somme.[33]

From the outset Marshall should have realized that he was waging a hopeless fight to save SLEDGEHAMMER. He may have sensed its futility, but he hoped to achieve his basic objective even if he lost the preliminary bout. Although in his first meeting with the British Chiefs of Staff he mentioned the critical necessity of keeping Russia in the fight and the importance of giving American troops experience in battle as soon as possible, his emphasis was on a prompt decision to stop the dispersion of Allied forces in secondary tasks.[34]

General Brooke strongly doubted SLEDGEHAMMER's chances for success. He declared flatly that not more than seven infantry and two armored divisions, a force insufficient to maintain the bridgehead against the forces the Germans would be able to muster against them, could be landed on the Continent in 1942. Worse still, the Allies would be unable to extricate the units if the Germans determined to expel them. Instead of embracing this unlikely adventure, he preferred to turn to the Middle East and the Indian Ocean area, where serious threats were developing from German and Japanese offensives.

Backing him in his opposition was Admiral Mountbatten, who was discouraged by the enormous difficulties of maintaining a force across the Channel and the virtual impossibility of gaining surprise. Even more serious was the fear, expressed by Chief of the Air Staff Portal, that they could not give air support to the bridgehead even if it were secured. Marshall in the first meeting failed to win support from the British Chiefs of Staff.[35]

In his initial talks with Hopkins and Marshall, Churchill was not as plain-spoken in his opposition to the 1942 plan as were some of his advisers. His reaction to proposals for 1943 even encouraged Hopkins to conclude that the Prime Minister was sympathetic.[36]

At Chequers over the weekend, the British leader continued to turn a hopeful face toward the American representative. Perhaps the pulse of spring was working its magic. The riot of blooming plants and budding trees moved the usually prosaic Hopkins to exclaim that he now understood "why the English have written the best goddam poetry in the world." [37] Despite a minor tempest when Churchill exploded to Hopkins over Roosevelt's urging that Britain back a national government for India, Marshall gathered that the Prime Minister and his advisers had agreed in principle to American proposals for 1942 and 1943. From Chequers he telephoned hopefully to his deputy chief of staff that Churchill had indicated "that he virtually accepted in toto the proposals I submitted to him. . . ." [38]

Talks with the British Chiefs of Staff and other advisers of the Prime Minister tempered Marshall's optimism. On his return to London he wrote McNarney: "It appears that our proposal will be accepted in principle, but relative to avoidance of future dispersions particularly of planes, such acceptance will have to be considerably and continuously bolstered by firmness of our stand. . . . Virtually everyone agrees with us in principle but many if not most hold reservations regarding this or that." [39]

On the 14th the British Chiefs of Staff replied favorably to Marshall's Memorandum. They agreed with his outlines for action in 1943 but held that action in 1942 would have to be governed by developments on the Russian front. They warned also of the necessity of safeguarding India and the Middle East. On the last day of the discussions, as Marshall urged that operations on the Continent not "be reduced to the status of residuary legatee," Brooke warned that only a small-scale attack could be made that year, and Mountbatten saw no easing of the landing-craft bottleneck until 1943. [40]

The meeting with the Prime Minister and his advisers late that evening was more encouraging. Exuding good fellowship, Churchill announced that "he had no hesitation in cordially accepting the plan." Although he asked help in meeting "the vital requirements of the Indian Ocean," where the Japanese were threatening British control, he insisted that there was "complete unanimity on the framework" of the plan for 1943. He added eloquently that the two nations would march ahead together "in a noble brotherhood of arms." Deeply moved, Marshall threw aside his earlier doubts and cabled Secretary Stimson that in an impressive statement the Prime Minister had declared his complete agreement with their plan. [41]

Brooke himself described the midnight session as a "momentous meeting at which we accepted their proposals for offensive action in Europe in 1942 perhaps, and in 1943 for certain." Churchill made this point explicit in a message to the President on April 17. While emphasizing the need to make provisions to prevent the junction of Japanese and German forces and to halt enemy advances in the Indian Ocean, he assured the President that "broadly speaking, our agreed programme is a crescendo of activity on the Continent. . . ." [42]

Marshall would have been spared the shock of the British shift to North African operations a few weeks later if he had been able to read Brooke's diary entry about him and his proposals:

> He is, I think, a good general at raising armies and at providing the necessary link between the military and political worlds, but his strategical ability does not impress me at all. In fact, in many respects he is a very dangerous man whilst being a very charming one. He has found that King, the American Navy Chief of Staff, is proving more and more of a drain on his military resources, continually calling for land-forces to capture and hold land-bases in the Pacific. . . . MacArthur in Australia constitutes another threat by asking for forces to develop an offensive from Australia. To counter these moves Marshall has started the European offensive plan and is going one hundred per cent all out on it. It is a clever move that fits in with present political opinion and the desire to help Russia. . . .[43]

Churchill later said that he had little faith in SLEDGEHAMMER and that if he had been free to choose he would have settled on operations in North Africa and Norway, using SLEDGEHAMMER only as a feint to deceive the enemy. But he did not judge it expedient to make this proposal to Marshall at a time when the BOLERO build-up was being planned. He wrote of his decision: "But I had to work by influence and diplomacy in order to secure agreed and harmonious action with our cherished Ally, without whose aid nothing but ruin faced the world. I did not therefore open any of these alternatives at our meeting on the 14th." [44]

His failure to make some of his reservations more explicit was to create bad feelings in the future. "Our American friends," wrote Ismay later, "went happily homewards under the mistaken impression that we had committed ourselves to both ROUNDUP and SLEDGEHAMMER. This misunderstanding was destined to have unfortunate results. For when we had to tell them, after the most thorough study of SLEDGEHAMMER, that we were absolutely opposed to it, they felt that we had broken faith with them." [45] Discussing the question in 1960, Ismay added that if they had known each other better, the British probably would have gone out to dinner with the Americans and have said, " 'Look here, old boy, this sounds lovely but surely we are talking in terms of the end of 1943. It isn't practical politics as far as we are concerned.' Also I think we should have come clean, much cleaner than we did, and said, 'We are frankly horrified because of what we have been through in our lifetime. . . . We, who had survived, had got that into our minds, never again, you see. We are not going into this until it is a cast-iron certainty.' " [46]

Disillusionment still lay several weeks ahead for Marshall and Hopkins as they left for home pleased with their mission's apparent success. The Chief of Staff broke his journey to the United States by stopping near Londonderry on the 18th to inspect recently arrived American units in Northern Ireland, commanded by Major General Russell P. Hartle.[47] He saw them as the first representatives of a million-man army that would be engaged in battle on the Continent within a few months. Indeed, before the year's end, many of these men would fight and die in action against the Germans. But it would be on the shores of North Africa and not under the skies of France.

XV

Marshall Loses a Fight

DURING the General's two-week absence in London, Mrs. Marshall prepared for him a great surprise at their home in Leesburg, thirty-five miles from Washington. Two years earlier she had bought Dodona Manor, a stately colonial home with fine old trees and a pleasant garden that had once been owned by George Washington's grandnephew. Marshall had spent some quiet weekends there before the spring of 1942 but much needed to be done to make it a truly comfortable residence. Rushing plans for painting and repair while her husband was away, Mrs. Marshall had the house and grounds ready for inspection when he returned. Costs for the job had completely outrun her estimates, and it was with some trepidation that she prepared him for a shock. Her worry in this case had been needless, her battle was quickly won. Contrasting the peaceful scene with the torn land that he had just left and recollecting the periodic uprootings that he had suffered in moving from Army billet to Army billet over the years, he gave way to the sentiment he usually disdained. "This is Home," he said, "a real home after forty-one years of wandering." [1]

Until the war's end Fort Myer—almost within sight of the War Department—would be the Marshalls' main residence. But to the house at Leesburg he gave his heart, and he stole away as often as possible for a few hours or a day to work with his roses and tomatoes. Although not reared as a farm boy Marshall loved the soil, and he managed occasionally to forget the problems of the war tending his plants and campaigning against Japanese beetles. Carefully preserved in his files are the annual orders he filled out for packets of Kentucky Wonder beans, Hubbard squash, and Wallace's hy-

brid corn. He liked to recount the story of the occasion on which
Lieutenant General Leslie R. Groves, the officer he had appointed
to supervise the atomic energy project, came in to ask for an additional hundred million dollars. He was writing busily when
Groves entered the office, and he continued to scribble as the subordinate waited. When he finished he turned quickly to the officer's project, approved it, and handed it back. As Groves started to
leave, he said, "It may interest you to know what I was doing. I was
writing the check for three dollars and fifty-two cents for grass seed
for my lawn." [2]

Had he wished to cultivate the legend of Cincinnatus, he could
not have succeeded better than by his life at Dodona Manor. Dropping his parade dress immaculateness for practical disarray, he misled more than one unwary visitor into assuming that he was an ancient family gardener intent on his crops. He complained often
that his visitors praised his handiwork but did nothing to help him
with his chores. General Arnold once rashly offered to be of assistance, and Marshall quickly set him to work with a shovel in a com-
post pile, a hot job that soon reduced Arnold's white collar to an
unsightly mess. Members of Marshall's staff who reported with official business were often interviewed in the garden, and natives of
Leesburg still treasure the tale that General Bedell Smith was once
welcomed by the Chief of Staff in his corn patch in the midst of a
fine drizzle that wrecked Smith's well-pressed uniform. To his subordinate's muttered question, "Do I have to stand here in the rain
to make my report?" Marshall blandly replied, "No, just turn over
that pail there and sit on it." [3] Few weekends were uninterrupted
by calls from the President or the War Department. Marshall's
publicized periods of relaxation as a country squire became as infrequent as the canoe rides with Mrs. Marshall on the Potomac that
earlier had been duly chronicled in the press and envied by his
associates in Great Britain.

He found that after even a short absence, his work piled up. In
late May, for example, the General flew with Mrs. Marshall to
Roanoke, where she spoke at the centennial celebration of Hollins
College, her alma mater. "We were back at Fort Myer at six o'clock
that evening," Marshall wrote Admiral Stark, "where we found a
considerable section of the War Department waiting for me with
sheaves of papers." The General was reminded of a song the sol-

diers had sung in Mindoro in 1902. "There was no town, no diversion, pretty much no nothing, but always they would be singing a song as they came in at night, which had one refrain, 'Every day will be Sunday Bye and Bye!' Now-a-days Sundays are like Mondays and every other day of the week." [4]

The problems that mounted on Marshall's desk bothered Secretary Stimson, who fretted continually about the General's inability to get sufficient relaxation. Foremost among Marshall's problems in May were the persistent calls by Admiral King and General MacArthur for greater emphasis on operations in the Pacific. Even before he had gone to London, the Chief of Naval Operations had urged Marshall to allocate additional air strength to the Pacific, and MacArthur and Australian officials were demanding protection against large-scale Japanese attacks on Australia that they believed to be imminent.[5] On the General's return King again strongly opposed diversion of United States forces to any other theater "to the extent that we find ourselves unable to fulfill our obligations to implement our basic strategic plan in the Pacific Theater, which is to hold what we have against any attack that the Japanese are capable of launching against us." [6]

In mid-May, Japanese naval movements aroused Washington's fears that the enemy fleet might be planning an attack on Midway or Dutch Harbor. Public jubilation over Colonel James H. Doolittle's spectacular air raid on Tokyo on April 18 soon gave way to private anxieties that the Japanese might retaliate against the west coast of the United States. When worried citizens began to demand that defenses of key cities in the area be strengthened, General Marshall decided to lend them a hand. Accompanied by Doolittle, who had recently been brought to Washington to receive the Medal of Honor and a promotion to brigadier general, he flew out to cut the official red tape that was choking the flow of equipment to the threatened centers.

The role of the man at the top in making things move was strikingly demonstrated in the next two days. With his usual energy he ordered in anti-aircraft batteries, established balloon barrages at San Francisco and Los Angeles, and saw to it that several squadrons of pursuit planes were made available. Long-dormant plans for closer defense coordination with Mexico came alive. Marshall's presence stimulated activity by subordinates at all levels and vastly relieved civilians in the coast areas easily inclined to panic at the thought of an enemy attack.[7]

The hasty measures of late May were intended as prudent protection against a possible surprise from the sea and not as a prelude to increased activities in the Pacific. Marshall stoutly declined to accept Admiral King's proposal that they rush air and sea reinforcements to the Fijis-Australia area—even at the expense of BOLERO—to avoid possible disaster in that area. Lest there be any doubt of his continued backing of the Europe First concept, he repeated it at West Point on May 29 in an address hailed by one news association as the most important speech by an American leader since the President appeared before Congress on December 8.[8]

For security reasons the General's participation in the graduation exercises at the United States Military Academy had received no advance publicity. His unheralded appearance as well as his statements created a considerable stir. During the presentation of diplomas he stepped forward to the microphone to announce that the father of Cadet Alexander M. Patch, Jr., was in New Caledonia and the father of Edgar Bergman Colladay, Jr., in the Aleutians, and that Olmedo Alfaro, son of the Ambassador from Ecuador, was the third member of his family to graduate from the Academy. When the turn of the lowest-ranking member of the class came, Marshall took him by the hand and proclaimed to the delighted audience, "In this war we need less mathematics and more powder."

His informality charmed the cadets. It was his statement that American troops were landing in England and "will land in France" that stole the headlines. His assurance that "no compromise is possible, and the victory of the democracies can only be complete with the utter defeat of the war machines of Germany and Japan," was backed up by his revelation that the Army had been increased by 300,000 in the past four weeks and that the previous estimate of Army strength by the end of the year had been raised from 3,600,000 to 4,500,000. Major George Fielding Eliot, a widely quoted military commentator, saw in the pronouncement the dashing of Axis hopes for a breathing spell or a chance at a new Axis peace offensive.[9]

As Marshall spoke, Japanese and American naval and air forces were converging in the Central Pacific for one of the war's decisive battles, which indirectly would aid his desire to continue the strategy of Europe First. Recent intercepts of the Japanese Navy's messages, sent in a code that had been broken a few weeks earlier, alerted the United States Navy to an enemy plan for attacking Midway near the end of May. The long-expected assault came on June 4. At daybreak the four carriers of the Japanese force launched an air strike—destined to be the only one it was able to make—against the American-held island. At almost the moment of the attack on Midway's installations, land-based Army and Marine aircraft were ordered out against the enemy carriers. The first round of the fight went to the Japanese; they shot down most of the American planes with little damage to themselves.

Meanwhile planes from the Navy's three carriers were seeking out the enemy force. Before noon they had wrecked three of the Japanese carriers. The fourth escaped long enough for its aircraft to inflict mortal damages on the *Yorktown*, which was later sunk by Japanese submarine fire. Long before the American ship went under, divebombers from the *Enterprise* had finished off the last enemy carrier. Although Admiral Isoroku Yamamoto, chief of the Japanese Combined Fleet, still commanded a powerful battle force in the Central Pacific, he decided shortly after three o'clock on the morning of June 5 to abandon the fight.[10]

"The closest squeak and the greatest victory [in the Pacific] was at Midway," said Marshall later. "The Navy performance there was magnificent and self-sacrificing to the last degree. . . . There, by a very fortunate series of events, and by very superb action by the Navy and its air—the ships were very much crippled at that time—the dominance of the Pacific was recaptured." [11]

To General Marshall's embarrassment the battle brought unpleasant bickering over the Army Air Force's premature claims of a large share of the credit for the enemy defeat. "Our people claimed everything, but did little. They were using pinpoint bombing, but were not ready to use it successfully. . . . Arnold complained on the publicity, but I [told him] you have no case." The Chief of Staff ordered that more careful checks be made in future before boastful claims were released to the public. General Arnold later declared: "The Battle of Midway was the reality which the Army Air Force had simulated for years. Yet, when the opportunity came, we did not measure up to the high standard we had set for ourselves." In the months that followed he took steps to see that the mistakes were set right.[12]

Marshall and Stimson both saw in the Navy's victory an opportunity to turn their main attention back to an offensive in Europe for 1942. As early as June 6 the Secretary of War declared that matériel diverted from BOLERO to protect the west coast could now be shifted again to the build-up in the United Kingdom. General MacArthur and Admiral King saw instead the opportunity to launch an offensive against the Japanese. Heavy pressure was thus brought to bear on Marshall to turn his main efforts to the Pacific at the very moment the Russians were demanding from Roosevelt and Churchill an operation in Europe for the summer or fall of 1942 to reduce German threats to the eastern front.

In late May, Foreign Commissar V. M. Molotov, on a trip to London, asked bluntly what could be done that year to divert forty German divisions from the Russian front. After concluding an Anglo-Russian treaty of alliance, the Soviet official left for Washington without getting a firm answer to his question. The Prime Minister had spoken of the difficulties involved and suggested they discuss it further on Molotov's return from the United States. Churchill hastened to warn President Roosevelt that the British were discovering complications in planning a cross-Channel attack for that year. He announced that he was sending Admiral Mountbatten to explain the difficulties and to outline a plan, called JUPITER, for landing in Norway. In closing, he reminded Roosevelt that they "must never let GYMNAST [a plan for invading North Africa] pass from our minds." [13]

In the talks with Molotov in Washington that followed, General Marshall cautioned the President against promising the Russians too much. At Roosevelt's prompting he informed the commissar that the Allies were preparing a second front. He held to his belief that events might force an emergency Channel crossing by late 1942, but he recognized the factors working against it. When Molotov asked for an effort capable of drawing forty German divisions from the eastern front, Marshall made no promises. Any operation that fall, he warned, would depend on the number of men the Allies could ship to France.[14]

General Marshall protested at the conference's end against the President's suggestion of an operation by August, indicating that it would arouse British fears. When Molotov proposed the release of a statement saying that "full understanding was reached with re- gard to the urgent tasks of creating a Second Front in Europe in 1942," the General urged that all references to a date be dropped. Although Hopkins called Marshall's warning to Roosevelt's at- tention, the President authorized the release of the statement. In so doing he implied a pledge to Stalin the British were not willing to underwrite.[15]

Apparently the President saw in the announcement nothing more than a word of good cheer for a weary comrade. But the situ- ation had the makings of a possible trap. From this public pledge of action to aid the Soviet Union by an operation in 1942 there could be no easy turning back. If the cross-Channel attack had to be ruled out for 1942, Churchill was in a perfect position to insist on GYMNAST.

Almost as if waiting in the wings until the stage was cleared, Admiral Mountbatten arrived in Washington near the end of Molotov's discussions with the Americans and as the Russian was preparing to return to London for further talks. Visiting Washing- ton to check on the current program for producing landing craft, the Combined Operations Commander lost no time in outlining for Roosevelt the drawbacks to a 1942 cross-Channel attack. Mar- shall and King were not only unhappy over the news; they were more distressed because Roosevelt failed to invite them to sit in on the discussions. They were not fully aware of the President's views until British members of the Combined Chiefs of Staff made avail- able Mountbatten's summary of the conversation that had been forwarded from London.[16]

Marshall and Stimson were jolted by the extent to which Roo- sevelt had shifted ground. The President had made an effort to con- vince Mountbatten that there was an agreement (a view Churchill declined to accept) to make a sacrifice landing in France that year if the war went badly for the Russians. Apparently shaken by Mountbatten's view that no landing the Allies could mount could draw off additional German divisions that year, the President ended by suggesting that American divisions might be sent to Libya or Morocco.

Before Mountbatten's final report on Roosevelt's views reached London the British War Cabinet had dealt a stunning blow to SLEDGEHAMMER. On June 10 Prime Minister Churchill explained to Molotov that the British were not committed to a cross-Channel operation for 1942. Next day he asked the cabinet to agree that there would be no substantial landing in France unless the Allies were prepared to remain and that there be no invasion in 1942 unless the Germans were demoralized by their operations against the Russians. The cabinet's acceptance of these reservations effectively ended SLEDGEHAMMER. It now remained for the British to convince the President that he should lose no time in adopting GYMNAST for 1942. They had to act quickly because General Marshall had selected General Eisenhower to command United States Forces in Europe and was soon to send him to London to plan for operations that summer.

When Field Marshal Dill confirmed Mountbatten's observations that Roosevelt was looking for an alternative to SLEDGEHAMMER and that the offensive in Europe was "losing ground" in his mind, the Prime Minister prepared for another trip to Washington. Fighting in the Western Desert was then reaching a dangerous climax, but Churchill and his advisers considered such a trip crucial to their future plans.[17]

Accompanied by Brooke and Ismay, Churchill set off by flying boat for the United States shortly before midnight, June 17. Twenty-eight hours later they put down in Washington, where the British Ambassador, Lord Halifax, and General Marshall bade them welcome. Early the next morning the Prime Minister flew up to Hyde Park for the weekend, leaving Marshall and Stimson uneasily wondering what new operations the British visitor would sell their chief.

The yeast of Mountbatten's suggestion that a North African landing be substituted for SLEDGEHAMMER for 1942 had already begun to work before Churchill appeared on American shores. At a White House meeting with his advisers on June 17 the President showed signs that he was "going to jump the traces." Having anticipated this move, Marshall came prepared with a blast against GYMNAST. Stimson vigorously supported the attack.[18]

After their meeting Stimson and Marshall made one last attempt to spike the President's guns. The Secretary of War on June 18 drew up a strong restatement of the SLEDGEHAMMER-BOLERO concept, which Marshall approved. The General then passed it around to his chief advisers, Arnold, McNarney, and Eisenhower, and wrote an accompanying letter saying that the statement had the concurrence of all the officers who had seen it. Stimson fired the message off to Hyde Park for Roosevelt to read before the Prime Minister arrived.[19]

While the political chiefs talked at Hyde Park, Marshall tried to sell his views to Brooke. Although the Chief of the Imperial General Staff still disliked SLEDGEHAMMER, he was willing to help Marshall head off GYMNAST. Vitally concerned with the dangers in the Middle East and fearful of any African operation that would draw troops and supplies away from that theater, Brooke encouraged continued planning for a 1943 cross-Channel attack.[20]

The temporary alliance against North Africa did not extend to a 1942 landing in France; on June 20 Brooke again turned his fire against the emergency cross-Channel effort. Marshall fell back to his fixed position: preparations for SLEDGEHAMMER in 1942 were necessary to save ROUNDUP for 1943. For reinforcement he called in General Eisenhower, who argued forcibly that there was a possibility of seizing a bridgehead in France and holding it through the winter as a desperate means of drawing German air forces from the eastern front. Brooke listened courteously but was not convinced.[21]

The day, as the British Army chief recalled it, was "stinking hot." Sweltering in a winterweight uniform, more suited to London than to Washington's tropical steam bath, Brooke was relieved to get away from the Munitions Building to the cooler environs of Marshall's Fort Myer quarters for lunch. Spoiling the day for both Marshall and Brooke, however, were visions they shared of what their chiefs "were brewing up together at Hyde Park." "We fear the worst," wrote Brooke, "and are certain that North Africa and North Norway plans for 1942 will loom large in their proposals." [22] Equally uneasy was Secretary Stimson, who recorded that Churchill and Roosevelt, despite their brilliance, were too much alike in lacking "the balance that has got to go along with warfare." [23]

Marshall later commented on his problems in the spring and summer of 1942: "We were largely trying to get the President to stand pat on what he had previously agreed to. The President shifted, particularly when Churchill got hold of him. . . . The President was always ready to do any sideshow and Churchill was always prodding him. My job was to hold the President down to what we were doing. It was difficult because the Navy was pulling everything toward the Pacific, and that's where the Marines were, and they got a lot of publicity. The President's tendency to shift and handle things loosely and be influenced, particularly by the British, was one of our great problems. . . ." [24] In 1956 General Marshall conceded: "We failed to see that the leader in a democracy has to keep the people entertained. (That may sound like the wrong word, but it conveys the thought.) The people demand action. We couldn't wait to be completely ready. Churchill was always getting into sideshows. If we had gone as far as he did we never would have gotten out. But I could see why he had to have something." [25]

The tolerant view was a postwar judgment. In 1942 Marshall still saw the meeting at Hyde Park as a definite danger to his proposals, and he soon found that he had not overestimated Churchill's influence. On June 20 the Prime Minister opened a frontal attack on SLEDGEHAMMER, throwing a series of hard questions at the President: Did they have a plan? What troops could be used? Where would they land? What shipping and landing craft were available? Who was to command the operation? What British aid was required? [26]

In Marshall's view, all the questions came back to landing craft and shipping. In a statement that oversimplified the problem, he put much of the blame for the landing-craft shortage on the Navy. "The reversal of the April decision about ROUNDUP was due to the Navy, particularly its construction department, and to the British Chiefs of Staff. It was a combined affair: the British on one slant and the Navy on another. I don't mean that it was King. It was the Yards and Construction people. They were so dominant that they told me when we were talking about making a mountain division with different equipment and numbers of men that they would only carry a standard-type division. I ignored them and went ahead." [27]

The United States had started late on a program of landing-craft production. In addition, as an official Army historian has written, "During the first year of the war the majority of naval leaders resisted the development of landing craft as a foolhardy gamble with an untried weapon and a waste of resources badly needed for naval construction." [28] General Marshall recalled earlier opposition from officers in the Bureau of Yards and Docks who didn't want anything to interfere with the enlargement of the Navy: "Officers of that type, considerably influenced by the British, felt that we couldn't possibly get an efficient mass Army. . . . I was accused of being in the horse-and-buggy days in proceeding to get a mass Army. They said we didn't know the score." As a result, "they poured icewater on everything about an Army in Europe. They got it into Congress and it was very hard to deal with. I tried not to get into a fight within the team." [29]

Mountbatten had gratified Marshall by giving the Army a helping hand on his trip in early June. In the course of a discussion with Mountbatten and Marshall, King had looked extremely sour when he was told that he would have to find and train crews of a great number of landing ships and craft. General Marshall had replied that if necessary he would train his own. After the discussion Mountbatten went to King. Speaking as one Navy man to another, he said, "You are selling the birthright of the Navy. We can't stop the invasion of Europe." He warned that if the Navy turned over its function to the Army, "the Army puts itself ashore, and in the long run you don't need a Navy." King took the lecture without blinking and asked for his recommendations. Mountbatten proposed that King send one of his best admirals to London for several weeks. Next day the Chief of Naval Operations produced Rear Admiral H. Kent Hewitt, who was to play a leading role in landing operations for the remainder of the war. "I told General Marshall what I had done," Mountbatten said later, "and he couldn't conceal his delight. He said to me, . . . this makes it 100 per cent." [30]

But the building of sufficient landing craft and the training of necessary crews still lay in the future. After putting the Americans on the defensive, Churchill declared on June 20 that no responsible British military authority believed that any plan for attack on the Continent in 1942 had a chance to succeed unless the Germans were in a state of collapse. Having struck down the French operation, he expressed concern about the beleaguered Russians. The alternative that he pulled out of his magician's bag was the North African landing.[31]

The trap contained in Roosevelt's pledge to Stalin had been sprung. The President promptly got in touch with Marshall and

King. He instructed them to be prepared to discuss with him next day at the White House the situation that must be faced in July if the Russian Army was hard-pressed and retreating and in August if the Germans were seriously about to take Leningrad or Moscow or had made a serious breakthrough on the southern front threatening the Caucasus.[32]

Having ruined the sleep of his advisers by throwing this problem to them, the President on the evening of June 20 joined Churchill and Hopkins in his private car to return to Washington. On their arrival at the White House the following morning the Prime Minister summoned his Army chief for an accounting of his discussions with Marshall. After an hour's talk he hauled Brooke off to the White House for his first meeting with Roosevelt.[33]

Shortly after his arrival with Ismay and Brooke in the President's office the Prime Minister received one of the heaviest blows he suffered during the war. As he talked with his host someone entered with a pink slip of paper and handed it to Roosevelt. He read it quickly and then silently extended it to the British leader. The chilling words of the message announced the fall of Tobruk— long the symbol of tough British resistance to the Germans in Libya. Unwilling to accept what he feared must be true, Churchill sent Ismay to check with London. In a few minutes Ismay returned with confirmation from the Commander-in-Chief of the Mediterranean Fleet, who declared that the situation in the Middle East had deteriorated seriously. It was then that the President made a spontaneous gesture of friendship that the Prime Minister was always to treasure. Making clear his sympathy in every word, he asked what the United States could do to help in the crisis. To stem the German attack that he knew would follow, Churchill asked for Sherman tanks to reinforce General Sir Claud Auchinleck's battered forces. Roosevelt at once summoned Marshall to see what could be done speedily to aid the British.

The offer of assistance was made promptly, but the working out of the details took longer than Churchill later recollected. General Marshall assessed British needs in the course of three meetings held during the afternoon and evening at the White House and finally offered to send an armored division, fully equipped with the most modern tanks and guns. To get the full complement of equipment he found it necessary to shift tanks from units that had only just received them. "It is a terrible thing to take the weapons out of a soldier's hands," he remarked to the Prime Minister but added, "If the British need is so great they must have them." [34]

To command the division the Chief of Staff called on an officer that he had long had in mind for a key combat assignment. General Patton was summoned from the Desert Training Center to Washington and told to prepare the 2d Armored Division for possible movement to Egypt.

Even as Patton hurried to carry out this directive, other advisers of Marshall became convinced that the division would be of little value to the British in their hour of greatest peril, inasmuch as it would be October or November before the unit could get into action. The Chief of Staff then proposed instead to send 300 tanks and 100 105-mm. guns by fast convoy to the Middle East. To Brooke's relief, Churchill accepted the substitution and immediate steps were taken to rush the matériel to Auchinleck's forces.[35]

In the end Marshall more than made good on his initial pledge. When one ship was sunk with heavy loss of equipment, the Chief of Staff quickly made available seventy additional tanks. As men of military experience, Churchill and Brooke valued deeply the Chief of Staff's willingness to go the extra mile, but even they did not appreciate the effort it cost him. In explaining his action to his advisers, Marshall found it advisable to avoid basing his assistance on the grounds of generosity. Instead, he accepted the explanation proposed by an aide that the tanks and guns were given to hold the British to their promise to mount ROUNDUP.[36]

As a tough realist, the Prime Minister did not permit gratitude to weaken the force of his battle against Marshall's war plans. All of his argumentative skill was now turned toward persuading the President to commit his efforts for 1942 to North Africa. Believing, as Stimson put it, that GYMNAST was the President's "great secret baby," he lavished his praises on it. Preparations begun after Arcadia for such an operation had been dropped when it appeared definite that the French would not invite the Allies to land in their North African territory, and when lack of shipping made such an operation inexpedient. Now Marshall feared that the interloper would inherit all the Allied fortunes.

On the "Day of the Dupes"—so dubbed by the British official historian of this period—Churchill and Roosevelt with gentle words quietly nullified all that Marshall and Brooke had carefully concocted the previous day. In a skillful exercise in semantics, carefully worked out by Ismay, the Allied leaders agreed that "operations in France or the Low Countries would, if successful, yield greater political and strategic gains than operations in any other theater." Included in this concession was the stinger that if the success of the operation appeared improbable an alternative must be ready for execution.[37]

It had been a trying day. Near midnight, at the conclusion of the fourth meeting with the British since morning, the President asked the Chief of Staff to stay after the others left. To Marshall's consternation, Roosevelt suggested sending a large American force to the Middle East to control the area between Tehran and Alexandria. "Terribly taken aback" by this new and unwelcome proposal, the General almost lost control of his temper. But he held his tongue. Not daring to trust himself, he declined to discuss the subject that evening. After a moment he turned and left the room.[38]

Despite the shock of Tobruk's fall Marshall proceeded with his plans to take the Prime Minister, Ismay, Brooke, Dill, and Stimson with him to Fort Jackson, South Carolina, on June 24 for carefully staged demonstrations by American armored, infantry, and parachute units. These arrangements were part of Marshall's campaign, begun earlier in the month, to impress British visitors with the fighting qualities of American soldiers. In early June he had taken Admiral Mountbatten and Field Marshal Dill to Fort Benning, Camp Gordon, Fort Bragg, and Fort Jackson. With customary attention to detail he had outlined what he wanted done and had penciled in numerous changes on plans submitted to him by officers in charge of the reviews. As soon as he learned that Churchill and his party were coming to Washington he proposed an even more impressive display. Disappointed in the lack of imagination shown in the earlier demonstrations, he selected Major General Robert L. Eichelberger, commander of I Corps (later chief of the Eighth Army in the Pacific), to plan the show and impressed on him the importance of an effective military performance.[39]

Marshall and his party left Washington by special train on the evening of June 23 for the overnight trip to Fort Jackson. The following day was incredibly hot, reminding Churchill of the furnacelike heat he had known on the plains of India. Despite the tropical blast a stirring show was staged by some 10,000 men and hundreds of tanks and vehicles of the 8th, 30th, and 77th Divisions. Churchill followed the demonstrations with eager interest, exhibiting boyish delight at being able to carry and operate a "walkie-talkie." He was especially pleased with the air drops, finding "impressive and convincing" the parachuting to earth of more than 600 soldiers.[40]

The British visitors expressed polite congratulations but still held serious reservations about the men's readiness for combat. General Brooke thought that the Americans had much to learn; the more genial Ismay remarked to his chief that it would be murder to put the young men they had just seen against trained continental troops. With the man who counted most General Marshall did win points. The Prime Minister recognized that the men were still green, but he was persuaded that they were wonderful human material and would learn quickly. Years later he recalled his surprise and wonder at "the mass production of divisions under General Marshall's organization and inspiration." His conviction that a fine American Army was in the making still did not change the fact that any attack on Europe in 1942 had to be carried out in the main by British troops. As he left South Carolina by plane to return to Washington and then, shortly afterward, to London, Churchill was more convinced than ever that Africa rather than France must be the scene of Allied fighting for the fall.[41]

Churchill returned to a noisy battle in the House of Commons. Pointing to Tobruk and other reverses, opponents of the government claimed that the organization for the conduct of the war was not effective. The Prime Minister counterattacked. After a powerful speech in which he taunted the opposition for undermining his efforts while abroad—tactics that failed "solely because our American friends are not fair-weather friends"—he won a smashing victory when the opposition mustered only 25 votes against 475 in his favor.[42] Yet even in his moment of triumph there was a warning. It was more dangerous than ever for him to launch an operation that might turn into a disastrous defeat. He was convinced, according to Lord Moran, his physician, "that his life as Prime Minister could be saved only by a victory in the field." There was less chance than before that he would send troops to the Continent that fall.[43]

At the moment, in fact, there seemed to be only a slight possibility that the British could mount an offensive anywhere in 1942. On June 28 the Prime Minister was forced to concede that the situation in Egypt could scarcely be worse and to admit that he did not see how it could end. On that day the British had fallen back to El Alamein, sixty miles from Alexandria. The Russian outlook seemed more serious. Sevastopol was now in German hands as Hitler's forces drove southward and westward, threatening to gain a foothold in the Middle East.

General Marshall's intelligence advisers could see only gloomy prospects ahead for the British. Toward the end of June they warned that a final decision might come within a week and that he could expect a catastrophe for British arms.[44] Recalling the wrong predictions he had received the previous summer on Russian chances of survival, General Marshall decided to take another reading. He got from Major General Thomas T. Handy, who had recently succeeded General Eisenhower as Chief of the Operations Division, and General Smith of his secretariat a far more optimistic view of the British position. He reflected their attitudes on June 30 in answering Roosevelt's anxious query from Hyde Park as to what immediate assistance the United States could send to the Middle East.

General Erwin Rommel, Marshall reminded the President, did not have everything going his way. Recent German advances had left his supply lines badly extended and open to British attacks. The Chief of Staff recommended that Washington await results of General Auchinleck's current battle with the enemy before giving up hope for the Middle East. At least he saw no possibility of affecting the current situation by increasing American efforts in that part of the world and he feared that major activity in that area "would bleed us white." [45] He proposed that the United States permit shipments for the Middle East to proceed but that such aid should not interfere with other plans for 1942. The only measures that would have an immediate effect on the situation—the arrangement to release to the British American planes at Basra intended for Russia and the prompt dispatch of an ammunition shipment to cover temporarily a shortage in certain calibers needed by the British—were promptly ordered by the President and the Chief of Staff.[46]

General Marshall's current efforts to build up American forces in Great Britain strengthened his determination to avoid further involvement in the Middle East. On June 23 he had sent General Eisenhower to London as "Commanding General, United States Forces, European Theater," with a directive to "prepare for and carry on military operations in the European Theater against the Axis Forces and their Allies." [47] He wanted nothing to interfere with the success of this mission.

In retrospect, Marshall's appointment of Eisenhower seems remarkably casual. No special delegation went to the airfield to see him off, and there was no fanfare on his arrival in the United Kingdom. But in elevating his Chief of the Operations Division to the post in London, the Chief of Staff set Eisenhower on the road to the supreme command in Europe and, indirectly, on the way to the Presidency.

As was his habit, General Marshall had been gathering information on his new commander for many years. Fox Conner thought well of him; he had worked with Pershing on the American Battle Monuments Commission. One of Marshall's friends from World War I, Major Ben F. Caffey, stationed in Manila, had written the Deputy Chief of Staff early in 1939: "Lieutenant Colonel D. D. Eisenhower, Infantry, familiarly known as 'Ike', has been an especially brilliant member of the [MacArthur] Mission. He is 'going places' or I miss my guess." [48]

Chance, of course, also played a part. General Marshall had planned several months before Pearl Harbor to shift Gerow to a field command and to bring Colonel Bundy in as his replacement. Bundy's death in early December left a vacancy that Eisenhower was called to fill. By the time Gerow left to command the 29th Division in mid-February, Eisenhower was ready to move up.

When General Marshall found an officer of promise, he handed him a task with few instructions and then checked carefully on what the officer turned up. In his first interview with his new assistant in December 1941, he said: "Eisenhower, the Department is filled with able men who analyze their problems well but feel compelled always to bring them to me for final solution. I must have assistants who will solve their own problems and tell me later what they have done." "I resolved then and there," Eisenhower said later, "to do my work to the best of my ability and report to the General only situations of obvious necessity or when he personally sent for me." [49]

If his subordinates met the challenges acceptably the Chief of

Staff tested them with a bigger job. Of Eisenhower, as of others he selected, he commented, "If he hadn't delivered he wouldn't have moved up." It was this emphasis on performance that led Marshall always to brush aside thanks from officers for their promotions. His typical reply was, "Thank yourself; if you hadn't earned it you would not have received it."

Like his colleagues, Eisenhower soon learned not to expect lavish praise. Marshall's reaction to Eisenhower's plan for a cross-Channel attack was typical. "When he studied it, he said, 'All right, it is persuasive to me and here is what we will do and we are going to stand for it.' " Marshall's acceptance of the paper constituted his acknowledgment of a job well done. "The nearest that he ever came to saying [anything I would call] complimentary directly to my face," Eisenhower remembered, "was, 'You are not doing so badly so far.' " But he was rewarded by a chance at a bigger job.

General Eisenhower believed that he unwittingly aided his own cause by an encounter with the Chief of Staff early in his service in the War Department. As he recalled it:

> I was in his office one day and he got on the [subject] of promotion. He said, "I want you to know that in this war the commanders are going to be promoted and not the staff officers." After letting go this homily for about two or three minutes, he turned to me and said, "You are a good case. General Joyce wanted you for a division commander and the Army commander said you should have corps command." He said, "Eisenhower"—this was a real loaded brick— "you're not going to get any promotion. You are going to stay right here on this job and you'll probably never move."
> Finally I said, "General, I don't give a damn about your promotion. I was brought in here to do a duty. I am doing that duty to the best of my ability and I am just trying to do my part in winning the war." And I got up and left. It was a great big test. And for some reason . . . it was just one of those things. . . . I happened to turn around and there was a little bit of quirk of a smile [on his face] and I grinned and left. I just had to grin." [50]

That was only one of several tests to which Marshall subjected Eisenhower. Perhaps the decisive one came in early May soon after Marshall returned from his conference with the British. During his short stay in the United Kingdom, Marshall had decided that he needed someone other than Chaney to plan the operations that he expected to launch against the Germans. On his return to Washington he asked his Chief of the Operations Division to study the type of organization needed and the type of officer qualified to boss the headquarters he proposed to establish in London.

Taking into consideration the possibility that Roosevelt and Churchill would select General Marshall to command the cross-Channel operation, Eisenhower suggested that the United States Theater Commander should be an officer capable of serving Marshall as deputy or as chief of staff. He declared: "He must enjoy the fullest confidence of the Chief of Staff in order that he may efficiently, and in accordance with the basic ideas of the Chief of Staff, conduct all the preparatory work essential to the successful initiation of BOLERO." Having drawn the picture, Eisenhower nominated no candidate for the job. This was done a few days later by a member of his staff, Colonel Wedemeyer, who saw Marshall as commander of the invasion and Eisenhower as his chief of staff.[51]

Marshall's next move was to send Eisenhower to London to look over the headquarters and to report back on the changes that should be made. Apparently the trip constituted still another test. "I sent Eisenhower and some others over so the British could have a look at them," Marshall said in 1956, "and then I asked Churchill what he thought of them. He was extravagant in his estimate of them, so then I went ahead with my decision on Eisenhower." [52]

Eisenhower's own nominee for the post in London was General McNarney, who had only recently completed the task of reorganizing the War Department and was now serving as General Marshall's Deputy Chief of Staff. To command the corps that would make preparations for the invasion Eisenhower suggested General Clark. The Chief of Staff studied his recommendation and then asked that Eisenhower prepare a directive for the new commander.

Believing that any officer sent to London should have broad strategical, technical, tactical, and administrative powers, the Chief of the War Plans Division wrote the type of orders that he would want if he held the position. When Eisenhower finished he suggested that it was important that Marshall read the directive before it went out. The Chief of Staff replied, "I certainly do want to read it. You may be the man who executes it. If that's the case, when can you leave?" [53]

A few days later Marshall told Clark of his selection. During the conversation he reminded Clark of the latter's earlier suggestion that Eisenhower be named theater commander, but, said Marshall, "I had already decided to send [him]." He added that Eisenhower, on being told of his new post, had said that he wanted Clark for his corps commander. "Marshall gazed at me speculatively," General Clark wrote later. "It looks to me as if you boys got together." [54]

Eisenhower and Clark landed in London on June 23 prepared to start preparations for a cross-Channel attack. They learned immediately that the British had no such plan in mind. This was made clear to Washington on July 8, when Prime Minister Churchill announced that SLEDGEHAMMER was definitely out for 1942 and that they should concentrate on GYMNAST instead.[55] Although General Marshall should have expected this reaction from the British he was "very stirred up," according to Stimson, to find GYMNAST back in the running for the fall. Determined to head off the North African operation and to save the BOLERO build-up, Marshall resorted to a desperate measure to influence the President.[56]

Nearly three months earlier, when General Eisenhower had outlined the advantages of a cross-Channel operation, he had suggested that if the plan was not adopted the United States should turn from the Atlantic and seek a decision against Japan. From Australia, General MacArthur continued to insist that a shift of the main effort to the Pacific would be popular in the United States and would aid the Russians by keeping the Japanese fully occupied. Drawing on these views, General Marshall on July 10 proposed to the Joint Chiefs of Staff that they offer the President a Pacific alternative to the GYMNAST operation.

Encouraged by Stimson, General Marshall and Admiral King presented Roosevelt with a memorandum in which a dash of solemn warning was well laced with bluff:

> If the United States is to engage in any other operation than forceful, unswerving adherence to BOLERO plans, we are definitely of the opinion that we should turn to the Pacific and strike decisively against Japan; in other words, assume a defensive attitude against Germany, except for air operations; and use all available means in the Pacific." [57]

Afterward there was always some question about the seriousness of the suggestion. General Marshall declared in 1956: "In my case

it was bluff, but King wanted the [Pacific] alternative." Secretary
Stimson explained in postwar additions to his diary: "It shows the
effect of [Churchill's] obstinacy on Marshall and me, for we were
both staunch supporters of the 'Europe First' plan and argued for
the Pacific only because we were desperate at British inaction." [58]

Scenting the strong element of bluff in the memorandum, the
President called from Hyde Park on Sunday morning, July 12, demanding by that afternoon a full statement of the Pacific alternative, with estimated times of landings, total numbers of ships,
planes, and men, proposed withdrawals of men, planes, and ships
from the Atlantic, and the effect of the change on the defense of
the Soviet Union and the Middle East. From Leesburg, where
Marshall hoped to spend a peaceful Sunday, he was summoned to
the War Department to aid members of his staff who had begun to
gather the information for the President.

The service chiefs had no detailed plan to submit. They also had
to admit that their proposed alternative would not improve the
strategic situation.[59] The President promptly disapproved their
proposal, summing it up as "taking up your dishes and going
away." Stimson argued the point, insisting that it was "absolutely
essential to use it as a threat of our sincerity in regard to BOLERO if
we expected to get through the hides of the British." The President, he recorded, "agreed to that." [60] But Roosevelt did not want
history to record that the British had been left in the lurch.

On July 14 Roosevelt notified Marshall that he was firmly opposed to the Pacific idea. Wanting a prompt settlement of the issue
of a 1942 operation, he decided to send Hopkins, Marshall, and
King to London to get the opinions of Eisenhower and the other
American planners and then come to some final agreement with
the British. Although he indicated his continued support of the
cross-Channel strategy, he gave Marshall the impression that he
was leaning toward the North African invasion. Presenting the
White House view to the Joint Chiefs of Staff later that day, the
General concluded that Roosevelt would insist on GYMNAST. His
colleagues agreed, saying that while operations in the Pacific would
be preferable, "apparently our political system would require major operations this year in Africa." [61]

Both Stimson and Marshall had a final go at Roosevelt on his
return to Washington on July 15. The Secretary of War had been
reading Field Marshal Sir William Robertson's Soldiers and

Statesmen, in which the World War I Chief of the British Imperial General Staff castigated Winston Churchill and other British leaders for the mistakes of the Dardanelles campaign. Stimson saw in Robertson's warnings against expeditions that shifted the emphasis away from the main front a frightening reminder that Churchill was addicted to "half-baked" schemes.[62] He brought a copy of the book to the conference and advised the President to read it carefully.

Marshall was alarmed by indications that the President might be considering intervention in the Middle East. In "a thumping argument" [Stimson's words] with Roosevelt, the General insisted that involvement in that part of the world was worse than a North African operation. It would knock out cross-Channel plans for 1942 and 1943 and put the United States in deadly peril in the Pacific. He suggested that if they swung over to the Pacific while preparing for a later cross-Channel operation they would at least be able to block the Japanese in the Indian Ocean and prevent a link-up between Japan and Germany. The President had already made clear that it was a waste of breath to talk of a major offensive in the Pacific. Marshall had to be content with Roosevelt's pledge of continued support for BOLERO and the intimation that he had given up his lingering hopes for the Middle East.[63]

As the Chief of Staff set off for the United Kingdom with Hopkins and King on July 16 he saw no reason to believe that he could win his battle. After seeing the party off at noon Stimson took a little comfort from the fact that Marshall would be able to appraise the situation at first hand and perhaps "put some inspiration into the rather lethargic and jaded minds of the British General Staff." [64]

In a determined effort to help Marshall in his arguments with the British, Dill warned Brooke that Marshall was almost at the end of his patience. Almost certainly with the encouragement of the American Chief of Staff, Dill wrote:

> Marshall is true to his first love, but he is convinced that there has been no real drive behind the European project. Meetings are held, discussions take place, and time slips by. . . . Marshall feels, I believe, that if a great businessman were faced with pulling off this *coup* or going bankrupt, he would strain every nerve to pull off the *coup,* and would probably succeed.

To still Marshall's fears Dill thought the British must show the Chief of Staff that they were determined to defeat the Germans, that they would strike them on the Continent at the earliest possible moment, even if on a limited scale, and that everything that detracted from the main effort would get "no support from you at all." [65]

As evidence that Marshall was in a fighting mood, Dill warned that the American Chiefs of Staff were reading Robertson's *Soldiers and Statesmen* and had sent him a marked copy. Churchill needed no reminder that he was one of the chief targets in the book. Accustomed to parrying rough blows, the old campaigner remained gracious, cabling his pleasure to hear that "our friends are coming" and adding, "Soldiers and Statesmen here are in complete agreement." [66]

Dill's warnings had little effect because Churchill sensed that the President had given up the fight. Although he still supported SLEDGEHAMMER and ROUNDUP, Roosevelt had let it be known weeks before that American forces had to be in action somewhere before the end of the year. The British were certain they faced a divided delegation. "Hopkins is for operating in Africa, Marshall wants to operate in Europe, and King is determined to stick to the Pacific," Brooke wrote even before the party arrived. If the British stood firm against the cross-Channel attack, there was no chance for Marshall to win. [67]

Realizing that he faced a solid British front in the approaching conversations, Marshall wanted to make certain of the views of his representatives in London before talking to the Prime Minister. Churchill, anxious to see the visitors just as soon as they arrived, learned that they would land in Prestwick, Scotland, on Saturday, July 18, in weather that would prevent their proceeding to London by air, and sent his private train to meet the Americans, instructing his representative, Commander Charles Thompson, to bring them to Chequers for the weekend. Ignoring the invitation, Marshall and King elected to go on to London, where the Chief of Staff had directed Eisenhower and his staff to be ready to start discussions at once.

The Prime Minister was not in a generous mood when he heard that his wishes had been flouted. Holding General Marshall mainly responsible for the decision, the Prime Minister growled to Brooke

that the Chief of Staff was trying to exercise the powers of the
Commander-in-Chief of the United States Army. He roared at
Hopkins over the telephone, refusing to be placated by the latter's
assurances that Marshall and King intended no rudeness by their
action. To calm his host Hopkins agreed to go to Chequers for the
weekend. In a show of temper, probably more histrionic than real,
Churchill strode up and down the room, declaiming that visitors
should see him first and that the British chiefs of staff were under
his command. According to one version of the story, the Prime
Minister brought out a book of Army regulations to prove his
point, tearing out each page as he read it and throwing it on the
floor. Long accustomed to petulance in high places, Hopkins dealt
with the angry statesman with great skill, administering equal
doses of soothing syrup and bitters.[68]

The most effective tranquilizer in calming the Prime Minister
seems to have been Hopkins' intimations that he brought concessions from the President. Unlike Hopkins' earlier trip, when he
had led the way in pressing the American case, his main concern
now was to carry out Roosevelt's instructions to agree speedily on
some operation that would put American troops into action in that
part of the world in 1942. Hopkins, engaged to be married to
Louise Macy as soon as he returned, was in no mood to draw out
the debate. In a revealing observation, Brooke later recalled that
once during the meeting when Hopkins was with Churchill and
Eden, "I was not allowed to join them for fear Marshall and King
should hear of it and feel that I had been briefed by Hopkins
against them according to the President's wishes." [69]

While Hopkins calmed the Prime Minister, Marshall was exploring the chances of SLEDGEHAMMER with Eisenhower and his associates. They were not unanimous in predicting success. The
Chief of Staff was influenced to some degree by the report of Brigadier General Lucian K. Truscott, whom he had sent over several
months earlier to work with Mountbatten's staff. In the course of a
long session Truscott revealed that, in contrast to senior officers at
Combined Headquarters, the younger planners believed that an
operation to seize the Cherbourg Peninsula "was not only practicable but within our means." After lengthy discussions in Marshall's suite at Claridge's on the 18th and 19th, the Americans decided to favor an attack on the Cotentin Peninsula (of which the

Cherbourg Peninsula is a part), which could be held as a bridge-head until the full-scale ROUNDUP operation could be launched in 1943.[70]

In tedious meetings from Monday until Wednesday, Marshall and King repeated their well-worn arguments for a cross-Channel attack in 1942 to aid the Russians and to prepare the way for a full-scale operation in 1943. The British Chiefs of Staff warmed over their familiar rejoinders that they could not make the operation on a scale to help the Russians or to remain on the Continent. On July 22 Marshall conceded most of the faults the British had found in the SLEDGEHAMMER operation, agreeing that it could not be launched before October, when bad weather and the likely shift of German planes from the Russian front to the west would increase the hazards of the attack. But he saw no alternative for 1942. "Time was temporarily against us," he insisted, "and without SLEDGEHAMMER we were faced with a defensive attitude in the European Theater." [71]

It was a strange way to argue for SLEDGEHAMMER. But it was ROUNDUP he was desperately trying to save. Without ROUNDUP, he believed, "we waited for Germany to disintegrate or starve" before acting. The pressures were already mounting to dispatch reinforcements to the Pacific-Alaska area, the Southwest Pacific, the west coast, the Middle East, North Africa, the Persian Gulf and elsewhere. Without a main goal for 1943 it would be the story of dispersion all over again. So he argued on for an unsatisfactory operation for 1942, hoping until the last that he could stave off GYMNAST, lest its demands at last destroy ROUNDUP.

Soon after Marshall made his final plea the Prime Minister and the British Chiefs of Staff brought the proposal before a formal meeting of the War Cabinet. Unanimously the members voted down a cross-Channel operation for 1942. Marshall and his associates promptly threw in the towel and cabled the President for instructions. Having lost a fight that he had realized he had little chance of winning when he left the United States, the General relaxed at the day's end at a dinner given by the British Chiefs of Staff at Claridge's. "On the whole," wrote Brooke, "the evening went well." [72]

Roosevelt showed no surprise at the news. Having kept his promise to fight for SLEDGEHAMMER, he now sought a course that would win firm British agreement. He gave top priority to a new plan with Algeria and/or Morocco as targets or the original GYM-NAST plan, to be carried out by American forces only in its first stages.[73]

The next move was up to General Marshall. According to his account, as given in 1956:

> The British staff and cabinet were unalterable in their refusal to touch SLEDGEHAMMER. It looked like the Russians were going to be destroyed. (I remember that one sentence in our argument was that it would be a historic blunder if we allowed the Russian Army to perish in the field.) The successful defense of Moscow had not yet occurred. . . . So we were at a complete stalemate. Churchill was rabid for Africa. Roosevelt was for Africa. Both men were aware of political necessities. It is something that we [in the military] fail to take into consideration. I told the National War College students [later on several occasions] that officers lack knowledge of political factors which political leaders must keep in mind.
>
> One morning at Claridge's I sat down in my room and began to write. I recognized we couldn't do SLEDGEHAMMER and that there was no immediate prospect of ROUNDUP. What was the least harmful diversion? I always had to bear in mind that we didn't have much and that much of what we had was in an amateurish stage—particularly Air. I started writing a proposal [on which we might agree]. It called for an expedition into North Africa with operations, limits, nature, and the like. Just as I was finishing, King came in. It is remarkable, but he accepted without a quibble. Usually he argued over all our plans.[74]

While agreeing to prepare for combined operations in North Africa before December 1942, General Marshall made a final effort to save ROUNDUP for 1943. For purposes of deception and to have a force available to take advantage of favorable openings on the Continent, he asked that preparations for SLEDGEHAMMER continue until the eve of the North African invasion. Planning for ROUNDUP was to continue so long as there was any reasonable hope of executing it before July 1943. If the situation on the Russian front in mid-September indicated that ROUNDUP could not be successfully executed, then the Americans would agree on North Africa.[75]

"In the paper," continued Marshall, "I made several stipulations which had interesting outcomes: (1) a certain number of heavy bombers [fifteen groups] were to go to the Pacific and (2) under these circumstances [invasion of North Africa] ROUNDUP could not be executed in 1943." A commitment to invade North Africa, he and King warned, rendered ROUNDUP "in all probability" impractical for 1943 and involved the acceptance of "a defensive, encircling line of action for the Continental European theater, except as to air operations." [76]

The British War Cabinet objected strenuously to Marshall's statement on the likely collapse of plans for 1943. "They didn't want it used against them politically if they prevented ROUNDUP in 1943, thus delaying the freeing of Europe," the General recalled. "The cabinet would not agree to the wording, but the Chiefs of Staff did accept. I blew the hell out of that and said unless the cabinet agreed I wouldn't go along. A compromise wording was worked out that was agreeable to me." [77]

The War Cabinet also worried over the failure to make absolutely clear that the North African operation would be launched. But General Brooke was satisfied. Having won a major concession from Marshall, he was not disposed to quibble over the fine print. He sighed happily when he succeeded in getting the War Cabinet to let well enough alone. Apparently Churchill persuaded Hopkins to get the agreement firmly nailed down in Washington. On the day after the cabinet acted Hopkins cabled Roosevelt that there was a tendency to postpone a final decision on GYMNAST until mid-September. He "strongly urged" the President to set a date not later than October 30. The President at once complied.[78]

Churchill's pleasure at the decision equaled the disappointment of the American service chiefs. In cabling the President of his satisfaction, he stressed Hopkins' helpfulness in reaching the final agreement. Roosevelt replied that "the past week represented a turning point in the whole war." [79] General Eisenhower, momentarily downcast, reflected the despair of the American military leaders when he said that the day of the decision, July 22, could well go down as "the blackest day in history." [80]

At their final meeting with Marshall and King on July 25 the British Chiefs of Staff accepted the American proposal to set up a planning and command organization for the three operations now being considered. The North African operation was rechristened TORCH, the name it would carry into the history books.[81] Inasmuch as it was thought necessary to reduce French opposition by putting

only American troops in the initial landings, they agreed to give
the command to an American. Since preparations were to proceed
simultaneously for cross-Channel and North African operations, it
appeared best to have the same commander in charge of both.[82]

Shortly after leaving the meeting of the Combined Chiefs of
Staff on July 25 Marshall called Eisenhower to his suite at Cla-
ridge's to discuss the command arrangements. He indicated that
Eisenhower would be in charge of planning for the TORCH opera-
tion and that he and King favored him for command of the joint
British-American expedition.[83]

The question of a supreme commander for cross-Channel operations had definitely not been settled when Marshall and his party
left London on the evening of July 25. (They stopped in Iceland
for a brief inspection of the forces there and then returned to
Washington for Hopkins' wedding at the White House on July 30,
with Roosevelt, Marshall, and King as witnesses.) In an effort to
regularize the situation, Dill proposed to Churchill at the end of
the month that Marshall be made supreme commander and that
Eisenhower act as his deputy until it was possible for the Chief of
Staff to leave Washington. On the eve of Churchill's departure
for Cairo and Moscow he cabled the President that he would be
glad to have General Marshall named as supreme commander for
the ROUNDUP operation with Eisenhower as his deputy in London.
As soon as TORCH was ready Eisenhower could command it, and
then Marshall or another deputy would carry on planning for BO-
LERO, ROUNDUP, and the like until it was time to launch the cross-
Channel operation.[84]

Although the President considered the North African operation
settled by his decision of July 25, Marshall and Stimson continued
throughout early August to speak of it as still not definite. Intimations of their views crept into the press with the result that some of
the newspapers charged that the President was failing to heed the
recommendations of his military advisers. At his cabinet meeting
on August 6 the President hotly denied the charge.[85]

Deciding that the President was unaware of the depth of feeling
in the War Department, Stimson sounded out Marshall, Lovett,
and Handy on their views and found that they were all "blue"
about the recent decision. He asked Marshall bluntly if he would
go on with the North African affair if he were President or a dicta-

tor and in a position to block it. The reply, "Frankly no," stimulated Stimson to draw up for the President another of his sharp lectures on presidential responsibilities. To his surprise, Marshall opposed sending the letter. Feeling that he should take the initiative if any protest was made, the Chief of Staff said that it would appear that he was "not being manly enough to do it himself." When Stimson suggested that the President was guilty of self-deception, the General replied sternly that Roosevelt had known exactly what he was doing at the cabinet meeting and had acted deliberately. He solemnly assured Stimson that "he and his staff would not permit GYMNAST to become actually effective if it seemed clearly headed to a disaster." With this understanding, the Secretary dropped the proposal to protest to the President.[86]

On no other issue of the war did the Secretary of War and the Chief of Staff differ so completely with the Commander-in-Chief. Their distrust of his military judgment, their doubts about the Prime Minister's advice, and their deep conviction that the TORCH operation was fundamentally unsound persisted throughout August. With the same kind of tenacity that Churchill was to use in 1944 in the hope of scuttling the landings in Southern France, they continued by a fine splitting of hairs to insist that the final decision for TORCH had yet to be made and that preparations for SLEDGE-HAMMER must be continued.

Stimson and Marshall felt frustrated because of their inability to convince the President that he was gaining nothing by following the Prime Minister's approach. So long as Churchill, with the aid of American forces, was winning a peripheral victory in North Africa, the Eastern Mediterranean, or the Middle East, he was gaining victories for the British Empire. But he was not necessarily hastening the final victory in Europe and he was definitely delaying the comeback fight in the Pacific for which the American public was clamoring. From the American standpoint, the Mediterranean road was not the shortest way to victory, and Marshall and his associates believed that it would be even slower than it proved to be. It was this fear of the long, tortuous approach that would leave his forces in the Pacific beleaguered and neglected for months and perhaps years that later prompted Marshall's fierce efforts to tie the British to a major offensive against the Germans.

XVI

Tyranny of the Weak

O F all the cluttered mazes of global strategy into which Marshall was drawn in World War II, he found most difficult and distasteful the China tangle. Here was no clear-cut American responsibility such as existed in the Philippines or the Southwest Pacific, where United States troops fought daily for their lives, or in Western Europe, the defense of whose shores strengthened barriers against further Nazi spread toward the west. Japan's aggression in the Southwest Pacific was clearly evident; the China battleground was distant and costly to contest, and there was little to spare from burdened stores. Yet out of a romantic interest in China, fed by stories of early Yankee merchants and missionaries—some of them Delanos—out of fury at repeated Japanese rape of Chinese cities and provinces, and out of a belief that Chiang Kaishek had carried on the fight against the Emperor's forces while the Western Powers sympathized from afar, the President was determined to assist the Generalissimo. As a means of encouraging a power for which he currently could do so little, Roosevelt enrolled China among the Great Powers and set the liberation of her borders as one of the pressing aims of the Western Alliance.

The British, cruelly pressed at home and in every corner of their realm, more fearful over India's plight than China's peril, found no romance and little military profit in efforts beyond those sufficient to keep Chiang's forces in the fight. If the Chinese could pull their weight, well and good, but the battling must be at Britain's convenience and under her command. This anachronistic reminder of treaty-port rudeness freshened China's memory of affronts by white men who had profited by her misery and awakened recollections of imperial arrogance that the British had in late years been at great pains to dispel. All too readily the Chinese forgot that the United States had stood apart from European designs on China and lumped America's policy with Britain's. As a result Roosevelt and his advisers had constantly to prove and prove again a good will that Americans had historically taken for granted.

China's weakness in World War II was compounded by her attempts to regain status that she had not in fact held for centuries and to set the building of her armies as an end in itself rather than a part of an over-all Allied victory effort. Chiang Kai-shek further strained a difficult relationship by his touchiness over delays in meeting his demands, his opposition to putting his forces under foreign leaders, and his readiness to resent slights to his dignity as head of state. Marshall learned the hard way that in a coalition the weakest ally causes less trouble by his impotence than by his insistence on being accorded a position in Allied councils that his strength cannot justify. So the American leaders in the Revolution, down-at-the-heels and running from the British, must have appeared to the elegant Frenchmen at Versailles. The precedent made China's actions no more palatable to her Allies.

Like many revolutionaries come to power, Chiang Kai-shek was certain of the rightness of his cause and the special claims of his mission. The long fight in which he had won his way to national dominance had been marked by ruthlessness, impatience with the views of others, and strong insistence on his own course of action. Although tempered to a degree by the influence of Madame Chiang, whose beauty, intelligence, and diplomatic skill constituted major assets of the regime, the Generalissimo's stubborn pride made him a difficult associate in military and political enterprises.

Acquainted with China through a favored position in special spheres of influence, the British were highly skeptical of National China's military potential. Like his predecessors, Winston Churchill was unable to visualize China as a power that should sit in Allied councils and he refused to consider changing his strategy to accommodate Chiang Kai-shek. Even less was he willing to shift dispositions of troops and allocations of supplies to the Far East or to entrust the command of British troops to a Chinese leader.

When the Chinese Government late in 1937 pressed Great Britain, France, and the United States for a $500,000,000 loan to buy armaments, Secretary of State Hull emphatically told the Chinese Ambassador that only Congress could authorize such a loan. Not until late 1938 did the United States make any material contribution. In mid-December of that year, Washington announced a $25,000,000 credit for the purchase of civilian supplies in this country. Further loans amounting to $45,000,000 followed in March and September 1940.[1] Military supplies and planes that Chiang wanted for his armies and air force were not available in 1939 as Marshall sought to strengthen the defenses of the mainland, ensure the safety of the Western Hemisphere, and spare something for Hawaii and the Philippines. Marshall was brought more fully into the China picture in the summer of 1940 and again in the fall of that year when the Generalissimo warned that his government faced possible collapse unless he could get additional economic aid and American aircraft with volunteer pilots from the United States to bolster his defenses. With proper support, he hoped to block Japanese expansion in China and establish bases from which Japan's naval concentrations and airfields could be attacked.

Advising Chiang in the development of an air program was an American, Captain Claire L. Chennault, a tough, leathery, square-jawed flier from the bayous of Louisiana who had won a reputation as a fighter pilot in the United States Air Corps before being retired for physical disability in 1935. Soon he had been sought out by representatives of Chiang, and he had gone almost at once to China as adviser to the fledgling air force. The Generalissimo's resources did not include trained pilots, and many of the first planes he managed to procure were frittered away for lack of proper handling and care.

Chinese Air Force development gained in impetus in December 1940 when the United States made available to China a 100-million-dollar credit, of which 25 per cent could be used to buy planes. The Generalissimo gave his permission for a recruiting program to get trained pilots and crews in the United States. Since the fliers capable of handling the tough missions that the new force would undertake were in the Navy and Army Air Forces, it was essential to gain backing at the highest levels in the United States. Secretary Knox was one of the first to give his unreserved approval,

and then in mid-February 1941 General Marshall began to explore
with the State Department the proper steps to be followed in recruiting American fliers. Taking the lead in the program to procure these officers were two salesmen for American airplane com-
panies, William D. Pawley, who had been in business in the Far
East and India for a number of years, and Bruce Leighton, a
retired Navy commander.

With the blessing of the President, the State, War, and Navy
Departments approved a nonprofit contract between a corporation
formed by Pawley and representatives of the Chinese government,
by which the former was to organize and supply an American Volunteer Group to China. Acting as supervisor was Chennault. With
Army and Navy sanction, Pawley and his associates visited government air bases throughout the United States, offering good pay,
adventure, and a hint of bonuses for men who would sign up. The
lure was irresistible, and the first pilot contingent of a total of 101
volunteers, sixty-three of whom were from the Navy, arrived in late
July in the Far East, where they were to fly 100 P-40s released by
the United States to China. The British did their part to aid this
enterprise by agreeing to make available in Burma training facilities for the group, soon to be christened the "Flying Tigers." A call
soon went out for a second volunteer group shortly before Pearl
Harbor, and ground personnel for this group were en route to
China when war began.[2]

The United States did more than help build China's air resources. When the Lend-Lease bill passed in the spring of 1941, it
sent extensive military and economic aid for Chiang's entire defense effort. As weapons and supplies began to flow toward the Far
East, American military leaders agreed that, without proper organization and advice, scarce items desperately needed on other fronts
would rot or rust in clogged ports or be improperly used when
finally delivered.

In July 1941 General Marshall approved sending an American
Military Mission to China to insure proper use of United States aid.
He named Brigadier General John Magruder, former military at-
taché in China, to head the group.[3]

As the mission focused the War Department's attention on
Chiang's problems, General Marshall had to take an increasing responsibility for China's defense. The more deeply he became in-

volved, the more he found himself frustrated. The Lend-Lease background of the mission blurred the military picture and created a complicated politico-military relationship that tangled ordinary command channels, resulting in extreme confusion and administrative cross-purposes.

Magruder's group, with its extensive control over Lend-Lease shipments, was only one entry in the field. Harry Hopkins, on whom the President depended to speed Lend-Lease to Britain, the Soviet Union, and China, appointed one of Roosevelt's administrative assistants, Dr. Lauchlin Currie, to expedite assistance to Chiang Kai-shek. Currie took as his first item of business the implementing of a program to equip, man, and maintain a 500-plane Chinese Air Force. Working directly with T. V. Soong, brother-in-law of the Generalissimo, chairman of the National Bank of China and later Foreign Minister, Currie was able to appeal to President Roosevelt against the War Department and its representatives. He soon became a strong supporter of Chiang's plans and the channel through which Chennault funneled his proposals to the White House. The absence of clear lines of authority meant that Chennault, even after he re-entered the United States Air Force as a brigadier general in the spring of 1942, could appeal successfully to the White House against his Air and Army superiors. When his policy was totally at variance with that of the War Department and its representatives in China, administrative chaos reigned.

"The President pursued a preposterous course for military operations," General Marshall believed. "He was selling down the river his commander and believing only the subordinate and didn't even talk to me about it." The General abhorred this type of command anarchy but found no easy way of challenging it. In the European debates he had often profited from Hopkins' assistance. In matters pertaining to China his old friend was on the other side. "Hopkins and I hit an unspoken understanding. He was representing the President's interest, and I was not in agreement." The time came when they avoided the subject altogether. "He and I didn't disagree violently at all. . . . I was just trying to work the thing out. I tried to keep clear of any personal feelings on any of these things." [4]

The effort was not always successful. Years later General Marshall was still indignant over the treatment he received from the

White House in matters pertaining to China. He recalled being summoned by the President one evening to discuss what the Army must do in the China-Burma-India Theater (CBI). To his annoyance the General found Dr. Currie sprawled across one of the chairs in the President's room. There he remained while Roosevelt gave his decision against Marshall and in favor of his assistant's proposal. It was a needless embarrassment and surprising in a person of the Chief Executive's diplomatic skill.

From the beginning of the mission in China, Marshall received a series of reports indicating that the Chinese Army lacked the will to fight an aggressive action—challenging the notion that Chiang's forces had battled the Japanese to a standstill. Although General Magruder had hoped for improvement, some of his staff concluded that China's interest in stockpiling arms was not for the purpose of defeating Japan but to make the central government "safe against insurrection after diplomatic pressure by other nations had forced Japan out of China." [5] Somewhat later a member of the mission's staff reported that T. V. Soong had predicted that the regime would be out of a job six months after the war's end.

After Pearl Harbor the American Military Mission changed profoundly. Chiang Kai-shek, now the commander-in-chief of the China Theater, wanted a senior commander of at least lieutenant-general rank who could serve as his chief of staff. If American troops were to be sent over, such an officer would be essential; he was also needed to act as intermediary with the British, who believed it necessary on political grounds for British and Indian troops to take the lead in defending Burma.

It seems likely that General Marshall thought of only one man—General Stilwell—as meeting the job's requirements of experience in troop training, knowledge of China, and rank. A graduate of West Point, Stilwell had served in China for nearly a decade—as an Army language student at Peking and as a construction engineer in Shansi province in the early 1920s, then as a battalion commander in Marshall's regiment in the late 1920s, and finally as military attaché in Peking in 1937-38 when the Japanese pushed into China. Marshall had been impressed by him in 1926 at Tientsin and had offered him the tactical section at Fort Benning when he became assistant commandant, holding the slot open for a year until Stilwell could return and take it. In this job Stilwell exhibited the independence for which he became famous in China. He exercised his right to criticize to the point that some of the assistant commandant's friends thought him disloyal to his superior. But Marshall prized his frankness and his abilities; after he became Chief of Staff the second colonel to receive stars was Joe Stilwell.

Lean to the point of gauntness, perpetually squinting through steel-rimmed glasses as a result of a near-blinded eye injured in a World War I explosion, profane, irascible, well disciplined in body, undisciplined in tongue, Stilwell was totally lacking in the art of diplomatic finesse. A man with a compulsion to speak and damn the consequences, he sounded off against colleagues and superiors with a zest that caused momentary amusement but ultimate dislike. The nickname "Vinegar Joe," applied in affection, became a damaging trademark. As a safety valve for his temper he poured part of his bile into his diary and personal letters. Unintended for publication and unedited by him, they appeared in the postwar years as the work of an amusing but temperamental officer, bedeviled by poor digestion and Job-like afflictions, who took peevish and childish revenge upon his contemporaries by characterizing them with ludicrous names and rude remarks.

Seeing Stilwell's task as one of training troops and reviving faltering spirits, Marshall overlooked his lack of a smooth touch. Formerly a division commander and more recently in charge of a corps, Stilwell had been summoned in mid-December to Washington to prepare plans for a proposed invasion of North Africa. To the Chief of Staff he appeared as a skilled student of his art, an excellent instructor, a fine soldier who welcomed the sweat and toil of preparation and was not frightened by those who sat in high places.

Left to his own choice, the Chief of Staff would probably have picked Stilwell at the outset, but Stimson had other ideas. "It was really my responsibility to handle the Chinese business, but the Secretary wanted to get in on it so I let him," Marshall later recalled.[6] On December 31, 1941, Stimson discussed the appointment with Assistant Secretary of War McCloy, and the two officials concluded that the "best available man at present" was General Drum, commanding general of the First Army. They drove over at once to Fort Myer to tell Marshall of their decision. It is doubtful if he welcomed the proposal, but his reply was cautious. "He was inclined to accept it favorably," wrote Stimson, "but of course we all want reflection." [7]

Marshall expressed his approval of Drum to Stimson on January 1; the Secretary informed the President, and the word was passed to Governors Island for the First Army commander to report to Stimson next day. Apparently impressed by a series of magazine articles that had appeared in recent months suggesting that he was the proper general to lead American forces in Europe, Drum seems to have arrived in Washington expecting the top field command in World War II.

For the misunderstandings that later developed and ended with Drum's being dropped from consideration for the China mission, Secretary Stimson may have been partly to blame. In his first interview with Drum, held with Marshall and Eisenhower present, he spoke in general terms of the China Mission, indicating problems that had arisen between the Chinese and the British and the need of someone to soothe the Generalissimo. Writing later that spring, General Drum recalled that the Secretary had stressed an active command role for the head of the mission. If so—though his diary entry for the day stresses the adviser phase—Stimson was not thinking of the current role of the mission. His chief worries on January 2 were how to deal with Japanese forces then entering Manila and current preparations for the invasion of North Africa. [8]

As Drum made the rounds of War Department offices to discuss plans for his mission he was dismayed. Not only had his hopes of being the Pershing of World War II gone down the drain, but he seemed fated to languish in the backwater of the war in a far-off place where it was easy to fail and even easier to be forgotten. It was not surprising that he complained.

After a short study of War Department plans for China, Drum reported to Stimson that the objectives of the proposed mission were "nebulous, uncertain, and indefinite." Marshall was merely sending out a new staff to deal with old conditions and imposing on the Magruder mission another military group that served no useful purpose. Stimson interrupted to say that he had given careful thought to the project and that it was the fulfillment of a policy that he had favored for years. Strangely enough Drum left the meeting thinking that he had gained ground with the Secretary. [9]

On January 8 Drum countered the War Department proposals

by submitting a plan foreshadowing the building of American
bases in Calcutta and Rangoon and the rapid development of
ground and air forces to support United States military operations
from India through Burma and the Kra Peninsula to China. He
thus assumed the shifting of a major American effort into the
China-Burma-India Theater and a position for himself only slightly
less than that of General MacArthur's.[10]

Marshall lost no time in setting Drum right on the War Department's concept of his mission. In a stormy meeting on January 8
the Chief of Staff ruled out any major effort in China at that time.
Perhaps needlessly blunt, he revealed that in forwarding a copy of
the War Department's views to Sir John Dill for consideration, he
had omitted any mention of Drum's proposals. When the First
Army commander suggested that his statement be studied as a basis
for later action, Marshall coldly replied that there was little use as
he doubted if the British would agree to any proposals about India
and Burma.[11]

Taking these remarks as a personal affront, Drum lost his head.
He attacked the War Department's concept of the new mission,
"its objectives being of a limited nature, of certain inconsistencies
and indignities relative to command arrangements." The China
Mission could succeed only if the United States expanded its
ground and air commitment in China and provided greater authority for the head of the China Mission, he declared.

Threading through his furious flow of words was the implication
that the entire offer was a trap. Marshall's temper flared. Hot with
anger, he denied any thought of sending Drum on a dead-end mission. In the present crisis, he roared, every officer was expected to
serve without regard to personal ambitions. The situation was too
grave to permit such factors to interfere. The First Army commander's own wrath mounted. He continued to argue until Marshall, with a sudden and disconcerting switch to his customary reserve, said shortly that he would recommend against Drum's
appointment as head of the mission. Returning from a short vacation, Stimson found the smoke still rising above the ruins of the
China plan he "had been so carefully working out." After hearing
Marshall he was convinced that the two men had lost their tempers
so completely in their encounter as "to have left an irreconcilable
obstacle to Drum's taking the position." [12]

In the belief that Stimson was basically sold on his approach, Drum turned to the Secretary of War, explaining that the War Department staff was destroying the concept of the mission as outlined by Stimson earlier. He made a mistake fatal to his hopes. Instead of urging a proper strategy for China, he spoke of a proper role for himself. With his experience, he declared, he would be "more valuable to the country and better fulfill my trust, in connection with a mission involving larger responsibilities than those contemplated by the memorandum of the General Staff." He foresaw the danger of being shut off in relatively unimportant duties and "not available to our nation for its real major effort in the war. I would be lost by being involved in the heart of China in a minor effort of little decisive consequence." [13]

In an uncomfortable interview on January 13 Drum repeated these arguments personally to the Secretary. He said too much. Not China's but General Drum's future appeared at stake. Stimson shook his head reprovingly. He contrasted Drum's position with his own when he had been offered the Governor-Generalcy of the Philippines, an appointment he had not wanted but one he had felt he must accept. He assured Drum that he personally had planned the mission offered him—one he thought "important work for his country." As to its importance, he had had confidence in Drum's abilities to seize the opportunities to expand his sphere.[14]

Evidently "scared at the effects of his recalcitrancy," the First Army commander frantically tried to repair the damage. In a letter, regarded by Marshall as "additional evidence of Drum's unfitness for the post," Drum deferred to Stimson's long experience in the Orient and contacts in Washington, saying smoothly, "Your judgment in these matters is superior to the conclusions we reach who have not served in those parts for more than thirty years and do not have the advantage of such contacts." He would be happy to follow the Secretary's advice if he deemed it in the best interest of the nation for him to undertake the China Mission.[15]

This astonishing performance did not work. On January 14 Drum sought an interview with the Secretary and "almost tearfully" assured him that he wanted to carry out Stimson's wishes. The old gentleman had hardened his heart and spoke sadly of seeing his plans fall like a house of cards. Under the circumstances, he said, he was inclined against assigning Drum to China.[16] The Secretary's distaste was unmistakable, but Drum sacrificed his pride to make a final plea. Declaring that he had been touched by Stimson's deep feeling in the matter, he urged him "to assign me the task you have in mind." He promised to enter on it whole-heartedly with every confidence of producing successful results.[17]

But the door was firmly shut when Marshall persuaded Stimson to see Stilwell that evening. In a quiet evening at Woodley, the vinegary general proved to be "quick-witted and alert-minded." In a half hour, Stimson wrote, Stilwell gave "a better firsthand picture of the valor of the Chinese armies than I had ever received before." The worries and confusions that had bothered him were swept away, and the Secretary went to bed relaxed, feeling that he had found a man who would be useful in time of troubles. On January 15, proud of his new discovery, he admonished Marshall to keep his eye on Stilwell. Too startled to gloat in silence over his triumph, the Chief of Staff retorted, "Hell, that's what I have been telling you." [18]

One final act remained in what Stimson now described as "the wretched Drum affair," and the Secretary handled it deftly. In a short note he thanked General Drum for his willingness to subordinate his views to those of others. The tone was friendly but the words were fatal: "I don't think I will ask you to make that sacrifice." [19]

In speaking of Stilwell's appointment in later years, Marshall said that it had been made by Stimson. But "Vinegar Joe" was clearly the Chief of Staff's choice, and he would not have had the place without Marshall's strong backing. It was this fact, even more than their long friendship or his loyalty to a subordinate, that made General Marshall stand firmly behind Stilwell in the tedious fight that developed in China—bucking the White House advisers, Chiang Kai-shek, the British, and the President himself before he was through. It was to tie him closely to Stilwell's kite and to make him a more determined partisan of that general's cause than that of any other officer in the war.

The Chief of Staff worked rapidly to settle the details of the new mission. He asked Stilwell to draft a statement of what he wanted, and this was sent over McCloy's signature to T. V. Soong. The Chinese representative agreed on January 21 that the mission head would have executive authority over Chinese and American units in Burma, and Stilwell would serve as chief of staff of Chiang Kai-shek's Allied headquarters. Told that the conditions had been met, Stilwell said simply, "I'll go where I'm sent." [20]

For better or worse Marshall had committed himself to Stilwell. He was sending out to Chungking a man who knew China better than any other high-ranking officer in the Army, but also a man repelled by the diplomatic niceties required for dealing with Chiang Kai-shek. In a spot where the United States depended on the British for bases, training facilities, and operational support, there was an officer who was convinced that the "Limeys" had sold Roosevelt a bill of goods and were intending to use American soldiers and resources to further their imperial interests. Sent as chief of staff to the Generalissimo, a thin-skinned autocrat accustomed to instant obedience from his staff, capable of ordering the execution of officers who failed in their campaigns, was an individualist who had scant respect for the rulers in Washington and who persisted, almost from the day of his arrival, in writing of his chief at Chungking as the "Peanut"—an attitude of derision and near contempt that he allowed his staff to share and that all too soon came to the Generalissimo's attention.[21]

Stilwell's weakness in personal contacts was intensified by his prickly relations with Americans allied to Chiang, for whom he had even less respect than he had for the Generalissimo. He was soon at odds with Chennault, and his mixed opinions of Roosevelt's judgments were evident to the President's representatives. In retrospect, it seems that General Marshall could have recommended few officers more likely to create trouble for himself and the Army in China. The Chief of Staff eventually conceded Stilwell's faults but he could never bring himself to agree that the initial selection was a mistake. What was needed early in 1942, he argued, was an officer who knew the Chinese soldier, who was skilled at training, and who was willing to fight. Stilwell was all of these. In the task at hand, where the forces and equipment he brought were scarce and where he often came empty-handed to a harassed Generalissimo, a smoother tongue and a lighter manner would have been better suited to the situation.

Had the new head of the China Mission possessed the amiable qualities of an Eisenhower, he would still have clashed with the

Generalissimo. Chiang Kai-shek wanted a major build-up in China of United States forces and matériel for a large-scale offensive against Japan, and he assumed that he had been promised that by the President. Some of the later misunderstandings were due to T. V. Soong's reluctance to inform the Generalissimo of all of the unfavorable answers he was given in Washington and some to the President's own shift in emphasis on the campaigns to which he wanted to grant priority. Much of Stilwell's trouble arose over the handling of Lend Lease supplies. As the Generalissimo's chief of staff he was in a subordinate position. As head of the China Mission he had special control over Lend-Lease affairs that permitted him to go counter to the wishes of Chiang Kai-shek.[22]

To add to the untenable situation, the British demanded assistance in the Middle East and India that might otherwise have gone to Chiang. The root of Stilwell's worst embroilment was Chennault's insistence that airpower could win the war against Japan without use of ground troops—a concept that suited Chiang Kai-shek's future planning and his desire to save his army for the postwar period. Although as avid as any member of the Generalissimo's staff for more planes and supplies and equipment, Stilwell was the whipping boy for American failure to rush more aid to Chungking. He would have had trouble if he could have filled all the Chinese demands; empty-handed, he had no chance.

Stilwell landed in India as the Japanese were driving into southern Burma, only ten days before they seized the key Burmese port of Rangoon. As the British position became desperate, Wavell asked for the Chinese forces he had once been reluctant to take. The Generalissimo offered two armies, the Fifth and Sixth, but insisted that they must be under Stilwell rather than a British commander. When the British leaders opposed this arrangement, preferring that they be placed under General Sir Harold Alexander, newly arrived commanding general of Burma, General Marshall appealed to Dill in Stilwell's behalf, describing him as "an immensely capable and remarkably resourceful individual [who] possibly understands more of how to do business with the Chinese, particularly in military matters, than any other individual in this country." The matter was settled when Stilwell declared that he had no objection to serving under Alexander and when Chiang Kai-shek reluctantly agreed to a command which Alexander described as "nominal." [23]

In the campaign that followed, Stilwell fought the battle more in consonance with Alexander's wishes than Chiang Kai-shek's. He faced serious problems caused by the Generalissimo's reluctance to hold certain strongpoints unless the British agreed not to withdraw, the flat refusal of certain Chinese commanders to move when they were told to advance, and the weakness of British and Chinese units as opposed to those of the Japanese. Better command organization and prompter obedience to orders might have improved the situation; it is doubtful if they could have saved it.

General Chennault, speaking as one closely acquainted with the Generalissimo's thinking, has charged that Chiang lost confidence in Stilwell as a result of his handling of the proposed offensive near Pyinmina. The American leader had prepared a counteroffensive in this area, which he intended to launch when the Japanese followed retreating Allied units northward. This plan was dropped when British units, defending oil fields along the Irrawaddy, called for help. Stilwell, apparently with Chiang's consent, rushed one of his divisions to their support.[24] The shift of troops took place just as the Japanese to the southeast attacked the Chinese Sixth Army, smashing part of it beyond repair and driving the Chinese back in disorder. Although Stilwell rushed his division back from the Irrawaddy, he was unable to stop the rout. General Chennault later wrote that Chiang considered Stilwell's action in aiding the British one "of the sheerest sentimentality and incredible military callowness." "If Stilwell had been a Chinese general," the airman added, "there seems little doubt that his performance would have ended with a firing squad." Since American generals were not expendable in this fashion, the Generalissimo was content to withdraw his support and to inform Chinese field commanders that they could no longer move their troops on Stilwell's orders without approval at Chungking. Except in the case of one group of troops, Chiang let the order stand. "It became a sore spot repeatedly rubbed raw during the bitter years that followed." [25]

General Marshall in mid-April contributed indirectly to Stilwell's problems with the Chinese. The Chief of Staff, in London to discuss plans for SLEDGEHAMMER and ROUNDUP, agreed to put the Tenth Air Force, then being organized under General Brereton for service in the China-Burma Theater, temporarily under British command in India. He ordered all available aircraft above the authorized strength of the American Volunteer Group to be released to Brereton. Unfortunately the Chief of Staff's deputy in Washington failed to inform Stimson. Not knowing of Marshall's order, the Secretary of War told T. V. Soong the following morning that the Tenth Air Force would be put at Chiang's disposal as soon as possible. "Angry and excited," the Generalissimo denounced Marshall's earlier action as a breach of faith and Madame Chiang protested to the President. Roosevelt replied soothingly that no further diversions would be made without Chiang's consent and agreed that aircraft already allocated would be speedily delivered. Although none of this mix-up was Stilwell's fault, he was around to receive the blame.[26]

As the situation in Burma became hopeless near mid-April, General Stilwell proposed that 100,000 Chinese troops be withdrawn to India where they could be trained for future operations to recapture Burma with the use of Lend-Lease stores accumulating there that could not now be transported to China. The Generalissimo gave "general approval" to the plan on April 27, and Washington was notified two days later. General Marshall welcomed the idea and promised Stimson that he would find the necessary support to permit Stilwell to carry it out. On April 30, during Marshall's absence on an inspection trip in the South with Dill and General McNair, Secretary Stimson authorized Stilwell's withdrawal to India.[27]

At the end of May, Burma was almost completely held by the Japanese. The road that had carried American aid to China was now cut, and there was a serious question as to how long it would be possible to keep even a small crumb of nourishment flying over the Hump. India itself was threatened with attack, and the possibility of safeguarding China from further Japanese expansion looked exceedingly grim. This was no time for excuses or apologies, and Stilwell made none. Instead he appealed to the Generalissimo for radical changes in military arrangements to permit an offensive in Burma in the coming months. To cure the impossible command situation, he asked that one individual be given responsibility for command in the field; to improve the efficiency of divisions, he asked for a drastic reduction in the number of units and the bringing up to full strength of those remaining; to deal with corruption and incompetence, he asked for a ruthless purge of commanders.[28]

In blunt talks with T. V. Soong, Marshall and Stimson supported Stilwell's plea for more effective command organization. Soong passed on the arguments to Chiang Kai-shek, who agreed near the end of June to accept some of the demands. Tediously and painfully a flimsy house of cards was built. Within days it would come fluttering down.

Again it was action in another theater that caused trouble. Tobruk fell on June 21, and Rommel threatened a sweep toward Cairo and the Suez Canal that would break Britain's hold on the Middle East. In the emergency General Marshall ordered General Brereton to transfer the heavy bombers of his Tenth Air Force, with supporting transports, to the Middle East, and he halted in Africa, for possible shift to support of the British, a number of light bombers then en route from the United States to China.

It was one of several actions that made Chiang increasingly dubious about American aid. Roosevelt's proposal to give the Generalissimo his own theater had not been followed by membership in the Combined Chiefs of Staff organization or a place on the Munitions Assignment Board. The Doolittle Raid, launched in April without consultation with China, had provoked a Japanese assault on Chekiang Province, where the wrecked American crews had been hospitably received. Action had been started in April to absorb the American Volunteer Group into the United States Air Force, with a promise of more planes and personnel. Not only had the delivery of additional support been delayed, but Chiang had been stunned to find that Chennault was to be reduced to a subordinate position in the new arrangement.

Stilwell was not surprised at the furious reception by the Generalissimo and his wife of his announcement on June 26 that the expected aircraft was to be diverted to the Middle East. Bitterly Chiang charged that the Allies had no regard for the Chinese Theater; Madame recalled that every British defeat ended with Chinese equipment being taken away. This being the case, "there is no need for China to continue the war." [29]

On June 29 Madame Chiang explained to Stilwell that prompt delivery of the planes originally intended for China was essential to prove American good faith. In a belligerent mood the Generalissimo laid down three minimum requirements, henceforth referred to by the Americans as "the Three Demands," that must be met if his country was to continue in the war. Showing little understanding of the problems involved in procuring and moving

men, equipment, and supplies more than 10,000 miles in two or
three months, Chiang Kai-shek insisted that three American divisions arrive in India between August and September to help
China reopen communications to India; that beginning in August
the air force should consist of 500 planes to be maintained with
continuous replacements; and that from August on, military transports sufficient to carry 5000 tons monthly to China should be
provided.[30]

The President now had to intervene. He had been asked by the
Generalissimo in late May to send Harry Hopkins to China
to investigate Lend-Lease arrangements and discuss the handling
of American aid. Because of other demands on Hopkins' time,
Roosevelt had suggested that Dr. Currie go instead. He now hastened Currie's departure, and the White House representative arrived in Chungking on July 20.

Marshall favored Currie's visit, cabling Stilwell that it should be
helpful rather than an added complication. He also approved Currie's suggestion that the President defer decision on Chiang's
Three Demands until after his return. Marshall turned out to be
only partly right about Currie's helpfulness. The President's representative got along well with Chiang, but his reports on Stilwell's
relations with the Chinese leader were almost fatal to Stilwell's
continued service in China.[31]

While favoring many of Chiang Kai-shek's demands, Stilwell insisted on being free from the Generalissimo's control in matters of
Lend-Lease assistance. More important, the American general recommended that the United States require reforms and promises to
fight before giving additional aid. As a way to test Chiang's intentions he proposed that the Generalissimo be told that he must segregate and equip thirty divisions, bring them to full strength, hold
Yunnan, and prepare to carry out an attack on Burma. In a bitter
indictment that convinced Currie that Stilwell should not remain
in China, the general added: "The probabilities are that the
Chiang Kai-shek regime is playing the USA for a sucker; that it
will stall and promise but not do anything; that it is looking for an
Allied victory without making any further effort on its part to secure it; and that it expects to have piled up at the end of the war a
supply of munitions that will allow it to perpetuate itself indefinitely." [32]

Currie was in a more amiable frame of mind. Feeling that it was not proper to insist on promises when the United States was in no position to grant most of Chiang Kai-shek's demands, the White House representative laid down no terms. He was pleased to find the Generalissimo in a reasonable mood. Chiang had already indicated that he was in full agreement with Stilwell's project for an attack on Burma. On August 1 he modified his Three Demands so far as to drop his request from three American divisions to one, and he agreed to set no deadline for the delivery of troops, planes, or supplies.

Returning to the United States near the end of August, Currie supported Stilwell's proposal for an offensive in Burma in the spring but informed Marshall and Stimson that relations between Stilwell and Chiang were apparently irreconcilable. He proposed that Major General Raymond A. Wheeler, the able engineer officer sent out by Marshall to handle supply problems in the China-Burma-India Theater, be made head of the mission.[33] Neither the Chief of Staff nor Stimson liked the suggestion. In fact, Marshall had boiled with fury over the Generalissimo's reported treatment of Stilwell. Recent reports had made him more suspicious than ever of China's willingness to fight.

In early August, T. V. Soong had ruffled Marshall's feelings by trying to slide over some of the points at issue. The Chief of Staff "turned on him with an extremely frank and forcible statement" of his opinion of China's recent actions and made "brutally plain" that he would not "tolerate much more of the current attitude." [34] In a mood to talk turkey himself, Marshall was not perturbed at Stilwell's reported solution to the stalemate in Chungking: "Either we stop fooling and get out of here entirely, or we should lay down certain conditions which they must meet." [35]

Stilwell's memorandum to Currie and another of similar tenor sent by one of his staff officers to General Handy during the same period contain the essence of the Stilwell tragedy. The American had reason to be bitter, but it was patently dangerous for him to treat the Generalissimo as an unruly child. Stilwell misread Chiang Kai-shek even as he did Lauchlin Currie. He assumed that it was possible to call the Chinese leader's bluff by saying if he wanted to make peace with the Japanese, "Go ahead."

Disturbed at the developments in China but still strongly sympathetic to Stilwell, General Marshall asked his angry protégé if he felt that the existing differences with Chiang were "too strong or deep rooted to expect a favorable readjustment." From Chungking in early September, Stilwell replied that his recent meetings with the Generalissimo had been pleasant and suggested that his problems could be traced to Soong's lack of frankness with the Generalissimo.[36]

By early September a reply to the Generalissimo's Three Demands had been readied for the President's signature. The proposed message, Marshall told the President, included definite conditions which Stilwell had "repeatedly advised" should be met by the Chinese government to make American aid effective. The message was promptly referred to Currie, who strongly objected to Stilwell's advice that Chiang be requested to reorganize and train thirty Chinese divisions in the province of Yunnan. This was not the time to press this program, for "after all we are not going very far to meet his request." Currie was also fearful of the effect of Marshall's recommendation that Chiang be asked to use Stilwell as his adviser in the reorganization. In the light of the Generalissimo's state of mind, made so clear to him, Currie was afraid this suggestion would be taken as a deliberate affront. Currie told Marshall frankly: "At the risk of being tiresomely insistent, I would again in all earnestness ask you to consider a shift in command. I am certain that the present arrangement cannot work." [37]

The worried President asked Marshall to discuss with Currie the form of the War Department's draft reply. "Perhaps you can tone it down. Will you send for him?" The final reply *was* toned down; the revised text omitted requests likely to offend.[38]

Possibly the President had hoped to make the answer to the Three Demands more palatable by prefacing it with the announcement that he was shifting Stilwell elsewhere, for his reply fell short of Chiang's modified requirements. It assured Chiang that the American Tenth Air Force would continue to support China and would reach full operational strength as soon after October 31 as possible. The message promised that the freight-carrying capacity of the China-India air line over the Hump would be developed to the maximum but avoided promises about combat planes for the Chinese Air Force. The most difficult "no" was drafted by Marshall himself: the "extremely serious shortage" of troop-carrying transports made it impracticable to send any American divisions to the China-India Theater that fall. "The United States is waging this war on far-flung fronts and demands for men and particularly materials and ship tonnage are now beyond our present capacity." [39]

The President did not let the subject of Stilwell's transfer drop. In early October he suggested to the Chief of Staff that apparently the matter between Stilwell and Chiang was so involved "that I suppose Stilwell would be more effective in some other field." It was a gentle hint that received a strong answer from Marshall. Burma required, he wrote, "a troop leader rather than a negotiator or supply man who would only serve to promote harmony at Chungking." He had searched his resources and found no one else with sufficient knowledge of the Chinese and standing as a troop leader to secure either British or Chinese acquiescence for control of the campaign. He reminded Roosevelt that Stilwell had spent nearly ten years in China and that without such experience any successor would be "utterly helpless in dealing with Chinese methods, particularly in resistance to Occidental methods." [40]

For the moment Marshall had his way. He followed up his advantage by calling in Soong and reminding him that the great issue was Burma, "which meant a properly trained force at Ramgarh, an improved or selected Chinese force in Yunnan, and a practical basis of cooperation with the British in such an operation—in other words, Stilwell." The pressure apparently paid off. Shortly afterward Soong returned to Chungking for a conference with the Generalissimo; in early November the Chief of Staff was able to report to Roosevelt that the situation in China had improved. Stilwell was delighted with the change of climate and grateful to the Chief of Staff. "I think I recognize your fine Italian hand," he wrote Marshall.[41]

In a protracted discussion that lasted until early in the New Year, involving Chungking, London, Washington, and New Delhi, plans for a Burma offensive in the spring continued to be advanced. After months of preparation the operation was dropped shortly before the Casablanca Conference in January 1943. Stilwell blamed the British, the Chinese, Chennault, and the advisers of "Big Boy" (the President). Yet he himself expressed relief that he didn't have to launch an attack in the spring. The basic problem—deeper than the temperamental clashes with the Generalissimo, the plans of Chennault, the shifts in British thinking, the amazing convolution of Chiang Kai-shek's policy—lay in Allied inability to launch a successful offensive in China so long as North Africa, the Pacific, and the long-range build-up in the British Isles had higher priority. This fact had been rubbed in on Stilwell during many months of correspondence. The status of his theater and the nature of his own dilemma were neatly summarized in his exchange of letters with the War Department in late November 1942.

Messages from the War Department to distant theaters were often drafted by officers who overlooked the immediacy of the problems of commanders on distant fronts. One such communication reached Stilwell. In a message signed "Marshall," written with an impersonality and in a jargon indicating that it had escaped the General's careful pen, the writer declared that in view of the magnitude of requirements for support of current offensives in other vital theaters, the War Department could not divert personnel and cargo ships to support the Chinese in Assam and Burma. Only a thin-lipped politeness was shown in the official reminder that "we cannot meet your full requirements now, but be assured that when the demands of the present situation are less exacting we will endeavor by all practicable means to progressively increase the effectiveness of our support of your theater." [42]

Suspecting that the message had been cranked out rather automatically, General Stilwell fired back a reply representative of the bile that rose in all fighting men when their imaginations played with the picture of well-fed officers with trim haircuts and spit shoeshines, comfortably ensconced in the Munitions Building or the newly built Pentagon, casually writing "no" on overseas requests. He dashed off a personal note to a friend, Colonel Thomas Timberman, who had served as a young lieutenant with Marshall and Stilwell in China in the middle 1920s and was now chief of the Asiatic Section of the Operations Division and incapable of writing the patronizing jargon of the cable. In one of the classic letters of the war, which won Marshall's warm approval, Stilwell released some pent-up frustrations of several angry months:

To wage war in this theater, I am promised the following support: First, Lend-Lease combat materials, which is now in India. Second,

U. S. instructor personnel. Very handsome. Third, engineer construction material. Maybe two wheelbarrows, and a bulldozer, with bull. Fourth, increased effectiveness of freight line. This last one gets me. This list of imposing support for China's war effort would look well in the newspapers. And wouldn't it please the Chinese. If this is the backing the War Department is going to give to an honest effort at a serious campaign, that is their business, but the bonus [sic] for failure cannot be ducked and I will be *God damned* if I like playing goat all the time. If nothing can be done, OK, but for Christ's sake don't let them go on telling me how they are going to back me up to the limit. This is the limit, already.[43]

The letter was too good to keep. It speedily came to Marshall's attention—as Stilwell probably knew it would when he wrote it. The Chief of Staff was aware of all that lay behind Stilwell's indignation—the fight with the Generalissimo, the struggle with Chennault, the opposition of the British, and the lack of supplies. Marshall sensed something of Stilwell's frustrations over a wretched year of defeats, deceptions, and disappointments, but there was little he could promise and no magic he could perform to change the situation in the China-Burma-India Theater. Lacking Stilwell's pungent vocabulary, he did not reply in kind. He could make clear that he loved a fighter, and he did that by cabling, "I read your profane message for 'Timberman's eyes only' and I sympathize with you in your reactions." [44] For the moment sympathy was all he had to give.

XVII

Troubled Pacific

ONE morning early in 1942 Admiral King, the new Chief of
Naval Operations, came to General Marshall's office in the
Munitions Building for a talk. While King waited in the reception
room, the Chief of Staff was in the midst of a heated exchange with
Dr. Herbert Evatt, the fiery Australian Minister for External
Affairs, who had gained a reputation for creating "a tempest wherever he came" and "for dressing down everybody he came in contact with." [1] By combining firmness and persuasion the General
transformed the dispute into a profitable session, but it took time.
While Marshall and Evatt were composing their differences King
had stalked out, obviously angry. Having quieted the storm of one
angry official, the Chief of Staff set off at once to try his hand anew
at peacemaking. He hastened to King's office, denied any intention
of being discourteous, and explained why he had not welcomed his
colleague.

Then he added: "I think this is very important. Because if you
or I begin fighting at the very start of the war, what in the world
will the public have to say about us. They won't accept it for a
minute. We can't afford to fight. So we ought to find a way to get
along together." King listened carefully and when Marshall had
finished sat silent for what seemed a minute or two. He finally
turned toward him and thanked him for coming over. "We will see
if we can get along," he said, "and I think we can." [2]

The two men never succeeded in developing the warm affection
Marshall and Stark had for each other, and they had what the
Chief of Staff described as "one or two pretty mean fights," but
each gained the other's respect and made honest efforts to reach

agreement when it seemed that further controversy would interfere seriously with the conduct of the war.

An unwritten agreement became apparent: King supported
most of Marshall's proposals for the European and the China-
Burma-India Theaters and in return asked for the main voice in
Pacific matters. Although far more conciliatory than his bleakness
of manner and rudeness in debate often indicated, he was less disposed than the Army chief to seek agreement and was extremely
jealous of the interests of the Navy.

Under normal conditions General Marshall would have accepted quietly Admiral King's proprietary attitude toward the operations projected for the Pacific. The miles of rolling ocean sepa-
rating San Francisco from Hawaii, the Philippines, Australia, and
other distant Allied outposts meant that any campaign waged by
the United States in that part of the world had to be amphibious
and that the Chief of Naval Operations would exercise prime responsibility for planning and mounting operations. But the tragedy
at Pearl Harbor and the unexpected and rapid expansion of Japanese control upset the assumptions on which all naval strategy for
the Pacific had been planned and imposed requirements for men
and planes and special equipment that the Navy could not meet
fully from its own reserves.

Complicating the situation further was the presence in Australia
of a senior United States Army commander whose strategic views
and wounded pride made him intent on personally conducting
prompt offensive action against the Japanese. His determined
efforts to advance the special claims of his Southwest Pacific Theater brought him into conflict with the designs of the Navy, forcing
Marshall to become deeply involved in interservice quarrels and
special problems. Thus, while committed to pressing offensive operations in northwest Europe, for which he was charged with special responsibilities by the Joint Chiefs of Staff, he had to serve as a
buffer between the Army and Navy leaders in the Pacific, helping
to provide a measure of unity that would otherwise have been lacking. On many issues Marshall found it simpler to achieve harmony
with Admiral King than with his own subordinate, General Mac-
Arthur.[3]

A man of profound belief in his own destiny and in the rightness
of his own judgments, MacArthur was convinced that the war must

be won in the Pacific, that it should follow strategic concepts that he had outlined while still in the Philippines, and that it should be conducted along lines that would make his theater the center of operations. This attitude not only ignored the broad decisions taken by the Combined Chiefs of Staff but overlooked the central role of the Navy in any operation planned for the Pacific.

Political opponents of the administration created problems by proposing that MacArthur be given his head, and friends of the President made difficulties by suggesting that the Southwest Pacific commander be selected as generalissimo of the Armed Forces of the United States. The latter prospect appealed neither to Roosevelt nor to Marshall. It is not clear how soon Roosevelt feared that his critics were grooming the Pacific leader as a possible McClellan for the election of 1944, but there is evidence that as early as February 1942 at least one powerful Republican senator, Arthur Vandenberg, was thinking of MacArthur as a candidate in the next presidential election.[4] In these circumstances MacArthur's allusions to the demands of American public opinion for certain operations he wanted to launch assumed political overtones that he probably did not intend.

In no other theater of war did Marshall have the constant hint of challenge to War Department policy that he sensed in messages from the Southwest Pacific. That no angry showdown came in the course of the war was due largely to his own forbearance and the conviction that MacArthur was especially fitted for the Pacific Command. Unfortunately his attitude was misunderstood; some of MacArthur's staff apparently concluded that Marshall was afraid to go to the mat with his former superior.

In talking after the war about operations in the Pacific, General Marshall emphasized repeatedly MacArthur's excellence as a commander and the fact that he often had to fight with almost nothing. But there were points on which the two men strongly disagreed. In speaking of his relationship with MacArthur, something he rarely did, Marshall said:

> He was of a very independent nature and he made himself a political factor from the start. . . . And the President was very careful in handling him because of that. . . . Over there [in Australia], he made beautiful use of what he got, but he spent so much time scrapping with the Navy. Halsey tried his best to please MacArthur. He

tried to cooperate all the way through. MacArthur was a very fine commander. He was . . . supersensitive about everything. He thought everybody had ulterior motives about everything. . . . He was conspicuous in the matter of temperament. With Chennault in China and MacArthur in the Southwest Pacific, I sure had a combination of temperament.[5]

Because of the potential clashes between services and personalities in the Pacific, General Marshall retained a special interest in the command organization in that area. He took the lead in securing MacArthur's appointment as the Southwest Pacific commander, winning British agreement to an arrangement whereby he exercised supreme command under the Combined Chiefs of Staff. In addition, the governments of Australia, New Zealand, and the Dutch Government-in-Exile granted MacArthur authority over their troops in the Pacific. Allied Land Forces were commanded by General Sir Thomas Blamey of Australia, Allied Naval Forces were under Vice Admiral Herbert F. Leary of the United States Navy, and Allied Air Forces were under General Brett. General Marshall twice indicated that MacArthur should emphasize the international nature of his headquarters by adding key Australian, New Zealand, and Dutch officers to his staff, but the suggestion was rather pointedly ignored.[6]

Had it been feasible, General Marshall would have liked to unite all American forces in the Pacific under one commander, an idea to which he returned as late as 1943. His stubborn fight had won Churchill's acceptance of the concept of unified command, but he was less successful when it came to bringing MacArthur and the Navy under the same arrangement. Here he was blocked by the fact that MacArthur was quite senior to Admiral Chester W. Nimitz, the ranking naval commander in the Pacific, and could not easily serve under him, and by the Navy's flat refusal to put its carriers under the Southwest Pacific commander. King agreed on the creation of a Pacific Ocean area headed by Admiral Nimitz, with headquarters at Pearl Harbor, and a Southwest Pacific area commanded by MacArthur, with headquarters first at Melbourne. The Navy area was divided into the Central and North Pacific areas commanded directly by Nimitz and the South Pacific Area commanded by an officer under Nimitz, Vice Admiral Robert L. Ghormley.[7]

Although less far-reaching than the Navy's three areas, MacArthur's sphere was quite extensive, including Australia, the Philippines, New Guinea, the Solomons, the Bismarck Archipelago, and most of the Netherlands East Indies. The continental United States could be set down in the area of his command, which ran from eastern Borneo to western Australia.[8]

Ghormley's South Pacific command, to the east of MacArthur, was marked by strings of small islands, which he attempted to oversee from his headquarters in New Zealand. Unfortunately the objectives of initial operations launched from his area were located either in MacArthur's theater or near enough that boundary to create questions of tactical support. For lack of a supreme commander, both questions of support and control had to be referred constantly to Washington for settlement.

The South Pacific command was at first made up mainly of naval and Marine units, plus a small ground force under Major General Alexander M. Patch in New Caledonia and Army Air Force units based on several nearby islands. Only after considerable discussion with King did Marshall manage to persuade the Navy chief to agree to the establishment of United States Army Forces in the South Pacific. In late July the Chief of Staff sent out Major General Millard F. Harmon, Arnold's chief of staff, to head the new headquarters.[9]

The Chief of Staff also took a lively interest in the organization of the Army and Air commands in the Southwest Pacific Theater. Finding that MacArthur wanted someone experienced in supply to head the United States Army Forces in Australia headquarters, temporarily under General Barnes, he recommended the Southwest Pacific commander's deputy chief of staff, Brigadier General Richard J. Marshall, a Virginia Military Institute graduate but no relation. Highly pleased with the idea, MacArthur quickly made the change, reorganizing the command as a Headquarters, Services of Supply.

The Chief of Staff was disturbed by MacArthur's proposal to replace General Brett as commander of Allied Air Forces in the Southwest Pacific Theater with one of Marshall's highly regarded protégés, General Andrews. It touched Marshall on a sore point, inasmuch as he had been defending Brett for many weeks against efforts by Secretary Stimson and members of his staff to transfer the air officer. All of them conceded Marshall's arguments in favor of Brett's fighting ability but held that he lacked the administrative qualifications needed for the post. The Chief of Staff at last agreed to remove Brett but declined to release Andrews—for whom he had other assignments. Instead he offered Major General George C. Kenney, a highly experienced officer, or Brigadier General Doolittle, who had recently gained fame for leading the raid against Tokyo. MacArthur decided in favor of Kenney on the basis of his excellent record and the fact that Doolittle's relatively junior rank might be held against him by senior Australians who would have to serve under him.[10]

As the new command structures were being perfected and Allied plans were taking shape in the Pacific, the Japanese continued to expand, threatening every unprotected island in the Central, South, and Southwest Pacific. For nearly six months victories mounted steadily on the enemy side of the ledger until some despairing persons in the States began to think the unthinkable, "What if we lose this war?" At last, in early May in the Battle of the Coral Sea and in early June at Midway, the orgy of Japanese conquest was brought to a halt. Although it was evident that the Japanese would still attempt to take Port Moresby and extend their holdings in the Solomons, the way was open in June for Nimitz and MacArthur to consider offensive action.

The course of strategy for the coming months had been considered since early spring by planners in Washington and the commanders in the Pacific areas. In March, Admiral King proposed to General Marshall that they establish a number of island strong points from which a step-by-step advance could be made through the New Hebrides, the Solomons, and the Bismarck Archipelago. His demands on the Army were modest, since he proposed to use Marines with naval support for the initial phases of operations and only then bring in Army units to occupy the islands. Although he estimated that two groups of heavy bombers, two groups of medium bombers, and four groups of fighters would be needed, he believed that the total Army requirements for the contemplated operations would be limited to two or perhaps three Army divisions.[11]

The War Department's initial approach was fundamentally defensive. Marshall's policy, as reflected in General Eisenhower's memorandum of April 21, stressed the earlier Allied agreement to adopt the strategic defensive in the Pacific and devote major offensive efforts to the Atlantic. General MacArthur could not have disagreed more completely with this policy. Not only would it have restricted him to a strictly limited role, but it would have relegated part of his forces to occupation duties for the Navy and Marines. In his early dispatches from Australia he warned that the Japanese were concentrating their main efforts on his area and insisted that the bulk of American resources in the Pacific be directed to his command.[12]

Still nervous in the face of enemy advances in the Southwest Pacific, Australian Prime Minister Curtin in April called on Churchill for increased assistance, citing MacArthur as his authority for the need. Already irritated at Curtin for suggesting earlier that Australia was looking to the United States rather than to Great Britain for support, the British Prime Minister ruled that the requirements of India were more pressing and turned down the plea. He also moved to scotch further maneuvering by the American commander. "I should be glad to know," Churchill wrote Roosevelt, "whether these requirements have been approved by you . . . and whether General MacArthur has any authority from the United States for taking such a line." [13]

Wanting no quarrel with MacArthur, the President brought Marshall into the imbroglio by directing him to deal with Churchill's complaint. The Chief of Staff's rather mild suggestion to the Southwest Pacific commander that the normal channel for transmission of requests was through the Joint Chiefs of Staff brought an angry rejoinder from MacArthur. Somewhat ingenuously, he explained that he had merely expressed his views to Curtin for the latter's personal information. He was annoyed, therefore, that "breach of frankness" was now implied. Having tried his hand, Marshall passed the reply on to Roosevelt, who carefully solicited MacArthur's aid in escaping Churchill's wrath. "I see no reason why you should not continue discussion of military matters with the Australian Prime Minister," wrote the President, "but I hope you will try to have him treat them as confidential matters, and not use them for public messages or for appeals to Churchill and me." [14]

Before any conclusions could be reached in Washington on plans for future action in the Pacific, the Japanese push into Tu-

Tagi in the Solomons, their unsuccessful effort to take Port Moresby, and their decisive reverse at Midway brought matters to a head. On June 8 General MacArthur sent General Marshall a plan for an attack against New Britain and New Ireland for the purpose of seizing Rabaul. For this he required, in addition to the three divisions he had, "one division trained and completely equipped for amphibious operations and a task force including two carriers." [15]

Marshall had anticipated MacArthur. "Prior to June 5," he wired, "I started Operations Division working on troop shipping logistics for operation of same general nature as you propose but with greater naval strength." He was preparing to ask the Navy to send two or three carriers into Australian waters and to persuade the British to send one or two carriers from the Indian Ocean. All of this would require careful negotiation. "Until I have had the opportunity to break ground with Navy and British [here] please consider all this personally confidential, not discussing it at present with Navy, British, or Australian officials," Marshall asked.[16]

The need for prudence in discussing the plans with the Navy soon became clear. Admiral King on June 11 indicated that his planners were already considering operations "against the objectives given in General MacArthur's dispatch." He emphasized that they would be "primarily of a naval and amphibious character supported and followed up by forces operating from Australia." [17]

King's letter was crossed by one from Marshall urging the acceptance of MacArthur's plan and the assignment of Marine units and two or three carriers for the operation. The ticklish point at issue was introduced with his statement: "The operation will require the closest coordination among all forces involved. There must be unity of command." [18]

Attempting to keep the command question at planning level, General Marshall directed General Handy to discuss arrangements with his Navy opposite, the Chief of Naval War Plans, Rear Admiral Charles M. Cooke. After a series of conferences Cooke spelled out the Navy's objections: it did not propose to entrust its carriers to the control of General MacArthur. Cooke made clear that he was speaking for Admiral King.

To the Chief of Naval Operations the solution was simple: direct Admiral Nimitz to command forthcoming operations to block

Japanese expansion in the South Pacific, with authority to draw on naval forces assigned to Ghormley and MacArthur. King cited Nimitz's initial directive of March 30 from the Joint Chiefs of Staff as authority for him to prepare operations for both the South and Southwest Pacific. In his most gracious manner the Navy chief reminded Marshall that the Navy had cheerfully accepted Army primacy in Europe, an arrangement admirably suited to a theater where the bulk of the forces were ground units. In the Pacific, where naval forces predominated, it was only proper that the Navy command. Thus far, he had been polite; he finished on a stronger note. In a take-it-or-leave-it gesture, he chopped off further debate by saying that if necessary he would open the offensive without "the support of Army forces in the Southwest Pacific." Then, to leave no doubt that he meant what he said, he ordered Nimitz to make his plans on the assumption that he must depend solely on the Navy and Marines in the coming attack.[19]

In the two weeks that passed after he submitted his plan, General MacArthur grew suspicious of Navy aims. Dramatically he warned Marshall on June 28 that the Navy obviously intended to assume "general command control of all operations in the Pacific theater," reducing the Army to a subsidiary role. Its whole policy, he hinted, was part of a grand design for "the complete absorption of the national defense function by the Navy," which he had discovered accidentally at least ten years earlier when as Chief of Staff he served on the Joint Army-Navy Board. "By using Army troops to garrison the islands of the Pacific under Navy command," he explained, "the Navy retains Marine forces always available, giving them inherently an army of their own and serving as the real bases of their plans by virtue of having the most readily available unit for offensive action." He urged Marshall to be watchful, lest King get presidential approval of his proposal without the Chief of Staff's knowledge.[20]

With two stubborn and touchy men to conciliate, Marshall took sweet reasonableness as the best course of action. He rewrote a strong rejoinder drafted by General Handy in reply to Admiral King to say that he was "greatly" disturbed by the Admiral's implication that he would go it alone and urged a meeting to work out differences. As a thought for the day for MacArthur, he suggested that it was more important for the Army and Navy to use their full

efforts against the enemy than on each other. The Pacific commander was therefore to plan on the assumption that he was to go
all out against the Japanese regardless of the settlement reached
with the Navy.²¹

Marshall's mild approach soon showed results. Willing to make
more concessions than he had implied in his earlier manifesto,
King recommended that Admiral Ghormley command during the
first part of the coming campaign during the assaults on Tulagi
and the Santa Cruz Islands and then hand over to MacArthur the
later operations against New Britain and New Guinea. The Southwest Pacific commander promptly found the flaw in this arrangement, pointing to the confusion that would follow the change of
commanders in the midst of an operation.²²

At this point General Marshall intervened. He accepted King's
compromise solution and carefully drafted a joint directive on this
basis. Twice again King came back with proposals for Naval control, postponing the decision on the later operations, but Marshall
remained firm. The final directive divided the coming offensive
into three parts: Task One, the attack on the Santa Cruz Islands,
Tulagi, and adjacent positions to be under the control of Admiral
Nimitz; Task Two, the capture of the remainder of the Solomon
Islands and the seizure of Lae, Salamaua, and northeast New
Guinea, and Task Three, the attack on Rabaul and adjacent positions, were to be under General MacArthur. Amphibious forces in
all three phases would be placed under naval task force commanders. The Joint Chiefs of Staff would decide on the composition of
forces to be used, the timing of tasks, and the passage of command
from Nimitz to MacArthur.²³

The directive issued by King and Marshall on July 2 represented the maximum that the Army could reasonably hope to get
from the Navy. Marshall cabled MacArthur that a workable plan
had been won at great effort and "a unity of command established
without previous precedent for an offensive operation." Therefore
he expected the Southwest Pacific commander to "make every conceivable effort to promote a complete accord throughout this
affair." He granted that difficulties and irritations would be inevitable under the arrangement, but the end in view demanded "a
determination to suppress these manifestations." ²⁴

The agreement was worked out just as civilian coast-watchers re-

ported that the Japanese were constructing an airfield on Guadalcanal. Admiral Ghormley flew at once to Australia to discuss with
MacArthur his plans for future offensive action. Both officers were
unhappy about the paucity of forces available for a campaign and
made clear to Washington that they had little liking for the Tulagi
operation. With a certain grim satisfaction Admiral King on July
10 informed Marshall of the situation. Only two weeks earlier Mac-
Arthur had said that with amphibious forces and two carriers he
could push through to Rabaul. Now, when "confronted with the
concrete aspects of the tasks, he . . . feels he not only cannot
undertake this extended operation but not even the Tulagi operation."

The Navy chief was displeased to find Ghormley agreeing with
the Southwest Pacific commander that Task One should be postponed until they had in hand the necessary aircraft and equipment to undertake all three tasks. Marshall agreed with King's
strong insistence on speedy action. The two service chiefs decided
that Ghormley should go ahead with Task One, concentrating on
Tulagi and Guadalcanal, and MacArthur should plan for the next
two tasks as if planes and supplies would be available when required.[25]

In later months when critics charged King with having pushed
in ahead of MacArthur, Marshall made clear that the Army had
not opposed the operation. After the war he declared: "The Marines went to Guadalcanal at my urging in a way, because if we lost
that field there we were pushed way to the south in trying to move
troops to Australia, . . . and so we went ahead and made do with
what we had." [26]

While the Americans talked the Japanese had not been idle. Before the Navy could launch its early August attack the enemy dispatched a force to northeast New Guinea. Buna was occupied quietly on July 22; by the end of the month troops marching overland
had taken Kokoda. These movements menaced both the Gona Bay
area and Port Moresby, posing a threat to operations in the South
Pacific as well as in MacArthur's theater.

As the time for the invasion of Guadalcanal and Tulagi drew
near, King became uneasy about a matter that he had not yet
fully explored with Marshall. He could not depend solely on the
Navy's air resources to protect ground forces sent to the islands

against planes from Japanese bases in the Solomons. Carrier-based planes could carry the burden in naval engagements but were not available for day-to-day support. From land bases in the South Pacific area, the Navy's planes lacked the range necessary to provide reconnaissance and support. It became necessary for King, who had been threatening to go it alone, to demand air reinforcements from the Army. While removing ships formerly allocated to MacArthur from that commander's control, he had to ask for increased air support from the Southwest Pacific.

When King appealed to Marshall at the beginning of August for more planes he reminded the Chief of Staff of his statement less than two weeks earlier that substituting the TORCH operation for a cross-Channel attack would release planes and shipping for the Pacific. King also recalled the agreement won from the Combined Chiefs of Staff that, after the needs of North Africa were supplied, a total of fifteen air groups could be withdrawn from the build-up in Britain and given to the Pacific. Exploring the question with Arnold, Marshall found that the North African invasion would require the maximum number of Army planes coming from the assembly lines. Under the circumstances he decided to delay his reply.[27]

Admiral Ghormley launched his attack on August 7. Led by Major General Alexander Vandegrift, Leathernecks of the 1st Marine Division swarmed ashore on Guadalcanal without opposition. Although other Marine elements ran into stubborn resistance on Tulagi and the two tiny islands nearby, there was no hint in the first hour of the invasion that six months of bloody fighting in the air, on the land, and especially in the troubled waters to the north would follow before the islands were securely in American hands. Recognizing the tremendous importance of airfields on Guadalcanal and Tulagi to their future operations in the South Pacific, the Japanese prepared to drive out the Americans. As soon as they could gather their forces they struck back at the American naval task force. After losing four cruisers, the American naval commander decided to withdraw his ships, leaving the Marines on the beaches.

Gone was the possibility of the short campaign on which King had counted, and with it Marshall's hope of being able to concentrate on his Europe First build-up. The Navy was in deep trouble and American prestige was at stake. The Chief of Staff found it increasingly difficult to deny King's demands for greater ground and air reinforcements in the South Pacific, especially when his own commanders, Harmon and Patch, added their voices to the growing clamor. The Chief of Naval Operations pressed unceasingly for ground forces, planes, weapons, and ammunition as the Japanese threw ships and planes and men into repeated efforts to drive the invaders from Guadalcanal. The realities of battle outweighed the theoretical outlines of future strategy and forced Marshall to become more deeply immersed in the Pacific adventure than he deemed wise.

To meet Ghormley's immediate needs, Marshall had to rob the Southwest Pacific. Unable to get additional aircraft to Harmon in time to affect the current fighting, the Chief of Staff accepted Admiral Nimitz's suggestion of diverting to the South Pacific fighter planes then being sent through that area to Australia. Marshall also urged MacArthur to support attacks against enemy airfields in the area and to be prepared to move a pursuit squadron if it was required. Above all, he stressed the importance of "an intimate cooperation between Ghormley and MacArthur as to the use of Army air," and kept at Harmon and the Southwest Pacific commander to see that this was achieved.[28]

Furnishing fighter support was more than a question of close coordination, MacArthur reminded Marshall. He offered nevertheless to risk the hazards imposed by distance and bad weather to go to Ghormley's aid if the Chief of Staff thought best. Accepting this answer as evidence that MacArthur would do everything possible to aid the South Pacific, Marshall left the matter of air reinforcements "completely" in his hands.[29]

Facing heavy United States losses in the islands, King warned Marshall that he would have to pull his carrier force away from Hawaii to protect Guadalcanal, a move that would require additional Army Air Force planes for both the Central and South Pacific. From every side Marshall heard renewed calls for aid: Ghormley saw the possibility of losing a foothold in the Solomons; Harmon warned that there must be a major increase in all forces if Ghormley and MacArthur were to succeed in their objectives; and Emmons echoed Nimitz's appeal, "Let's not let this offensive die on the vine." [30]

At a time when Marshall was fully occupied with the task of

preparing for the invasion of North Africa, some ten weeks away, an operation that he considered risky at best, he faced constant drains on his reserves. "My struggle," he afterward said of this period, "was to see that the main show went on and the later show was not washed out." [31] In his determination to protect the main production he was backed solidly by General Arnold, who was dismayed by competitive efforts to establish aerial superiority in Alaska, Hawaii, the Southwest Pacific, Australia, India, the Near East, and North Africa. Running through the list of planes already allocated to various commands in the Pacific, Arnold was convinced that sufficient aircraft had been sent to the area to do what was needed if they were properly used. "Even though everyone agrees that success in the Pacific Theater will not win the war," he complained to Marshall, "we are planning to concentrate more airplanes there in spite of the very serious shortage which will exist in our North African operations." Only by pushing offensive operations against industrial Germany "relentlessly *from now on*" was there a chance of obtaining decisive results in the war. The situation, as he saw it, was "very, very grave"; instead of sending more planes to the Pacific, the Allies should be moving aircraft from that area to the North African and European Theaters.[32]

Arnold was less alarmed about the needs of the European area than about the fact that the Navy was getting more and more deeply involved in the Pacific fight and expecting the Army to bail it out. "King never lets up," he told Stimson. "He has not receded one inch from any of his demands upon us and I prophesy that he will eventually get them all." [33]

Bright thumbtacks on charts in War Department offices, showing clusters of aircraft in the Pacific, were more impressive in their Washington surroundings than they were to troops fighting in the jungles. Indeed, as the Japanese prepared to brush away the forces that dared to strike at them, it seemed that Allied resources would prove unequal to the challenge. Although a strong Japanese naval force was driven back from Guadalcanal on August 23-24, the enemy returned with reinforcements a few days later. The enemy also stepped up activities in New Guinea. One Japanese force continued its plodding advance along the Kokoda Trail while a second expedition was landed on the north shore of Milne Bay. MacArthur's forces repulsed this group but still faced a renewed strike at

Port Moresby. He wired Washington that withdrawal to the South Pacific of naval forces that had been assigned his theater left his position exposed to actions from Rabaul. MacArthur urged Marshall to persuade the Navy to add the protection of the Milne Bay area to Ghormley's over-all mission.[34]

The Southwest Pacific commander followed this grim report with dire predictions. No longer optimistic about his ability to launch an offensive, he feared that the Japanese had now been stung into making their main efforts in the South and Southwest Pacific. Unless the Joint Chiefs of Staff changed their commitments and met the mounting challenge, MacArthur warned Marshall, they must expect "a disastrous outcome" within a short time. Choosing his words for maximum shock effect, he prophesied that if the United States failed to match the enemy in air, sea, and ground forces, it faced the repetition of a situation "similar to those which produced the disasters that have successively overwhelmed our forces in the Pacific since the beginning of the war." The President and the Joint Chiefs of Staff must review this "momentous question . . . lest it become too late." [35]

To MacArthur, facing new attacks in New Guinea and fuming at Washington's indifference, it seemed that Marshall purposely ignored him. Actually the Chief of Staff promptly informed the President of the Pacific commander's appeal and then laid it before the Joint Chiefs of Staff. He had already ordered the transfer of an infantry division to the Pacific. Arnold now began a search for additional planes, and King directed Ghormley to return a naval contingent borrowed from the Southwest Pacific. Lacking anything more to send, Marshall reminded MacArthur that the defense of the Pacific areas still depended heavily on the carefully coordinated use of forces that had already been dispatched.[36]

Marshall's homily failed to impress his commander in Australia. Although MacArthur again assured Ghormley that he was willing to assist him, "even to the jeopardy of my own safety," he saw no sense in transferring reinforcements at a time when both areas were under attack. He warned Marshall of the dangers that faced him. "If New Guinea goes," he forecast, "the results will be disastrous." [37]

From Admiral King, Marshall got equally positive warnings, reinforced by an appeal to the Army chief's sense of fairness. In other days the Navy had aided Allied efforts in the Atlantic at the expense of its position in the Pacific; it was proper that the Navy's needs be considered now. The Army, he said, should find air reinforcements for the South Pacific to "the extent found necessary, regardless of interference with 'commitments' for the eastern Atlantic." [38]

The message revealed to Marshall how far King was willing to go to save the Navy's show. No longer was he asking for a larger effort in the entire Pacific or for a secondary operation that would keep up the fight against Japan while the major battle was being fought in Europe. To save Guadalcanal he was prepared to divert further resources from MacArthur and ignore the demands of the European area. Patiently the Army chief described for his Navy colleague the significance of his requests. The planes for which King asked could be found only by taking them from the North African build-up. "If we withdraw these planes we, in effect, impose a drastic change, if not the abandonment of TORCH." [39]

To officers and men fighting in the South Pacific, Europe seemed "remoter than the stars." One Marine historian has noted that to some of his colleagues "the prime culprits" who deprived them of needed fighters were "MacArthur, Arnold, and Marshall." Short of supplies and pounded constantly by enemy air forces, they had no time for the subtleties of global strategy, of agreed-on allocations of items in short supply, and of arranged priorities. [40]

For Marshall the issue was clearly drawn. The North African operation, warmly endorsed by the President and Prime Minister and less enthusiastically concurred in by the Combined Chiefs of Staff, was already straining the Army's resources. For more than a month Army and Navy planners had disagreed over priorities in planes, supplies, and shipping. At stake were fifteen air groups held back from North Africa that King wanted for the Pacific and Arnold wished to keep for the BOLERO build-up or for a strategic reserve.

Arnold wondered whether the Pacific commanders were really short of planes in the fighting areas or were using what they had uneconomically and failing to construct adequate airfields. The Navy argued forcefully that attrition, fatigue, distance, and need of 100 per cent replacement outweighed lack of proper coordination between theaters as causes of its troubles. General Marshall decided it was necessary to send General Arnold to the Pacific to appraise the situation.

On September 15, the day Marshall directed Arnold to make his trip,[41] the Joint Chiefs of Staff examined the effect on accepted Allied strategy of continued diversion of aircraft from the North African venture and the build-up in Britain. King asked for more planes for the South Pacific, and Arnold insisted that the principal needs were improved airfields and a better supply organization. At last Admiral Leahy intervened to propose that a decision be postponed until Arnold had a chance to make his tour of inspection. His suggestion was at once adopted, and the debate over priorities was delayed for three weeks.[42]

Marshall realized that the Air Chief's views would not be popular in the Pacific. Hoping to forestall arguments, the Chief of Staff called Arnold in before he left for a word of advice. His capsule prescription for a successful visit was: "1. Listen to the other fellow's story. 2. Don't get mad. 3. Let the other fellow tell his story first." [43]

In a striking demonstration of ocean-hopping possibilities at this stage of the war, Arnold sped over 21,000 miles in twelve days, visiting Nimitz and Emmons in Hawaii, Ghormley, Harmon, and Patch in Noumea, MacArthur and Kenney in Brisbane, returning by Port Moresby for a chat with Eichelberger, and stopping again in Hawaii to get further reactions from Nimitz and Emmons. He was back in Washington on October 2, prepared to give Marshall the results of the first visit by a member of the Joint Chiefs of Staff to that fighting area since the outbreak of war.

To the surprise of no one, the Chief of Staff for Air returned home still convinced that sufficient aircraft had been allotted to the Pacific to perform the operations that had been planned. He charged that poor handling of supplies, inadequate airfield construction, and wretched administrative organization were responsible for difficulties in Guadalcanal. In his judgment, the Navy had failed to demonstrate its ability to conduct air operations or handle logistical matters.

Navy leaders believed that Arnold was unduly hard on Admiral Ghormley and that officers "in their snug offices" in Washington were more to blame than those in the Pacific, but the airman's picture of the chaotic supply situation left a lasting impression on Marshall. Long after the war he still recalled that ships had been tied up at the docks at Noumea when they were desperately needed for North Africa or elsewhere in the Pacific.

General Arnold also gave the Chief of Staff fresh insight into General MacArthur's state of mind by reconstructing his interview with the Southwest Pacific commander at Brisbane. MacArthur staged for the Air Chief one of his famous monologues, pacing up and down the room, pouring forth strong and often brilliant opinions without pausing for a response. Either in the hope of making his hearer's flesh creep or because he was too close to the situation to see all of its aspects clearly, he imparted a strangely pessimistic tone to his recital of the dangers threatening various parts of the Pacific. The Japanese, he thought, could take New Guinea almost at will. Apparently no longer worried about Hawaii, as he had been a few weeks earlier, he now saw the Japanese preparing a general move into Alaska.[44]

Warming to his subject, he scornfully swept aside the puny measures being considered for winning the war in Europe. There was little possibility of establishing a second front in England, inasmuch as it was a "besieged citadel" and there was no possibility of providing air cover from those islands for an invasion effort. It was far better, he insisted, to look to Russia as a base and to give the Soviet Union additional supplies and troops to work from interior lines within that vast domain against Germany and Japan. The chief Allied center for operations was Australia, for which he asked planes, men, and equipment that could be sent out in any direction.

On his way to Australia, Arnold had stopped in Hawaii for a talk with General Emmons, who had seen General MacArthur a short time before. Emmons said that he did not believe that the Pacific commander was in good health. After getting a sample of MacArthur's strategic views at first hand, Arnold, who had always considered him one of America's great leaders, reported that he "was very battle weary; he had not, as yet, had a chance to recover nor to get the whole world picture." The Air Chief declared that he was certain MacArthur would not make the same statements six months later and that they should therefore be ignored.

Arnold's belief that MacArthur could take the offensive, securing bases at Lae and Salamaua and striking at Rabaul, impressed the Chief of Staff. The only hope for an immediate effective counterblow against the Japanese, Marshall reasoned, was by air from New Guinea. A sudden dash by MacArthur, who had been proceeding methodically and carefully, to oust the Japanese from northeast New Guinea, would permit bombers to be shifted from Australia to Port Moresby. From there they could hit Japanese concentrations at Bougainville, hold up enemy forces, and allow aid to be sent to United States forces in the Solomons.[45]

Arnold returned more convinced than ever that the primary need in the Pacific was the unified command that Marshall and MacArthur had frequently recommended. In view of past arguments, his proposals were not realistic. Overlooking the Navy's strong views on the subject, he ruled out a naval officer for the supreme command, listing as alliterative alternates, MacArthur, McNarney, or McNair.[46]

Marshall handled the proposal as if it were a hot potato, dropping it into the Operations Division's lap for study. First of the planners to react was General Wedemeyer, who readily accepted the concept of a unified command. The commander, he added, should be capable of firm and tactful dealings with other services and nations, be a man of high professional attainment, and come from the service that would exercise the strongest influence in "the consummation of our plans for the entire area." First choice for the appointment was General Arnold; second, General McNarney. Influenced by his strong commitment to the Europe First concept, he concluded that a commander such as he named would cease "to piddle our resources away in dangerous piecemeal actions throughout the area." [47] Apparently his supreme commander was to be chosen less for what he might win in the Pacific than for his sympathy with the build-up in Europe.

Brigadier General St. Clair Streett, an able airman who had accompanied Arnold on his trip, came up with the most astounding proposal of the lot. In his opinion, the "chief obstacles to a sane military solution" to the Pacific "mess" were "the political implications that revolve around MacArthur." He felt that "the sooner MacArthur comes out of the place and out of the entire military picture, the sounder we are going to be allowed to be in our solution of our Pacific problem." [48] As an assignment important enough for General MacArthur, he suggested the post of Ambassador to Russia. The Pacific commander's admirers had varied in their estimates of General MacArthur's worth in the Pacific. Some said two divisions, a corps, or even an Army. Streett was the first to consider him as a substitute for Lend-Lease. "In view of the Russian claims they are being short-changed [on the matter of supplies]," he argued, the appointment of a major military commander "might have a mollifying effect on them." Oddly enough, Streett was less air-minded than infantryman Wedemeyer. If naval forces were to predominate in the Pacific, then Nimitz should have the nod; if air forces were to have primacy, then McNarney was the choice.

Many such bizarre proposals were circulating around the War Department, providing merriment for the staff, but it is not likely that these found their way to Marshall's desk. They have persisted as historical curiosities, interesting mainly because of the implication that General MacArthur's presence made unification impossible in the Pacific.

On the basic recommendation Marshall left no doubt. He told the President on October 26 that there should be a unified command in the South and Southwest Pacific. "The present complication in the employment of air in the Pacific emphasizes the necessity." [49]

Unified or not, the services now had to pull together if they were to beat off renewed Japanese efforts to destroy the American hold on Guadalcanal. On October 3 the Chief of Naval Operations warned Marshall that the Japanese were gathering their forces for a new assault on New Guinea or the Solomons. A week later, in the face of a spirited naval attack, the enemy managed to put 3000 troops and additional supplies ashore on Guadalcanal. More menacing was a heavy concentration of ships near the Shortland Islands, southwest of the Solomons. In order to insure the South Pacific Army commander of full support from General MacArthur's theater, the Chief of Staff asked Harmon if he was getting from General Kenney, commander of the air forces in the Southwest Pacific, the air support he had requested. If not, he asked what instructions Admiral Ghormley would like the Joint Chiefs of Staff to issue General MacArthur. Although Ghormley reassured him by reporting that Kenney had cooperated so far as difficult communications, logistics, primitive operating conditions, enemy action, and violent weather conditions would permit, Marshall asked MacArthur to go further still.

From naval charts that he had just checked, showing Japanese concentrations at Bougainville and in ports to the south, he believed that "supporting action of some sort must be taken immediately and at the moment we can only see possibility of increased frequency of bomber activity from New Guinea directed against Naval Task Forces referred to." He recognized that the Southwest Pacific commander would weaken support of his own ground operations in New Guinea, but Marshall believed the sacrifice imperative. At the President's request he asked MacArthur if anything could be done to expedite the operation to seize the airfields of northeast New Guinea.[50]

Marshall's coupling of a request for increased air support to the South Pacific theater with a demand that MacArthur advance his own ground attack was more than the Pacific commander could take. He grasped the opportunity to voice some of his deep-held grievances. He was already supporting Ghormley to the capacity of his air forces, using all the planes that could reach the targets. His chief anxieties, however, were for the consequences of the expected debacle in the South Pacific, which, he emphasized, he had predicted earlier.

"If we are defeated in the Solomons," he told Marshall, "as we must be unless the Navy accepts successfully the challenge of the enemy surface fleet, the entire Southwest Pacific will be in gravest danger." Enemy sources, he declared, indicated an attack on Milne Bay, showing that his own theater rather than the South Pacific was the area most seriously threatened. Therefore he urged "that the entire resources of the United States be diverted temporarily to meet the critical situation; that shipping be made available from any source; that one corps be dispatched immediately; that all available heavy bombers be ferried here at once; that urgent action be taken to increase the air strength at least to the full strength allotted for this area; that immediate action be taken to prepare bases for naval operations on the east coast of Australia; that the British Eastern Fleet be moved to the west coast of Australia." [51]

This picture of desperation, little more than two weeks before MacArthur's troops in New Guinea retook Kokoda from the Japanese, explains why Arnold thought he was battle-weary. Stimson commented tartly that the recent cables were not "as wholehearted as a less selfish man would send." Sorting out the positive elements of MacArthur's reply, Marshall informed the President that MacArthur's air forces were apparently doing everything possible to cripple the Japanese naval force between Rabaul and the Shortland Islands and that the commander was keenly aware of the possibilities of an attack on Japanese-held positions on the northeast coast of New Guinea. The critical situation in the Solomons had prevented the Navy from furnishing Marine units previously intended to spearhead the infiltrations northward, but the War Department was dispatching a parachute regiment and troop carrier squadrons for the Southwest Pacific commander's use.[52]

Marshall in the meantime was moving rapidly to reinforce the South Pacific. Fighters were transferred from Hawaii and Christmas Island to that area, and a division in Hawaii was alerted to go either to the South or Southwest Pacific theater.[53] The Navy also took additional measures to strengthen General Vandegrift's forces on Guadalcanal. At the end of the first week of October, Ghormley ordered forward a regiment of General Patch's Americal Division; and in mid-October, Nimitz transferred a patched-up carrier, a battleship, and a complement of destroyers. Perhaps more important still was the change in command.

On October 18 King selected Admiral William F. Halsey, already known for his fighting style, to succeed Ghormley. The situation seemed to improve at once as this aggressive and able sea dog gave new energy and zest to the command. Marshall, who frequently showed a fondness for rough-and-ready fighters (Halsey, Patton, and Terry Allen were all favorites of his), was delighted with the change. "Halsey seemed to be the easiest [naval commander] to do business with. He was always trying to smooth out things instead of arousing things. I always thought if Halsey had been given a more leading role he could have gotten along with General MacArthur because he very much wanted to. In the single practice of taking the tie off the shirt he made a move to broaden general unanimity." [54]

But even the new commander could not work instant miracles. As the Japanese continued to flex their muscles, the President became seriously alarmed over the situation on Guadalcanal. On October 24, little more than a week before the fall election, he directed the Joint Chiefs of Staff to make sure "that every possible weapon gets into that area to hold Guadalcanal." When Marshall told him that shipping was the chief bottleneck, Roosevelt arranged for the War Shipping Administration to provide twenty additional vessels, at the expense of neither TORCH nor Russia, for use in the Pacific.[55]

The President's directive, while it was important to long-range reinforcement of the South Pacific, has often been incorrectly credited with breaking the deadlock between the Army, Navy, and Air Force over support for Guadalcanal. General Marshall's report to the President on the 26th indicated that steps had already been agreed on to resolve the principal difficulties before the directive was issued. Additional Army units were already en route to the South Pacific to reinforce the Marines. Marshall estimated that there were 72,000 ground troops in the South Pacific area and that some 23,000 of these could be moved forward as soon as shipping was available. He had already alerted the 25th Division to be prepared to sail from Hawaii for the South or Southwest Pacific in mid-November.[56]

Probably even more important than the movement of troops was the agreement on air reinforcements for the South Pacific reached on October 16 and quickly approved by the Joint Chiefs of Staff. After long discussions Arnold and Rear Admiral John S. McCain, naval air commander for the South Pacific, had agreed to substantial increases in bombers and fighters. The Navy failed in its efforts to get the fifteen groups that Arnold wanted to save for BOLERO after satisfying the demands for TORCH. On this issue a compromise was reached, and the planes were established as a strategic reserve.[57]

As so often happens when help is on its way and light at last seems about ready to break through a cloudy sky, the demands for immediate action now were at their loudest. Before the new commander and his reinforcements could affect the situation in the Guadalcanal fight, press criticism of the Navy grew so strident that Stimson described it as "unfair and dangerous" and reported, perhaps even more significantly, that King was "in a humble frame of mind because of the pounding." Several anti-administration newspapers opened fire on Roosevelt for refusing to let MacArthur fight. The entire Pacific stalemate was laid at the President's door, just as he was charged with dividing the ocean area in an effort to block MacArthur's presidential aspirations. The Navy was assailed for insisting on the Guadalcanal operation instead of allowing the Southwest Pacific commander to make his New Guinea attack.[58]

The attacks reopened an old sore that Marshall hoped he had healed in August. At that time an article, giving MacArthur's headquarters as the dateline and based on information attributed to "authoritative military and civilian circles" in Australia, criticized Washington for its failure to give adequate support to the Southwest Pacific commander. At once Marshall had informed MacArthur that the article implied "that you are objecting to our strategy by indirection." He assumed that this must be erroneous inasmuch as the commander was fully aware of the complex problems that faced American authorities. MacArthur promptly agreed that he had made no attempt to bring pressure on the administration. All information released at his headquarters, he insisted, was intended to counteract Australian resentment against the United States for failure to take a more aggressive policy in the Southwest Pacific by showing "that sufficient resources were not available to do what was believed possible by the public and demanded by the opposition." Newspaper attacks abated temporarily, but the feeling persisted in the War Department that MacArthur and his friends were over-willing to fish in troubled waters. The recurrence of attacks in October again raised this suspicion.[59]

Resolved to stop the revival of attacks on the President's policy and on the Navy, General Marshall outlined statements for his press chief, Major General Alexander D. Surles, to release and for Secretary Stimson to discuss in his October 29 press conference. He emphasized that the Guadalcanal operation was decided on by the Joint Chiefs of Staff and not by the Navy independently, and that no one had proposed that the New Guinea operation be launched first. As background for Stimson, he challenged the suggestion "that the President, fearing MacArthur's political future, decided to limit his sphere of activity." "I doubt," he said, "if the President even knew of the subdivision at the time it was made." [60]

Marshall was careful to make no accusation against MacArthur and no deprecatory remarks by him found their way to paper in this stormy period. Stimson was blunt in his comments. "MacArthur," he confided to his diary after hearing from Marshall, "who is not an unselfish being and is a good deal of a prima donna has himself lent a little to the story by sending people here who carry a message that he is not a presidential candidate, thereby playing into the hands of people who would really like to make him a candidate instead of treating the matter, as a soldier like Marshall would treat it, [by] never saying a word on the subject and assuming that all talk of one's candidacy is nonsense. These statements of MacArthur have served to keep the story going." [61]

Washington's irritation with MacArthur's political activities, real or imagined, did not lessen the War Department's admiration for his generalship. As the Navy continued to meet reverses in late October, the Southwest Pacific commander's drive in New Guinea was paying dividends. In briefing Stimson for his press conference, Marshall informed him of the splendid fight being waged by MacArthur's forces. Happy at being able to bear glad tidings, the Secretary of War praised MacArthur's work at the cabinet meeting that day. Roosevelt was favorably impressed. For once out of patience with his favorite service, he complained to Stimson that the Navy had belittled MacArthur's work.[62]

In New Guinea, MacArthur pressed his advantage, sending two regiments of the 32nd Division to aid the Australians in an effort to seize Gona and Buna on the coast. Then, to his dismay, the Americans faltered, and Blamey suggested that he preferred to bring up Australian reserves. Fighting mad, the Pacific commander summoned General Eichelberger and gave him power to remove officers in order to achieve victory. He enjoined the officer to take Buna or not return.

The Chief of Staff watched attentively as Australian and American forces closed in on Gona, Buna Village, and Buna Mission, tiny dots on the northeast coast of New Guinea, which were to be inscribed in history's pages because of the blood that bought them. On the fall of Buna Village in mid-December, General Marshall cabled MacArthur his heartiest congratulations: "The amount that has been accomplished with the very limited means available is a tribute to your leadership and to the fortitude and fighting qualities of the Australian and American soldiers. Quite evidently the wonderful support given by the air forces contributed in large measure to the success of the operations." [63]

The long struggle for Guadalcanal was meanwhile in its final stages. In early December the Army took over from the weary Marines the task of clearing the enemy from the island. For the last phase General Patch was given fresh Army and Marine units and made commander of a new corps, the XIV, which General Marshall activated for this purpose.

By the end of the month the Army's effort in the Pacific far surpassed anything originally expected. The number of troops in the various areas was almost equal to the total forces sent to North Africa and the United Kingdom. Nine of the seventeen American divisions that had been sent overseas and nineteen of sixty-six air combat groups were in the Pacific.[64] As late as the first of November the outcome seemed still in doubt; by mid-month it was clear that the battle would be won.

For the High Command in Tokyo, the Allied victories accompanied by increased reinforcements contained a bitter message. The cost in men and planes and ships to continue the fight for Guadalcanal and northeast New Guinea was too great for the Japanese to bear. So the word went out to their subordinates in the Pacific that they were to evacuate Guadalcanal and to fall back in New Guinea on Lae and Salamaua and strategic points north of the Owen Stanley Range. Fighting desperately to cover their withdrawal, they were dangerous until the end. By the end of January the enemy had been cleared out of New Guinea east of Gona; a few days later, on February 9, General Patch signaled the end of hostilities on Guadalcanal.

The bitter six months of conflict had secured the lines of communications from the United States to Australia and had halted at least temporarily Japan's expansion to the south. Marshall and King now had to decide where they would go next in the Pacific, what forces they would commit, and under whose command the operations would be placed. More important, those decisions had to be fitted into a broader Allied strategy to be discussed by the President, Prime Minister, and Combined Chiefs of Staff in late January at Casablanca.

XVIII

"End of the Beginning"

GENERAL MARSHALL went to bed early on the evening of October 31. Next morning before dawn he planned to be off for a rare day of duck shooting down the Potomac. Urged on by his wife, he had agreed to relax for a few brief hours after his long summer of debating European strategy, rushing men and planes to the Pacific, and struggling vainly against the North African venture named TORCH.

Near midnight Mrs. Marshall heard the telephone ring in his bedroom and then his tired voice as he carried on a long and muffled conversation. From long experience she knew that the duty officer at the War Department was at the other end of the line, and as soon as the call was over she came to the General's room to plead that he not allow some new development to upset his outing the following day. "You are tired," she said, "and must get some relaxation." "This matter is very important," he replied. In her exasperation she retorted, "Oh! Every little thing is important but you," and flounced out of the room, closing the door "rather firmly" behind her. The General, acting toward his wife as he did toward anyone who did not "need to know," made no further explanation and left her wondering what new matter had upset his plans.

Several nights later as she sat in Griffith Stadium in Washington, watching a football game from which he had excused himself, again on the grounds of important business, the mystery was solved. In the middle of a play the loudspeaker crackled with an unexpected interruption as the announcer broke into his description of the game with a plea for attention. He declared to an excited audience: "The President of the United States of America announces the successful landing on the African coast of an American Expeditionary Force. This is our Second Front." When Mrs. Marshall came home that evening she asked the General softly, "Was this the important thing you were talking about?" It was.[1]

On the night before the blighted hunting trip a message had come from Robert Murphy, consul general in Algiers, arguing that the landing date for North Africa should be postponed for three weeks to give General Henri Giraud time to prepare for his part in the invasion.[2] Both Marshall and Eisenhower immediately balked at the suggestion and held firm to November 8, a date set after weeks of disagreement and debate. The weather charts later proved their decision sound.

Murphy's eleventh-hour jitters were natural enough under the circumstances, but the plea for delay was totally unrealistic; the initial convoys from American and British ports had already sailed. His appeal was another manifestation of the uncertainty, delay, political complication, and general confusion that had marked the progress of Operation TORCH since the heated July meetings in London when General Marshall and Admiral King had reluctantly agreed to undertake planning for an invasion of North Africa.

For the British, as well as for the President, the memorandum in which the American service chiefs had signaled their capitulation in late July effectively ended the debate about Allied action for the fall of 1942. But to Marshall and King this view overlooked not only the contract's fine print but the main clauses as well. Although the service chiefs were aware that only TORCH had a chance of being executed in 1942, the formula worked out by the Chief of Staff at Claridge's stipulated that a final decision between Europe and Africa would be made in mid-September. General Marshall continued to press this point in an effort to remind the President and Prime Minister that their acceptance of TORCH meant the end not only of the weak SLEDGEHAMMER invasion of Europe in 1942 but of the more ambitious ROUNDUP return to the Continent the following year.

Roosevelt blandly ignored these reservations. He decided on July 25 that October 30 would be the target date for the landings in North Africa. Five days later Marshall and King tried again. When Admiral Leahy, acting for the first time as a member of the

Joint Chiefs of Staff, told them that Roosevelt and Churchill considered the agreement on TORCH firm, the service chiefs insisted that no final decision had been made.

Leahy dutifully promised to tell the President what they thought and gave them hope that the decision was still negotiable. Roosevelt was less obliging. That evening, July 30, he stated, in the words of the official record, "very definitely that he, as Commander-in-Chief, had made the decision that TORCH would be undertaken at the earliest possible date. He considered that this operation was now our principal objective and the assembling of means to carry it out should now take precedence over other operations as, for instance, BOLERO." [3]

The President had made his views clear enough, but he had not specifically acknowledged that his decision had killed ROUNDUP for 1943. Marshall held out for the positive *coup de grâce*. The result was a curious contretemps between him and the President that lasted through much of August. The Chief of Staff told members of his staff as late as August 19 that the operation in North Africa was still subject to the vicissitudes of war. Roosevelt held firm to his earlier pronouncement.

The July meetings between the American and British representatives had terminated with the understanding that a supreme commander to handle the planning for both SLEDGEHAMMER and TORCH would soon be named. Eisenhower was to carry on the planning for the North African landings as deputy, but it was generally understood that he would lead the TORCH operation. In late July the Prime Minister indicated his willingness to have Marshall as the over-all commander. The President made no reply. Nearly a month later, in mid-August, Eisenhower asked the Chief of Staff for a definite statement as to Marshall's role in SLEDGEHAMMER-ROUNDUP planning. In some embarrassment the Chief of Staff replied that so far as he knew, Roosevelt had never so much as commented on the Prime Minister's proposal. "Just why the President has given no expression of his view or concurrence I do not know, but I must not under any circumstances in any way be put in the position of seeking his favorable action, or even of suggesting that he make a decision." [4] For lack of a final decision, Marshall and Eisenhower had to proceed on the assumption that the latter was to continue planning for both operations until the emphasis was clearly set on one or the other.

No matter how much the President was committed to TORCH, planning for the operation could not get thoroughly on its way until those responsible for its execution were completely pledged to it. The British knew that both Marshall and King disliked TORCH and did not accept it as a final commitment for 1942. The delicate task of conveying the feeling of the British Chiefs of Staff that Marshall was dragging his feet was left to Dill. In a masterpiece of subtlety he gently chided his American friend while professing to be disturbed solely with the attitude of the United States planners in London. "For good or ill it has been accepted," he declared, "and therefore I feel that we should go at it with all possible enthusiasm and give it absolute priority. If we don't it won't succeed." He questioned whether CCS 94 (basically General Marshall's memorandum on future operations) had altered ABC-4/CS.1 (the January 1942 Anglo-American agreement on war aims). He personally thought that the ABC document still held the field as a guide to "our major strategical policy" but felt that everyone should be clear on the subject. "At present," he quipped, "our Chiefs of Staff quote ABC-4/CS.1 as *the* Bible whereas some of your people, I think, look upon CCS 94 as the revised version!" [5]

In London, Eisenhower became increasingly uneasy. On August 17 he assured Marshall that he was thoroughly committed to TORCH. As if unaware of the Chief of Staff's doubts, he announced that he had informed his subordinates that the time for doubting the wisdom of the original decision had passed—that they were going to accept without question whatever the two governments could make available and do everything possible to ensure success. [6]

Before Eisenhower's message arrived Marshall had sent a carefully worded letter to Dill designed to put at rest the latter's fears about future cooperation while warning him that he wanted no juggling with CCS 94. In contrast to Dill's warm and personal note, Marshall's reply—drafted by members of his staff—was formal and almost cold in tone. Putting first things first, he agreed that "the execution of TORCH must have the complete support and most energetic cooperation of those charged with its implementation," and he ended by assuring Dill that the United States planners would "enthusiastically and effectively support decisions made by the Commander-in-Chief." But he reminded the Field Marshal that the commitment to TORCH rendered ROUNDUP an impracticable venture for 1943. TORCH therefore scuttled for two years a return to Europe.[7]

Marshall's letter made no impression on Prime Minister Churchill—if indeed he read it. For the moment his chief interest, like the President's, was to determine how soon the grand adventure in North Africa could be launched. Willing to take great risks in order to have the landings as early as October 7 and in no case later than October 30, he and Roosevelt urged maximum speed on their advisers.

For planners and commanders on both sides of the ocean October was soon regarded as unrealistic; November 7 seemed the earliest date by which a practical operation could be mounted. Any effort to stage the invasion before then meant that landing craft and men would not be available for all of the proposed points of landing. Since a scaling down of resources would rule out the British demand that troops be put ashore between Algiers and the Tunisian border, the Chiefs of Staff in London expressed immediate disapproval of the October date.

As a shrewd politician, President Roosevelt believed that the public demanded a major American military effort before the crucial congressional elections of November 3. "When I went in to see Roosevelt and told him about [planning for] TORCH," Marshall recalled in 1956, "he held up his hands in an attitude of prayer and said, 'Please make it before Election Day.' However, when I found we had to have more time and it came afterward, he never said a word. He was very courageous. Steve Early, Roosevelt's press secretary, who was told only an hour before the attack, blew up about it because it came after the elections."[7]

Marshall found this emphasis on political considerations distasteful but was pleased that the President did not complain at the postponement. This was the more remarkable in view of the fact that an earlier landing might have lessened the anti-administration swing that reduced the Democratic seats in the Senate by ten and decreased the majority of 101 held by the Democrats in the House of Representatives to fourteen.

To Marshall and his colleagues the chief point at issue with the British during August and September was the decision on the places at which landings would be attempted. Long before TORCH was thought of, American planners had toyed with the idea of seizing a foothold on the northwest corner of Africa to forestall German threats to South America. Because neither the Army nor the Navy liked the prospect of putting large forces ashore east of the Straits of Gibraltar, a landing near Casablanca was favored for American forces. General Marshall saw the possibility of a German drive from France into Spain or a move by General Francisco Franco to slam the door behind an American force. But he and King wanted a strong base for their lines of communication that could not be easily destroyed by the enemy. Neither officer wanted to become heavily involved in the central or eastern Mediterranean. On the other hand, the British wanted to land as far east as possible so as to give maximum assistance to the forthcoming campaign of the British Eighth Army and to clear the enemy from the whole of the African coast from Morocco to Egypt. When it developed that there was insufficient shipping to permit American landings at Casablanca and Oran and additional assaults at Algiers, Philippeville, and Bône, the British Chiefs of Staff proposed that the Casablanca attack be dropped or at least staged after the initial landings.[8]

General Marshall led the American bloc solidly opposed to dropping Casablanca. His determination was increased when General Eisenhower agreed that TORCH was risky, and General Handy, sent to London to make a special study, judged that at best it was a fifty-fifty gamble. In the face of extremely strong pressure the British at last agreed to the Casablanca landing. The Americans in turn gave in to their pleas for two landings east of Algiers by agreeing to make available troops and shipping from their task forces for operations near Philippeville and Bône.

The Chief of Staff liked no part of the TORCH operation, but if it had to be staged he was determined that it should succeed. In discussing the landings with the British Joint Staff Mission in late August, he reiterated the importance of success in the first large United States expedition. "A failure in SLEDGEHAMMER, for which the public has been adequately prepared, could have been accepted," he insisted, "but failure in TORCH would only bring ridicule and loss of confidence."[9]

General Marshall remembered with pain the incredulous and even sorrowful looks the French had given the first American troops, untrained and undisciplined, who had arrived in 1917 talking about repayment of America's debt to Lafayette. He had no illusions about the readiness of many American divisions and he realized that they would face severe pressure in their early trials in Africa. He resolved therefore that Eisenhower should have the best officers the Army could provide. The little black book which he had kept for years was now carefully consulted.

In later years some critics of the Chief of Staff would say that he did not always pick good men, that he formed quick impressions, made snap judgments and sometimes serious mistakes. Perhaps as good a test as any is to examine his selections for the North African operation. He began by choosing Dwight D. Eisenhower and Mark W. Clark and ended with Omar N. Bradley.

One of his early selections to command one of the task forces in the landing was General Patton. Eisenhower accepted him gladly, writing his chief in mid-August: "I am delighted you fixed upon him as your choice for leading the American venture." [10] Shortly after the maneuvers in Arkansas and Louisiana in the summer of 1941 and in North Carolina in the late fall, the Chief of Staff had given Patton a corps and put him in charge of the Desert Training Center at Indio, California. It was from here in June 1942 that he summoned the armored commander when he considered the possibility of sending a division to the Middle East.

In one of his favorite stories about Patton, General Marshall recalled: "I brought Patton in and sent him down to the War College to make plans for moving a division into [the Middle East]— hoping against hope that I wouldn't have to do it, but feeling I should be prepared in case the President ordered the move. I told Patton we were opposed to this, but it was necessary to make the plans. I said there had been a big discussion about it, particularly what to send, and the decision was final that it would be a division with some special troops or a total of 18,000 (a division was then about 12,000). This was all the special troops we would send. I didn't want anything said about a corps. That was settled. So I told him to get down to the War College and get to work. He went down and, to my intense surprise, early the next morning I had a letter from him vigorously proposing that we send an additional division. So I sent one of my staff to get General Patton and put him on a plane and send him back to California that morning."

Back in Indio, General Patton had time to reflect on Marshall's warnings. After a day or two he called General Marshall's office, only to be told that the General was in conference. Several more calls proved equally futile. He then telephoned the deputy chief of staff, General McNarney. He explained that he had been thinking matters over and had decided that he could do the job with the troops that had been provided. When McNarney reported the call to the Chief of Staff, Marshall had the armored commander ordered back to Washington. "And that," General Marshall liked to say, "is the way to handle Patton." [11]

There were also problems between Patton and the Navy later when the armored commander, whose earlier assignment was dropped, began to assemble ground elements of the Western Task Force that was to sail from the United States. "Patton and the Navy were in a scrap all the time. He would get off a wild punch and the Navy would fire up." Apparently at one point King asked Marshall to replace Patton with another commander. The Chief of Staff insisted that the same qualities that made the armored commander difficult to work with also made him successful in battle. With Marshall's help, the Navy-Patton combination worked beautifully. Two days before the North Africa invasion Patton wrote the General: "I should like to call your attention to the fact that the relations between the Army and Navy in this convoy could not possibly be more satisfactory. Admiral Hewitt and his Chief of Staff, Admiral John L. Hall, [have] shown the utmost cooperation and the finest spirit. My doubts have been removed." [12]

There was, as Marshall realized, no easy way of handling this unpredictable genius. From observing Patton and from talking to his friends, he knew that Patton was obsessed with war and was not quite rational on the subject. Patton boasted of the two Mexicans he had killed personally during the Pershing expedition into Mexico and persistently pressed his former chief, General Pershing, to have Army records amended to give Patton full credit for the exploit.

Independently wealthy through inheritance and married to a member of an even wealthier family, he was oblivious to the normal inhibitions imposed by the Army on its officers. Marshall recalled that Patton was encouraged in his antics by a fiercely devoted wife. The armored commander apparently believed seriously in reincarnation and was persuaded that he had fought with

Alexander's hosts and Caesar's legions, but the spirit that damaged him was not that of a hero from the past but of a wild demon who took control at unguarded moments.

General Marshall had many memories of the man. He recalled years later:

> I had known Patton for a long time. I lived at Fort Myer when he was stationed there. Mrs. Marshall told him once when he was swearing and going on (he would say outrageous things and then look at you to see how it registered; curse and then write a hymn) that it was surprising to hear such things from a man who wanted to be at the top. She said a major could get by with this, but for a man who wants to be a general it was serious. "You have no balance at all." And she was right. . . . He was not only indiscreet but he descended almost to buffoonery at times.
>
> I remember a colonel of his who wrote some sharp criticisms of the War Department—wholly unjustifiable. I knew that Patton had encouraged him. [Patton] liked the idea of taking slaps at the War Department people while he was striding about with two revolvers on his hip in the field. It wasn't right because a lot of these people he was criticizing would have given anything to be in a command. Later when I was overseas he asked me to promote the colonel. I said no. Then at the table one night he pressed the matter. I said to him, "This is not the time to bring this up. This is a social gathering not a business meeting. But since you brought it up, I will make it a business meeting. I am speaking now as the Chief of Staff to General Patton and not to my friend, General Patton. You have encouraged the colonel in his attacks and you have destroyed him. I will not promote him; never mention it to me again." [13]

In General Marshall's book, Patton's love of violence, his needless profanity and obscenity, and his gaudy showmanship were all serious defects in a commander. But the Chief of Staff saw behind the officer's adolescent caperings the skill of a professional, who added to years of training a natural talent for fighting and the ability to make men go beyond what they believed themselves capable of doing in battle. Perhaps it was a sign of some inner regret in Marshall that he would never have a chance to prove himself in conflict that he prized the eccentrics like Patton and Wingate who were difficult to live with but who exulted in the fray. Or it may have been the temper and the fury of his own nature, rigidly disciplined and long pent up, responding sympathetically to natures that were never curbed. Whatever his reason, he called Patton to fighting command and saw that he had his chance. In time he would become weary of Patton's bombast and escapades and skill at grabbing headlines from those who performed ably but quietly, but he did not regret his choice. Twice when it seemed that public indignation would require Patton's relief, General Marshall helped save the general from himself.

Another swashbuckler who gladdened Marshall's heart was Major General Terry de la Mesa Allen, whose fondness for fighting made enemies in peacetime but friends in battle. Orthodox leaders of the Army never understood why Marshall gave his backing to the doughty cavalryman, and they liked to repeat the story that only the timely announcement of Allen's promotion to general saved him from court-martial. Allen had produced a paper at Fort Benning that Colonel Marshall liked, and he picked a day to show his dash and gumption when the "old man" was watching. After that he could do no wrong. The Chief of Staff suggested his name when early units were being formed for Africa, and Allen ended as commander of Marshall's World War I division (the 1st) which won new glory for itself and for its commander. Although he was a good fighter, his weakness as a disciplinarian and as a team player led to his relief. On Allen's return to the United States, General Marshall gave him another division in time for him to have another fling at combat before the war's end.

It was Marshall, perhaps on McNair's recommendation, who pressed Eisenhower to replace the officer he had in mind for the Central Task Force with a general of more recent field experience. The Chief of Staff suggested eight top officers, including Courtney H. Hodges, William H. Simpson, and John P. Lucas, whom he was prepared to make available. From the list General Eisenhower took Major General Lloyd R. Fredendall, a short, tough-talking, belligerent infantryman, who had succeeded Stilwell as planner of the original GYMNAST operation. Shortly after the landings the TORCH commander-in-chief wrote Marshall: "I bless the day you urged Fredendall upon me and cheerfully acknowledge that my earlier doubts of him were completely unfounded." [14] Later, when Fredendall commanded II Corps, he ran into serious difficulties. He was replaced with Patton and returned to the United States where General Marshall gave him command of Second Army.

In the selection of Walter Bedell Smith and Omar N. Bradley, as well as in the appointment of General Clark, General Marshall must have a share of the credit, although General Eisenhower would probably have chosen all three without the Chief of Staff's intervention. Both Clark and Bradley were classmates and old friends, and he and Smith had been colleagues in the War Department. But they were all Marshall men.

The Eisenhower-Smith combination became so well known in World War II that it is often forgotten that Marshall and Smith worked closely together long before Smith went to Europe. They had met at Fort Benning, where Smith served as secretary of the school, quickly winning his boss's admiration. The younger officer had come into the Army by way of the National Guard, which he had joined at sixteen. He had a sense of humor and could be conspicuously successful as a diplomat, but the hard fight upward and an intestinal disorder that bit like an ulcer had left an angry streak in him that made him ugly and even brutal when crossed. He had a passion for order and tidiness in organization and an unreasoning insistence on speed in meeting his requests. Those who worked under him dreaded both his tongue and exactions. On reaching a newly established headquarters, he liked to pull out his watch and give the staff two minutes to produce a given paper or put through an important telephone call. His harried subordinates attempted to outwit him by special improvisations or by delaying his arrival until they were ready to operate, but they ended by having the best-run office in any headquarters.

Smith was the lean and hungry type Marshall needed for a ruthlessly efficient office, and he leaned on him heavily as Secretary General Staff and Secretary of the Combined Chiefs of Staff in 1941-42. In an Army where he depended on officers like Eisenhower and Bradley to do their jobs quietly, to conciliate, to persuade, he required others like Smith who could hack a path through red tape and perform hatchet jobs when time and tradition and the dead hand of the past threatened to block progress. Smith was the perfect complement to Eisenhower. In organizing his headquarters for a trying assignment, the TORCH commander asked for his boss's handyman to serve as his chief of staff. Marshall was persuaded to release him, but he delayed the process, pleading the pressure of this or that crisis, and it was mid-September before he sent Smith to London.

Part of the reason for the almost perfect understanding between Eisenhower's headquarters in Europe and the War Department was, of course, the personality of the supreme commander, but equally important was the role of the man called "Beetle." Months of practice enabled him to understand the nuances of a message composed by Washington officialdom, whether it was the White House, State Department, or Marshall's inner staff. He could tell who wrote it and just how seriously it should be taken. He knew the right man to call and whether to talk softly and say "yes, sir" or berate him as if he were a pickpocket. He knew just how to deal with the Chief of Staff. In time Smith learned his way around 10 Downing Street and gained expertise in the techniques of dealing with the Prime Minister.

Of all the officers sent to Eisenhower by Marshall none brought stronger recommendations than General Bradley. As a member of General Marshall's instructional staff at Fort Benning, this soft-spoken, modest, diligent officer won the Chief of Staff's lasting praise. "Bradley was a major [and lieutenant colonel] there and very competent and very quiet. . . . He was conspicuous for his ability to handle people and his ability to do things very simply and clearly." [15] Unlike the Pattons and Allens who won the General's eye by dash and color, or the Eisenhowers who gained attention by personal charm and geniality, the undramatic, somewhat diffident Bradley was likely to be overlooked by anyone giving a quick appraisal of a group of potential leaders. Those who accused Marshall of snap judgments in selecting officers forgot the men who gained his approval by steady performances of high quality. Completely dependable, thoroughly loyal, uncomplaining, Bradley excelled at explaining a soldier's duty to the officers and men doing a job. In 1936 Marshall had written him: "I very much hope we will have an opportunity to serve together again; I can think of nothing more satisfactory to me." [16]

In 1940 the Chief of Staff had directed Colonel Bradley's transfer from the G-1 division of the War Department to the post of Assistant Secretary General Staff. The following February he jumped him from lieutenant colonel to brigadier general and put him in charge of the Infantry School at Fort Benning. Less than a year later he gave him command of the 82d Division. When Bradley had organized that unit to General Marshall's satisfaction, he was sent to the 28th Division. On Bradley's fiftieth birthday—it coincided with Lincoln's 134th—the Chief of Staff wired: "It is only fitting that your birthday should precede by only a few days your transfer to command a corps which comes as a long-delayed acknowledgment of your splendid record with the 28th Division. Congratulations and best wishes." [17]

Before Bradley could get the corps he was ordered overseas. General Marshall, growing increasingly worried over the situation in Tunisia, had decided that Eisenhower needed a highly competent officer who could serve as his "eyes and ears" and had selected Bradley for this job. Instead of assuming command of X Corps, for which he was listed, Bradley was told he was going to join his classmate—Ike Eisenhower, class of 1915.

General Marshall's efforts to provide General Eisenhower with the best field commanders available were matched by his efforts to provide the troops, supplies, and planes needed for success. He later described some of his problems:

> The decision having been made to go into Africa, a great effort was made to get what we needed. Some of the divisions were only partly trained and badly trained. The equipment was hard to get together. Eisenhower thought he had the necessary equipment in warehouses in the United Kingdom. It was scattered in small warehouses all over the country. When Eisenhower came to ship the stuff to Africa he couldn't find it. The British didn't have our experience with large warehouses and improvised them. So we had to ship matériel to Africa from the United States when it was in the United Kingdom.[18]

Shortly before the landings the Chief of Staff summed up for Eisenhower what Washington had done to meet his requirements:

> In the mounting of TORCH I have had the War Department do everything in its power to provide what you have asked for. We have stripped units of men, reduced eight or nine divisions to such low levels in personnel it will require from six to eight months to restore them to their former state of efficiency, and we have scalped the troops in this country for equipment to meet your requirements. I intend to see that this attitude is maintained in the approved program for the build-up of your forces by succeeding convoys.[19]

Marshall's watchfulness also extended to early promotions. He heartily approved Eisenhower's suggestion that Clark and two colonels on the TORCH staff be promoted on the day of attack. The Chief of Staff already had in mind the advancement of Smith. But he did not stop there. If either or both corps commanders gave good performances, he wanted to submit their names at once. "I would be particularly anxious to pick up a regimental commander who does an unusually fine job regardless of whether or not there is a vacancy." A week before the landings he advised: "If battle tests cause you to alter your views or disclose outstanding leadership under adversity, radio me accordingly that first list may not involve us in regrets or failure to take account of outstanding performance." [20]

In a message typical of others he would send Eisenhower during the remaining months of the war—indicative of almost paternal interest on the part of the Chief of Staff—Marshall asked the TORCH commander to deal with him on the frankest possible basis: "When you disagree with my point of view, say so, without an apologetic approach; when you want something that you aren't getting, tell me and I will try to get it for you. I have complete confidence in your management of the affair, and want to support you in every way practicable." [21] Before many weeks Eisenhower was to be especially grateful for the solid backing he received from the War Department.

The troubles that hit the TORCH commander hardest in the early weeks of the invasion were not military operations—although he had his share of them. It was in the realm of politics, to which he was a newcomer, that severe complications set in. From the beginning of planning for the invasion of North Africa, Eisenhower and his superiors in London and Washington had assumed that if the Allies played their cards right, French leaders in Morocco and Algeria would welcome an Anglo-American force. They recognized as well that there might be problems if British troops were in the van of the invading forces. The French in North Africa still smarted under the memories of British attacks on their ships at Mers-el-Kebir and Alexandria and the more recent British support of de Gaulle's attempt to seize Dakar. In an effort to reduce French resistance to a minimum, the fiction had to be maintained that all of the task forces were American. This fact had dictated the appointment of an American as TORCH commander-in-chief. Not only did Americans lead the Western and Central Task Forces, made up principally of United States ground forces with British and American naval support, but an American general had nominal command of the Eastern Task Force, which was more than two to one British.[22]

Throughout the late summer and early fall of 1942 representatives of the United States in North Africa attempted to find a French leader around whom his countrymen would rally for the November landing. Robert Murphy, former United States Minister at Vichy and currently consul general in Algiers, believed that the Allies could win over French support in North Africa by finding a man of stature whom they could trust and follow.

To some degree the British found themselves embarrassed by their past encouragement of the Free French Committee and their strong support of the chief opponent of the Vichy regime, General Charles de Gaulle, who claimed to speak for the French not under the influence of the Axis Powers. Despite his evident loyalty to the cause of France, no one but a dedicated Gaullist could have believed that the solemn Frenchman who ruled the destinies of the Free French could rally to his standard the civil and military leaders in control of Vichy's armed forces in North and West Africa. If he was a loyal Frenchman, these leaders reasoned, they were disloyal. It was essential to them, therefore, that he be considered a foe of France.

Even the British and Americans found it difficult to be a friend of the tall, mournful-visaged patriot who had defied the Germans and his own superiors when the moment of truth arrived for his country in the summer of 1940. Refusing to surrender, he had escaped to London, where he condemned Pétain's act of capitulation and proclaimed that France had lost a battle but not the war. In ringing terms of defiance he had asked the support of courageous countrymen in the effort to restore the prestige of France. Capable of breaking with old friends and of flinging down the gauntlet to the masters of Vichy in the face of a death sentence, he had icy self-confidence and an iron arrogance that submitted ill to tempering. Having defied Hitler and Pétain, he disdained petty compromises that might win the friendship of generals who still paid allegiance to Vichy.

He was not an easy ally for Churchill and Roosevelt. Paradoxically he combined a belief in the most modern methods of warfare with an anachronistic idea that France should exercise the power she enjoyed in the age of Louis XIV. To purge himself of the taint of the *émigré* who returns home in the baggage of a foreign army, he coolly bit the hands that attempted either help or restraint. His efforts to assume the rank of a head of a government-in-exile irritated the British Prime Minister and the American President.

Knowing of Washington's coolness toward de Gaulle, General Marshall stayed clear of him during his visit to London in April 1942.[23] Ambassador Winant in June tried to promote a meeting, telling de Gaulle that he was certain that the Chief of Staff would see eye to eye with him if the two men had a chance to discuss plans for the future. Assistant Secretary of War McCloy, responsible for War Department Civil Affairs arrangements, in July urged Stimson to persuade Marshall to see de Gaulle on his next visit to London. The Secretary agreed, then promptly dropped the idea when McNarney informed him that Marshall had deliberately shunned the French leader in April.[24]

By mid-July 1942 de Gaulle knew that plans were being discussed for a cross-Channel attack and visibly resented being left out of Allied planning discussions. Unable to get any information from Eisenhower and members of his staff, he told an aide that he intended to stop talking to underlings, "looking as it were through the wrong end of the telescope," and would insist instead on discussing operational plans with the governments and high commands of Great Britain and the United States. When General Marshall and Admiral King arrived the French leader promptly asked for an interview, and a meeting was arranged on July 23.[25] To de Gaulle's displeasure, the gathering included three "underlings," Eisenhower, Clark, and Smith.

The conference that followed was one of the stuffier confrontations of the war. Any hope of a fruitful meeting was dashed by the British request that General Marshall avoid revealing details of future plans to the French leader. In the strained atmosphere Marshall's manner became ultra polite and stiff. Speaking through an interpreter, he conducted the interview as if it were a formal exchange of credentials. Someone had thoughtfully provided champagne, but de Gaulle declined it, and that attempt at geniality went by the board.[26]

General Marshall announced that he was happy to meet the

French leader and that he admired the bravery of the French. General de Gaulle expressed his thanks. Then, in the words of the French recorder, "a somewhat lengthy silence ensued." Finally the French general outlined details on the forces under his command throughout the world. When that presentation failed to elicit any information, he again fell silent. But realizing that it was up to him to keep the discussion alive, he indicated his willingness to give his opinion on the opening of a second front. The Americans expressed a polite interest but volunteered no information. At last, seeing that his hosts had no intention of revealing their future plans, de Gaulle broke the silence by saying that he was pleased to have made the acquaintance of the chiefs of staff. He then withdrew, and a frustrating session ended.

The Americans were unfavorably impressed; King noted that de Gaulle's approach was "scarcely calculated to make friends." In view of his disappointment at learning nothing of Allied intentions, the French leader managed to put a good face on the meeting. He cabled his representative in Washington, Adrien Tixier, that Marshall and King "gave me the impression of being men of good faith and value, but without any definite ideas and embarrassed by the complexity of the business, vast and new to the United States, that is a world war." He added that Admiral Stark and General Eisenhower were similarly limited and that "the installation of Admiral Leahy in the White House will certainly not contribute to creating order out of this confusion or to shedding light on this darkness." [27]

By failing to win General Marshall's sympathy and, indeed, by buttressing some of the unfavorable views that Roosevelt and Hull had passed on to the Chief of Staff, General de Gaulle lost the backing of one of the few officials who might have been able to soften the President's antagonism. It was unfortunate for the Free French and for the United States that General Marshall's impressions confirmed the anti-Gaullist attitude already prevalent in Washington official circles.

In October, General Marshall was informed that a man had been found who seemed capable of bringing the French leaders in North Africa into line. General Giraud, hero of the First World War and an Army commander in the Second, had escaped from a German prison some months before and was now living in Unoccupied France. Unembarrassed by political ties with the Vichy government or by association with the Gaullists, he appeared to be a likely candidate to lead a pro-Allied regime in North Africa after the landings.

As unofficial discussion proceeded with Giraud's representative, officials in London and Washington were startled to learn that the commander of Vichy's armed forces, Admiral Jean Darlan, regarded as a bitter enemy of the British and a leading pro-German collaborator in France, might be willing to play along with the Allies if he were made commander of French forces in North Africa. Impressed by the prospects of lining up two powerful French factions, General Eisenhower outlined to General Marshall a scheme to make Giraud governor of French North Africa, responsible for all civil and military affairs, and to appoint Darlan commander-in-chief of French armed forces there. He suggested that after the landings, when Clark would be given an army, that Clark might be succeeded as deputy commander-in-chief by Giraud or Darlan.[28]

The introduction of Darlan's name raised bitter controversies, even stronger in Great Britain than in the United States. The admiral's forebears had fought the British at Waterloo, and he supposedly traced his animus toward Great Britain to the London Naval Conference of 1930 and the evacuation of Allied forces from Dunkerque. The British press had bitterly attacked him for his anti-Allied role in the Vichy government. To reward him for turning his coat was to create a storm of protest. Churchill in his zeal to put Allied troops ashore in North Africa was willing to explore the proposition. Although the full onus of dealing with the hated admiral would later fall on the Americans, who ultimately went further in their dealings with Darlan than the Prime Minister may have intended to go, Churchill did not in October 1942 shun the prospect of transferring considerable power to a man who was anathema to most pro-Allied circles in the west.[29]

At the moment the Darlan proposal was something to be considered for the future. The big game seemed to be Giraud. A cloak-and-dagger expedition developed in mid-October when Murphy forwarded word to Eisenhower that General Charles E. Mast, representative of Giraud, wished to discuss future plans with representatives of the Allied commander at Cherchel, some seventy-five miles west of Algiers. Arrangements were quickly worked out for

General Clark and a small party to go by submarine to the rendezvous. For reasons of security, the messages between London and
Algiers went through the War Department. General Marshall followed with interest the planning of the daring trip, sharing Eisenhower's concern for the safety of the party and his relief at their
safe return.[30] Because of the demands of secrecy, the group withheld from Mast news of the approaching attack, leaving him to
suppose that the invasion was some months away.[31]

As General Clark was concluding his conference at Cherchel,
General Montgomery's Eighth Army was preparing to open its successful attack against Axis forces at El Alamein. On the same day
ships bearing elements of General Patton's Western Task Force
began moving out of Hampton Roads bound for the west coast of
Africa. Elements of the Central and Eastern Task Forces, assigned
to objectives near Oran and Algiers, were assembling on the Clyde
in western Scotland.

Both Marshall and Eisenhower watched nervously as the various
pieces of the complicated operation began to fall into place. In the
final days before the attack the TORCH commander unburdened
himself of dozens of ideas about the landings and their aftermath,
as if writing to the Chief of Staff somehow made his problems easier
to bear. The menace of enemy submarines, obstacles to daylight
bombing, the difficulty of bringing Giraud and Darlan together,
the probability that Giraud would demand the supreme command,
future operations in Europe—these and many more topics filled
his messages to Marshall.

The mounting tension reached a peak on the morning of November 7 as Eisenhower, now at Gibraltar, awaited Giraud's arrival from France and scanned anxiously the reports from the convoy still steaming eastward from the United States. Murphy, he
radioed Marshall, again had the jitters and wanted diversionary
landings in southern and western France and in Norway. The
enemy had sighted Patton's force south of the Azores, and there
was a possibility of a concentration of German submarines off the
African coast. "We are standing, of course, on the brink and must
take the jump—whether the bottom contains a nice feather bed or
a pile of brickbats." [32]

As Eisenhower finished his message to Marshall, Giraud arrived,
upset at having been so long left in the dark about Allied plans. In

a postscript the TORCH commander indicated that brickbats were beginning to fly. At ten that evening, after four hours of steady argument with the French commander, Eisenhower added another note: "He so far says 'Either I'm Allied commander-in-chief or I won't play.' He threatens to withdraw his blessing and wash his hands of the affair. I'm weary! But I'll send you a radio later to-night, after the thing is finished." [33]

No message of final settlement went out that evening. The tired but stubborn "Kingpin," as Giraud was called in code language, went to bed still insisting that he would not cooperate. Not until the next day, after the landings had begun, did he consent to do what he could without being given the supreme command.

While Eisenhower and Clark were arguing with Giraud over his proper command role, combined British and United States forces transformed George Marshall's theory of unified Allied command into reality. In the early hours of November 8 attacks began on an extended front, with Casablanca, Oran, and Algiers as the main objectives. Three amphibious forces, totaling 35,000 to 40,000 each, had sailed hundreds of miles through submarine-infested waters and had arrived almost precisely on schedule off West and North Africa prepared to launch their surprise attack.

General Marshall had worried most over the landings off West Africa. Although he and his colleagues had insisted on the operation against strenuous British protests, they recognized the serious problems that could easily develop as a result of heavy surfs that could normally be expected in November. Weather predictions on the 7th were highly unfavorable, threatening danger to landing craft and a possible shift to other targets. When later readings showed that the weather might moderate, the commander of the Western Naval Task Force, Admiral Hewitt, decided to gamble. His daring paid off. Instead of hitting a heavy surf, the troops landed in a flat calm, the quietest sea seen by the inhabitants in many years. Writing to Marshall a week later, General Patton explained why: "In spite of my unfortunate proficiency in profanity, I have at bottom a strongly religious nature. It is my considered opinion that the success of the operation was largely dependent on what people generally call 'luck,' but what I believe to be Divine help." [34]

General Marshall was quite willing to credit the aid of Providence in calming the waves, but he believed that part of the success of the early stages of the operation was due to Anglo-American collaboration. In the last hours before the attack General Eisenhower had described for the Chief of Staff how British and American staff members had "slaved like a dog" and "established a pattern for Combined Staff operations that might well serve as a rough model [for] the future." Even if the operation of the morrow should by some mischance go wrong, it should not be allowed to "blind us to the fact that before this war is won the type of thing that we have been doing for the past many weeks will have to become common practice between the British and American services." [35]

The words moved the man who had made a virtual fetish out of interservice cooperation and unified Allied command. Three days later, in an address before the American Academy of Political Science in New York City, General Marshall described the means by which the British and American armed services had created a working partnership:

> In the past two days, we have had a most impressive example of the practicable application of unity of command, an American Expeditionary Force . . . supported by the British fleet, by British fliers, and by a British Army, all controlled by an American commander-in-chief, General Eisenhower, with a deputy commander also an American officer, General Clark. . . . The instructions of the British Cabinet to guide their Army commander serving under General Eisenhower furnish a model of readiness of a great nation to cooperate in every practicable manner. I go into detail because this should not be a secret. It will be a most depressing news to our enemies. It is the declaration of their doom.[36]

Marshall was strongly bent on making the public aware of American contributions to victory. On the second day of the invasion he informed Eisenhower that he wanted "a wonderful press kept at its same tone by filling in gaps in communiqué business with details regarding personal items." The details of Clark's submarine adventure, he believed, would help make up for lack of information on the development of the fighting. As a good feature, he suggested the story of the battalion commander who shifted his men from a torpedoed ship to small landing craft and set off for his objective more than 100 miles away under the protection of a British warship. Admitting the danger of releasing stories before all the information was in, he recalled from experience "that if we wait for perfection somebody else will nominate the individual for press heroics." He insisted that Eisenhower's public-relations people give an exposure to worthy combatants, "enough so that one man is not starred at ridiculous elevation." [37]

The Chief of Staff soon found that his problem was not one of getting information on the fighting into the headlines but of offsetting the press criticism of the Army's political activities in North Africa. The efforts of General Eisenhower and his colleagues to find a French leader threatened to get out of hand. In discussing the North African political imbroglio after the war, General Marshall described the situation succinctly: "Eisenhower's first troubles in North Africa were political. Clark did well at the start. He made the initial decision. The British were united against Darlan. His appearance was a complete surprise. . . . We found that Giraud had no influence with the French commanders, especially Juin." [38]

When the first British and American ships appeared off Algiers, Oran, and the beaches of Mehdia, Fedala, and Safi, the Allies learned that they had been wrong in assuming that French authorities in Africa were anxiously awaiting the expeditionary force. Consul General Murphy, who had sought an interview with General Alphonse Juin, commander of French armed forces in North Africa, shortly after the landing parties had started ashore on the coast near Algiers, was told bluntly by the general that there would be no surrender without an order from Marshal Pétain. Juin revealed, however, that Admiral Darlan, commander of all French armed forces, was at that moment in Algiers. Darlan had recently returned as the result of the serious illness of his son and was then staying with Admiral Raymond Fenard. At Juin's request for guidance, Darlan—accompanied by Fenard—joined the French commander and Murphy. After some discussion the admiral agreed in midafternoon of November 8 to order a cease-fire in Algiers. On November 10 he ordered it for all North Africa with varying success. Meanwhile Hitler rushed his troops into Unoccupied France and Marshal Pétain denounced Darlan's action. Although resistance continued in Morocco and Algeria, the Allies hoped to win the full cooperation of the French forces throughout North Africa.

On the afternoon of November 9 General Clark followed Giraud by plane to Algiers from Gibraltar. After a night's rest he joined a sleepless Murphy in lengthy negotiations with representatives of the French factions in Algiers. In the next two days Clark and Murphy concluded that Giraud did not command the allegiance of French officers in Africa and that Darlan, out of opportunism or in response to Allied pressure, might be able to win the support of French forces in Tunisia and persuade the French fleet at Toulon to join the Allies. On November 12 the American representative outlined an arrangement by which Darlan would serve as high commissioner in North Africa with Giraud as commander-in-chief of French forces. When the details were complete General Eisenhower flew into the Algerian capital. On November 13 he met with Darlan and Giraud to confirm the agreement.

As soon as details of the preliminary draft reached the American and British press, loud outcries were raised against any traffic with Darlan. Secretary Stimson heard from McCloy that the "starry-eyed circles," as Secretary Hull called the liberal adherents in the State Department, were angered by the deal with Darlan and that Washington was rocked by the news. In a meeting at Woodley, Secretary Morgenthau attacked the "deal," declaring that he was almost in favor of giving up the war, which had lost all interest for him.

Word had reached McCloy that Wendell Willkie was scheduled to appear that evening on the radio and intended to blast the "Darlan deal." Stimson promptly telephoned Roosevelt's 1940 Republican opponent and, after a lively conversation in which Willkie flew into a "terrible rage" and asked if Stimson was trying to control his freedom, managed to persuade the stubborn orator to water down his attack.

General Marshall, who had accepted Eisenhower's arrangement as a means of saving American lives, promptly assured the TORCH commander that he was doing his utmost to support him by meetings with the press, members of Congress, representatives of the State Department, and the President. The Secretary of War, he added, was equally aggressive. "Do not worry about this, leave the worries to us, and go ahead with your campaign," he urged.[39]

While backing the deal with Darlan, the Chief of Staff urged his own staff to promote friendlier relations with the Free French leaders. He notified the War Department Chief of Intelligence,

General Strong, on November 17 that he thought they should change their policy immediately in dealing with Free French representatives in Washington. Formerly they had feared loose talk and diplomatic involvements by dealing freely with this group. "It seems to me," he wrote, "that we should now change our tune, our courtesies and so forth." The following day he added: "What I am talking about is what we do here in Washington. I understand that you have had virtually no contacts with the Free French, the de-Gaullists. They have been barred from everything. At the same time in the field we are doing business and must continue to do so in Central Africa, New Caledonia, etc." [40]

Foreign Minister Anthony Eden protested strongly against the arrangement with Darlan. Churchill, although sympathetic with Eisenhower, went so far as to warn Roosevelt that public opinion would oppose a permanent arrangement with Darlan or the formation of a Darlan government in North Africa. To quiet critics in the United States and Great Britain, President Roosevelt on the 17th helped to reduce some of the adverse reaction by announcing that he had accepted "the present temporary arrangement" in North and West Africa only as "a temporary expedient, justified solely by the stress of battle." [41] Privately he made clear that he supported Eisenhower but wanted him to keep in mind that the United States did not trust Darlan and that it would be impossible to keep the admiral in authority indefinitely. A day or two later General Marshall informed General Eisenhower that the President agreed with the TORCH commander's draft protocol but wanted it handled on a military rather than a diplomatic basis.[42]

In London, Churchill and Eden disagreed over the draft protocol. Churchill wanted to inform Roosevelt of his agreement but the Foreign Secretary objected sharply. They finally decided to send no statement and to wait for a message from the President. Eden commented: "I cannot get W. [Winston] to see the damage Darlan may do the Allied cause if we don't watch it. He can make rings, diplomatically, round Eisenhower. At a moment of the shouting match W. said: 'Well D. [Darlan] is not as bad as de Gaulle, anyway!' " [43]

The Prime Minister and the Foreign Secretary continued their arguments until the agreement was signed in final form by General Clark and Admiral Darlan on November 22. After studying

the text, Eden declared that the arrangement seemed to contradict
the President's earlier assurances. He believed it dangerous militarily to deal with men who could not be wholly trusted and wrong
morally to accept their leadership. In his opinion: "Our appeal to
the French people, whose resistance has been steadily stiffening, is
now stultified. In Europe as a whole the 'filthy race of quislings,'
as you [Churchill] once so aptly called them, will take heart since
they now have reason to think that if only they happen to be in
authority when the forces of the United Nations arrive, they will
be treated as being the government of the country." [44]

The developments in North Africa prompted Eden to write on
December 5 that the "Americans seem completely to ignore political issue at stake." He persuaded Churchill to suggest to Roosevelt
that Eisenhower be provided with political representatives who
would aid him in arrangements having diplomatic overtones. Murphy was thus appointed as the President's Personal Representative
at Eisenhower's headquarters and Harold Macmillan as Minister of
State at Algiers. Eden also insisted on a secret debate in the House
of Commons, which Churchill vainly tried to postpone. On December 10 the Prime Minister declared his belief that under the circumstances Eisenhower was right. Churchill thought it was fortunate that as a result of the arrangements that had been made "the
French troops in Northwest Africa have pointed and fired their
rifles against the Germans and Italians instead of continuing to
point and fire their rifles against the British and Americans." [45]

As the outcry against the Darlan agreement continued to run its
course publicly and privately, General Marshall stood firmly by his
commander. On December 8 he wrote Eisenhower: "I want you to
feel that you had not only my confidence but my deep sympathy in
conducting a battle, organizing a fair slice of the continent, and at
the same time being involved in probably the most complicated
and highly supervised negotiations in history, considering the time
element and other circumstances." [46]

The Chief of Staff did not stop there. A few days later he asked
Elmer Davis, chief of the Office of War Information, to do what he
could to help out Eisenhower with the press. "I am very much
worried over the terrific pressure being put on him . . . to do the
impossible," he wrote, "when what we want him to do is win the
battle in Tunisia." Forwarding a copy of the correspondence to

Eisenhower, Marshall added: "I intend to give you every support in this difficult situation." [47]

By mid-December, Eisenhower had his hands full with the duel with the Axis for control of Tunisia. Enemy forces that had streamed into Tunisia from across the Mediterranean in the days following the initial landings had managed to extend their lines around Bizerte and Tunis and to occupy Sousse, Sfax, and Gabes along the eastern coast of Tunisia. Axis troops, retreating through Libya and Tripoli in the face of British Eighth Army, now could fall back on friendly ports.[48]

General Kenneth A. N. Anderson's force, soon to be organized as British First Army, attacked on November 25 in an effort to separate enemy forces in Bizerte and Tunis as a preliminary to later capture of the cities. After some initial successes the Allies were driven back on December 1. On the 10th, Anderson was forced to shorten his line.

Hoping to gain a victory before the year's end, Eisenhower rushed airfield construction, brought in additional ground elements for an offensive, and ordered a series of attacks beginning December 22. General Marshall suggested to Eisenhower that "you delegate your international diplomatic problems to your subordinates and give your complete attention to the battle in Tunisia." The TORCH commander should feel free to concentrate on the fighting, said Marshall, and depend on Washington to protect his interests. The Chief of Staff advised Eisenhower that lengthy justifications of his position were unnecessary and added, "You are doing an excellent job and I want you to feel free to give your exclusive attention to the battles particularly as German intentions against your right flank seem evident." [49]

Events in Algeria soon intruded on Eisenhower's activities in the field. On Christmas Eve, while the TORCH commander was in Tunisia with his troops, a young monarchist, Fernand Bonnier de la Chapelle, shot Darlan as he entered his office. The admiral died a few hours later.

Although Darlan's death eliminated a man who, while at first useful, had become an embarrassment to the Allied cause, it thrust new political problems on General Eisenhower. General Marshall promptly sent the TORCH commander the President's authority to appoint General Giraud as high commissioner in the event that the French Council, organized by Darlan, attempted to take other action. Since it was evident that Eisenhower wanted Giraud to have the status he had been promised earlier, the council unanimously named Giraud. From London, General de Gaulle, who had earlier informed Eden that the death of Darlan had cleared the way for him to cooperate with General Giraud in North Africa, asked for talks with the new French leader.[50]

In the Darlan affair Marshall stanchly backed Eisenhower and Clark in their argument that political expediency could be used to save American lives. It was a philosophy that Churchill and Roosevelt approved throughout the war. But the formula did not easily square with bold pronouncements about a democratic postwar world. The fact that Marshal Stalin approved of the Darlan deal troubled many idealists.

The outraged explosion of many segments of American and British public opinion left its mark on Marshall and Eisenhower. It was not enough to say, they learned, that expediency saved lives. The means of gaining victory had to be proved undamaging to the principles for which the Allies were fighting. The Darlan affair apparently made Marshall more reluctant than ever to become involved in political issues. It seems likely that his later tendency to leave politics to Churchill and Roosevelt was influenced by the North African experience.

Darlan's death came at a time of great disappointment for General Eisenhower. Heavy rains and increased Axis reinforcements stalled his offensive just at Christmas. Shortly after the holiday he and General Anderson concluded that the Germans had won the first round in Tunisia and that the Allies must wait at least two months before resuming the attack.

The British were convinced that the United States Chiefs of Staff had prevented a prompt seizure of Tunisia by insisting on a landing on the Atlantic coast of Morocco. General Marshall and his colleagues persisted in their view that untried American forces, traveling more than 4000 miles for their first battle, had to play a cautious game. Convinced that his troops must be successful in their first major test, both from the standpoint of their morale and the acceptance of future American strategy by the British, he refused to concede that he erred in taking the careful approach and declining to overextend his forces in the Mediterranean.[51]

Although resistance had ceased completely in French Morocco and Algeria, the year's end found victory in North Africa incomplete. In Tripoli the Eighth Army still pursued the Afrika Korps, causing it to fall back rapidly on Tunisia. At Stalingrad, after a long siege, the Russians had struck back, encircling the Sixth Army of General von Paulus and opening the way for a powerful Soviet offensive in the coming year. In the Pacific, success was near at hand for American forces in Guadalcanal and in northeast New Guinea.

As Marshall looked about him near the end of 1942 he could see mistakes, lost opportunities, and disappointments. But despite the wreckage of BOLERO and ROUNDUP and the setbacks in Tunisia, there was a tremendous record of solid achievement. He had established a claim to his later title of "organizer of victory." From 1,686,000 troops (37 divisions and 67 air combat groups) on December 31, 1941, the Army had risen by the end of 1942 to 5,397,-000 (73 active divisions and 167 air combat groups). Outside the United States the number of American troops had increased from 192,000 to 1,065,000 in the twelve months since Pearl Harbor. Nearly 20 per cent of the Army's total strength was now abroad.

The large-scale mobilization of America's young men for action was reflected in the military service of members of General Marshall's own family. Picking up the story of a draft dodger who claimed to be exempt from service because he was General Marshall's nephew, a columnist attacked the Chief of Staff. The writer was promptly advised that the General's only nephew, son of Stuart Marshall, had enlisted in the Regular Army before the war and was then serving as a sergeant. Molly's husband, Major Winn, was training a field artillery battalion in the South; Mrs. Marshall's brother, Tristram Tupper, an officer in World War I and later a successful magazine and screen writer, was back in the Army as a public relations officer; Clifton had finished recruit training and was now in Officers' Candidate School; and, finally, Allen, the last to go in, was taking training as a private at the Armored School at Fort Knox. His younger stepson had enlisted in September, saying fiercely that he wanted no special treatment, as if daring his mother or "George," as he always called the Chief of Staff, to suggest a different course.

The demands of the service prevented Allen from coming home

for Christmas. In a letter intended to lessen his loneliness at the separation from wife and baby at holiday time, General Marshall contrasted his stepson's lot with that of others in the service:

This is a note of Christmas greetings. I know you will have a full dinner, and probably a very good dinner, but I also know that you will miss Madge and Tupper very much. However, until we straighten out this world I am afraid a great many separations must be involved.

I have tried to send a note to the commander and men in each isolated outpost, particularly the little islands in the Pacific, and in Labrador, Greenland, and the Hudson Bay region. We have these garrisons all over the world and in many of the posts they have not only a great deal of loneliness to combat and lack of action, but extreme discomforts of heat and cold, or wind and rain, as in the Aleutians. The men across the ice cap of Greenland, with literally no diverting facilities and Arctic winter darkness to combat, have a very hard role to play. There are others manning look-out towers in the peaks of the Himalayan Mountains between India and China who have a fearfully trying task to perform. It makes a very moving picture to one who is aware of the conditions.[52]

On the last day of the year General Marshall's colleagues arranged a surprise birthday party for him. Field Marshal Dill and Secretary Stimson were invited to meet with the chief staff officers in General McNarney's office for sherry and cake. When they had all gathered, Stimson proposed a toast.

The Secretary of War had already paid General Marshall his tribute for the year, privately, a few days after it was clear that the Allies were ashore in North Africa to stay. At that time he had said "it seemed to me that this plan, which was the most difficult and complex and large expeditionary plan that the United States had ever tackled in its history, . . . had been planned for execution and carried out in a most wonderful and perfect manner, and that . . . the chief credit belonged" to the Chief of Staff. Marshall seemed touched but replied that he thought they had better wait and see how things went.[53]

Now, six weeks later, the Secretary thought that the events justified congratulations and reflections. In drinking Marshall's health, he dwelt on the character of the man he was about to honor. Throughout his own life, Stimson declared, he had found that public figures fitted into two classes, "first, those who are thinking primarily of what they can do for the job which they hold, and second, those who are thinking primarily of what the job can do for them." At the end of this early foreshadowing of John Kennedy's more famous remark about public service, he added: "General Marshall stands at the very top of my list of those I would place in the first category. . . . I feel, General Marshall, that you are one of the most selfless public officials that I have ever known." [54]

No record was kept of General Marshall's response. But he had summed up his reaction to the changes wrought in a busy year in his Christmas message to Prime Minister Churchill. Sending the British leader a fifty-inch globe—twin of one the War Department was giving President Roosevelt—"so that you may better follow the road to victory," he recalled that the Allies had much to be thankful for. "The skies have cleared considerably since those dark weeks when you and your chiefs of staff first met with us a year ago. . . . Today the enemy faces our powerful companionship in arms which dooms his hopes and guarantees our victory." [55]

The most difficult phase of the long ordeal for the Allies was nearing its end. With recent gains in the Pacific, Africa, and on the eastern front, the British, American, and Russian forces had come, as Churchill had said only a few weeks before, "to the end of the beginning." To Marshall, as he celebrated his sixty-second birthday and completed his third strenuous year as Chief of Staff of the United States Army, the future hinted of promise and of hope.

Appendices

APPENDIX I: MARSHALL AND PEARL HARBOR

Shortly after World War II a revisionist interpretation of the origins of the war evolved in which President Roosevelt's whole diplomatic policy in the later 1930s and early 1940s was seen as a great conspiracy to involve the United States in war with Germany. In its most extreme form, Marshall and Stark were described as willing pawns in this grand design. According to this view, the President finally despaired of his ability to get full American backing for aid to the Western Powers against Germany and decided to bring the United States into the war through the back door by goading the Japanese into making an attack. By placing the fleet at Pearl Harbor and refusing to make concessions to Japan, he would entice that country into an assault on Hawaii. An aroused and unified country would demand war and would then accept the conflict with Japan's ally, Germany, that was bound to follow. This took delicate handling as it was necessary to leave the Hawaiian commanders in ignorance of Japan's hostile movements lest they take action that would frighten the enemy away and spoil the plot. As a result President Roosevelt directed his Army and Navy Chiefs of Staff to withhold information and to remain where they could not be found in the last hours before the attack so that there would be no interference with Japan's planned attack. In leaving Pearl Harbor in ignorance of its fate the President took the calculated risk of suffering the complete destruction of the fleet on which he had lavished his attention and on which he had to depend for future aid to Great Britain as well as the protection of American interests in the Pacific. So runs the astounding argument, which also implies that Marshall and Stark would willingly permit the wrecking of an Army garrison and the backbone of the fleet.

In the summer and fall of 1944 the Army and the Navy, at the direction of Congress, conducted secret investigations into the background of Pearl Harbor. The Navy Board found no basis for further action against Admiral Kimmel and indeed implied that he was more sinned against than sinning. When the Navy's report was presented to Admiral King in 1944, he concluded that both Kimmel and Stark had indicated lack of superior judgment necessary for exercising command commensurate with their rank and suggested that both men be relegated to positions in which this lack of superior judgment would not result in future error. In view of the fact that Kimmel was retired and Stark had been shifted to London early in 1942, the recommendation had the effect of closing the door to future punishment. After further investigations on certain points in the inquiry, Secretary of Navy James Forrestal confirmed King's recommendation.

The Army Board's findings were handled in a different manner. Inasmuch as Marshall's own actions were included in the investigation, he carefully refrained from any part in selecting members of the board and passing on its findings. "I gave no instructions about the Army inquiry except that there must be no friend of mine on the board." [1]

The Army Board held that General Short had been remiss in his duties by failing (a) to place his command in state of readiness in face of a war warning by adopting an alert against sabotage only; (b) to reach or attempt to reach an agreement with Admiral Kimmel for implementing joint Army and Navy plans and agreements; (c) to inform himself of the effectiveness of long-distance reconnaissance being conducted by the Navy; and (d) to replace inefficient staff officers. On the basis of testimony, some of which was later seriously challenged and changed, the Board included in its criticisms various officials in Washington. It declared that General Marshall in his relations with the Hawaiian Command had failed (a) to keep General Short fully informed of the growing tenseness of the Japanese situation; (b) to send additional instructions to Short when it was clear that he had failed to understand that the warning of November 27 extended beyond the alert against sabotage; (c) to warn Short on the evening of December 6 and the early morning of the 7th of critical information indicating an almost immediate break with Japan, although there was ample time to have accomplished this; and (d) to investigate the state of readiness of the Hawaiian Command between November 27 and December 7, 1941.[2]

When the report was completed General Handy warned the Chief of Staff that inasmuch as Marshall was criticized in the findings he should avoid reading it and leave the matter entirely in the hands of the Secretary of War. Stimson ordered additional investigations of points brought out in the testimony and had all the evidence carefully reviewed by the Judge Advocate General. In addition, he read the testimony carefully with the aid of a member of his law firm, who served as a special assistant, Allen Klots, and Harvey Bundy. On finishing his study he wrote a statement in which he concluded that General Short's errors of judgment were of such a nature as to demand his relief from command status and that this was sufficient action to be taken against a conscientious officer with a long record of excellent service. In the matter of General Marshall's responsibility for the failures of the War Department to take proper action in relation to the Hawaiian Command, he took complete exception to the board's findings. He ruled that the shortcomings could not "in any fairness be attributed to the Chief of Staff. On the contrary, throughout this matter, I believe that he acted with his usual great skill, energy, and efficiency." [3]

The Secretary believed that his lengthy statement, going into the ramifications of the hearings, should be released. The Navy Department held that this was not wise, and the President held that the less said while the war was in progress the better. Stimson therefore prepared a shorter statement, which was issued in December 1944. Before releasing it he showed the text of the longer statement to General Marshall. "And he, the person who has most to lose by the publicity which would come out of it, favored mine as altogether the wisest thing. He was very sorry, he said, that I had been forced out of the longer one which I had drawn . . . by the President's deciding with the Navy. . . ." [4]

A short time earlier, when the Chief of Staff had been told of the Army Board's report, he discussed the findings with Stimson. "As usual he was so modest that he admitted to me that he thought his usefulness to the Army had been destroyed by this Board's report that had come along," the Secretary wrote in his Diary. "I told him that was nonsense, to forget it. But he was very grateful for the work I had done on it and the fight that I was making for him." [5]

The full-dress inquiry conducted by a distinguished Joint Committee of Congress, consisting of five senators and five representatives, six of whom were Democrats and four Republicans, presided over by Senator Alben W. Barkley, conducted hearings from mid-November 1945 until the end of May 1946. General Marshall and Admiral Stark found that with President Roosevelt dead, it was inevitable that his subordinates should be caught in the cross fire. To his amazement, the former Chief of Staff discovered that what he had assumed would be an inquiry into his exercise of proper military judgment and the efficient functioning of his staff was marked by attacks on the policy of the former President and that his own personal actions, which he was prepared to defend on military grounds, were to be examined for sinister political implications. "Remember that the investigation was intended to crucify Roosevelt," he told the author in 1956, "not to get me. There was no feeling in the War Department that we had anything to hide." [6]

Some of the more lengthy discussions pertaining to General Marshall's role revolved around the alleged delivery of the thirteen-part message to him on the evening of December 6, the receipt of a genuine "winds" message in the week before Pearl Harbor, and his whereabouts on the evening of December 6 and the morning of December 7.[7] [The last question has been discussed in Chapter X. The others have been reserved for this appendix.]

The Army Board's grounds for criticizing General Marshall and members of his staff for failure to send information of an impending attack on Pearl Harbor rested in part on the testimony of Colonel Rufus Bratton, a member of the War Department Intelligence Division charged with delivery of PURPLE intercepts to Secretary of State Hull, Secretary Stimson, General Marshall, General Gerow, and General Miles. Bratton declared in 1944 that he had delivered the intercept of the first thirteen parts of the Tokyo message to offices of all individuals on his list on the evening of December 6. In so testifying, he followed a pattern almost universally observed during the investigations by witnesses who had had a set duty to perform. Relying on their memories as to their actions several years earlier, they all tended to describe their normal routine and to say that was what they had done. When pressed, for example, on the details of delivering the intercepts to General Marshall's office, Bratton spoke of handing the locked pouch with MAGIC material to General Smith, Secretary General Staff, with the admonition that it was important to get the information to General Marshall.[8] When confronted later by Smith's testimony that Smith was not in his office after 10 p.m. on December 6—at a time before Bratton said he began his deliveries—by other officers' statements that they had not received the intercepts that evening, and by the reminder that his own testimony was contradicted by that of his chief assistant, Colonel Carlisle Dusenbury, Bratton assumed that his memory was at fault. He then concluded that Dusenbury had delivered all the intercepts except those to Hull's office, adding that Dusenbury had dropped the intercepts off for General Marshall on his way home to Virginia. The assistant denied delivering intercepts to anyone that evening, saying that Bratton had said that there was no need of delivering the first thirteen parts until the final one came in. Bratton himself later admitted that he did not become concerned, even on the morning of December 7, until a message arrived setting the time for the delivery of the fourteen-part message to Hull.

General Smith in 1958 told the author that, after reviewing the situation, he believed that Bratton or his assistant had delivered a pouch to him either in the afternoon of December 6 or before he went home later that evening.

Since Smith was not one of the officers permitted to read the PURPLE intercepts, he had no knowledge of what was in the locked pouch or its importance and had to depend entirely on the intelligence officer's advice as to the necessity of sending the message out to General Marshall at Fort Myer. He insisted that the officer who had delivered the message had said only that the pouch contained something that was being decoded and was not "all in yet." Smith therefore locked the pouch in the safe for General Marshall to read when all the message had arrived.[9]

Smith's testimony is of interest for the postwar admission that he had received something from the G-2 Division at some time on December 6. Unfortunately he was not certain of the time of receipt or the nature of the message. It could therefore have been either the pilot message or the first thirteen parts. Whatever it was, he did not deliver the message to General Marshall, who became aware of it only after 10 a.m. the following day.

The only points in Bratton's testimony that were corroborated as to his delivery of messages on the evening of December 6 were his statements that he left a copy at the State Department and that he spoke with his superior, the Chief of the Intelligence Division, General Miles, that evening and found that he had seen the message while visiting the Chief of Naval Intelligence. It was Miles's belief that there was no necessity for disturbing General Marshall with the message at that late hour in view of Bratton's statement that the message was incomplete. His lack of any feeling of urgency may have been partly inspired by the attitude of Colonel Bratton. Although Bratton was the expert on Japan in the Intelligence Division and the officer most concerned with impending difficulties with that country, he later conceded that he attached no undue importance to the first thirteen parts on the evening of December 6. No one to whom he talked was impressed by any sense of urgency.[10]

The controversy over the receipt of a "winds" message was even more muddled. Tokyo had advised its representatives several days before Pearl Harbor that in the event of a break in diplomatic relations or a serious emergency with the United States, Great Britain, or the Soviet Union, there would be included in regular weather broadcasts a statement or statements concerning "winds" from various directions that would indicate a crisis. There were no indications that the messages would actually mean the immediate outbreak of war or would specify the place or date of attack. In its 1944 inquiry the Army Board had given special weight to the testimony of a naval intelligence expert, Captain Laurence F. Safford, that an authentic execute of the "winds" message had been received several days before Pearl Harbor and that its contents had been shown to various admirals in the Navy Department and were known to several officers in the War Department, including Colonel Otis F. Sadtler, operations officer of the Signal Corps. In his first statement Captain Safford suggested that the message definitely meant war and indicated that it would come at Pearl Harbor. Although he never conceded that he was mistaken about the receipt of the message, he did admit later that nothing in the intercepts specified an attack at Pearl Harbor.

Before the congressional hearings opened in the latter part of 1945, earlier investigations had thrown doubt on the likelihood that a genuine "winds execute message" had been received. It was considered significant that Captain Safford, the one Navy officer who never ceased to maintain that the message had arrived and that war would come on December 6 or December 7, had left his office while the first parts of the Japanese message were coming in on

the afternoon of December 6 and did not come to his office at all the following day.[11] One of the few Army witnesses to testify that he had heard of the
receipt of the "winds message" by the Navy, Colonel Sadtler, declared that he
had never seen it and that it had never come to the War Department. He also
admitted that although he had believed as early as December 4 that war would
come within forty-eight hours, he had not come to his office on December 7.[12]
All Army witnesses denied any knowledge other than hearsay of the receipt of
the message, and all agreed that no information on such a message had been
delivered to General Marshall.

In the course of his earlier testimony Captain Safford indicated that he had
heard that General Marshall had ordered the burning of Army files containing the "winds" message. When pressed, he gave as his source Lieutenant Colonel William F. Friedman, the War Department expert who had broken the
Japanese code. Friedman testified that he had never given any credence to the
statement and attributed it to Colonel Sadtler, who had picked it up secondhand. Sadtler categorically denied that he had made the statement, since the
"winds" message had never been sent to the War Department and he had
never heard anyone say that Marshall had ordered it destroyed. He admitted
that he might have mentioned hearing Brigadier General Isaac Spalding say
that he had been told by Colonel J. T. B. Bissell, formerly of the Military Intelligence Division of the War Department, that everything pertaining to Pearl
Harbor was being destroyed or had been destroyed. When questioned, Spalding declared that some mention had been made of papers being burned on
Bissell's initiative but that General Marshall's name had never been mentioned. Bissell, in turn, denied the statement attributed to him.[13]

One rumor that was alluded to in passing in the hearings and quickly
dropped has proved to have a healthy constitution. It was repeated on a national television hook-up as late as December 1962 by a highly reputable historian, who later explained that he had been misled by false sources handed
him by an informant on whom he thought he could rely. The story, initially
given wide currency by Senator Joseph R. McCarthy, suggested that General
Marshall could not be found on the morning of December 7 because he had
gone to the National Airport to welcome Soviet Ambassador Maxim Litvinov,
who was arriving that morning. The Senator gave as his source a biography of
the Russian envoy by Arthur Upham Pope. Pope later made a special effort to
correct the account, saying that he had based his statement on incorrect information. His correction was made public in 1952 during a heated session of
"Author Meets the Critics," a television program, in which Senator Mc-
Carthy's book attacking General Marshall was reviewed. Apparently no one
who repeated the story troubled to check various Washington and New York
newspapers, which listed the names of those who welcomed Litvinov and published photographs of the reception at the airport. In no case was Marshall's
name listed, nor did he appear in the photographs.[14]

Even if one could accept the argument that President Roosevelt was capable
of issuing an order to his Chiefs of Staff to withhold information of a Japanese
attack from their commanders overseas, the character and public record of
Marshall and Stark constitute their strongest defense against the truth of the
allegation that they carried out such a directive. No reward the President
could offer them in the way of promotion would have been sufficiently alluring to sway men who already stood at the peak of their professions. Nothing
in their careers suggests that even at executive command would they stifle all

the instincts of forty years of service to plot deliberately to allow their forces to be attacked without a chance to defend themselves. On the contrary, the record shows that they made numerous attempts to alert all of their commanders to approaching danger. One can argue that they might have done even more, but it is impossible to say that they did not cry warning.

For the record, it is worth saying that both General Marshall and Admiral Stark categorically denied the existence of a conspiracy. After the appearance of Admiral Robert A. Theobald's *The Final Secret of Pearl Harbor* in 1954, suggesting that they had been prevented by President Roosevelt from sending information to Pearl Harbor, Hanson Baldwin of *The New York Times* asked them separately two questions: (1) "Did you ever receive from President Roosevelt, or any other source, direct or indirect orders or intimations directing you to withhold intelligence information from the commanders in Hawaii or from our commanders in any other areas?" and (2) "Did you ever gain any direct or indirect impression that President Roosevelt or anyone else in the United States Government planned deliberately to expose the United States Fleet at Pearl Harbor and our military installations in Hawaii to Japanese attack? In other words, was our fleet used as a deliberate decoy in order to incite the Japanese to attack?" At a period of their lives when men begin to put their final accounts in order, Marshall and Stark left no doubt on the points raised by the newsmen. In his response General Marshall answered, "*No,* emphatically," to both questions, and Admiral Stark said, "The answer to both your questions is *no.*" [15]

In the matter of responsibility, the majority report of the congressional inquiry repeated a number of charges assessed against the Hawaiian commanders by earlier boards of inquiry but declared them to be errors of judgment and not derelictions of duty, thus softening the findings of the Roberts Commission. They blamed the War Plans Division for failure to advise General Short that he had not carried out the War Department directive; the Intelligence and War Plans Divisions of both Army and Navy Departments for failure to give proper attention to intercepted messages from Tokyo to Honolulu in September and November, asking for information on the Pacific Fleet's base, and for failure to be on the alert to receive the "one o'clock" intercept and to recognize the fact that some Japanese action would probably occur somewhere at that hour on December 7; and the War and Navy Departments for not being sufficiently alerted on December 6 and December 7 in view of the imminence of war. These conclusions were signed by the six Democrats and two Republicans, including one who submitted additional critical remarks.[16]

The minority report (signed by Republican Senators Homer Ferguson and Owen Brewster) concluded that "the tragedy of Pearl Harbor was primarily a failure of men and not of laws or of powers to do the necessary things, and carry out the vested responsibilities." They felt that the members of the High Command both in Washington and Hawaii were at fault and listed among the culpable Roosevelt, Stimson, Knox, Marshall, Stark, Gerow, Short, and Kimmel.

On the broader matter of conspiracy, there remains for the record thirty-nine volumes of testimony and contradictory statements. When the committee of inquiry had completed its hearings in 1946, the six Democrats and two of the four Republicans (one of whom submitted more critical additional views of his own) stated that there was no evidence to support the charges that American officials "tricked, provoked, incited, cajoled, or coerced Japan into attacking this Nation in order that a declaration of war might be easily obtained from the Congress." Although the minority report by the two Republican senators, as well as the additional remarks by the House Republican member, who had voted with the majority, was highly critical of President Roosevelt's diplomacy and of the failure of the administration to supply the committee with everything pertinent to the background of the war, it made no effort to dispute the basic conclusion.

APPENDIX II:
RELIEF OF GENERAL WALTER C. SHORT

Shortly after the news arrived in Washington of heavy losses in ships and lives at Pearl Harbor, wild rumors—subsequently proved false—multiplied that Army and Navy commanders were at odds, that most of the troops and crewmen were drunk, and that no effort had been made to carry out orders from Washington. Inasmuch as the Navy had been hardest hit, President Roosevelt sent Secretary Knox to make a preliminary investigation.

The Secretary of Navy reported his findings to the President on December 15. On leaving this conference Knox informed Secretary Stimson that the Chief Executive wanted an investigation by a special commission consisting of a civilian chairman and two officers each from the Army and Navy. He proposed Rear Admiral Joseph M. Reeves and Rear Admiral William H. Standley as the Navy representatives and Federal Judge Philip L. Sullivan of Chicago as the civilian member. Secretary Stimson accepted the Navy officers but objected to the civilian nominee as not sufficiently well known nationally, and he suggested instead Associate Justice Owen J. Roberts, who had won fame as an investigator in the Black Tom and Teapot Dome cases before being appointed to the Supreme Court by President Hoover in 1930. The Secretary was also dissatisfied with a list of Army members suggested by General Marshall and said that he wanted Major General Frank R. McCoy as one of the panel members. At Stimson's request for an air member, General Marshall proposed Brigadier General Joseph T. McNarney, who had recently returned from duty in Great Britain and was, therefore, not directly concerned with events leading up to Pearl Harbor.[1]

The Roberts Commission reported its findings in January 1941, declaring that "in the light of the warnings and directions to take appropriate action, transmitted to both commanders between November 27 and December 7, and the obligation under the system of coordination then in effect for joint cooperative action on their part, it was a dereliction of duty on the part of each of them not to consult and confer with the other respecting the meaning and intent of the warnings, and the appropriate measures of defense required by the imminence of hostilities." The commission made clear that the War Department had failed to note that General Short was taking precautions only against sabotage and that his failure and that of Admiral Kimmel to take all the defensive actions required under the messages received "resulted largely from a sense of security due to the opinion prevalent in diplomatic, military, and naval circles, and in the public press, that any immediate attack by Japan would be in the Far East. The existence of such a view, however prevalent, did not relieve the commanders of the responsibility for the security of the Pacific Fleet and our most important outpost." [2]

The release of the Roberts Commission findings on January 25 reached General Short at his home in Oklahoma City. He was stunned by the charge that he was guilty of dereliction of duty and telephoned General Marshall at once to inquire what action he should take, asking if he should retire. The Chief of Staff, who had just returned from New York, replied that he had not read the report and had not discussed the matter with anyone. He advised him to stand pat, adding that he would use the telephone call as an application for retirement if that should be necessary. In a memorandum for record made at the time, General Marshall added that he would withhold acceptance pending consideration of the matter with the Secretary of War. After leaving the telephone, General Short prepared a formal application for retirement and sent it to Marshall later the same day. In recalling the conversation in 1946, however, he implied that General Marshall had left him with the impression that he did not intend to accept the application and thus trapped him into submitting the request, which was promptly accepted.[3]

On the following morning General Marshall discussed the situation with Admiral Stark, who suggested that if Short retired it would be possible to use this action to persuade Kimmel to do the same. At the moment, as a result of the finding of dereliction of duty, speedy retirement seemed a means of barring unjust punishment for the two officers. This obviously occurred to Stimson when General Marshall discussed with him Short's call and Stark's suggestion. The Secretary at once warned that they must not permit the retirement to be made too hastily lest it appear that they were trying "to let off these people without punishment because we felt guilty ourselves." At the same time Stimson hesitated to hold a court-martial because he feared that Congress and the press were showing signs of going through "a ghost hunt" and that the men might be excessively punished as a result of the great excitement being generated by the disaster and the Roberts Commission report. He related to Marshall how as a young United States District Attorney in New York he had once delayed the trial of a banker until the hot public temper, fanned by a bank failure in which the man was involved, had been allowed to cool.[4]

After talking with Stimson and checking with the Judge Advocate General, Major General Myron Cramer, on the action that could be taken against Short on the basis of the Roberts Commission charges, Marshall told Stimson that he now believed they should accept Short's application for retirement and "do this quietly without any publicity at the moment." [5] Cramer's memorandum of the following day, apparently spelling out in detail what he had outlined earlier, reported that Short could be tried by a general court-martial or dismissed summarily by the President under the articles of war. Cramer argued in Short's defense that his derelictions were those of omission rather than commission and that his failures to take action were based on an estimate of the situation shared "by all those officers in Hawaii best qualified to form a sound military opinion." He warned (1) that if a trial was held and Short was found guilty, anything less than dismissal would bring the accusation that the War Department was engaged in whitewashing the General, and if he was acquitted the same charge would be made; and (2) that the trial would have to be in open court or the War Department would be charged with whitewashing if he was acquitted or with persecuting if he was found guilty. If an open trial was held, however, some secret plans and orders would have to be introduced, which would clearly be opposed to public interest while the war was in progress.[6]

Cramer added a final plea for permitting retirement to close the books against General Short in his statement: "The career of General Short as an active Army officer is finished and closed. Because of the lack of confidence which the public now has in him, which lack of confidence would no doubt be shared by his future subordinates, it is unthinkable that any command should again be entrusted to him. General Short knows this. That in itself is a severe punishment. Furthermore, General Short has been relieved of his command which reduces him from a lieutenant general to a major general. The addition to that punishment of any punishment other than dismissal, such as a reprimand, loss of files, forfeiture of pay, or suspension from a command, would be inappropriate." [7]

Two days later Secretary Stimson consulted with the President about the action that should be taken in the face of the findings of the Roberts Commission in regard to Short and Kimmel. Roosevelt suggested that the Army and Navy act on parallel lines, first announcing that the officers had applied for retirement and then, after a week, adding that the applications had been approved but that this action would not be a bar to later court-martial if that proved necessary. Stimson warned that it was essential to postpone any such action in the interest of giving the men a fair trial and of avoiding disclosures of secret information.[8]

On February 17 the War Department informed General Short that he would be retired at the end of the month. In the three weeks that had passed since his talk with the President, Stimson had worked out a phrase that would satisfy the President that there would be no attempt to dodge a later court-martial. The order for retirement contained the statement that Short was retired "without condonation of any offense or prejudice to any future disciplinary action." Short considered this wording unnecessarily damaging and incorrectly attributed it to General Marshall.[9]

Having worked out a formula that he believed would be fair to General Short and avoid a controversy over a future court-martial, Stimson was startled a week later when the President informed him and Secretary Knox that the temper of the people demanded a court-martial in view of the Roberts Commission's findings. He proposed that the two officers request a court-martial but that the hearings be delayed until they could be held without damaging public interest. Concerned once more over the imposition of excessive punishment, the Secretary reminded the President that the two officers had merely reflected the general attitude of the country in not expecting an attack. Roosevelt replied that he realized this fact and that they should not be severely punished, adding that he would have final control over any sentence that was imposed. Stimson concluded that the President was thinking of a severe reprimand for the two men but was still troubled about "the situation of doing justice." On the way home Stimson stopped at the War Department to tell General Marshall of the developments and found him also "rather staggered by the President's change." [10]

Still disturbed over the situation, Stimson discussed the court-martial with

Marshall, Cramer, and Major General Hilldring, the G-1 of the War Department, on February 26. They suggested that the Secretary rather than the President handle Short's court-martial, since it would appear that Roosevelt was guilty of bias if he acted as reviewing officer in the case. Later in the day, when Secretary Knox reminded Stimson that the President wanted the officers to request a court-martial, the Secretary of War warned that if such action was taken it would appear either that a bargain had been struck with them or that they had been dragooned into it. He pressed on the President instead the arrangement that was finally approved on February 28. Explaining that he was having charges drawn for the trial of General Short, based on the Roberts Commission findings, he specified that the trial would not be held until such time as the public interest and safety would permit. Stimson then asked Marshall to call Short so that Short would not first hear the announcement from the press, tell him what had been proposed and the reasons why.[11] This was apparently the basis for Short's conclusion that Marshall had engineered the whole affair.

From the entries in Stimson's Diary of this period and the opinions of the Judge Advocate General rendered at Marshall's request, it is evident that General Short had the sympathy of the officials of the War Department and that they were prepared to protect him, so far as it was possible, against a damaging court-martial. In view of the inflamed state of public opinion, it must have appeared to Short, temporarily at least, that this was a satisfactory way out of a difficult situation. Later when he and Kimmel were told that vital information had been withheld from them, they concluded that they had been rushed into retirement and their careers untimely ended. In an indignant statement to the Pearl Harbor Inquiry in January 1946, General Short charged that the War Department had "singled him out as an example, as the scapegoat for the disaster." [12]

Acknowledgments

On pages 444-46 I have listed the individuals who contributed directly to the book in the form of interviews or other materials pertinent to the biography. Here I wish to list some of those who helped in other ways to make this life of General Marshall possible.

Funds earmarked for research and writing of the biography were contributed by John D. Rockefeller, Jr., his widow, the Rockefeller Brothers Fund, the Ford Foundation, and a contributor who asked to remain anonymous. Part of the money from the large gifts made by the three Mellon foundations of Pittsburgh and the Mary W. Harriman Foundation was used in the research program. A liberal advance from The Viking Press added to these funds. Thousands of contributors, including the General Assembly of the Commonwealth of Virginia, supplied the funds to build the George C. Marshall Research Library, dedicated at Lexington, Virginia, in 1964 by President Johnson, General of the Army Eisenhower, General of the Army Bradley, the Hon. Robert A. Lovett, and Governor Albertis Harrison of Virginia. The drive for funds in Virginia was headed by former Governor John Battle, with Mr. Joseph D. Neikirk, Executive Vice-President of the Virginia Military Institute Foundation, directing the over-all drive for the Marshall Foundation. As a private, non-profit foundation, dependent on gifts for our continued existence, we gratefully acknowledge the support of many friends in Virginia and throughout the nation.

The George C. Marshall Research Foundation, initially organized through the tireless efforts and able leadership of the late John C. Hagan, Jr., who served for six years as its first president, has been headed since 1959 by General Bradley. It holds title to the papers of Gen. Marshall and exercises general supervision over the research program. I was employed by the Foundation to write the biography along lines laid down by the directors. In giving his papers to the Foundation, General Marshall stipulated that all funds received from writings based on his interviews and papers should go to the Marshall Foundation to support future research. My salary is paid from Foundation grants, including a special ten-year fund from the Ford Foundation earmarked to supplement the salary of "the chief research scholar" of the Marshall Library. In addition to Mr. Hagan, Gen. Bradley, and the author, the following have been connected with the Foundation as officers or members of its board of directors, giving generously of their time: J. Clifford Miller, Jr., Maj. Gen. William M. Stokes, John C. Parker, former Supt. William H. Milton, the late Dr. Francis P. Gaines, Brig. Gen. Frank McCarthy, Harry A. deButts, Lt. Gen. Milton G. Baker, Carter Burgess, H. Merrill Pasco, Giles Miller, Jr., Dr. Fred C. Cole, Edmund Pendleton, Maj. Gen. George R. E. Shell, Robert A. Lovett, L. Elmon Gray, Col. C. J. George, Joseph D. Neikirk, and Royster Lyle, Jr. Gen. Bradley, Mr. Miller, Mr. deButts, and Gen. Shell make up the Executive Committee. Gen. Shell, Dr. Cole, and I have served as members of the special committee in charge of Library building and development.

Four Presidents of the United States—Harry S. Truman, Dwight D. Eisenhower, John F. Kennedy, and Lyndon B. Johnson—have granted access to official documents and given their backing to our project. We have had excellent relations with government archivists and historians. Dr. Rudolph Winnacker, historian in the Department of Defense, has served faithfully and effectively since 1953 as the liaison between the Foundation and various government departments and agencies. At the National Archives we have been aided by Dr. Wayne Grover, former Archivist of the United States, his successor, Dr. Robert H. Bahmer, and by Dr. Herman Kahn, Sarah Jackson, and Garry Ryan. At the World War II Reference Branch of the National Archives we are deeply indebted to its former head, Sherrod East (now Assistant Archivist, Office of Military Archives), the present chief, Wilbur J. Nigh, and Hazel Ward. Others in the Branch who assisted us were: Morton Apperson, Helen McCrehan, Edna Self, Louise Branham, Virginia Jezierski, Lois Aldridge, Joseph Avery, Thomas Hohmann, Henry Williamson, Hildred Livingston, Caroline Moore, Ellenor Burchell, Mae Moore, and Maxine Kimball.

In the Department of the Army we have been aided by the following from the Office of the Chief of Military History: in particular by the Chief of Military History, Brig. Gen. Hal C. Pattison, and the Chief Historian, Dr. Stetson Conn; and by Charles F. Romanus, Israel Wice, Dr. Maurice Matloff, Charles B. MacDonald, and Royce L. Thompson. In the Adjutant General's Office we have worked with Ollon D. McCool and Robert Ballentine. In the Department of State we wish to acknowledge the assistance of Dr. William M. Franklin, Historical Officer, Bureau of Public Affairs, and the late Dr. E. Taylor Parks, formerly Chief, Research Guidance and Review Division.

Mrs. George C. Marshall has been especially helpful in answering questions about the General and herself. She forwarded many items sent to her regarding the General. She made no attempt to influence the writing of the manuscript, nor did she read it before publication.

Several members of General Marshall's former personal staff have been especially helpful. This group includes Brig. Gen. Frank McCarthy, Col. C. J. George, and Lt. Gen. Marshall S. Carter. To Miss Alma Hickey, secretary to General Bradley, the Foundation and I owe a special debt of appreciation. General Bradley has made a tremendous effort to get funds for the Foundation and support for its program. I wish to acknowledge my special appreciation to him for his advice and personal backing in every phase of our work.

I cannot speak too highly of the members of my staffs in Arlington and Lexington. Miss Eugenia Lejeune, the Archivist-Librarian, has been of great assistance to me at every stage of my work. She has helped on research, compiled and checked footnotes, searched newspaper files, run down references in books and periodicals, read proof, prepared the index and bibliography, and in many ways proved herself to be an invaluable assistant. In this work she has been aided particularly by Mrs. Juanita Pitts, who has ably shared in many of these undertakings. Mrs. Pitts has been mainly responsible for selecting documents for microfilming and in preparing the reference cards. Mary Ann Knight and Diane Strickland worked tirelessly on many other clerical duties. Mrs. Arline Van B. Pratt, who has worked with me as research assistant since early in the history of the project, did extensive work in newspaper files and collected and checked material on chapters dealing with the Far East and the Pacific operations. Former staff members, Mrs. Helen Roepke and Mrs. Patty Kornell, transcribed many of the interviews and typed some of the draft chapters of the book. Coming in as Mrs. Roepke's successor as my secretary at a hectic stage in the book's development, Mrs. Dorothy Dean has proved calm and especially capable in coping with my handwriting and demands for speed. All of the staff members have been unusually long suffering in the face of heavy pressures, tight deadlines, and last-minute changes.

Assistants who have since taken other jobs include: Helen Bailey, Norma Kennedy,

Peggy Saunders, Dr. E. M. Coffman, and John H. Gauntlett. Myles Marken, a part-time assistant until recently, selected a number of documents for microfilming and checked newspapers for me.

In addition to my Arlington staff, concerned directly with the research activities of the Marshall Foundation, I must express my thanks to members of my staff in Lexington. Their untiring efforts in dealing with the detailed operations of the Library and Foundation have given me additional time for research and writing. I am especially indebted to Mr. Royster Lyle, Jr., my assistant and Curator of the Museum. He has been ably assisted by Mrs. Suzanne Lipscomb, Mrs. Louise Stuart, Mrs. Judith Cash, Chester Goolrick, and Jorge Piercy.

The Foundation has been aided in great measure by the personal efforts and financial contributions of the members of its Advisory Board, headed by Robert A. Lovett. The members include: James Bruce, Ward M. Canaday, Lewis W. Douglas, Gordon Gray, Maj. Gen. John H. Hilldring, Mrs. Oveta Culp Hobby, Paul Gray Hoffman, Mrs. Anna Rosenberg Hoffman, George M. Humphrey, Harrison Jones, Dan A. Kimball, Frank Pace, Jr., William D. Pawley, Mrs. Philip W. Pillsbury, John Lee Pratt, Edward V. Rickenbacker, Mrs. Mary G. Roebling, Spyros Skouras, Robert T. Stevens, Adm. Lewis L. Strauss, Juan T. Trippe, Thomas J. Watson, Jr., Charles E. Wilson, and Erskine Wood. Former board members, now deceased, were Robert Woods Bliss, Bernard Baruch, Gen. Walter Bedell Smith, Will L. Clayton, and Maj. Gen. Chester R. Davis.

Through regrettable inadvertence on my part, the contributions of Dr. Lloyd Davidson of the Virginia Military Institute were not mentioned in Volume I of the biography. As adviser to the directors of the Foundation, Dr. Davidson played a key role in the selection of the director and in drawing up basic guide lines for the research program.

In addition to the staffs of libraries mentioned elsewhere, I should like to acknowledge in particular the assistance of Paul Burnette, Director, Army Library, the Pentagon; Miss Judith Schiff and the late Mrs. Bess Henken of the Historical Manuscripts and University Archives of Yale University; and Miss Elizabeth Drewry of the Franklin D. Roosevelt Library.

For aid to the Foundation in the organization of its early program, plans for the Library, access to records, and the furnishing of government publications for research, we are indebted, in addition to those mentioned above, to the late Joseph Short, Carlisle Humelsine, Dr. L. Arthur Minnich, G. Bromley Smith, Alonzo H. Gentry, Dr. Philip Brooks, Maj. Gen. Chester V. Clifton, Col. James M. Connell, former Sen. Earle Clements, and Rep. Robert A. Everett.

The following have read the book in whole or in part: Dr. William Franklin, Vernon Davis, Dr. Stetson Conn, Dr. Maurice Matloff, Charles B. MacDonald, Martin Blumenson, my wife, and members of my staff. They aided by correcting errors and suggesting new material but are in no sense responsible for the errors that remain or for the nature of my interpretations.

—F.C.P.

Bibliographical Note

MARSHALL INTERVIEWS

In 1956-57 General Marshall recorded on tape some forty hours of answers and comments in response to questions submitted by me. This material was recorded in sessions at the Pentagon, at Leesburg, and at Pinehurst. Some of the comments were recorded without my being present, with his orderly, Sergeant William Heffner, running the machine. In addition, General Marshall talked to me about fifteen hours without a tape recorder. Part of the comments in these sessions was recorded by his secretary, Miss Mary Louise Spilman, and part by me.

The interviews and this biography began with a project first suggested in 1951 by friends and admirers of General Marshall. In 1953 a group of graduates of his alma mater, the Virginia Military Institute, headed by the late John C. Hagan, Jr., established the George C. Marshall Research Foundation to collect material on the General's career which would furnish information for a definitive biography and for numerous special studies on the period in which Marshall served as soldier and statesmen. Earlier the group had been assured of the backing of President Harry S. Truman in the collection of documents and the development of a Research Center. Shortly before leaving office, Mr. Truman issued a directive to the General Services Administrator, the Secretary of State, and the Secretary of Defense "to cooperate with Virginia Military Institute and the proposed George C. Marshall Research Foundation in procuring documentary material relating to the activities of General Marshall as a soldier, as Secretary of State, and as Secretary of Defense." In 1956 President Eisenhower wrote a similar letter, and this official support was reaffirmed by President Kennedy in 1962 and President Johnson in 1965.

In 1956 funds to start the collection of documents and the writing of a biography were provided by a generous personal gift from John D. Rockefeller, Jr. Impressed by the actions of President Truman and President Eisenhower and the urgings of many friends, General Marshall agreed in 1956 to cooperate with a biographer in recording, on tape, information on high points of his career.

In the late summer of 1956 I was employed to head the project and was directed to begin at once with the interviews. I hoped that it would be possible to conduct the interviews so that the General would virtually write his own memoirs. Unfortunately he did not feel up to these demands on his time and energies. Instead he suggested that I prepare, on the basis of his personal and official papers, rather detailed questions which would furnish a general outline to be filled out by his dictated comments. Following his advice, I prepared summaries of information from documents and official histories and listed questions raised in the summaries. I would say, "The authors indicate that it is not clear why General Marshall took this step," "General Marshall was criticized for this action," "Information is lacking on the background of this decision," "Is this summary of your action in the official history accurate," "In retrospect do you feel that your decision was correct," and the like.

I was given a desk in his Pentagon office, where part of his papers were kept and where the remainder was brought, and began at once the research necessary to prepare the outlines and questions he requested. As a means of expediting this work the General handed me a manuscript copy of Matloff's *Strategic Planning for Coalition*

Warfare, 1943-44, which he had been asked to review for the Department of the Army, and asked that I base some of my questions on material cited in that work. I proposed that I follow the same procedure on earlier periods of his career, using references from Matloff and Snell's *Strategic Planning for Coalition Warfare, 1941-42,* Watson's *Chief of Staff, Prewar Plans and Preparations,* and materials collected by Mr. Watson and his assistants for a projected volume (never published) covering the Chief of Staff's office during the war years.

Since the citations in these and other volumes made frequent references to General Marshall's handwritten accounts of meetings at the White House, to the minutes of meetings of the Combined Chiefs of Staff and the Joint Chiefs of Staff in which the General took part, and to folders of material the General had taken with him to the great conferences, to White House meetings, and to congressional hearings, it was possible for me to locate documents he had used and to base my outlines and questions on these. Much of the material was already in the General's personal files; additional information was delivered to his office for my use. In some cases I went over papers with former members of his staff, such as Gen. John E. Hull, who would check on documents they had prepared for the Chief of Staff, identifying specimens of handwriting and giving the background of some of them. General Marshall's appointment books, memoranda for the record prepared by members of his staff, his corrected drafts of key papers, his copies of minutes of the great conferences, and correspondence with key political and military leaders were drawn on.

I was also aided by earlier research that I had conducted between 1946-52 while preparing the Department of the Army's *The Supreme Command,* the official account of Eisenhower's command in Northwest Europe, 1944-45. I had collected hundreds of pages of notes in the United States and Great Britain, which I left with the Office of the Chief of Military History when I completed the volume. These papers were sent to the General's office for my use. Since the collection included my notes on Allied planning from January 1941 through Casablanca and Yalta to Potsdam, this phase of preparation was simplified.

General Marshall was quite willing to deal with specific statements or charges, but he declined to accept my suggestion that he comment generally on a number of public figures that I listed for his consideration. He declared: "You give a long list of names of officers and others to have me analyze them and comment on their efficiency. I am not going to do this. I think if this got into the book in any way, the books rather, all the attention would go to that, and all the acrimonious debate would go to that and nothing to the really important part of the text. I don't think it would be quite fair because the officers would have no chance to answer it at all." He did agree to comment on views or actions of individuals in those cases where they or their biographers had raised questions concerning Marshall's decisions. His purpose here was to give additional background on which I could judge the points at issue. In this connection he said to me on another occasion: "The accusations are so numerous, so altogether remarkable at the time, that you can hardly believe what you read. But, of course, you have a number who want to get into public print. And you have others who feel very deeply and are quite prejudiced. And you have other historians who really try to get at basic truths in the matter. Unless you diagnose which crowd you are dealing with, it is very hard."

Aware of the limitations of interviews and of the skepticism that might greet the accuracy of his recollections, General Marshall once remarked: "I am dictating this without a mass of records about me. . . . I am doing this out of hand—off the cuff, as it were—and it should be . . . checked for that reason. You must be very careful not to publish in any way or broadcast or arrange for later publication just out of hand what I say here—speaking off the cuff and at considerable length and of course at times when I'm a little bit tired. I am covering a vast amount of ground in a short time." Some of the General's comments have been quoted for their flavor and as guides to problems that he considered vital during the war, but at his insistence I have rested the main narrative on his personal and official records.

The General's interest in getting the record straight led to his expression of considerable interest in historical methods. He asked one day: "How do you know whether you can depend on what I tell you?" I replied that from time to time I gave him "loaded" questions to which I already had the answer from his papers. I discovered that if he had ever testified on a subject or had drafted a paper on it, he was likely to remember exact statistics and repeat the same illustrations he had used ten or fifteen years earlier.

Inasmuch as General Marshall had no opportunity to check the transcripts of his interviews and perform the careful editing at which he excelled, I have taken the liberty of making occasional slight corrections in the text without in any way altering the sense or flavor of the language. Exact transcriptions will be placed on file with the Marshall papers. (It should be noticed that in those cases where I have quoted from my handwritten notes, the quotation marks denote the language of my transcription of his remarks rather than an exact reproduction of his statements.)

LETTERS

The General's personal files contained copies of much of his correspondence for the years 1939-42. I have supplemented these by papers from the official files. Bernard M. Baruch permitted the author to copy all letters pertaining to General Marshall in his files. I was able to supplement these from notes on General Eisenhower's correspondence with General Marshall, which I had taken from the former's files in 1946.

OTHER INTERVIEWS

More than three hundred friends and former associates of the General's have granted the interviews. Of these, 163 pertain to the period covered by this book. Individuals whose names are starred gave material on General Marshall both in interviews and in the form of letters, photographs, clippings, newspapers, and the like: Dean G. Acheson,* Gen. Sir Ronald Adam, Brig. Gen. and Mrs. Claude M. Adams,* Field Marshal Lord Alanbrooke, Mrs. H. H. Arnold,* Lord Attlee, Bernard M. Baruch,* Col. William Baumer, Brig. Gen. T. J. Betts, Gen. Charles Bolté, General of the Army Omar N. Bradley,* Lt. Gen. Lewis H. Brereton,* Lt. Gen. George H. Brett,* Rear Adm. R. V. Brockman,* Lt. Gen. E. H. Brooks,* Maj. Gen. William Bryden,* Maj. Gen. Kenneth Buchanan,* Lt. Gen. Harold R. Bull, Harvey Bundy, Lady Mary Burghley, Maj. Gen. James H. Burns, Brig. Gen. Frederic B. Butler, James F. Byrnes, Brig. Gen. B. F. Caffey, Lt. Gen. Marshall S. Carter,* Maj. Gen. James G. Christiansen, Gen. Mark W. Clark,* Brig. Gen. Carter Clarke, Henry C. Clausen, Gen. J. Lawton Collins, Philip E. Connelly, Adm. C. M. Cooke, Jere Cooper, Col. William Couper,* Maj. Gen. Frank L. Culin, Adm. of the Fleet Lord Cunningham of Hyndhope, Ralph A. Curtin, Gen. John E. Dahlquist, Maj. Gen. John R. Deane, Gen. Jacob L. Devers,* Lady Dill, Lewis W. Douglas,* Sgt. George E. Dumcke, Col. R. E. Dupuy,* Lt. Gen. Ira C. Eaker, Sir Anthony Eden, Gen. of the Army Dwight D. Eisenhower,* Lt. Gen. Delos Emmons, Sgt. William Farr, Leo Farrell,* Brig. Gen. Louis J. Fortier,* Justice Felix Frankfurter, Col. William F. Friedman, William Frye,* Maj. Gen. Philip E. Gallagher, Frederick V.

Geier, Col. C. J. George,* Gen. Leonard T. Gerow,* Gerhard A. Gesell, Dr. Kent R. Greenfield,* Maj. Gen. C. C. Haffner, Gen. Wade Haislip,* Gen. Thomas T. Handy, Maj. Gen. H. S. Hansell, Maj. Gen. E. F. Harding, William D. Hassett, Maj. Gen. Charles D. Herron,* Lt. Gen. Lewis B. Hershey, Maj. Gen. John H. Hilldring, Mrs. Oveta Culp Hobby, Gen. Courtney Hodges, Gen. William M. Hoge,* Gen. Sir Leslie Hollis, Mrs. Nan Wood Honeyman, Charles R. Hook,* Gen. John E. Hull,* Carlisle Humelsine, Gen. Lord Ismay, Lt. Gen. Reuben E. Jenkins, Louis Johnson, Thomas M. Johnson,* Lt. Gen. C. E. Kilbourne, Capt. T. B. Kittredge,* Gen. Walter Krueger, Gen. Laurence S. Kuter, Maj. Gen. Charles T. Lanham, Maj. Gen. Samuel T. Lawton, Gen. Ben Lear, Maj. Gen. H. B. Lewis, Col. G. A. Lincoln, Robert A. Lovett,* Scott Lucas, General of the Army Douglas MacArthur, Col. J. E. McCammon, Brig. Gen. Frank McCarthy,* John J. McCloy, Mrs. Frank R. McCoy,* Maj. Reginald Macdonald-Buchanan,* Gen. Joseph T. McNarney, Donald Mace,* Mrs. George C. Marshall,* Brig. Gen. S. L. A. Marshall, John Martyn, Maj. Gen. Russell L. Maxwell, Mrs. Henry F. Meyer,* Maj. Gen. Sherman Miles, Francis Pickens Miller, Maj. Gen. Luther D. Miller, Brig. Gen. H. M. Monroe, Field Marshal Lord Montgomery of Alamein, Maj. Gen. Richard C. Moore,* Lt. Gen. Sir Frederick Morgan,* Admiral of the Fleet Lord Mountbatten of Burma, Miss Mona Nason, Fleet Adm. Chester W. Nimitz, Maj. Gen. Thomas North, Brig. Gen. Frederick Osborn, Arthur W. Page, Gen. Sir Bernard Paget, H. Merrill Pasco,* William D. Pawley, Marshal of the Royal Air Force Lord Portal of Hungerford, Sgt. James Powder,* John Lee Pratt,* Sam Rayburn,* Col. Russell P. Reeder,* Gen. Matthew B. Ridgway,* Walter S. Robertson, Brig. Gen. Paul McD. Robinett,* Mrs. George H. Rockwell,* Mrs. Eleanor Roosevelt, Maj. Gen. H. M. Roper, Brig. Gen. Charles H. Royce (interviewed by Dr. E. M. Coffman), Maj. Gen. William T. Sexton,* Field Marshal Lord Slim, Col. Truman Smith,* Gen. Walter Bedell Smith,* Maj. Gen. Howard M. Snyder, Gen. Carl Spaatz, Col. William Spencer,* Adm. Harold R. Stark, Maj. Gen. M. C. Stayer,* Adlai Stevenson, Mrs. Joseph Stilwell, Lt. Gen. Richard K. Sutherland, Charles P. Taft, Gen. Maxwell Taylor, Miss Cora Thomas, Maj. Gen. Thomas S. Timberman, President Harry S. Truman, Gen. L. K. Truscott,* Brig. Gen. H. A. Twitchell, Maj. Gen. Fred L. Walker, Maj. Gen. Orlando Ward,* Mrs. E. M. Watson,* Mark S. Watson,* Gen. A. C. Wedemeyer, Maj. Gen. Lawrence Whiting, Field Marshal Lord Wilson, and Col. and Mrs. J. J. Winn.

For background I have used notes on interviews that I conducted in 1946-47 while gathering material for *The Supreme Command*. In addition to Alanbrooke, Betts, Bradley, Cunningham, Eisenhower, Morgan, Mountbatten, Portal, and Smith, listed above among those I interviewed later, I received information pertinent to this volume from Maj. Gen. Ray W. Barker, Maj. Gen. Robert W. Crawford, Gen. Charles de Gaulle, Brig. Gen. Thomas J. Davis, Maj. Gen. Julius Holmes, Marshal Alphonse Juin, Fleet Adm. Ernest J. King, Capt. C. E. Lambe, Fleet Adm. William D. Leahy, Henry Cabot Lodge, and Brig. Gen. Arthur S. Nevins.

ADDITIONAL SOURCES OF INFORMATION

The following have supplied information in various forms, such as letters, photographs, clippings, speeches, articles, or general information pertaining to General Marshall or the events covered by this volume: Lt. Gen. Edward M. Almond, N. J. Anthony, Ray H. Balken, M. K. Barber, Brig. Gen. Clifford Bluemel, Edward L. Bowles, F. Gorham Brigham, Jr., Jack Burness, John M. Camp, Leo Cherne, Robert Coakley, Brig. Gen. Robert F. Cocklin, Hugh M. Cole, Richard C. Corbyn, John DeM. Cine Crane, Brig. Gen. Robert Cutler, Willis J. Dance, C. E. Dornbusch, L. M.

Dorsch, Mrs. Louise B. Duntze, Col. Trevor Dupuy, Sherrod East, Rear Adm. E. M. Eller, Stanley Falk, Detmar Finke, Mrs. Hazel W. Frese, Col. J. J. Fulmer, Ward Gibson, Brig. Gen. Raymond E. Goodridge, R. L. Gorny, Lt. Gen. Leslie Groves, Rep. Kenneth Hechler, Sgt. William Heffner, Col. R. D. Heinl, Jr., Maj. Gen. Guy V. Henry, Lt. Gen. Thomas F. Hickey, Miss Cynthia Hill, Brig. Gen. C. C. Hillman, Wilber Hoare, Maj. Gen. J. L. Homer, Col. Morgan Hudgins, Bert Ivry, Gen. Harold K. Johnson, Lt. Col. Robert A. Johnston, Col. Bertram Kalisch, Col. Joseph C. King, Col. Herman O. Lane, Richard Leighton, Misses Eugenia and Laura Lejeune, Sir Basil Liddell Hart, Ernest K. Lindley, Russell Lynes, Speaker John McCormack, L. A. Minnich, Jr., Louis Morton, Miss Buell Mullen, Col. Homer C. Munson, Col. R. V. Murphy, Richard Newman, Eugene Overstreet, John C. Parker, Lt. Gen. W. S. Paul, Milton F. Perry, Irving Peterfreund, Robert Proenneke, Capt. Edgar F. Puryear, Jr., Col. Julian E. Raymond, Thomas B. Rogers, Charles F. Romanus, R. G. Ruppenthal, Don Russell, E. A. Sale, Jr., Robert Sherrod, Mrs. James W. Simpson, Col. Frank S. Singer, Mrs. Brehon B. Somervell, John P. Spore, Brig. Gen. Alexander N. Stark, Rep. Frank A. Stubblefield, Riley Sunderland, Gen. W. C. Sweeney, Jr., Col. Arthur Symons, Marcel Vigneras, Col. John M. Virden, Arthur Webb, Lt. Gen. Walter L. Weible, Egon Weiss, Lt. Col. C. W. Westlund, James T. Williams, Col. F. H. Wilkerson, Lyle Wilson, Rudolph H. Winnacker, William H. Worrilow, Jr., Mrs. Harry Wright, Donna H. Traxler, J. E. Hughes, and Ted Wycoff.

DIARIES

I have drawn heavily on the Diary of Secretary of War Henry L. Stimson, which is at the Yale University Library. Since Stimson saw General Marshall almost daily, when the two men were at the War Department, and made frequent summaries of their conversations, it is an invaluable source on the wartime Chief of Staff. Unquestionably the Diary contains comments by both men, made when they were tired or angry, which later they would have preferred to revise. In fact, Secretary Stimson omitted many of them from *On Active Service*, which he wrote in collaboration with McGeorge Bundy. I have included some of these on the ground that they reflected War Department thinking at the time. (Quotation marks around statements from the Stimson Diary may refer to the Secretary of War's paraphrase rather than to General Marshall's exact words.)

Material from the Morgenthau Diaries, to which I was directed by John Blum's *Years of Urgency*, was furnished me by the Franklin D. Roosevelt Library, Hyde Park, New York. For those portions of the Diary entries not open to the public, I have relied on Blum's book.

Brig. Gen. Paul McD. Robinett, who served as a member of General Marshall's staff during the first half of 1941 and as Chief of Intelligence of General Headquarters during the last half of 1941 and the first few weeks of 1942, kept a diary during this period which he kindly permitted me to use. It is valuable not only for information on the workings of the office of the Chief of Staff and GHQ but for insight on problems he gained as Assistant Secretary, WDGS, and from attending and recording the proceedings of the Standing Liaison Committee and of the Combined U.S.-U.K. Chiefs of Staff at the Arcadia Conference.

MEMOIRS, AUTOBIOGRAPHIES, AND BIOGRAPHIES

The best volumes on British policies and the views of Prime Minister Churchill and the British Chiefs of Staff in the 1939-42 period are Churchill's three volumes, *Their Finest Hour, The Grand Alliance,* and *The Hinge of Fate,* and Sir Arthur

Bryant's *Turn of the Tide,* based on the diaries of General Sir Alan Brooke (later Lord Alanbrooke).

Sherwood's *Roosevelt and Hopkins,* based on Hopkins' personal papers and notes and many official files, British and American, is particularly valuable on American military and political leaders and policies during the war period.

Two excellent volumes, *On Active Service,* written by Secretary Stimson and McGeorge Bundy, and Elting Morison's *Turmoil and Tradition, A Study of the Life and Times of Henry L. Stimson,* are especially valuable for the background of the period, the workings of the War Department, 1940-45, and the relationship between Secretary Stimson and General Marshall.

In addition to General MacArthur's *Reminiscences,* the following books are valuable for the Pacific commander's views and policies: Hunt, *The Untold Story of Douglas MacArthur,* Willoughby and Chamberlain, *MacArthur, 1941-1951;* and Whitney, *MacArthur, His Rendezvous with Destiny.* Hunt's volume was based in part on material gathered during several months at General MacArthur's headquarters during the war. Willoughby, General MacArthur's chief of intelligence, drew on the "MacArthur Histories," written after the war under Willoughby's supervision. He indicates that his book was expanded from an original group of ten chapters read and annotated by General MacArthur. General Whitney, aide to General MacArthur for many years and at the time he wrote the book, had full access to his superior's files. General MacArthur said that "his actual participation in the events and his intimate knowledge of the concepts underlying my actions cannot fail to ensure the historical accuracy and corresponding value of the book."

Mrs. George C. Marshall's *Together* has many delightful anecdotes on the General during the war period and gives valuable insights into his thinking. The only two biographies of General Marshall, those by William Frye and Robert Payne, while containing some material taken from interviews with General Marshall's colleagues, were written without access to the Chief of Staff's papers. DeWeerd's collection of General Marshall's speeches for the war years is valuable for the student of the period.

The Stilwell Papers contains colorful extracts from General Stilwell's diary and letters for the war period.

My Three Years with Eisenhower by Butcher is based on the "Diary, Commander-in-Chief," which he kept for General Eisenhower from 1942-45. I was permitted by General Eisenhower to make notes from the manuscript diary in 1946.

Sir John Kennedy's *The Business of War,* based on his diary, Leasor's *The Clock with Four Hands,* based on the diary of Sir Leslie Hollis, and Lord Moran's *Churchill* contain valuable material on personalities in the war period.

Volumes by some of the other key figures of the war years include: Leahy, *I Was There;* Arnold, *Global Mission;* King and Whitehill, *Fleet Admiral King, A Naval Record;* Lord Ismay, *Memoirs;* Wedemeyer, *Wedemeyer Reports;* Eisenhower, *Crusade in Europe;* Clark, *Calculated Risk;* Murphy, *Diplomat Among Warriors;* Cunningham, *A Sailor's Odyssey;* Truscott, *Command Missions;* de Gaulle, *War Memoirs.*

ARCHIVES AND LIBRARIES

General Marshall's personal papers were given to the George C. Marshall Research Library before his death and title was confirmed by Mrs. Marshall. Many of the papers are now deposited in the Marshall Library at Lexington, Virginia. Others are still in Washington being processed for shipment to Lexington. These files are not yet open to researchers.

The principal official records pertaining to the Chief of Staff's activities for the period 1939-42 are in the custody of the National Archives. Record collections that have been used for this volume include:

RECORD GROUP 319—*Records of the Army Staff, 1939:* Office of the Chief of Staff (OCS)—to March 1942; War Department Chief of Staff Army (WDCSA)—after March 1942; War Plans Division (WPD)—to March 1942; Operations Division (OPD) —after March 1942; Personnel Division (G-1); Intelligence Division (G-2); Operations Division (G-3).

RECORD GROUP 94—*Records of the Adjutant General's Office (TAG).*

RECORD GROUP 337—*Records of Headquarters, Army Ground Forces (AGF).*

RECORD GROUP 339—*Records of Army Air Force Headquarters.*

The author has drawn on material from the National Archives, the World War Records Division (Alexandria, Virginia), The Office of the Chief of Military History, The Department of the Army Library, The National War College Library, The Library of Congress, The Franklin D. Roosevelt Library, The Office of Naval Records and Library, U. S. Marine Corps Historical Section, The Yale University Library, and The Virginia Military Institute Library. I wish to thank their directors and staffs for their willing cooperation.

OFFICIAL HISTORIES

I am heavily indebted to the Department of the Army's official volumes in the *United States Army in World War II* series. Based on all of the available official records and presented in great detail, they were invaluable for background information and for guides to the official sources. Although I have attempted to check the original sources wherever available to me, I have been influenced in my selection of material and in my interpretations in many cases by these volumes. Although I have listed the location of original sources as a means of indicating to the reader the nature of the material, I have noted in a master copy of the manuscript, filed with the Marshall Library, the citations to the official volumes. Volumes that were espe cially valuable are listed in notes to the chapters to which they pertain.

For the British side of the story I have relied heavily on *Grand Strategy* by Sir J. R. M. Butler and J. M. A. Gwyer.

Pertinent volumes by Samuel E. Morison on the operations at sea and the Air Force volumes edited by Craven and Cate, in the *Army Air Forces in World War II* series, were frequently consulted.

NEWSPAPERS AND PERIODICALS

Miss Lejeune, Mrs. Pratt, Mrs. Pitts, Mr. Marken, and Mr. Gauntlett have checked the files of the following newspapers and periodicals for the period 1939-42 for editorial and general comments: *New York Times; Washington Post; Washington Star; Chicago Tribune; The Times of London; Army and Navy Journal; Army and Navy Register; Time; Newsweek;* and *Life.* Several years ago the Marshall Library acquired the *New York Times'* own clipping file of its stories on World War II, arranged by topic. This collection, now at Lexington, fills some 164 boxes. The Library also has an extensive clipping collection on General Marshall from the UPI collection at the *New York World Telegram and Sun;* a collection made by Don Russell and presented to the Library; and a collection made over a number of years by Arthur Webb, former U. S. correspondent for the *London Mail.*

Also of assistance was the annotated bibliography of articles, editorials, and books pertaining to General Marshall for the war years which was prepared by my wife, Christine Pogue, as her Master's thesis at Catholic University. Copies are on file at the university, at the Department of Army Library, and at the George C. Marshall Library.

Selected Bibliography

Acheson, Dean G. *Sketches from Life of Men I Have Known*. New York: Harper and Brothers, 1961.

Alexander of Tunis, Earl of. *The Alexander Memoirs, 1940-1945* (edited by John North). New York: McGraw-Hill Book Co., 1962.

Arnold, Henry H. *Global Mission*. New York: Harper and Brothers, 1949.

Baldwin, Hanson W. *Great Mistakes of the War*. New York: Harper and Brothers, 1950.

Barber, Noel. *How Strong is America?* London: George Harrap and Co., 1942.

Baruch, Bernard M. *The Public Years*. New York: Holt, Rinehart and Winston, 1960 (vol. 2 of *Baruch*).

Beard, Charles A. *President Roosevelt and the Coming of the War, 1941, a Study in Appearances and Realities*. New Haven: Yale University Press, 1948.

Bernardo, C. Joseph, and Bacon, Eugene H. *American Military Policy, Its Development since 1775*. Harrisburg, Pa.: Military Service Publishing Co., 1946.

Biddle, Francis. *In Brief Authority*. Garden City, N.Y.: Doubleday and Co., 1962.

Blum, John Morton. *From the Morgenthau Diaries*. Boston: Houghton Mifflin Co., 1959-1965. 2 vols. Vol. 2, *Years of Urgency*.

Bradley, Omar N. *A Soldier's Story*. New York: Henry Holt and Co., 1951.

Brereton, Lewis H. *The Brereton Diaries, the War in the Air in the Pacific, Middle East and Europe, 3 October 1941-8 May 1945*. New York: William Morrow and Co., 1946.

Bryant, Sir Arthur. *The Turn of the Tide, a History of the War Years Based on the Diaries of Field-Marshal Lord Alanbrooke, Chief of the Imperial General Staff*. Garden City, N.Y.: Doubleday and Co., 1957. Vol. II: *Triumph in the West*, 1959.

Buchanan, Albert R. *The United States and World War II*. New York: Harper and Row, 1964. 2 vols.

Burtness, Paul S., and Ober, Warren U., eds. *The Puzzle of Pearl Harbor*. Evanston, Ill.: Row, Peterson and Co., 1962.

Buss, Claude A. *The Far East, a History of Recent and Contemporary International Relations in East Asia*. New York: Macmillan Co., 1955.

Butcher, Harry C. *My Three Years with Eisenhower, the Personal Diary of Captain Harry C. Butcher, USNR, Naval Aide to General Eisenhower, 1942 to 1945*. New York: Simon and Schuster, 1946.

Butler, J. R. M., and Gwyer, M. A. *Grand Strategy*. London: Her Majesty's Stationery Office, 1964. (History of the Second World War; United Kingdom Military Series.) Vol. 2, *September 1939-June 1941*—by Butler; Vol. 3, *June 1941-August 1942*—pt. 1 by Gwyer, pt. 2 by Butler.

Butow, Robert J. C. *Tojo and the Coming of the War*. Princeton, N.J.: Princeton University Press, 1961.

Byrnes, James F. *All in One Lifetime*. New York: Harper and Brothers, 1958.

Catton, Bruce. *The War Lords of Washington*. New York: Harcourt, Brace and Co., 1948.

Chennault, Claire Lee. *Way of a Fighter, the Memoirs of Claire Lee Chennault*, edited by Robert Hotz. New York: G. P. Putnam's Sons, 1949.

Churchill, Winston S. *My Early Life: A Roving Commission*. New York: Charles Scribner's Sons, 1958.

————. *The Second World War*. Boston: Houghton Mifflin Co., 1949-1960, 6 vols. Vol. 2, *Their Finest Hour;* Vol. 3, *The Grand Alliance;* Vol. 4, *The Hinge of Fate*.

Clark, Mark W. *Calculated Risk*. New York: Harper and Brothers, 1950.

Cline, Ray S. *Washington Command Post, the Operations Division*. Washington: Office of the Chief of Military History, Dept. of the Army, 1951. (United States Army in World War II: The War Department.)

Cole, Wayne S. *America First, the Battle against Intervention, 1940-1941*. Madison, Wis.: University of Wisconsin Press, 1953.

Coles, Harry L., ed. *Total War and Cold War; Problems in Civilian Control of the Military*. (Conference on Civil-Military Relations, Ohio State University, Columbus, 1959.) Columbus: Ohio State University Press, 1962.

Compton, Arthur H. *Atomic Quest, a Personal Narrative*. New York: Oxford University Press, 1956.

Conn, Stetson, and Fairchild, Byron. *The Framework of Hemisphere Defense*. Washington: Office of the Chief of Military History, Dept. of the Army, 1960. (United States Army in World War II: The Western Hemisphere.)

————, Fairchild, Byron, and Engelman, Rose C. *Guarding the United States and Its Outposts*. Washington: Office of the Chief of Military History, Dept. of the Army, 1964. (United States Army in World War II: The Western Hemisphere.)

Craven, Wesley F., and Cate, James L.

(eds.). *See* U.S. Air Force, USAF Historical Division.

Cunningham of Hyndhope, Viscount. *A Sailor's Odyssey, the Autobiography of Admiral of the Fleet Viscount Cunningham of Hyndhope.* New York: E. P. Dutton and Co., 1951.

Davis, Kenneth S. *Experience of War, the United States in World War II.* Garden City, N.Y.: Doubleday and Co., 1965.

————. *Soldier of Democracy, a Biography of Dwight Eisenhower.* Garden City, N.Y.: Doubleday, Doran and Co., 1945.

Dawson, Raymond H. *The Decision to Aid Russia, 1941, Foreign Policy and Domestic Policies.* Chapel Hill, N.C.: University of North Carolina Press, 1959.

de Gaulle, Charles. *War Memoirs.* Vol. 1, *The Call to Honour, 1940-42.* New York: Viking Press, 1955. Vol. 2, *Unity, 1942-44,* and Vol. 4, *Unity, 1942-44, Documents.* New York: Simon and Schuster, 1960.

de Seversky, Alexander P. *Victory through Air Power.* New York: Simon and Schuster, 1942.

Divine, Robert A. *The Reluctant Belligerent, American Entry into World War II.* New York: John Wiley and Sons, 1965. (*America in Crisis.*)

Dupuy, Richard E., and Dupuy, Trevor N. *Military Heritage of America.* New York: McGraw-Hill Book Co., 1956.

Dziuban, Stanley W. *Military Relations between the United States and Canada, 1939-1945.* Washington: Office of the Chief of Military History, Dept. of the Army, 1959. (United States Army in World War II: Special Studies.)

Eden, Earl of Avon. *The Reckoning, the Memoirs of Anthony Eden, Earl of Avon.* Boston: Houghton Mifflin Co., 1965.

Eichelberger, Robert L. *Our Jungle Road to Tokyo* (with Milton Mackaye). New York: Viking Press, 1950.

Eisenhower, Dwight D. *Crusade in Europe.* Garden City, N.Y.: Doubleday and Co., 1948.

Fairchild, Byron, and Grossman, Jonathan. *The Army and Industrial Manpower.* Washington: Office of the Chief of Military History, Dept. of the Army, 1959. (United States Army in World War II: The War Department.)

Falk, Stanley L. *Bataan, the March of Death.* New York: W. W. Norton and Co., 1962.

Farago, Ladislas. *Patton: Ordeal and Triumph.* New York: I. Obolensky, 1964.

Feis, Herbert. *Churchill, Roosevelt, Stalin, the War They Waged and the Peace They Sought.* Princeton: Princeton University Press, 1956.

————. *The Road to Pearl Harbor, the Coming of the War between the United States and Japan.* New York: Atheneum, 1962.

Fergusson, Bernard. *The Watery Maze, the Story of Combined Operations.* New York: Holt, Rinehart and Winston, 1961.

Friend, Theodore. *Between Two Empires, the Ordeal of the Philippines, 1929-1946.* New Haven: Yale University Press, 1965. (Yale Historical Publications Studies 22.)

Frye, William. *Marshall, Citizen Soldier.* Indianapolis: Bobbs-Merrill Co., 1947.

Fuchida, Mitsuo, and Okumiya, Masatake. *Midway, the Battle that Doomed Japan; the Japanese Navy's Story.* Annapolis: U.S. Naval Institute, 1955.

Ganoe, William A. *The History of the United States Army.* New York: D. Appleton-Century Co., 1943.

George C. Marshall Research Library. *Addresses Delivered at the Dedication Ceremonies of the George C. Marshall Research Library, May 23, 1964, Lexington, Va.* 1964.

Green, Constance (McLaughlin). *The Ordnance Department.* Washington: Office of the Chief of Military History, Dept. of the Army, 1955. (United States Army in World War II: The Technical Services.)

Greenfield, Kent Roberts. *American Strategy in World War II, a Reconsideration.* Baltimore: Johns Hopkins Press, 1963.

————, Palmer, Robert R., and Wiley, Bell I. *The Organization of Ground Combat Troops.* Washington: Historical Division, Dept. of the Army, 1947. (United States Army in World War II: The Army Ground Forces.)

Grew, Joseph C. *Ten Years in Japan, a Contemporary Record Drawn from the Diaries and Private and Official Papers of Joseph C. Grew.* New York: Simon and Schuster, 1944.

————. *Turbulent Era, a Diplomatic Record of Forty Years, 1904-1945.* Boston: Houghton Mifflin Co., 1952. 2 vols.

Griffith, Samuel B. *The Battle for Guadalcanal.* New York: J. B. Lippincott Co., 1963.

Gwyer, M. A. *See* Butler, J. R. M., and Gwyer, M. A.

Halifax, Lord. *Fullness of Days.* New York: Dodd. Mead and Co., 1957.

Hall, Hessel D. *North American Supply.* London: Her Majesty's Stationery Office, 1955. (History of the Second World War: United Kingdom Civil Series: War Production Series.)

Halsey, William F. *Admiral Halsey's Story* (with Lieutenant Commander J. Bryan III). New York: Whittlesey House, 1947.

Hammond, Paul. *Organizing for Defense, the American Military Establishment in the Twentieth Century.* Princeton, N.J.: Princeton University Press, 1961.

Harrison, Gordon A. *Cross-Channel Attack.* Washington: Office of the Chief of Military History, Dept. of the Army, 1951. (United States Army in World War II: The European Theater of Operations.)

Hatch, Alden. *The de Gaulle Nobody Knows, an Intimate Biography of*

Charles de Gaulle. New York: Hawthorn Books, 1960.

————. *The Mountbattens, the Last Success Story.* New York: Random House, 1965.

Heckstall-Smith, Anthony. *Tobruk, the Story of a Seige.* New York: W. W. Norton and Co., 1960.

Heinl, Robert D. *Soldiers of the Sea, the United States Marine Corps, 1775-1962.* Annapolis: U.S. Naval Institute, 1962.

Hicks, John D. *The American Nation, a History of the United States from 1865 to the Present.* Boston: Houghton Mifflin Co., 1949.

Hoehling, Adolph A. *The Week before Pearl Harbor.* New York: W. W. Norton and Co., 1963.

Holley, Irving B. *Buying Aircraft: Matériel Procurement for the Army Air Forces.* Washington: Office of the Chief of Military History, Dept. of the Army, 1964. (United States Army in World War II: Special Studies 7.)

Howe, George F. *Northwest Africa, Seizing the Initiative in the West.* Washington: Office of the Chief of Military History, Dept. of the Army, 1957. (United States Army in World War II: The Mediterranean Theater of Operations.)

Hull, Cordell. *The Memoirs of Cordell Hull.* New York: Macmillan Co., 1948. 2 vols.

Hunt, Frazier. *MacArthur and the War against Japan.* New York: Charles Scribner's Sons, 1944.

————. *The Untold Story of Douglas MacArthur.* New York: Devin-Adair Company, 1954.

Huzar, Elias. *The Purse and the Sword, Control of the Army by Congress through Military Appropriations.* Ithaca, N.Y.: Cornell University Press, 1950.

Ickes, Harold L. *The Secret Diary of Harold L. Ickes.* New York: Simon and Schuster, 1953-54. 3 vols. Vol. 2, *The Inside Struggle, 1936-1939;* Vol. 3, *The Lowering Clouds, 1939-1941.*

Ismay, Baron. *The Memoirs of General Lord Ismay.* New York: Viking Press, 1960.

Johnson, Walter. *Battle against Isolation.* Chicago: University of Chicago Press, 1944.

Karig, Walter. *Battle Report.* Prepared from official sources by Walter Karig [and others]. New York: Published for the Council on Books in Wartime by Farrar and Rinehart, 1944-52. 6 vols. Vol. 1, *Pearl Harbor to Coral Sea;* Vol. 2, *The Atlantic War.*

Kennedy, Sir John. *The Business of War, the War Narrative of Major General Sir John Kennedy* (edited by Bernard Fergusson). New York: William Morrow and Co., 1958.

Kimmel, Husband E. *Admiral Kimmel's Story.* Chicago: Henry Regnery Co., 1955.

King, Ernest J. *Fleet Admiral King, a Naval Record* (with Walter Muir Whitehill). New York: W. W. Norton and Co., 1952.

Kirby, Stanley W. *The War against Japan.* London: Her Majesty's Stationery Office, 1957-58. (History of the Second World War: United Kingdom Military Series.) Vol. 1, *The Loss of Singapore;* Vol. 2, *India's Most Dangerous Hour.*

Kreidberg, Marvin A., and Henry, Merton G. *History of Military Mobilization in the United States Army, 1775-1945.* Washington: Dept. of the Army, 1955. (Dept. of the Army Pamphlet no. 20-212.)

Krueger, Walter. *From Down Under to Nippon, The Story of the Sixth Army in World War II.* Washington, D.C.: Combat Forces Press, 1953.

Langer, William L. *Our Vichy Gamble.* New York: Alfred A. Knopf, 1947.

————, and Gleason, S. Everett. *The Challenge to Isolation, 1937-40.* New York: Published for the Council on Foreign Relations by Harper and Brothers, 1952.

————, and Gleason, S. Everett. *The Undeclared War, 1940-41.* New York: Published for the Council on Foreign Relations by Harper and Brothers, 1953.

Leahy, William D. *I Was There, the Personal Story of the Chief of Staff to Presidents Roosevelt and Truman, Based on his Notes and Diaries Made at the Time.* New York: Whittlesey House, 1950.

Leasor, James. *The Clock with Four Hands, Based on the Experiences of General Sir Leslie Hollis.* New York: Reynal and Company, 1959.

Leighton, Richard M., and Coakley, Robert W. *Global Logistics and Strategy, 1940-1943.* Washington: Office of the Chief of Military History, 1955. (United States Army in World War II: The War Department.)

Leopold, Richard W. *The Growth of American Foreign Policy, a History.* New York: Alfred A. Knopf, 1962.

Lincoln, George. *Economics of National Security, Managing America's Resources for Defense.* New York: Prentice-Hall, 1954.

Linebarger, Paul M. A. *The China of Chiang K'ai-shek, a Political Study.* Boston: World Peace Foundation, 1941.

Lohbeck, Don. *Patrick J. Hurley.* Chicago: Henry Regnery Co., 1956.

Lord, Walter. *Day of Infamy.* New York: Holt and Co., 1957.

MacArthur, Douglas. *Reminiscences.* New York: McGraw-Hill Book Co., 1964.

————. *A Soldier Speaks, Public Papers and Speeches of General of the Army Douglas MacArthur.* New York: Frederick A. Praeger, 1965.

McCarthy, Dudley. *South-west Pacific Area—First Year: Kokoda to Wau.* Canberra: Australian War Memorial, 1959. (Australia in the War of 1939-1945. Series I [Army], no. 5.)

McCarthy, Joseph R. *America's Retreat from Victory, the Story of George Catlett Marshall.* New York: Devin-Adair Co., 1951.

McClendon, Robert E. *Autonomy of the Air Arm* (rev. ed.). Maxwell Air Force Base, Ala.: 1954. (U.S. Air University Documentary Research Study.)

McCloy, John J. *The Challenge to American Foreign Policy.* Cambridge, Mass.: Harvard University Press, 1950.

McNeill, William H. *America, Britain and Russia, Their Cooperation and Conflict.* London: Oxford University Press, 1953. (*Survey of International Affairs,* 1939-1946.)

Marshall, George C. *Selected Speeches and Statements of General of the Army George C. Marshall, Chief of Staff, U.S. Army* (edited by Major H. A. DeWeerd). Washington: Infantry Journal, 1945.

Marshall, Katherine T. *Together, Annals of an Army Wife.* Atlanta: Tupper and Love, 1946.

Marshall, Samuel L. A. *Armies on Wheels, the First Two Years of the Greatest World War.* New York: William Morrow and Co., 1941.

Matloff, Maurice, and Snell, Edward M. *Strategic Planning for Coalition Warfare, 1941-1942.* Washington: Office of the Chief of Military History, Dept. of the Army, 1953. (United States Army in World War II: The War Department.)

Miller, John. *Guadalcanal, the First Offensive.* Washington: Historical Division, Dept. of the Army, 1949. (United States Army in World War II: The War in the Pacific.)

Millett, John D. *The Organization and Role of the Army Service Forces.* Washington: Office of the Chief of Military History, Dept. of the Army, 1954. (United States Army in World War II: The Army Service Forces.)

Millis, Walter. *This is Pearl! The United States and Japan in 1941.* New York: William Morrow and Co., 1947.

Milner, Samuel. *Victory in Papua.* Washington: Office of the Chief of Military History, Dept. of the Army, 1957. (United States Army in World War II: The War in the Pacific.)

Moffat, Jay Pierpont. *The Moffat Papers. Selections from the Diplomatic Journals of Jay Pierpont Moffat, 1919-1943* (edited by Nancy Harrison Hooker). Cambridge, Mass.: Harvard University Press, 1956.

Moran, Lord. *Churchill: Taken from the Diaries of Lord Moran: The Struggle for Survival, 1940-1965.* Boston: Houghton Mifflin Co., 1966.

Morgenstern, George Edward. *Pearl Harbor, the Story of the Secret War.* New York: Devin-Adair Co., 1947.

Morison, Elting E. *Turmoil and Tradition, a Study of the Life and Times of Henry L. Stimson.* Boston: Houghton Mifflin Co., 1960.

Morison, Samuel Eliot. *History of United States Naval Operations in World War II.* Boston: Little, Brown and Co., 1947-1960. 15 vols. Vol. 1, *The Battle of the Atlantic, September 1939-May 1943;* Vol. 2, *Operations in North African Waters, October 1942-June 1943;* Vol. 3, *The Rising Sun in the Pacific, 1931-April 1942;* Vol. 4, *Coral Sea, Midway, and Submarine Actions, May 1942-August 1942;* Vol. 5, *The Struggle for Guadalcanal, August 1942-February 1943.*

———. *Strategy and Compromise.* Boston: Little, Brown and Co., 1958.

Morton, Henry C. V. *Atlantic Meeting, an Account of Mr. Churchill's Voyage in H.M.S. Prince of Wales in August 1941, and the Conference with President Roosevelt which Resulted in the Atlantic Charter.* New York: Dodd, Mead and Co., 1943.

Morton, Louis. *The Fall of the Philippines.* Washington: Office of the Chief of Military History, Dept. of the Army, 1953. (United States Army in World War II: The War in the Pacific.)

———. *Pacific Command, a Study in Interservice Relations.* Colorado Springs: U.S. Air Force Academy, 1961. (The Harmon Memorial Lectures in Military History, no. 3.)

———. *Strategy and Command, the First Two Years.* Washington: Office of the Chief of Military History, Dept. of the Army. (United States Army in World War II: The War in the Pacific.)

Motter, Thomas H. V. *The Persian Corridor and Aid to Russia.* Washington: Office of the Chief of Military History, Dept. of the Army, 1952. (United States Army in World War II: The Middle East Theater.)

Murphy, Robert D. *Diplomat Among Warriors.* Garden City, N.Y.: Doubleday and Co., 1964.

Nelson, Otto Lauren, Jr. *National Security and the General Staff.* Washington: Infantry Journal Press, 1946.

Ney, Virgil. *Evolution of the U.S. Army Field Manual, Valley Forge to Vietnam.* Ft. Belvoir, Va.: U.S. Army Combat Development Command, 1966.

Overseas Press Club of America. *I Can Tell It Now,* by members of the Overseas Press Club of America (edited by David Brown and W. Richard Bruner). New York: E. P. Dutton and Co., 1964.

Palmer, Robert R., Wiley, Bell I., and Keast, William R. *The Procurement and Training of Ground Combat Troops.* Washington: Historical Division, Dept. of the Army, 1948. (United States Army in World War II: The Army Ground Forces.)

Parkes, Henry B., and Carosso, Vincent P. *Recent America, a History.* New York: Thomas Y. Crowell Company, 1963.

Payne, Robert. *The Marshall Story, a Biography of General George C. Marshall.* New York: Prentice-Hall, 1951.

Perkins, Dexter. *The New Age of Franklin Roosevelt, 1932-1945.* Chicago: University of Chicago Press, 1957.

Phillips, Cecil Ernest Lucas. *Alamein.* Boston: Little, Brown and Co., 1962.

Pogue, Christine B. "General George C. Marshall as Chief of Staff, a Selected and Annotated Bibliography." Unpublished Master's thesis. Washington: Catholic University, 1960.

Pogue, Forrest C., with the editorial assistance of Gordon Harrison. *George C. Marshall, Education of a General, 1880-1939.* New York: Viking Press, 1963.

Pomeroy, Earl S. *Pacific Outpost, American Strategy in Guam and Micronesia.* Stanford: Stanford University Press, 1951.

Potter, John Deane. *Yamamoto, the Man Who Menaced America.* New York: Viking Press, 1965.

Pratt, Julius W. *Cordell Hull, 1933-44.* New York: Cooper Square Publishers, 1964. 2 vols. (*The American Secretaries of State and Their Diplomacy,* edited by Samuel Flagg Bemis and Robert H. Ferrell.)

Public Opinion, 1935-1946, under the editorial direction of Hadley Cantril; prepared by Mildred Strunk. Princeton: Princeton University Press, 1951.

Reeder, Russell P. *Born at Reveille.* New York: Duell, Sloan and Pearce, 1966.

Riddle, Donald H. *The Truman Committee, a Study in Congressional Responsibility.* New Brunswick, N.J.: Rutgers University Press, 1964.

Ridgway, Matthew B. *Soldier, the Memoirs of Matthew B. Ridgway.* New York: Harper and Brothers, 1956.

Riker, William H. *Soldiers of the States, the Role of the National Guard in American Democracy.* Washington: Public Affairs Press, 1957.

Rollins, Alfred Brooks, ed. *Franklin D. Roosevelt and the Age of Action.* New York: Dell Publishing Company, 1960.

Romanus, Charles F., and Sunderland, Riley. *Stilwell's Mission to China.* Washington: Office of the Chief of Military History, Dept. of the Army, 1953. (United States Army in World War II: China-Burma-India Theater.)

Roosevelt, Eleanor. *This I Remember.* New York: Harper and Brothers, 1949.

Roosevelt, Franklin Delano. *F.D.R., His Personal Letters* (edited by Elliott Roosevelt). New York: Duell, Sloan and Pearce, 1947-50. 4 vols. Vol. 3-4, *1928-1945.*

———. *The Public Papers and Addresses of Franklin D. Roosevelt,* with a special introduction and explanatory note by President Roosevelt, compiled by Samuel I. Rosenman. New York: Random House, 1938-1950. 13 vols. Vol. 8, *War—and Neutrality, 1939.* Vol. 9, *War—and Aid to Democracies, 1940.* Vol. 10, *The Call to Battle Stations, 1941.* Vol. 11, *Humanity on the Defensive, 1942.*

Sayre, Francis B. *Glad Adventure.* New York: Macmillan Co., 1957.

Schroder, Paul W. *The Axis Alliance and Japanese-American Relations, 1941.* Ithaca, N.Y.: Published for the American Historical Association by Cornell University Press, 1958.

Sherwood, Robert E. *Roosevelt and Hopkins, an Intimate History.* New York: Harper and Brothers, 1948.

Shugg, Roger W., and DeWeerd, H. A., Maj. *World War II, a Concise History.* Washington: Infantry Journal, 1946.

Slessor, Sir John Coatsworth. *The Central Blue, Autobiography.* New York: Frederick A. Praeger, 1957.

Slim, Lord. *Defeat into Victory.* New York: David McKay, 1961.

Smith, Ralph E. *The Army and Economic Mobilization.* Washington: Office of the Chief of Military History, Dept. of the Army, 1959. (United States Army in World War II: The War Department.)

Snell, John S. *Illusion and Necessity, the Diplomacy of Global War, 1939-45.* Boston: Houghton Mifflin Co., 1963.

Snyder, Louis L. *The War, a Concise History, 1939-1945.* New York: Julian Messner, 1960.

[Soviet Commission on Foreign Diplomatic Documents]. *Correspondence between the Chairman of the Council of Ministers of the USSR and the Presidents of the USA and the Prime Minister of Great Britain during the Great Patriotic War of 1941-1945.* English translation. Moscow: Foreign Languages Publishing House, 1957. 2 vols.

Stalin, Iosif. *The Great Patriotic War of the Soviet Union.* New York: International Publishers, 1945.

Stein, Harold, ed. *American Civil-Military Decisions, a Book of Case Studies.* University, Ala.: Published in cooperation with the Inter-University Case Program by University of Alabama Press, 1963.

Stettinius, Edward R. *Lend-Lease Weapons for Victory.* New York: Macmillan Co., 1944.

Stilwell, Joseph W. *The Stilwell Papers* (arr. and ed. by Theodore H. White). New York: W. Sloane Associates, 1948.

Stimson, Henry L. *On Active Service in Peace and War* (with McGeorge Bundy). New York: Harper and Brothers, 1947.

Storey, Robert C. "Some Attributes of Military Leadership." Unpublished Master's thesis, Syracuse University, 1945.

Tansill, Charles C. *Back Door to War, the Roosevelt Foreign Policy, 1933-1941.* Chicago: Henry Regnery Co., 1952.

Taylor, Telford. *The March of Conquest, the German Victories in Western Europe, 1940.* New York: Simon and Schuster, 1958.

Theobald, Robert A. *The Final Secret of Pearl Harbor, the Washington Contribution to the Japanese Attack.* New York: Devin-Adair Co., 1954.

Toulmin, Henry A. *Diary of Democracy, the Senate War Investigating Committee.* New York: Richard R. Smith, 1947.

Truscott, Lucian K. *Command Missions, a Personal Story.* New York: E. P. Dutton and Co., 1954.

Tuleja, Thaddeus V. *Statesmen and Admirals, Quest for a Far Eastern Naval*

Policy. New York: W. W. Norton and Co., 1965.

U.S. Air Force, USAF Historical Division. *The Army Air Forces in World War II* (prepared under the editorship of Wesley F. Craven and James L. Cate). Chicago: University of Chicago Press, 1948-1958. 7 vols. Vol. I, *Plans and Early Operations, January 1939 to August 1942,* by Office of Air Force History. Vol. II, *Europe—Torch to Pointblank, August 1942 to December 1943,* by Air Historical Group. Vol. IV, *The Pacific—Guadalcanal to Saipan, August 1942 to July 1944,* by Air Force Historical Division.

U.S. Army Air Forces. Office of Air Comptroller. *Army Air Forces Statistical Digest, 1946.* Washington: 1947.

U.S. Army Service Forces, Control Division. *Statistical Review, World War II; a Summary of ASF Activities.* Washington: Statistics Branch, Control Division, Headquarters, Army Service Forces, War Dept., 1946.

U.S. Congress. *Biographical Directory of the American Congress, 1774-1961; The Continental Congress, September 5, 1774, to October 21, 1788 and the Congress of the United States, from the First to the Eighty-sixth Congress, March 4, 1789, to January 3, 1961, Inclusive* (rev. ed.). Washington: U.S. Govt. Print. Off., 1961.

U.S. Congress, Joint Committee on the Investigation of the Pearl Harbor Attack. *Report . . . Pursuant to S. Con. Res. 27, 79th Congress; a Concurrent Resolution to Investigate the Attack on Pearl Harbor on December 7, 1941, and Events and Circumstances Relating Thereto and Additional Views of Mr. Keefe Together with Minority Views of Mr. Ferguson and Mr. Brewster.* Washington: U.S. Govt. Print. Off., 1946.

————. *Pearl Harbor Attack.* Hearings . . . 79th Congress, 1st Session, Pursuant to S. Con. Res. 27, a Concurrent Resolution Authorizing an Investigation of the Attack on Pearl Harbor on December 7, 1941, and Events and Circumstances Relating Thereto. Washington: U.S. Govt. Print. Off., 39 vols.

U.S. Congress, House Committee on Appropriations. *Defense Aid Supplemental Appropriation Bill, 1941.* Hearings before the Subcommittee of the Committee on Appropriations, 77th Congress, 1st Session, March 13, 1941. Washington: U.S. Govt. Print. Off., 1941.

————. *Emergency Supplemental Appropriation Bill, 1940.* Hearings before the Subcommittee of the Committee on Appropriations, 76th Congress, 3d Session, November 27-30, 1939. Washington: U.S. Govt. Print. Off., 1939.

————. *Fifth Supplemental National Defense Appropriations, 1941.* Hearings before the Subcommittee of the Committee on Appropriations, 77th Congress, 1st Session, March 5-11, 1941.

Washington: U.S. Govt. Print. Off., 1941.

————. *Military Establishment Appropriations for 1941.* Hearings before the Subcommittee of the Committee on Appropriations, 76th Congress, 3d Session, February 23-March 19, 1940. Washington: U.S. Govt. Print. Off., 1940.

————. *Second Supplemental National Defense Appropriation Bill for 1941.* Hearings before the Subcommittee of the Committee on Appropriations, 76th Congress, 3d Session, July 22-26, 1940. Washington: U.S. Govt. Print. Off., 1940.

U.S. Congress, House Committee on Military Affairs. *Joint Resolutions Declaring a National Emergency, Extending Enlistments, Appointments and Commissions in the Army of the U.S. . . . And for Other Purposes.* Hearings . . . 77th Congress, 1st Session, on H.J. Res. 217, 218, 220, 222, July 22, 25, 28, 1941. Washington: U.S. Govt. Print. Off., 1941.

————. *Promotion of Promotion-List Officers of the Army.* Hearings . . . 76th Congress, 2d Session, on H.R. 9243, April 9, 1940. Washington: U.S. Govt. Print. Off., 1940.

————. *Selective Compulsory Training and Service.* Hearings . . . 76th Congress, 3d Session, on H.R. 10132, July 10-August 14, 1940. Washington: U.S. Govt. Print. Off., 1940.

U.S. Congress, Senate Committee on Appropriations. *Defense Aid Supplemental Appropriation Bill, 1941.* Hearings before the Subcommittee on Appropriations, 77th Congress, 1st Session, on H.R. 4050, March 20, 1941. Washington: U.S. Govt. Print. Off., 1941.

————. *Second Supplemental National Defense Appropriations Bill, 1941.* Hearings before the Subcommittee of the Committee on Appropriations, 76th Congress, 3d Session, on H.R. 10263, August 5, 6, 15, 1940. Washington: U.S. Govt. Print. Off., 1940.

————. *Compulsory Military Training and Service.* Hearings . . . 76th Congress, 3d Session, on S. 4164, July 3, 5, 10-12, 1940. Washington, D.C.: U.S. Govt. Print. Off., 1940.

————. *Ordering Reserve Components and Retired Personnel into Active Military Service.* Hearings . . . 76th Congress, 3d Session, on S.J. Res. 286, July 30, 1940. Washington: U.S. Govt. Print. Off., 1940.

————. *Promotion of Promotion-List Officers of the Army.* Hearings . . . 76th Congress, 3d Session, on S. 3712, April 8, 1940. Washington: U.S. Govt. Print. Off., 1940.

————. *Retention of Members and Units of Active Reserve Components in Active Military Service Beyond Twelve Months.* Hearings . . . 77th Congress, 1st Session on S.J. Res. 92 and 93, July 17, 18, 21, 22, 23, 24, 1941.

Washington: U.S. Govt. Print. Off., 1941.

U.S. Dept. of State. *Foreign Relations of the United States, Diplomatic Papers.* (24 vols.) *1939,* 5 vols.; *1940,* 5 vols.; *1941,* 7 vols.; *1942,* 7 vols., including *China, 1942.* Washington: U.S. Govt. Print. Off., 1955-1963.

U.S. Dept. of the Army, Office of Military History. *Command Decisions* (edited with introductory essay by Kent Roberts Greenfield. The Authors: Martin Blumenson and Others. Washington: 1960.

U.S. Laws, Statutes, etc. *Acts and Resolutions Relating to the War Department.* Washington: U.S. Govt. Print. Off., 1941. (2 vols.) 76th Cong., 2d and 3d Sessions, September 21, 1939-January 3, 1941; 77th Cong., 1st and 2d Sessions, January 3, 1941-December 16, 1942.

U.S. Library of Congress, Legislative Reference Service. *Conduct of the War* (*April 1941-March 1942*), *Selected and Annotated Bibliography on the Operations of the Armed Forces in the War.* Washington: 1942. (*Bibliographies of the World at War,* no. IX).

U.S. Marine Corps. *The Guadalcanal Campaign,* by John L. Zimmerman, USMCR, Historical Division, Headquarters, U.S. Marine Corps. Washington: 1949.

U.S. Navy Dept. *Annual Report of the Secretary of the Navy to the President, 1939-1942.* Washington: U.S. Govt. Print. Off., 1939-1942.

U.S. War Dept. *Annual Report of the Secretary of War to the President, 1939-1941.* Washington: U.S. Govt. Print. Off., 1939-1941.

———. *Prelude to Invasion, an Account Based on the Official Reports of Henry L. Stimson, Secretary of War.* Published with the cooperation of the American Council on Public Affairs. Washington: Public Affairs Press, 1944.

U.S. War Dept., General Staff. *Biennial Report of the Chief of Staff of the U.S. Army, July 1, 1939 to June 30, 1941, to the Secretary of War.* Washington: U.S. Govt. Print. Off., 1942.

Vandenberg, Arthur H. *The Private Papers of Senator Vandenberg* (edited by Arthur H. Vandenberg, Jr., with the collaboration of Joe Alex Morris). Boston: Houghton Mifflin Co., 1952.

Viorst, Milton. *Hostile Allies: FDR and Charles de Gaulle.* New York: Macmillan Co., 1965.

Wainwright, Jonathan M. *General Wainwright's Story* (edited by Robert Considine). Garden City, N.Y.: Doubleday and Co., 1946.

The War Reports of General of the Army George C. Marshall, Chief of Staff, General of the Army H. H. Arnold, Commanding General, Army Air Forces, Fleet Admiral Ernest J. King, Commander-in-Chief, United States Fleet and Chief of Naval Operations. Philadelphia: J. B. Lippincott Co., 1947.

Watson, Mark S. *Chief of Staff, Prewar Plans and Preparations.* Washington: Historical Division, Dept. of the Army, 1950. (United States Army in World War II: The War Department.)

Webster, Sir Charles Kingsley. *The Strategic Air Offensive against Germany, 1939-1945.* London: Her Majesty's Stationery Office, 1961. (History of the Second World War: United Kingdom Military Series.) 4 vols. Vol. 1, *Preparation, 1939-1942.*

Wedemeyer, Albert C. *Wedemeyer Reports.* New York: Henry Holt and Co., 1958.

Weigley, Russell F. *Towards an American Army: Military Thought from Washington to Marshall.* New York: Columbia University Press, 1962.

Welles, Sumner. *Seven Decisions that Shaped History.* New York: Harper and Brothers, 1951.

———. *Where Are We Heading?* New York: Harper and Brothers, 1946.

Wheeler-Bennett, John W. *King George VI; His Life and Reign.* New York: St. Martin's Press, 1958.

Wheeler-Nicholson, Malcolm. *Battle Shield of the Republic.* New York: Macmillan Co., 1940.

Whitney, Courtney. *MacArthur; His Rendezvous with History.* New York: Alfred A. Knopf, 1956.

Wiley, Bell I., and Govan, Thomas P. *History of the Second Army.* Washington: Historical Section, Army Ground Forces, 1946. (U.S. Army Ground Forces, Study no. 16.)

Williams, Mary H., comp. *Chronology, 1941-1945.* Washington: Office of the Chief of Military History, Dept. of the Army, 1960. (United States Army in World War II: Special Studies.)

Willoughby, Charles A., and Chamberlain, John. *MacArthur, 1941-1951.* New York: McGraw-Hill Book Co., 1954.

Wilmot, Chester. *The Struggle for Europe.* New York: Harper and Brothers, 1952.

Wohlstetter, Roberta. *Pearl Harbor, Warning and Decision.* Stanford, Calif.: Stanford University Press, 1962.

Woodward, Sir Ernest Llewellyn. *British Foreign Policy in the Second World War.* London: Her Majesty's Stationery Office, 1962. (History of the Second World War: United Kingdom Military Series.)

Notes

Unless otherwise specified:

1. Interviews were conducted by the author, Forrest C. Pogue.
2. Citations of letters to and from General Marshall are to copies found in the General's Pentagon files. Originals or copies will ultimately be deposited in the Marshall Research Library.
3. General Marshall's speeches are from Marshall's typewritten reading copies of speeches, hereinafter cited as *Marshall Speech Book*. Secondary source is cited if available.

ABBREVIATIONS*

ABC American-British Conversations
ActACofS Acting Assistant Chief of Staff
ACofS Assistant Chief of Staff
ABDA Command of American, British, Dutch, and Australian Forces in the Pacific
AG Adjutant General (used for file location of documents)
AGF Army Ground Forces
ALUSNA U.S. Naval Attaché
AsstSecWar Assistant Secretary of War

BrCOS British Chiefs of Staff
BurBud Bureau of Budget Director

CCS Combined Chiefs of Staff
CDC Caribbean Defense Command
Cdrs. Commanders
CG Commanding General
CinCAF Commander-in-Chief, U.S. Asiatic Fleet
CinCLant Commander-in-Chief, U.S. Atlantic Fleet
CinCPac Commander-in-Chief, U.S. Pacific Fleet
CM-IN (or OUT) Cable Message, Incoming or Outgoing
CNO Chief of Naval Operations
CofS Chief of Staff
CsofS British and U.S. Chiefs of Staff at conferences
Cominch Commander-in-Chief, U.S. Fleet
CO Commanding Officer
Conf. Conference
COS Chiefs of Staff (British)

DCofS Deputy Chief of Staff
DSM Distinguished Service Medal

Exec. Executive File (OPD) (used for file location of documents)

G-1 Personnel Division
G-2 Intelligence Division
G-3 Operations Division

G-4 Supply Division
GHQ General Headquarters
GHQ Air Force U.S. Air Force. General Headquarters

HawDept Hawaiian Department

int. interview

JAG Judge Advocate General
JB Joint Board
JCS Joint Chiefs of Staff
JPC Joint Planning Committee

OCMH Office of the Chief of Military History
OCS SGS Office of the Chief of Staff, Secretary General Staff
OpNav Office of the Chief of Naval Operations

POA Pacific Ocean Area

RG Record Group
ROTC Reserve Officers' Training Corps

SecNavy Secretary of the Navy
SecWar Secretary of War
SGS Secretary General Staff
So Pac South Pacific Area
SWPA Southwest Pacific Area

TAG The Adjutant General of the Army

UndSecWar Under Secretary of War
USA United States Army
USAAF United States Army Air Forces
USAF United States Air Force
USAFBI United States Army Forces in the British Isles
USAFFE United States Army Forces in the Far East
USAFIA United States Army Forces in Australia
USN United States Navy

VMI Virginia Military Institute

WD   War Department (used for file location of documents)

WDCSA   War Dept. Chief of Staff Army

(used for file location of documents)

WPD   War Plans Division

* Documents have special nomenclature which does not always agree with approved abbreviations but it has been used for quick identification.

GLOSSARY OF CODE NAMES

BOLERO Build-up of U.S. forces and supplies in United Kingdom for cross-Channel attack.

GYMNAST Early plan for invasion of North Africa, referring to either the American idea of landing at Casablanca or the British proposal for landing farther eastward on the Mediterranean coast. SUPERGYMNAST was a plan for Anglo-America invasion of French North Africa, combining U.S. and British plans and often used interchangeably with GYMNAST.

JUPITER Plan for operations in northern Norway.

MAGIC American term for all Japanese diplomatic codes and ciphers.

PURPLE American term for the top-priority Japanese diplomatic cipher.

RAINBOW Various plans prepared between 1939 and 1941 to meet Axis aggression involving more than one enemy.

ROUNDUP Plan for major U.S.-British attack across the Channel in 1943.

SLEDGEHAMMER Plan for limited cross-Channel attack in 1942.

TORCH Allied invasion of North and Northwest Africa, November, 1942.

I: THE NEW CHIEF

For the background of Chapters I, II, and III, I found especially helpful Langer and Gleason, *Challenge to Isolation* and *The Undeclared War;* Conn and Fairchild, *The Framework of Hemisphere Defense;* Watson, *Chief of Staff: Prewar Plans and Preparations.* Helpful interview material was collected from Generals Bradley, Ward, Robinett, Taylor, Collins, Walter Bedell Smith, Bull, Adams, Buchanan, Kuter, Sexton, Haislip, Hilldring, and McCarthy; and from John Martyn, Col. and Mrs. Winn, Merrill Pasco, Sgt. Powder, and Sgt. Farr. Interviews with Gen. and Mrs. Marshall have been helpful throughout the book.

1. Gen. Dwight D. Eisenhower to Gen. George C. Marshall, 15Apr45.
2. K. T. Marshall, *Together,* p. 290. Presentation of Oak Leaf Cluster to DSM to Gen. Marshall by President Truman at the Pentagon, 26Nov45.
3. Marshall to the Rev. G. E. Mac-Girvin, 6Sept39.
4. Marshall int., 15Nov56.
5. *Ibid.,* 22Jan57.
6. Marshall to Gen. Malin Craig, 21-Aug39; Marshall to Craig, 19Sept39.
7. *Ibid.,* 5Sept39.
8. Marshall to Brig. Gen. Lorenzo D. Gasser, 4Aug39.
9. Marshall to Craig, 19Sept39.
10. Senate Appropriations Subcomm., *2d Suppl. Nat. Def. Appro. Bill 1941,* 5Aug40, p. 2.
11. House   Appropriations   Subcomm., *Emer. Suppl. Appro. Bill 1940,* 27-Nov39, pp. 11-13.
12. Marshall to Mrs. Claude Adams, 2Jan40.
13. Marshall to Brig. Gen. Bruce Magruder, 7Aug39.
14. *Supra,* note 12.
15. Maj. Gen. John H. Hilldring int., 30-Mar59.
16. *Ibid.*

17. *Supra,* note 12.
18. Gen. Albert C. Wedemeyer int., 1-Feb58; Wedemeyer, *Wedemeyer Reports,* p. 121.
19. General Marshall continued to encourage officers on duty in the War Department to wear civilian clothes until the day after Pearl Harbor. Sec-War Stimson, who took a contrary view, promptly directed all officers into uniform. Marshall said: "I was in favor of remaining in civilian clothes at the War Department and the big city headquarters as long as possible though I was much opposed on this. I know how quickly the worm turns on this, and while I was asking for billions, I didn't want a lot of uniforms plastered around Washington. I remember in the First World War we came back and found one of the acrid comments on the Army was the number of officers around Washington. . . , and I was trying to play that down as much as possible." Marshall int., 14Feb57.
20. Davis, *Experience of War, the U.S. in World War II,* p. 254.
21. Dean G. Acheson int., 2Oct57.

22. Conn and Fairchild, *Framework of Hemisphere Defense* (hereafter cited as *Framework*), pp. 26-27.
23. Marshall said: "Military history, since it deals with wars, is unpopular, and probably more so today than at any other time. Yet I believe it is very important that the true facts, the causes and consequences that make our military history, should be matters of common knowledge. War is a deadly disease, which today afflicts hundreds of millions of people. It exists; therefore, there must be a reason for its existence. . . . A complete knowledge of the disease is essential before we can hope to find a cure." Speech before Jt. Mtg. of Amer. Mil. Inst. and Amer. Hist. Assn., 28Dec39, *Marshall Speech Book*. See also De-Weerd, *Selected Speeches and Statements of General of the Army George C. Marshall*, pp. 36-39.
24. Marshall radio address to ROTC, 16-Feb40, *Marshall Speech Book*.
25. CofS Conf., 19Feb40, *OCS SGS, 1939-42*, *CofS Misc. Conf., 1938-42*.
26. Marshall to Dr. Douglas S. Freeman, 27Feb40.
27. House Appropriations Subcomm., *Mil. Est. Appro. Bill 1941*, 23Feb40, p. 3.
28. Marshall to Maj. Gen. Charles D. Herron, 1Apr40.

II: EUROPE BLAZES

In addition to books listed under Chapter I, I have found especially valuable for this chapter: Morison, *Turmoil and Tradition;* Stimson, *On Active Service;* and Blum, *From the Morgenthau Diaries, The Years of Urgency.* In addition to some of the individuals listed in the first chapter who provided information, I wish to include: James F. Byrnes, Bernard M. Baruch, Robert A. Lovett, John J. McCloy, Harvey Bundy, Arthur W. Page, Louis Johnson, and Lt. Gen. Brooks.

1. E. E. Morison, *Turmoil and Tradition; a Study of the Life and Times of Henry L. Stimson,* pp. 477-78; Ickes, *The Inside Struggle,* p. 718.
2. Ickes, *ibid.,* p. 718.
3. *Ibid.,* p. 717.
4. Blum, *From the Morgenthau Diaries: The Years of Urgency, 1938-1941* (hereafter cited as *Years of Urgency*), pp 153-54.
5. Marshall int., 14Nov56.
6. *Ibid.,* 11Feb57.
7. *Ibid.,* 29Oct56.
8. *Ibid.,* 14Nov56.
9. *Ibid.*
10. *Ibid.,* 22Jan57.
11. Marshall to Harry Hopkins, 24Dec41, 18Dec42, 24Dec43.
12. *Ibid.,* 22Dec44.
13. Marshall int., 14Feb57.
14. Bernard M. Baruch to Marshall, 5-Apr40; Marshall to Baruch, 9Apr40; Lt. Col. Orlando Ward to Marshall, 9Apr40; Baruch, *The Public Years,* pp. 274-78.
15. Marshall int., 29Oct56; Baruch, *op. cit.,* pp. 274-78.
16. Morgenthau Diary, 11May40, Book 261, pp. 279-331; Blum, *op. cit.,* p. 139.
17. Marshall int., 15Nov56; Morgenthau Diary, *loc. cit.,* p. 292; Blum, *op. cit.,* p. 139.
18. Morgenthau Diary, *loc. cit.,* p. 329; Blum, *op. cit.,* p. 140.
19. Marshall memo, 12May40, on additional national defense requirements, with notation "File as original proposal to President May 12th or 13th, leading up to special message of May 16th," *OCS SGS, 1939-42, Binder 2.*
20. Blum, *op. cit.,* pp. 140-41.
21. Blum, *op. cit.,* p. 141; Marshall int., 15Nov56.
22. Blum, *op. cit.,* p. 141.
23. Marshall to Baruch, 14May40.
24. Ward memo for record on White House Conference, 14May40, with attached papers, *OCS SGS, 1939-42, Binder 2.*
25. Marshall int., 15Nov56.
26. *Ibid.,* 28Feb57; Blum, *op. cit.,* pp. 143-44.
27. Senate Appropriations Subcomm., *Mil. Est. Appro. Bill 1941,* 1May40, p. 65; 17May40, pp. 403, 414.
28. Marshall int., 22Jan57.
29. Marshall to Lt. Gen. Stanley D. Embick, 1May40.
30. Marshall to Col. Morrison C. Stayer, 22Apr40.
31. Marshall to Allen Brown, 2Jan40.
32. *Ibid.,* 13Jun40.
33. *Ibid.,* 17Jul40.
34. Marshall address at VMI, Lexington, Va., 12Jun40, *Marshall Speech Book.* See also DeWeerd, *Selected Speeches . . . ,* p. 55.
35. Former SecWar Harry Woodring to Bob Harris, 23Jun54, in *Congressional Record,* v. 100, pt. 10, 83d Cong., 2d sess., 2Aug54, p. 1296.
36. Stimson Diary, 25Jun40; E. E. Morison, *op. cit.,* pp. 481-82.
37. Marshall int., 13Nov56.
38. *Ibid.,* 22Jan57.

III: "THE HUNGRY TABLE"

In addition to books listed in Chapters I and II, I have found especially valuable Leighton and Coakley, *Global Logistics and Strategy;* Greenfield, *Organization of Ground Combat Troops;* Holley, *Buying Aircraft.* I have also used articles by Dr. John McVicker Haight, "Roosevelt as Friend of France," and "Les Négotiations Françaises pour la Fourniture d'Avions Américain." See also *Foreign Relations, 1941, The American Republics,* Vol. VI. Interviews giving special background on this period were held with Maj. Gen. Burns and Lt. Gen. Hershey.

1. Marshall to Lt. Col. Harold R. Bull, 1Sept39.
2. Holley, *Buying Aircraft; Matériel Procurement for the Army Air Forces,* p. 202. See also Hall, *North American Supply,* pp. 105-120; Leighton and Coakley, *Global Logistics and Strategy,* pp. 36-37.
3. Leighton and Coakley, *ibid.;* Hall, *op. cit.,* p. 127; Holley, *op. cit.,* p. 355.
4. Watson, *Chief of Staff; Prewar Plans and Preparations,* p. 302 (hereinafter cited as *Chief of Staff*).
5. Morgenthau Diary, 17May40, Book 263, pp. 247-48; Blum, *Years of Urgency,* p. 150.
6. Morgenthau Diary, Book 265, p. 86; Blum, *op. cit.,* pp. 150-51.
7. Hall, *op. cit.,* pp. 134-35. Ultimately amounts well in excess of the surpluses listed were shipped. See Leighton and Coakley, *op. cit.,* pp. 32-36.
8. Blum, *op. cit.,* p. 153.
9. Maj. Walter Bedell Smith for info of CofS, 11Jun40, *OCS SGS, 1939-42, Binder 4.*
10. Conn and Fairchild, *Framework . . . ,* chap. xi.
11. *Ibid.,* pp. 273, 333.
12. *Ibid.,* pp. 284-302.
13. Marshall int., 22Jan57.
14. Unsigned memo, "Basis for immediate decisions concerning the national defense," 22Jun40; Marshall's notes taken to White House, *WPD 4250-3.* Marshall to Brig. Gen. George V. Strong, 24Jun40, giving the President's action, comments, and amendments.
15. Senate Comm. on Mil. Aff., *Compulsory Military Training and Service,* 12Jul40.
16. House Appropriations Subcomm., *2d Suppl. Nat. Def. Appro. Bill 1941,* 24Jul40, pp.123-24, 129.
17. House Comm. on Mil. Aff., *Selective Compulsory Training and Service,* 4-Jul40.
18. Watson, *op. cit.,* p. 216. Although he must have doubted that the crisis would be ended in the fall of 1941, he said later on that "the final decision will depend on the world situation as it exists at that time."
19. Senate Comm. on Mil. Aff., *Ordering Reserve Components and Reserve Personnel into Active Military Service,* 30Jul40, p. 4.
20. Senate Appropriations Subcomm., *2d Suppl. Nat. Def. Appro. Bill 1941,* 5, 6, 15Aug40, pp. 1, 21, 244.
21. *Chicago Tribune,* 13Aug40, editorial.
22. Polls taken in late June showed 63 per cent of those expressing an opinion favoring such legislation. The percentage rose to 71 in July and 73 in late August. *Public Opinion,* 1935-46, under the editorial direction of Hadley Cantril, pp. 458-89. See also Langer and Gleason, *The Challenge to Isolation, 1937-40,* p. 680 (hereinafter cited as *Challenge . . .*); *New York Times,* 17Sept40, p. 25.
23. Stimson Diary, 22Aug40; Marshall int., 22Jan57.
24. *New York Daily News,* 31Oct40.
25. Buchanan, *The United States and World War II,* Vol. I, p. 123. The selectees plus other troops gave the Army 1,400,000 in July 1941. The Air Corps had 167,000 of these. See *War Reports of Marshall, Arnold and King,* pp. 28, 36, 44.
26. Watson, *op. cit.,* p. 201; Greenfield, Palmer, and Wiley, *The Organization of Ground Combat Troops,* pp. 10-12.
27. Stimson Diary, 24Sept40.
28. *Ibid.,* 27Sept40.
29. Blum, *op. cit.,* pp. 188-90.
30. Watson, *op. cit.,* pp. 316-19; Leighton and Coakley, *op. cit.,* pp. 37-39.
31. Watson, *ibid.,* p. 306.
32. CofS Conf., 7Nov40, *OCS SGS, 1939-42, Conferences (15Nov38-14Jan42), Vol. I.*
33. Stimson Diary, 12Nov40.
34. *Ibid.;* Marshall int., 15Nov56; CofS Conf., 13Nov40, *OCS SGS, 1939-42, Binder 6;* CofS Conf., 14Nov40, *OCS SGS, 1939-42, Conferences (15-Nov38-14Jan42), Vol. I.*
35. Marshall int., 15Jan57.
36. CofS Conf., 2Dec40, *OCS SGS, 1939-42, Conferences (15Nov38-14Jan42), Vol. I.*
37. Langer and Gleason, *The Undeclared War, 1940-41,* pp. 234-36; Stimson Diary, 13Dec40.
38. Morgenthau Diary, 3Dec40, Book 335, p. 121; Blum, *op. cit.,* p. 203.
39. Blum, *ibid.*
40. Langer and Gleason, *Challenge . . . ,* pp. 239, 247-49.
41. Stimson Diary, 2Mar41; Marshall int., 15Jan57.
42. Marshall int., 22Jan57.

43. Roosevelt to Adm. William D. Leahy, 26Jun41, in Roosevelt, *FDR, His Personal Letters*, p. 1177.
44. SecWar Conf., 23Jun41, *OCS SGS, 1939-42, Binder 1*.
45. CofS Conf., 2Aug41, *OCS SGS, 1939-42, Conferences (15Nov38-14Jan42), Vol. II*.
46. Stimson Diary, 1Aug41.
47. *Ibid.*, 4, 5Aug41.
48. *Ibid.*, 1, 4, 5Aug41.
49. Watson, *op. cit.*, pp. 329-30.
50. Stimson Diary, 10Sept41.
51. Watson, *op. cit.*, p. 329-30.
52. Sherwood, *Roosevelt and Hopkins*, p. 398; Marshall to Maj. Gen. Richard C. Moore, 3Dec41.
53. Marshall int., 14Nov56, 22Jan57.
54. Marshall to Hopkins, 10Oct41.
55. *New York Herald Tribune*, 20Sept41, article by Walter Lippmann.
56. Stimson Diary, 1Oct41.
57. Marshall int., 15Jan57.
58. Watson, *op. cit.*, pp. 363-64; "Morale of the country": notes on the Lippman-Lindley theory. Pencil notation "Reply of McCloy and Lovett." *OCS Conferences, 9-21-41*.
59. Stimson Diary, 1Oct41.

IV: THE POWER TO LEAD

Of special assistance in this and the following chapter were: Greenfield, Palmer, and Wiley, *The Organization of Ground Combat Troops;* Palmer, Wiley, and Keast, *The Procurement and Training of Ground Combat Troops;* Watson, *Chief of Staff.* . . . Helpful interviews included those with Gen. Clark, Mrs. H. H. Arnold, Bernard M. Baruch, Maj. Gen. Christianson, Gen. Lear, Gen. Krueger, Brig. Gen. Osborn, Charles P. Taft, and Gen. Buchanan. I also gained background on Army training by a year's work (1943-44) on a history of the Second Army when I acted as research assistant to Bell I. Wiley and, later, Thomas P. Govan.

1. Marshall radio address, 29Nov40, *Marshall Speech Book.* See also De-Weerd, *Selected Speeches*, pp. 90-91.
2. Cline, *Washington Command Post, the Operations Division*, pp. 8-19.
3. Marshall int., 22Jan57.
4. *Ibid.*
5. Fortune also favored him and his fellow graduates of the West Point class of 1915 ("the class the stars fell on"), which produced sixty generals out of its roll of 164—a list that included Eisenhower, Bradley, Clark, Van Fleet, McNarney. Just the right age to reach top field command in World War II, Clark rose rapidly in the course of the war to hold corps, army, and army group command.
6. Although one of the few qualified pilots in the Air Section of the Signal Corps of the Army, Arnold discovered that he was still regarded as a foot soldier, and he was back at his old infantry duties in 1914 in the Philippines. On this tour, he arrived in time to observe a bright young first lieutenant named Marshall dictating field orders for maneuvers in Batangas Province. At the end of the exercises he told his wife that he had just seen a future Chief of Staff of the United States Army. He omitted any prophecy that young "Hap" Arnold would be the top air officer of World War II. See Arnold, *Global Command*, p. 44.
7. Marshall int., 22Jan47.
8. *Ibid.*
9. Arnold, *op. cit.*, pp. 163-64.
10. Gen. Laurence S. Kuter int., 10-Nov60; Gen. Kuter gave the number mentioned by Gen. Marshall as 86, but I have used the smaller number as the one initially proposed.
11. Marshall int., 7Dec56. Similar views given in interviews of 15Jan57 and 14Feb57. He believed that "part of our trouble goes back to the days of our ancestors being expert with the rifle and the rifle being on the conventional deer horns over the fireplace. Every man in those days, certainly every man on the frontier, was expert in handling a gun. He knew how to track, he knew how to screen himself. . . . Now practically all that has vanished, and the major part of the forces are city boys. I know that when we went into the First World War, I went over with the first unit and there was much talk then about the troops being trained marksmen and trained woodsmen. Most of them hadn't seen a weapon except in a shooting gallery and never had been in the woods in their life, other than in a park."
12. Marshall to Mrs. Marshall, 9, 15-Aug40.
13. There were many variations to this order, such as: "no honors, no special announcements, no aide, and no entertainment," Marshall to Brig. Gen. Asa L. Singleton, 23Apr40; or "no honors, no changes [of clothes], and no parties," Marshall to CG, Fort Sill, Okla., 8Apr41, both in *OCS Misc. Corres.*
14. Marshall int., 15Feb57.
15. *Ibid.*, 14Feb57.
16. *Ibid.*, 22Jan57.
17. When a prominent attorney warned

the Chief of Staff that such criticism increased the difficulties of congressmen who were pushing the Selective Service Act, Marshall passed the message on to Maj. Gen. H. J. Brees for a reply. The Third Army Commander took back nothing but indicated that he was trying to make people face facts and "cease to emulate the ostrich" by burying their heads in the sand. J. C. McManaway to Marshall, 23Aug40, with notes by Marshall; Brees to McManaway, 31Aug40. For nature of maneuvers, see Lt. Gen. Lesley J. McNair, "Comments on Army Maneuvers, 1940," 7Jan41, *AGF 354.2/1.*

18. Maj. Gen. Fox Conner to Marshall, 15Sept40; Marshall to Conner, 20-Sept40.
19. Marshall int., 15Nov56.
20. *Ibid.* Obviously the point about Union commanders still weighed on Connally's mind some years later. When the Senate debated the question of how many four-star generals should be kept, Connally was moved to wrath. In full voice, he asked his colleagues to survey the galleries and behold the officers come there in uniform to intimidate them. He ridiculed the need for four-star generals, reminding his fellow senators that Robert E. Lee, the greatest commander in American history, had been defeated by a lieutenant general named Grant.
21. Marshall int., 19Nov56.
22. *Ibid.* Marshall added, "And he was a very dear friend of mine. That was a result, I suppose, of arteriosclerosis."
23. This story was related by Marshall himself, although he did not concede that he made the mistake. Certainly there was pleasant correspondence as late as 1939 to show that Marshall knew who he was. Whatever the mix-up, Marshall later saw to it that Van Fleet headed the Mission to Greece in 1947, and later Van Fleet commanded the Eighth Army in Korea.
24. Marshall int., 15Feb57.
25. Senate Comm. on Mil. Aff., *Promotion of Promotion-list Officers of the Army,* 8Apr40, p. 13.
26. House Comm. on Mil. Aff., *Promotion of Promotion-list Officers of the Army,* 9Apr40, pp. 18-19.
27. *Supra,* note 25.
28. Marshall int., 19Nov56.
29. ACofS G-1 Lt. Col. John H. Hilldring

to CofS, 21Aug41, *G-1/3615-24;* Watson, *Chief of Staff,* pp. 242-45. In the first six months of its activities, the board removed by discharge or forced retirement some 195 officers or a number slightly over the one per cent of the Regular Army strength that Marshall had estimated would be affected. But to many of the 31 colonels, 117 lieutenant colonels, 31 majors, and 16 captains the action was "ruthless." Seventeen years later, when reminded of the strong criticism that greeted this initial action and the later removals of more than 500 colonels, Marshall agreed that he and the board had been ruthless, but insisted that their action had paved the way to victory.

30. Byrnes, *All in One Lifetime,* pp. 113-14. General Marshall said, "Byrnes was very fine. . . . He did me proud." Marshall int., 29Oct56.
31. Marshall int., 14Nov56, 15Feb57.
32. The story has been told the author by several people. In mid-May 1966, Maj. Gen. Charles Saltzman related the incident, saying that he had heard it from Gen. Frederick Osborn, and asked if I planned to include it. On digging through my notes, I found a brief confirmation of it by General Marshall. Marshall int., 14Feb57.
33. Marshall int., 22Jan57 says: "I did something at [this] stage which I think is very reprehensible on the part of a government official—the more so when it is a military official. . . . I went to Mr. Stimson and told him I had done my best and said the entire staff is with me on this. 'I will tell you now I am going to resign the day you do it.' As I say, I consider this reprehensible . . . but nothing else would stop this thing. So I decided I would just take that stand. If they were going to do it—and I considered it a colossal mistake—they could do it without me." Stimson Diary, 27Mar41; Marshall int., 22-Jan57; Robinett Diary, 28Mar41; CofS Conf., 28Feb41, *OCS SGS,* 1939-42, *Conferences (15Nov38-14Jan42),* Vol. II; Stimson, *On Active Service in Peace and War,* pp. 348-49.
34. Marshall address to graduates of the first Officer Candidate School, Fort Benning, Ga., 18Sept41, *Marshall Speech Book.* See also DeWeerd, *op. cit.,* pp. 175-77.

V: CIVILIANS IN UNIFORM

1. Marshall to Craig, 3Sept40.
2. Marshall to Gen. John J. Pershing, 31Jan41.
3. Senate Appropriations Subcomm., *2d Suppl. Nat. Def. Appro. Bill 1941,* 5Aug40, p. 4; Marshall to Stimson, 1Apr41.
4. Marshall int., 20Feb57.

5. K. T. Marshall, *Together,* pp. 118-19.
6. Marshall to DCofS, 18Apr41.
7. Riddle, *The Truman Committee: a Study in Congressional Responsibility,* chap. 1.
8. Forty-two-year-old Sgt. James W. Powder, nearly 6 feet 4¾ inches tall, and skilled at the tricks of getting

things done in an Army that he had entered as a boy of fifteen, was a driver for the office of the DCofS when Marshall assumed that post in 1938. By 1939 Powder began accompanying the General as his orderly, ultimately going with him to most of the great conferences in the course of the war. Thrice declining a commission at Marshall's hands, on the ground that he would be embarrassed as an officer because of his lack of sufficient formal education, he remained with the General until the war's end. Normally too busy to see much of the posts he visited, Powder on this rare occasion passed on to Marshall the request for blankets.

9. Based on interview with Sgt. Powder, 19Oct59; Marshall int., 20Feb57; Maj. Gen. Kenneth Buchanan int., 3Oct58.

10. On the blanket shortage, see Buchanan int., 3Oct58; Marshall to Maj. Gen. Asa Singleton, 23Mar40. For statement on "pinchpenny" policy, see Marshall int., 20Feb57. For Marshall's fight with senior colonels over equipment for soldiers in 1917, see Pogue, *George C. Marshall: Education of a General*, pp. 140-42.

11. General Council Mtg., 19Feb41, *OCS SGS, 1939-42, Conferences (15-Nov38-14Jan42), Vol. II.*

12. Marshall to Senator Harry Byrd, 16-May 41, *OCS Misc. Corres., 1939-42.* Marshall speech to American Legion, Milwaukee, Wis., 15Sept41, *Marshall Speech Book.* See also DeWeerd, *Selected Speeches,* p. 172.

13. Marshall to UndsecWar Robert P. Patterson, 30Sept41.

14. Senate Special Comm. to investigate the Nat. Def. Program, *Investigation*

of National Defense Program, 22-Apr41, p. 175.

15. Marshall to William R. Mathews, 31-Aug39.

16. *New York Times,* 14Jul40.

17. Stimson Diary, 3Mar41.

18. Marshall int., 15Feb57.

19. Charles P. Taft int., 19Apr59; Stimson Diary, 7Feb41; Frederick Osborn int., 18Feb59; Marshall to Cdrs., 1st, 2d, 3d Armies, GHQ Air Force, and Armored Force, 18Feb41, *OCS 19246-21.*

20. Taft int., 19Apr59; Marshall to Cdrs., 1st, 2d, 3d Armies, GHQ Air Force, and Armored Force, 18Feb41, *OCS 19246-21;* TAG Adams to Cdrs., 14-Mar41, *OCS 15473-6;* Marshall to Patterson, 30Sept41.

21. Marshall to Maj. Gen. W. S. Key, 14Apr41.

22. Various memos, Marshall to G-3, G-4, around middle of Apr41; Marshall to Maj. Gen. Ernest D. Peek, 3Apr41.

23. Marshall to Mrs. Peter G. Gerry, 17-Apr41.

24. Marshall to CO, Fort Hancock, N.J., 18Sept41.

25. Kent Roberts Greenfield, "Impressions of General George C. Marshall, Notes on his addresses to the '91 Dinner Club," Baltimore, Spring 1941.

26. Marshall to Maj. Gen. Frederic H. Smith, 7Nov40.

27. Marshall to Brig. Gen. Alexander M. Patch, 6Dec41.

28. Gen. Ben Lear int., 9May57; Marshall to Maj. Gen. Campbell King, 19Aug41.

29. Marshall speech at Trinity College, Hartford, Conn., 15Jun41, *Marshall Speech Book.* See also DeWeerd, *op. cit.,* pp. 122-24.

30. *Supra,* note 25.

VI: IF WAR CAME

Especially helpful for this and the following chapter were: Conn, Fairchild, and Engelman, *Guarding the United States and Its Outposts;* Morton, *Fall of the Philippines* and *Strategy and Command;* Matloff and Snell, *Strategic Planning for Coalition Warfare, 1941-42;* Morison, *Battle of the Atlantic;* Churchill, *The Grand Alliance;* Arnold, *Global Mission;* Sherwood, *Roosevelt and Hopkins;* Langer and Gleason, *The Undeclared War;* Watson, *Chief of Staff.* . . . Helpful interviews were those with Adm. Stark, Lt. Gen. Emmons, Maj. Gen. Bryden, Maj. Gen. Moore, Capt. Kittredge, Generals Ridgway, Gerow, Wedemeyer, Bolté, Burns, Robinett, and Ward.

1. Kennedy, *The Business of War; the War Narrative of Sir John Kennedy,* pp. 160-61; Robinett Diary, 7Feb41.

2. Robinett Diary, 16Apr41.

3. JPC to JB, 21Jan41, *JB 325, Ser. 674;* L. Morton, "Germany First: the Basic Concept of Allied Strategy in World War II," in U.S. Dept. of the Army, Office of the Chief of Military History, *Command Decisions,* pp. 41-42.

4. The Joint Board, established by a joint order of the Secretaries of War and Navy in 1903, had been reorganized and furnished with a supporting Joint Planning Committee in 1919. The Deputy Chief of Staff for Air and the Navy's Chief of the Bureau of Aeronautics were added to the Joint Board in July 1941. In 1942 the board's functions were largely assumed by the Joint Plan-

ning Committee. Cline, *Washington Command Post*, chaps. iii and iv; Watson, *Chief of Staff*, chap. iii; Morton, *op. cit.*, pp. 22-41.

5. CofS Conf., 17Jun40, *OCS SGS, 1939-42, Binder 3*. See also Morton, *op. cit.*, pp. 11-47; Matloff and Snell, *Strategic Planning for Coalition Warfare, 1941-42*, p. 17 (hereinafter cited as *Strategic Planning*); Watson, *op. cit.*, p. 108.

6. CofS Conf., 17Jun40, *OCS SGS, 1939-42, Binder 3*.

7. Stark to SecNavy Frank Knox, 12-Nov40, *WPD 4175-15*.

8. Marshall testimony, *Pearl Harbor Hearings*, pt. 3, p. 1052; Marshall int., 15Jan57.

9. CofS to CNO, 29Nov40, *WPD 4175-15*.

10. JPC to JB, 21Dec40, "National Defense Policy for the U.S." and a study of JPC, 12Dec40, *JB 325, Ser. 670;* see Watson, *op. cit.*, pp. 122-23.

11. CofS to Brig. Gen. Leonard T. Gerow, 17Jan41, "White House Conf., 16-Jan41," *WPD 4175-18;* Watson, *op. cit.*, p. 125; Matloff and Snell, *op. cit.*, p. 32.

12. Marshall int., 15Jan57.

13. Sherwood, *Roosevelt and Hopkins*, p. 273.

14. S. E. Morison, *The Battle of the Atlantic, September 1939-May 1943*, p. 56; *Pearl Harbor Hearings*, pt. 16, p. 2161, and pt. 11, p. 5502.

15. The entire question of the use of the fleet in the Atlantic is discussed in Robert J. Quinlan, "The United States Fleet: Diplomacy, Strategy and the Allocation of Ships, (1940-1941)," in Stein, ed., *American Civil-Military Decisions*, pp. 155-201; Conn and Fairchild, *Framework*, chap. v; Stimson Diary, 15Apr41.

16. Stimson Diary, 15Apr41; CofS Conf., 16Apr41, *OCS SGS, 1939-42, Binder 13*.

17. CofS Press Conference, 17Apr41, *Sexton Collection;* Robinett Diary, 15-Apr41.

18. CofS Conf., 16Apr41, *OCS SGS,* 1939-42, *Binder 13;* Robinett Diary, 16Apr41.

19. Stimson Diary, 15Apr41.

20. *Ibid.*, 17Apr41.

21. CofS Conf., 3Apr41, *OCS SGS, 1939-42, Conferences (15Nov38-14Jan42), Vol. II;* CofS Conf., 16Apr41, *OCS SGS, 1939-42, Binder 13*.

22. CofS Conf., 16Apr41, *OCS SGS, 1939-42, Binder 13*.

23. *Ibid.;* Robinett Diary, 16Apr41.

24. Embick to Marshall, 12Apr39.

25. Robinett Diary, 16Apr41; CofS Conf., 11:25 a.m., 16Apr41, *OCS SGS, 1939-42, Conferences (15Nov38-14Jan42), Vol. II*.

26. Marshall to Stimson, 16Apr41, *OCS SGS, 1939-42, Binder 13;* Stimson Diary, 16Apr41, says Roosevelt called Marshall and Embick to a White House meeting at two o'clock; he added that some Navy representatives would probably be there.

27. Conn and S. E. Fairchild, *Framework*, pp. 107-108; Morison, *op. cit.*, p. 61; Watson, *op. cit.*, pp. 390-91. In May the Army sent instructions to its base commanders in Newfoundland, Bermuda, and Trinidad saying that if forces of any belligerent power other than those having sovereignty over Western Hemisphere territory attacked or threatened British possessions on which the United States had bases, the commander of the Army base should resist the attack with all means at his disposal.

28. Stimson Diary, 23, 24Apr41.

29. Stimson Diary, 24Apr41.

30. *Ibid.*

31. Stimson Diary, 7, 8May41. Stimson wrote: "Marshall stands very high in Hull's estimation and he has a very forceful, able way of stating his points of military and naval strategy." Among others with whom Stimson talked in an effort to reach Hull was Dean Acheson.

32. Conn and Fairchild, *Framework*, pp. 109-110.

33. SecWar Conf., 3Jun41, *OCS SGS, 1939-42, Binder 1*.

VII: PLAN FOR VICTORY

1. Maj. Gen. Haywood S. Hansell int., 9Jul59. The other was Harold L. George, later a lieutenant general. Gen. Kuter told the author in an interview, 10Nov60, that he had taken the two officers to see the Chief of Staff. "General Marshall was quite polite to them and sent them out and then worked on me: 'Don't you ever let any half-baked magazine type proposal of that sort get this high again.'"

2. Leighton and Coakley, *Global Logistics*, p. 128.

3. Patterson to Stimson, 18Apr41, *WPD 4494;* Watson, *Chief of Staff*, pp. 332-33.

4. Leighton and Coakley, *op. cit.*, p. 128.

5. Wedemeyer, *Wedemeyer Reports*, chaps. iii and iv.

6. For general details of the Argentia meeting, see King, *Fleet Admiral King, a Naval Record*, pp. 331-37 (hereinafter referred to as *Fleet Admiral King*); Arnold, *Global Mission*, pp. 246-56; H. C. V. Morton, *Atlantic Meeting; an Account of Mr. Churchill's Voyage . . . in August 1941 and Conference with President Roosevelt . . . ;* Sherwood, *Roosevelt and Hopkins*, chap. xvi; Welles, *Where Are We Heading?*, pp. 3-18; Churchill, *The Grand Alliance*, pp.

427-50; Langer and Gleason, *Undeclared War*, ch. 16. Brig. Gen. James H. Burns and Lt. Col. Charles W. Bundy accompanied Generals Marshall and Arnold. Harriman and Welles flew to Argentia.

7. Marshall int., 15Jan57.
8. Stimson Diary, 14 and 19Aug41.
9. House Appropriations Subcomm., *5th Suppl. Nat. Def. Appro. Bill 1941*, p. 16.
10. Stimson Diary, 21Jun41. Note that Stimson told Hopkins the statement was being made on his responsibility. See also Langer and Gleason, *Undeclared War, 1940-41*, p. 570.
11. U.S. War Dept. General Staff. *Biennial Report of the Chief of Staff of the U.S. Army, July 1, 1939 to June 30, 1941, to the Secretary of War*, pp. 10-12.
12. Stimson Diary, 8, 9Jul41.
13. Stimson Diary, 10, 11Jul41 and entry for period 13-21Jul41.
14. Senate Comm. on Mil. Aff., *Retention of Members and Units of Active Reserve Components in Active Military Service beyond Twelve Months*, 17-Jul41, pp. 6-8.
15. *Ibid.*, pp. 10, 32-33.
16. House Comm. on Mil. Aff., *Providing for the Nat. Def. by Removing Restrictions on Numbers and Length of Service of Draftees*, 22Jul41, pp. 17, 35.
17. Grenville Clark to Marshall, 7Aug41; Stimson Diary, 23Jul41, said Marshall "had made another admirable witness"; *supra*, note 16, p. 41.
18. Cole, *America First, the Battle Against Intervention, 1940-42*, pp. 101-102.
19. Martin, in an amazingly candid statement about his tactics, said that he believed he had to go along with the violent opponents of Roosevelt in order to keep his group under control. He also believed that there were other ways of getting men for the Army. After explaining his basic political reasons noted above, he added, "Thus, while as leader I voted against it myself, I hoped it would pass." Martin, *My First Fifty Years in Politics*, pp. 96-98.
20. Marshall int., 22Jan57; James W. Wadsworth to Marshall, 25Aug41.
21. *Supra*, note 16, p. 5; Stimson Diary, 24Jul41; "If This Be Treason," *Time*, 4Aug41.
22. Stimson Diary, 6, 7Aug41.
23. "Problem of Morale," *Time*, 18-Aug41, p. 36; "This is What Soldiers Complain About," *Life*, 18Aug41, pp. 17-18.
24. "This Is What Soldiers Complain About," *Life* 25Aug41, pp. 30-36.
25. Marshall to Baruch, 19Aug41.
26. Blum, *Years of Urgency*, pp. 275-76.

27. "War and Peace," *Time*, 18Aug41, pp. 27-32; "Critical Areas in the War Effort," *Fortune*, Aug. 1941, pp. 42-43.
28. Watson, *op. cit.*, pp. 353-55; SecWar and SecNavy to President, 25Sept41, *WPD 4494-13*.
29. SecWar and SecNavy to President, 25Sept41, *WPD 4494-13;* JB Report attached to Victory Program Estimate, *WPD 4494-13*.
30. Strategic Estimate of Oct41, *WPD 4494-21*, Sec. 1; Conn and Fairchild, *Framework*, pp. 146-47.
31. Strategic Estimate of Oct41, *WPD 4494-21, Sec. 1.*
32. Watson, *op. cit.*, pp. 343-46; Wedemeyer, *op. cit.*, pp. 65-67.
33. *Chicago Tribune*, 4Dec41, p. 1; Wedemeyer, *op. cit.*, chap. ii; Capt. Tracy B. Kittredge, "A Military Danger; the Revelation of Secret Strategic Plans," *U.S. Naval Institute Proceedings*, July 1955, pp. 731-43.
34. Stimson Diary, 5Dec41.
35. In addition to *Tribune* attacks against Roosevelt, Stimson, and Marshall, which lessened somewhat after Col. McCormick's death, see the books and articles of Chesly Manly, Walter Trohan, and George Morgenstern.
36. Senator Burton K. Wheeler, *Yankee From the West*, pp. 32-36, says that an Air Force captain brought a copy of the plan to his home in Washington and that he showed it to Chesly Manly, who came to his house to copy the pertinent pages. Cf. Waldrop, *McCormick of Chicago*, pp. 256-57, 267-68.
37. "There were those who felt politically that we should do nothing—that we must be utterly defenseless—or we were plotting war. That would have been suicidal. The fact that we made ourselves capable of exerting military influence made the Germans very much more cautious in their [actions]." Marshall int., 15Jan57.
38. Wedemeyer, *op. cit.*, pp. 17-20.
39. *New York Times*, 22Aug41, p. 7.
40. Wiley and Govan, *History of the Second Army* (U.S. Army Ground Forces Study no. 16), pp. 23-26.
41. Krueger to Marshall, 11Jun41; Marshall to Krueger, 13Jun41.
42. Marshall to Lt. Col. George S. Patton, 29Sept36.
43. Marshall speech to American Legion Convention, Milwaukee, Wis., 15-Sept41, *Marshall Speech Book*. See also DeWeerd, *Selected Speeches*, p. 169.
44. McNair critique of 1st and 2d phases of maneuvers, Carolina area, 16-21-Nov, 25-28Nov41, *McNair Personal File, AGF*.
45. *Ibid.*

VIII: PACIFIC OUTPOSTS

The basic source on Pearl Harbor consists of the testimony and exhibits of the thirty-nine-volume Pearl Harbor Hearings and the one-volume final Report of the Joint Congressional Committee on Pearl Harbor. Especially valuable secondary sources and memoirs were: Wohlstetter, *Pearl Harbor;* Langer and Gleason, *The Undeclared War;* Feis, *Road to Pearl Harbor;* Butow, *Tojo and the Coming of War;* Hull, *Memoirs;* Conn, Fairchild, and Engelman, *Guarding the United States . . . ;* Morton, *Fall of the Philippines* and *Strategy and Command;* Morison, *Rising Sun in the Pacific;* Craven and Cate, *Army Air Forces in World War II,* Vol. I; MacArthur, *Reminiscences;* Whitney, *MacArthur.* Col. Dupuy's article "Pearl Harbor: Who Blundered?" *American Heritage* (Feb. 1962), pp. 64-81, gives a careful and accurate summary of events. A. H. Hoehling's *Week Before Pearl Harbor* has interesting material on the individuals and the atmosphere of the period. For detailed coverage of diplomatic dealings with Japan during the period, see *Foreign Relations, Japan, 1931-1941,* Vol. II, and *Foreign Relations, The Far East, 1941,* Vol. V. Helpful interviews were those with Maj. Gen. Herron, Adm. Stark, Gen. Gerow, Lt. Gen. Brereton, Lt. Gen. Brett, Maj. Gen. Miles, Brig. Gen. Betts, Col. Friedman, Gen. Smith, Maj. Gen. Deane, Mrs. Eleanor Roosevelt, Brig. Gen. Clarke, Henry C. Clausen, Sen. Scott Lucas, and Harvey Bundy.

1. CofS Conf., 17Jun40, *OCS SGS, 1939-42, Binder 3.*
2. Marshall to Herron, 17Jun40, *WPD 4322.*
3. Stark to Adm. James O. Richardson, 27May40, *Pearl Harbor Hearings,* pt. 1, p. 261.
4. Marshall to Herron, n.d., and not used, *WPD 4322.*
5. *Ibid.*
6. *Washington Post,* 3Mar40, Sec. 8, p. 5; Conn, Fairchild, and Engelman, *Guarding the U.S. and Its Outposts,* p. 13.
7. *Honolulu Advertiser,* 6Mar40, p. 4; *Washington Star,* 16Mar40.
8. See Wohlstetter, *Pearl Harbor, Warning and Decision,* pp. 74-98, on background of this alert and its importance.
9. Marshall to Herron, 19Jun40, 16-Jul40, and 28Aug40, *WPD 4322;* Herron to Marshall, 6Sept40; *Pearl Harbor Hearings,* pt. 15, pp. 1599-1600.
10. Marshall to ACofS WPD Strong, 6-Feb41, *WPD 3583-1.*
11. Marshall to Lt. Gen. Walter C. Short, 7Feb41, *WPD 4449-1.*
12. Short to Marshall, 19Feb41, *AG 318 (2-19-41).*
13. Short to Marshall, 5Mar41, *Pearl Harbor Hearings,* pt. 15, p. 1605; Short to Marshall, 15Mar41, *OCS 21105-20.*
14. Col. E. M. Markham to CofS, 10-Jan38, *WPD 3878-9;* Conn, Fairchild, and Engelman, *Guarding the U.S. and Its Outposts,* pp. 154-55.
15. Joint Estimate Covering Army and Navy Action in the Event of Sudden Hostile Action against Oahu or Fleet Units in the Hawaiian Area, 31-Mar41, *AG 601.5 (4-14-41).*
16. Maj. Gen. Frederick L. Martin to Short, "Study of the Air Situation in Hawaii," 20Aug41, *Pearl Harbor Hearings,* pt. 14, pp. 1029-30.
17. Marshall to Short, 7Feb41, *WPD 4449-1.*
18. Marshall Aide-Mémoire to President, 24Apr41, *OCS 19741-53.* Date penciled in. Copy printed in *Pearl Harbor Hearings,* pt. 15, p. 1635, is undated with remark "come to file 5/3/41." See also Stimson Diary, 23 and 24Apr41.
19. Stark Testimony, 3Jan46, *Pearl Harbor Hearings,* pt. 5, p. 2213. In his plans to make the Hawaiian Islands impregnable, Gen. Marshall included thirty-five heavy bombers for Hawaiian defense. Of this number only 21 were delivered in May 1941, the others being held back for use in the Atlantic area. Of the twenty-one, nine were sent to the Philippines in September. At the time of the Japanese attack in December only six of the remaining twelve were in commission. War Department planners provided for the delivery of 200 bombers to the Hawaiian Department by mid-year, 1942, but on the eve of Pearl Harbor, its needs were still secondary to the Atlantic area and the Far East (Conn *et. al., op. cit.,* pp. 166-67). In speaking of his problems of this period, Gen. Marshall said: "In regard to Hawaii we were always worried because they did not have enough bombers of the long range to set up adequate reconnaissance. . . . It is almost impossible to realize now how little we possessed, particularly in the air. I think it is best explained by something I mentioned to you before —that we had fifteen Flying For-

tresses (to send to Hawaii) and didn't have money to service them, to maintain them—fifteen! One of my last acts as Chief of Staff was to co-operate with some of the authorities in approving the condemnation of 2500 Flying Fortresses and stacking them out in Arizona." Marshall int., 7Dec56.

20. Endorsement by Maj. Gen. Ewing E. Booth on memo of Embick to Booth, 19Apr33, *WPD 3251-15*.

21. L. Morton, *Strategy and Command, the First Two Years* (hereinafter cited as *Strategy and Command*), p. 35.

22. ACofS WPD Brig. Gen. Charles E. Kilbourne to CofS, 27Apr34, *WPD 3251-17;* Watson, *Chief of Staff*, p. 415.

23. L. Morton, *The Fall of the Philippines*, pp. 9-12; Watson, *Chief of Staff*, p. 426.

24. ACofS WPD Strong to CofS, 21-Aug39, *WPD 4192;* ACofS WPD Strong to CofS, 2Mar40, *WPD 4192-3;* Watson, *Chief of Staff*, p. 416.

25. Butow, *Tojo and the Coming of the War*, pp. 103-105, 141-42 (hereinafter cited as *Tojo*).

26. Feis, *The Road to Pearl Harbor*, chap. 15.

27. Stimson Diary, 26Sept40.

28. Maj. Gen. George Grunert to Marshall, 2Nov40, *WPD 3251-39;* Act-ACofS WPD Gerow to CofS, 20-Nov40, *WPD 3251-39*.

29. Grunert to Marshall, 1Sept40, *AG 093.5 Philippines (7-2-40)*, gives convenient summary of eight messages.

30. ActACofS WPD Gerow to CofS, 20-Nov40, *WPD 3251-39;* Watson, *op. cit.*, pp. 422-23.

31. Marshall to Stark, 29Nov40, *WPD 4175-15*.

32. Stimson Diary, 16Sept., 13, 22, 23-Dec40; CofS Conf., 23Dec40, *OCS SGS, 1939-42, Binder 6;* Romanus and Sunderland, *Stilwell's Mission to China*, pp. 11-13; Army and Navy Conf., 16Dec40, *OCS SGS, 1939-42, Binder 6*.

33. ActACofS WPD Gerow to CofS, 26-Dec40, approved by Marshall, *WPD 3251-39*.

34. K. T. Marshall, *Together*, pp. 80-81.

35. Stimson Diary, 2Jan41.

36. Stimson Diary, 10Feb41; Marshall to Grunert, 27Mar41, *OCS 18812-51;* Marshall to ACofS G-1 Brig. Gen. Wade Haislip, 13Feb41, *OCS 15036-9*. See also Langer and Gleason, *Undeclared War*, pp. 322-24.

37. Marshall to Brig. Gen. Douglas MacArthur, 20Jun41, *WPD 3251-50*. Marshall indicated that he had spoken to Stimson some three months earlier. Stimson's only reference to such a conversation is in his entry for May 21, 1941. On May 29 the Chief of Staff advised Grunert to keep in close

touch with MacArthur, adding that "by virtue of his own ability as well as his position as Military Advisor for the Philippine forces, his support will be invaluable to you in the accomplishment of the difficult task with which you are confronted." Marshall to Grunert, 29May41, *WPD 3251-49*.

38. Langer and Gleason, *Undeclared War*, pp. 629-41; Feis, *Road to Pearl Harbor*, ch. 27; *U.S. Foreign Relations, Japan, II*, pp. 502-503 (hereinafter cited as *For. Rels.*).

39. Stark in name of CNO and CofS to Navy Commands to be delivered to Army Commands, 25Jul41, *WPD 4544-3*. See also Wohlstetter, *Pearl Harbor*, pp. 98-131.

40. Marshall testimony before Naval Court of Inquiry 2Sept44, *Pearl Harbor Hearings*, pt. 32, p. 560.

41. Despite Marshall's letter of May to Gen. MacArthur indicating the War Department's intention to make him commanding general, his biographer Frazier Hunt, in *The Untold Story of Douglas MacArthur*, p. 208, says that MacArthur later learned that the President waited until he had left for Hyde Park and was "well away from the War Department and General Marshall" before he directed the sending of the cables calling the Philippine forces into service and appointing MacArthur to head the command. Although emergency orders drawn up in December 1940 proposed to put Commonwealth troops under the Philippine Department commander, the draft orders prepared by WPD on July 17 included an order calling MacArthur to duty as Commanding General of U.S. Army Forces in the Far East. Recalled to duty in his permanent rank of major general, MacArthur was quickly promoted to lieutenant general on Marshall's recommendation. BurBud Harold D. Smith to Stimson, 11Dec40, *AG 093.5 (7-2-40)*; ActACofS WPD Gerow to CofS, 17Jul41, *WPD 3251-52*.

42. Hunt, *op. cit.*, pp. 27, 38, 113, 121-22, 167-69.

43. Marshall to Robert Ward Johnson, 1Nov42, *Sexton Collection*. The portrait had been painted at the request of Marshall's onetime VMI roommate Leonard Nicholson.

44. Morton, *The Fall of the Philippines*, pp. 37-39; Craven and Cate, *The Army Air Forces in World War II*, Vol. I, pp. 178-79.

45. Craven and Cate, *op. cit.*, pp. 178-79; Stimson, *On Active Service*, pp. 388-89; Stimson Diary, 4, 25Aug41 and 12Sept41.

46. ActACofS WPD Gerow to TAG, 30-Sept41, approved by Marshall and sent by SecWar to CG, USAFFE, *OCS 18136-67*.

47. Brereton, *The Brereton Diaries: the*

War in the Air in the Pacific, pp. 5-9 (hereinafter cited as *Diaries*).

48. Marshall to MacArthur, no. 137, 9-Sept41, *AG 320.2 (7-28-41)*; MacArthur to TAG, 1Oct41, *WPD 4175-18*, Sec. II.
49. ActACofS WPD Gerow to SecWar, 8Oct41, *WPD 3251-60;* Marshall to MacArthur, 18Oct41, *WPD 4178-18;* Watson, *op. cit.*, pp. 445-46.
50. Brereton, *op. cit.*, p. 19.
51. *Ibid.*, pp. 20-24.
52. CofS Conf., 26Nov41, *WDCSA 381 Philippines (12-4-41)*.
53. Unsigned memo CofS to Stark, 25-Sept41, *OCS 17396-56B;* Marshall comments on DCofS for Air Maj. Gen. Henry H. Arnold to CofS, 8-Oct41, *OCS 18136-72;* ActACofS WPD Gerow to AsstSecWar John J. McCloy and DCofS Moore, 10Nov41, *WPD 2789-17*.
54. Craven and Cate, *op. cit.*, p. 176. General Marshall later said of the problems and efforts in this period: "There were certain things started to increase the defensive power of the Philippines but they had not yet gotten well underway and they would proceed very slowly. The quantity production of material had not yet developed. That refers to airplanes, ammunition, anti-aircraft material, [everything] of that general nature that was so necessary in the Philippines. . . . Now the question was whether we could find time to build up the defenses in the Philippines.

"There was General MacArthur's plan to raise an army in the Philippines that had been started. But it takes a long time to develop an army —it takes a great deal of time to develop the discipline and training of such an army. . . . The only successful development that we achieved was by doubling the Philippine Scouts. . . .

"The development of supply [production] was really tragic as regards Hawaii and the Philippines because these things came into quantity production at the very last minute. We started to get material to them—some little bit we did get out—but there was a great deal on shipboard in the process of being sent out when the war came. . . .

"The lack of anti-aircraft guns was tragic and particularly for the naval anchorage and bases at Cavite and other places in the Philippines. We just didn't have them at all." Marshall int., 15Jan57.
55. CofS Conf., 3Nov41, *OCS SGS, 1939-42, Conferences (15Nov38-14Jan42)*, *Vol. II*. See ch. XIII for Marshall's remedy.
56. K. T. Marshall, *Together*, pp. 124-26; Marshall to Mrs. J. J. Winn, 20-Oct41.
57. Marshall to Mrs. Winn, 20Oct41.
58. Marshall to Mrs. Winn, 29Oct41.
59. Stimson Diary, 21, 28Oct41.
60. CNO to CinCLant, CinCPac, CinCAF, 16Oct41, *Pearl Harbor Hearings*, pt. 14, p. 1402. See Wohlstetter, *Pearl Harbor*, pp. 131-66.
61. Short testimony before Naval Court of Inquiry, 12Aug44, *Pearl Harbor Hearings*, pt. 32, p. 191.

IX: SO LITTLE TIME

The sources for Chapter VIII were also helpful here.

1. Herron to Marshall, 24Jun40, *Pearl Harbor Hearings*, pt. 15, p. 1596; JB Minutes, 3Nov41, *JB Records*. Gen. Marshall said this was not his direct statement but the sense of it. *Pearl Harbor Hearings*, pt. 3, p. 1260.
2. Marshall Testimony before the Joint Committee, 7Dec45, *Pearl Harbor Hearings*, pt. 3, p. 1119.
3. Marshall Testimony before the Naval Court of Inquiry, 2Sept44, *Pearl Harbor Hearings*, pt. 32, p. 560; JB Minutes, 3Nov41, *JB Records*.
4. ActACofS WPD Gerow to Marshall, 3Nov41, *WPD 4389-29;* JB Minutes, 3Nov41, *JB Records*.
5. Marshall and Stark to President, 5-Nov41, Serial 0130012, *WPD 4389-29*.
6. *Ibid.* The build-up would have been impressive if completed. Near the end of November there were 35 B-17s in the Philippines and 48 more scheduled to arrive by the first of January; 81 P-40s and 101 scheduled to ar-rive by the first of the year; and 52 A-24s were en route and expected to arrived by Christmas. Feis, *Road to Pearl Harbor*, p. 313, fn. 13.
7. *Supra*, note 5.
8. Stimson Diary, 6Nov41.
9. Grew, *Turbulent Era, a Diplomatic Record of Forty Years, 1904-45*, p. 1281; JB Minutes, 3Nov41, *JB Records; For. Rels., Japan, II*, p. 704. For date of outbreak of war, Langer and Gleason, *Undeclared War*, p. 854; Feis, *Road to Pearl Harbor*, pp. 294-97.
10. CofS Conf., 26Nov41, *WDCSA 381 Philippines (12-4-41)*. On this whole problem of intelligence, see the excellent treatment in Wohlstetter, *Pearl Harbor*, pp. 75ff.
11. Marshall int., 14Nov56.
12. Brig. Gen. Sherman Miles testified proudly before the Pearl Harbor Joint Committee that he served "as an assistant chief of staff to General Marshall something between two and

three times as long as any other officer." *Pearl Harbor Hearings*, pt. 3, p. 1583.

13. Photostat of notes taken by Robert Sherrod, then head of the *Time-Life* Bureau in Washington, 15Nov41. He also made available photostat of his Diary entry for 7Dec41, in which he recapitulated the points about the build-up but not some of the more amazing statements relating to the Navy and the bombings. For an account of the interview, see Sherrod's article, "Secret Conference with General Marshall," in Overseas Press Club book, *I Can Tell It Now*, pp. 39-45. After the war Sherrod showed his notes to Hanson Baldwin of *The New York Times*, who summarized the main points and sent them to General Marshall for comment. Warning that he wrote without checking any documents, the former Chief of Staff explained that he had been mistaken because of the extravagant claims advanced by the Air Corps for the performance of its heavy bombers. General Marshall's statement of the Navy's role in the Far East was at a Joint Board meeting on November 3, 1941. The new directive then being drawn up for General MacArthur provided for "offensive air operations in furtherance of the strategic defensive," a requirement that included cooperation by the Army with the U.S. Asiatic Fleet and with British ground and naval forces. The revised RAINBOW plan that MacArthur was to put into effect on the outbreak of hostilities stressed Army support of the Navy in raiding Japanese sea communications. Gen. Brereton wrote the author, 2July64, that there were no plans in 1941 for attacks on Japanese cities. For Plans A and B, see *For. Rels., Japan, II*, pp. 706-10, 715-19, 729-37, 753-57.

14. Intercepted diplomatic messages Tokyo to Washington, no. 812, 22-Nov41, *Pearl Harbor Hearings*, pt. 12, p. 165.

15. Stark to CinCAF and CinCPac, 24-Nov41, *WPD 4544-12*.

16. Stimson Diary, 25Nov41.

17. *Ibid.*

18. Marshall Testimony before the Joint Committee, 10Dec45, *Pearl Harbor Hearings*, pt. 3, p. 1257. Gerow Memo, 27Nov41; *Pearl Harbor Hearings*, pt. 15, p. 1471; and Gerow Testimony, *Pearl Harbor Hearings*, pt. 4, p. 1664.

19. Hull, *Memoirs*, Vol. II, pp. 1083-84; Pratt, *Cordell Hull, 1933-44*, Vol. II, pp. 509-15; Stimson Diary, 25, 26, 27Nov41.

20. Pratt, *op. cit.*, p. 515.

21. This and following four paragraphs from CofS Conf., 26Nov41, *WDCSA 381, Philippines (12-4-41)*.

22. Stimson Diary, 27Nov41.

23. *Ibid.*

24. ActACofS WPD Gerow to TAG, 27-Nov41, *AG 381 Gen. (11-27-41)*.

25. *Ibid.;* Marshall to MacArthur, no. 624, 27Nov41, *AG 381 Gen. (11-27-41)*.

26. Stark to CinCAF and CinCPac, 27-Nov41, *WPD 4544-16*.

27. Short to Marshall, no. 959, 27Nov41, *AG 381 Gen. (11-27-41)*.

28. Miles to Short, 27Nov41, *Exec. 10, Item 7a. Pearl Harbor Hearings*, pt. 18, p. 2962. See also Wohlstetter, *op. cit.*, pp. 403-404 on Short's change in alert numbers.

29. Marshall Testimony before Joint Committee, 12Dec45, *Pearl Harbor Hearings*, pt. 3, p. 1434.

30. *Ibid.*, p. 1425.

31. *Ibid.*, pp. 1420, 1422, 1424.

32. *Ibid.*, p. 1422.

33. Marshall and Stark to President, 27-Nov41, *OCS 18136-125*. The memorandum appears to have been drafted by the Army and Navy staffs by 26-Nov and may have been signed by General Marshall before he left for the maneuvers.

34. Statement by Stimson to Joint Committee, Mar46, *Pearl Harbor Hearings*, pt. 11, p. 5436; Stimson Diary, 28Nov41.

35. Marshall to Mrs. Allen Brown, 5-Dec41.

36. Marshall to Col. Ralph H. Goldthwaite, 1Dec41.

37. Marshall to Mrs. Winn, 6Dec41.

X: THE FATAL WEEK

The sources for Chapter VIII were also helpful here.

1. Capt. Charles H. McMorris, USN, Testimony before the Roberts Commission, 30Dec41, *Pearl Harbor Hearings*, pt. 22, p. 526.

2. Capt. Edwin Layton, USN, Testimony before the Joint Committee, 18Feb46, *Pearl Harbor Hearings*, pt. 10, p. 4839.

3. Army Pearl Harbor Board conclusions of Marshall's Testimony, JAG

Cramer to SecWar, n.d., *Pearl Harbor Hearings*, pt. 3, p. 1470.

4. Marshall Testimony before Joint Committee, 10Dec45, *Pearl Harbor Hearings*, pt. 3, p. 1247.

5. Stimson Diary, 1Dec41.

6. Raymond A. Esthus, "President Roosevelt's Commitment to Britain to intervene in a Pacific War," *Mississippi Valley Historical Review*, June

1963, pp. 28-34; Woodward, *British Foreign Policy in the Second World War*, pp. 186-87.
7. CNO to CinCAF, CinCPac, Com14 and 16, 3Dec41, *Pearl Harbor Hearings*, pt. 14, p. 1407.
8. Wohlstetter, *Pearl Harbor*, p. 50; Stark to CinCPac and CinCAF, 6-Dec41, *Pearl Harbor Hearings*, pt. 14, p. 1408.
9. Butow, *Tojo*, pp. 387-401; *For. Rels. Japan, II*, pp. 784-86.
10. Lt. Col. Charles K. Gailey, Memo for Record, 15Jan42, *Exec. 4, Bk. 1;* Col. John R. Deane Memo to W. B. Smith, 8Jun42, *WDCSA Hawaii.* Still bound together in their original folder, the documents may be seen in the files of The National Archives. The papers Marshall requested for the discussion at the White House on the 7th concerned with the Philippines and the Far East: Philippine troop lists; sailing dates for reinforcements; location of transports; maps of the Indian Ocean, Indochina, Thailand, and Malaya; locations of Japanese, Russian, British, Dutch, and United States forces in the Far East; locations of United States, British, Dutch, and Japanese naval forces in the Far East; a report from the Commander-in-Chief of the Far Eastern Fleet listing the convoys sighted on December 6; an aviation map showing status of planes and the radii of operations; location of British air forces in the Far East; that portion of the RAIN-BOW plan showing Army and Navy tasks in the Philippines; draft orders for the Commanding General, U.S. Army Forces in the Far East, and "proposed instructions to Army commanders other than the Commanding General, U.S. Army Forces in the Far East."
11. Stimson Diary, 6Dec41; Arnold, *Global Mission*, pp. 268-69.
12. Marshall to Mrs. Winn, 6Dec41.
13. Marshall to Mrs. Allen Brown, 5-Dec41.

14. See Appendix 1 of this volume on Marshall Testimony.
15. Marshall Testimony before the Joint Committee, 7Dec45, *Pearl Harbor Hearings*, pt. 3, p. 1110.
16. For testimony on delivery and receipt of thirteen-part message, see testimony in *Pearl Harbor Hearings* by Marshall, Miles, Gerow, Walter B. Smith, Ralph Smith, Gailey, and Dusenbury. Bratton's various statements are in *Pearl Harbor Hearings*, pt. 9, pp. 4512-15; pt. 29, 2335-55; pt. 34, pp. 10-30; pt. 35, pp. 96-98.
17. *Supra*, note 15, p. 1108.
18. The more usual version based on Kramer's later testimony, is that Knox called Stimson and Hull the evening of December 6 to arrange for the meeting. I have preferred Stimson's Diary entry of December 7, indicating that he and Knox arranged the meeting apparently after they reached their offices on the morning of the 7th.
19. Marshall int., 14Nov56.
20. Marshall to CGs USAFFE, CDC, HawDept, and 4th Army, 7Dec41, *AG 381 Gen (12-7-41)*.
21. Lord, *Day of Infamy*, pp. 174-75; Trevor Dupuy, "Pearl Harbor, Who Blundered?" *American Heritage*, February 1962, p. 65.
22. Stimson Diary, 7Dec41. Marshall later testified that one of his aides thought he stayed at the War Department and another reported that he went home for lunch. Mrs. Marshall after the war, *Together*, p. 99, thought he did not come home until that evening. Col. Deane in a memorandum (*supra*, note 10), written at Gen. Marshall's request shortly after the event, says that the General went to Fort Myer and that he called him there. He is also the authority for the statement that the General notified him on reaching the office that morning that he was going to a conference at the White House that afternoon.

XI: PACIFIC ORDEAL

In addition to volumes by Morton, Morison, MacArthur, Whitney, and Conn, Fairchild, and Engelman, I also found helpful the work of Craven and Cate. Interviews that helped on background were those with Gen. MacArthur, Lt. Gen. Sutherland, Gen. Brett, Gen. Brereton, Gen. Eisenhower, and Gen. Gerow.

1. Telephone conversation, Gerow and MacArthur, 7Dec41 (8Dec, Manila time), *WPD 4622;* MacArthur, *Reminiscences*, p. 117; Brereton, *Diaries*, p. 38; Arnold, *Global Mission*, p. 272.
2. Marshall to MacArthur, 27Nov41, *AG 381 Gen. (11-27-41);* MacArthur, *op. cit.*, p. 113; Whitney, *MacArthur: His Rendezvous with History*, p. 10; Hunt, *Untold Story of MacArthur*, pp. 227-28.

3. Overseas Press Club, *I Can Tell It Now*, p. 44.
4. Deane int., 31Oct60.
5. K. T. Marshall, *Together*, p. 99.
6. L. Morton, *Strategy and Command*, pp. 140-41; Marshall handwritten memo, 12Dec41, informing WPD of "presence of Japanese force . . . in area . . . of San Francisco and Cape Mendocino," *WPD 4622*.
7. Stimson Diary, 15Dec41. Secretary

Stimson, in noting the preparation of a public statement on the reliefs on December 17, wrote: ". . . and in that announcement I, according to my promise, took my position side by side with Knox as to the absence of preparedness on December 7." Gen. Marshall testified in 1945 that the relief was based on a directive from the SecWar. *Pearl Harbor Hearings*, pt. 3, pp. 1528-31. See also Appendices 1 and 2 of this volume.

8. Morton, *Fall of the Philippines*, p. 151; Hunt, *Untold Story of MacArthur*, pp. 440-41.

9. Stimson Diary, 10Dec41; JB Minutes, 10Dec41, *JB Records*. Stimson Diary, 14Dec41. He noted that entries in the Diary for the past six days had given "a very inadequate view of this struggle and of the affirmative efforts which Marshall and I have been making. . . . We have apparently gotten the President firmly on our side."

10. CofS Conf., 10Dec41, *OCS SGS, 1939-42, Binder 29*.

11. Stimson Diary, 11Dec41.

12. Eisenhower, *Crusade in Europe*, pp. 16-18 (hereinafter cited as *Crusade*); Eisenhower int., 28Jun62.

13. Stimson Diary, 14Dec41.

14. *Ibid.*

15. Eisenhower, *op. cit.*, pp. 21-22.

16. Stimson Diary, 10Dec41; ActACofS WPD Gerow to CofS, 17Dec41 [not used] with Marshall's forwarding note [to be attached to Stark's memo to President, 13Dec41], *WPD 4557-32*; ActACofS G-2 Miles to CofS, 15Dec41, *Exec. 8, Bk. 1;* MacArthur to Marshall, 10Dec41, *WPD Msg. File no. 1.* Unsigned memo, 17-Dec41, "Assistance to the Far East," attributed to Eisenhower by Matloff and Snell, *Strategic Planning*, p. 87, fn. 88(2).

17. Marshall to Stark, 18Dec41, *Exec. 8, Bk. 1, Tab Misc.;* SecWar to Col. Philip R. Faymonville, no. 114, 16-Dec41, giving contents of msg. sent by President to Stalin, with rough draft corrected by Marshall, *WPD 4557-31;* Churchill, *Grand Alliance*, pp. 627-28; Eden, *The Reckoning*, pp. 342, 344-49; *For. Rels., 1941, IV*, pp. 752, 760; *Correspondence between Stalin and Franklin D. Roosevelt . . . ,* II, p. 18.

18. Robert A. Lovett to author, 1Sept64; Arnold, *op. cit.*, p. 290.

19. Lovett int., 14Oct57; Arnold, *op. cit.*, pp. 290-91.

20. Arnold to Marshall, 15Dec41, *WPD Msg. File no. 1;* Marshall to MacArthur, no. 824, 18Dec41, *WPD 4622-38;* Marshall to Brig. Gen. Julian F. Barnes, 12Dec41, *WPD 4628.*

21. Gerow to CofS, 17Dec41, *Exec. 8, Bk. 1;* DCofS Maj. Gen. Richard C. Moore to Maj. Gen. George H. Brett, 19Dec41, *OCS 18136-161;* Whitney, *MacArthur*, p. 34.

22. Stark to CofS, 23Dec41, Marshall to Brett, no. 856, 21Dec41, Marshall to MacArthur, no. 855, 22Dec41, all in *AG 381 Gen. (11-27-41) Far Eastern Situation.*

23. MacArthur, *op. cit.*, p. 127.

24. White House Conf., 11:45 a.m., 28-Dec41, *WDCSA 334 Mtgs. and Confs. (1-28-42).*

25. L. Morton, *Fall of the Philippines*, p. 162, estimates that MacArthur had from 75,000 to 80,000 as against 43,000 for the Japanese during this period, although MacArthur reported only 40,000 as against 80,000 to 100,000 Japanese.

26. L. Morton, *Strategy and Command*, pp. 186-87; MacArthur to Marshall, 1Jan42, Marshall to MacArthur, 2-Jan42, both in *WPD 4639-2;* Gerow to CofS, 3Jan42, *WPD 4639-3;* MacArthur to Marshall, 27Dec41, *AG 381 Gen. (11-27-41) Far Eastern Situation.*

27. Marshall to Brett, no. 26, 17Jan42, Marshall to MacArthur, no. 949, 17-Jan42, with rough draft corrected by Marshall, both in *WPD 4560-9.* It should be noted that within a period of a few months, as a result of the rapid changes in the Southwest Pacific, the command of U.S. Army Forces in Australia was held briefly by Generals Barnes, Clagett, Brereton, and Brett.

28. Marshall int., 20Nov56; Lohbeck, *Patrick J. Hurley*, pp. 159-60, has a different account, indicating that Hurley was given the temporary military mission first and notified of the New Zealand appointment after he reached the west coast. Eisenhower, *op. cit.*, p. 25, indicated that the War Department was looking for someone who would expedite shipments to MacArthur. Stimson Diary, 17Jan42, says Hurley called to say good-by. "We are promoting him . . . to Brig. Gen. and he is going to be . . . Minister [to] New Zealand."

29. Marshall to Maj. Gen. Lewis H. Brereton, nos. 134 and 152, 17, 19-Jan42, *AG 381 (11-27-41) Sec. 1, Far Eastern Situation.*

30. Morton, *Fall of the Philippines*, chap. xxii.

31. Lohbeck, *op. cit.*, p. 164.

32. MacArthur to Marshall, no. 201, 4-Feb42, *WDCSA 381 (2-17-42) Philippines.*

33. Marshall to MacArthur, no. 1024, 8-Feb42, *WDCSA 381 (2-17-42) Philippines.*

34. Morton, *Strategy and Command*, pp. 189-90; MacArthur to Marshall, nos. 226 and 227, 8Feb42, *WPD 3251-78;* MacArthur, *op. cit.*, pp. 138-39; Whitney, *op. cit.*, pp. 42-43; Sayre's *Glad Adventure* does not mention the incident.

35. Stimson Diary, 8, 9Feb42; Marshall int., 14Nov56.

36. President to MacArthur, no. 1029, 9-

Feb42, *AG 381 (11-27-41) Sec. 2A;* MacArthur, *op. cit.,* p. 139; Stimson Diary, 9Feb42.

37. MacArthur to Marshall, no. 252, 11-Feb42, *AG 381 (11-27-41) Sec. 2B.*

38. Whitney, *op. cit.,* pp. 41-42; Morton, *Strategy and Command,* pp. 193-94; Marshall to MacArthur, no. 919, 4-Feb42, *Exec. 10, Item 7a.*

39. Whitney, *op. cit.,* pp. 39-40; Hunt, *op. cit.,* p. 250, says that MacArthur's "resentment" was "far from placated" by Marshall's suggestions that orders would come from the President.

40. Hunt, *op. cit.,* p. 250; Hurley to Marshall, 21Feb42, cited in Lohbeck, *op. cit.,* p. 167.

41. Whitney, *op. cit.,* pp. 42-43; Hunt, *op. cit.,* pp. 255-58.

42. *Congressional Record,* 77th Cong., 2d sess., Vol. 88, pt. 1, p. 1249; pt. 2, p. 1666.

43. Stimson Diary, 18, 20, 21, 22, 23-Feb42; Marshall to MacArthur, no. 1078, 22Feb42, containing Roosevelt's order, *WDCSA Philippines, MacArthur's move from Philippines to Australia.*

44. MacArthur to Marshall, no. 358, 24-Feb42, *WDCSA Philippines, MacArthur's move from Philippines to Australia;* MacArthur, *op. cit.,* p. 140; Whitney, *op. cit.,* pp. 45-46; Hunt, *op. cit.,* pp. 256-58.

45. MacArthur, *op. cit.,* p. 140, says: "The same day (Feb. 21) the cabinet in Canberra had requested my immediate assignment to Australia as commander of the newly formed Southwest Pacific. When Prime Minister Curtin's recommendation reached the White House, President Roosevelt personally sent me a message to proceed as soon as possible in Mindanao." On p. 151 he calls Curtin "the man who had been instrumental in having me brought to Australia."

46. Morton, *Strategy and Command,* p. 245.

47. Marshall to Brett, no. 543, 5Mar42, *War Dept. Outgoing Msg. File Australia, Sec. 2;* Brett to Marshall, no. 550, 8Mar42, *OPD Msg. File;* Morton, *Strategy and Command,* p. 242.

48. President to Churchill, no. 115, 9-Mar42, *ABC 371 (3-5-42).*

49. *New York Times,* 18Mar42, p. 1; D. McCarthy, *South-west Pacific Area—First Year: Kokoda to Wau,* pp. 17-18.

50. Marshall to Brig. Gen. Richard K. Sutherland, 30Jan42, 12Mar42, Sec-War to Congressman Andrew May, 6Mar42 [apparently not sent], Marshall to SecWar, 24Mar42, all from *WDCSA 210.522 (3-2-42); Congressional Record,* Vol. 88, pt. 1, p. 1088, pt. 2, p. 1724, pt. 8, pp. A392, A803.

51. Sutherland to Marshall, no. 497, 16-Mar42; ACofS G-1 Hilldring to Marshall, 19Mar42, proposes award, with approval of Marshall and SecWar, 25Mar42, *WDCSA 210.522 (3-2-42);* this file includes Stimson's handwritten statement praising the language of the citation. For statements by Marshall and Eisenhower stating their roles in writing the citation, see Marshall to SecWar, 24Mar42, *WDCSA 210.522 (3-2-42);* Marshall to President, 22Aug44, *WDCSA 201, Ma-Mag (1944-45);* Eisenhower int., 28Jun62. Marshall also wrote the citation for an Oak Leaf Cluster to MacArthur's DSM in 1944. See Col. Frank McCarthy to G-1, 2Feb44, saying: "General Marshall disapproves of what he calls 'canned language,' used in most citations. I suggest that you write a good, strong, dignified citation without the usual stock phrases. For example, see Gen. MacArthur's recent DSM citation, which was written by Gen. Marshall himself." *WDCSA 201, Sti-Stz (1944-45).*

52. Marshall to SecWar, 24Mar42, forwarding proposed citation; Marshall to President, 25Mar42, Marshall to Sutherland, 25Mar42, Stimson to May, 7Apr42, all in *WDCSA 210.-522 (3-2-42); New York Times,* 26-Mar42, p. 5. In view of Marshall's initiative, it is startling to read in Hunt's biography of MacArthur that pressure by Congress on Roosevelt to grant the medal "was further to widen MacArthur's already strained relations with the White House." "On March 25," Hunt wrote, "a resolution was introduced in the Lower House that MacArthur be voted a Congressional Medal of Honor. It was passed with applause and three days later the President duly bestowed the highest decoration the nation possessed. The significance of the incident lay in the fact that, despite its name, the medal is actually proposed and given by the President and not by Congress. Rarely had Congress openly prodded a President to bestow the Congressional Medal of Honor." Hunt, *op. cit.,* p. 281.

53. Marshall to MacArthur, no. 739, 18Mar42, *OCS Incoming and Outgoing Msgs., USAFIA, 1941-42.*

54. Whitney, *op. cit.,* pp. 62-63; Morton, *Strategy and Command,* pp. 220-21.

55. Stimson Diary, 23Feb42.

56. Morton, *Fall of the Philippines,* pp. 360-63; Hunt, *op. cit.,* pp. 259-60.

57. Morton, *Fall of the Philippines,* pp. 363-65.

58. *Ibid.,* pp. 364-65; Marshall int., 14-Nov56; Marshall to President, 22-Mar42, *Exec. 10, Item 7d;* Marshall to MacArthur, 22Mar42, *Exec. 10 Item 7d;* MacArthur to Marshall, no. 19, 24Mar42, *OCS 201-M (MacArthur).*

59. Wainwright, *General Wainwright's Story,* pp. 83-85.

60. MacArthur, *op. cit.,* p. 146.

61. President to Wainwright, 5May42, *Exec. 10, Item 9.* See also Baldwin, "The Fall of Corregidor," *American Heritage* (Aug. 1966), pp. 16-23, 84-90.
62. MacArthur to Marshall, no. C-183, 1Aug42, *WDCSA 201 Wainwright (8-1-42).* Gen. MacArthur earlier gave Wainwright a DSC and later recommended him for a DSM and Legion of Merit.
63. Marshall int., 14Nov56; Stimson Diary, 8Sept42, 28Feb43.
64. SecWar to MacArthur, WAR 51945, 20Aug45, *OPD Msg. File;* MacArthur to SecWar, no. C35492, 21-Aug45, *OPD Msg. File.*

XII: ARCADIA

Many of the sources for Chapters XIV and XV were also helpful here.

1. Sir John Dill to Gen. Sir Alan Brooke, 3Jan42, in Bryant, *The Turn of the Tide, a History of the War Years Based on the Diaries of Field-Marshal Lord Alanbrooke, Chief of the Imperial General Staff,* p. 234.
2. *Washington Post,* 23Dec41; Churchill, *My Early Life, a Roving Commission,* pp. 76-77.
3. Marshall int., 5, 29Oct56.
4. *Ibid.,* 5Oct56.
5. *Ibid.*
6. Stimson Diary, 25Dec41.
7. "Immediate Military Measures," Tab ii, in Notes on Agenda Proposed by British, 21Dec41, *Exec. 4, Bk. 2.*
8. Churchill minutes of BrCOS on Atlantic front, cited in Gwyer, *Grand Strategy,* Vol. III, pt. 1, pp. 325-29. Marshall notes of meeting at White House with President and British Prime Minister presiding, 23Dec41, *WPD 4402-136;* also in *WDCSA 334 Mtgs. (12-23-41).* Handwritten draft on White House stationery attached.
9. Gwyer, *op. cit.,* p. 329.
10. Marshall notes of meeting at the White House . . . , *supra,* note 8.
11. Robinett Diary, 24Dec41, pp. 160-64.
12. Leasor, *The Clock with Four Hands,* pp. 4, 6; Marshall int., 29Oct56.
13. Robinett Diary, 24Dec41, p. 161; Marshall int., 29Oct56.
14. Leasor, *op. cit.,* p. 6; Robinett Diary, 24Dec41, p. 161; Kuter int., 10-Nov60.
15. Dill to Marshall, 20Aug41, 3Sept41, 13Nov41; Marshall to Dill, 7Nov41, 2Dec41.
16. Halifax, *Fullness of Days,* p. 268.
17. Executive Order 8984.
18. 1st Mtg. CsofS Conf., 24Dec41, *ABC 337, Arcadia (24Dec41), Arcadia Development File, Sec. II.*
19. Churchill, *Grand Alliance,* pp. 669-70; *Washington Post,* 25Dec41; Sherwood, *Roosevelt and Hopkins,* p. 443.
20. K. T. Marshall, *Together,* p. 100-102; Marshall int., 20Feb57.
21. Robinett Diary, 20Dec41; SecWar to CG, CDC, no. 7, 19Dec41; *WPD 2917-37;* MA no. 135, Lt. Col. Francis G. Brink to Marshall, 21Dec41, *OCS 18136-179.*
22. Robinett Diary, 25Dec41, p. 163.
23. 2d Mtg., CsofS Conf., 25Dec41, *ABC 337, Arcadia (24Dec41), Arcadia Development File, Sec. II.*
24. *Ibid.*
25. *Ibid.;* Marshall int., 5Oct56. At the close of the meeting Admiral Pound discussed the matter at some length with Col. Robinett of the American secretariat. He told him he was afraid of the unity of command proposal. Robinett Diary, 25Dec41, p. 164.
26. Eisenhower memo for file, "Notes taken at Jt. Conference of Chiefs of Staff, on afternoon, 25Dec41," 28Dec 41, *WPD 4402-136.*
27. Stimson Diary, 27Dec41.
28. Speaking of the fight waged by Marshall, Stimson said that the President on the 28th spanked the Navy for its lack of initiative and enterprise. The blame, Stimson added, did not fall on King, who "backed up Marshall in regard to this question of united command against practically all of his fellows. Knox has also been perfectly strong and loyal in his support of united command. But the bulk of the admirals have evidently been pretty stubborn and I think the future has some dark days for them." Stimson Diary, 28Dec41.
29. Conf. in Stark's office, 27Dec41, *WDCSA 334 Mtgs and Conf. (1-28-42).*
30. Robinett Diary, 27Dec41, p. 166.
31. Stimson Diary, 27Dec41.
32. 4th Mtg., CsofS Conf., 27Dec41, *ABC 337, Arcadia (24Dec41),* Arcadia Development File, Sec. II.
33. *Ibid.;* Robinett Diary, 27Dec41; Marshall int., 5Oct56. Dill did not imply by this action any approval of the appointments of Wavell.
34. Sherwood, *op. cit.,* pp. 456-57.
35. *Ibid.,* p. 457; Churchill, *Grand Alliance,* pp. 673-74; Stimson Diary, 26, 27, 28Dec41. Sherwood gives the meeting with the President as 26 Dec but references in Churchill, p. 674, and Stimson Diary, 28Dec41, point to the 27Dec.
36. Marshall int., 5Oct56, 21Nov56. See also Lord Moran, *Churchill,* p. 18.
37. Churchill to Lord Privy Seal Clement R. Attlee, 28Dec41, in Churchill, *Grand Alliance,* p. 674.
38. Churchill to Attlee, 29Dec41, in Churchill, *Grand Alliance,* pp. 675-76.

39. *Ibid.*
40. Stimson Diary, 29Dec41.
41. Dill to Brooke, 28Dec41, 3Jan42, and Brooke entry, in Bryant, *Turn of the Tide*, p. 235.
42. Robinett Diary, 31Dec41.
43. Marshall int., 5Oct56, 21Nov56.
44. Bryant, *Turn of the Tide*, p. 254.
45. Gwyer, *op. cit.*, pp. 386-87.
46. Marshall int., 13Nov56.
47. Wedemeyer, *Wedemeyer Reports*, pp. 164-67, 187-88.
48. Marshall int., 13Nov56.
49. Leighton and Coakley, *Global Logistics*, p. 250; Gwyer, *op. cit.*, p. 396.
50. Leighton and Coakley, p. 251; Gwyer, p. 397.
51. 11th Mtg., CsofS Conf., 13Jan42, *ABC 337*, *Arcadia (24Dec41)*, *Arcadia Development File*, Sec. *II and IV*; Gwyer, *op. cit.*, p. 397.
52. Sherwood, *op. cit.*, pp. 470-71; Leighton and Coakley, *op. cit.*, p. 251; Gwyer, *op. cit.*, p. 397.
53. Sherwood, *op. cit.*, pp. 471-72.
54. White House Conf., 14Jan42, *WDCSA 334 Mtgs. and Confs.* (*1-28-42*); Sherwood, *op. cit.*, p. 472.
55. Stimson Diary, 5Jan42. Stimson said grumpily that it was thoughtless of the President to let Marshall be deprived of his only chance for rest. See Moran, *op. cit.*, p. 22. Moran wrote that Churchill realized that Marshall was "the key to the situation." The Prime Minister felt that the American general "in his quiet unprovocative way" meant business and might take a strong line if the British were too obstinate. Neither the President nor Churchill, he said, could think of "going forward without Marshall."
56. *Supra*, note 32.
57. Marshall notes of meeting at White House . . . , *supra*, note 8. A slightly different version used by Matloff and Snell, *Strategic Planning*, p. 105.

XIII: STREAMLINING FOR ACTION

I have drawn heavily on articles by Col. Stansfield Haydon, which I read in manuscript form; on Otto Nelson, *National Security and the General Staff;* and on Greenfield, Palmer, and Wiley, *The Organization of Ground Combat Troops.* Valuable interviews were those with Generals McNarney, Kuter, Spaatz, Haislip, and Hilldring. Dr. J. E. Hughes, of the Office of the Chief of Military History, made a number of valuable suggestions for this study.

1. Kuter int., 10Nov60.
2. Marshall to Col. Hjalmar Erickson, 18Mar42.
3. Marshall Statement, 5Sept45, *Patch-Simpson Board Proceedings*, 1945, *OCS RG 110 58-85.*
4. Gen. Joseph T. McNarney Statement, 26Sept45, *Patch-Simpson Board 1945*, *loc. cit.*
5. Marshall int., 14Feb57.
6. Marshall to Brig. Gen. John McA. Palmer, 12Mar42.
7. McNarney int., 2Feb66.
8. *Ibid.*
9. *Ibid.*
10. Marshall to Palmer, 12Mar42.
11. Mtg. in Off. of DCofS attended by CofS, 5 Feb42, *OCS SGS, 1939-42*, *Binder 32.*
12. Marshall to Palmer, 12Mar42.
13. Minutes of the opening session, Special Committee on Reorganization of the War Dept., 16Feb42, *WDCSA 020, 1942-43.*
14. Frederick S. Haydon, "War Department Reorganization, Aug. 1941-Mar. 1942," *Military Affairs*, XVI, Spring and Fall 1952; See also Haydon, "War Department Reorganization," Aug. 41-Mar. 42, manuscript, Office of the Chief of Military History.
15. Gen. Marshall attributed this to Maj. Gen. Brehon B. Somervell. McNarney says he was the man involved. The author is inclined to agree with McNarney. McNarney int., 2Feb66.
16. Marshall to Palmer, 12Mar42.
17. Millett, *Organization and Role of the Army Service Forces*, pp. 1-42.
18. Marshall int., 13Nov56.
19. *Ibid.*, 14Feb57.
20. Charles Murphy, "Somervell of the SOS," *Life*, 8Mar43, pp. 82-84.
21. Marshall int., 14Feb57.
22. Marshall to Palmer, 12Mar42.
23. Stimson understood the proposal as the selection of a single chief of staff over the Army and Navy with power to issue orders without reference to the President except in matters of broad policy. This is somewhat at variance with Marshall's later description of what he had in mind. Stimson Diary, 25Feb42, 20Mar42; Marshall int., 14Feb56.
24. Marshall int., 14Feb57.
25. Stimson Diary, 25Feb42.
26. Stimson says in his Diary, 25Feb42, that the President was apparently intrigued but could not resist trying to twist it into a less important position.
27. Roosevelt's letter of 20July called him to duty as "Chief of Staff to the Commander-in-Chief of the United States Army and Navy." He announced it at his press conference the next day. Leahy, *I Was There*, pp. 94, 96-98.
28. Marshall int., 14Feb56.

XIV: LONDON IN THE SPRING

Valuable books on this period that were used in this chapter and the following are: Butler and Gwyer, *Grand Strategy;* Matloff and Snell, *Strategic Planning for Coalition Warfare;* Churchill, *Hinge of Fate;* Leighton and Coakley, *Global Logistics and Strategy;* Bryant, *Turn of the Tide;* Ismay, *Memoirs;* Wedemeyer, *Wedemeyer Reports;* and *Foreign Relations, 1942,* Vol. III. Interviews include: Field Marshal Lord Alanbrooke, Adm. Lord Mountbatten, Sir Anthony Eden (Lord Avon), Marshal of the RAF Lord Portal, Gen. Sir Leslie Hollis, Gen. Lord Ismay, Lord Attlee, Adm. Stark, Generals Wedemeyer, Handy, Hull, McCarthy, Robinett, Eisenhower, Clark, Smith, and Truscott, Lady Dill, Lt. Gen. Sir Frederick Morgan, Col. Truman Smith, Maj. MacDonald-Buchanan. An interview I conducted with Fleet Adm. Ernest J. King in 1947 for another book proved of some aid in writing this chapter.

1. Stimson Diary, 24Mar42: "I pointed out that we couldn't delay any longer in trying to bolster up the President from giving away what might be fatal amounts of our munitions and men."
2. Marshall to Allen Brown, 7Jan42, 23Mar43.
3. K. T. Marshall, *Together*, p. 39.
4. Felix Frankfurter int., 20Feb58.
5. K. T. Marshall, *op. cit.*, p. 110.
6. Churchill, *Hinge of Fate*, pp. 189-94.
7. Eisenhower notes, 22Jan42, author's personal notes from Eisenhower Diary taken in 1946.
8. Eisenhower to CofS, 28Feb42, *Exec. 4, Env. 35;* Matloff and Snell, *Strategic Planning*, p. 177.
9. Eisenhower to CofS, 28Feb42, *loc. cit.;* Eisenhower to CofS, 25Mar42, *OPD 381, Bolero, Sec. 1, Case 6;* Matloff and Snell, *op. cit.*, pp. 177, 181-82.
10. Marshall int., 5Oct56.
11. Stimson Diary, 25Mar42; Stimson, *On Active Service*, pp. 416-17.
12. Eisenhower to CofS, 25Mar42, *OPD 381, Bolero, Sec. 1.*
13. Stimson Diary, 27Mar42; Stimson, *On Active Service*, p. 413.
14. Stimson Diary, 1Apr42; Stimson, *On Active Service*, p. 419. Marshall to the President [n.d.], "Basis for preparation of attached outline plan for invasion of Western Europe," *Roosevelt Library*. Several versions of this plan exist, some with the date 2Apr42, others without dates. The fifth version, entitled "Operations in Western Europe," is marked as the one having been taken to London by Marshall, *ABC 381, Bolero (3-14-42), Bolero Development File, Sec. 4, Bk. 1.*
15. Marshall to Mrs. Frederick M. Ayres, 14Sept42; Marshall to Troup Miller, 2May43; K. T. Marshall, *op. cit.*, pp. 111-12, *Wedemeyer Reports*, pp. 100-101, have slightly different accounts.
16. Marshall to Erickson, 22Sept42.
17. Marshall to Churchill, 28Apr42; Marshall int., 15Jan57. General Marshall said: "There was no getting away from the fact that Mr. Churchill was the buoyant force in maintaining the Empire, together with the characteristic attitude of the British to hold out under very difficult circumstances."
18. *New York Times*, 9Apr42; *Times of London*, 9Apr42; Sherwood, *Roosevelt and Hopkins*, p. 523; Bryant, *Turn of the Tide*, p. 284.
19. Sherwood, *Roosevelt and Hopkins*, p. 523.
20. Bryant, *Turn of the Tide*, p. 285. Brooke made handsome amends for some of his disparaging remarks about Gen. Marshall but left others intact. Thus he went out of his way to praise as the greatest strategist of the war an officer, Gen. MacArthur, with whose global strategy he consistently disagreed. The chief burden of the Pacific commander's discontent with Marshall and Eisenhower was their support of British policy in the European Theater.

Perhaps Brooke assumed that the Pacific commander would have changed his views completely had he again become Chief of Staff. He left in his diary, apparently as a final and considered judgment: "He is head and shoulders bigger than Marshall, and if he had been in the latter's place the last four years I feel certain that my task in the Combined Chiefs of Staff would have been far easier." This pronouncement belongs in the same class as the statement Brooke attributes to Gen. MacArthur, when they met in Tokyo shortly after the end of the war, that MacArthur was especially grateful for the visit "as it was the first time during the war that he had ever been visited by any of the Chiefs of Staff." The book containing those remarkable words was published in 1959 after the appearance of volumes by Gen. Arnold and Adm. King, indicating their meetings with Gen. MacArthur, and after the publication of Hunt's biography in which he tells of Gen. Marshall's trip to the Pacific. Hunt

declares that when the Pacific commander heard that the Chief of Staff was coming to see him, "MacArthur seriously considered conducting the Gloucester operations in person, thus relieving Marshall of his presence." Hunt, *Untold Story of MacArthur*, p. 313.
21. Bryant, *Turn of the Tide*, pp. 6-9.
22. Brooke incorrectly says Marshall commanded a company in World War I, Bryant, *Turn of the Tide*, p. 74.
23. Brooke int., 18Apr61.
24. Ismay, *The Memoirs of General Lord Ismay*, p. 318.
25. After the war Ismay went to India as Chief of Staff to Lord Mountbatten at the time of the partition. Later, when the North Atlantic Treaty Organization was established, Ismay was chosen as its first Secretary General, a post he held from 1952-57.
26. Marshall int., 13Nov56.
27. Lord Louis Mountbatten int., 5-May61; Fergusson, *The Watery Maze, Story of Combined Operations*, pp. 149-50. Cf. Wedemeyer, *Wedemeyer Reports*, p. 109.
28. Bryant, *Turn of the Tide*, p. 242.
29. War Cabinet, COS Minutes, 9 Apr42 —part of COS (42) 112 Mtg. (Min. 5), *Exec. 1, Item 5d.* See also Sherwood, *Roosevelt and Hopkins*, p. 523.
30. Fergusson, *op. cit.*, p. 148.
31. Butler, *Grand Strategy*, Vol. III, pt. 2, pp. 565, 568-69.
32. *Ibid.*, pp. 569-72.

33. Marshall int., 5Oct56.
34. *Supra*, note 29.
35. *Ibid.*; Slessor, *Central Blue*, p. 397.
36. Sherwood, *Roosevelt and Hopkins*, pp. 525-26.
37. *Ibid.*, p. 529.
38. Extracts from telephone conversation, Marshall to McNarney, 12Apr42, *Exec. 1, Item 5d.* Others at Chequers over the weekend included Brooke, Lord Mountbatten, Rt. Hon. Oliver Lyttelton, Rt. Hon. A. V. Alexander, Lord Leathers, and Lord Cherwell.
39. Marshall to McNarney, No. 2387, 13Apr42, *Exec. 1, Item 5c.*
40. Sherwood, *op. cit.*, p. 533; War Cabinet, COS Minutes, 14Apr42—part of COS (42) 118th Mtg. (Min. 5); also, War Cabinet, COS, Comments on General Marshall's memorandum, 13Apr42—COS (42) 97 (0). General Marshall's copy is in the file. Both in *Exec. 1, Item 5d.*
41. War Cabinet Defence Committee, Minutes of Mtg., 14Apr42, sent by Ismay to Marshall, 17Apr41, *Exec. 1, Item 5d;* Marshall to SecWar, no. 2412, 15Apr42, *Exec. 1, Item 5c.*
42. Churchill to Roosevelt, 17Apr42, quoted in Churchill, *Hinge of Fate*, pp. 320-21. Cf. Bryant's *Turn of the Tide*, p. 287.
43. Bryant, *Turn of the Tide*, pp. 288-89.
44. Churchill, *Hinge of Fate*, p. 324.
45. Ismay, *op. cit.*, pp. 249-50. See also Lord Moran, *Churchill*, p. 51.
46. Ismay int., 18Oct60.
47. *Times of London*, 20Apr42, p. 2.

XV: MARSHALL LOSES A FIGHT

1. K. T. Marshall, *Together*, pp. 115-19.
2. Compton, *Atomic Quest*, pp. 166-67.
3. Acheson, *Sketches from Life of Men I Have Known*, p. 159.
4. Marshall to Stark, 20May42.
5. King to Marshall, 29Mar42, *Navy File A16-3(1)*, cited in Matloff and Snell, *Strategic Planning*, p. 211; MacArthur to Marshall, CM-IN-1070 (R), *OPD Msg. File.*
6. King to JCS, 4May42, *OPD 381, Gen. Sec. II, Case 62.*
7. Stimson Diary, 27May42; General Council Mtg., 27May42. Pt. 1 contains remarks by McNarney and Crawford on Marshall trip on which he was accompanied by Doolittle, Maj. Frank McCarthy and Col. S. H. Sherrill.
8. Cominch and CNO to CofS, 24-May42, CofS to Cominch and CNO, n.d., comment on 24May42 memo, both in *Exec. 10, Item 67a; News Syndicate*, 2Jun42.
9. *New York Times*, 30May42; *Washington Times*, 29May42; *News Syndicate*, 30May42.
10. S. E. Morison, *The Coral Sea, Midway and Submarine Actions, May 1942-August 1942*, chaps. vi-viii; Pot-

ter, *Yamamoto, the Man Who Menaced America*, chaps. 16-20; Fuchida and Okumiya, *Midway, the Battle that Doomed Japan.*
11. Marshall int., 14Nov56, 29Oct56, 20-Feb57.
12. Marshall int., 14Nov56; Arnold, *Global Mission*, pp. 378-79; *For. Rels. 1942*, III, 566ff.
13. Sherwood, *Roosevelt and Hopkins*, p. 556; Churchill, *Hinge of Fate*, p. 340.
14. Sherwood, *op. cit.*, pp. 564-69; *For. Rels., Europe, 1942, III*, pp. 566ff.
15. *Ibid.*, p. 577.
16. *Ibid.*, pp. 582-83; Wedemeyer, *Wedemeyer Reports*, pp. 136-39.
17. Butler, *op. cit.*, pp. 622-23; Churchill, *Hinge of Fate*, pp. 374-76.
18. Stimson Diary, 17Jun42.
19. *Ibid.*, 18, 19Jun42.
20. Minutes of an informal meeting between Marshall, members of his staff, and Dill, Brooke, and Ismay, 19-Jun42, *Exec. 1, Item 4;* Bryant, *Turn of the Tide*, pp. 324-25.
21. CCS 28th Mtg., 20Jun42, *ABC 334, CCS Minutes (1-23-42), Sec. 2.*
22. Bryant, *op. cit.*, p. 325.
23. Stimson Diary, 20Jun42.

24. Marshall int., 5Oct56.
25. Marshall int., 13Nov56.
26. Prime Minister to President, 20-Jun42, *Exec. 8, Book 5, Tab. Misc.*
27. Marshall int., 5Oct56.
28. For excellent short studies of the landing-craft situation, see Harrison, *Cross-Channel Attack*, pp. 60-63, from which the quotation is taken, and Matloff and Snell, *op. cit.*, pp. 192-94.
29. Marshall int., 5, 29Oct56.
30. Mountbatten int., 5May61; Ferguson, *Watery Maze*, p. 154.
31. *Supra*, note 26.
32. Capt. John L. McCrea, Presidential naval aide, forwarding President's queries to Marshall and King, sent by Hopkins to McCrea, 20Jun42, *Exec. 10, Item 32.*
33. Bryant, *op. cit.*, p. 328.
34. Churchill, *Hinge of Fate*, p. 383.
35. Butler, *op. cit.*, p. 607; Churchill, *Hinge of Fate*, p. 383.
36. *Supra*, note 34.
37. Butler, *op. cit.*, pp. 627-28. Conclusions of meeting at White House, 21Jun42, between President and Prime Minister, and W. B. Smith to CofS, 21Jun42, forwarding Draft of notes by Ismay on White House meeting, 21Jun42, both in *Exec. 1, Item 4.*
38. Marshall's account to Stimson as given in Stimson Diary, 22Jun42. Stimson in talking of his own meeting with Roosevelt on the 22nd said that the President spoke "with the frivolity and lack of responsibility of a child."
39. Tentative Schedule of Inspection Trip Outlined by General Marshall, 31-May42; handwritten notes by General Marshall stating: "I wish Sir John to see the type of men, state of discipline and apparent morale and training of our infantry divisions"; Schedule for visit to 9th Division, Fort Bragg, N.C., *Folder Fort Bragg Trip, Marshall Files*, Lt. Gen. James M. Gavin to Col. John H. Virden, 14Sept63, on his experience in the demonstration; Clark, *Calculated Risk*, pp. 8-9; Eichelberger, *Our Jungle Road to Tokyo*, pp. xxiv-xxv.
40. Eichelberger, *op. cit.*, pp. xxiv-xxv; Churchill, *Hinge of Fate*, p. 386.
41. *Washington Times Herald*, 27Jun42, describes June 24 demonstration; Churchill, *Hinge of Fate*, pp. 386-87; Bryant, *op. cit.*, pp. 331-33; Ismay, *Memoirs*, pp. 256-57; Stimson Diary, 24Jun42.
42. Churchill, *Hinge of Fate*, pp. 391-409.
43. Lord Moran, *Churchill*, p. 51. See also his statement, pp. 49-50, on the effect of the Prime Minister's actions following Tobruk.
44. ActACofS G-2 Strong to CofS, 29-Jun42, *ABC 381, Middle East (3-10-42), Sec. 1-B, Item 3.*
45. Sherwood, *op. cit.*, p. 595. Believing

the British incapable of saving the situation in the Middle East, Col. Bonner Fellers, U.S. military attaché in Cairo, proposed to Marshall the formation of an international corps under American command. The Chief of Staff made clear that he did not want to get involved in purely British affairs.
46. President to Marshall, 30Jun42 (telephoned by Hopkins), Marshall to President, 30Jun42, both in *Exec. 10, Item 53.*
47. Marshall to CG, USAFBI, no. 1120, 8Jun42, *ABC 381, Bolero (3-16-42) Sec. II.*
48. Maj. Ben F. Caffey to Marshall, 9-Feb39.
49. Eisenhower's address in *Addresses Delivered at the Dedication Ceremonies of the George C. Marshall Research Library, May 23, 1964, Lexington, Va.*, p. 14.
50. Eisenhower int., 28Jun62. Gen. Eisenhower recalled that Gen. Marshall once called him "Ike." "In the next two sentences, I'll bet he said 'Eisenhower' five times to make sure that I understood it was just a slip of the tongue."
51. Eisenhower to Marshall, 11May42, *Exec. 1, Item 4;* Wedemeyer to Marshall, 22May42, *WDCSA 570, pt. 1.* For the job of corps commander to plan the details of the operation, Wedemeyer suggested Gen. Patton or General Terry de la Mesa Allen.
52. Marshall int., 29Oct56. In a meeting with the British Chiefs of Staff, Eisenhower had made a favorable impression on Mountbatten. Inasmuch as Mountbatten reported to Roosevelt on his arrival in Washington and a few days later accompanied Marshall and Dill on a trip to camps in the South, he had an opportunity to impress Gen. Marshall with British views of Eisenhower's qualities. He definitely discussed appointments with Marshall, since it was he who first told Clark that Clark was to have the corps command in Great Britain. The author has found no basis for Marquis Child's view that Gen. Marshall sent the personal files of Eisenhower and two or three other officers to Churchill, who was allowed to take his pick. Arnold, *Global Mission*, p. 315; Clark, *Calculated Risk*, p. 20. Apparently Churchill did not meet Eisenhower on this trip, but it seems he was impressed by reports from Mountbatten and other British officials who met him.
53. Eisenhower, *Crusade*, p. 50; Davis, *Soldier of Democracy, a Biography of Dwight Eisenhower*, p. 302, has a slightly different version, which he apparently got from Eisenhower.
54. Clark, *Calculated Risk*, p. 20.
55. Churchill, *op. cit.*, p. 434.
56. Stimson Diary, 10Jul42.

57. Marshall and King to President, 10-Jul42, *Exec. 5, Item 1.*
58. Stimson Diary, 12Jul42.
59. Marshall, King, and Arnold to President, 12Jul42, *Exec. 5, pt. 1, Tab 8.*
60. Stimson Diary, 15Jul42. See other entries, 12, 13 July, which tend to support view that Marshall and Stimson intended the Pacific alternative as a bluff.
61. Telegram, President to Marshall, 14-Jul42, *WDCSA, Bolero, 1942-43;* Wedemeyer to Maj. Gen. Thomas T. Handy, 14Jul42, *Exec. 5, Item 1, Tab 10.* See Matloff and Snell, *op. cit.,* p. 272, for detailed statement of President's instructions and his viewpoint on operations in 1942.
62. Stimson Diary, 12Jul42.
63. *Ibid.,* 15Jul42.
64. *Ibid.,* 16Jul42.
65. Churchill, *Hinge of Fate,* pp. 439-40.
66. Butler, *op. cit.,* pp. 632-33. Butler notes that Churchill omits the reference to Robertson in his reprinting of Dill's letter in *Hinge of Fate,* pp. 439-40.
67. Bryant, *Turn of the Tide,* p. 341.
68. Butler, *My Three Years with Eisenhower,* pp. 24-25 (hereinafter cited as *Eisenhower*); Sherwood, *Roosevelt and Hopkins,* p. 607, quotes Hopkins as saying Churchill threw the British Constitution at him.
69. Bryant, *op. cit.,* p. 343.
70. Sherwood, *op. cit.,* p. 608; Butler, *op. cit.,* pp. 25-26; Truscott, *Command Missions, a Personal Story,* p. 49.
71. Marshall and King to President, 28-Jul42, *WDCSA 319.1 (7-29-42).*
72. Bryant, *op. cit.,* p. 343.
73. Roosevelt suggested: 1. an offensive against Algeria and/or Morocco; 2. the original North African operation; 3. an operation into Northern Norway; 4. U.S. reinforcement of British in Egypt; 5. American operations through Iran into the Caucasus. Sherwood, *op. cit.,* p. 610.
74. Marshall int., 28Sept56.
75. U.S. CsofS to COS, 24Jul42, included in Marshall and King to President, 28Jul42, *WDCSA 319.1 (7-29-42).*
76. *Ibid.*
77. Marshall int., 28Sept56; Butler, *op. cit.,* pp. 635-36.
78. Bryant, *op. cit.,* pp. 345-46. Brooke in his diary entry for 24 July said: "The Americans had gone a long way to meet us, and I should have hated to ask them for more." He

added: "A very trying week, but it is satisfactory to feel that we have got just what we wanted out of the U.S. Chiefs." On Hopkins' message and Roosevelt's reply, see Sherwood, *op. cit.,* p. 611. Although Marshall and King may have believed that a choice still remained to be made, the President had no such illusion. Mc-Narney to Marshall, no. 2569, 25-Jul42, *WDCSA 381 War Plans, pt. 2;* Stimson Diary, 25Jul42.
79. Churchill, *op. cit.,* pp. 448-49.
80. Butcher, *op. cit.,* p. 29.
81. The practice of changing code names for plans shortly before an operation, as a security measure, became common, confusing not only the enemy but the unwary historian. There had already been some confusion between SUPERGYMNAST and GYMNAST. Now there was TORCH to look out for.
82. CCS 33d Mtg., London, 25Jul42, *WDCSA 319.1 (7-29-42).*
83. Eisenhower to Maj. Gen. Orlando Ward, 15Apr51, *OCMH files,* quoted by Matloff and Snell, *op. cit.,* p. 286; Butcher, *op. cit.,* p. 32; Eisenhower, *op. cit.,* p. 71. Eisenhower's accounts in his letter and book incorrectly give the date as the 26th. He told Butcher that Marshall said that King proposed him for the command. Oddly enough this is not mentioned in King's book.
84. Dill to Churchill, 30Jul42, Churchill to Roosevelt, 21Jul42, in Churchill, *Hinge of Fate,* pp. 449-50. Sherwood later cited the Prime Minister's cable as indicating that he was wedded to ROUNDUP for 1943. Members of Marshall's staff in the War Department saw it differently. The suggestion had been mentioned in the American press before Marshall left for London. His Chief of the Operations Division, Gen. Handy, warned him that Churchill possibly wanted "to place you as 'Supreme Commander' in order to control you which so far he has been unable to do"—Handy to Marshall, 14Jul42, initialed by Marshall, *Exec. 5, Item 1, Tab 3.* Dill also suggested on 1 Aug. that Marshall might be made commander of the TORCH operations—Churchill, *Hinge of Fate,* p. 451. Marshall later made clear that he had no interest in that command and seemed surprised at the suggestion.
85. Stimson Diary, 6Aug42.
86. *Ibid.,* 9, 10Aug42, draft of letter.

XVI: TYRANNY OF THE WEAK

I drew heavily on Romanus and Sunderland, *Stilwell's Mission to China. The Stilwell Papers* and Chennault, *Way of a Fighter* were also helpful. See also *Foreign Relations, 1942, China.* Valuable interviews included those with former Ambassador William D. Pawley, Field Marshal Lord Slim, and Mrs. Stilwell.

1. Hull Memo, 3Jan38, Press Releases, For. Rels.: *1938*, III, 519, 586; *1940*, IV, 647; *Japan: 1931-41*, II, 222.
2. William D. Pawley int., 9Nov62; Romanus and Sunderland, *Stilwell's Mission*, pp. 11, 18-19, 24.
3. Romanus and Sunderland, *Stilwell's Mission*, pp. 29-30. Magruder was directed to advise and assist the Chinese government on all matters pertaining to procurement, transport, and maintenance of materials, equipment, and munitions needed to prosecute the war effort; to aid in training in the use and maintenance of these materials; to aid personnel of other United States government departments in carrying out the Lend-Lease provisions relating to China; to aid in insuring the flow of materials and munitions from Lend-Lease agencies to Chinese military forces; and to explore vital port, road, and rail facilities with a view to establishing and maintaining an adequate line of communications. Marshall int., 20Oct56.
4. Marshall int., 20Oct56.
5. Lt. Col. George W. Sliney to Brig. Gen. John Magruder, 10Dec41, cited in Romanus and Sunderland, *op. cit.*, pp. 43-44.
6. Marshall int., 29Oct56.
7. Stimson Diary, 31Dec41. On New Year's Day, the Chief of Staff mentioned the mission to Stilwell, along with the hint that it would go to Drum. Stilwell confided in his Diary: "George looking for a high-ranking man to go [to China]. Drum? Pompous, stubborn, new to them, high rank. Me? No, thank you. They remember me as a small-fry colonel that they kicked around. They saw me on foot in the mud, consorting with coolies, riding soldier trains. Drum will be ponderous and take time through interpreters; he will decide slowly and insist on his dignity. Drum by all means." Stilwell, *The Stilwell Papers*, p. 19.
8. *Ibid.*, 2Jan42. Marshall and his staff had no doubts concerning Drum's limited role. One member of the Ground Forces staff, who was working closely with Stilwell on a plan to invade North Africa, suggested that the whole China project was a device of Marshall's to get Drum out of the country by handing him a minor assignment in an unimportant theater.
9. *Ibid.*, 6Jan42; Lt. Gen Hugh A. Drum to SecWar and CofS, 5Jan42, *WDCSA Far East, 1942-43*.
10. Drum to SecWar and CofS, 8Jan42, *WDCSA Far East, 1942-43*.
11. Drum to SecWar and CofS, 10Jan42, with covering letter to SecWar, *WPD 4389-71*.
12. Stimson Diary, 11Jan42.
13. Drum to SecWar and CofS, 10Jan42, *WPD 4389-71*.
14. Stimson Diary, 13Jan42.
15. Drum to SecWar, 13Jan42; Stimson Diary, 14Jan42.
16. Stimson Diary, 14Jan42.
17. Drum to SecWar, 15Jan42.
18. Stimson Diary, 14Jan42. Stimson gave Marshall the go-ahead sign on Stilwell and on the 16th the Chief of Staff offered the post to the old China hand. The task as Marshall outlined it, translated into picturesque Stilwellese, was to "co-ordinate and smooth out and run the road, and get the various factions together and grab command and in general give 'em the works. Money no object." Stilwell, *op. cit.*, pp. 25-26.
19. Drum to SecWar, 13, 15Jan42; SecWar to Drum, 17Jan42.
20. Romanus and Sunderland, *op. cit.*, pp. 72-73.
21. General Marshall said later: "It was a fact that Stilwell was very much at fault in his tactlessness. He was referring openly to the Generalissimo as the 'Peanut.' " Marshall int., 29-Oct56.
22. See Romanus and Sunderland, *op. cit.*, chap. v, for details of controversies over this in the summer and fall of 1942.
23. Marshall to Dill, 19Mar42, (2 memos), both in *WDCSA, China, 1942-43;* Romanus and Sunderland, *op. cit.*, pp. 94-96.
24. Romanus and Sunderland, *op. cit.*, pp. 121-27; Chennault, *Way of a Fighter*, pp. 158-59.
25. Chennault, *op. cit.*, p. 159.
26. Stimson Diary, 14, 15Apr42; Romanus and Sunderland, *op. cit.*, pp. 114-15.
27. Stimson Diary, 27, 30Apr42; Romanus and Sunderland, *op. cit.*, pp. 135-36.
28. Stilwell to Stimson, 25May42, cited in Romanus and Sunderland, *op. cit.*, p. 151; Notes for Generalissimo, 26-May42 (Hoover Library, Palo Alto, Calif.), quoted *ibid.*, pp. 153-54.
29. Chinese Minutes of Conf., 26Jun42 (Hoover Library); American Minutes recorded by Bissell (Kansas City Records Center), both cited in Romanus and Sunderland, *op. cit.*, p. 171.
30. Chiang Kai-shek to Stilwell, 28-Jun42, encl. 2 to Handy to Marshall, 4Sept42, *OPD 381, CTO, Sec. II, Case 74*.
31. Marshall to Stilwell, no. 960, 4-Jul42, *OPD Msg. Log;* President to Lauchlin Currie, 28Jul42 (drafted in OCS), OPNAV 290059 to ALUSNA, Chungking, *Presidential File, China Policy, To CKS, Tab 5*.
32. Stilwell to Currie, 1Aug42, *OPD 381, CTO, Sec. II, Case 82*.
33. Stimson Diary, 26Aug42.
34. Handwritten note, Marshall to McCloy, 3Aug42, Marshall to Stilwell, no. 5, 1Sept42, both in *WDCSA China, 1942-43*.
35. Stilwell to Currie, 1Aug42, *OPD 381, CTO Sec. II, Case 82*.
36. Marshall to Stilwell, no. 5, 1Sept42,

Stilwell to Marshall, AMMISCA 1115, 4Sept42, *Exec. 10, Item 22.*

37. Marshall to President, 11Sept42, encl. 4 to Handy to Marshall, 4-Sept42, *OPD 381, CTO Sec. II, Case 74;* Currie to Marshall, 14Sept42, with brief handwritten notes from CofS to OPD; and SecWar to Marshall, *loc. cit., Case 82;* Currie to President, 12Sept42, *WDCSA China, 1942-43.*

38. President to Marshall, 15Sept42, Handwritten note, Marshall to Handy, n.d., Marshall to Currie, 18-Sept42, all from *WDCSA China, 1942-43.*

39. Marshall to Stilwell, no. 1469, 10-Oct42, *SecWar Safe File, Folder China;* Handy to Marshall, 18Sept42, *WDCSA China, 1942-43.* Stilwell had the last word. Before sending the final draft to the White House, Marshall radioed the text to Stilwell for comment. One of his suggestions was that Chiang be queried about the progress of the thirty division plan. This was included in the President's reply in tactful phrases: ". . . in order to reappraise on a practical basis your requirements in Lend-Lease combat material, it would

be most helpful if you advise me of the progress being made with the Yunnan group." Stilwell was pleased with the reply to Chiang: it was "exactly as I had recommended." Marshall to Stilwell, no. 1398, 25Sept42, Stilwell to Marshall, no. 1196, 28-Sept42, both in *Exec. 10, Item 22.* Romanus and Sunderland, *op. cit.,* p. 224.

40. President to Marshall, 3Oct42, Marshall to President, 6Oct42, both in *OPD 381, CTO, Sec. II, Case 82.*

41. Marshall to President, 5Nov42, quoting Stilwell to Marshall, 4Nov42; Stimson in earlier letter to Stilwell, 13Oct42, says he has talked with Soong and that he and Marshall "fully appreciate your trying and difficult situation"; both in *WDCSA China, 1942-43.*

42. Marshall to Stilwell, WAR 1724, 21-Nov42 (sent 23rd), *OPD 381, CTO, Sec. III, Case 100.*

43. Stilwell to Col. Thomas S. Timberland, AMMISCA no. 1463, 28Nov42, *Exec. 10, Item 22.*

44. Marshall to Stilwell, 7Dec42, (Hoover Library), quoted in Romanus and Sunderland, *op. cit.,* pp. 246-47.

XVII: TROUBLED PACIFIC

In addition to books by Morton, MacArthur, Whitney, and Matloff and Snell, I made use of Morison, *Coral Sea, Midway, and Submarine Actions* and *The Struggle for Guadalcanal;* Milner, *Victory in Papua;* and Miller, *Guadalcanal: The First Offensive.* Interviews used included those with Generals MacArthur, Sutherland, and Harding.

1. Marshall int., 14Feb57. Marshall recalled that when Evatt started in on a "tirade," he stopped him and said: "You are not going to get anywhere by storming in here at me. In the first place, I won't accept it. I won't have you in the office if you do it. So let's get down to business and find a way to get along without this tempestuous performance." Stimson later mentioned the episode and noted that Evatt worked quite well with them.

2. Marshall int., 14Feb57.

3. Professor Louis Morton thinks that the key to King's behavior may be found in the statement of an unidentified naval officer who declared: "I have come to the conclusion that Adm. King considers his relations with Gen. Marshall on such a successful plane . . . that there are some matters in which he will not proceed to their logical accomplishment, believing that even if he succeeded he would damage the relationship mentioned beyond repair." Morton, *Strategy and Command,* p. 399.

4. Vandenberg, *The Private Papers of Senator Vandenberg,* p. 76.

5. Marshall int., 29Oct56.

6. *Ibid.,* 14Nov56.

7. Morton, *Pacific Command, a Study in Interservice Relations.*

8. In Professor Morton's effective reminder, "The headquarters in Melbourne would be equivalent to one in South America directing operations against Boston and New York, and planning for an invasion against northwest Canada"—Morton, *Strategy and Command,* p. 252.

9. *Ibid.,* pp. 260-61.

10. Stimson Diary, 1Jul42; Marshall to MacArthur, no. 347, CM-OUT 1475, 6Jul42, MacArthur to Marshall, no. C-38, 7Jul42, both in *Exec. 10, Item 7b.*

11. King to Marshall, 2Mar42, *ABC 381 (3-2-42);* King to President, 5-Mar42, *ABC 323.31, POA (1-29-42), Sec. 1-A.*

12. Eisenhower to CofS, 21Apr42, *Exec. 10, Item 56.*

13. Churchill to President, no. 73, 29-Apr42, *Exec. 10, Item 62;* Milner, *Victory in Papua,* pp. 28-29.

14. Marshall to MacArthur, no. 8, 30-Apr42, MacArthur to Marshall, no. 151, 3May42, both in *Exec. 2, Item 1i;* Marshall to MacArthur, no. 31, 6May42, *Exec. 10, Item 7a.*
15. MacArthur to Marshall, no. 913, 8-Jun42, *Exec. 2, Item 1i.*
16. Marshall to MacArthur, no. 204, 10-Jun42, *Exec. 2, Item 1i.*
17. King to Marshall, 11Jun42, *WDCSA SWPA, 1942-43.*
18. Marshall to King, 12Jun42, *OPD 381, SWPA, Sec. II, Case 73.*
19. Handy to Marshall, 24Jun42; King to Marshall, 25Jun42 (with proposed directive) and 26Jun42; Marshall to King, 26Jun42; King to Adm. Chester Nimitz, no. 271415, 27Jun42; all from *OPD 381, SWPA, Sec. II, Cases 76, 80.*
20. MacArthur to Marshall, no. 254, CM-IN 9329, 28Jun42, *OPD Msg. Log.*
21. Marshall to King, 29Jun42, Marshall to MacArthur, no. 300, 28Jun42, both from *OPD 381, SWPA, Sec. II, Case 80.*
22. Marshall to MacArthur, no. 306, 29-Jun42, MacArthur to Marshall, no. 261, 1Jul42, both in *OPD Msg. Log.*
23. Marshall to King, 1Jul42, submitting proposed draft of joint directive for SWPA operations; King's proposed joint directive, 30Jun42; King to Marshall, 2Jul42; final text signed by King, Marshall, 2Jul42, "Joint Directive for Offensive Operations in SWPA," *OPD 381, SWPA, Sec. II, Cases 80, 83; Exec. 10, Item 67a; Exec. 8, Bk. 6.*
24. Marshall to MacArthur, no. 334, 3-Jul42, *OPD Msg. Log.*
25. Marshall and Ghormley to Marshall and King, no. 1012, 8Jul42, *Exec. 2, Item 1i;* King to Marshall, 10Jul42, *OPD 381, SWPA, Sec. II, Case 87;* Marshall and King to MacArthur and Ghormley, no. 2100, 10Jul42, *WDCSA SWPA, 1942-43.*
26. Marshall int., 21Nov56.
27. Craven and Cate (eds.), *The Army Air Forces in World War II*, Vol. IV, pp. 44-45; King to Marshall, 1Aug42; handwritten note, Marshall to Handy, n.d., attached to Handy to CofS, 5Aug42, both in OPD *320.2, PTO, Sec. II, Case 37.*
28. Marshall to King, 20Aug42, *OPD 320.2, PTO, Sec. II, Case 37;* Marshall to MacArthur, no. 658, 9Aug-42, *OPD 381, SWPA, Sec. II, Case 97;* Marshall to Harmon, no. 906, 10-Aug42, *OPD 452.1, PTO, Sec. I, Case 6;* Marshall to MacArthur no. 690, 10Aug42, *OPD Msg. Log;* Marshall to Harmon, no. 913, 11Aug42, *OPD 381, PTO, Sec. II, Case 82;* Harmon to Marshall, nos. 768, 770, 12Aug42, both in *OPD Msg. Log.*
29. MacArthur to Marshall, no. C-253, 12Aug42, Marshall to MacArthur, no. 796, 13Aug42, both in *OPD Msg. Log.*
30. King to Marshall, 20Aug42, with

paraphrases of Rear Adm. Robert L. Ghormley msg., 17Aug42, *OPD 381, PTO, Sec. II, Case 84;* Emmons to Marshall, No. 2504, 25Aug42, *OPD Msg. Log;* Harmon to Handy, 20-Aug42, *OPD 381, PTO, Sec. III, Case 91.*
31. Marshall int., 21Nov56.
32. Arnold to CofS, 21Aug42, *OPD Exec. 10, Item 67b.* Information furnished Marshall showed that available to Nimitz in the Central and South Pacific were 100 bombers and 273 fighters with 86 fighters en route to the area and a heavy bombardment group (35 planes) being prepared for shipment. MacArthur had in his theater 283 bombers and 327 fighters with 127 fighters on the way to him by boat and 40 bombers and 44 fighters being prepared for shipment. In addition, 24 bombers were being sent from Hawaii. Marshall to King, 25-Aug42, *OPD 452.1, PTO, Sec. I, Case 8.* In *Global Mission*, p. 336, Arnold says that in the Central, South, and Southwest Pacific areas, there were 1314 airplanes available for use with 302 more en route—a total of 1616 to the 554 available to the Japanese.
33. Stimson Diary, 2Sept42.
34. MacArthur to Marshall, no. C-367, 28Aug42, *OPD Msg. Log.*
35. MacArthur to Marshall, no. C-381, 30Aug42, *OPD Msg. Log.*
36. Marshall to MacArthur, no. 1320, 31Aug42, *OPD Msg. Log;* Marshall to President, 2Sept42, *Exec. 10, Item 23a.*
37. MacArthur to Marshall, no. C-436, 6Sept42, MacArthur to Marshall, no. C-411, 3Sept42, both in *OPD Msg. Log*, quoting MacArthur and Ghormley messages.
38. King to Marshall, 3Sept42, *WDCSA SWPA, 1942-43.*
39. McNarney to King, 5Sept42; Arnold to King, 3Sept42, both in *OPD 452.1, PTO, Sec. I, Cases 12, 18.*
40. Griffith, *The Battle for Guadalcanal*, pp. 180, 261, fn. 20.
41. Arnold says Sept. 16, but he also says that he attended the meeting of the Joint Chiefs of Staff the same day, which was definitely the 15th. See Arnold, *op. cit.*, p. 338, JCS 33d Mtg., 15Sept42, *ABC 334, JCS Minutes, Sec. II.*
42. Morton, *Strategy and Command*, pp. 335, 337-38; references are to Minutes of JCS Mtgs., 15Sept42 and 6Oct42; Ct. Griffith, *op. cit.*, pp. 137-38.
43. Arnold, *op. cit.*, p. 338-39.
44. *Ibid.*, p. 344.
45. Stimson Diary, 16Oct42.
46. Arnold to Marshall, 6Oct42, *OPD 384 (4-3-42).*
47. Wedemeyer to Brig. Gen. St. Clair Streett, 11Oct42, *OPD 384 (4-3-42).*
48. Streett to Wedemeyer, 9Oct42, *OPD 384 (4-3-42);* Streett to Handy, 31-

Oct42, *OPD 384, PTO, Sec. II, Case 43.*

49. Marshall to President, 26Oct42, *WDCSA South Pacific Area, 1942-43.*

50. King to Leahy and Marshall, 3Oct-42, *OPD 381, PTO, Sec. III, Case 102;* Capt. J. L. McCrea (for Roosevelt) to Marshall, 14Oct42, *WDCSA South Pacific Area, 1942-43;* Marshall to Harmon, no. 1695, 15Oct42, *OPD Msg. File;* Marshall to Mac-Arthur, no. 2716, 16Oct42, *Exec. 10, Item 23b.*

51. MacArthur to Marshall, no. C-731, 17Oct42, *OPD Exec. 10, Item 23a.*

52. Stimson Diary, 18Oct42; Marshall to President [New Guinea], 19Oct42, Marshall to President [Solomons], 19-Oct42, both in *WDCSA South Pacific Area, 1942-43.*

53. Marshall to President [Solomons], 19-Oct42, *WDCSA South Pacific Area, 1942-43;* Marshall to Emmons, no. 720, 16Oct42, in which Marshall asked Emmons to pick a division from his command and to make Maj. Gen. J. Lawton Collins commander of the one that was chosen, and Marshall to Emmons, no. 802, 20Oct42, both in *OPD Msg. Log.*

54. One of Halsey's first actions after assuming command was to order "all Navy men and Marines in the area to leave off their neckties" in an effort to conform to Army practice. Halsey, *Admiral Halsey's Story,* p. 139. See Marshall int., 21Nov56.

55. President to Leahy, King, Marshall, and Arnold, 24Oct42, *WDCSA South Pacific Area, 1942-43;* Leahy to Lewis W. Douglas, 26Oct42, *OPD 565.4, Sec. I, Case 16.*

56. Marshall to President, 26Oct42, *WDCSA South Pacific Area, 1942-43.*

57. JCS 97/4, 16Oct42, JCS 97/5, 22-Oct42, both in *ABC 381 (9-25-41) Sec. III;* Minutes JCS Mtg., 27Oct-42, *ABC 334, JCS Minutes (2-14-42), Sec. II.* The Joint Chiefs of Staff, in order to expedite action, directed (13Oct) that the recommendations of Air Force strength in the South Pacific be circulated among the Chiefs of Staff for approval as soon as reached. The partial report, 16Oct, on deployment was incorpo-rated in the report of 22Oct, approved by the JCS at their meeting on 27Oct. Marshall could tell King, 24Oct, that action had already been started to fulfill the Army's commit-ment. The 52 heavy bombers and the 29 medium bombers now in the area or en route from the U.S. would reach the recommended strengths of 70 and 52 respectively before the specified date of 1Jan43. Even more immediate would be the increase in fighter strength: 145 fighters of the recommended 150 were now in the area, and 48 fighters now on their way from the Central Pacific area would more than fulfill the fighter aircraft requirement. Marshall to King, 24Oct42, Handy to Marshall, 22Oct42, both in *OPD 452.1, PTO, Sec. I. Case 23.*

58. Stimson Diary, 29, 31Oct42.

59. Lee Van Atta, "U.S. Force in Australia Small," *Washington Post,* 7-Aug42, p. 2. MacArthur to Marshall, no. C-219, 8Aug42, complained that an editorial in *The New York World-Telegram* had damaged morale in Australia by saying that "Australia no longer can count on priority"—*OPD Msg. Log;* Marshall to MacArthur, no. 664, 10Aug42, MacArthur to Marshall, no. Q-321, 11Aug42, Marshall to President, 12Aug42, all in *WDCSA Australia, 1942-43.*

60. Marshall to Stimson, 29Oct42, *WDCSA South Pacific Area, 1942-43;* Marshall to Maj. Gen. Alexander D. Surles, 28Oct42, *WDCSA Solomon Islands, 1942-43.*

61. Stimson Diary, 29Oct42. References to MacArthur's political ambitions prompted Hanson Baldwin to deny in his column of 26Oct42 that they were serious. When these continued, MacArthur issued a public state-ment, saying: "I have no political ambitions whatsoever. . . . I started as a soldier and I shall finish as one. . . . If I survive the campaign, I shall return to that retirement from which this great struggle called me" —*New York Times,* 26, 29Oct42.

62. Stimson Diary, 29, 30Oct42.

63. Marshall to MacArthur, no. 4539, 15Dec42, *OPD Msg. Log.*

64. Matloff and Snell, *Strategic Planning,* p. 359.

XVIII: "END OF THE BEGINNING"

In addition to the books by Eisenhower, Clark, and Churchill listed earlier, I drew on Langer, *The Vichy Gamble;* Murphy, *Diplomat Among Warriors;* Howe, *Northwest Africa: Seizing the Initiative in the West;* and Morison, *Operations in North African Waters.* See also *Foreign Relations, 1942,* Vol. II. Interviews especially useful for this period were held with Generals Eisenhower, Clark, Smith, Bradley, and Truscott. I received some background material from interviews conducted in 1946 and 1947 with Gen. de Gaulle, Marshal Juin, and Adm. Leahy.

1. K. T. Marshall, *Together*, pp. 128-29.
2. Robert Murphy [signed for Cole] to Handy or Leahy, no. 749, 31Oct42, *WDSCA 381 Torch, File II, 1942-43.* See Clark, *Calculated Risk*, p. 91; Murphy, *Diplomat Among Warriors*, pp. 140-41.
3. W. B. Smith to JCS, Notes of 30-Jul42 Conference at White House, 1Aug42, *Exec. 5, Item 1, Tab 14.*
4. Marshall to OPD, 19Aug42, *Exec. 5, Item 1;* Eisenhower to Marshall, no. 1153, 14Aug42, *OPD Msg. Log;* Marshall to Eisenhower, no. 3332, 14Aug42, *Exec. 10, Item 36a.*
5. Dill to Marshall, 8Aug42, *Exec. 5, Item 1.*
6. Eisenhower to Marshall, 17Aug42, *WDCSA 381, Torch, 1942-43.*
7. Marshall to Dill, 14Aug42, *WDCSA 381, Torch, 1942-43.* Marshall int., 5Oct56. The President carried his concern to the point of trying to postpone the British attack at El Alamein. "When Roosevelt heard that Montgomery was going to attack in late October, he said, 'Stop it, the British always get licked.' "
8. BrCOS to U.S. CsofS, 27Aug42, *ABC 381 (7-25-42), Sec. I;* S. E. Morison, *Operations in North African Waters, October 1942-June 1943.* U.S. planners and Adm. Sir Andrew Browne Cunningham felt Casablanca must be secured in order to possess an Atlantic port for reinforcements.
9. CCS 38th Mtg., 28Aug42, *ABC 334, CCS Minutes, Sec. 2.*
10. *Supra*, note 6.
11. Marshall int., 19Nov56, based on author's notes; Frye, *Marshall; Citizen Soldier*, pp. 321-33; Farago, *Patton: Ordeal and Triumph*, pp. 176-78. Frye and Farago put the incident in July.
12. Marshall int., 28Sept56; Farago, *op. cit.*, pp. 186-87; Patton to Marshall, 6Nov42.
13. The author has combined statements from two interviews with Gen. Marshall, 28Sept56 and 19Nov56.
14. Eisenhower to Marshall, 11Nov42; Marshall to Eisenhower, 28Sept42.
15. Marshall int., 19Nov56.
16. Marshall to Col. Omar N. Bradley, 29Sept36.
17. Bradley, *A Soldier's Story*, p. 16.
18. Marshall int., 28Sept56. Marshall added: "I was to learn the vital importance of having a checking system at the beaches. They not only had trouble in Africa, but were to have trouble again on the Normandy beaches and at Antwerp. We got into a hell of a plight at the time of the Battle of the Bulge. Of course it is hard to do these things right. You are landing, fighting the surf, and carrying on the battle. As a result, the only reason we got through some of these battles with enough equipment was that the G-4 planners had asked for so much more than we needed. . . . We had an enormous problem of supply. If we didn't check where it was, we lost it. Beach organization was very important. I am reminded of Teddy Roosevelt in World War II. He had been appointed to organize the beach; instead he went into the fight and let the beach go. However, it was probably good at this point because they were in a rough fight." See also Eisenhower, *Crusade*, chap. 16.
19. Marshall to Eisenhower, no. R-2593, 30Oct42, *Exec. 5, Item 7.*
20. Eisenhower to Marshall, 3Oct42, *WDCSA Torch, 1942-43;* Marshall to Eisenhower, 1Nov42.
21. Marshall to Eisenhower, 28Sept42.
22. Maj. Gen. Patton had the Western Task Force, Maj. Gen. Lloyd R. Fredendall, the Center Task Force, and Maj. Gen. Charles W. Ryder, the Eastern Task Force. Lt. Gen. Kenneth A. N. Anderson commanded the British elements of Gen. Ryder's force. The entire naval operation was under Adm. Sir Andrew Browne Cunningham. Brig. Gen. Doolittle commanded the U.S. Air Forces in support of the U.S. forces, and Air Marshal William L. Welsh, the British. Adm. H. Kent Hewitt commanded U.S. Forces in the Mediterranean. Patton's force had approximately 35,000 U.S. troops; Fredendall's some 39,000 troops; and Ryder's some 10,000 American and 23,000 British troops.
23. de Gaulle, *The Call to Honour*, p. 241.
24. Notes drawn up by René Pleven after the meeting of Gen. Charles de Gaulle and U.S. Ambassador John G. Winant, 30Jun42 in de Gaulle, *War Memoirs: Unity, 1942-44; Documents*, pp. 16-17; Col. de Chevigné, head of the Fighting French Military Mission to the USA, to French National Committee in London, 1Jul42, in *Documents*, p. 18; Stimson Diary, 23Jun42.
25. de Gaulle, *Unity, 1942-44*, p. 8, says that Marshall and King asked to see him, but King's recollection, supported by Clark, is that de Gaulle sought the interview. King says that de Gaulle thought that Marshall and King should come to see him but was finally convinced that two stars (a French brigadier general) should go to four stars.
26. Notes drawn up by de Gaulle's office after his interview with the heads of the American Army and Navy, 23-Jul42 in de Gaulle, *Unity, 1942-44; Documents*, pp. 26-28; Clark, *Calculated Risk*, pp. 36-37; Viorst, *Hostile Allies: FDR and Charles de Gaulle*, p. 93; King, *Fleet Admiral King*, p. 406.
27. de Gaulle to Adrien Tixier in Washington, 31Jul42, in de Gaulle, *War*

Memoirs: Unity, 1942-44; Documents, pp. 30-31.

28. Eisenhower to Marshall, no. 3711, 17Oct42, *OPD Exec. 5, Item 8;* Langer, *Our Vichy Gamble,* pp. 325-26.
29. Eisenhower to Marshall, no. 3730, 17Oct42, *Exec. 5, Item 8;* Butcher, *Eisenhower,* p. 146; Eden, *The Reckoning,* p. 399, gives a slightly different view.
30. Maj. Gen. Mark Clark was accompanied by Brig. Gen. Lyman L. Lemnitzer, Col. Julius C. Holmes, Navy Capt. Jerauld Wright, and Col. Archelaus L. Hamblen. Cole to War Dept., 15Oct42, in *For. Rels., Europe, II,* pp. 394.
31. Clark, *op. cit.,* pp. 67-89, stresses the importance of the expedition; Murphy, *op. cit.,* pp. 137-39, claims less for the meeting; Viorst, *op. cit.,* p. 103, calls it "one of the most dramatic, most foolhardy, most meaningless exploits of the entire war."
32. Eisenhower to Marshall, 7Nov42, *Exec. 5, Item 2, Tab 31.*
33. *Ibid.*
34. Patton to Marshall, 15Nov56. Patton added: "I regret that I had no chance to personally distinguish myself, but I assure you that I did my best to get shot at. In fact, I was under fire on several occasions but only in line of normal duty."
35. *Supra,* note 32.
36. Marshall speech to American Academy of Political Science in New York City, 10Nov42, *Marshall Speech Book.* See also DeWeerd, *Selected Speeches,* p. 216.
37. Marshall to Eisenhower, 9Nov42. Later he deprecated "cheap details" of Clark's submarine mission. "There was more about the loss of pants and of his money than there was of the serious phase of the matter"—Marshall to Eisenhower, 20Nov42.
38. Marshall int., 28Sept42.
39. Marshall to SecWar, 17Nov42; Marshall to Eisenhower, 20Nov42.
40. Marshall to Strong, 17, 18Nov42.
41. Sherwood, *Roosevelt and Hopkins,* p. 653; Prime Minister to President, 17Nov42, with annex to memo by Sumner Welles, 18Nov42, *For. Rels., Europe, 1942, II,* pp. 445-46.

42. Marshall to Eisenhower, 20Nov42.
43. Eden, *op. cit.,* p. 406.
44. *Ibid.,* pp. 409-410.
45. Churchill, *Hinge of Fate,* p. 641.
46. Marshall to Eisenhower, no. 63, 8-Dec42.
47. Marshall to Eisenhower, 13Dec42, enclosing letter to Elmer Davis. Marshall described the situation in an interview, 15Feb57: "In the Darlan episode I brought down a group of members of Congress, particularly of the Senate, very carefully selected men, and explained to them what the situation was and read to them a message I had just gotten from Gen. Eisenhower that day which explained his point of view, which helped a great deal because it gave us defenders on the floor of the Senate and the House. And they were very loyal in the fact that they didn't spread this all over the place. . . . We had about as much difficulty with English opinion as we did with American press opinion, and Eisenhower and Clark had a very difficult time. It was hard enough fighting on about a 600 mile front with only 105,000 troops. But when you have to fight all the editorial press . . . that was a difficult proposition. I thought Gen. Eisenhower carried it off very, very well and with great restraint."
48. Howe, *Northwest Africa: Seizing the Initiative in the West,* chap. xv.
49. Marshall to Eisenhower, 22Dec42.
50. Marshall to Eisenhower, 26Dec42; Murphy, *op. cit.,* p. 183; Eden, *The Reckoning,* p. 416.
51. S. E. Morison, *Operations in North African Waters . . . ,* p. 183; Cunningham, *Sailor's Odyssey,* p. 501.
52. Marshall to Allen Brown, 17Dec42.
53. Stimson Diary, 9Nov42.
54. Remarks by SecWar at Marshall's birthday party, 31Dec42, *OCS 201-M (Marshall, G.C.);* Stimson Diary, 31Dec42, had a slightly different paraphrase. In his Diary, Stimson said that he thought the proverb of Solomon that "he that ruleth his spirit is better than he that taketh a city" applied in particular to the General.
55. Marshall to Churchill, 12Dec42.

APPENDIX I

1. Marshall int., 14Nov56.
2. Report of Army Pearl Harbor Board, 20Oct44, in *Pearl Harbor Hearings,* pt. 39, pp. 175-76.
3. Stimson statement, 30Nov44, *Pearl Harbor Hearings,* pt. 19, pp. 3895-3897. See views of JAG Myron C. Cramer on errors in Army Board finding, pt. 39, pp. 231-296. There are almost daily entries in Stimson's Diary on report for month of December 1944.

4. Stimson Diary, 22Nov44.
5. Stimson Diary, 14Nov44.
6. Marshall int., 14Nov56.
7. In 1955, Virginius Dabney, editor of the *Richmond Times Dispatch,* suggested to Gen. Marshall that he permit an answer to be made on the various attacks on him concerning Pearl Harbor.—Virginius Dabney to Marshall, 16May55. Marshall replied, "The Pearl Harbor incident, for example—as to where I was and

the political purpose to embroil President Roosevelt—after my first day's testimony in the hearings, I checked up carefully and found that I spent the evening in Mrs. Marshall's bedroom, she being ill at the time. This I stated publicly several times, but this was overwhelmed by political assaults for purely political purposes.

"Practically anything I wrote now would be brought immediately into the coming political campaign, perverted or otherwise. . . . I have testified for as much as a week at a time to committees or joint committees of Congress. All that is in the record and was mulled over in the press at the time."

8. Affidavit of Lt. Gen. W. B. Smith, 15Jun45, *Pearl Harbor Hearings*, pt. 35, pp. 90-91.
9. W. B. Smith int., 29Jul58.
10. Miles Testimony before the Joint Committee, 13Dec45, pt. 3, pp. 1554-55, Col. Rufus S. Bratton testimony before the Joint Committee, 14Feb-46, pt. 9, pp. 4515-16, both in *Pearl Harbor Hearings*.
11. Capt. Laurence F. Safford Testimony before the Joint Committee, 1Feb46, *Pearl Harbor Hearings*, pt. 8, p. 3574.
12. Col. Otis K. Sadtler testimony before the Joint Committee, 15Feb46, *Pearl Harbor Hearings*, pt. 10, pp. 4633, 4637.
13. See *Pearl Harbor Hearings*, pt. 34, Proceedings of Col. Carter W. Clarke Investigation, 20Sept44, for testimony of Sadtler, pp. 67-69, 85-89; Lt. Col. William F. Friedman, pp. 34-36, 77-85; Brig. Gen. Isaac Spalding, pp. 89-93; Col. John T. Bissell, pp. 7-10, 99-102. George Morgenstern,

in his *Pearl Harbor, the Story of the Secret War*, pp. 215-17, a book sharply critical of Gen. Marshall, makes no mention of Sadtler's denial that the message was even in the War Department nor of the fact that Friedman, Spalding, and Bissell all made sworn statements in an investigation conducted by Clarke. No mention is made of the fact that Friedman's specific testimony was read to Col. Sadtler during the congressional hearings and that the latter made clear that he had been misunderstood in quoting secondhand testimony. Nor does the author make clear that the testimony of all witnesses concerned in the incident was made part of the record of the *Pearl Harbor Hearings*. Instead, he stresses that neither Friedman nor Bissell "was ever called as a witness by the New Deal majority of the congressional committee."

14. Arthur Upham Pope to Marshall, 6-Apr52; "TV Panel Makes More Noise than Sense," *Life*, 14Apr52, pp. 101-110.
15. *New York Times*, 18Apr54, p. 31; Marshall to Hanson Baldwin, 15-Apr54.
16. The Democrats signing were Senator Alben W. Barkley (Kentucky), chairman; Representative Jere Cooper (Tennessee), vice-chairman; Senators Walter George (Georgia), Scott W. Lucas (Illinois), Representatives J. Bayard Clark (North Carolina), John W. Murphy (Pennsylvania). The Republicans were Representatives Bertrand W. Gearhart (California) and Frank B. Keefe (Wisconsin). Keefe filed a separate statement.

APPENDIX II

1. Stimson Diary, 15 and 16Dec41.
2. Reprint of Roberts Commission Report, 23Jan42, *Pearl Harbor Hearings*, pt. 39, pp. 20-21.
3. Short Testimony before the Joint Committee, 25Jan42, including request for retirement, 25Jan42; Short to Marshall, 25Jan42, *Pearl Harbor Hearings*, pt. 7, pp. 3133-35. A vast amount of material relating to the relief of General Short may be found in *Pearl Harbor Hearings*, pt. 19, pp. 3789-3941.
4. Stimson Diary, 26Jan42.
5. Marshall to Stimson, 26Jan42, *Pearl Harbor Hearings*, pt. 7, p. 3139.
6. JAG Cramer to Marshall, 27Jan42,

Pearl Harbor Hearings, pt. 7, pp. 3145-46.
7. *Ibid.*
8. Stimson Diary, 28Jan42.
9. Stimson Diary, 17Feb42; ACofS G-1 Hilldring to TAG, 17Feb42, and Retirement of Major General Walter C. Short, 17Feb42, *Pearl Harbor Hearings*, pt. 7, pp. 3141-42.
10. Stimson Diary, 25Feb42.
11. Stimson Diary, 26Feb42.
12. Maj. Gen. Short Testimony before Joint Committee, 22 and 26Jan46, *Pearl Harbor Hearings*, pt. 7, pp. 2964, 3169; *New York Times*, 1-Mar42, p. 1.

Index

Officers' ranks used in this index are those attained at the end of December 1942

485

The European Theater
Mediterranean and North Africa

NORWAY
Oslo
SWEDEN
Stockholm

NORTH
SEA

DENMARK
Copenhagen
BALTIC

NORTHERN
IRELAND

IRELAND

GREAT
BRITAIN
Amsterdam
London
NETH.
Berlin
GERMANY

ATLANTIC

OCEAN

Dunkerque
Antwerp
Brussels
BELG.
Rhine R.
COTENTIN
PENINSULA
NORMANDY
LUX.
Prague
CZECHOSLO

Paris

FRANCE
Munich
Vienna
AUSTRIA
HU
Berne
SWITZERLAND
Vichy

ITALY
YUGOS

PORTUGAL
Madrid
Florence
Adriatic
Sea
Lisbon
SPAIN
CORSICA
Rome
Anzio
Naples
Salerno
SARDINIA

GIBRALTAR
Tangier
Strait of
Gibraltar
MEDITERRANEAN
Palermo
SICILY

Rabat
Fez
Algiers
Philippeville
Bizerte
Casablanca
Melilla
Oran
Cherchel
Bougie
Bône
Tunis

MOROCCO
Sousse
Kasserine
MALTA
ALGERIA
Sfax

TUNISIA
Gabes
Tripoli

LIBYA

HS